MAC GAME
PROGRAMMING

PREMIER PRESS

GAME DEVELOPMENT

Mac Game Programming

Mark Szymczyk

PREMIER PRESS

GAME DEVELOPMENT

Premier

p

Press

Publisher: Stacy L. Hiquet

Marketing Manager: Heather Buzzingham

Managing Editor: Sandy Doell

Acquisitions Editor: Emi Smith

Series Editor: André LaMothe

Editorial Assistant: Margaret Bauer

Marketing Coordinator: Kelly Poffenbarger

Technical Reviewer: Darrell Walisser

Copy Editor: Alice Martina Smith

Interior Layout: LJ Graphics

Cover Design: Mike Tanamachi

CD Producer: Darrell Walisser

Indexer: Johnna VanHoose Dinse

Proofreader: Kim Benbow

ISBN: 1-931841-18-7

Library of Congress Catalog Card Number: 2001096218

Printed in the United States of America

02 03 04 05 RI 10 9 8 7 6 5 4 3 2 1

This book is dedicated to the memory of Jeff Bilicki.

Foreword

So you want to be a Mac game programmer? This book is a great place to start. Whether you are interested in how games work, want to learn to write shareware games, or want to become the next great commercial game developer, this book will show you some of the key technologies and techniques required to make your dream game.

Through the years, I've worked on many Mac games, from *Duke Nukem 3D* to *Tomb Raider* and *Unreal Tournament*. When I began writing Mac games in 1985, I would have loved to have access to a reference like this one. In those early years, Mac game developers learned tricks from anywhere they could find them—late nights pouring over Apple documentation, swapping ideas with other developers, and a lot of trial and error.

As president of Westlake Interactive, I'm often asked by people how to break into the Mac game business. My first answer is to get experience any way you can. Anything from writing simple 2D games to working on flashy demos will show potential employers that you have the drive and knowledge to make it in the game business. Mac game programmers are incredibly difficult to find these days, so the market for people with the interest and talent to work in the industry is very strong.

Writing Macintosh games can be some of the most exciting, challenging, and rewarding work a programmer can tackle. You have in your hands the perfect starting point to enter the world of game programming; with hard work and determination, you'll be well on your way to writing that next great Mac game!

Glenda Adams

President, Westlake Interactive

May 2002

Acknowledgments

It pains me to admit it, but I did not single-handedly create this book. Many people helped make this book a reality, and I'd like to thank them here.

First, I'd like to thank my editors at Premier Press—and I worked with many editors on this book. I would like to thank my original acquisitions editor, Jody Kennen, for discovering me and for putting the book deal together. I would also like to thank my original project editor, Brian Thomasson, for his help as I wrote the first chapters of this book. He helped me get up to speed quickly on writing the chapters.

While I was writing this book, both Jody and Brian left to take other positions. Emi Smith became my new acquisitions editor. I need to thank Emi for gathering all the permissions necessary to include all the programs on the CD-ROM and for putting up with delays in the project. Thanks to my copy editor, Alice Martina Smith, for cleaning up some of my grammar and for bringing up questions that made the text of this book easier for you to understand. I would also like to thank my Tech Editor, Darrell Walisser, for reviewing all the source code in this book and making sure it all runs well.

Next, I owe a huge Thank You to Carlos Camacho, the editor of the Mac game programming site iDevGames, for two reasons. First, he let me write some articles for his site, which is how Premier Press found me. Without his Web site, I wouldn't be writing this book. Second, he donated artwork, music, and sound effects for the CD-ROM that accompanies this book. His donation will make it easier for you to make your own games, improving the book in the process.

I had many programming questions as I wrote the code for the book. I would like to thank everyone who answered my questions on various mailing lists and message boards. I don't have a list of individuals who helped, but you know who you are.

The CD-ROM that is with this book comes packed with development tools, games, source code, and game assets. I would like to thank everyone who graciously let me include their programs on the CD-ROM. You have helped make this book as good as it can possibly be.

Finally, I want to thank my family for helping keep me sane while I wrote the book. To my parents Stan and Mary, my brothers Dave and Steve, my sister Kathy, her husband John, and my nephews Zachary and Christian, thank you.

About the Author

When he graduated with a computer science degree from John Carroll University, **Mark Szymczyk** set out on a career in software development. After bouncing around among various corporate programming positions, he decided to go into game development, starting his own shareware game company, Black Apple Software. While working on his first game, he wrote some game development articles for the iDevGames Web site, which led to a request to write this book. Now that the book is completed, he can finish up work on his first game.

Mark currently lives in the Cleveland, Ohio area. When he's away from his Mac, he enjoys playing basketball, listening to underground music from the 80s and 90s, and hanging out with his nephews.

Contents at a Glance

Contents

CHAPTER 1
INTRODUCTION TO THE MAC AND TO
GAME PROGRAMMING 1

CHAPTER 3
C++ FOR C PROGRAMMERS 59

CHAPTER 4
INTRODUCTION TO
MACINTOSH GRAPHICS. 77

CHAPTER 10
SOUND· · · · · · · · · · · · · · · · 345

Chapter 12
Beginning Artificial Intelligence . . 455

CHAPTER 13
PATHFINDING 491

Chapter 16
Putting It All Together 639

CHAPTER 17
UNDERSTANDING THE GAME'S SOURCE
CODE • • • • • • • • • • • • • • • • • • • 675

CHAPTER 18
OPTIMIZATION • • • • • • • • • • • • • • • 717

CHAPTER 19
GAME DEVELOPMENT TIPS 763

APPENDIX B
GAME DEVELOPMENT RESOURCES . . . 801

Letter from the Editor of *Mac Game Programming*

Let's face it. Macs have never been the world's greatest game programming platform. The reasons are many: Macs have never had the penetration the PCs had in the hobbyist market, Macs are expensive, and Macs tend to be used only for high-end design, layout, and publishing.

However, with the entry of the iMac into the market and Apple's persistence in changing the mindset of the masses (or at least Steve Jobs's persistence), Macs now have the power to play any 2D/3D game a PC does—in addition, the prices of the machines are comparable to PCs, and they sure do look a lot better!

These days, everyone is starting to buy Macs—college students, moms, and hobbyists of all sorts—so the commercial opportunities for creating games on these machines are finally a reality. The only problem, of course, is that Macs have never been "programmers' machines." The tools for game development on Macs are few and far between, there aren't many books on Mac programming (let alone Mac game programming), and all this has contributed to a big black hole of knowledge as far as Mac game development goes.

However, this is all about to change! *Mac Game Programming* is the first-ever Mac game programming book that covers game programming for the Mac at this level of detail. This isn't just a graphics book, this is a high-performance, professional-level book designed to teach you all the facets of Mac game development. Mark Szymczyk has taken some time writing this book so that you will really get a lot out of it. If you're a C/C++ programmer on any platform, you will be able to read through this book and develop a complete Mac game with all the bells and whistles—from artificial intelligence to networking.

Additionally, this book covers operating system issues and various I/O libraries (such as the "sprocket" API) and more to give you a repertoire of tools to use when developing your Mac games with features appropriate

for your application. To tell you the truth, I am quite excited about
this book.

There are a zillion iMacs out there now, and with the help of this book,
you can create games to be played on them! Moreover, if you're a PC or
Linux game programmer who is interested in porting to the Mac platform,
this book is for you. You can jump to the areas in the book you're interested in—such as input, graphics, sound, networking, and so forth—and
use the libraries and techniques to port your games.

Even if you're never going to develop Mac games professionally, this book
is a great read. And if you are going to develop Mac games professionally,
this book should be a requirement!

Sincerely,

André LaMothe
Series Editor, Premier Game Development Series

Introduction

Welcome to the world of Macintosh game programming. This is the first book on Macintosh game programming to be published since 1996, so I know you're eagerly anticipating it. I hope this book meets your expectations and provides the information you need to program games for the Mac.

System Requirements

To install the CodeWarrior demo on the CD-ROM, your system must meet the following requirements:

- A Macintosh with a Power PC processor running Mac OS 8.6 or higher
- 64MB of RAM, 128MB if running Mac OS X
- 150MB of hard disk space

In addition, to take full advantage of the code in this book, you need the following:

- A Macintosh with a Power PC processor running Mac OS 8.1 or higher
- A C++ compiler, such as CodeWarrior or Project Builder.

If you have an older Macintosh that does not meet the system requirements, don't chuck this book into the garbage. Most of the topics I cover in the book apply to older Macs, but you will have more work to do:

- You will have to find a compiler that will run on your computer. You can download MPW (Macintosh Programmer's Workshop) for free from Apple's Web site, or you can scour the Internet looking for an older version of CodeWarrior.
- You will have to find older versions of the Game Sprockets; the versions I include on the accompanying CD-ROM are intended for Power PC–based Macs running Mac OS version 8.1 and higher. The versions to look for are DrawSprocket version 1.1.3 or 1.1.4 , InputSprocket version 1.3 or 1.4, and NetSprocket version 1.1.1. These are the only versions of the Game Sprockets that will run on 68K Macs (68K chips are the chips Apple used to make Macs until 1994; they are the main category of Macs that do not meet this book's system requirements).

- You will have to make some minor code changes to the source code examples on the CD-ROM that comes with this book. Carbon, the programming model I use in the book, contains some functions that will not run on older Macs. You will have to change those functions to code that will run on older Macs.

I know it's a pain to do all that, but consider it an opportunity to learn—or an excuse to buy a new computer.

What the Reader Needs to Know

This book assumes that the reader has intimate knowledge of multivariable calculus, linear algebra, rigid body dynamics, control theory, 3D graphics, neural networks, and genetic algorithms. Readers without this knowledge will find the book to be incomprehensible.

HA HA HA! You really don't have to know all that stuff to understand the topics in this book. I wrote the book figuring that many people new to game programming would be reading it. The only thing you really have to know to benefit from this book is a knowledge of programming. C or C++ are the ideal languages to know, but if you are familiar with a different language, you shouldn't have a problem reading the source code listings in the book. If you don't know how to program, you're going to find the program listings in the book and the source code on the CD-ROM nearly impossible to understand.

What This Book Will Teach You

Games take separate components—such as graphics, sound, player input, and artificial intelligence—and combine them to provide an entertaining and interactive experience for the player. This book will cover the separate components that make up a game and teach you to program these components for use on Macintosh computers running Mac OS 8, 9, and X. In the process of covering the components that make up a game, we will develop a complete game. The following sections go into more detail about what I cover in the book.

Preliminary Information

The first three chapters of the book will bring less-experienced programmers up to speed so that they can handle the rest of the book. To paraphrase George W. Bush, I want to ensure that no reader is left behind. Chapter 1 provides a general intro-duction to programming Mac games and introduces some Mac terminology. Chapter 2 familiarizes the reader with the Project Builder development environ-ment, showing how to create projects and compile programs. Chapter 3 gives an introduction to the C++ programming language so that C programmers can better understand the source code in the book and on the accompanying CD-ROM.

Graphics

After providing the preliminary material, I spend the next three chapters covering graphics. Chapter 4 introduces Macintosh graphics. In that chapter, I will explain how QuickDraw, the Mac OS graphics manager, stores colors and images. The chapter also shows you how to use offscreen buffers for flicker-free drawing and how to draw from these buffers to the screen. Chapter 5 demonstrates the use of tiles for drawing backgrounds and storing game levels. In addition, I show you how to scroll the screen so that you can create huge game levels in your games. Chapter 6 covers animation so that your games can have moving characters and fast action.

Reading Player Input

I move from discussions on rendering graphics to reading input from the player in the next three chapters. Chapter 7 explains InputSprocket, the Mac OS 8 and 9 method of supporting joysticks and gamepads in your games. Chapter 8 covers the HID Manager, which is the Mac OS X equivalent of InputSprocket. Chapter 9 pro-vides techniques for reading the keyboard and mouse directly as well as through Mac OS events. I cover event handling with both the Classic Event Manager and the Carbon Event Manager.

Sound

After reading Chapter 10, you'll know how to add audio support to your games. I show you how to use the Sound Manager to play, pause, resume, and stop sound effects. I also teach you ways to play longer musical sequences by using QuickTime.

Physics

Chapter 11 covers physics, which will add to the realism of your game's world. As part of this chapter, I will show you how to accurately detect collisions and respond realistically to them.

Artificial Intelligence

The next two chapters cover artificial intelligence so that the enemies in your game will provide a suitable challenge to the player. Chapter 12 shows some low-level AI routines, such as chasing, evading, patrolling, and moving randomly. Chapter 13 covers pathfinding so that your computer-controlled enemies can move intelligently from one place to another without getting stuck.

Changing the Screen Resolution

Many types of games must hide the menu bar to take over the entire screen; they also must switch the resolution of the screen. Chapter 14 shows you how to use DrawSprocket to change the monitor resolution and provide a full-screen gaming experience.

Files

Every game must deal with files in some way, even if it's just loading the game's graphics and sound files. In addition, most games should allow the player to save his game so that he can pick up and play it where he left off at another time. Chapter 15 demonstrates how you can load your game's data and assets from disk as well as how to permit the player to save games and resume playing them later.

Bringing Everything Together

Chapter 16 covers all the little details that aren't big enough for their own chapter, but are necessary for a finished game. It covers topics such as initializing the game, ensuring that the user has the necessary system components to play your game, and making all the components discussed in the previous sections work together. After finishing Chapter 16, you will have a working game.

Classes

Many game companies are releasing the source code of their old games to the game development community. For example, Bungie released the source code to

Marathon, and id Software did the same with *Quake*. When I downloaded some of these games' source code, I found the source code nearly impossible to comprehend. I don't want you to feel the same way about the source code I wrote for this book, so I have included a chapter to explain the source code for the game we'll develop as we work through the book. Chapter 17 gives you a picture of how all the objects and classes in the game interact so that you can better understand the source code for the game that I put on the accompanying CD-ROM.

Improving Your Game

The last two chapters focus on improving your game. Chapter 18 shows you ways to optimize your game so that it will run faster on the player's machine. Chapter 19 gives you some techniques to write better code so that you can finish your game sooner.

What This Book Will Not Teach You

Programming is just one part of making a successful game. Because this is a programming book, I can cover only the programming aspects of game development. The following sections cover briefly the aspects of game development this book will *not* teach you.

Tool Creation

Most games require a number of tools to create the content for the game. First-person shooters such as *Quake* and *Unreal* use level editors to create the levels for the game. Real-time strategy games such as *Starcraft* use map and mission editors to make the game's maps and missions.

Although creating tools is part of the game programming process, I chose not to write about it in this book. I wanted to focus the book on game programming; I didn't want to hear readers complain that "He spent a third of the book showing us how to write a level editor. I wanted more game programming information." In addition, game tools tend to be game specific. The techniques I cover in the book are applicable to multiple game genres.

The tools you write will depend on the type of game you create. Most games require some sort of map/level editor to create the game's world. Mission-based games, such as war games, strategy games, and military simulations are much easier to make with a mission editor. Adventure and role-playing games can have tools to make puzzles and traps. Programming game tools on the Macintosh involves GUI programming. If you're unfamiliar with Macintosh GUI programming, pick up a book on GUI programming, such as *Beginning Mac Programming* (published by Prima Tech).

Game Design

This book will show you how to create a game, but it will not show you how to make a *fun* game. It will not show you how to design a game. It will not show you how to design a level. It will not show you how to create challenging puzzles for a game. Good game design makes a game fun to play. If I had the magic formula for designing fun games, I'd be too busy designing best-selling games to write this book. You are on your own with regard to game design, but I'm sure you have your own game ideas, so this should not be a problem.

Creating Artwork

Modern games require a great deal of artwork: backgrounds, characters, animation frames, and items. Good games require teams of artists to make all the game's assets. I am not a graphic artist, so I'm not qualified to teach you how to make artwork. Believe me, I am the last person who should be teaching the graphical arts. The CD-ROM that comes with this book contains game graphics you can use in your games as well as tools to help you create your own artwork.

Creating Audio

Audio is a major component of games (along with the graphics). I am not a musician, so I cannot teach you how to make music and sound effects for your games. You can find some music and sound effects on the accompanying CD-ROM that you can use in your games. The CD-ROM also includes tools to help you make your own audio effects.

On to Chapter 1!

I know you are anxious to begin your game programming journey. It is going to be a long journey, so keep your spirits up and don't get discouraged. If you're ready, let's move on to Chapter 1.

CHAPTER 1

Introduction to the Mac and to Game Programming

Many of you reading this book are either new to programming for the Macintosh or new to game programming. You are the people for whom I am writing this chapter. This chapter covers some basic concepts in Macintosh programming and game programming so that we're all on the same page when I begin covering Macintosh game programming in Chapter 4, "Introduction to Macintosh Graphics."

A Brief History of the Mac OS

In 1984, Apple introduced the Macintosh and changed the face of personal computing forever. With the introduction of the Macintosh came version 1.0 of the Mac OS. Apple designed the Mac OS to work with the original Macintosh. As with all personal computers at the time, the Macintosh let one user run one application at a time. The original Macintosh had black-and-white graphics, an 8MHz processor, 128KB of RAM, one floppy disk drive, and no hard drive. This was considered powerful hardware at the time, but it was still limiting for Apple. Apple had to make a graphical user interface and an operating system that would fit on a floppy disk, fit in 128KB of RAM, and run on an 8MHz processor.

As you probably know, the computer industry changes rapidly. Computing power doubles every two years, and with that increased power, things that were impossible to do ten years ago can work today. Throughout the 1980s and 1990s, users demanded more from their computers. They wanted color graphics and stereo sound. They wanted to run multiple programs at once. They wanted to network computers together so that they could share information. They wanted to use their computers to go on the Internet. To keep up with users' computing demands, Apple made many changes and released many updates to the Mac OS, finishing with Mac OS 9.1 in 2001. Updates to Mac OS after 9.1 are bug fixes that add no new functionality to the operating system.

Apple did their best in updating the Mac OS, but design flaws in the original Mac OS made it difficult to update the operating system. What Apple needed was a new operating system, one that they could update more easily. Apple attempted to write a new operating system called Copland in the early 1990s, but Copland didn't work.

In late 1996, Apple bought the company Next from former Apple CEO Steve Jobs and used Next's operating system as the basis for its new operating system. Jobs became CEO of Apple shortly after the acquisition. After a great deal of effort, Apple released its new operating system, Mac OS X (the X stands for 10) on March 24, 2001.

Mac OS X has several features that differentiate it from previous versions of the Mac OS:

- **The Aqua interface, shown in Figure 1-1.** Contrast Aqua with the Platinum interface that older versions had, which you can see in Figure 1-2. Notice that the text and graphics look much clearer in Aqua. Observe the row of icons at the bottom of the screen in Figure 1-1. That row is the Dock, which contains commonly used programs and documents. Aqua has greater impact for developers of other types of software than it does for game developers. Most games take over the entire screen so the players won't even see Aqua.

- **Protected memory.** If a program crashes in Mac OS X, you just restart the program that crashed. On pre-OS X systems, a program crash also brought down all the other programs that were running, forcing you to restart the computer.

- **Preemptive multitasking.** With preemptive multitasking, the operating system decides how much time to give to each application, making it easier for the user to do multiple tasks at the same time.

- **Multithreading.** Multithreading allows you to split your program up into threads that run simultaneously. A thread is a separate program inside an application with its own stack and set of registers. For a game, you could have each component of the game (such as the game loop, physics engine, AI engine, and network code s) in a separate thread. All these threads would run at the same time along with the game itself.

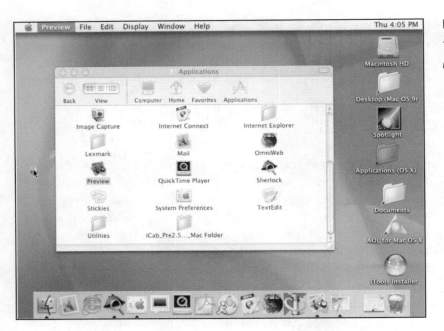

Figure 1-1

The Aqua interface used in Mac OS X

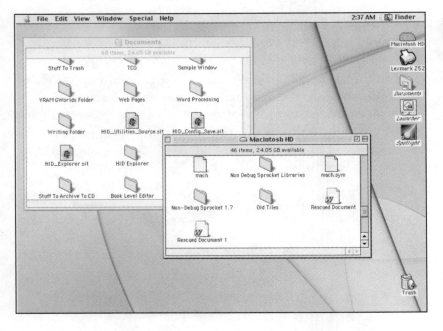

Figure 1-2

The Platinum interface used in Mac OS 8 and 9

NOTE

Although it's true that Mac OS 8.6 and 9 have multithreading capability, the support for it is not as good as it is in OS X. On Mac OS X, the operating system schedules time for all the threads. On Mac OS 8 and 9, your game is responsible for scheduling time for all the running threads.

Mac OS X introduces many new technologies that run only in Mac OS X. Table 1-1 lists the technologies of greatest interest to game developers.

Table 1-1   Mac OS X Technologies

Technology	Description
Quartz	A technology for 2D graphics based on the Adobe PDF (Portable Document Format) model. Quartz provides rendering of much higher quality than QuickDraw, Apple's previous 2D technology. Quartz also gives your games access to 2D acceleration and direct access to the video frame buffer.
HID Manager	The HID Manager provides support for gamepads and joysticks in your games.
Core Audio	An audio technology that allows the programmer to access the audio hardware at the lowest possible level for maximum performance.

Mac OS X can run in two modes. When running natively in OS X—also called *the Yellow Box*—a program can take advantage of all OS X's features and uses the Aqua interface. To maintain backwards compatibility with old programs, Mac OS X also can run in Classic mode—also called *the Blue Box*. Classic mode is just Mac OS 9.1, and it runs as one program among many in OS X. For example, you could have an Internet browser and a spreadsheet running natively while running five programs in Classic mode. To OS X, there are eight programs running: the Internet browser, the spreadsheet program, Classic (Mac OS 9.1), and the five programs running in Classic. A program running in Classic looks and behaves just as it would in Mac OS 9.1. If a program crashes in Classic, you must reload Classic, but you do not have to restart the entire machine.

Although Classic mode is Mac OS 9.1, Mac OS X runs Mac OS 9.1 in emulated mode—which is how a Mac runs Windows using a program such as Virtual PC or SoftWindows. The emulated version of Mac OS 9.1 sits on top of Mac OS X, which means that there are two layers of operating system between your code and the Mac hardware. Code running in Classic mode in OS X runs slower than equivalent code running natively in Mac OS 9.1 because there's an extra layer of operating system to go through in Classic mode. The extra layer of operating system also means that programs running in Classic mode run slower than programs running natively in Mac OS X.

Mac Programming Models

Mac programmers have three ways to write programs that take advantage of Mac technologies: the Mac Toolbox, Carbon, and Cocoa. The next three sections explain each of these programming models.

Mac Toolbox

If you're writing programs intended for pre–Mac OS X systems, the Mac Toolbox provides the functions you need to write Mac programs. The Toolbox is composed of dozens of managers, each of which handles one particular aspect of the Mac OS. For example, the Window Manager contains the functions and data structures you need to use windows in a program. Some of the major managers used for games are listed here:

- QuickDraw for 2D graphics
- OpenGL for 3D graphics
- Sound Manager for sound
- OpenTransport for networking
- InputSprocket for supporting game controllers
- DrawSprocket for monitor resolution switching and hiding the menu bar
- QuickTime for multimedia

The weakness of the Mac Toolbox is that it does not support Mac OS X directly. A program written with the Mac Toolbox can run in Classic mode on an OS X system, but that means it cannot use the Aqua interface or protected memory. A game running in Classic mode on Mac OS X runs slower than a game running natively in OS X. This sluggish behavior will annoy the OS X users who play your game.

You should use the Mac Toolbox for your game only if you want your game to run on 68K machines, that is, computers using the Motorola 680x0 family of processors that Apple built in the 1980s and early 1990s. Programming with the Toolbox is the only way users of these machines can play your game because Carbon and Cocoa run only on Macs with Power PC processors. If your game is not too technically demanding, you should consider supporting 68K machines, even if your intended audience is users of Mac OS X. Supporting 68K machines could mean selling an extra 500 copies of your game.

Carbon

No matter how great an operating system you have, nobody will use that operating system unless there's software to run on the system. Apple had to make it easy for software developers to update their existing programs to Mac OS X. If they did not, Apple would fall victim to this vicious cycle: Users don't upgrade to OS X because there is no software for OS X, and developers don't create OS X versions of their software because no customers are using OS X. Software companies would not be thrilled to throw away code that took years to write and have to totally rewrite their applications to run on a new operating system.

Apple created Carbon so that software developers could easily migrate their programs from Mac OS 8 and 9 to OS X. If you see that a piece of software has been *Carbonized,* it means that the software has been converted from the Mac Toolbox to Carbon. Carbon contains the most frequently used functions in the Mac Toolboxes well as many additions. The result is a massive collection of functions and data structures you can use to write programs for Mac OS 8, 9, and X. Think of Carbon as a Mac OS X–compatible version of the Mac Toolbox. If you already know how to program with the Toolbox, learning Carbon should be no problem. You can use the same technologies and most of the same code you used with the Mac Toolbox. For example, when coding with Carbon, you can still use the Sound Manager to program audio and QuickDraw to program 2D graphics.

Unfortunately, most of the Apple Game Sprockets did not survive the transition from the Mac Toolbox to Carbon. The Game Sprockets are a collection of Software Development Kits (SDKs) that simplify game development for Macs. The Game

Sprockets are the Mac equivalent of Microsoft's DirectX toolkit for Windows. There are four Game Sprockets in the Macintosh Toolbox:

- DrawSprocket makes it easy to switch screen resolutions, go into full-screen mode (by hiding the menu bar), and perform 2D graphics.
- InputSprocket provides support for joysticks and gamepads.
- NetSprocket simplifies the process of game networking.
- SoundSprocket provides support for 3D sound.

Here's how each of the Game Sprockets looks in Carbon:

- DrawSprocket kept its screen-resolution-switching and full-screen mode functions.
- InputSprocket is not a part of Carbon, but a Carbon program running in Mac OS 8 or 9 can use InputSprocket functions. To support joysticks in OS X, use the HID Manager, described in Chapter 8, "HID Manager."

F I N D I T

ONLINE

Apple's NetSprocket page:
http://www.opensource.apple.com/projects/openplay

- NetSprocket was open sourced, which means that volunteers maintain and improve the NetSprocket code instead of Apple. You can still use the original NetSprocket in your Mac OS 8 and 9 games. The open source version of NetSprocket is Carbon compatible so the open source version is what you want if you want your NetSprocket code to run natively in OS X. You can download the open source version of NetSprocket from Apple's Web site.
- SoundSprocket is not included in Carbon. Unfortunately, Apple has no 3D sound technology at this time. If you want 3D sound in your game, you can go with Open AL, which is an open source, cross-platform audio library, or you can roll your own 3D sound solution.

F I N D I T

ONLINE

Open AL site: http://www.openal.org
Mac Open AL download: http://developer.creative.com

There are two types of Carbon programs you can develop: CFM Carbon programs and Mach-O Carbon programs, as discussed in the following two sections.

CFM Carbon Programs

CFM (Code Fragment Manager) Carbon programs run on Mac OS 8 and 9 and run natively in Mac OS X. With one set of code, your game can take advantage of OS X features such as protected memory while maintaining backwards compatibility with Mac OS 8 and 9 (very cool for us as programmers). Because CFM Carbon programs are the only Carbon programs that will run in Mac OS 8 and 9, you will probably be writing CFM Carbon games.

The one weakness of CFM Carbon programs is that it is difficult to take advantage of the new Mac OS X–only technologies. If you want to use Mac OS X–only technologies such as the HID Manager and Core Audio in a Mach-O Carbon game, you just call the appropriate functions. To use these technologies in a CFM Carbon game, you must write a bunch of glue code to access each technology's framework before you can access each technology's functions.

Carbon version 1.0.4 is the oldest version of Carbon, and it supports Mac OS 8.1 and above. Any versions of Carbon higher than 1.0.4 run on Mac OS 8.6 and above. Carbon is constantly evolving, so I cannot tell you what the most recent version of Carbon is. Check Apple's Developer Web site to find the most recent version. Ninety-nine percent of the Carbon code I write in this book will run with Carbon version 1.0.4. The only technology I cover that is not part of Carbon version 1.0.4 is the Carbon Event Manager, discussed in Chapter 9, "Reading the Keyboard and Mouse Plus Event Handling."

NOTE

Although code written for Carbon version 1.0.4 supports Mac OS 8.1 and above, specific technologies introduced in later versions of Mac OS require the later version of Mac OS. For example, in Mac OS 9, Apple made it possible to create offscreen buffers in the memory of a 3D graphics accelerator to speed up drawing. This ability to create offscreen buffers in video memory is part of Carbon version 1.0.4, but it still requires Mac OS 9 and above. Computers running Mac OS 8.1, 8.5, and 8.6 will not be able to create offscreen buffers in video memory. Being able to run Carbon programs does not magically give computers running Mac OS 8.1, 8.5, and 8.6 the ability to use technologies that require Mac OS 9 and above.

Mach-O Carbon Programs

Mach-O Carbon programs can directly take advantage of Mac OS X–only technologies, meaning that you can easily use Quartz, the HID Manager, and Core Audio in your Mach-O Carbon games. Mach-O Carbon programs will also load a little faster than CFM ones. The major disadvantage of Mach-O Carbon programs is that they will not run on Mac OS 8 and 9.

The type of Carbon games you choose to write depends on which versions of Mac OS you want to support, your development environment, and the technologies you want to use in your game. If you want to support Mac OS 8, 9, and X, have CodeWarrior, and don't care about the new Mac OS X technologies, write a CFM Carbon game. If you use Project Builder, Apple's development environment that ships with every copy of Mac OS X, you must write a Mach-O Carbon game because Project Builder cannot make CFM Carbon programs. If you don't care about supporting Mac OS 8 and 9, write a Mach-O Carbon game.

If you want to support Mac OS 8, 9, and X and use the new Mac OS X technologies, you have two choices. First, you can write two versions of your game, a CFM Carbon version that runs on Mac OS 8 and 9 and a Mach-O version that runs on Mac OS X. Second, you can write a CFM Carbon version and write special code to call Mach-O frameworks from a CFM Carbon program. Both options are equally valid. You just have to decide whether you prefer to maintain two versions of your game's source code or prefer to write code to call Mach-O frameworks from a CFM Carbon program.

Cocoa

If you don't care about supporting older versions of the Mac OS, you may be interested in Cocoa. Cocoa is a class library that makes it easy to write OS X programs. It is much easier to create user interfaces in Cocoa than in Carbon or the Mac Toolbox because you can make user interfaces visually rather than having to write a lot of code. Cocoa is great for creating your game's tools, such as level and mission editors. You could write the level editor for your game in Cocoa, and then use Carbon to make the game itself. You probably won't be releasing your game's level editor to the public, so having the level editor run on only Mac OS X won't alienate your customers.

Another advantage of Cocoa is that its development tools come with OS X so you don't have to pay for another compiler. A final advantage of Cocoa is that you can use it to easily support OS X–only technologies.

There are two main problems with using Cocoa for game development. The first is that Cocoa is for OS X–only development. The second is that you must use Objective C or Java as your programming language. Objective C is an object-oriented language built on top of the C language. Next invented Objective C and used it to write their class frameworks; Cocoa is the Mac OS X version of those frameworks. Because most game programmers use C or C++, using Cocoa means learning a new programming language.

Programming with Carbon

I'm going to be using Carbon throughout this book to develop the code examples and the game. By using Carbon, I ensure that the greatest number of readers will be able to use this book. If you have a compiler with built-in Carbon support (CodeWarrior Pro 6 and later versions have built-in Carbon support along with Project Builder), you can just create a new Carbon project in the compiler and begin coding. For those of you with old versions of CodeWarrior, there's some preliminary work you must do so you can program with Carbon.

What to Place in Your System Folder

To program with Carbon, you must place the Carbon library inside your System folder. Without the Carbon library, the computer won't know what Carbon is, and your code will not run. Apple provides two versions of the Carbon library as part of the Carbon SDK, a debug version (DebuggingCarbonLib) and a release version (CarbonLib). The debug version provides information when something goes wrong in your program so that you can fix what's wrong with your code.

Place either the debug or release version of the Carbon library inside the System folder. If you have both versions in the System folder, your program will crash. I suggest using the debug version during development. If you are running Mac OS 8 or 9, place the Carbon library in the Extensions folder. If you are running Mac OS X, place the Carbon library in the CFMSupport folder, which is located in the Library folder of the System folder.

What to Place in Your Compiler

After you have your System folder set up for Carbon development, you must set up your compiler for Carbon. Here's what you must do to have your Carbon code compile properly:

1. Add the library CarbonLib to your project.
2. Copy the Carbon Support folder from the Carbon SDK to the folder containing your compiler.
3. Add access paths to the CarbonLib library and Carbon Support folder so that the compiler knows where to find the Carbon libraries and header files.

A Description of the Game We Will Develop

In the course of this book, we will develop a complete game that incorporates all the concepts covered in the book. The game, titled MyGame, is a 2D game combining action and role-playing in the spirit of the old *Zelda* games on the Super Nintendo console.

While developing the game in the book, I will be creating C++ classes for the various components in the game, such as graphics, sound, physics, and artificial intelligence. These classes can be the basis for your own games. Even though I'm writing code for an action/RPG, you can modify the code to write role-playing (the *Baldur's Gate* series), platform (*Super Mario Brothers*), arcade (*Pac Man*), strategy (the *Civilization* series), board (checkers), card (poker), and puzzle (*Tetris*) games.

Elements of a Computer Game

Webster's—or whatever dictionary Microsoft Word uses—defines a game as "an activity that people participate in, together, or on their own, for fun." In addition to being fun, computer games have specific elements, which I detail in the following sections. I will be covering each of these elements in much greater detail in individual chapters of the book.

Player Input

All computer games must have a way to read input from the player. If you don't allow the player to interact with the computer, you don't have a game; you have a movie. The type of game you develop will determine what input devices you must support, but some examples of input devices include keyboards, mice, joysticks, gamepads, and steering wheels.

Challenges

For your game to be fun, it must present some challenges for the player. Challenges can come in many forms. For board and card games, the challenges come from the rules of the game. Computer-controlled enemies provide the challenge in action and role-playing games. Adventure games use puzzles to present their challenges.

Many computer games use artificial intelligence to give a challenge to game players. The computer plays against the player in board and strategy games. The computer moves the monsters around and coordinates their actions in action and role-playing games. Even the best artificial intelligence is no match for human players, so most modern games provide online play so that humans can play each other. In this case, the other people playing online supply the challenge for the player.

Graphics

Virtually every computer game uses graphics to show the current state of the game world. Graphics can be simple 2D graphics, such as the falling pieces in *Tetris* or the game board in *Risk*. The graphic can be a massive world map that spans several screens in a strategy game such as *Civilization*. The graphic can be a 3D underground dungeon common to first-person shooters such as *Quake* and *Unreal*. In addition to showing the environment of the game world, games use graphics to show the creatures and items the player can interact with in the game world.

A lot of games also use graphics to help the player keep track of what's happening in the game. First-person shooters such as *Doom* use a status screen to tell the player how healthy he is and how much ammunition he has left. Arcade games such as *Pac Man* use graphics to tell the player his current score and how many lives he has left.

Although most games use graphics in one form or another, it's possible to make a game with no graphics. Infocom made a series of text adventure games that were very popular in the early 1980s. Multi User Dungeons (MUDs) use text to play *Dungeons and Dragons*–style role-playing adventures online. If you want to do something different, you can make a text-based game with no graphics.

Sound

Many games use sound to enhance the game playing experience. Background music can add to the game's atmosphere in much the same way that movie scores do. The music in a game can improve its gameplay (what the player gets to do in the game) as well as the atmosphere. In the classic arcade game *Ms. Pac Man*, the game music changes when Ms. Pac Man eats a power pellet. The music changes back when the power pellet wears off, giving the player an audio cue that the pellet has expired.

Sound effects work with the background to provide an enticing audio experience. One of the cool things about playing first-person shooters is hearing the machine gun fire while you pump your enemies full of lead. Playing with the sound turned off makes the game less fun. Shooters that involve stealth use sound to enhance the gameplay of the title. In *Deus Ex*, for example, the faster you move, the more noise you make, making it more likely that the guards will notice you. By moving slowly and crouching while you move, you can move silently and get to where you want to go without resorting to violence. If there were no audio in *Deus Ex*, the player would have no idea whether he were moving quietly enough to avoid detection.

Physics

Card and board games don't have to deal with physics, but other types of games must have physics. Physics makes the game world you create with your game's graphics behave in a manner that your players can anticipate. Physics makes the player character come down when he jumps up in a side-scrolling platform game such as *Super Mario Brothers*. Physics keeps the characters from running through walls in action and role-playing games. Physics makes the airplane behave like an airplane in a flight simulator.

The physics in your game can be as complicated as you want. You could crack open some textbooks on mechanics, kinematics, and dynamics to design a mathematically correct physics engine. Or you can fudge the numbers and test your game to check whether the physics "looks" right. Don't worry about the details of physics right now; I will cover that in Chapter 11, "Physics." The important thing is about your physics engine is that it meets the player's expectations of the game world and that it doesn't hurt the gameplay. Some physics engines are too accurate; they make the game so difficult to play that players get frustrated and stop playing. If you make a 100-percent physically accurate flight simulator, only professional pilots will be able to play the game. Remember the last word of the dictionary definition of game: *fun*.

Game Event Loop

At its heart, a game is not that complicated from a programming point of view. The core of a game is its main event loop, which runs as fast as possible, usually 30 to 60 times per second. The following code shows what a typical event loop looks like:

```
while (gameInProgress) {
     ReadPlayerInput();
     DetermineOpponentsMove();
     UpdateGameWorld();
     RenderFrame();
}
```

The guts of the ReadPlayerInput() function vary depending on the type of game you write. A chess game would simply read the player's move. An action game would determine whether the player fired a weapon or moved. A racing game would see which way the player turned. The ReadPlayerInput() function also provides a way to break out of the game loop; if the player pauses the game, the gameInProgress variable would be set to false, and the game would break out of the event loop.

The DetermineOpponentsMove() function normally falls in the realm of artificial intelligence. In a board game, the computer would make a move in this function. In a strategy game, the computer would move the units it controls. In a first-person shooter, the computer would determine what the individual enemies do. The DetermineOpponentsMove() function is the computer player's equivalent of the ReadPlayerInput() function. The computer uses artificial intelligence instead of a mouse and keyboard.

The UpdateGameWorld() function changes the state of the game world based on the inputs from the player and the computer. In an action game, this function would move the characters, determine whether the weapons hit any characters, and update the characters' health if they were hit. In a board game, this function would change the state of the board.

The `RenderFrame()` function redraws the screen to reflect the changes in the game world.

Usually a game's background music starts playing outside the game loop. When the music starts playing, the game installs a callback function that the operating system calls when it reaches the end of the music file. The callback function normally replays the music so that the music loops indefinitely with no pauses in the sound's playback. The `ReadPlayerInput()` and `UpdateGameWorld()` functions will undoubtedly trigger sound effects. For example, if the player fires a weapon in a shooting game, the firing of a weapon will spawn the sound effect of a weapon firing.

Your game event loop may not take exactly the same form as what was just shown. Action games normally change the `UpdateGameWorld()` function to look like this:

```
MovePlayer();
MoveEnemies();
DetectCollisions();
```

How you write your game event loop will depend on the type of game you're developing and your personal preferences. The sample one I wrote earlier in this section should show you that it's not as difficult as it sounds.

I Want to Be a Professional Game Developer

The dream of many teenage boys is to make video games for a living. I had the same dream myself. Although I'm not a career counselor, I can give you some tips to help make the dream a reality.

Landing a Job as a Game Programmer

The most common way to break into the game industry is by securing a job as a game programmer or artist. Because this is a game programming book, the following sections will focus on securing a game programming job. How do you get that first job? What skills and educational background do you need? Read on.

Go to College

If you're a high school student who wants to work as a game programmer, you should go to college. Major in computer science and minor in math. If the school you choose to attend has any game development classes, take them. Take classes in graphics, artificial intelligence, networking, and compiler design in your computer science coursework. The compiler design class will show you what you need to know to make scripting languages for a game. Take classes in calculus, linear algebra, and numerical analysis as part of your math minor. With this foundation, you will have the educational background to become a game developer.

While you're spending your four years in college getting your degree, develop some games and demos on the side. You don't have to write the most technically advanced first-person shooter. A 2D side-scrolling game or a board game will work, but the important thing is to finish the game. There are tons of half finished games on programmers' hard drives around the world. Finishing a game separates the men from the boys. Having a finished game will show a prospective employer that you have a love of game programming—and prove that you have what it takes to complete a game.

DigiPen Game Programming School

If the thought of going to a traditional four-year college is unbearable, there is an alternative. DigiPen has a game programming school located in Redmond, Washington, just outside of Seattle. At DigiPen, you can get a two- or four-year degree in game development. Instead of taking classes that you have no interest in just to fulfill requirements at a four-year college, you can focus strictly on game development. My brother attended DigiPen when it was in Vancouver, British Columbia, and he now works as a game programmer, so I can vouch for the program's effectiveness. Attending DigiPen is no guarantee of employment in the game industry, but it won't hurt your chances of working in the industry.

Before you start packing for Seattle, there are some things you need to consider:

- Enrollment is limited. When my brother went, DigiPen accepted only about 75 people a year out of 12,000 applicants. I'm not sure of the exact number of people they admit now, but they do not take in thousands of new students every year.

- It's expensive. At the time I'm writing this, it costs $300 a credit hour to attend, which is more than $10,000 a year. Plus, you need to pay for an apartment and food. To make matters worse, there are no scholarships or financial aid (which you can receive from a traditional college). My parents had to make some extreme financial sacrifices to let my brother attend.

- You had better be sure you want to program games. If you go to college and find that you don't like programming, you can switch majors. If you don't like the courses at DigiPen, you have to transfer to another school, and the courses you took most likely will not transfer with you.

To learn more about DigiPen and their programs, check out their Web site.

F I N D   I T

ONLINE

DigiPen Game Programming School:
http://www.digipen.edu

Finding the Jobs

The Internet is your best resource for finding game programming jobs. The Gamasutra Web site has lots of game development job listings. Many game development companies have job listings on their company Web sites.

To meet recruiters face to face, there's the Game Developers' Conference. It's an annual conference (usually held in March) in Silicon Valley where game developers meet to exchange information and schmooze. If you can afford to attend, the Game Developers' Conference is a good way to come into contact with companies looking to hire game developers.

F I N D   I T

ONLINE

Game Developers' Conference:
http://www.gdconf.com

Making Your Own Games

An alternative to working for a game development company is to start your own company and make your own games. By starting your own company, you don't have to worry about impressing employers. You can develop the types of games you want rather than working to fulfill someone else's vision. The freedom and power that owning your own company brings comes with a price. Owning your own company is a tremendous financial risk if you're using it as your sole source of income. If your game is a flop, you may not have enough money for food, clothing, and rent. In addition, as a company owner, you have to be concerned with things other than game development, such as paying bills, marketing, and accounting.

Finding a Team

Unless you have the rare multiple talents to program, create great visual art, and create stirring music, you will need to find people to help you make your game. I'm going to assume that you don't have millions of dollars to hire an in-house development team. Now you're probably wondering how you find a team.

The best situation is to have friends who have the talent to help you. These friends would be willing to be partner with you and develop the game without you having to pay them. When you sell the game, you split the revenues with your friends. By working with friends, you can keep your development costs low—plus you know the character of the people on your development team. You don't have to worry as much about somebody quitting three quarters of the way through the project.

I've seen tons of posts on Internet message boards asking for team members. The posts tend to sound like this: "I'm working on a really great game. I need programmers, artists, and musicians to help finish the game. I don't have any money to pay you, but when the game is finished, you'll get to split the profits." Don't make a post like this. Strangers are not going to want to work for free on your game. If they're not going to get paid, they're going to work on their own projects.

If you're going to get a stranger to do work for your game, have some money to offer him. Even if it's just a few hundred dollars plus a piece of the revenues, the financial commitment shows you're serious. For artwork, students are a good option for low-cost help. Students are willing to take less money to get experience. For my first game, I found a recent art school graduate to do the artwork for $1,500 and a royalty on every copy over 2,500 the game sold. This arrangement ended up being a lot less expensive than hiring a full-time employee or contracting a graphic design firm.

Before you meet with an artist, you must prepare by determining your artwork needs. Some things you should decide before meeting with the artist include

- The number of backgrounds, with a description of each. For a board game, this will be easy: You will have one background for the board. A fantasy role-playing game will require more backgrounds. At a minimum, you will want backgrounds for wilderness, towns, dungeons, and castles.

- The size of each background.

- The list of items, with a description of each for the artist. In a role-playing game, each character, monster, weapon, and magic item should be in the list. A military strategy game's list would include the game's units.

- If any of the game's items move, list the possible animation states for the item. For example, the main character in an action game may be standing, running, jumping, fighting, and crouching. If that character can use a number of different weapons, list the weapons he can use. The artist will have to draw the character fighting with each of the weapons.

- The number of frames for each animation state. How many frames of animation do you want for running, jumping, and fighting? More frames of animation look better, but it's more work for the artist (and probably more costly for you).

- The directions the characters can face. If the player can face up, down, left, and right, the artist has to draw the character facing in all those directions.

- The size of each of the game's items.

- The color depth for the backgrounds and items (8-bit, 16-bit, or 32-bit). Chapter 4, "Introduction to Macintosh Graphics," explains each of the color depths and their strengths and weaknesses.

- The file format for the graphics. Some popular graphics file formats are PICT, GIF, JPEG, and TIFF. For Mac games, the PICT file format is usually a good choice.

If you meet with a musician, you must do your homework as well and come up with a list of music and sound effects. In addition, you should figure out the sampling rate you want for the sounds and the file format you want to use to store the sounds. Chapter 10, "Sound," provides more detailed information on sampling rates and file formats.

I bet you didn't realize how many little details you had to be aware of just to have someone else create your game's graphics and audio. It's a lot of preparation to do, but it's a good idea to know your game's art and sound needs before you meet with an artist or musician to discuss the game. If you meet with an artist or musician and don't know what you want, he will think that you are an amateur and might not want to do business with you. You will look really stupid if you answer all his questions by saying, "I don't know." Knowing what you need tells the artist or musician that you've done your homework, and that will make a good impression on him. A detailed list of requirements will let the artist or musician know the amount of work you require, and he will be able to provide a better estimate of how long the work will take.

Landing a Publishing Deal

Whenever an interesting scandal occurs in Hollywood or Washington, it seems that somebody is selling their story for big money. You might be thinking, "I have a great idea for a game. Maybe a publisher will give me a bunch of money to turn my idea into a game." Dream on. The game industry does not buy game ideas the way movie studios buy stories.

To get a major publisher to give you a deal, you need one of two things: a track record for making hit games or a finished game. The odds are you haven't yet made a blockbuster game. If you want a publishing deal where the publisher funds the game's development, you'll have to work for a game development company that makes commercial games and get yourself a reputation first.

If you want a major publisher to publish your game, it had better run on Windows. Games that run only on the Mac do not sell enough copies for a major publisher to be interested. The company might publish a Mac/Windows hybrid CD game, but it must run on Windows or a game console for the publisher to be interested. It sounds harsh, but you must remember that the major publishers spend millions of dollars up front to develop their games. The games must sell hundreds of thousands of copies for the publisher to make any money on the game. I wish Mac games sold that well, but unfortunately they do not. Few Windows games sell that well either, but it doesn't stop the publishers from funding Windows games.

The previous paragraph may have terrified you about the Mac gaming market, but I would argue that the Mac is a better market for the new game developer than Windows. Windows may have 80 to 90 percent of the computer gaming market, but they also have 99 percent of the game developers, which means there is less competition writing Mac games. Game players with Macs are more hungry for original games than game players with Windows computers. Windows gamers can walk into any store that sells computer software and find shelves stacked with the latest games. The same store may not carry any Mac games, and if they do, they carry ports of old Windows games that cost more than the Windows version. If a new company writes an original game for the Mac, people will try the demo because of the lack of original Mac games. Assuming the game is good, they will buy it so the company will continue to make Mac games. If the same company develops a Windows game, it will probably be drowned out by all the other games crowding the market, and game players won't even be aware of the game's existence. With less competition, powerful hardware, and a market eager for new games, the Mac is a new game developer's dream.

When you have your game finished and you're shopping it around, it's best to avoid the big Mac publishers. The largest Mac publishers tend to port Windows games rather than publish original Mac games. Look for publishers on the Internet that publish original Mac games, such as Ambrosia , Delta Tao, Freeverse, and Spiderweb. See what kinds of games they publish. Would your game fit in with their game lineups? For example, Spiderweb Software publishes role-playing games. If you've written a role-playing game, Spiderweb is a good publisher to approach.

It's very difficult for a Mac game developer to get his game on retail store shelves. The publishers that can get a game on the store shelves focus on ports of Windows games; the publishers who are interested in original Mac games don't have the financial muscle to get games on the store shelves. Don't despair. There's always electronic distribution through the Internet.

Self-Publishing

A lot of people will tell you that publishing your own game is unfeasible, but a lot of times it's your only option. If no publishers want to publish your game, you'll have to do it yourself. It's also a fact that most publishers take 80 to 90 percent of the game's revenue, leaving with you with an income of 2 or 3 dollars for a game that sells for 30 or 40 dollars. If you write a smaller game that will sell only a few thousand copies, you have to publish it yourself to make any money.

Self-publishing will not get your game on the shelves at Comp USA, but you can use the Internet to sell your game. Build a Web site for your game where people can go to download it. You can have a Web site with your own URL (www.your-company.com) for $20 a month.

F I N D I T

ONLINE

Inside Mac Games:
http://www.insidemacgames.com
MacGamer: http://www.macgamer.com
Kagi: http://www.kagi.com

Write some press releases hyping up your game and send them to Internet gaming sites. Macintosh gaming sites such as Inside Mac Games and MacGamer are interested in any Mac games, and the press release will help bring people to your site. You can use a service like Kagi or eSellerate to handle

FIND IT

ONLINE

eSellerate: http://www.esellerate.net

credit card orders. Self-publishing using these services allows people to buy your game online, and you get to keep 85 percent of the game's sale price.

The question you must ask yourself is whether you can handle the business side of publishing. Are you willing to answer customers' technical support questions? Can you write press releases? Can you manage a business and its finances? If the answer to these questions is no, find somebody else to publish your game. If the answer is yes, you're ready for self-publishing.

Advice for New Game Developers

After reading this book, you'll be eager to start developing your own games. The following sections provide some pointers for programmers embarking on their first game project.

Pick a Project You Can Handle

Many first-time game developers want to make a masterpiece for their first game. They play big-budget computer and console games and want to make a game that blows those games away. Although the desire to make an outstanding game is commendable, resist the urge to compete technically with the big boys for your first game. Commercial games have teams of programmers, artists, musicians, and designers working full time for two years on a title. Their games' budgets run into the millions of dollars, and it shows when you play them.

Now compare your own situation. Chances are you're the only programmer working on the game, and you're probably working part-time on it while going to school or working at a "real" job. If you're lucky, you have someone to do your artwork and somebody else to make your music. You're going to have a difficult time going head-to-head with John Carmack and id Software. Plan a smaller game that you have a chance to finish. Keep in mind that a *smaller* game does not necessarily mean a *bad* game. *Tetris* and *Bomberman* are small games, but they are better than many games with huge budgets. Good first-game projects include the following:

- Board games
- Card games
- Side-scrolling platform games such as the old *Super Mario Brothers* games
- 2D shooters reminiscent of the old arcade games *Asteroids*, *Centipede*, and *Space Invaders*

Choose a Project You Enjoy

That statement sounds obvious, but you'd be surprised how many people work on projects they don't enjoy. If you're creating an entire game from scratch, it will take a minimum of a year—and as long as several years—to finish. You're going to have to play your game thousands of times to make sure that it plays perfectly. If you don't like the type of game you're developing, it's going to be very difficult to stay interested long enough to finish making the game.

Choose a game genre you enjoy playing. If you've played enough games of that type, you'll already know what it takes to make a great game in that genre. If you love strategy games, make a strategy game. If you hate racing games, don't make one just because you think the Mac needs a racing game.

Use Placeholder Assets at First

It can take a while to find the right people to help develop the artwork and music for your game. If you don't start working on the game until you get the art and music, you'll end up wasting a lot of time. Start developing your game, using placeholders for the art and music. Placeholder art is crude backgrounds and characters you can whip up in a couple of hours. Placeholder music might involve sampling one of your favorite compact discs. Record yourself saying the word *boom* as a placeholder for an explosion sound effect. When you find an artist and composer who provide you with the final artwork and music, you can get rid of the placeholders and use the final assets.

Design First

Before you sit down in front of your Mac and start cranking out code, do some design first. It's a lot easier to figure out that something won't work in the design phase than after writing the code. There's nothing more aggravating than having to rewrite some code because you didn't take the time to plan things before writing the code.

Figure out what gameplay elements your game will have. If you're writing an action or role-playing game, make a list of the enemies the player will encounter, the weapons he can use, and the items he can acquire. If you're writing a strategy game, make a list of the units in the game along with their strengths and weaknesses. After assembling a list of the elements you want in your game, use them to design the game's data structures (C language structures or C++ classes) and routines. Break up the programming tasks into small chunks so that you don't get overwhelmed. Implement one feature of the game at a time. When problems occur (believe me, they will occur) it will be easier for you to find the problem area than if you try to add five features at once.

Know the Lingo

To make sure that you know what I'm talking about when I mention Mac OS terms later in this book, take a look at Table 1-2, which contains a list of these terms.

Table 1-2   Mac Terminology

Term	Description
Carbon	A collection of Application Programming Interfaces (APIs) used to write programs that run on Mac OS 8, 9, and X.
Carbon-compatible	A Carbon-compatible program uses 100 percent Carbon code, meaning that it does not call old Mac Toolbox functions that did not make it into Carbon.
Cocoa	A class library used to develop Mac OS X programs and user interfaces.
Classic	A mode in Mac OS X that allows OS X to run older programs. Programs running in Classic mode look and behave like Mac OS 9.1 programs.
Running natively	A program that runs natively in Mac OS X looks and behaves like a Mac OS X program, complete with the Aqua interface, protected memory, and preemptive multitasking.
Pre-Carbon	Code that uses the Mac Toolbox, the predecessor to Carbon. Mac Toolbox programs run in Classic mode on Mac OS X.
Mac OS x.x and above	The designated code or technology that will run on Mac OS version x.x and later versions of the Mac OS. For example, a game that runs on Mac OS 8.6 and above will run on Mac OS 8.6, 9.0, 9.1, and OS X.

Summary

This chapter provided an introduction to a variety of topics. I began by describing the three models for Mac OS programming. The Mac Toolbox model lets you write code that will run on versions of Mac OS up to 9.1. Mac Toolbox code runs in Classic mode, which emulates Mac OS 9.1 on OS X. The Carbon model lets you use most of the functions you use for Mac Toolbox programming. Carbon code can run on Mac OS 8 and 9, and run natively in Mac OS X. The Cocoa model is an object-oriented class framework for writing Mac OS X programs. You can develop programs quickly in Cocoa, but you must program in Objective C or Java.

After introducing the Mac programming models, I moved on to introducing game programming. I described the elements that make up a computer game. After that, I gave some tips for new game developers on how to get a job as a game programmer and how to sell their games. Finally, I gave some advice for those of you working on your first game. In the next chapter, you will enter the magical world of the compiler, where you will learn how to compile, run, and debug programs.

CHAPTER 2

PROJECT BUILDER

It sounds strange for me to be writing a chapter on Project Builder instead of CodeWarrior when a 30-day demo of CodeWarrior appears on the book's CD-ROM, but I have my reasons. First, almost every person running Mac OS X has Project Builder (some Macs that shipped with Mac OS X did not include a Developer Tools CD-ROM), and the fact that Project Builder is free means more people will develop with Project Builder than CodeWarrior. Second, Project Builder's documentation is much worse than CodeWarrior's, which necessitates a chapter on using Project Builder. The CodeWarrior demo on the CD-ROM comes with extensive documentation that will get you up to speed on CodeWarrior quickly.

Project Builder is Apple's Integrated Development Environment (IDE) for developing C, C++, Objective C, and Java programs on Mac OS X. You probably have a Developer Tools CD-ROM with Project Builder on it if you use Mac OS X. Every copy of Mac OS X on store shelves includes the Developer Tools CD-ROM, and Apple started shipping the Developer Tools CD-ROM with every new Mac in 2002. Should you be one of the unlucky people who bought a Mac that shipped with OS X, but no Developer Tools CD-ROM, you can sign up as an online member of

Apple's Developer Connection and download the Developer Tools for free or you can pay the shipping and handling for Apple to ship you a Developer Tools CD-ROM. If you've already installed Project Builder and know how to use it, you can skip this chapter.

F I N D   I T

ONLINE

Apple's Developer Page:
http://www.apple.com/developer

If you haven't installed the developer tools, read Appendix A, "Installing Programs from the CD-ROM," for instructions on how to install them. If you do not run any version of Mac OS X, you must find another compiler for your programs, such as CodeWarrior, and you can skip this chapter.

Creating Your First Project

Project Builder makes it very easy to have a program up and running quickly. To test this ease, run Project Builder and select New Project from the File menu. The New Project dialog box shown in Figure 2-1 will appear. Choose Carbon Application as the type of project you want to build and click the Next button.

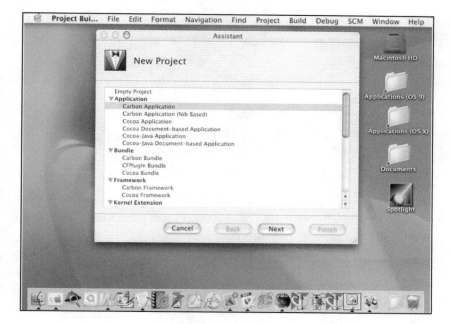

Figure 2-1

Choosing a project type in Project Builder

The New Carbon Application dialog box shown in Figure 2-2 appears. Type a name for the project you are going to create; I typed the name MyFirstProject. Then click the Set button to choose the location on disk where you want to store the project. Finally, click the Finish button to create the Project Builder project.

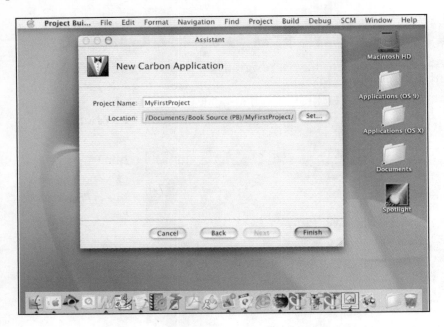

Figure 2-2

Specifying your project's name and location in Project Builder

After you create the project, a project window like the one in Figure 2-3 appears on the screen. From the Build menu, choose Build and Run. Project Builder will compile the source code files, link them, and run the program.

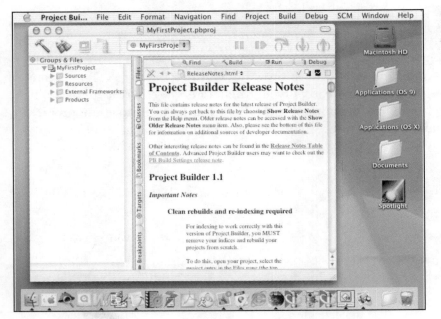

Figure 2-3

A Project Builder project window

When your program runs, it will open in a window that looks like the one in Figure 2-4. Without writing any code, you just created a working program in Project Builder. It's not much of a program, but you cannot expect too much from a program for which you didn't do any programming.

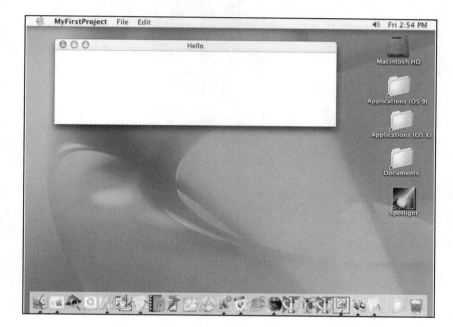

Figure 2-4

The program you built.

Your First Real Project

Now it's time to create a program that actually does something. We're going to build the program I wrote for Chapter 4 of this book. The program creates a window the size of the screen and draws a picture into that window. To begin, we must create another project in Project Builder, which involves the following steps:

1. Choose New Project from the File menu.
2. Choose Carbon Application as the project type and click the Next button.
3. Name your project (I named my project Chapter02).
4. Select the storage location for your project and click the Finish button.

Figure 2-5 shows the project window that Project Builder creates along with the files that Project Builder includes when it starts a Carbon Application project.

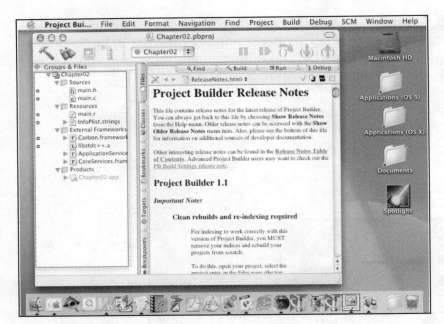

Figure 2-5

The Project Builder project window after creating a Carbon Application project.

You may be wondering what type of project is best for the game you want to develop. Project Builder offers you choices in several project categories: Application, Bundle, Framework, and Kernel Extension, among others. You want to create an application project for your game. The type of application project you choose depends on the technology you want to use for your game. If you use Carbon for your game and make your user interface with Interface Builder (a program that comes with Apple's Developer Tools to create user interfaces visually), choose the Carbon Application (Nib Based) option. If you use Carbon but not Interface Builder, choose the Carbon Application option. If you're writing your game in Objective C, choose Cocoa Application. If you're writing your game in Java, choose Cocoa-Java Application. All the projects I make in this book will be Carbon Application projects.

Creating Source Code Files

When programming a game, sooner or later you must create a source code file and type some source code in the file. To create a source code file, choose New File from the File menu; you'll see a dialog box with a list of file types you can create, as shown in Figure 2-6. Choose either Empty File or C++ File (Choosing C++ File will create some introductory comments with the program name and copyright notice) and click the Next button.

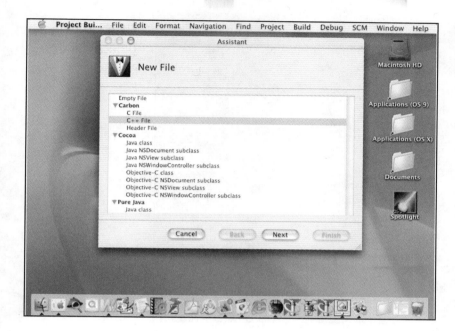

Figure 2-6

The New File dialog box

After clicking the Next button, you will see the dialog box shown in Figure 2-7. Type the name you want to give the file (I used main.cpp) in the File Name text box. Project Builder will use the location of your project as the default location. If you want to change the location of the file, click the Set button and choose the project to which you want to attach the file you are creating. The Add to Project popup menu contains a list of open projects. Choose the project you created in the last section (Chapter02 in my case) and click the Finish button.

Figure 2-7

Specifying a file's name and location in Project Builder

The name of the file you just created appears in the Groups & Files list on the left, and the file appears in the project window on the right so that you can type in it. Figure 2-8 shows what the file would look like if you chose to create a C++ file; if you chose to create an empty file, the file would be blank.

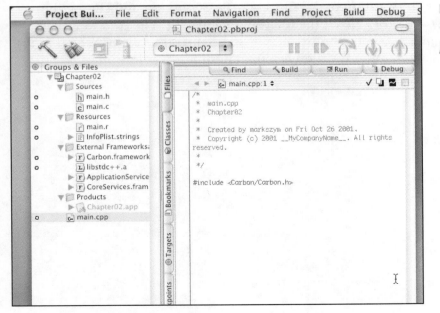

Figure 2-8

The source code file in the project

Now we have to type some source code. If you made a C++ file, delete the following line:

```
#include <Carbon/Carbon.h>
```

Other files that we will be adding to the project later in this chapter include the Carbon header file, therefore we don't need to include it in the main.cpp file. Type the following code in the editor and then save the file:

```
#ifndef GAME_APP

        #include "GameApp.h"
#endif

int main (void)
{
        GameApp theGame;

        theGame.InitApp();
        theGame.EventLoop();
        theGame.CleanUpApp();

        ExitToShell();
        return 0;
}
```

If that's too much typing for you, I included the file lazymain.cpp (which contains the preceding code) on the CD-ROM that accompanies this book. You can cut and paste the code from the lazymain.cpp file into the file you are creating in Project Builder.

Adding Files to a Project

Obviously, it's going to take more than six lines of code to make a full-screen window and draw a picture into it; we'll have to add some files to our project. Before we can add files to our project, we must first remove some of the files that Project Builder created when it made the project. In this example, we must remove the files main.h and main.c from the Sources folder along with the file main.r from the Resources folder. To remove these files from the project, click the file name in the Groups & Files list on the left side of the window and choose Edit, Delete. Project Builder will display a dialog box asking whether you want to remove the files from disk as well. You can go either way; it doesn't really matter whether you remove the files from disk in this case. For files you create, you most likely will not want to remove the files from disk.

Second, we must find the files we want to add to the project. On the CD-ROM that comes with this book, I put the following files in the Chapter02 folder:

- `Blitter.cpp`
- `Blitter.h`
- `GameApp.cpp`
- `GameApp.h`
- `GameOffscreenBuffer.cpp`
- `GameOffscreenBuffer.h`
- `Chapter02 Resources`

Copy these files to the folder containing your project. You can give the `Chapter02 Resources` file a new name to match the name of your project, if you want.

Now we're ready to add the files to the project in Project Builder. To do this, choose Add Files from the Project menu, navigate to the directory containing the files you copied from the CD-ROM, and select the files. The newly added files should appear at the bottom of the Groups & Files list on the left side of the project window (see Figure 2-9).

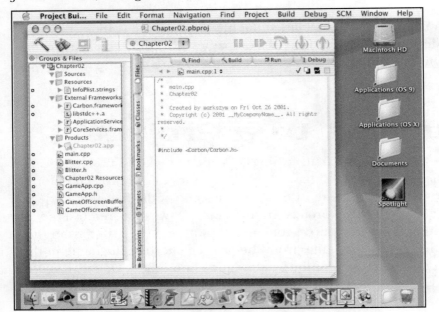

Figure 2-9

The project window after adding files to it

We should add a new folder in which we can store the header files to keep them separate from the source code files. To add a new folder, choose New Group from the Project menu. This command creates a new folder titled New Group, from which you can rename Headers. Now you can drag all the files you added that end in `.h` to the Headers folder; drag all the files that end in `.cpp` to the Source folder. Drag the `Chapter02 Resources` file (or whatever you decided to name it) to the Resources folder. Now our project is neatly organized, as you can see in Figure 2-10.

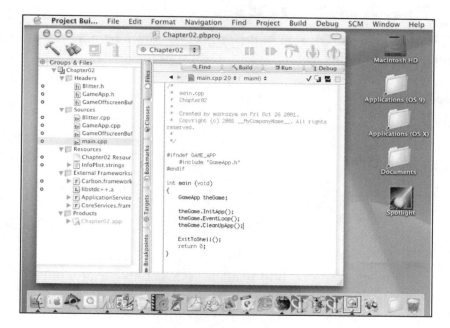

Figure 2-10

A perfectly organized project window

Adding Frameworks to a Project

To hide the menu bar so that the window covers the whole screen, we will use QuickTime, Apple's toolkit for multimedia applications. To use QuickTime functions in our program, we must add the QuickTime framework to our project. Mac OS X uses frameworks for its technologies. The framework contains all the libraries and header files you need to use a particular technology in your programs. For example, the QuickTime framework contains all the QuickTime header files and libraries. Using frameworks makes it easy for programmers; just add the framework to the project, and you're ready to code. In Mac OS 8 and 9, you must add each individual library you want to use in your games. It's easy to forget one library, and that will lead to a slew of compiler error messages. Select Add Frameworks from the Project menu to display a list of frameworks installed on your computer. Choose the framework `QuickTime.framework`; it will appear in the list of files on the left side of the project window. Drag the file into the Frameworks folder.

Contents List Tabs

If you look at the list of files on the left side of the Project Builder screen, notice the five tabs running from top to bottom:

- Files
- Classes
- Bookmarks
- Targets
- Breakpoints

These tabs let you look at various aspects of your project. The next few sections detail each of these tabs.

Files Tab

The Files tab is the tab with which you're most familiar at this point because we haven't looked at any other tab. The list you see contains all the files involved with the project: header files, resource files, source code files, and frameworks. To edit a file, select it in the Contents list. The contents of the file will appear in the project window on the right side of the screen, and you will be able to type in the file. If you double-click a file in the list, Project Builder will create a separate window for the file in which you can type source code. Creating a new window makes it easy to look at two files at once, one file in the project window and one file in the new window.

Classes Tab

Click the Classes tab to display Project Builder's class browser, which contains a list of all the classes in your project. If you do your programming in C, you will have no use for the class browser because the C language has no classes. However, C++,

Objective C, and Java programmers will benefit from the class browser because it allows you to look at any member function or data member for your game's classes.

If you click the Classes tab and look at the class browser right now, you will notice that it is empty. You must build your project to generate a list of classes for the class browser. Figure 2-11 shows Project Builder's class browser for the completed project we're making in this chapter.

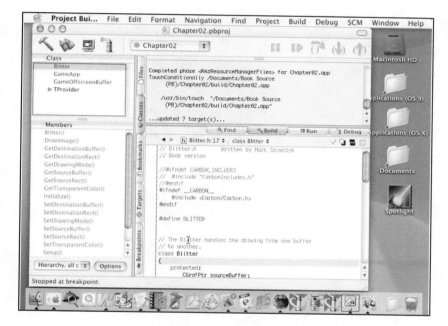

Figure 2-11

Project Builder's class browser

By default, Project Builder's class browser displays only member functions of a class, but not data members. Click the Options button at the bottom of the window to display a dialog box that lets you choose what information will appear in the class browser.

Bookmarks Tab

If you click the Bookmarks tab, Project Builder will display a list of bookmarks for your project. Bookmarks work like bookmarks in an Internet browser; they list the files you use often. If you have a project with lots of files, bookmarks provide a way for you to quickly access the files you use most.

At this point in the development of our project, the Bookmarks list is empty because we haven't added any files to the bookmark list. To add a bookmark, click the Files tab and select a file. From the Navigation menu, choose the Add to Bookmarks option. This command adds the file you selected to the Bookmarks list. Figure 2-12 shows that I bookmarked the `GameApp.cpp` file. You can also bookmark multiple locations in the same file so you can quickly reach a particular line in the file. To bookmark a particular line in a file, move to the line you want to bookmark and choose the Add to Bookmarks option in the Navigation menu.

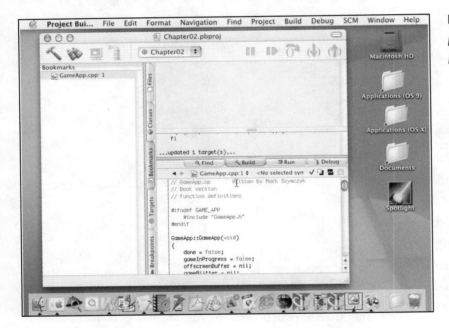

Figure 2-12

Project Builder's Bookmarks list

Targets Tab

Clicking the Targets tab brings up your project's Targets list, which should consist of one target at the moment: the name of your project. The Targets list lets you edit your project's settings, such as code optimization settings, search paths, compiler options, and linker options. If you click a target in the list, you can edit the target's settings. When you do so, the project window will look similar to the one shown in Figure 2-13.

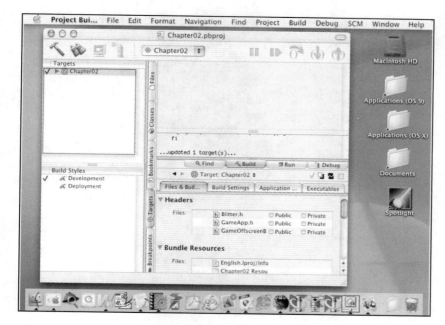

Figure 2-13

*Project Builder's
Targets list*

There are four categories of project settings, represented by the tabs above the word Headers in Figure 2-13:

- Files & Build Phases
- Build Settings
- Application Settings
- Executables

Files & Build Phases

The Files & Build Phases category tab displays a list of all the files in the project. Figure 2-14 shows the list for the project we're developing in this chapter. As you can see, there are five categories of files, and Table 2-1 describes them.

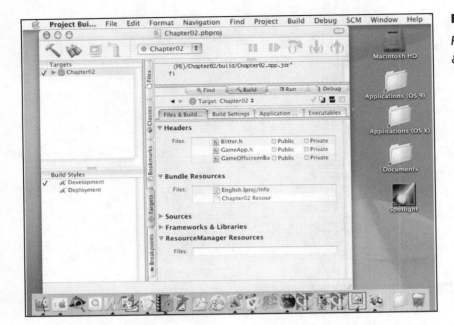

Figure 2-14

Project Builder's Files & Build Phases tab

Table 2-1   Files & Build Phases File Categories

Category	Description
Headers	The header files you created for the project
Bundle Resources	Files to copy into the application's resource folder
Sources	The source code files for your project
Frameworks & Libraries	External frameworks and libraries you compile with your source code
ResourceManager Resources	Resource files that use the Resource Manager to access the resources in the file. Refer to Chapter 15, "Files," for details about the Resource Manager.

In Figure 2-14, notice that the resource file we added to the project, Chapter02 Resources, appears in the Bundle Resources category. We must move the resource file to the ResourceManager Resources list if the program is to run properly. If we keep the resource file in the Bundle Resources category, the program will launch and then quit immediately. That's because our program expects its resources (window, picture, and menus) to be automatically loaded when the application loads, either as the resource fork of the application file or as a resource file that shares your application's name (depending on your linker settings) . If we keep the resource file Chapter02 Resources in the Bundle Resources category, the resources will not automatically load. The program will look for the program's resources (window, picture, and menus) and not find any resources. The program will be unable to find the window to load from disk, forcing the program to quit. To move the resource file, drag it from the Bundle Resources category to the ResourceManager Resources category, and everything should work properly.

I am sure you are wondering which resource files should go in the Bundle Resources area and which should go into the ResourceManager Resources area. Nib files (files that you will have if you use Interface Builder to construct your user interface) go in the Bundle Resources area. External files like QuickTime movie files, sound files, and graphics files (JPEG, TIFF, and PICT files) also should go in the Bundle Resources area. Resource files you create with a resource editor like ResEdit or Resorcerer belong in the ResourceManager Resources section. Resource files you create with Rez (a resource compiler that lets you create resources that look remarkably like C language structs) also belong in the ResourceManager Resources section. As a rule of thumb, if the file stores all of its data in resources, place it in the ResourceManager Resources section. If not, place it in the Bundle Resources section.

Looking at the Headers category in Figure 2-14, I'm sure that you noticed the Public and Private check boxes next to each header file. Those check boxes let you determine who can access and modify the header files. The check boxes matter only on Framework projects and only if multiple programmers are working on the project; you can give the junior programmers public access to the files on which they're working and mark the other header files as private to keep them away from header files they shouldn't be touching. Because we are creating an Application project, we do not need to worry about the Public and Private check boxes.

By default, Project Builder builds projects in the order listed in Table 2-1: Headers, Bundle Resources, Sources, Frameworks & Libraries, and finally Resource Manager Resources. This build order should work well for you, but you can change the order if you wish. To change the build order, click the name of one of the five phases (Headers, Bundle Resources, Sources, Frameworks, or Libraries) and drag it to where you want it to be built. Project Builder builds the phases from top to bottom in the Files & Build Phases window.

Build Settings

The Build Settings tab contains the settings for compiling and linking your project. Figure 2-15 shows you the Build Settings tab. It will look different on your computer because the settings do not fit on one screen. There are seven categories of build settings, as described in Table 2-2.

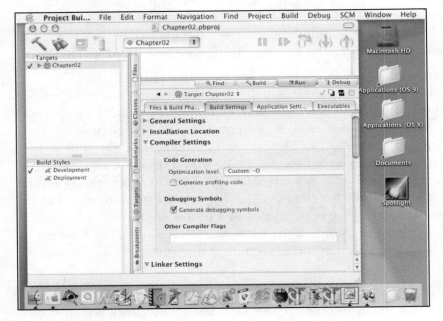

Figure 2-15

Project Builder's Build Settings tab

Table 2-2   Build Settings Categories

Category	Description
General Settings	This category lets you change the name of the application that Project Builder creates.
Installation Location	This category lets you specify where to install your game.
Compiler Settings	Compiler settings such as code optimization level
Linker Settings	Linker settings for your project
Headers to Implicitly Include	Precompiled headers for your project. For example, in a Carbon project, you might want to precompile the Carbon header file to speed up the compilation of your program.
Search Paths	Locations where Project Builder will look for header files, frameworks, and libraries
Build Settings	The total list of build settings. The other categories will fill these settings for you, so you shouldn't have to do anything with this category.

The category you will find most interesting is the Compiler Settings category. Use the Compiler Settings category to choose the optimization level for your code, to choose whether or not to generate profiling information, and to choose whether or not to generate debugging symbols. During development, you want no optimization, no profiling, and debugging symbols. When your code works, you will want to generate profiling information so that you can determine where your code runs slowly. Chapter 18, "Optimization," shows you how to use the profiling information that Project Builder generates. At that point, you will want to turn on compiler optimization to increase the speed of your code.

In the Linker Settings category, you have two ways to deal with resources. You can either put them in the data fork of a separate resource file, or you can place them in the resource fork of the application file. Normally, you should tell the linker to put resources in the data fork of a separate resource file. Project Builder will create a file called `ApplicationName.rsrc` (where `ApplicationName` is the name of your application) and place your resources in the newly created file. To learn more about all the possible compiler and linker settings, select the Developer Tools Help option from the Help menu. Then click the GNU C/C++/Objective C Compiler link, and your mind can be blown away by all the available settings for compiling and linking programs.

Application Settings

The Application Settings tab lets you customize information about your application. You can do such things as specify the version number of your game, the name of your game, and the icon for your game. Figure 2-16 shows as much of the Application Settings tab as can fit on the screen.

Version Numbers for Your Game

Software releases normally use a three number versioning system separated by decimal points with the following form:

major version.minor version.release

Games will usually have a major version of either 0 or 1. Versions of your game before you ship have a major version of 0, and versions after shipping the game have a major version of 1. An update to a game that would have a major version of 2 would end up being a sequel and a separate product. Other types of software (operating systems, Internet browsers, compilers) update the major version number when they ship a new version of their product.

Minor version numbers start at 0 and increment each time you add a feature to the game. When the major version changes, the minor version resets to 0. The release number starts at 0 and increments each time you make a minor update to the software, such as a bug fix. When the release number is 0, it does not appear in the version. When the minor version changes, the release number resets to 0.

Now let's look at an example. Suppose you develop a game "The Greatest Game Ever," and you're ready to release the single-player version of the game. The version number at the ship date will be

1.0

Remember that the release number does not appear in the version number when it is 0. After people purchase "The Greatest Game Ever," they find some bugs in the game, which you fix, then release a new version. The new version number will be

1.0.1

Suppose you then add a multiplayer option to "The Greatest Game Ever." The new version number will be

1.1

After releasing version 1.1, Apple releases an update to Mac OS that causes an error in your game, forcing you to release a bug fix to the game. The new version will be

1.1.1

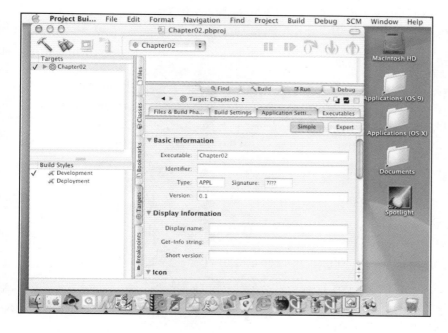

Figure 2-16

Project Builder's Application Settings tab

For now, you shouldn't have to change any application settings. When you write your game, you will want to change the signature from the four question marks that appear in Figure 2-16. The signature is a four-character code that uniquely identifies your game. Chapter 15, "Files," contains information on which character codes are valid as identifiers for your game. You attach this signature when saving games so that the player can launch your game by double-clicking the saved game file. Having a signature also keeps players from accidentally opening files not related to your game, like spreadsheet files and word processing documents.

Related to the Signature field is the Document Types category (which does not appear in Figure 2-16 because it didn't fit on the screen). This category lets you create a list of file types with which your application can work. For example, in a game, you would add your file type for saved game files to the Document Type list. The Project Builder documentation explains how you add document file types to an application.

Executables

The Executables tab lets you specify information such as command-line arguments and the debugger to use. As you can see from Figure 2-17, there are five different tabs in the Executables tab: Arguments, Env Vars, Source Dirs, Debugger, and Runtime. The Runtime tab is the one you are most likely to edit, which is why I chose the Runtime tab to display in Figure 2-17.

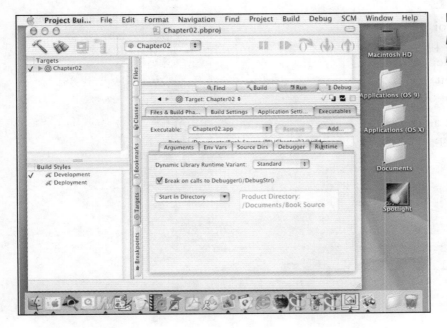

Figure 2-17

Project Builder's Executables tab

The Arguments tab lets you add command-line arguments that are passed to the application when it launches. Mac programs normally do not use command-line arguments, so you will not use this tab much.

The Env Vars tab allows you to add environment variables to your program. You shouldn't need to add environment variables to your game. Environment variables are useful if you want to write Unix programs with Project Builder, which we are not doing in this book.

The Source Dirs tab lets you add directories to the project. For example, if you have a directory of data files containing your game's graphics, sounds, and levels, you can add this directory to the project using the Source Dirs tab.

The Debugger tab allows you to choose the debugger you want to use. There are only two options: Gdb (GNU debugger) and Java Debugger. We're not programming in Java, so we'll use Gdb, which is the default choice.

The Runtime tab lets you choose a dynamic runtime library and the starting directory for your program. Your dynamic runtime library choices are Standard, Debug, and Profile; you will usually choose Standard or Debug. Use the Standard library for normal cases, the Debug library for debugging, and the Profile library for profiling.

Breakpoints Tab

Click the Breakpoints tab to display a list of breakpoints you have set in any source code files in your project. You set a breakpoint on a line of code; when you run the program in the debugger, the program will stop executing momentarily at the line of code where you set the breakpoint. At this point, you can step through the code line by line in the debugger to see how your program is running.

Notice that there are no breakpoints in the list at the moment. I will show you how to add breakpoints to your program in the "Debugging" section later in this chapter.

Action Panel Tabs

The Project Builder has four Action Panel tabs running from left to right about a
third of the way down the project window:

- Find
- Build
- Run
- Debug

The next few sections provide details about the Action Panel tabs.

Find Tab

Click the Find tab to display a find window in the upper-right portion of the project window (see Figure 2-18). You can use the find window to find things such as
function and variable names in your project's files. You can find function names in
your source code files and in Apple header files. Not sure of the parameters that
the function CopyBits() takes? Type the word **CopyBits** in the Find text box, and
Project Builder will show you where CopyBits() appears in your source code and system header files. The function will appear in the header file Quickdraw.h, where you
can look at the parameters for CopyBits().

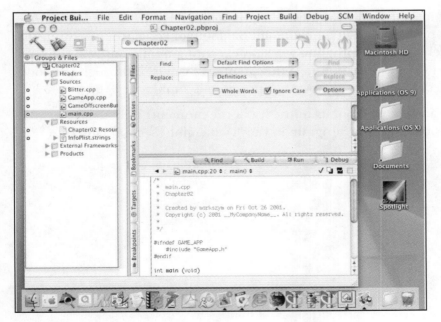

Figure 2-18

*Finding information in
Project Builder*

The find window also lets you replace text in a file. Do you want to change a variable name? Type the old variable name in the Find text box and the new variable name in the Replace text box, and you can replace any or all of the old instances of the variable name with the new one.

Build Tab

Click the Build tab to change the upper-right corner of the project window to the build window (see Figure 2-19). If you do this, you will get a blank gray window instead of the information shown in Figure 2-19. That's because you haven't compiled the project yet. When you compile your project, information about the build appears in the build window. The information about the build is lengthy (way too big to fit in the window) and difficult to read, showing you every header file and library included with the project, the status of each source code file's compile, and the status of linking each file to the project. What's important is that no error messages appear in the build window.

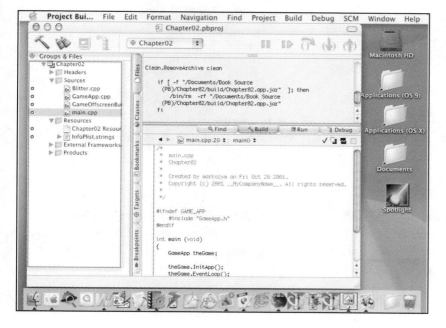

Figure 2-19

Project Builder's build window

Run Tab

Click the Run tab to change the upper-right corner of the project window to the run window (see Figure 2-20). In the figure, all that appears is a blank white window. The run window works with standard C and C++ console functions such as printf(), scanf(), cin(), and cout(). When your program calls the standard console functions, the results will appear in the run window. If you don't use these functions in your program, you won't be making any use of the run window.

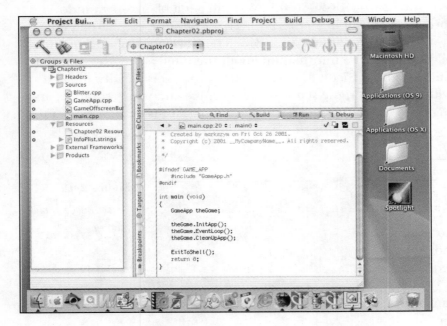

Figure 2-20

Project Builder's run window

Debug Tab

Click the Debug tab to change the upper-right corner of the project window to a debugger window (see Figure 2-21). You will see the debug window a lot if you use Project Builder to make your game. The debug window in Figure 2-21 is empty right now because we're not debugging, but it won't be empty for long.

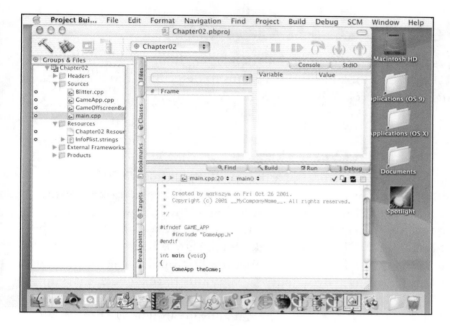

Figure 2-21

Project Builder's debug window

Compiling a Project

Now we're ready to compile our project. You have three choices: Build, Build and Run, and Build and Debug. The Build option compiles and links your program and creates an executable file that you can run from the Finder. The Build and Run option builds your program and launches it. The Build and Debug option builds your program and runs it in the debugger. You can choose your option from the Build menu, or you can use the toolbar at the top of the project window. The hammer icon in the upper-left corner will build the program. The computer monitor icon will build and run the program, and the spray can icon will build and debug the program. The whisk broom icon cleans the project, which means it removes any object code created by any previous compiles. When you clean the project, you must recompile every source code file so it's not something you want to do often.

After you build your program, you can use the Debug menu to run or debug the program. The Run Executable menu item runs the program; the Debug Executable menu item runs the program in the debugger.

Debugging a Program

Game programmers spend a great deal of time debugging their programs. The debugger is a tool they use to look at their programs to determine the location and cause of their game's errors. Project Builder includes a debugger, and I will show you how to use it in the next two sections.

Setting Breakpoints

Breakpoints let you pause the execution of a program at a particular line of code so that you can examine your program at the breakpoint. In Project Builder, you set a breakpoint at a particular line of code by clicking in the margin to the left of the line in the source code file. This action positions a black arrow pointing to the line and adds the breakpoint to the list of breakpoints. Figure 2-22 shows a sample breakpoint list. The Breakpoints list shows the file, the line number of the file, and whether or not the breakpoint is active. Active breakpoints have a check mark in the right column; inactive breakpoints do not have this check mark. You can move to the breakpoint line by clicking the line. You can activate an inactive breakpoint by clicking the Use column for the breakpoint. Clicking the Use column for an active breakpoint deactivates it, turning the black arrow to gray in the margin of the source code file. Selecting a breakpoint and choosing Delete from the Edit menu removes the breakpoint from the Breakpoints list and removes the arrow from the margin of the file.

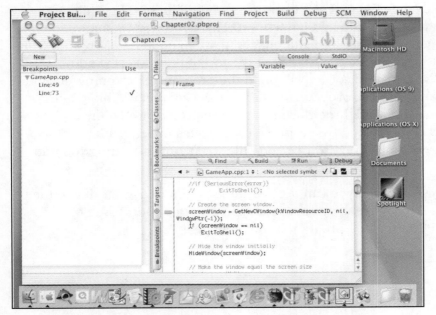

Figure 2-22

Project Builder's Breakpoints list

A Debugging Example

To demonstrate Project Builder's debugger, I've created a brief example that covers the basic elements of using the debugger. As a start, we need a breakpoint in our program. For this example, I want you to set a breakpoint at the following statement in the GameApp class's InitApp() function (It should be line 58 in the file GameApp.cpp):

```
offscreenBuffer = new GameOffscreenBuffer;
```

Feel free to set any additional breakpoints in the program.

If you haven't built your project already, choose Build and Debug from the Build menu. Otherwise, select Debug Executable from the Debug menu. This command runs your program, stops at the breakpoint we set, and fills the debugger window with information about the program. Figure 2-23 shows the debugging window at the moment it hit the breakpoint.

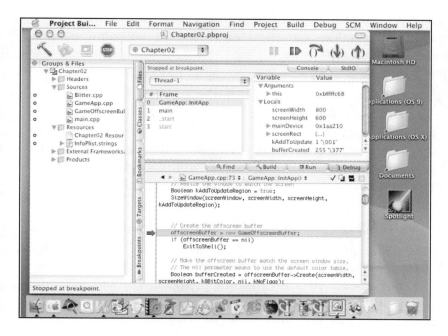

Figure 2-23

Project Builder's debugging window upon reaching a breakpoint.

Debugger Window Elements

The debugging window in Project Builder contains three elements: a thread viewer, a stack frame viewer, and a variable viewer.

The *thread viewer* allows you to view different threads of an application. Our program has only one thread, so the only choice is Thread-1.

The *stack frame viewer* lets you view the stack frame, which contains the call chain of functions. The top of the stack contains the current function. The second element is the function that called the current function. The third element is the function that called the second element, and so on.

In our example, the InitApp() function in the GameApp() class resides at the top of the stack. Below that is the main() function that calls InitApp(). If you click main() in the stack frame viewer, the main.cpp window will open, and the following statement will be highlighted:

```
theGame.InitApp();
```

This makes sense because we set the breakpoint at a line inside the InitApp() function. The two start() functions at the bottom of the stack have nothing to do with our code. Clicking them won't do anything.

The *variable viewer* lets you view the contents of all your variables. Let's see what the value of the variable offscreenBuffer is before we allocate memory for it. To do this, click the triangle next to the variable this (the second line from the top). This action displays the variable name protected. Click the triangle next to protected to display more variables. The third variable from the top should say offscreen, which is the offscreenBuffer variable (the full name doesn't fit in the window). Notice that the value is zero, which means that we have a null pointer right now.

Debugger Window Navigation Buttons

Before we do any actual debugging, let's go over the five debugging navigation buttons that appear in the upper-right corner of the project window. The first button is the pause button, which pauses a currently running program. The second button is the continue execution button, which resumes a paused program. Games have thousands of lines of code, and stepping through an entire game line by line can be excruciatingly slow. Pressing the continue execution button runs the program and stops at the next breakpoint you set.

The third button (the arrow over parentheses) steps over the current line of code. If the current line of code calls another function, the debugger will execute the function and move to the next line of code. The fourth button (the downward-pointing arrow in parentheses) steps into a function call. If the current line of code calls a function, stepping into the function will take you into the newly called function. The last button (the upward pointing arrow in parentheses) steps out of a function and moves to the function that called the current line's function.

Consider a current line of code that looks like this:

```
CallAFunction();
```

The next line of code looks like this:

```
NextLine();
```

Stepping over the current line moves the debugger to the statement NextLine(). Stepping into the function will move you into the CallAFunction() function so that you can step through the code in that function. If you want to jump out of the CallAFunction() function, do so by clicking the button on the far right. This action will take you to the statement NextLine().

Stepping Through the Code

Let's begin by stepping over (click the middle debugging button) the function to allocate memory for an offscreen buffer. Notice that the offscreenBuffer variable's value changed and is now red. This is a good thing. It means that the computer has allocated the buffer. Now step over again. You should be at the following line of code:

```
if (offscreenBuffer = nil)
```

Step over again, which will take you to the next line of code:

```
Boolean bufferCreated = offscreenBuffer->Create(screenWidth, screenHeight,
                             k8BitColor, nil, kNoFlags);
```

I'm tired of stepping over functions. Three times is the limit for me. Let's step into a function by clicking the fourth button. This action will transfer you to the GameOffscreenBuffer class's Create() function. Now click the last button to step out of the function; we're back in the InitApp() function. If you want to step through any more code, feel free to do so; but if you want to see the program run, click the second button. Click the application's button in the Dock (when the program launches in the debugger, its icon appears in the Dock, the collection of icons that appear on the bottom of the screen in Mac OS X) to run the program, choose Start from the File menu; a picture covers the entire screen. Press the Esc key to bring back the menu bar.

Summary

This chapter introduced Project Builder, Apple's program for developing programs on Mac OS X. We covered basic Project Builder tasks such as creating projects, creating source code files, adding files to projects, compiling programs, running programs, and debugging programs.

In addition to learning how to perform basic programming tasks in Project Builder, we also learned about the Project Builder development environment. Project Builder's Contents list lets you access source code, view classes, bookmark frequently used files, set breakpoints in your program for debugging purposes, and edit project settings. Project Builder's Action tabs let you search for text in your source code listings as well as build, run, and debug programs.

For more information on Project Builder, choose Project Builder Help from the Help menu. In Project Builder, you can also find documentation on other developer tools, Carbon function calls, and core OS X technologies. It's really nice to be able to look at documentation without having to leave Project Builder.

CHAPTER 3

C++ FOR C PROGRAMMERS

In the game development community, most programmers write their games in either the C or C++ programming languages. Because this book is about game programming, I had two choices for the programming language to use in the book. I chose to use C++ because it better suits the way I program. My decision to use C++ doesn't mean that C is a bad programming language. If you want to use C, or any other language, to program your games, go ahead. When I made the decision to use C++ in the book, I realized that readers would know C, but be unfamiliar with C++. I want everybody who reads this book to be able to understand the material in the book, including the source code. As a service to all the readers who are not fluent in C++, I wrote this chapter to show you enough about C++ so that you'll be able to follow the source code examples in this book.

C++ is a superset of the C language, as Figure 3-1 shows. This means that C++ contains the entire C language and adds to it. Don't forget all the C programming you have learned; it still applies when you program in C++. You still declare variables, write functions, and have if-then-else statements and loops. This chapter describes some of what C++ adds to the C language.

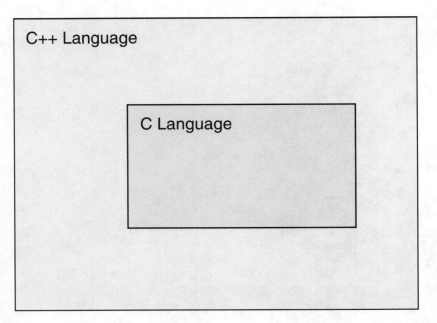

Figure 3-1

The relationship between C and C++

Structured vs. Object-Oriented Programming

In the software development world, companies use development *methodologies*. Methodologies make it easier for developers to manage, understand, debug, and maintain the programs they write. The two major programming methodologies are *structured programming* and *object-oriented programming*. Because game development is a portion of the software development world, the following sections explain both the structured and object-oriented programming methodologies.

Structured Programming

If you're programming in C, you're most likely using structured programming techniques. (If you're not, you should be.) What the structured programming model does is break up a large program into two parts: data and subroutines. Breaking up the large program into smaller subroutines makes the code modular and easier to understand and modify. The subroutines work with, modify, and manipulate the data. The data and the subroutines are separate in structured programming.

In the C language, you would use structures to store your game data and functions for your subroutines. In a game, you might use a GameSprite structure like this one to store your sprites:

```
struct GameSprite
{
        int worldX;
        int worldY;
};
```

The functions for your game might look like this:

```
void DrawSprite(GameSprite* theSprite);
void MoveSprite(GameSprite* theSprite, int amountToMove);
```

Obviously, a real game using sprites would have more in the GameSprite structure than I have shown here, but I'm simplifying things to make my explanations easier to understand.

The subroutines you write using the structured programming methodology can contain one of three components. The first component is *sequences*, which are sets of statements executed in order. Assignment statements and function calls are C language examples of sequences, as you can see in the following sample code:

```
worldX = 30;
worldY = 50;
DrawSprite(mySprite);
```

The second component of structured programming is *selections*. A selection is a control structure that executes statements conditionally. C language examples of selections are if-then-else statements and switch statements.

The final component of structured programming is *iterations*. An iteration is a control structure that executes statements multiple times. C language examples of iterations include for loops and while loops.

People have written entire books about structured programming; obviously this short introduction hasn't exhaustively covered the topic of structured programming. But I am sure you're not too upset, because this is a game programming book.

Object-Oriented Programming

Rather than working with data and subroutines, object-oriented programming works with objects. Objects can contain both data and subroutines. Object-oriented programming provides several advantages over structured programming.

- **Abstraction**—Abstraction lets you think of your program in terms of the problem you're trying to solve instead of in computer science terms. By using object-oriented programming for your game, you can think of your game in terms of game-specific entities, such as players, enemies, and levels rather than in computer science terms, such as arrays, pointers, and linked lists.

- **Encapsulation**—Object-oriented programming encapsulates both data and subroutines into an object. The only way to manipulate the data in the object is through the object's subroutines. Encapsulation protects the object's data from unauthorized access, making your code more stable.

- **Inheritance**—Inheritance allows an object to inherit the data and subroutines of another object. If object A inherits from object B, you just have to write the code in object A where object A differs from object B, saving you time as a programmer.

- **Polymorphism**—Polymorphism allows one subroutine to be implemented in different ways in different classes. C++ uses virtual functions to apply polymorphism. You can learn more virtual functions in the section "Virtual Functions" later in this chapter.

In the C++ language, you use classes to define your objects. A C++ class works like a structure does in C language. The main difference is that you can put functions in a C++ class, whereas a C structure can contain only data.

Classes

Recall the C language structure and functions presented in the "Structured Programming" section earlier in this chapter. The C++ class equivalent looks like this:

```
class GameSprite
{
        protected:
                int worldX;
                int worldY;

        public:
                // Constructor
                GameSprite(void);

                // Destructor
                virtual ~GameSprite(void);

                // Accessors
                int GetWorldX(void);
                void SetWorldX(int x);

                int GetWorldY(void);
                void SetWorldY(int y);

                // Other member functions
                void Draw(void);
                void Move(int amountToMove);
};
```

Now let's create a GameSprite object by declaring a GameSprite variable:

```
GameSprite playerSprite;
```

The variable playerSprite is an object of the GameSprite class. Declaring a variable of a class creates an object of that class. GameSprite is the class and playerSprite is the object. The `worldX` and `worldY` variables are the data members of the `GameSprite` class, and the `Draw()` and `Move()` functions are the member functions of the `GameSprite` class.

To the C++ class, a member function is the same as a data field in a structure in C language. To draw the `playerSprite` object, you use the *dot operator* to access the `Draw()` function in the `GameSprite` class. The dot operator works like this:

```
playerSprite.Draw();
```

A C++ class has two major components: data members and member functions. There are three special instances of member functions: constructors, destructors, and accessors. The following sections describe these components of a C++ class.

Data Members

Remember that C++ classes contain both data and functions. The data variables of the class are the class's data members. C++ class data members are equivalent to the fields of a C language structure. Our `GameSprite` class has just two data members: `worldX` and `worldY`. The keyword `protected` means that outside classes (classes other than `GameSprite` that do not inherit from `GameSprite`) cannot directly access the contents of the data members. You'll learn more about the `private`, `protected`, and `public` keywords later in this chapter.

Member Functions: Constructors

When you create an object of a particular class, the compiler calls the class's constructor function. A *constructor function* has the same name as its class. You use the constructor to initialize the data members of the class. Here's an example of a constructor for our `GameSprite` class:

```
GameSprite::GameSprite(void)
{
        worldX = 0;
        worldY = 0;
}
```

A class can have more than one constructor. In our `GameSprite` example, we could add another constructor that has parameters that allow a program to pass initial values for the `worldX` and `worldY` data members:

```
GameSprite::GameSprite(int x, int y)
{
```

```
        worldX = x;
        worldY = y;
}
```

Suppose that we declare two sprite objects, like this:

```
GameSprite playerSprite;
GameSprite enemySprite(64, 32);
```

Because the `playerSprite` declaration did not include any parameters, the compiler would use the constructor with no parameters. The `playerSprite` object would have a `worldX` value of 0 and a `worldY` value of 0.

Because I supplied initial `worldX` and `worldY` values for the declaration of the `enemySprite` object, the compiler would use the second constructor. It would set `enemySprite`'s `worldX` value to 64 and its `worldY` value to 32.

Member Functions: Destructors

When you destroy an object of a particular class, the compiler calls the class's destructor function. A class's destructor function has a tilde (~) preceding the name of the class. If the class allocated any memory when it created the object, the destructor must dispose of the allocated memory. Because we don't allocate any memory in the `GameSprite` class, the `~GameSprite` destructor is empty.

```
GameSprite::~GameSprite(void)
{
}
```

You should declare your destructors to be *virtual functions*. That way if you create any subclasses, the memory will be disposed of properly. Suppose that you create a class, `GameItem`, that inherits from the `GameSprite` class. A `GameItem` object is both a `GameItem` and a `GameSprite` in this case. When you dispose of a `GameItem` object, you want to dispose of the `GameSprite` too so that you dispose of all the memory used by the `GameItem` object. If you declare the `GameSprite` class's destructor to be a virtual function, the compiler automatically calls the `GameSprite` destructor when it calls the `GameItem` destructor. Making all your destructors virtual functions ensures the proper disposal of every object's memory.

Member Functions: Accessors

Because the data members of our `GameSprite` class are `protected`, outside classes cannot directly access them through a statement like this one:

```
worldX = 50;
```

To access the data members of the GameSprite class, you must call accessor functions. Accessors are functions the programmer writes to provide a safe way to access the data members of a class. Accessors make it easy to make changes to the data members of the class. If you need to change your class's data members and you use accessors, all you need to modify is the accessor. Without accessors, you would have to wade through all your source code and make changes to reflect the change you made to that data member. To change the value of worldX to 50, you use a statement like this one:

```
SetWorldX(50);
```

Here are the accessor functions I wrote for the GameSprite class:

> **NOTE**
> You can use accessor functions in C, too. Accessor functions provide clean access to the fields of your C data structures.

```cpp
int GameSprite::GetWorldX(void)
{
        return worldX;
}

void GameSprite::SetWorldX(int x)
{
        worldX = x;
}

int GameSprite::GetWorldY(void)
{
        return worldY;
}

void GameSprite::SetWorldY(int y)
{
        worldY = y;
}
```

Member Functions: General

The functions declared inside a class are that class's member functions. Constructors, destructors, and accessors are special instances of member functions, but you can have member functions that are not constructors, destructors, or accessors. If the only member functions you could have were constructors, destructors, and accessors, using classes would be pointless. In the GameSprite example, the Draw() and Move() functions are examples of member functions. Here's the Move() function for the GameSprite class example:

```
void GameSprite::Move(int amountToMove)
{
        worldX = worldX + amountToMove;
}
```

The GameSprite:: reference preceding the Move() function tells the compiler that this is the Move() function for the GameSprite class. Other classes may have their own Move() functions; without the reference to the class, the compiler would have no way of knowing which Move() function belonged to which class.

Member functions have access to the class's data members without having to use accessor functions. The Move() function knows about the GameSprite class's worldX data member as well as all the other data members of the class. I don't have to pass the worldX member as a parameter to a member function. The member function can just use the worldX data member directly.

Inheritance

In C++, it's possible to create a class that inherits the members of another class. For example, we could make a GamePlayer class that inherits from the GameSprite class we created in the previous section. Here's how such a GamePlayer class would be created:

```
class GamePlayer: public GameSprite
{
        protected:
                int hitPoints;

        public:
                // Constructor
                Player(void);
```

```
// Destructor
virtual ~Player(void);

// Accessors
int GetHitPoints(void);
void SetHitPoints(int hp);
};
```

The new GamePlayer class has its own members and all the members of the original GameSprite class. The GamePlayer class has the data members worldX, worldY, and hitPoints. It has accessors for all three data members plus the Draw() and Move() functions from the GameSprite class. If you declared a variable player1 of type GamePlayer, the following statements would be legal:

```
player1.SetWorldY(100);
player1.Draw();
player1.Move(20);
```

Even though I did not declare the SetWorldY(), Draw(), and Move() functions in the GamePlayer class, I can use them because the GamePlayer class inherited these functions from the GameSprite class. You must remember that a GamePlayer object is both a GamePlayer and a GameSprite. Let me repeat that: *A GamePlayer object is both a GamePlayer and a GameSprite.* If you wrote a function that took a Game Sprite object as a parameter, you could call that function and pass a GameSprite object to it.

Now let me explain the following line:

```
class GamePlayer: public GameSprite
```

This line of code states that the new GamePlayer class *publicly inherits* from the original GameSprite class. When you create a class with public inheritance, the protected and public members of the original GameSprite class remain protected and public in the new GamePlayer class. In C++ terminology, GameSprite is known as the *base class* and GamePlayer is known as the *derived class* or the *subclass* of GameSprite.

The other type of inheritance is private inheritance. In *private inheritance,* all the members of the base class are private in the derived class, meaning that an outside class has no way of accessing the members the GamePlayer class inherited from the GameSprite class—not even by using the accessor functions. Private inheritance would cause big problems in this scenario. For a game, suppose that we have this

GamePlayer object:

`GamePlayer player1;`

Suppose that, in the main loop of the game (called from an outside `GameApp` class), we constantly read user input and move the player:

`ReadInput();`
`MovePlayer();`

In the `MovePlayer()` function, we want to use the `Move()` function the `GamePlayer` class inherited from `GameSprite` like this:

`player1.Move(howMuchToMove);`

But with private inheritance, the preceding statement is illegal and will generate a compiler error. With private inheritance, the `Move()` function is `private` in the `GamePlayer` class, and the game loop cannot access it because the game loop is outside the `GamePlayer` class. Now you can see why I chose to use public inheritance. With public inheritance, the `Move()` function is `public` in the `GamePlayer` class so the game loop can access it.

Virtual Functions

Closely related to inheritance is the topic of virtual functions. A *virtual function* is a member function in a class that can be redefined in any derived classes. Virtual functions allow a subclass to override member functions of its base class. You use virtual functions when a class hierarchy (a base class and its subclasses) performs the same high-level behavior but has different low-level implementations of that behavior.

As an example, let's create two subclasses, `GamePlayer` and `GameMonster`, from the `GameSprite` class. Suppose that we want to draw a `GamePlayer` object differently than we draw a `GameSprite` object. The high-level behavior, drawing, is the same, but the low-level details of drawing differ. To do this, we declare the `Draw()` function as `virtual` in the `GameSprite` class. Then, we declare a `Draw()` function in the derived `GamePlayer` class that has the same parameters as the `Draw()` function in the `GameSprite` class.

CAUTION

When declaring virtual functions, the return type and the parameters must be exactly the same in all the classes using that virtual function. If the return type or parameters differ, you have two different functions with the same name, not a virtual function.

Here's an example of the class declarations of a virtual function with unnecessary details omitted:

```
class GameSprite
{
        public:
                virtual void Draw(void);
};

class GamePlayer : public GameSprite
{
        public:
                // Notice that the return type and parameters are the
                // same as the GameSprite's Draw() function.
                virtual void Draw(void);
};

class GameMonster : public GameSprite
{
        // GameMonster uses GameSprite's Draw function
};
```

Now suppose that we declare objects of the GameMonster and GamePlayer classes, and draw them like this:

```
GameMonster myMonster;
GamePlayer player1;

myMonster.Draw();
player1.Draw();
```

Because we did not override the Draw() function in the GameMonster class, the myMonster.Draw() statement uses the GameSprite class's Draw() function. The player1.Draw() statement uses the GamePlayer class's Draw() function because we *did* override the Draw() function in the GamePlayer class.

It's possible for a subclass to call the base class's function as part of the overridden function. For example, if we want the GamePlayer class's Draw() function to do everything the GameSprite class's Draw() function does plus some extra stuff, we would write the GamePlayer class's Draw() function like this:

```
void GamePlayer::Draw(void)
{
```

```
                // Call the GameSprite's Draw function
                GameSprite::Draw();
                // Do extra stuff here
        };
```

TIP

To use virtual functions, you must declare the function `virtual` in the base class. You don't have to declare the function virtual in the derived class, but doing so makes it easier for you to determine which functions are `virtual` and which ones are not.

Private, Protected, and Public Keywords

All the data members and member functions of a C++ class have their own access levels. They can be `private`, `protected`, or `public`. Figure 3-2 shows the differences between `private`, `protected`, and `public` members of a class.

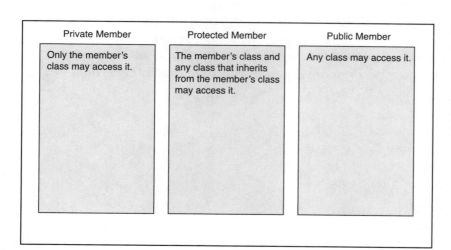

Private Member	Protected Member	Public Member
Only the member's class may access it.	The member's class and any class that inherits from the member's class may access it.	Any class may access it.

Figure 3-2

The differences between `private`*,* `protected`*, and* `public` *members of a class*

Also suppose that we have a `Player` class that inherits from the `GameSprite` class:

```
Class Player : public GameSprite
{
        protected:
                int hitPoints;
}
```

Finally, suppose that we have a `Game` class outside of the `GameSprite` and `Player` classes. Table 3-1 shows which classes can directly access the members of the `GameSprite` class. Note that the `speed` data member is `private`; only the `GameSprite` class can directly access it. Because `Player` is a subclass of `GameSprite`, it can directly access the `protected worldX` data member. Because the `Move()` function is `public`, all three classes can directly call it.

Table 3-1   Directly Accessing Members

Member	GameSprite	Player	Game
speed	yes	no	no
worldX	yes	yes	no
Move	yes	yes	yes

Dynamic Memory Allocation

Dynamic memory allocation differs from normal memory allocation in that dynamic memory allocation occurs while the program is running. The most common example of dynamic memory allocation is creating a variable-sized array. Suppose that you create an array to store your enemies in the game. In each level, you will have a different number of enemies, so it can be difficult to determine how many elements you'll need in the array before you run the game. By using dynamic memory allocation, you can count how many enemies are in a level when you load that level and make an array with enough elements to store all the enemies.

In the C language, you use the `malloc()` function to dynamically allocate memory; you use the `free()` function to free the dynamically allocated memory. Here's some C code that dynamically allocates a `GameSprite` structure and then frees the memory:

```
GameSprite* playerSprite;
playerSprite = malloc(sizeof(GameSprite));
free(playerSprite);
```

In the C++ language, you use the new() function to dynamically allocate memory and the delete() function to free the dynamically allocated memory. Here's the C++ equivalent of the preceding code example:

```
GameSprite* playerSprite;
playerSprite = new GameSprite;
delete playerSprite;
```

When allocating memory dynamically, you first need a pointer variable. Then you call the new() function using this form:

```
variable = new DataType;
```

When you dynamically create an object of a class, use your class name as the data type in the new() statement. To free the memory you allocated, call the delete() function on the pointer variable.

Remember from the "Member Functions: Constructors" section that you can have multiple constructors for a class. To call a specific constructor, pass the appropriate parameters when you call the new() function. In the "Member Functions: Constructors" section, I wrote two constructors for the GameSprite class. The first constructor takes no parameters and sets the worldX and worldY data members to 0. The second constructor takes two parameters, x and y, and sets the worldX and worldY data members to the values of x and y, respectively. Dynamically allocating a GameSprite object like this calls the constructor that takes no parameters and sets the worldX and worldY data members to 0:

```
playerSprite = new GameSprite();
```

Declaring the object like this calls the constructor that takes two parameters and sets worldX to 50 and worldY to 75.:

```
playerSprite = new GameSprite(50, 75);
```

To dynamically allocate an array, you call the new [ ] and delete [ ] functions. Here's some code that dynamically allocates an array of 12 GameSprite objects and then deletes the array:

```
GameSprite* enemySprites;
enemySprites = new GameSprite[12];
delete [ ] enemySprites;
```

Keep in mind that you have to call `delete [ ]` to delete an array of objects. Just calling `delete()` deletes just one object, not the whole array.

Converting the Book Code to C from C++

Nothing can start a flame war on Usenet or a mailing list like a question over which language is superior, C or C++. I prefer using C++ because I like object-oriented programming, and I find that it's easier to do object-oriented programming with C++ than it is with C. C++ has built-in language support for object-oriented programming, and C doesn't, which means you have to do extra work to do object-oriented programming in C. My selection of C++ over C is just my personal preference. Program in whatever language you feel comfortable using.

If you despise C++, you will want to convert the source code in this book to C. Here's what you'll have to do:

- Change all the classes in the header files to structures.
- Eliminate all the `public`, `private`, and `protected` keywords in the class declarations.
- Move all the class's functions outside the structure. You will have to change some function names to avoid having duplicate function names.
- Eliminate the constructor and destructor functions, replacing them with your own initialization and cleanup functions.
- Add a parameter of the appropriate structure to all your functions.
- In your source code files, eliminate the `<Class Name>::` reference preceding all the member functions.
- Because member functions have automatic access to the data members of a class, you may have to change some variables from `<data member>` to `<structure variable>.<data member>`.
- Change the end line `//` comments to C-style `/* */` comments.
- Move all the variable declarations to the beginning of the function. C++ lets you declare a variable anywhere in a function, but C does not.

Summary

In this chapter, I covered the basics of the C++ language—at least enough of it so that you can read and understand the source code examples in the rest of the book and on the accompanying CD-ROM. It would be impossible to completely cover the C++ language in this chapter; I've seen C++ programming books that are larger than this entire book. I'm sure that you would prefer to see more game programming information in this book than more C++ language information.

At this point, we are finished covering the preliminary material. We can move on to some actual game programming. In the next chapter, we start our game programming journey by discussing graphics.

CHAPTER 4

Introduction to Macintosh Graphics

Now that we've gotten the preliminary material out of the way, we're ready to begin our game programming odyssey. I can't think of a better place to begin than with graphics. This chapter introduces you to the fundamentals of Macintosh graphics programming using QuickDraw, the Macintosh graphics manager in Carbon. After finishing this chapter, you'll be able to make graphics appear on the screen, and you will have the foundation you need to implement graphics in your game.

Macintosh Color

The Macintosh stores color in an RGBColor structure. The structure consists of three 16-bit integers, one for the red component, one for the green component, and one for the blue component of the color. This 48-bit number represents a pure color, which QuickDraw must translate into a pixel value. How QuickDraw converts the RGBColor value to a pixel value depends on whether you have 8, 16, or 32-bit color pixels.

As the programmer, you get to decide what color depth your game will use, 8-bit color, 16-bit color, or 32-bit color. When making your decision, you have to decide between the number of colors you can display at one time and the size of your graphics. Higher color depths let you show more colors at once, but they take up a lot of space, and they take more time to draw. If you're going to have people download your game from the Internet, then you have to consider the size of your graphics. Not many people are going to want to download a 50 MB game, even if it does look magnificent in 32-bit color.

8-Bit Color Pixels

Table 4-1   8-Bit Color Lookup Table Entries

Entry	Color	Red	Green	Blue
0	White	65535	65535	65535
5	Yellow	65535	65535	0
17	Orange	65535	39321	0
102	Purple	39321	0	65535
255	Black	0	0	0

For game development purposes, 8-bit color is the minimum color depth you should use. QuickDraw stores 8-bit color in color lookup tables. Because 8-bit color uses color lookup tables, it is called indexed color. Each entry in the table is an index to an RGBColor structure. The 8-bit color lookup table contains 256 entries. Each entry contains an entry value and the RGBColor structure that makes up that entry value's color. Table 4-1 shows some entries in the standard 8-bit color table. The entry value in the color table is the pixel value when using 8-bit color. As you can see in Table 4-1, an orange pixel has the pixel value 17 when using the default color table.

Apple supplies a standard color table, which you will get by default if you create a window or offscreen buffer that uses 8-bit color. To see the colors in the default color table, run Apple Works (Claris Works for those of you with older computers) and create a painting with 8-bit color. Greens, reds, and purples dominate the default color table, but the default color table gives you a mix of colors that works well for general use. If the default color table does not fit your game's color scheme, you can create customized color tables. You would go into a resource editor like ResEdit or Resorcerer and create a color table (CLUT) resource. In the color table resource, you would fill out the 256 entries with the colors you want in your color table. In Chapter 16, "Putting It All Together," I show you how to work with color tables.

An 8-bit color picture would be stored in the computer as an array of numbers ranging from 0 to 255. The colors that show up on the screen depend on the active color lookup table. If you drew the picture where the value 74 represented orange and showed it in a program that used a color table where 74 represented pink, all the orange pixels you drew would show up as pink on the screen.

The advantage of 8-bit color is that drawings with 8-bit color take up less space. Each pixel in an 8-bit color drawing takes up one byte, which is half the memory a pixel in a 16-bit color drawing takes. Taking up less space means the computer has to move less data when drawing, which results in faster drawing.

> **NOTE**
>
> This fact bears repeating. An 8-bit color graphic consists only of a group of numbers ranging from 0 to 255. It does not contain any actual colors. The color lookup table determines what color the numbers represent, and thus determines what colors will appear on the screen.

The main disadvantage of 8-bit color is that you're limited to 256 colors at one time. However, it's possible to have one color table for each level in the game. If your game has 20 levels, for example, and each level used a completely different color table, your game would have 5120 different colors, but the game can still display only 256 colors at one time. Another disadvantage of 8-bit color is that Mac OS X is not a big fan of 8-bit color. The only way a native Mac OS X game can use 8-bit color is if the game hides the menu bar and takes over the entire screen. If your game uses standard Mac windows and has the menu bar visible, you must use 16-bit or 32-bit color if you want your game to run natively in Mac OS X.

> **CAUTION**
>
> While you technically could have 256 different colors for each level in your game, you can change only 254 of them if you use CopyBits() for your drawing. CopyBits() demands that the first entry in a color table be white and the last entry be black. You are free to place whatever colors you want in the rest of the color table.

16-Bit Color Pixels

Table 4-2 Composition of a 16-Bit Color

Bits	Description	Bits of the RGBColor Structure Used
1-5	Blue component	Bits 12-16 (The highest five bits)
6-10	Green component	Bits 28-32 (The highest five bits)
11-15	Red component	Bits 44-48 (The highest five bits)
16	Empty	

Rather than using color lookup tables, 16-bit color pixels use a 16-bit integer to store a color. Because 16-bit color does not use a lookup table, it is called direct color. Each color value directly refers to a color. Table 4-2 shows the composition of a 16-bit color. As you can see from the table, the red, green, and blue components of a 16-bit color take up five bits each. This arrangement gives 32 levels of red, 32 levels of green, and 32 levels of blue for a total of 32768 possible colors. QuickDraw translates the 16-bit components of the RGBColor structure to the 5-bit components of a 16-bit color pixel by copying the highest five bits of each color component in the RGBColor structure to the pixel.

The computer stores a 16-bit color picture as an array of numbers ranging from 0 to 32767. The main difference between 16-bit and 8-bit color pixels is that a 16-bit color's color is fixed depending on the value it has. A 16-bit color pixel with value 0 will always be black because the value 0 means that the red, green, and blue components will all be 0, which yields the color black. You cannot make the value 0 represent a different color in a 16-bit color system. With an 8-bit color pixel, you can create a custom color lookup table that assigns the value 0 to any color you choose.

One advantage of using 16-bit color instead of 8-bit color is that you don't have to worry about color lookup tables. Many programmers consider not putting up with the aggravation of color tables reason enough to use direct color. Another advantage of 16-bit color over 8-bit color is the greater number of colors you can show at one time, 32768 versus 256. This greater color variety comes at the expense of added space. 16-bit graphics take up twice the space of 8-bit graphics, two bytes per pixel.

32-Bit Color Pixels

Table 4-3	Composition of a 32-Bit Color	
Bits	**Description**	**Bits of the RGBColor Structure Used**
1-8	Blue component	Bits 9-16 (The highest eight bits)
9-16	Green component	Bits 25-32 (The highest eight bits)
17-24	Red component	Bits 41-48 (The highest eight bits)
25-32	Empty	

A 32-bit color pixel uses a 32-bit integer to store a color. Since 32-bit color does not use a lookup table, it is called direct color, just as 16-bit color is. Table 4-3 shows the composition of a 32-bit color. As you can see from the table, the red, green, and blue components of a 32-bit color take up eight bits each. This gives 256 levels of red, 256 levels of green, and 256 levels of blue for a total of 16,777,216 possible colors. Remember that the RGBColor structure contains 48 bits: 16 bits of red, 16 bits of green, and 16 bits of blue. QuickDraw translates the 16-bit components of the RGBColor structure to the 8-bit components of a 32-bit color pixel by copying the highest eight bits of each color component in the RGBColor to the pixel.

The computer stores a 32-bit color picture as an array of numbers ranging from 0 to 16,777,215. Like a 16-bit color, a 32-bit color's color is fixed depending on its value. A 32-bit color pixel with a value of 0 will always be black, and a pixel with a value of 16,777,215 will always be white.

Table 4-4 Storage Requirements for 8-Bit, 16-Bit, and 32-Bit Color

Picture Size	8-Bit Color	16-Bit Color	32-Bit Color
640 by 480 pixels	307,200 bytes	614,400 bytes	1,228,800 bytes
800 by 600 pixels	480,000 bytes	960,000 bytes	1,920,000 bytes
1024 by 768 pixels	786,432 bytes	1,572,864 bytes	3,145,728 bytes

The advantage of 32-bit color over 16 and 8-bit is that you can show a greater number of colors at one time, 16,777,216 versus 32768 in a 16-bit color system and 256 in an 8-bit color system. This greater color variety comes at a price. 32-bit color takes up four bytes per pixel, four times the space of 8-bit color and double the space of 16-bit color. Table 4-4 details how much memory pictures require in 8-bit, 16-bit, and 32-bit color.

QuickDraw Introduction

Before I can move on to drawing with QuickDraw, there are some QuickDraw basics I need to cover. In the next few sections, I cover these basics, including pixel maps, graphics ports, graphics devices, and the QuickDraw coordinate system.

Pixel Maps

A pixel map is a rectangular array of pixels where each entry in the array is the pixel's color. For an 8-bit color pixel map, each entry in the pixel map is a value from 0 to 255. For a 16-bit color pixel map, each pixel has a value ranging from 0 to 32767. Each pixel in a 32-bit color pixel map has a value ranging from 0 to 16,777,215. Figure 4-1 shows how a five pixel square pixel map in 16-bit color would be stored in the computer and shown on the screen.

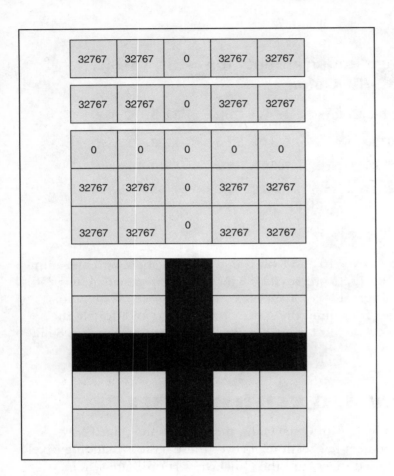

Figure 4-1

How the computer stores a pixel map and displays it on the screen.

If you're writing a 2D game, you will make extensive use of pixel maps. You will use them to store your backgrounds and game characters. If you're writing a 3D game, you will use pixel maps to store your game's texture maps. 3D games normally use polygons for the backgrounds and game characters so 3D games use pixel maps less than 2D games.

Table 4-5 PixMap Fields

Field	Description
baseAddr	The location of the first pixel in the pixel map.
rowBytes	The number of bytes in one row of the pixel map.
bounds	The boundary rectangle of the pixel map.

QuickDraw supports pixel maps through the PixMap data structure. The PixMap structure contains 15 fields, but there's only three you need to be concerned about. Table 4-5 lists these fields. If you are intellectually curious and want to

CAUTION

You cannot take the number of pixels in a row, multiply it by the number of bytes per pixel, and use that result as a substitute for the rowBytes field. Always use the function GetPixRowBytes() to determine the number of bytes in one row of the pixel map.

It can be difficult to predict the number of bytes in one row of a pixel map because QuickDraw may pad the end of a row with zeroes. For example, on Power PC-based Macs, QuickDraw can move eight bytes at a time. If you had 75 pixels per row in a 16-bit color pixel map, you would have 150 bytes in a row. Since 150 is not a multiple of eight, QuickDraw pads the pixel map with two bytes of 0 to bring the number of bytes in a row to 152, which is a multiple of eight. Without row padding, the drawing would screech to a halt at the end of each row when trying to draw the last pixels in the row. Because of the difficulty in trying to predict the number of bytes in a row, you should call GetPixRowBytes() to find the number of bytes in one row of the pixel map.

know all the fields of the PixMap data structure, read the book *Inside Macintosh: Imaging With QuickDraw*. You can download an electronic version from Apple's developer Web site.

In the pre-Carbon days, you could access the fields of the PixMap structure directly. For example, to set the variable sourceRect to the boundary rectangle of myPixelMap, you would write a statement like this.

```
sourceRect = myPixelMap.bounds;
```

Carbon does not allow you to access the fields of a pixel map directly. Instead you have to use accessor functions that return the contents of a field. Using Carbon, you set the source rectangle like this.

```
GetPixBounds(myPixelMap, &sourceRect);
```

To access the base address of a pixel map, call the accessor function `GetPixBaseAddr()`. Call the accessor function `GetPixRowBytes()` to access the `rowBytes` field of a pixel map.

Why Doesn't Apple Call Them Bitmaps?

If you've done any work with computer graphics, my description of pixel maps should sound familiar to you, but you're probably thinking "You were describing bitmaps, why does Apple call them pixel maps?"

The original Macintosh computers had only black and white graphics. Apple created the `BitMap` structure to store the graphics on the early Macintosh. Later on, color came to the Macintosh. Apple couldn't change the `BitMap` structure to store color graphics because doing so would break old software that used the `BitMap` structure. Apple had to create another data structure to store color bitmaps while maintaining backward compatibility with the black and white bitmaps. The designers came up with the `PixMap` structure to store the color bitmaps.

Graphics Ports

A graphics port defines a complete drawing environment that specifies where and how graphics operations take place. Each graphics port has its own coordinate system, foreground color, background color, and pixel map. QuickDraw stores graphics ports either in video memory (VRAM) or in system memory. Every window and dialog box has a graphics port. If you go into a word processor and open three documents, you have just created three graphics ports. You also can create offscreen graphics ports, which are called offscreen GWorlds. I discuss offscreen GWorlds later in the chapter.

The screen itself has its own graphics port, and while it's possible to draw to the screen directly, Apple discourages the practice. The person playing your game may have other programs running at the same time, all of which share the same screen. Drawing directly to the screen could cause your game to draw into another application, messing up that application in the process. Apple can make internal changes to QuickDraw in future versions of Mac OS. These changes could break your game if you draw directly to the screen. You don't want to be forced to patch your games years from now because your graphics code that draws directly to the screen doesn't work on a new version of Mac OS. It is much safer to create a window with no title bar or grow icon, cover the screen with this window, and do your drawing in the window.

Creating a window to do your drawing does not involve a lot of code. Most of your work will be in a resource editor like ResEdit or Resorcerer. You go into the resource editor and create a resource file for your game. Add a window to the resource file and remember the ID you gave it. Add the resource file to your game's project in the compiler, then compile and run your program. Your game will have a window ready.

Creating the window in your game requires a call to NewCWindow() as shown in the following code. Calling ShowWindow() will make the window appear on the screen.

```
WindowPtr screenWindow;
screenWindow = GetNewCWindow(kWindowResourceID, nil, WindowPtr(-1));
ShowWindow(screenWindow);
```

kWindowResourceID is the resource ID of the window you created in the resource editor. The nil parameter tells the operating system to allocate the window's memory for you. The WindowPtr(-1) parameter tells the operating system to place screenWindow in front of any other windows that may be open. I explain how you draw into a window in the "Drawing to the Screen" section later in this chapter.

Table 4-6   CGrafPort Fields

Field	Description
portPixMap	The graphics port's pixel map containing the image the port displays.
portRect	The graphics port's boundary rectangle.
visRgn	The graphics port's visible region.
clipRgn	The graphics port's clipping region.
fgColor	The graphics port's foreground color.
bkColor	The graphics port's background color.

You use graphics ports in QuickDraw by accessing QuickDraw's CGrafPort structure. This structure has 31 fields, but I describe the most important ones in Table 4-6. You do not directly create CGrafPort structures. You either create a window or an offscreen GWorld, which create the graphics ports when creating the window or GWorld.

Just like with pixel maps, you cannot directly access the fields of the CGrafPort structure. You have to use accessor functions. Here's a list of the accessor functions.

- GetPortPixMap()
- GetPortBounds() to retrieve the portRect field
- GetPortVisibleRegion()
- SetPortVisibleRegion()
- GetPortClipRegion()
- SetPortClipRegion()
- GetPortForeColor()
- RGBForeColor() to set the port's foreground color
- GetPortBackColor()
- RGBBackColor() to set the port's background color

QuickDraw Coordinate System

If you've ever taken an algebra course, you're familiar with coordinate systems (a set of numbers used to specify the location of a point in space). QuickDraw has its own coordinate system, but it differs from the one you learned in algebra class. In algebra, the point (0, 0) is the center of the graph. Values below and to the left of the center are negative, and values above and to the right are positive. In QuickDraw, the point (0, 0) is the upper-left corner of the coordinate system. As you move down and right, the values increase. Figure 4-2 shows the difference between the two coordinate systems.

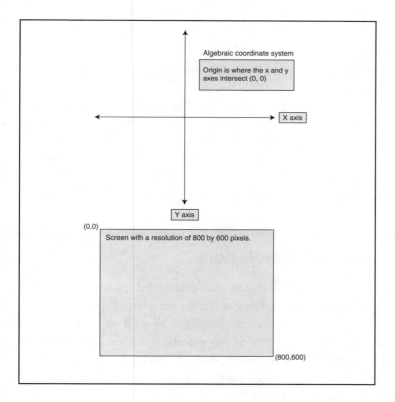

Figure 4-2

Algebraic and QuickDraw coordinate systems

Each graphics port has its own local coordinate system with the upper-left corner at point (0, 0). In addition, QuickDraw has a global coordinate system for the entire screen (or screens, if the user has multiple monitors). Figure 4-3 shows how the local and global coordinate systems interact.

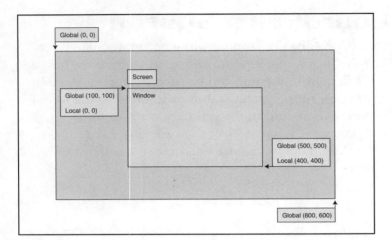

Figure 4-3

Local and global coordinate systems

If your computer has only one monitor, QuickDraw will have no negative coordinates. The upper-left corner of the screen will have global coordinates (0, 0) with the coordinates increasing as you move down and right. The only way to have negative coordinates is having a multiple monitor system where the main screen is not the leftmost one. Suppose you have three monitors running on your system, and the main screen, the one with the menu bar, is the center monitor. The upper-left corner of the center monitor will have global coordinates (0, 0). The left monitor will have a negative horizontal global coordinate since the monitor is to the left of the main screen.

Screen Resolutions

How far down and right the QuickDraw global coordinate system will go depends on the resolution of the screen. The user chooses what screen resolution he will use out of a list of available resolutions. The list of available screen resolutions depends on the size of the monitor and the amount of video memory in the computer. The absolute smallest screen resolution is 512 pixels wide and 384 pixels high, which was the screen resolution on the earliest Macs that were built in the mid 1980s. You can assume that the user has at least a 640-by-480-pixel screen resolution. The largest possible screen resolutions change rapidly. I've seen monitors with a 2048-by-1536-pixel resolution, and by the time you read this, there will be larger screen resolutions. Common screen resolutions include 640-by-480 pixels, 800-by-600 pixels, and 1024-by-768 pixels.

You will do your drawing using the local coordinates of the window or offscreen GWorld, depending on the destination of your drawing. The only way you would use global coordinates for drawing would be if you drew directly to the screen. In the "Graphics Ports" section earlier in this chapter, I advised against direct to screen drawing so you most likely will use local coordinates for your drawing. Situations where you would use global coordinates include positioning a window on the screen and reading the location of the mouse.

Graphics Devices

A graphics device is a final destination for QuickDraw. Examples of graphics devices are screens, printers, and offscreen GWorlds.

For game development, you don't need to do a whole lot with graphics devices. The only function you need to know is GetMainDevice(), which returns the main screen. Once you have the main device, the only field in the graphics device structure, GDevice, that you really need to know is gdRect, which is the boundary rectangle of the graphics device. If you wanted to make a window as large as the main screen for drawing, you would create a window, call GetMainDevice(), find the boundary rectangle of the main device, then resize the window to match the boundary rectangle. The following code shows how to make a window as large as the main screen.

```
void FitWindowToScreen(WindowPtr screenWindow)
{
        // Make the window equal the screen size
        short screenWidth;
        short screenHeight;

        // Get the current screen resolution
        GDHandle        mainDevice = nil;
        mainDevice = GetMainDevice();
        Rect screenRect = (**mainDevice).gdRect;
        screenWidth = screenRect.right - screenRect.left;
        screenHeight = screenRect.bottom - screenRect.top;

        // Resize the window to match the screen
        Boolean kAddToUpdateRegion = true;
        SizeWindow(screenWindow, screenWidth, screenHeight, kAddToUpdateRegion);
}
```

Offscreen GWorlds

Every graphical game has some kind of movement that requires portions of the screen to be erased and redrawn. If we do all this erasing and drawing directly on the screen, the screen will flash constantly. The term for this flashing is *flicker*, and games that have flicker look terrible. To avoid flicker, we'll do all our drawing off-screen and then copy the data to the screen. To do offscreen drawing, we need to use offscreen graphic worlds, known as offscreen GWorlds in QuickDraw.

An offscreen GWorld is a graphics port, just like a window. It has its own local coordinate system, pixel map, foreground color, and background color. The only difference between an offscreen GWorld and other graphics ports is that the offscreen GWorld is not visible on the screen. Because offscreen GWorlds are offscreen, they're perfect for updating the changed portions of the screen, which happens quite often in game development. Offscreen GWorlds allow you to make your erasing and redrawing invisible to the player, avoiding the flicker that occurs when you erase and redraw directly to the screen.

The GameOffscreenBuffer Class

I created the GameOffscreenBuffer class to handle offscreen GWorlds. Here are the data members — or should I say data member — of the class.

```
class GameOffscreenBuffer
{
    protected:
        GWorldPtr bufferStorage;
}
```

I needed only one data member, bufferStorage, for the offscreen buffer. The bufferStorage variable has type GWorldPtr, which just means that bufferStorage is a pointer to a graphics port. Refer to Table 4-6 for a description of the most important fields in QuickDraw's CGrafPort structure.

I created the GameOffscreenBuffer class to isolate the Mac-specific code. If I wanted to convert my code to another operating system, such as Windows, Linux, or BeOS, I would just need to change the GameOffscreenBuffer class to use that operating system's equivalent of GWorlds. My game code, which makes use of the GameOffscreenBuffer class, won't have to change.

Even if you don't plan on porting your game to another operating system, it's still a good idea to isolate operating system specific code. Apple could create a cool graphics technology five years from now that uses a different way of storing graphics offscreen. If this were to occur, you would just have to change the GameOffscreenBuffer class rather than changing a whole bunch of classes that directly used GWorlds to store graphics offscreen.

Creating Offscreen GWorlds

Table 4-7   NewGWorld() Parameters

Parameter	Description
offscreenGWorld	The newly created GWorld
pixelDepth	The color depth of the GWorld. You can pass the values 0, 1, 2, 4, 8, 16, or 32. If you pass the value 0, QuickDraw will use the color depth of the screen with the highest pixel depth whose boundary rectangle intersects the boundary rectangle of the GWorld.
boundsRect	The boundary rectangle of the GWorld.
cTable	The color table for the GWorld. If you pass nil, QuickDraw uses the default color table for the pixel depth you selected. If you passed 0 as the value of pixelDepth, QuickDraw ignores this parameter and uses the color table of the screen with the highest pixel depth whose boundary rectangle intersects the GWorld's boundary rectangle. Pass nil if you're creating a 16 or 32-bit color GWorld since those pixel depths don't use color tables.
aGDevice	The graphics device associated with the GWorld. If you pass the flags noNewDevice, useDistantHdwrMem, or useLocalHdwrMem, you need to supply a GDevice in this parameter. If you use a custom color table, you must pass nil. Otherwise, you should pass nil to let QuickDraw create a GDevice to associate with the GWorld.
flags	Options you can add to the GWorld. Table 4-8 lists some of the most common flags. Pass 0 if you don't want to pass any flags to NewGWorld().

Table 4-8   GWorld Flags

Flag	Description
pixPurge	Tells QuickDraw to create the GWorld in a purgable block of memory.
noNewDevice	Tells QuickDraw to not create a GDevice for the GWorld.
useTempMem	Tells QuickDraw to create the GWorld in temporary memory. I would recommend that you not use this flag.
keepLocal	Tells QuickDraw to keep the offscreen pixel image in main memory.
useDistantHdwrMem	Tells QuickDraw to store the GWorld in the video memory of a graphics accelerator card.
useLocalHdwrMem	Tells QuickDraw to store the GWorld in AGP memory.
clipPix	Tells QuickDraw to update the pixel image and clip it to the GWorld's boundary rectangle. You cannot use this flag when calling NewGWorld().
stretchPix	Tells QuickDraw to stretch the pixel image.

To create an offscreen GWorld, call the function NewGWorld(). The NewGWorld() function takes six parameters, shown in Table 4-7. The following sample code creates a GWorld.

```
Boolean GameOffscreenBuffer::Create(short width, short height, short colorDepth,
CTabHandle colorTable,
                        GWorldFlags flags)
{
    // Creates an offscreen buffer with the supplied
    // width, height, color depth, color table, and flags.
    // If you are using a color depth of 16 or 32, pass nil
    // for the color table.
    // Returns true if the buffer is created successfully.
```

```
    QDErr error;

    // NewGWorld() takes a rectangle rather than width and height.
    // Convert the width and height to a rectangle.
    Rect bufferRect;
    bufferRect.top = 0;
    bufferRect.bottom = height;
    bufferRect.left = 0;
    bufferRect.right = width;


    // The nil means there's no GDevice, which there shouldn't
    // be because the buffer is offscreen.
    error = NewGWorld(&bufferStorage, colorDepth, &bufferRect, colorTable,
                nil, flags);

    if ((error == noErr) && (bufferStorage != nil))
            // Buffer created successfully
            return true;
    else
            return false;

}
```

It's possible to create GWorlds in video memory (VRAM) so that you can take advantage of any graphics accelerator the user has on his machine. To create a GWorld in video memory, you call NewGWorld(), passing the value useDistantHdwrMem in the flags parameter.

Here are some things to keep in mind when creating offscreen GWorlds in video memory.

- VRAM-based GWorlds are currently available only on Mac OS 9. Mac OS X support for VRAM based GWorlds is forthcoming.

- You cannot use a custom color table with VRAM-based GWorlds. Custom color tables require you to pass nil as the aGDevice parameter to NewGWorld() while VRAM-based GWorlds require an existing GDevice in the aGDevice parameter. You can avoid this problem by using 16-bit or 32-bit color or by using the default color table in 8-bit color.

- Writing from system memory to VRAM is slow and vice versa. Writing from VRAM to VRAM is fast. Use VRAM-based GWorlds to store graphics you plan to use the entire game. Swapping graphics images in and out of VRAM will slow your game's drawing.

- You must do your drawing using CopyBits() to take advantage of having the GWorlds in VRAM. I discuss CopyBits() later in this chapter. If you use another method for drawing, such as using Open GL, the graphics data must move across the PCI or AGP bus to the CPU and back to the graphics card, negating the speed advantage of using VRAM-based GWorlds. Figure 4-4 shows the relationship between the CPU and the graphics accelerator.

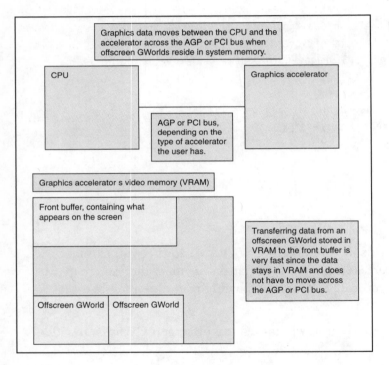

Figure 4-4

Relationship between the CPU and graphics accelerator

Updating Offscreen GWorlds

There will come times when you will want to make changes to a GWorld. Suppose we're making a time travel game, and the game begins in the present. The player enters the time machine and transports himself into another era, such as ancient Egypt. In the game, we want to erase the present day backgrounds and place the ancient Egyptian backgrounds in the GWorld. A couple of problems arise. The ancient Egyptian backgrounds are too large and won't fit in the GWorld. The backgrounds also have their own color scheme, and we would like to place the color table containing the new color scheme into the GWorld. How do we solve these problems?

One solution to the problem would be to dispose of the GWorld, create a new GWorld, and draw the ancient Egypt backgrounds into the GWorld. This solution will work, but it takes time to create a new GWorld. Fortunately, there's a faster way. QuickDraw has an UpdateGWorld() function that allows you to make changes to an existing GWorld without having to make a new one from scratch. The UpdateGWorld() function takes the same parameters as the NewGWorld() function, which you can see in Table 4-7.

NOTE

If you're updating a GWorld to change the GWorld's color table, you should pass either clipPix or stretchPix in the flags parameter to UpdateGWorld(). Passing either of those flags will update the pixel image to use the new color table.

The following function shows how you can update a GWorld to reflect a change in size, color depth, or color table.

```
Boolean GameOffscreenBuffer::Update(short width, short height, short colorDepth
CTabHandle colorTable,
            GWorldFlags flags)
{

        // Update an existing offscreen buffer with the supplied
        // width, height, color depth, color table, graphics device, and flags.
        // If you need to resize an offscreen buffer or change the
        // color table, updating the buffer is faster than creating
        // a new one.

        // Returns true if the buffer is updated successfully.

        GWorldFlags error;

        // Convert the width and height to a rectangle for UpdateGWorld()
        Rect bufferRect;
        bufferRect.top = 0;
        bufferRect.bottom = height;
        bufferRect.left = 0;
        bufferRect.right = width;
```

```
// Check if the buffer exists. If not, we'll create a buffer.
if (bufferStorage == nil)
        Create(width, height, colorDepth, colorTable,  flags);



// The nil means there's no GDevice, which there shouldn't
// be because the buffer is offscreen.
error = UpdateGWorld(&bufferStorage, colorDepth, &bufferRect, colorTable,
                nil, flags);

if ((error == noErr) && (bufferStorage != nil))
        // Buffer updated successfully
        return true;
else
        return false;


}
```

Drawing a Picture into an Offscreen GWorld

Now that we've created an offscreen GWorld, we have to put some graphics into it. The easiest way to get graphics into an offscreen GWorld is to use pictures. A picture contains a series of QuickDraw commands. For game development, most pictures will just be pixel maps. Here are the steps you have to take to draw a picture into an offscreen GWorld.

1. Read a picture from disk by calling the function GetPicture().
2. Save the previous drawing area by calling GetGWorld().
3. Set the drawing area to be the offscreen GWorld by calling SetGWorld().
4. Call GetGWorldPixMap() to gain access to the GWorld's pixel map.
5. Call LockPixels() to lock the pixel map's pixels so that they don't move during drawing.
6. Call DrawPicture() to draw the picture into the GWorld.
7. Unlock the pixel map's pixels by calling UnlockPixels().
8. Restore the previous drawing area with a call to SetGWorld().

Here's the code to draw a picture into an offscreen GWorld.

```
void GameOffscreenBuffer::Draw(short pictureResourceID)
{
        // Draws the picture into storage.


        PicHandle picToOpen = GetPicture(pictureResourceID);

        CGrafPtr oldPort;
        GDHandle oldGDevice;
        Boolean canLockPixels;

        // Save previous drawing area.
        GetGWorld (&oldPort, &oldGDevice);

        // Have drawing done to bufferStorage.
        SetGWorld(bufferStorage, nil);

        // Lock the buffer storage
        PixMapHandle thePixMap = GetGWorldPixMap(bufferStorage);
        if (thePixMap != nil)
                canLockPixels = LockPixels(thePixMap);
        else
                canLockPixels = false;

        // Draw the image in the offscreen buffer.
        Rect portRect;
        if (canLockPixels){
                GetPortBounds(bufferStorage, &portRect);
                DrawPicture(picToOpen, &portRect);
                UnlockPixels(thePixMap);
        }

        // restore graphics port and GDevice
        SetGWorld(oldPort, oldGDevice);

        // Clean Up
        ReleaseResource(Handle(picToOpen));
}
```

Disposing of Offscreen GWorlds

When we're finished with our offscreen GWorlds, we must dispose of them. If we do not dispose of our GWorlds, we will create a memory leak. A memory leak occurs when you allocate memory and fail to free the memory you allocated. The leaked memory is in limbo, unusable to any other program. If you keep leaking memory, you will run out of memory, and your computer will crash. It is especially important to dispose of offscreen GWorlds you allocate in video memory. Most users have less video memory than system memory so a crash will occur quicker. Video memory is not protected in OS X like system memory is so if you run out of video memory, you have to restart the computer.

Disposing of offscreen GWorlds involves a call to `DisposeGWorld()`. Here's the sample code to dispose of a GWorld and free the memory the GWorld used.

```
void GameOffscreenBuffer::Dispose(void)
{
        if (bufferStorage != nil) {
                DisposeGWorld(bufferStorage);
                bufferStorage = nil;
        }
}
```

Using OS X's Built-In Double Buffering

On Mac OS X all windows have double buffering, which means the operating system automatically creates an offscreen GWorld for the window when you create a window.

To draw into a Mac OS X window's back buffer, you need to do the following:

1. Call `GetWindowPort()` to get the window's drawing port.
2. Call `LockPortBits()` to have the drawing sent to the back buffer.
3. Do your drawing.
4. Call `UnlockPortBits()` so the contents of the back buffer can be moved to the front buffer.
5. Call `QDFlushPortBuffer()` to draw the contents of the back buffer to the screen.

The following code demonstrates how to draw a picture into an OS X window's backbuffer.

```
void DrawToBackBuffer(WindowPtr theWindow, short pictureResourceID)
{
        // Draws the picture into an OS X window's back buffer.

        OSStatus error;
        PicHandle picToOpen = GetPicture(pictureResourceID);

        CGrafPtr oldPort;
        GDHandle oldGDevice;
        OSError lockPixelsError;
        Boolean canLockPixels;

        // Save previous drawing area.
        GetGWorld (&oldPort, &oldGDevice);

        // Have drawing done to bufferStorage.
        SetGWorld(theWindow, GetMainDevice);

        // Get the window's port
        CGrafPtr windowPort = GetWindowPort(theWindow);

        // Lock the port's pixel map so the drawing will go to the backbuffer
        lockPixelsError = LockPortBits(windowPort);
        if (lockPixelsError == noErr)
                canLockPixels = true;
        else
                canLockPixels = false;

        // Draw the image in the back buffer.
        Rect portRect;
        if (canLockPixels){
                GetPortBounds(windowPort, &portRect);
                DrawPicture(picToOpen, &portRect);
                lockPixelsError = UnlockPortBits(windowPort);
        }

        // OS X windows are double buffered. We check if the destination
        // is double buffered. If so, we flush the port buffer so the
        // drawing will show on the screen in OS X.
```

```
    RgnHandle theVisibleRegion;

    if (QDIsPortBuffered(windowPort)) {
            theVisibleRegion = NewRgn();
            GetPortVisibleRegion(windowPort, theVisibleRegion);
            QDFlushPortBuffer(windowPort, theVisibleRegion);
            DisposeRgn(theVisibleRegion);
    }

    // Restore graphics port and GDevice
    SetGWorld(oldPort, oldGDevice);

    // Clean Up
    ReleaseResource(Handle(picToOpen));
}
```

Drawing to the Screen

Now that we have some graphics in an offscreen buffer, we need to draw the graphics to the screen. With no graphics on the screen, our game will be very dull and difficult to play. Luckily, the remainder of this chapter shows you how to make graphics appear on the screen.

The CopyBits() Function

Table 4-9   CopyBits() Parameters

Parameter	Description
srcBits	The source bitmap
dstBits	The destination bitmap
srcRect	The rectangular area of the source bitmap we're copying.
dstRect	The rectangular area we're copying to.
mode	A transfer mode for copying. I discuss the transfer modes later in this chapter. To do a straight copy, use the mode srcCopy.
maskRgn	An optional region you can specify as a clipping mask. If you don't want a clipping mask, pass nil.

For game development, CopyBits() is the most important call in QuickDraw. CopyBits() moves graphical data from one pixel map to another. CopyBits() takes six parameters, listed in Table 4-9. The main advantage of using CopyBits() for drawing is that CopyBits() can take advantage of hardware acceleration. If the player of your game has a 3D accelerator, CopyBits() automatically uses it for drawing, without you having to write any additional drawing code.

In the pre-Carbon days, you were forced to typecast your pixel maps to bitmaps to get your pixel maps to work properly as the srcBits and dstBits parameters to CopyBits(). This requirement gave you a messy looking CopyBits() call, which looked something like this.

```
CopyBits((BitMap*)&(theSource->portPixMap), (BitMap*)&(theDestination->portPixMap),
&sourceRect, &destinationRect, srcCopy, nil);
```

In Carbon, Apple added the call GetPortBitMapForCopyBits(). This function gives you the bitmap for a graphics port that you can pass as the srcBits or dstBits parameter to CopyBits(). Now our CopyBits() call looks like this.

```
CopyBits(GetPortBitMapForCopyBits(theSource),
GetPortBitMapForCopyBits(theDestination), &sourceRect, &destinationRect, srcCopy,
nil);
```

I'm sure you'll agree that the Carbonized CopyBits() call is much easier to read and understand.

Boolean Transfer Modes

One of the parameters to the CopyBits() function is a mode for the transfer. There are two types of transfer modes: Boolean and arithmetic transfer modes. There are eight types of Boolean transfers, and Figure 4-5 shows what an image looks like after each type of transfer.

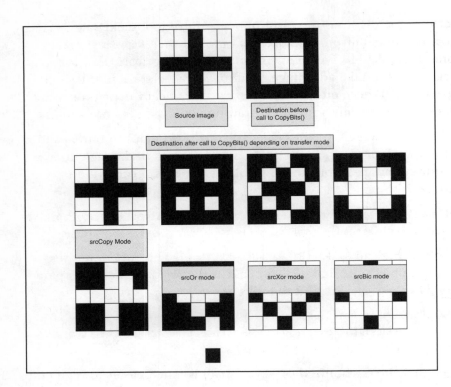

Figure 4-5

The ways the different Boolean transfer modes draw an image.

The srcCopy transfer mode is the Boolean transfer mode you will use most for your games. The srcCopy mode copies the entire source image to the destination, wiping out whatever was in the destination, making it ideal for drawing your game's backgrounds.

As you can see from Figure 4-5, the notSrcCopy transfer mode inverts the source image and copies it to the destination. If the source pixel is black, the notSrcCopy transfer mode copies the source's background color to the destination pixel. If the source pixel is white, the notSrcCopy transfer mode copies the source's foreground color to the destination pixel.

The srcOr transfer mode performs a Boolean OR operation between the source and destination pixels. If the source pixel is black, the srcOr transfer mode copies the source's foreground color to the destination pixel. If the source pixel is white, the srcOr transfer mode leaves the destination pixel alone.

The notSrcOr transfer mode leaves the destination pixel alone if the source pixel is black. If the source pixel is white, the notSrcOr transfer mode copies the source pixel's foreground color into the destination pixel.

The srcXor and notSrcXor transfer modes only apply to black and white pixels. The srcXor transfer mode performs an exclusive OR operation on the source and destination pixels. If one of the source and destination pixels is black, the destination pixel ends up black. If both pixels are black or both pixels are white, the destination pixel ends up white. The notSrcXor transfer mode works in the opposite way. If both pixels are black or both pixels are white, the destination pixel ends up black. Otherwise the destination pixel ends up black.

If the source pixel is white, the srcBic transfer mode leaves the destination pixel untouched. If the source pixel is black, the srcBic transfer mode copies the source pixel's background color to the destination pixel.

If the source pixel is black, the notSrcBic transfer mode leaves the destination pixel untouched. If the source pixel is white, the notSrcBic transfer mode copies the source pixel's background color to the destination pixel.

Arithmetic Transfer Modes

Table 4-10   Arithmetic Transfer Modes

Transfer Mode	Replaces Destination Pixel With
blend	A blend of the source and destination pixel colors.
addPin	The sum of the source and destination pixel colors.
addOver	The sum of the source and destination pixel colors. If one of the components of the color exceeds 65536, subtract 65536 from that value.
subPin	The difference of the source and destination pixel colors.
transparent	The source pixel if the source pixel does not equal the background color.
addMax	The color, either the source or destination pixel color, containing the higher red, green, and blue components.
subOver	The difference of the source and destination pixel colors. If one of the color's components is less than 0, take the negative number and add 65536 to it.
adMin	The color, either the source or destination pixel color, containing the lower red, green, and blue components.

There are eight arithmetic transfer modes you can use in `CopyBits()`. Table 4-10 lists the possible arithmetic transfer modes. Arithmetic transfer modes make me wish I had color figures in this book. Black and white figures do not paint an accurate picture of arithmetic transfer modes. For game development, the `transparent` mode is the one you will use most. The `transparent` node provides a neat way to draw sprites.

Steps to Take

Drawing to the screen is similar to drawing to an offscreen GWorld. Instead of calling `DrawPicture()` to do the drawing, however, you call `CopyBits()`. Here are the steps to take to draw from an offscreen GWorld to a window on the screen.

1. Save the previous drawing area by calling `GetGWorld()`.
2. Set the drawing area to the window by calling `SetGWorld()`.
3. Call `GetGWorldPixMap()` to gain access to the GWorld's pixel map.
4. Call `LockPixels()` to lock the pixel map's pixels so they don't move during drawing.
5. Call `CopyBits()` to draw from the offscreen GWorld to the window.
6. Flush the port buffer after drawing by calling `QDFlushPortBuffer()`. OS X windows are double buffered. If you don't call `QDFlushPortBuffer()`, only the back buffer will be updated, and your drawing will not display on the screen. To see if a window has two buffers, call the function `QDIsPortBuffered()`.
7. Unlock the pixel map's pixels by calling `UnlockPixels()`.
8. Restore the previous drawing area with a call to `SetGWorld()`.

The following code draws an image from an offscreen buffer to the screen.

```
void Blitter::DrawImage(void)
{
        // Make sure the source and destination buffers exist.
        CGrafPtr theSource = GetSourceBuffer();
        CGrafPtr theDestination = GetDestinationBuffer();
        if ((theSource == nil) || (theDestination == nil))
                return;

        CGrafPtr oldPort;
        GDHandle oldGDevice;
```

```
// Save previous drawing area
GetGWorld (&oldPort, &oldGDevice);

// Set drawing area to the screen
SetGWorld (theDestination, GetMainDevice());

// Lock the pixels
PixMapHandle thePixMap = GetGWorldPixMap(theSource);
Boolean canLockPixels = LockPixels(thePixMap);

// Draw from the offscreen GWorld to the window
if (canLockPixels){
        // Source and destination rectangles are data members
        // of the Blitter class. srcCopy means a straight copy
        // from the offscreen buffer to the screen.
        CopyBits(GetPortBitMapForCopyBits(theSource),
                GetPortBitMapForCopyBits(theDestination),
                &sourceRect, &destinationRect, srcCopy, nil);
}

// OS X windows are double buffered. We check if the destination
// is double buffered. If so, we flush the port buffer so the
// drawing will show on the screen in OS X.
RgnHandle theVisibleRegion;

if (QDIsPortBuffered(theDestination)) {
        theVisibleRegion = NewRgn();
        GetPortVisibleRegion(theDestination, theVisibleRegion);
        QDFlushPortBuffer(theDestination, theVisibleRegion);
        DisposeRgn(theVisibleRegion);
}

// restore graphics port and GDevice
SetGWorld(oldPort, oldGDevice);


}
```

Making CopyBits() Run at Its Best

Because you will call CopyBits() 30 or more times per second in your game, it's important to use CopyBits() properly. CopyBits() can do many things, but some of the things it can do will slow your game down to a crawl.

Figure 4-6 shows the steps CopyBits() goes through when copying an image. It's a lot of steps, but you can cut out several of the steps and improve your drawing performance.

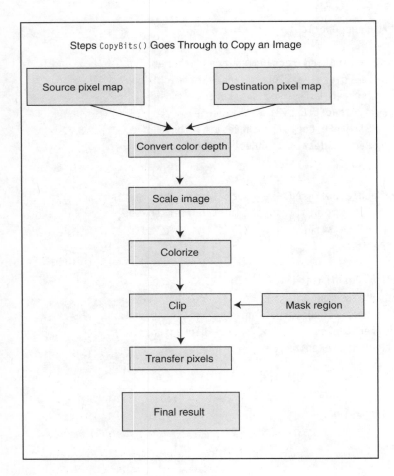

Figure 4-6

Steps involved when transferring an image with CopyBits().

Make Sure the Source and Destination Rectangles Are the Same Size

When the source and destination rectangles are the same size, all `CopyBits()` has to do is move the pixels from the source to the destination. If the source and destination rectangles have different sizes, `CopyBits()` will scale the source image to fit in the destination rectangle. This scaling takes time as QuickDraw must calculate the color for each pixel in the destination image. Scaling an image also makes it less likely that your `CopyBits()` call will be hardware accelerated. By using same-sized rectangles in `CopyBits()`, you eliminate the stretch or shrink image step.

Use the Same Color Depth

Use the same color depth for all your windows and offscreen GWorlds. If you do this, you eliminate the Convert color depth step shown in Figure 4-6. Using different color depths forces `CopyBits()` to do color conversions for each pixel. Suppose you called `CopyBits()` to draw an image from a 16-bit color GWorld to an 8-bit color window. For each pixel in the image, `CopyBits()` has to take the 16-bit color and determine which color in the window's color table comes closest to matching the 16-bit color. As you can imagine, this color matching consumes a lot of time, and your drawing will slow to a crawl. Having different color depths also makes it less likely that your `CopyBits()` call will be hardware accelerated. Being consistent in your color depths will speed up your game.

Set the Foreground Color to Black and the Background Color to White

When you set the foreground color to black and the background color to white, you eliminate the Colorize step shown in Figure 4-6. All `CopyBits()` has to do is move the pixels from the source to the destination in this case because black has zero percent intensity in its red, blue, and green components, and white has 100 percent intensity in its red, blue, and green components.

If you change the foreground and background colors from black and white, `CopyBits()` has to apply weighted portions of the new foreground and background colors to each pixel. These calculations will slow your drawing, but you can obtain some interesting color effects. Changing the graphics port's foreground and background colors will warp the image's colors from the version your artist gave you, which normally isn't what you want.

Since QuickDraw uses black as the default foreground color and white as the default background color for its graphics ports, this CopyBits() optimization is the easiest one to perform. In this case, you have to go out of your way to slow down your drawing.

Don't Use a Mask Region

You have the option of supplying a mask region as the last parameter to CopyBits(), as you can see in Table 4-9. If you supply a mask region, CopyBits() will clip the image it draws to the mask region and the bounding rectangle of the destination pixel map. The clipping takes time, and this time can be eliminated by not using a mask region. If you do not use a mask region and are careful when determining your source and destination rectangles, you can eliminate the Clip step in Figure 4-6.

Draw Wide Rectangles

Figure 4-7 shows the order the nine pixels in a 3 by 3 pixel map would be stored in memory. As you can see, the Macintosh stores the pixels in the first row from left to right, moves to the next row and stores those pixels consecutively from left to right, and repeats the process for all the rows in the pixel map.

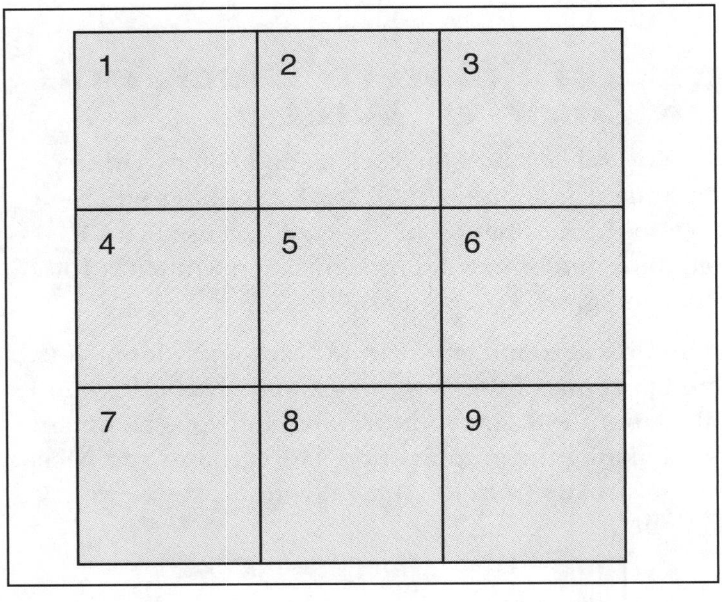

Figure 4-7

The order of the pixels in a 3 by 3 pixel map in memory.

If you were drawing the entire image from a pixel map, there would be no advantage to using wide rectangles over tall ones. CopyBits() would just move from pixel to pixel in memory, copying the entire image. However, in game development you will usually copy only part of an image in one CopyBits() call. Figure 4-8 shows a situation where you're drawing the upper 128 by 128 pixel area of a 256 by 256 pixel map. In the scenario in Figure 4-8, all the pixels in a row will be stored consecutively, but there's a 128 pixel gap in the last pixel in a row and the first pixel in the next row. It takes time for the computer to calculate the gap and move the 128 pixels to the next row. Drawing a row is fast since the pixels are right next to each other in memory. Moving from one row to the next is slow because the computer must determine how far to move in memory, then make the move to the location of the next row in memory. With wide rectangles you don't have to move from one row to the next as often as with tall rectangles so you're drawing will go faster. Drawing a rectangular image 200 pixels wide and 50 pixels tall will be faster than drawing an image 50 pixels wide and 200 pixels tall. You will have four times as many row transitions in the 200 pixel tall rectangle as you will in the 50 pixel tall rectangle, resulting in slower drawing in the 200 pixel tall rectangle.

128 by 128 pixel portion of a 256 by 256 pixel map. When QuickDraw reaches the end of one of these 128 pixel rows, it must skip 128 pixels in the full image to move on to the next row.

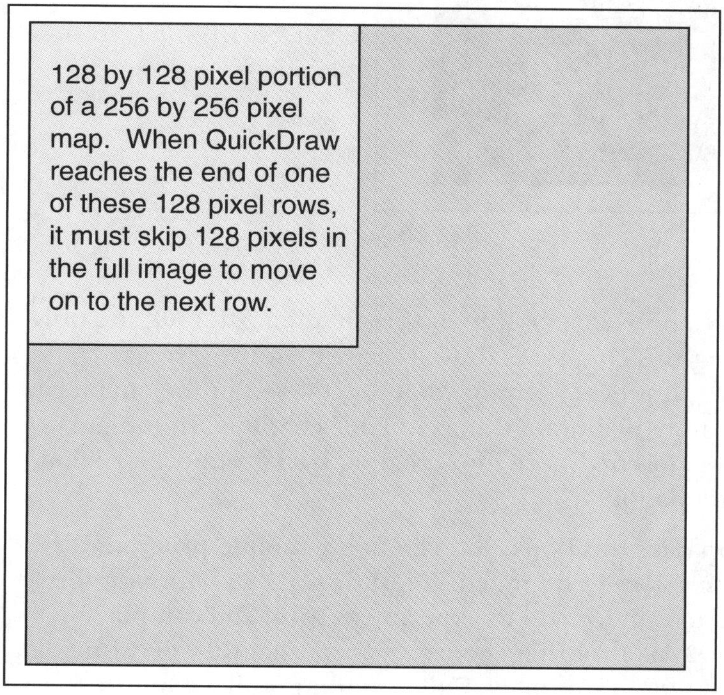

Figure 4-8

The gap between the last pixel in one row and the first pixel in the next row.

Draw Large Rectangles

When drawing a small image, CopyBits() spends more time in function overhead than drawing the image. Each time you call a C or C++ function, the computer needs to do things like pass the parameters you supply to the function, and CopyBits() is no different. If you have lots of small rectangles to draw, the overhead from calling CopyBits() dozens of times will slow your drawing.

To speed things up, you can combine smaller rectangles into one large rectangle. Figure 4-9 shows how you can combine five smaller rectangles into one large rectangle. Even though the larger rectangle is roughly double the size of the five smaller rectangles, it will draw faster because you call CopyBits() once rather than five times.

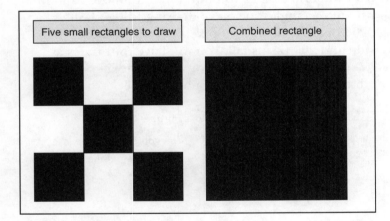

Figure 4-9

Combining smaller rectangles into one large rectangle.

Summary

At first glance, it looks like we covered very little in this chapter. After all, the only thing you can do after reading this chapter is draw a picture on the screen. Appearances can be deceiving, however. Most of what we covered in the chapter provides a foundation to do more elaborate things in later chapters. In the next two chapters, we'll put what we learned here into creating backgrounds, scrolling the screen, and producing animation.

On the CD-ROM that accompanies this book, you can find a sample program for this chapter. The program itself doesn't do much. It just displays a picture on the screen, but it's a nice small program for you to experiment with. You can play around with the different CopyBits() transfer modes and see what they do with color images. Future chapters will build on this meek little program until a game appears.

CHAPTER 5

TILES AND SCROLLING

After learning how to draw to the screen, we need to learn how to draw something interesting on the screen. In this chapter I teach you techniques for using tiles to create levels and maps in a game. I also show how to scroll the screen so that you can create huge worlds that span multiple screens.

Introduction to Tiles

A tile is a reusable piece of artwork, usually a pixel map. You can build game levels out of tiles in the same way you would build a tile floor in your kitchen. You lay the tiles on the screen using a level editor, a tool you will write for your game to speed up the process of building game levels. Figure 5-1 shows how you can make a brick wall using two tiles. Another way to think of tiles is as reusable jigsaw puzzle pieces. The level or map is the puzzle and the tiles are the individual pieces. Instead of having 20 physical jigsaw puzzle pieces that look alike, you can use one tile in the 20 places in the level that need that particular tile.

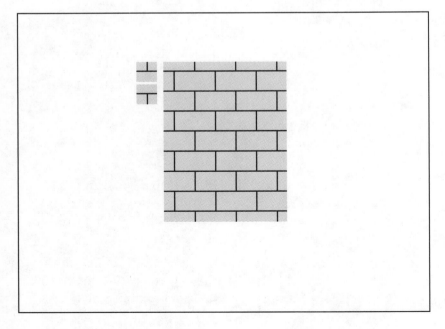

Figure 5-1

Building with tiles

Tiles work best with interior settings containing walls, floors, and doors because interior settings normally are rectangular. I'm sure most of the rooms in your house or apartment are rectangular. If you have octagon-, triangle-, or trapezoid-shaped rooms in your house, I apologize. You can use any shape for your tiles, but most games that use tiles use rectangular ones. QuickDraw's pixel maps and off-screen buffers are rectangular, and virtually all computer screens also have a rectangular shape. Using rectangular tiles allows your game to work most efficiently with QuickDraw for the fastest possible drawing performance.

By using tiles you can make large levels without taking up a lot of memory. Let's say you have a game playing at an 800-by-600–pixel screen resolution with 16-bit color. You want the level to be five screens wide and five screens high. If you chose not to go with tiles, you would have to create an offscreen buffer that was 4,000 pixels (five screens) wide and 3,000 pixels (five screens) high. This buffer would take up 4,000 times 3,000 times two bytes (16-bit color equals two bytes per pixel) or 24 million bytes of memory.

Now let's see how much space a 4000-by-3000–pixel level would take up using tiles. Let's use an 800-by-640–pixel offscreen buffer to store the tiles. This will give us 500 tiles that are 32 pixels tall and 32 pixels wide. This buffer would take up 800 times 640 times two bytes (for 16-bit color) or 1,024,000 bytes of memory.

We're not done yet. We still have to store the level. To store the level, we will use a 2D array. Each value in the array will be a number between 0 and 499, which corresponds to the appropriate tile in the offscreen buffer. To store a 4000-by-3000–pixel level, the array needs to have 125 rows (4000 pixels divided by 32 pixels per tile) and 94 rows (3000 pixels divided by 32 pixels per tile rounded up to the next highest integer). The space to store this array is 125 times 94 times 2 bytes (values between 0 and 499 take up two bytes), or 23,500 bytes. The total space to store the level using tiles is 1,024,000 bytes for the tiles plus 23,500 bytes for the level, or 1,047,500 bytes. By using tiles, we reduced our memory requirements by over 90 percent.

If you wanted to double the width and double the height of the level using tiles, all you would have to do is quadruple the level storage to 94,000 bytes. If you didn't use tiles, you'd have to quadruple the size of the offscreen buffer to 96 million bytes. Now you should be able to see the benefits of using tiles.

The challenge of tiles is using them in such a way that it does not look like you're using tiles. Used poorly, tiled levels can look flat and boring. Using tiles for outdoor levels is difficult because outdoor settings like forests, mountains, meadows, and beaches are not naturally rectangular like indoor settings. However, a good artist can construct outdoor scenes with tiles that look natural.

Storing Tiles

Because QuickDraw has no built in support for tiles, we must create our own class to store tiles, as you can see in the class declaration below:

```
class GameTile
{
        protected:
                short tileNumber;
                GameTileType tileType;

};
```

Storing an individual tile does not require many data members. The `tileNumber` data member uniquely identifies an individual tile in a group of tiles. The game engine uses the tile number to draw the correct tiles when drawing a level.

The `GameTileType` data type is an enumerated data type I created to store the different types of tiles in the game. I defined the following data types for the game in this book:

```
enum GameTileType{
        kWallTile = 1,
        kFloorTile,
        kDoorTile,
        kForegroundTile,
        kExitTile
};
```

As you can see from the list above, I defined five tile types: wall tiles, floor tiles, door tiles, foreground tiles, and exit tiles. Wall tiles behave like a wall (strangely enough), meaning that characters cannot pass through them. Floor tiles allow characters to walk over them. Door tiles are a combination of wall and floor tiles. They are solid so you couldn't shoot through them to hit somebody on the other side of the door, but you can open the door and walk through it to enter the room. Foreground tiles make it possible for characters to walk behind objects in the game world. Exit tiles tell the game that the player reached the end of a level and that it's

time to load a new level. Feel free to add any tile types for your own games.

The `tileType` data member stores what type of tile that particular tile is. The `tileType` data member transforms the tile from a pixel map to a living, breathing part of our game world. You can have a tile that looks like a brick wall, but if we don't tell the game engine that the tile should behave like a wall, characters will be able to walk through the wall. The `tileType` data member tells the engine that the tile should behave like a wall.

The `GameTile` class we created stores information about one tile. Our game is going to have more than one tile or else it will look pretty strange. We need a way to store a group of tiles on disk. We're going to create our own tile resource to store our tiles on disk. The tile resource has two parts.

- A picture containing the graphical tiles.
- An array of `GameTile` objects containing all the information about that particular group of tiles.

Figure 5-2 shows how the computer arranges the tiles for a tile space of Y rows and X columns.

Figure 5-2

Storing tiles

	Columns							
	0	1	2	3				X
	1							
Rows	2							
	3							
	Y							

For more information on resources, refer to Chapter 15, "Files."

When dealing with tiles in your game, you have two major decisions to make.

- How big should I make my tiles?
- How big a tile storage space should I use?

When choosing a tile size, there's a tradeoff between graphic quality and speed. Smaller tiles look better, but they're slower since you have to draw more of them on the screen. Good choices would be 16-by-16 pixel and 32-by-32 pixel tiles. You can also use non-square tiles where the width and height of the tiles differ.

When selecting the size of your tile storage space, you must choose between quality and size. Storing more tiles will give your levels more variety, but if you have too many tiles, you defeat the purpose of using them. I used an 800-by-640–pixel storage space in my example earlier in this chapter, giving enough storage space for 500 32-by-32–pixel tiles, which should provide enough space. Keep in mind that this storage space does not limit me to 500 tiles in the game. It just limits me to 500 tiles to display at one time. I could have a dozen groups of tiles in my game, giving me a total of 6000 tiles. I could use different tile groups for different levels of the game. For example, if I had a time travel game that transported the player to ancient Egypt, ancient Greece, ancient Rome, Victorian England, and modern-day New York City, I could have a different group of tiles for each time period. When the player traveled to a new time period, I would load the appropriate set of tiles from disk.

It's a good idea to use the same size tile space for all your sets of tiles. Suppose that you are developing a fantasy role-playing game, and you have three sets of tiles, one for the wilderness, one for towns, and one for dungeons. If the player moves from the wilderness to a town, you'll want to load the town tiles from disk. If the wilderness, town, and dungeon tiles all have different amounts of tile space, you would have to delete the old tile space, allocate new tile space, and then load the new tiles. By using a uniform amount of tile space for all your tile sets, all you have to do is load the new tiles into the same tile space to change the scene, resulting in a faster load time for the player.

Storing Levels

Now that we've come up with a way to store our game's tiles, we need a way to store the levels in our game. To do this, we must create a class to store our levels, as you can see in the class declaration below:

```
class GameLevel
{
        protected:
                short levelWidth;        // in tiles
                short levelHeight;       // in tiles
                short tileID;            // Resource ID of the tiles this level uses

        public:
                // Normally you do not want to make data members public, but
                // using accessor functions to retrieve arrays is a pain. It's
                // easier to just make the array public and read it directly.
                MapElementPtr levelMap;        // Used as a 2D array

}
```

The levelWidth and levelHeight data members store the level's width and length in tiles, not pixels. The tileID data member stores which set of tiles the level uses. This level design limits an individual level to one group of tiles. Multiple levels may use the same set of tiles, but one level may not use multiple sets of tiles.

The levelMap data member is a 2D array that tells us which tiles to draw in the level. I created a MapElement class to store this information, which looks like this:

```
class MapElement
{
        protected:
                short value;
                Boolean visibleToPlayer;
}
```

The value data member contains the tile number of the tile to draw. The visibleToPlayer data member is used by the game itself. If the player should not be able to see this tile, because it's in a room the player has not explored, for example, the visibleToPlayer value will be false, and a black tile will be drawn instead

NOTE

In the actual game, the GameLevel **class will also include things like the monsters in the level, the goodies the player can pick up in the level and the traps and puzzles in the level. I'm simplifying to make the discussion easier to understand here. Refer to Chapter 16, "Putting It All Together," to learn about loading a game's monsters and goodies.**

of the actual tile. When the player does enter the room, the visibleToPlayer value will be set to true, and the actual tile will be drawn.

You may be wondering why I used a pointer to store the level map instead of using the traditional method of allocating a 2D array, which would look like this:

```
MapElement levelMap[rows][columns];
```

I have two reasons for using a pointer. First, I have no idea how large a level is until I read it from disk so I don't know what values to use for the rows and columns in the array brackets. By using a pointer, I can read the level from disk, determine how large the level is, then allocate an array the size of the level. The technical term for this type of allocation is dynamic allocation.

The second reason for using a pointer to store the level map involves a limitation in CodeWarrior on versions of Mac OS prior to OS X. In the older versions of Mac OS, the size of your local variables cannot exceed 32KB if you use CodeWarrior. If I tried to allocate a 2D array of shorts in the GameLevel class like this:

```
short myArray[100][200];
```

I would receive a compiler error saying that I exceeded the 32KB limit for local data. The reason for the error is that the array takes up 40,000 bytes of space (100 rows times 200 columns times 2 bytes for each element in the array), which is greater than the limit of 32,768 bytes. I have three options for allocating the array:

- I can declare the array to be static in the GameLevel class. This means all the GameLevel objects must use the same array. If I have three GameLevel objects open in my game and I want each object to have its own array, I cannot use static arrays.
- I can declare the array to be a global variable. Using a global variable has the same problems that using a static array does. In addition, global variables are a coding nightmare; using global variables makes code difficult to read and understand.
- I can dynamically allocate the array using a pointer.

You will never guess which option I think is best.

We're going to create our own level resource to store our levels. The level resource contains a GameLevel object containing the data we need to store in the level.

To create the resources for your game's levels and resources, you have two choices: write a program to make the resources, or use Rez. Rez is a resource compiler that lets you create a resource with code in much the same way you would create a structure or class in a traditional programming language. After trying to create a level in Rez by typing in number after number, I am sure you will want to make a level editor for your game. Chapter 15, "Files," explains resources and shows you what you need to know to create resources.

The following code shows you how to allocate a level map:

```
Boolean GameLevel::ReadLevelData(short levelID)
{
        // WARNING
        // This snippet has some details stripped away for clarity.
        // This code as is would not compile. It's for explanation only.
        // Look at the Chapter 5 source code on the CD-ROM for
        // the entire code to this function.

        Handle savedLevel;

        // Assume we read the level resource from disk so that
        // savedLevel contains the level data.
        // Chapter 17 shows the process of reading resources from disk.

        // Now let's set the level data
        short theLevelWidth;
        short theLevelHeight;
        short theTileID;        // The set of tiles this level uses.
        Size offset = 0;

        // Read the level's width, height and tile ID
        BlockMoveData(*savedLevel + offset, &theLevelWidth, sizeof(short));
        offset = offset + sizeof(short);
        BlockMoveData(*savedLevel + offset, &theLevelHeight, sizeof(short));
        offset = offset + sizeof(short);
        BlockMoveData(*savedLevel + offset, &theTileID, sizeof(short));
        offset = offset + sizeof(short);

        SetLevelWidth(theLevelWidth);
        SetLevelHeight(theLevelHeight);
        SetTileID(theTileID);

        // Now that we have the level width and level height, allocate
```

```
            // the level map.
            AllocateLevelMap();

            // Read in the level map
            UInt32 mapIndex;
            for(short row = 0; row < theLevelHeight; row++) {
                    for(short column = 0; column < theLevelWidth; column++) {
                            mapIndex = (row * theLevelWidth) + column;
                            BlockMoveData(*savedLevel + offset, &(levelMap[mapIndex]),
                    sizeof(MapElement));

                            offset = offset + sizeof(MapElement);
                    }
            }

            return true;
    }

void Level::AllocateLevelMap(void)
{
        size_t levelMapSize = levelWidth * levelHeight * sizeof(MapElement);
        levelMap = (MapElementPtr)NewPtr(levelMapSize);
}
```

I stored the data on disk in this order:

- Level width
- Level height
- Tile ID
- Level map

So I must read the data in this same order. I need to read the level's width and height first so I can allocate the correct amount of space for the level map. After reading the width and height, I read the tile ID, then I allocate the level map. Allocating the level map is not too difficult, as you can see in the AllocateLevelMap() function. I just calculate how much space I need and call NewPtr() to allocate a pointer with the amount of space I need. The offset variable keeps track of where we are in the block of level data.

After allocating the level map, I read the data into the level map, which you can see in the `for` loop at the end of the `ReadLevelData()` function. The complicated thing is that I allocated a 2D array, but I'm treating it as a 2D array. The statement

```
mapIndex = (row * theLevelWidth) + column;
```

Converts the logical 2D array index `[row][column]` to the physical 1D array index `mapIndex`. Dynamically allocating a 2D array is a pain in the butt. It's a lot easier to allocate a 1D array and treat it like it has two dimensions.

Table 5-1 BlockMoveData() Parameters

Parameter	Description
srcPtr	The address of the first byte to copy
destPtr	The destination of the copy
byteCount	The number of bytes to copy

I am sure you have already guessed what the `BlockMoveData()` function does, but I'll explain it just in case you haven't. `BlockMoveData()` is a Mac Toolbox (and Carbon) function that copies data from one location in memory to another. The function takes three parameters, as you can see in Table 5-1.

Finding a Tile's Type

It's very important to be able to find a tile's type when using tiles for games. For example, you will want to periodically check if the player is standing on an exit tile. If he is, you will load the next level from disk. If the player moves the joystick left, you must check if the tile to the left of the player is a wall. If it is, don't move the player or he'll go through the wall.

You must perform the following steps to find a tile's type:

1. Find the location in the level map that you want to check. Usually this will involve taking the player's (or other character's) current position in the game world, which is in pixels, and dividing by the tile size to get a row and column in the level map.

2. Find the tile number of the location you found in Step 1. I wrote an accessor function for the GameLevel class, GetValue(), which returns the tile number of a given location in the level map.

3. Find the tile type of the tile number you found in Step 2. I wrote an accessor function for the GameTile class, GetTileType(), which returns the tile type of a given tile.

The following function checks whether the player has reached the exit of a level:

```
Boolean ReachedExit(short playerX, short playerY, GameLevelPtr theLevel,
GameTileListPtr theTiles)
{
        short tileNum;
        GameTileType tileAttribute;
        short theLevelWidth = theLevel->GetLevelWidth();
        UInt32 mapIndex;

        // Find where the player is on the tile grid.
        short rowToTest = playerY / kTileHeight;
        short columnToTest = playerX / kTileWidth;

        // Find the tile that's at the player's location on the tile grid.
        mapIndex = (rowToTest * theLevelWidth) + columnToTest;
        tileNum = theLevel->levelMap[mapIndex].GetValue();

        // Check if the tile is an exit tile.
        tileAttribute = theTiles->tileTable[tileNum].GetTileType();
        if (tileAttribute == kExitTile)
                return true;
        else
                return false;

}
```

Checking for other tile types would result in similar code. You would substitute the desired type for an exit tile in the if statement at the end of the ReachedExit() function.

Drawing Tiles

To draw the tiles in the level, we do the following.

1. Read the tile number in the level map
2. Find where that particular tile is in the tile space.
3. Draw the tile from the tile space to the level.

Figure 5-3 shows what it takes to draw a tile. To draw a particular tile from the level map (the tile in the upper right corner in the case of Figure 5-3), we first find the tile number we want to draw. In the case of Figure 5-3, the tile number is 49. Next, we must locate tile number 49 in the tile space. In the way I've chosen to store the tiles in Figure 5-3, tile 49 is in the last column (column number 24) of the second row (row number 1). If you choose to store your tiles in a different manner or choose different size tiles, tile 49 would be in a different location. Now that we've found the location of the tile in tile space, we must find the rectangle containing the tile in the picture that holds all the tiles. I made the picture match the tile space, 25 columns of tiles and 20 rows of tiles, so finding the rectangle to draw is easy; the shaded portion of the picture shown in Figure 5-3. We calculate the rectangle using the location of the tile in tile space, as you can see below:

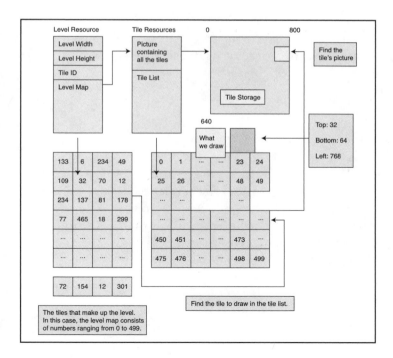

Figure 5-3

How our game draws a tile. The figure assumes 32-by-32–pixel tiles with 25 columns of tiles and 20 rows of tiles in the tile space.

- The top of the rectangle is the tile's row, 1, multiplied by the height of the tile, 32, giving the value 32.
- The bottom of the rectangle is the top of the rectangle, 32, plus the height of the tile, 32, yielding the value 64.
- The left edge of the rectangle is the tile's column, 24, multiplied by the width of the tile, 32, giving us the value 768.
- The right edge of the rectangle is the left edge of the rectangle, 768, plus the width of the tile, 32, which equals 800.

To draw the tile, we will call CopyBits() to draw the tile from the offscreen buffer containing the picture with all the tiles to the offscreen buffer storing the game's background. You would then call CopyBits() again to draw the tile on the screen from the offscreen buffer holding the game's background, like I showed you in Chapter 4, "Introduction to Macintosh Graphics." When drawing tiles with CopyBits(), we will use the srcCopy transfer mode for drawing. The srcCopy transfer mode will copy all the pixels from the source to the destination, which is what we want when drawing tiles.

Here's some code to draw a tile:

```
void GameContext::DrawTileFromLevelMap(GameLevelPtr theLevel, short theRow, short
theColumn)
{
        // The parameters theRow and theColumn are in screen space.
        // We need to convert them to world space. hOffset and vOffset
        // are data members of the GameContext class.
        short worldRow = theRow + vOffset;
        short worldColumn = theColumn + hOffset;

        // Find the tile number to draw
        short theLevelWidth = theLevel->GetLevelWidth();
        UInt32 mapIndex = (worldRow * theLevelWidth) + worldColumn;
        short tileNumber = theLevel->levelMap[mapIndex].GetValue();

        // Find the tile to draw in the level's tile space
        Point tileGridLocation = GetGridLocation(tileNumber);
        Rect tileRect = GetRectFromGridLocation(tileGridLocation);

        // Determine where to draw the tile on the screen
        Point backgroundLocation;
        backgroundLocation.h = theColumn;
```

```
        backgroundLocation.v = theRow;
        Rect backgroundRect = GetRectFromGridLocation(backgroundLocation);

        // Draw the tile. tileBlitter is a data member of the GameContext class
        tileBlitter.Setup(background->GetBufferStorage(), tileRect, backgroundRect);
        tileBlitter.DrawImageToOffscreenBuffer();

}


Point GameContext::GetGridLocation(short tileNumber)
{
        // Given a tile number from the level map, return
        // the grid location of the tile on the tile board.
        Point result;

        result.h = tileNumber % kTilesInRow;
        result.v = tileNumber / kTilesInRow;

        return result;
}


Rect GameContext::GetRectFromGridLocation(Point theGridLocation)
{
        Rect result;

        result.top = theGridLocation.v * kTileHeight;
        result.left = theGridLocation.h * kTileWidth;
        result.bottom = result.top + kTileHeight;
        result.right = result.left + kTileWidth;

        return result;
}
```

Isometric Tiles

If you've ever played the games *Diablo*, *Fallout*, and *Civilization 2*, then you have seen isometric tiles in action. Rather than being rectangular, isometric tiles have a diamond shape. This diamond shape provides the illusion of depth in a 2D tile.

Isometric tiles work well in environments that contain a lot of walls, which makes them a good choice for role-playing games. Role-playing games normally involve a lot of dungeon digging, and these dungeons have lots of walls. The major problem with isometric tiles is that they make life difficult for the artist who is making the tiles. Paint programs like Photoshop have a rectangular painting area so it's easier to draw rectangular tiles with an isometric perspective than draw pure isometric tiles. This difficulty in generating the artwork is the reason I chose not to use isometric tiles for the game in the book. However, isometric tiles could be just what your game needs so I'm providing you this introduction to isometric tiles.

Storing Tiles

Rectangular tiles have two dimensions, width and height, which you can see in Figure 5-4. Isometric tiles have three dimensions, length, width, and height. The length of an isometric tiles is the distance from the leftmost part of the tile to the rightmost part. It corresponds to the width of a rectangular tile. The width of an isometric tile is the distance from the top of the tile to the bottom. It corresponds to the height of a rectangular tile. The height of an isometric tile measures the thickness of the tile. Figure 5-4 shows the three dimensions of an isometric tile.

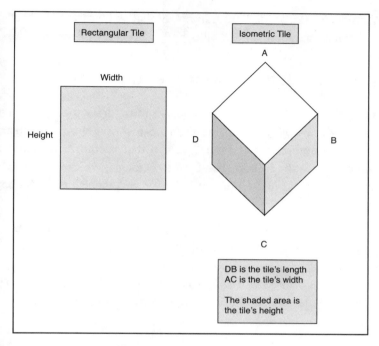

Figure 5-4

The dimensions of a rectangular and an isometric tile

When using isometric tiles, you will choose a tile length and width in much the same way you chose a rectangular tile's width and height. All the isometric tiles will have the same length and width, but the height can be different. Figure 5-5 shows tiles of differing heights. Because isometric tiles have different heights, you will need to store the tile's height as a data member of the GameTile class.

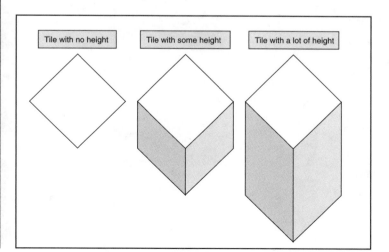

Figure 5-5

Isometric tiles can have different heights. The tile on the left has a height of 0. The tile in the middle has a height greater than 0, and the tile on the right is even taller.

You can store isometric tiles on disk the same way that you store rectangular tiles. You have a picture containing all the tiles, and a 2D array describing the isometric tiles.

Drawing Tiles

Even though isometric tiles are diamond shaped, we must draw them using rectangles because QuickDraw uses rectangles. Figure 5-6 shows the rectangular area an isometric tile encompasses and what part of that rectangle we must draw. Because we do not want to copy the entire rectangle, we cannot use the srcCopy transfer mode for CopyBits() like we did for rectangular tiles. We have two choices:

- We can use a mask that tells us what part of the rectangle to draw. For more detailed information on using masks, refer to Chapter 6, "Animation."
- We can specify a color to use as a transparent color then use CopyBits'() transparent transfer mode to avoid drawing the transparent pixels.

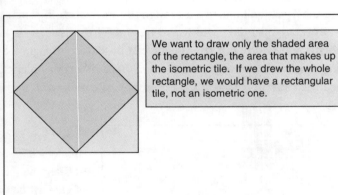

We want to draw only the shaded area of the rectangle, the area that makes up the isometric tile. If we drew the whole rectangle, we would have a rectangular tile, not an isometric one.

Figure 5-6

The shaded area shows the part of a rectangular pixel map that an isometric tile takes up.

In addition to drawing an individual tile, filling the screen with tiles requires more work when using isometric tiles. With rectangular tiles, you just start at the upper-left corner of the screen and draw tiles until you reach the lower-right corner of the screen, as you can see in the following code:

```
for (row = 0; row < screenRows; row++) {
        for(column = 0; column < screenColumns; column++) {
                DrawTile(row, column);
        }
}
```

With isometric tiles, things get more complicated. If you start at the left edge of the screen each row and start drawing tiles, the tiles won't line up, as you can see in Figure 5-7(a). What you need to do to align the tiles is alternate the starting point every other row of tiles. You would start drawing the first row of tiles at the left edge of the screen. For the second row, you would start drawing half a tile in. You would continue this pattern for all the rows, as you can see in Figure 5-7(b).

If we start at the left edge of the screen and start drawing isometric, as in (a), the tiles don t line up properly. The white diamond areas in (a) represent portions of the screen where tiles will not be drawn.

The solution is to move in half a tile every other row before you begin drawing that row, as you can see in the dark gray tiles in (b). By moving in half a tile, the tiles line up properly.

Figure 5-7

Drawing rows of isometric tiles on the screen

Another thing to keep in mind with isometric tiles is there will be twice as many rows to draw than with rectangular tiles. In Figure 5-7(b), a light gray row followed by a dark gray row corresponds to one rectangular row. When you move down one row, you move down half a tile (16 pixels for a 32-by-32–pixel tile) instead of a full tile (32 pixels for a 32-by-32–pixel tile),

Most of the steps I described to draw a rectangular tile in the section "Drawing Tiles" (Refer to Figure 5-3 for a picture of the steps involved and the function `DrawTileFromLevelMap()` for source code) are the same when drawing an isometric tile. The only difference occurs when drawing the tile from tile storage to the game background. Calculating the destination rectangle is what's different because the destination rectangle depends on whether the current row number is even or odd.

If the row number is even, we start drawing at the left edge of the screen (or the offscreen buffer that corresponds to the screen in this case), and the destination rectangle looks like this:

```
destRect.top = row * (kTileWidth / 2);
destRect.bottom = destRect.top + kTileWidth;
destRect.left = column * kTileLength;
destRect.right = destRect.left + kTileLength;
```

If the row number is odd, the code to compute the left component of the destination rectangle changes to look like this:

```
offset = kTileLength / 2;
destRect.left = column * kTileLength + offset;
```

My calculation of the destination rectangle assumes a flat tile with a height of zero. To draw a taller tile you would move the top of the destination rectangle up by the height of the tile. Here's the new calculation of the top of the rectangle:

```
destRect.top = row * (kTileWidth / 2) - tileHeight;
```

To draw an isometric tile instead of a rectangular one, the following section of code in the `DrawTileFromLevelMap()` function would change from this

```
Point backgroundLocation;
backgroundLocation.h = theColumn;
backgroundLocation.v = theRow;
Rect backgroundRect = GetRectFromGridLocation(backgroundLocation);
```

to this:

```
Boolean isRowOdd;
Rect backgroundRect;
```

```
short oddRowOffset;

oddRowOffset = kTileLength / 2;

// If the last bit is one, then we have an odd number.
rowIsOdd = theRow & 1;

if (rowIsOdd)
        backgroundRect.left = (theColumn * kileLength) + oddRowOffset;

backgroundRect.right = backgroundRect.left + kTileLength;

// Each isometric tile has its own tile height
backgroundRect.up = theRow * (kTileWidth / 2) - tileHeight;
backgroundRect.down = backgroundRect.up + kTileWidth;
```

Scrolling Backgrounds

Because the whole point of using tiles is to create large worlds that span multiple screens, we will have to scroll the background to show the appropriate part of the game world to the player.

For our scrolling examples, we will use 32-by-32–pixel tiles. We will use a screen resolution of 640-by-480 pixels. The game world is 100 tiles high and 100 tiles wide. Figure 5-8 shows how the screen shows only part of the game world at a time. The scrolling examples in the chapter will scroll one tile at a time, but that's for the purposes of explanation only. In a game, you will probably want to scroll a larger area of the screen so that you don't have to scroll as often. The scrolling functions we will develop in this chapter allow you to specify the number of tiles you want to scroll.

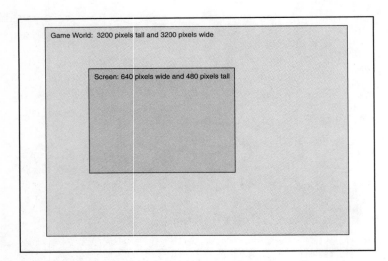

Figure 5-8

The screen and our game world

Games typically scroll the screen in one of two ways. The first method scrolls the screen whenever the player moves, keeping the player centered on the screen. The second method scrolls the screen only when it needs to, such as when the player comes close to the edge of the screen. I employ the second method in this chapter and in the game for this book because it involves less redrawing of the screen, resulting in faster drawing.

The GameContext Class

To make the scrolling code easier to read, here are the data members for the GameContext class we'll create to handle scrolling:

```
class GameContext
{
    protected:
        GameOffscreenBufferPtr background;
        GameOffscreenBufferPtr tileStorage;

        short screenWidth;
        short screenHeight;

        short hOffset;          // In tiles
        short vOffset;          // In tiles
        Blitter tileBlitter;
}
```

The `GameContext` class contains buffers to store the tiles and the background. The class also stores the screen width and height to make scrolling simpler. It contains horizontal and vertical offsets to make it easy to keep track of where we are in both world space and screen space. The upper left corner of the screen is at `((hOffset * kTileWidth), (vOffset * kTileHeight))` in world space coordinates. The offsets are in tiles so you must multiply them by the tile width and tile height to get the coordinates in pixels.

If you remember from Chapter 4, "Introduction to Macintosh Graphics," there are many little steps you must take to draw from one off-screen buffer to another (or to the screen) using `CopyBits()`. I wrote a `Blitter` class to hide many of these little details so you can focus on higher-level concepts. The `tileBlitter` data member will allow us to draw tiles from `tileStorage`, the location of the tiles, to the `background` so the tiles will appear on the screen.

> **NOTE**
>
> The term *blit* is shorthand for a block transfer. A block transfer occurs when you move data from one location to another in memory, which is the way most games draw 2D graphics. When you call `CopyBits()` to copy an image from an offscreen buffer to the screen, you are performing a block transfer. A *blitter* is a function that performs a block transfer for drawing graphics.

Scrolling Right

To avoid any confusion, let me explain how I'm going to define the phrase scrolling right in this chapter. Scrolling right is what happens when we reach the right edge of the screen, and we want to scroll to show what's located to the right of the screen. The background actually moves to your left, with the impression that you are moving to your right.

Before the scroll, the screen shows the upper-left portion of the game world, as shown in Figure 5-9. In a horizontal scroll, only the columns change, not the rows. That's why I show only the columns in Figure 5-9.

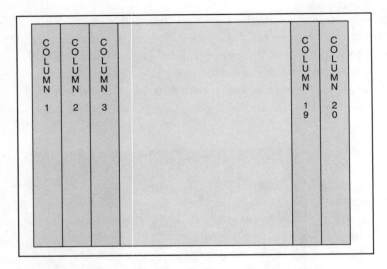

Figure 5-9

The screen before the scroll

To scroll one tile to the right, we have to do the following:

1. Move all the tiles on the screen except for the leftmost column one column to the left. Moving the tiles in this way obliterates the leftmost column. We can accomplish this with one call to `CopyBits()`.

2. Fill in the rightmost column of the screen with new tiles. This process involves calling the `DrawTileFromLevelMap()` function I wrote in the "Drawing Tiles" section earlier in this chapter.

Figure 5-10 shows how the screen looks after the scroll. Here's the code to scroll to the right by the number of tiles of your choice:

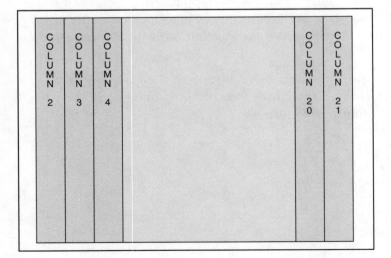

Figure 5-10

The screen after the scroll

```
void GameContext::ScrollRight(GameLevelPtr theLevel, short tilesToScroll)
{
        // Bounds checking. If we've hit the right edge of the level, don't
        // bother scrolling.
        short rightEdge = theLevel->GetLevelWidth() - (screenWidth / kTileWidth);
        if (hOffset >= rightEdge)
                return;

        // If a full scroll puts us past the right edge of the level
        // then only scroll to the edge.
        if ((hOffset + tilesToScroll) > rightEdge) {
                short amountToScroll = rightEdge - hOffset;
                ScrollRight(theLevel, amountToScroll);
                return;
        }

        CGrafPtr oldPort;
        GDHandle oldGDevice;

        // save previous drawing area
        GetGWorld (&oldPort, &oldGDevice);

        // Set drawing area to the background
        SetGWorld (background->GetBufferStorage(), nil);

        // Draw the portion of the background that remains after the scroll
        // For a scroll right, we move the rightmost columns that remain to
        // the left edge of the screen.
        Rect sourceRect;
        Rect destRect;

        sourceRect.top = 0;
        sourceRect.left = tilesToScroll * kTileWidth;
        sourceRect.bottom = screenHeight;
        sourceRect.right = screenWidth;

        destRect.top = 0;
        destRect.left = 0;
        destRect.bottom = screenHeight;
        destRect.right = screenWidth - (tilesToScroll * kTileWidth);
```

```
Blitter theBlitter;
theBlitter.SetSourceBuffer(background->GetBufferStorage());
theBlitter.SetDestinationBuffer(background->GetBufferStorage());
theBlitter.SetSourceRect(sourceRect);
theBlitter.SetDestinationRect(destRect);
theBlitter.SetDrawingMode(srcCopy);
theBlitter.DrawImageToOffscreenBuffer();



    // Update the origin to reflect the scroll
    hOffset = hOffset + tilesToScroll;

    // Fill in the new tiles. For a scroll right, it will be
    // the rightmost columns
    short rowsInContext = screenHeight / kTileHeight;
    short columnsInContext = screenWidth / kTileWidth;

    for (short column = columnsInContext - tilesToScroll; column <
columnsInContext; column++) {
            for (short row = 0; row < rowsInContext; row++) {
                    DrawTileFromLevelMap(theLevel, row, column);
            }
    }

    // restore graphics port and GDevice
    SetGWorld(oldPort, oldGDevice);


}
```

I wrote the DrawTileFromLevelMap() function in the section "Drawing Tiles" earlier in this chapter, so I won't repeat the code listing here. You can read the source code for the function there. The DrawTileFromLevelMap() function shows the GameContext class' tileBlitter data member at work.

Scrolling Left

Scrolling left is what happens when we reach the left edge of the screen, and we want to scroll to show what's located to the left of the screen. The background actually moves to the right, with the impression that you are moving to the left. Figure 5-11 shows the screen before the scroll.

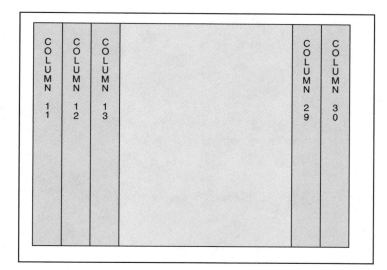

Figure 5-11

The screen before the scroll

To scroll one tile to the left, we have to do the following:

1. Move all the tiles on the screen except for the rightmost column one column to the right. Doing this obliterates the rightmost column. We can accomplish this movement with one call to CopyBits().

2. Fill in the leftmost column of the screen with new tiles. This process involves calling the DrawTileFromLevelMap() function I wrote in the "Drawing Tiles" section.

Figure 5-12 shows how the screen will look after the scroll. Here's the code to scroll left by the number of tiles of your choice:

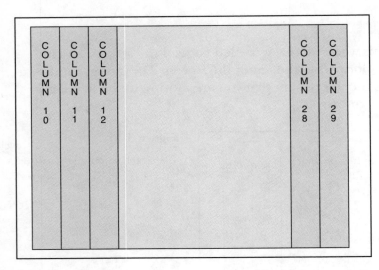

Figure 5-12

The screen after the scroll

```
void GameContext::ScrollLeft(GameLevelPtr theLevel, short tilesToScroll)
{
        // Bounds checking. If we've hit the left edge of the level, don't
        // bother scrolling.
        short leftEdge = 0;
        if (hOffset <= leftEdge)
                return;

        // If a full scroll puts us past the left edge of the level
        // then only scroll to the edge.
        if ((hOffset - tilesToScroll) < rightEdge) {
                short amountToScroll = hOffset;
                ScrollLeft(theLevel, amountToScroll);
                return;
        }

        CGrafPtr oldPort;
        GDHandle oldGDevice;

        // save previous drawing area
        GetGWorld (&oldPort, &oldGDevice);

        // Set drawing area to the background
        SetGWorld (background->GetBufferStorage(), nil);
```

```
    // Draw the portion of the background that remains after the scroll
    // For a scroll left, we move the leftmost columns that remain to
    // the right edge of the screen.
    Rect sourceRect;
    Rect destRect;

    sourceRect.top = 0;
    sourceRect.left = 0;
    sourceRect.bottom = screenHeight;
    sourceRect.right = screenWidth - (tilesToScroll * kTileWidth);

    destRect.top = 0;
    destRect.left = tilesToScroll * kTileWidth;
    destRect.bottom = screenHeight;
    destRect.right = screenWidth;

    Blitter theBlitter;
    theBlitter.SetSourceBuffer(background->GetBufferStorage());
    theBlitter.SetDestinationBuffer(background->GetBufferStorage());
    theBlitter.SetSourceRect(sourceRect);
    theBlitter.SetDestinationRect(destRect);
    theBlitter.SetDrawingMode(srcCopy);
    theBlitter.DrawImageToOffscreenBuffer();

    // Update the origin to reflect the scroll
    hOffset = hOffset - tilesToScroll;

    // Fill in the new tiles. For a scroll left, it will be
    // the leftmost columns
    short rowsInContext = screenHeight / kTileHeight;

    for (short column = 0; column < tilesToScroll; column++) {
        for (short row = 0; row < rowsInContext; row++) {
            DrawTileFromLevelMap(theLevel, row, column);
        }
    }

    // restore graphics port and GDevice
    SetGWorld(oldPort, oldGDevice);

}
```

Looking through the source code to scroll left and right, I'm sure you noticed the code at the start of the functions to make sure we don't scroll past the end of the level like the following:

```
if ((hOffset - tilesToScroll) < rightEdge) {
      short amountToScroll = hOffset;
      ScrollLeft(theLevel, amountToScroll);
      return;
}
```

The scrolling functions let you as the programmer decide how many tiles to scroll rather than just scrolling by one tile like I have been in this chapter. Let's say you wanted to scroll left by a quarter of the screen, which is five tiles in the scrolling examples in this chapter. Further, let's say you can scroll only three tiles left before you reach the left edge of the level. In this case, you want to scroll only three tiles. If you scroll the full five tiles left, you cannot be sure of the exact result, but it will most likely be disastrous. Garbage graphics may appear in the first two columns on the screen, or your game may crash. The source code above makes sure you don't scroll past the edge of the level.

Scrolling Down

Scrolling down is what happens when we reach the bottom edge of the screen, and we want to scroll to show what's located below the screen. The background actually moves up, with the impression that you are moving down. Figure 5-13 shows how the screen looks before the scroll. In a vertical scroll, only the rows change, not the columns. That's why I show only the rows in Figure 5-13.

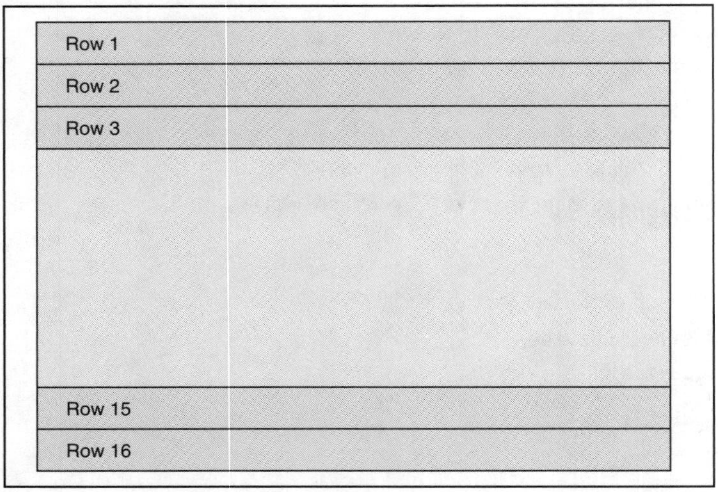

Figure 5-13

The screen before the scroll

Row 1
Row 2
Row 3

Row 15
Row 16

To scroll one tile down, we have to do the following:

1. Move all the tiles on the screen except for the top row one row up. Moving the tiles in this way will wipe out the top row of tiles. We can accomplish all this with one call to `CopyBits()`.

2. Fill in the bottom row of the screen with new tiles. This involves calling the `DrawTileFromLevelMap()` function I wrote in the "Drawing Tiles" section earlier in this chapter.

Figure 5-14 shows how the screen looks after the scroll. Here's the code to scroll down by the number of tiles of your choice:

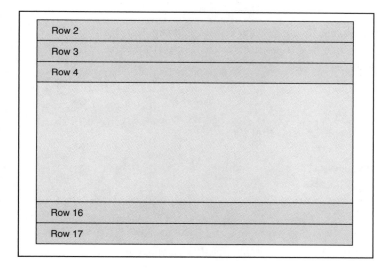

Figure 5-14

The screen after the scroll

```
void GameContext::ScrollDown(GameLevelPtr theLevel, short tilesToScroll)
{
        // Bounds checking. If we've hit the bottom edge of the level, don't
        // bother scrolling.
        short bottomEdge = theLevel->GetLevelHeight() - (screenHeight / kTileHeight);
        if (vOffset >= bottomEdge)
                return;

        // If a full scroll puts us past the bottom edge of the level
        // then only scroll to the edge.
        if ((vOffset + tilesToScroll) > bottomEdge) {
                short amountToScroll = bottomEdge - vOffset;
                ScrollDown(theLevel, amountToScroll);
```

```
        return;
    }

    CGrafPtr oldPort;
    GDHandle oldGDevice;

    // save previous drawing area
    GetGWorld (&oldPort, &oldGDevice);

    // Set drawing area to the background
    SetGWorld (background->GetBufferStorage(), nil);

    // Draw the portion of the background that remains after the scroll
    // For a scroll down, we move the lowest rows that remain to
    // the top edge of the screen.
    Rect sourceRect;
    Rect destRect;

    sourceRect.top = tilesToScroll * kTileHeight;
    sourceRect.left = 0;
    sourceRect.bottom = screenHeight;
    sourceRect.right = screenWidth;

    destRect.top = 0;
    destRect.left = 0;
    destRect.bottom = screenHeight - (tilesToScroll * kTileHeight);
    destRect.right = screenWidth;

    Blitter theBlitter;
    theBlitter.SetSourceBuffer(background->GetBufferStorage());
    theBlitter.SetDestinationBuffer(background->GetBufferStorage());
    theBlitter.SetSourceRect(sourceRect);
    theBlitter.SetDestinationRect(destRect);
    theBlitter.SetDrawingMode(srcCopy);
    theBlitter.DrawImageToOffscreenBuffer();

    // Update the origin to reflect the scroll
    vOffset = vOffset + tilesToScroll;

    // Fill in the new tiles. For a scroll down, it will be
    // the lowest columns
```

```
short rowsInContext = screenHeight / kTileHeight;
short columnsInContext = screenWidth / kTileWidth;

for (short row = rowsInContext - tilesToScroll; row < rowsInContext; row++) {
        for (short column = 0; column < columnsInContext; column++) {
                DrawTileFromLevelMap(theLevel, row, column);
        }
}

// restore graphics port and GDevice
SetGWorld(oldPort, oldGDevice);

}
```

Scrolling Up

Scrolling up is what happens when we reach the top edge of the screen, and we want to scroll to show what's located above the screen. The background actually moves down, with the impression that you are moving up. Figure 5-15 shows how the screen looks before the scroll.

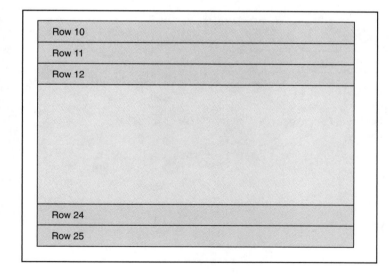

Figure 5-15

The screen before the scroll

To scroll one tile up, we have to do the following:

1. Move all the tiles on the screen except for the bottom row one row down. Doing this annihilates the bottom row of tiles. We can perform this movement with one call to CopyBits().

2. Fill in the top row of the screen with new tiles. This involves calling the DrawTileFromLevelMap() function I wrote in the "Drawing Tiles" section earlier in this chapter.

Figure 5-16 shows how the screen looks after the scroll. Here's the code to scroll up by the number of tiles of your choice:

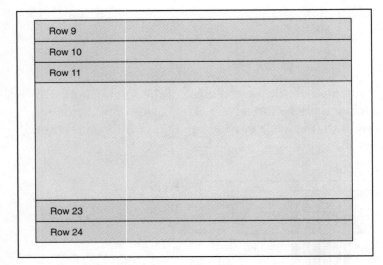

Figure 5-16

The screen after the scroll

```
void GameContext::ScrollUp(GameLevelPtr theLevel, short tilesToScroll)
{
        // Bounds checking. If we've hit the top edge of the level, don't
        // bother scrolling.
        short topEdge = 0;
        if (vOffset <= topEdge)
                return;

        // If a full scroll puts us past the top edge
        // then only scroll to the edge.
        if ((vOffset - tilesToScroll) < topEdge) {
                short amountToScroll = vOffset;
                ScrollUp(theLevel, amountToScroll);
```

```
        return;
    }

CGrafPtr oldPort;
GDHandle oldGDevice;

// save previous drawing area
GetGWorld (&oldPort, &oldGDevice);

// Set drawing area to the background
SetGWorld (background->GetBufferStorage(), nil);

// Draw the portion of the background that remains after the scroll
// For a scroll up, we move the highest rows that remain to
// the bottom edge of the screen.
Rect sourceRect;
Rect destRect;

sourceRect.top = 0;
sourceRect.left = 0;
sourceRect.bottom = screenHeight - (tilesToScroll * kTileHeight);
sourceRect.right = screenWidth;

destRect.top = tilesToScroll * kTileHeight;
destRect.left = 0;
destRect.bottom = screenHeight;
destRect.right = screenWidth;

Blitter theBlitter;
theBlitter.SetSourceBuffer(background->GetBufferStorage());
theBlitter.SetDestinationBuffer(background->GetBufferStorage());
theBlitter.SetSourceRect(sourceRect);
theBlitter.SetDestinationRect(destRect);
theBlitter.SetDrawingMode(srcCopy);
theBlitter.DrawImageToOffscreenBuffer();

// Update the origin to reflect the scroll
vOffset = vOffset - tilesToScroll;

// Fill in the new tiles. For a scroll up, it will be
// the highest rows
```

```
short columnsInContext = screenWidth / kTileWidth;

for (short row = 0; row < tilesToScroll; row++) {
        for (short column = 0; column < columnsInContext; column++) {
                DrawTileFromLevelMap(theLevel, row, column);
        }
}

// restore graphics port and GDevice
SetGWorld(oldPort, oldGDevice);

}
```

Tile Layering

So far all the tile drawing I've done has been drawing background tiles. It's possible to draw tiles in the foreground that allow the characters in a game to walk behind them. For example, in a game in a wilderness setting, you could draw bushes in the foreground and have the player walk behind them. Adding foreground tiles to your game's world will give the world more visual depth.

To draw with multiple levels, here's how you have to do your drawing.

1. Draw the background tiles first.
2. Draw the characters in the game.
3. Draw the foreground tiles last. This will make the characters appear behind the foreground tiles.

Storing the Foreground Tiles

I chose to lump the foreground tiles with the background tiles in the same set of tiles. Foreground tiles have the tile type kForegroundTile; all other tile types are background tiles. Combining the foreground and background tiles in one tile group simplifies the storing of the tiles on disk. If I put the foreground tiles in their own group, then each level would have to store a set of tiles on disk for both the background and the foreground.

Putting the background and foreground tiles together simplifies the tile storage, but we lose a little flexibility. The foreground tiles can be used only with the background tiles in their tile group. Separating the background and foreground tiles would allow a group of foreground tiles to be used with multiple sets of back-

ground tiles. I chose simplified storage over flexibility. I can just copy the foreground tiles to other tile sets if I want to use some foreground tiles with multiple sets of background tiles.

Adding Foreground Tiles to a Level

To use foreground tiles in our game's levels, we must add a data member to the GameLevel class, which you can see listed below:

```
MapElementPtr foregroundTileMap;
```

The foregroundTileMap data member is a 2D array containing the foreground tiles to draw in the level. The array of foreground tiles will be the same size as the level map, but most of the entries will be empty since most levels will not have many foreground tiles. I use the tile number -1 (constant kNoForegroundTile) to designate an empty foreground tile. The game engine will not draw foreground tiles with a value of kNoForegroundTile.

Allocating the foreground tile map and reading it from disk involve code similar to the ReadLevelData() and AllocateLevelMap() functions I wrote earlier in the chapter. You would add another for loop to the ReadLevelData() function to read the foreground tiles from disk. You would write a function AllocateForegroundMap() that uses the same code as AllocateLevelMap(), but substitutes the variable foregroundTileMap for levelMap. I'm not going to waste trees by rehashing the code here, but you can see the source code on the CD-ROM that comes with the book.

Drawing Foreground Tiles

As I mentioned earlier in this chapter, you draw the foreground tiles after you draw the background tiles and the characters in the game. Drawing the foreground tiles after the characters makes the tiles appear in front of the characters, making it look like the character is walking behind the foreground image.

Drawing a foreground tile is similar to drawing a background tile. You must take the following steps to draw a foreground tile:

1. Read the tile number in the array of foreground tiles. If the tile number is kNoForegroundTile, we will stop without drawing the tile.

2. If there is a foreground tile to draw, find where that particular tile is in the tile space.

3. Draw the tile from the tile space to the level.

We will use CopyBits() to draw foreground tiles, just like we did with background tiles. There is one difference in how we call CopyBits(). When drawing tiles with CopyBits(), we will use the transparent transfer mode for drawing instead of the srcCopy mode. Foreground tiles may have transparent pixels that allow the player to see the background through those pixels in the game. The transparent transfer mode will not draw the transparent pixels, which is what we want.

Because we use the transparent transfer mode for CopyBits() instead of the srcCopy mode, the tileBlitter data member of the GameContext class will not be suitable for drawing foreground tiles. We will have to add another Blitter object to the GameContext class to draw foreground tiles.

```
Blitter foregroundTileBlitter;
```

The following function draws a foreground tile from the foreground tile map:

```
void GameContext::DrawForegroundTileFromMap(GameLevelPtr theLevel, short theRow,
short theColumn)
{
        // The parameters theRow and theColumn are in screen space.
        // We need to convert them to world space. hOffset and vOffset
        // are data members of the GameContext class.
        short worldRow = theRow + vOffset;
        short worldColumn = theColumn + hOffset;

        // Find the tile number to draw
        short theLevelWidth = theLevel->GetLevelWidth();
        UInt32 mapIndex = (worldRow * theLevelWidth) + worldColumn;
        short tileNumber = theLevel->foregroundTileMap[mapIndex].GetValue();

        // See if there is an actual foreground tile to draw.
        // If not, exit the function
        if (tileNumber == kNoForegroundTile)
            return;

        // Find the tile to draw in the level's tile space
        Point tileGridLocation = GetGridLocation(tileNumber);
        Rect tileRect = GetRectFromGridLocation(tileGridLocation);

        // Determine where to draw the tile on the screen
        Point foregroundLocation;
```

```
        foregroundLocation.h = theColumn;
        foregroundLocation.v = theRow;
        Rect foregroundRect = GetRectFromGridLocation(foregroundLocation);

        // Draw the tile. foregroundTileBlitter is a data member of the GameContext
class

        foregroundTileBlitter.Setup(background->GetBufferStorage(), tileRect,
foregroundRect);
        foregroundTileBlitter.DrawImageToOffscreenBuffer();

}
```

Parallax Scrolling

When I described using multiple layers of tiles in the section "Tile Layering" earlier in this chapter, I had one background layer and one foreground layer. You can take multiple background and foreground layers and scroll these layers at different speeds to create a parallax effect. The term for doing this is parallax scrolling.

Figure 5-17 shows how an outdoor scene in a side scrolling game looks with multiple tile layers. In the figure, there are four layers. At the top of the screen is the sky layer. Below that is the mountain layer. Below that is the main background layer, and at the bottom is the foreground layer. If you wanted, you could add even more background and foreground layers.

Figure 5-17

Using multiple tile layers for parallax scrolling

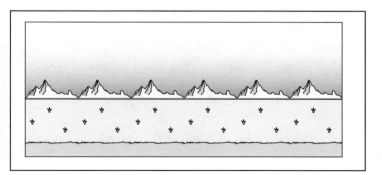

Multiple tile layers are one half of the parallax scrolling equations. Scrolling the layers at different speeds is the other half. You scroll the foreground layer closest to the screen the fastest, and then scroll each successive layer slower until you get to the point where the farthest background layer barely scrolls at all. In the outdoor scene shown in Figure 5-17, the mountain layer would scroll slowly, and the sky layer would scroll even slower. This is what you would expect in the physical world. If you take a walk down your street, the immediate scenery (houses, buildings, trees) changes as you walk. Your view of the sky is not going to change much.

Parallax scrolling works best if your game scrolls mainly in two directions, either vertically or horizontally, and if your game scrolls whenever the player moves. Our game in the book scrolls in all four directions so parallax scrolling doesn't work well, but it doesn't mean you can't use parallax scrolling for your game.

Storing Tile Layers

While it's possible to use the same architecture I used in this chapter (a GameTile class, a GameLevel class, and a GameContext class) for parallax scrolling and just add the extra layers to the classes and functions, I would advise against it. Things will get unwieldy in a hurry. Each layer is going to have its own scrolling speed. Because of this, each layer is in a different position in world space, so having two offsets, hOffset and vOffset, like I had for the GameContext class will not work. The solution is to create a class to store tile layers. Here's how such a class might look:

```
class GameTileLayer
{
        protected:
                short hOffset;
                short vOffset;
                float scrollSpeed;
                short layerWidth;
                short layerHeight;

        public:
                MapElementPtr layerMap;

}
```

A `GameTileLayer` object has its own offsets and scrolling speed. The `scrollSpeed` data member is a percentage of how much to scroll; a value of .5 means to scroll this layer at half the normal speed. The `layerWidth` and `layerHeight` data members tell us the layer's width and height so we don't accidentally scroll past the edge of the layer. The `layerMap` data member is a 2D array containing all the tiles to draw for the tile layer.

Using `GameTileLayer` objects changes the composition of the `GameLevel` class. Instead of having maps to contain the background and foreground tiles, the `GameLevel` class contains a collection of `GameTileLayer` objects. For the example I used in this sidebar, the `GameLevel` class would look like this:

```
class GameLevel
{
    protected:
        short tileID;
        GameTileLayer skyLayer;
        GameTileLayer mountainLayer;
        GameTileLayer backgroundLayer;
        GameTileLayer foregroundLayer;
};
```

The `GameContext` class would be mostly unchanged. We just get rid of the `hOffset` and `vOffset` data members because the `GameTileLayer` class stores the offsets.

Doing the Scrolling

The non-parallax method of scrolling we used in this chapter involved the following steps:

- Update the offsets to reflect the scroll.
- Move the portion of the screen that remains after the scroll.
- Fill the new tiles.

Parallax scrolling requires one more step at the beginning of the scroll; we must calculate the number of tiles to scroll for each layer. To do this, we multiply the base number of tiles to scroll by the layer's scrolling speed.

After calculating how much to scroll each layer, we update the offsets for each layer to reflect the scroll. Next it's time to move the portion of the screen that remains after the scroll. The question is, "How much of the screen remains after the scroll?" This is a very important question to answer because each layer scrolls a different number of tiles. The answer to the question is to use the layer that scrolled the largest number of tiles. It involves a little redundant drawing, but by going with the largest scroll value, we ensure that we will redraw the screen properly to reflect the scroll.

Finally, we fill the screen with new tiles. Using parallax scrolling requires more work. We must fill each layer with new tiles. This will involve a function that is very similar to the `DrawTileFromLevelMap()` function we wrote earlier in the chapter. The main difference is that we use a `GameTileLayer` object to store the layer's map instead of the level storing the map like it does in the `DrawTileFromLevelMap()` function.

Summary

Now we can do much cooler things than just show a picture on the screen. At this point, we have something that's starting to look like a game. We learned how to use tiles to create game levels, and we learned how to scroll the screen. We learned about foreground tiles, which you draw in front of the characters in the game to make the characters walk behind objects in the game. In addition, I introduced the topics of isometric tiles and parallax scrolling.

The program on the accompanying CD-ROM for this chapter displays a tiled background on the screen. You can use the arrow keys on the keyboard to scroll the background so you can get a feel for how scrolling works.

CHAPTER 6

ANIMATION

In the last chapter, you learned how to create game worlds using tiles. Now we must populate the world with a player character, creatures the player can encounter, and items he can acquire. Without these things, the player has nothing to control, making for a very dull game. This chapter shows you how to create creatures and items and provides you with some techniques to animate them.

Introduction to Sprites

Games with 2D graphics and some 3D games use *sprites* to display the objects that can move in the game and the items the player can interact with in the game. Examples of sprites include the player character, enemies, bullets, and health packs.

At a low level, a sprite is simply a rectangular pixel map. All it contains is a bunch of numbers representing color values. Entities in the game that can move contain multiple sprites while inanimate game objects have just one sprite.

Generating Animation

Animation in a computer game works similarly to an animated cartoon. You draw a series of animation frames and play them one after the other, providing the illusion of movement. You can tell I'm an animation scholar, can't you? In games, animation sequences loop to provide continuous movement. For example, if you have a ten-frame running animation, you would draw frame 1, then frame 2, then frame 3, and so on up to frame 10. After playing frame 10, you would go back to frame 1 and repeat the sequence as long as the player continues moving.

You need one sprite for each frame of animation in your game. Depending on your game, a human character could require sequences for running, jumping, kicking, and fighting. If your game has numerous enemies and many weapons for the player to use, you will need a lot of animation frames. Consider a fantasy role-playing game. Let's say that the player can carry a sword or a crossbow, and he can wear chain mail armor. If we allow the player to move in four directions, and give him an eight-frame walking sequence and a four-frame fighting sequence, we get the following sequence requirements:

- Four directions (up, down, left, and right)
- Three weapons (fist, sword, crossbow)
- Two types of armor (no armor, chain mail)
- Eight walking frames
- Four fighting frames

To calculate the total number of frames required for the player, we must multiply the number of directions by the number of weapons by the number of armor types by the number of walking frames by the number of fighting frames. This gives us a total of 768 animation frames for one character—and that's for a character with only two weapons and one set of armor. If you let the player have a dozen weapons and six different types of armor, you would need over 11,000 sprites. Add some monsters, and you'll be keeping your artist (or artists if you're fortunate) extremely busy.

Creatures with limbs, such as people, humanoids, and animals require the most animation frames. These creatures require frames in which their arms and legs move to give the appearance of realistic movement. If you use just one frame, the creature would appear to float across the screen, which looks good only if the creature is levitating. Spaceships and airplanes can get away with fewer animation frames. An airplane's wings don't move when it's flying the way a bird's wings do, so an airplane doesn't need a sequence to simulate wing flapping. If an aircraft floats across the screen, it looks okay because spaceships and airplanes appear to float in the physical world.

Storing Sprites

You can use any method you want to store your sprites, but the easiest way is to store a collection of sprites in one picture, as we do to store tiles. The way I store the sprites for the game we're developing is to have one picture for the player character's sprites, one picture for each monster's sprites, one picture for the missiles' sprites, and one picture containing all the sprites for inanimate objects such as ammunition, health packs, and treasure. Giving each animation frame its own picture involves too much overhead: You would need hundreds or even thousands of offscreen buffers to hold the frames. Each offscreen buffer incurs some storage overhead, and having thousands of them would make the overhead unbearable. On the other hand, stuffing all the game's sprites into one picture makes organization difficult if your game has many sprites.

How you arrange the individual sprites in each picture is up to you. Any way that makes it easy for you to remember the arrangement will work. Here's one way you could arrange the sprites for a monster, assuming that each individual monster uses the same weapon:

Row 1: Monster facing up

Row 2: Monster facing down

Row 3: Monster facing left

Row 4: Monster facing right

Column 1: Monster standing

Columns 2 to X: The monster's moving frames

Columns (X+1) to Y: The monster's fighting frames

Storing the sprites this way makes it relatively painless to support animation. If the sprite's direction changes, you change the sprite row to the new direction. When the sprite changes actions—such as going from standing to moving—you change the sprite column to reflect the change. When the sprite performs a multiframe action—such as moving or fighting—you just increment the sprite column.

Creating Transparency

Because the computer stores sprites as rectangles, you may be wondering how games make sprites look like people, animals, aircraft, tanks, or bullets instead of like rectangles. They do it by using transparency. The computer does not draw the pixels in the rectangle that are not part of the image, so the image appears on the screen as a person, spaceship, or arrow. The pixels the computer does not draw are the transparent pixels.

The easiest way to implement transparency is to reserve one color as the transparent color. Pixels with the transparent color are not drawn to the screen. In Figure 6-1, the gray pixels are transparent and do not appear on the screen. Most games use white as the transparent color, but using gray illustrates the point better in the figure. To use a transparency color on the Mac, call `CopyBits()`, using the `transparent` transfer mode. Refer to Chapter 4 for an explanation on all the transfer modes you can use with `CopyBits()`.

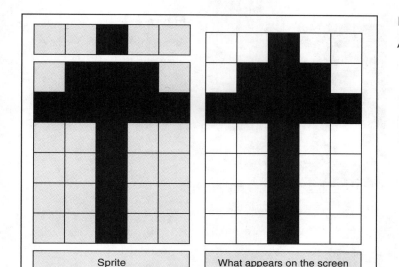

Figure 6-1

An example of transparency

Another way to implement transparency is by using masks. A *mask* is a pixel map through which you run your sprite (or any other pixel map) to transform the sprite. To implement transparency for sprites, you would supply a black-and-white (1-bit color) mask that is the same size as your sprite. Wherever the mask has a value of 1, the computer draws that pixel in the sprite. The computer will not draw pixels in the sprite if the corresponding pixel in the mask has a value of 0. Figure 6-2 provides an illustration of the workings of a mask. In the figure, the sprite pixels where the mask is black appear on the screen in the sprite's color (the gray and black pixels in the "What appears on the screen" figure). The gray pixels on the sprite appear as gray pixels on the screen, and the black pixels on the sprite appear as black on the screen. The sprite pixels that correspond to the white pixels in the mask are transparent pixels. They do not appear on the screen. In Figure 6-2, the transparent pixels are the white pixels in the picture above the caption "What appears on the screen.

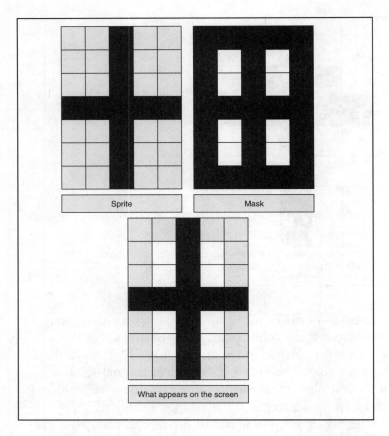

Figure 6-2

An example of transparency using masks

If all you are interested in is simple transparency, a transparency color works better than masks. If you use masks, you'll need a mask for every sprite; if you have a lot of sprites, the masks will consume a lot of memory. In addition, drawing with masks is slower than using a transparency color, and speed is of the essence in game development.

Masks can be useful if you need to apply other graphic effects in addition to transparency. For example, you might want the player character in the game be able to turn invisible, like Bilbo Baggins did in *The Hobbit* by wearing the invisibility ring. On the screen, you want to show an outline of the player so that the person playing the game knows where the character is to control the character properly. By creating a mask containing the outline of the player character sprite, you can achieve the invisibility effect without having to create separate sprites showing the character when he is invisible. Masks give you more graphical options at the expense of slower drawing.

Color Masks

Another useful tactic for masks is to create color masks. By using color masks, you can blend colors to transform your sprite and create special effects. What happens with a color mask is the color of a pixel in the sprite combines with the color of the corresponding pixel in the mask to make a new color appear on the screen.

The color in the mask determines how much of the source image (the sprite) appears in the destination image (the screen). Recall from Chapter 4 that a QuickDraw color consists of red, green, and blue components. Each component is a 16-bit value ranging from 0 (0 percent intensity) to 65535 (100 percent intensity). For each color component, the final value that appears on the screen uses the following formula (assuming the color intensity is a value between 0 and 1):

$$((1 - - - \text{mask intensity}) * \text{source intensity}) + (\text{mask intensity} * \text{destination intensity})$$

This formula says that as the intensity of the mask color increases, the amount of the source image's color that appears on the screen decreases.

Let's work through an example of using color masks. Suppose we have a yellow pixel in the sprite with 100 percent intensity and a corresponding blue pixel in the mask with 100 percent intensity. The sprite's pixel has 100 percent intensity in the red and green components and 0 percent intensity in the blue component because the pixel is yellow. The mask's pixel has 0 percent intensity in the red and green components and 100 percent intensity in the blue component because the pixel is blue.

When the sprite and the mask blend, the pixel that appears on the screen will have 100 percent intensity in the red and green components. This is because the mask pixel has 0 percent intensity in both the red and green components, which means the sprite pixel's original intensity makes it to the screen. The blue component of the mask has 100 percent intensity, which means none of the sprite pixel's blue component makes it to the screen. The final color that appears on the screen depends on the intensity of the blue component of the color that is currently on the screen. In most cases, the final color will be yellow. The higher the intensity of the blue component, the lighter the shade of yellow. At intensities close to 100 percent, the final color will be white. With color masks, when you blend yellow and blue, you usually get yellow as a result, not green as your art teacher taught you. It sounds strange, but that's the way color masks work.

I'd love to provide a figure to show color blending, but I'm limited to grayscale figures, and a grayscale figure would not show the effect properly. You will have to experiment with color masks on your own.

To draw with masks in QuickDraw, you can call two different functions, CopyMask() and CopyDeepMask(). CopyMask() copies a pixel map from one graphics port to another using a mask. CopyDeepMask() does the equivalent of calling CopyBits() and CopyMask() in one function. Table 6-1 lists the parameters for CopyMask(), and Table 6-2 lists the parameters for CopyDeepMask(). Because CopyMask() uses the srcCopy transfer mode, there's no need to provide a mode parameter to CopyMask(). If you want to use a transfer mode and a mask, use CopyDeepMask() to do your drawing.

Table 6-1   CopyMask() Parameters

Parameter	Description
srcBits	The source bitmap
maskBits	The mask bitmap
dstBits	The destination bitmap
srcRect	The rectangular area of the source bitmap we're copying.
maskRect	The mask rectangle. It must be the same size as the source rectangle.
dstRect	The rectangular area we're copying to.

Table 6-2   CopyDeepMask() Parameters

Parameter	Description
srcBits	The source bitmap
maskBits	The mask bitmap
dstBits	The destination bitmap
srcRect	The rectangular area of the source bitmap we're copying.
maskRect	The mask rectangle. It must be the same size as the source rectangle.
dstRect	The rectangular area we're copying to.
mode	A mode for copying. To do a straight copy, use the mode srcCopy.
maskRgn	An optional region you can specify as a clipping mask. If you don't want a clipping mask, pass nil.

Recall this CopyBits() call we used to draw to the screen in Chapter 4, "Introduction to Macintosh Graphics":

```
CopyBits(GetPortBitMapForCopyBits(theSource),
                GetPortBitMapForCopyBits(theDestination),
                &sourceRect, &destinationRect, drawingMode, nil);
```

This call looks like the following when using CopyMask():

```
CopyMask(GetPortBitMapForCopyBits(theSource), GetPortBitMapForCopyBits(theMask),
        GetPortBitMapForCopyBits(theDestination), &sourceRect, &maskRect,
        &destinationRect);
```

The call looks like this using CopyDeepMask():

```
CopyDeepMask(GetPortBitMapForCopyBits(theSource),
                GetPortBitMapForCopyBits(theMask),
                GetPortBitMapForCopyBits(theDestination), &sourceRect,
                &maskRect, &destinationRect, drawingMode, nil);
```

Even though the function name is `GetPortBitMapForCopyBits()`, you can use the function call to retrieve the bitmaps to supply to `CopyMask()` and `CopyDeepMask()`. Because more Mac programmers use `CopyBits()` more than `CopyMask()` or `CopyDeepMask()`, Apple chose to name the function `GetPortBitMapForCopyBits()`. It would be redundant to write functions called `GetPortBitMapForCopyMask()` and `GetPortBitMapForCopyDeepMask()` that did exactly the same thing that `GetPortBitMapForCopyBits()` does.

Drawing Sprites

The actual drawing of the sprites is pretty easy. You copy the sprite from its storage to the background, and then make another copy from the background to the screen, as shown in Figure 6-3. The difficult part is figuring out which sprite to draw, but I will cover that shortly.

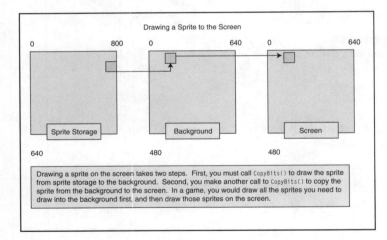

Figure 6-3

Drawing a sprite to the screen

The GameSprite Class

To draw our sprites, we need to create some new classes. The first class is the `GameSprite` class, whose data members look like this:

```
class GameSprite
{
        protected:
                short worldX;
                short worldY;
                float xSpeed;
```

```
            float ySpeed;
            float maxSpeed;
            float acceleration;

            SpriteDirection direction;

            // Pointer to the buffer holding the entity's sprites
            GameOffscreenBufferPtr spriteStorage;
            GameContextPtr destination;

            short spriteRow;            // Where the sprite is in spriteStorage
            short spriteColumn;
            short spriteWidth;          // Width and height of sprites for the
entity
            short spriteHeight;

            SpriteAction action;   // The action the entity is performing
            short frame;           // For Multi-Frame actions

            Blitter spriteBlitter; // A blitter to draw the sprites
}
```

The worldX and worldY data members store the sprite's current location in the game world. The xSpeed, ySpeed, maxSpeed, and acceleration data members help with moving the sprite. They won't have much of an impact for drawing sprites, but the classes for our game's players and enemies inherit from the GameSprite class, and they need those data members for movement.

The spriteDirection data member tells us which direction the sprite is currently facing. Here's a list of the possible sprite directions:

```
enum SpriteDirection {
      kUp = 1,
      kDown,
      kLeft,
      kRight
};
```

You can add your own directions—such as diagonal directions—to the SpriteDirection enumeration.

The spriteStorage data member contains the offscreen buffer that holds all the GameSprite object's sprites. The destination data member tells us where to draw the sprite. The `spriteRow` and `spriteColumn` data members tell us which sprite in the sprite storage we should draw. The `spriteWidth` and `spriteHeight` data members store the sprite's width and height. These data members are used to calculate the source and destination rectangles for sprite drawing.

The `action` data member tells us what action the sprite is performing. Here are the possible actions:

```
enum SpriteAction {
    kSpriteStanding,
    kSpriteMoving,
    kSpriteFighting
};
```

In our game, the entities in the game can be standing, moving, or fighting. The `frame` data member tells us which frame we're in if the sprite is moving or fighting. The `spriteBlitter` data member makes it simple to draw the sprite.

The Blitter Class

In the previous two chapters and the start of this one, I've hinted about the `Blitter` (refer to Chapter 5 for an explanation of the term blitter) class, and I'm sure you are dying of curiosity. I will end the suspense now and show you the data members of the `Blitter` class:

```
class Blitter
{
    protected:
            CGrafPtr sourceBuffer;
            CGrafPtr destinationBuffer;
            Rect sourceRect;
            Rect destinationRect;
            short drawingMode;
            long transparentColor;
}
```

The `Blitter` class simplifies the call to `CopyBits()` for performing the drawing. The first five data members correspond to the first five parameters of the `CopyBits()` function. The `transparentColor` data member specifies which color is transparent if we choose to use the `transparent` transfer mode for `CopyBits()`. For the purposes of sprite animation, we will be drawing from the offscreen buffer containing the sprites (the `spriteStorage` data member of the `GameSprite` class) to the offscreen buffer containing the game's background.

Finding the Sprite to Draw

For the example in this section, I will assume a sprite-storage arrangement like the monster sprite example described in the section "Storing Sprites" earlier in this chapter. Rows 1 through 4 store the sprite facing up, down, left, and right, respectively. The first column stores the sprite standing. The next columns store the sprite's movement frames, and the final columns store the sprite's fighting frames.

In this example, calculating the sprite row is simple: Find the direction the sprite is facing and set the row to match the direction. Computing the sprite column is slightly more complicated. You must find what action the sprite is performing—standing, moving, or fighting—and what frame the sprite is in for a multiframe animation sequence such as moving or fighting. The following function calculates which sprite should be drawn:

```
void GameSprite::DetermineSpriteToDraw(void)
{
        // Calculate sprite row
        short currentRow;

        switch (direction) {
                case kSpriteFacingUp:
                        currentRow = kPlayerUpFrame;
                        break;

                case kSpriteFacingDown:
                        currentRow = kPlayerDownFrame;
                        break;

                case kSpriteFacingLeft:
                        currentRow = kPlayerLeftFrame;
                        break;

                case kSpriteFacingRight:
                        currentRow = kPlayerRightFrame;
                        break;

                default:
                        break;

        }
```

```
        SetSpriteRow(currentRow);

        // Now calculate sprite column
        short currentColumn;

        switch (action) {
                case kSpriteStanding:
                        currentColumn = kPlayerStandFrame;
                        break;

                case kSpriteMoving:
                        currentColumn = kPlayerMoveFrame + frame;
                        break;

                case kSpriteFighting:
                        currentColumn = kPlayerAttackFrame + frame;
                        break;

                default:
                        break;

        }

        SetSpriteColumn(currentColumn);
}
```

Drawing the Sprite

Drawing the sprite involves filling the sprite's `spriteBlitter` data members and then calling `CopyBits()` to do the actual drawing. At the beginning, we set the data members that will stay the same for every frame, as you can see in the following source code:

```
void GameSprite::InitializeSpriteBlitter(void)
{
        // Sets up the parts of the sprite blitter that
        // stay the same from frame to frame. For sprite animation,
        // we want to use CopyBits'() transparent drawing mode.
```

```
        spriteBlitter.Initialize(spriteStorage, transparent);
}
void Blitter::Initialize(CGrafPtr theBuffer, short transferMode)
{
        // Sets up the parts of the sprite blitter that
        // stay the same from frame to frame.
        SetSourceBuffer(theBuffer);
        ForeColor(blackColor);
        BackColor(whiteColor);
        SetTransparentColor(whiteColor);
        SetDrawingMode(transferMode);


}
```

To do transparent drawing with CopyBits(), we must set the background color to the transparent color before calling CopyBits(). CopyBits() uses the background color as the transparent color when drawing using the transparent transfer mode; if you specify the wrong background color, the sprite will not appear correctly on the screen.

When I use the term background color in this section, I mean QuickDraw's background color, not the color of your game's background. Your game's background will contain multiple colors (or it will look terrible), and your artist predetermined which colors will make up the background. QuickDraw requires you to designate one color as the foreground color and one color as the background color. The colors you specify as the foreground and background colors determine the colors that appear on the screen. By default, the foreground color is black, and the background color is white. I strongly recommend you stick with the default and use white as the transparent color for your sprites. If you select a different transparent color for your sprites, purple for example, it will warp the colors in your background tiles. When drawing the tiles, we just perform a straight copy of pixels, and this copy relies on the background color being white and the foreground color being black. To prevent the color warping, we would have to explicitly set the background to color to white (by calling the function BackColor()) when drawing tiles and setting the background color to the sprite's transparent color when drawing sprites. Using white as the background color will spare you many headaches.

After initializing the sprite blitter, we set the parts of the blitter that can change from frame to frame and then actually do the drawing, as shown in the following code:

```
void GameSprite::Draw(void)
```

```
{
        spriteBlitter.DrawImageToOffscreenBuffer();

}
void GameSprite::SetupSpriteBlitter(CGrafPtr destBuffer)//(void)
{
        // Sets up the parts of the sprite blitter that
        // change from frame to frame
        SetupSourceRect();
        SetupDestinationBuffer(destBuffer);
        SetupDestinationRect();
}
```

Sprite Management

The preceding "Drawing Sprites" section has undoubtedly raised a bunch of questions. How do you handle a change in direction? How do you handle a change of action, such as going from moving to attacking? How do you move to the next frame of animation? How do you loop animations? The sections that follow answer all these questions and more.

Creating the AnimationController Class

To make sprite management easier, I created an AnimationController class, which has the following data members:

```
class AnimationController
{
        protected:
                GameSpritePtr modelToControl;
};
```

All the AnimationController class needs is a GameSprite object, the modelToControl data member. You may be wondering why the modelToControl data member is a pointer to a GameSprite object instead of a regular GameSprite object. The purpose of the AnimationController class is to determine the appropriate sprite to draw for a character in the game. We store the sprite to draw by updating the model's spriteRow and spriteColumn data members. With a pointer to a GameSprite object, we can just set the character's `spriteRow` and `spriteColumn` data members, and the changes will stick. If we did not use a pointer, the changes would apply only to a copy of the character, not the character itself. Without a pointer, the character's animation would never change; it would use the `spriteRow` and `spriteColumn` values we set in the `GameSprite` class's constructor.

Updating the Animation

To properly update the animation, you must figure out what the sprite did (move left, fire, move right, or do nothing are examples) and act appropriately. For the player character, we read the player's input from the keyboard or game controller to determine the action to perform. For enemy characters, the artificial intelligence system determines the action for the creature to perform. Here's the code that accomplishes this:

```
void AnimationController::UpdateAnimation(InputControllerAction theAction)
{
        switch(theAction) {
                case kMoveUp:
                        HandleMoveUp();
                        break;

                case kMoveUpAndLeft:
                        HandleMoveUp();
                        break;

                case kMoveUpAndRight:
                        HandleMoveUp();
                        break;

                case kMoveDown:
                        HandleMoveDown();
                                break;

                case kMoveDownAndLeft:
                        HandleMoveDown();
                        break;

                case kMoveDownAndRight:
                        HandleMoveDown();
                        break;
```

```
        case kMoveLeft:
                HandleMoveLeft();
                break;

        case kMoveRight:
                HandleMoveRight();
                break;

        case kAttack:
                HandleAttack();
                break;

        case kNoMovement:
                // The attack sequence consists of multiple frames.
                // If the player was attacking, we need to finish
                // the attack animation. Otherwise, only one
                // frame in the attack will be animated, which looks
                // really bad.
                if ((modelToControl->GetAction() == kSpriteFighting) &&
                            (modelToControl->GetFrame() <
                            modelToControl>GetFramesInSequence())) {
                    HandleAttack();
                }
                else {
                    HandleStand();
                }
                break;
        default:
                break;
    }
}
```

This code performs a `switch` statement on all the animation options: movement in eight directions, attacking, and no movement. The players and monsters can move in eight different directions, but the sprites have only four directions: up, down, left, and right. For diagonal movement, we must decide which sprite to use. I chose to use the moving-up sprite for upward diagonal movement and the moving-down sprite for downward diagonal movement. You could change that to suit your needs or display your sprites in eight directions; it's up to you.

The other interesting piece of the code is what happens when no movement occurs. If the sprite is fighting, we want to finish the fighting animation. For example, if the player presses the fire button and releases it, the release occurs before the animation finishes. If we don't finish the animation, every attack would be only partially animated, which would look bad. If the sprite is not fighting, we treat the sprite as if it were standing.

Handling Movement

Handling sprite movement in a particular direction depends on the direction the sprite is facing at the moment. If the current direction is different from the movement direction, we change the sprite's direction to reflect the movement. The sprite will begin moving in the next frame. Each frame is only a fraction of a second, so the player won't notice whether the movement begins one frame later.

If the current direction is the same as the movement direction, the sprite is moving. We move to the next frame in the movement animation sequence and set the sprite's action to moving.

The following function handles the situation in which the sprite is moving up:

```
void AnimationController::HandleMoveUp(void)
{
        if (modelToControl == nil)
                return;

        SpriteDirection creatureDirection = modelToControl->GetSpriteDirection();

        if (creatureDirection == kSpriteFacingUp) {
                // Have creature walk up
                MoveToNextFrame();
                modelToControl->SetAction(kSpriteMoving);

        }
        else {
                // Change creature direction
                modelToControl->SetSpriteDirection(kSpriteFacingUp);
        }
}


void AnimationController::MoveToNextFrame(void)
{
```

```
if (modelToControl == nil)
        return;

short framesInSequence = modelToControl->GetFramesInSequence();

short currentFrame = modelToControl->GetFrame();
currentFrame++;
modelToControl->SetFrame(currentFrame);

// If we hit the end of the animation sequence, go to first frame
if (currentFrame > framesInSequence)
        modelToControl->SetFrame(kFirstFrame);

}
```

The code is virtually the same to handle movement in the other three directions. A major portion of the movement code involves the function MoveToNextFrame(). In this function, we increment the sprite's frame number. Then we check to see whether that number is greater than the number of frames in the animation sequence. If it is, we go back to the first frame, looping the animation. The function GetFramesInSequence() depends on the entity and the action. The following is a sample GetFramesInSequence() call for a player character:

```
short GameSprite::GetFramesInSequence(void)
{
        SpriteAction playerAction = GetAction();

        switch (playerAction) {
                case kSpriteMoving:
                        return kPlayerMoveFrames;
                        break;

                case kSpriteFighting:
                        return kPlayerFightFrames;
                        break;

                default:
                        return 0;
        }
}
```

Handling Attacks

When handling fighting animation, we must check whether or not the sprite is already fighting. If it is, we move to the next frame in the animation. If not, we set the sprite's action to fighting, which starts the fighting animation sequence.

```
void AnimationController::HandleAttack(void)
{
        if (modelToControl == nil)
                return;

        SpriteAction creatureAction = modelToControl->GetAction();

        if (creatureAction == kSpriteFighting) {
                // Move to next frame in attack sequence
                MoveToNextFrame();
        }
        else {
                modelToControl->SetAction(kSpriteFightomg);

        }
}
```

Handling Standing

Handling a standing sprite is pretty easy; you set the sprite's action to stand and the frame to the sprite's standing frame.

```
void AnimationController::HandleStand(void)
{
        if (modelToControl == nil)
                return;

        modelToControl->SetAction(kStand);
        modelToControl->SetFrame(kStandFrame);
}
```

Maneuvering the Sprite through the Game World

Now that we have sprites moving, we must move them through the game world in a realistic manner. If the characters walk through walls, the player's suspension of disbelief will disappear, and the fanciest animation in the world will not restore it. Another way to think of this topic is collision detection between sprites and tiles. Detecting collisions between sprites and tiles falls into a gray area between the fields of computer graphics and physics, but I'm covering it here. This is information that cannot wait until Chapter 11, "Physics." The sections that follow show you what you need to do to determine whether a sprite can move in a particular direction.

Moving Up

To determine whether a sprite can move up x pixels, we take the upper-left corner of the sprite's boundary rectangle and move it up x pixels. Then we check the tile at that location. If the tile is a wall tile, we can't move. If the upper-left corner of the sprite has not encountered a wall tile, then we check the upper-right corner of the sprite. Figure 6-4 shows a situation in which part of the sprite is blocked. In this case, the sprite cannot move up. If both corners of the sprite are clear, then the sprite can move up.

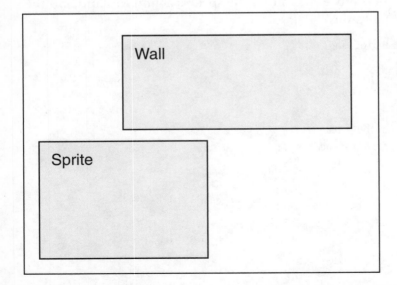

Figure 6-4

A situation in which the left half of the sprite can move up, but the right half cannot. In this case, the sprite cannot move up.

NOTE

In the code that follows, I assume that all doors are unlocked, and that the sprite can pass through the doors. If you want doors to be impassable, you must check for door tiles as well as wall tiles.

The following function checks whether or not the sprite can move up:

```
Boolean PhysicsController::CanMoveUp(short distance, GameLevelPtr currentLevel,
                                      GameTileListPtr theTileList)
{
        // Distance is the number of pixels we want to move.
        // modelToControl is the sprite we're checking.

        short tileNum;
        GameTileType tileAttribute;
        short theLevelWidth = currentLevel->GetLevelWidth();
        UInt32 mapIndex;

        // Test if the tile distance pixels above is a wall
        short rowToTest = (modelToControl->GetWorldY() - distance) / kTileHeight;
        short columnToTest = modelToControl->GetWorldX() / kTileWidth;

        mapIndex = (rowToTest * theLevelWidth) + columnToTest;
        tileNum = currentLevel->levelMap[mapIndex].GetValue();
        tileAttribute = theTileList->tileTable[tileNum].GetTileType();
        if (tileAttribute == kWallTile)
                return false;

        // We've just tested the left edge of the sprite.
        // Now test the right edge.
        short rightEdge = modelToControl->GetWorldX() +
                            modelToControl->GetSpriteWidth();
        columnToTest = rightEdge / kTileWidth;
        mapIndex = (rowToTest * theLevelWidth) + columnToTest;
        tileNum = currentLevel->levelMap[mapIndex].GetValue();
        tileAttribute = theTileList->tileTable[tileNum].GetTileType();
        if (tileAttribute == kWallTile)
```

```
                return false;

        // At this point, there are no walls blocking us
        return true;
}
```

If the `CanMoveUp()` function returns `false`, we may still be able to move. For example, we might want to move 15 pixels, but the wall is 11 pixels away. In this case, we'd want to move 10 pixels instead of 15. The following function calculates how far the sprite can move up:

```
short PhysicsController::HowFarUp(void)
{
        // This function is called after CanMoveUp() fails. So we can assume
        // that the adjacent tile is a wall. We just check how many pixels
        // y is from the next tile.

        short pixelsToNextTile;
        short result;

        pixelsToNextTile = modelToControl->GetWorldY() % kTileHeight;
        if (pixelsToNextTile == 0)
                result = pixelsToNextTile;
        else
                // Make sure the sprite doesn't go through the wall
                result = pixelsToNextTile - 1;

        return result;
}
```

The `HowFarUp()` function takes advantage of the fact that `CanMoveUp()` returned `false`. Because of this, we know the tile above the sprite is a wall so we calculate the distance between the top of the sprite and the next tile. Fortunately, it's a modulus operator between the sprite's `worldY` data member and the tile height, which gives us a value between 0 and the tile height. Calculating how far the sprite can move left works similarly; just substitute `GetWorldX()` for `GetWorldY()` and `kTileWidth` for `kTileHeight`.

Let's work through an example to see that using the modulus operator does give the correct distance between the top of the sprite and the next tile. Suppose that the top of the sprite (its `worldY` data member) is 167 pixels above the top edge of the game world and the tile height is 32 pixels in the example. In this case, the distance the sprite can move is 7 pixels; the bottom of the tile above the sprite is 160 (160 is the nearest multiple of 32), and 167 [ms] 160 = 7. Now let's try the modulus operator: 167 % 32 = 7. It works.

Moving Down

To determine whether a sprite can move down x pixels, we take the lower-left corner of the sprite's boundary rectangle and move it down x pixels. Then we check the tile at that location. If the tile is a wall tile, we can't move. If the lower-left corner of the sprite has not encountered a wall tile, then we check the lower-right corner of the sprite. Figure 6-5 shows a situation in which part of the sprite is blocked. In this case, the sprite cannot move down. If both lower corners of the sprite are clear, then the sprite can move down.

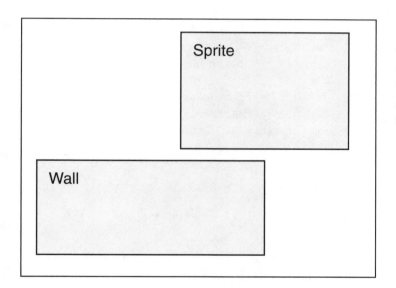

Figure 6-5

A situation in which the right half of the sprite can move down, but the left half cannot. In this case, the sprite cannot move down.

The following function checks whether or not the sprite can move down:

```
Boolean PhysicsController::CanMoveDown(short distance, GameLevelPtr currentLevel,
                          GameTileListPtr theTileList)
{
        // Distance is the number of pixels we want to move.

        short tileNum;
        GameTileType tileAttribute;
```

```
        short theLevelWidth = currentLevel->GetLevelWidth();
        UInt32 mapIndex;

        // Test if the tile distance pixels below is a wall
        short rowToTest = (modelToControl->GetWorldY() +
                modelToControl->GetSpriteHeight() + distance) / kTileHeight;
        short columnToTest = modelToControl->GetWorldX() / kTileWidth;

        mapIndex = (rowToTest * theLevelWidth) + columnToTest;
        tileNum = currentLevel->levelMap[mapIndex].GetValue();
        tileAttribute = theTileList->tileTable[tileNum].GetTileType();
        if (tileAttribute == kWallTile)
                return false;

        // We've just tested the left edge of the sprite.
        // Now test the right edge;
        short rightEdge = modelToControl->GetWorldX() +
                            modelToControl->GetSpriteWidth();
        columnToTest = rightEdge / kTileWidth;
        mapIndex = (rowToTest * theLevelWidth) + columnToTest;
        tileNum = currentLevel->levelMap[mapIndex].GetValue();
        tileAttribute = theTileList->tileTable[tileNum].GetTileType();
        if (tileAttribute == kWallTile)
                return false;

        // At this point, there are no walls blocking us
        return true;
}
```

If the CanMoveDown() function returns false, we may still be able to move. For example, we might want to move down 13 pixels, but the wall is only 10 pixels away. In this case, we'd want to move 9 pixels instead of 13. The following function calculates how far the sprite can move down:

```
short PhysicsController::HowFarDown(void)
{
        // This function is called after CanMoveDown() fails. So we can assume
        // that the adjacent tile is a wall. We just check how many pixels
        // y is from the next tile.

        short result;
```

```
    short pixelsToNextTile;

    short bottomEdge = modelToControl->GetWorldY() +
                modelToControl->GetSpriteHeight();
    pixelsToNextTile = kTileHeight - (bottomEdge % kTileHeight);
    if (pixelsToNextTile == kTileHeight)
            // There's nowhere to move
            result = 0;
    else
            // Make sure the sprite doesn't go through the wall
            result = pixelsToNextTile - 1;

    return result;
}
```

The `HowFarDown()` function takes advantage of the fact that `CanMoveDown()` returned `false`. We know that the tile below the sprite is a wall so we calculate the distance between the bottom of the sprite and the next tile. Calculating the distance works a little differently than it does when computing how far the sprite can move up. You still take the modulus operator between the sprite's `worldY` data member and the tile height, but you take that value and subtract it from the tile height. Calculating how far the sprite can move right works similarly; just substitute `GetWorldX()` for `GetWorldY()`, `GetSpriteWidth()` for `GetSpriteHeight()`, and `kTileWidth` for `kTileHeight`.

Let's work through an example to see whether my method gives the correct distance between the bottom of the sprite and the next tile. For this example, assume that the bottom of the sprite is 119 and the tile height is 32. In this case, the distance is 9: The top of the tile below the sprite is 128 (128 is the nearest multiple of 32), and 128 [ms] 119 = 9. Now let's try the modulus operator: 119 % 32 = 23. Now subtract the modulus operator from the tile height: 32 [ms] 23 = 9. It works.

Moving Left

To determine whether a sprite can move left x pixels, we take the upper-left corner of the sprite's boundary rectangle and move it left x pixels. Then we check the tile at that location. If the tile is a wall tile, we can't move. If the upper-left corner of the sprite has not encountered a wall tile, then we check the lower-left corner of the sprite. Figure 6-6 shows a situation in which part of the sprite is blocked. In this case, the sprite cannot move left. If both corners are clear, then the sprite can move left.

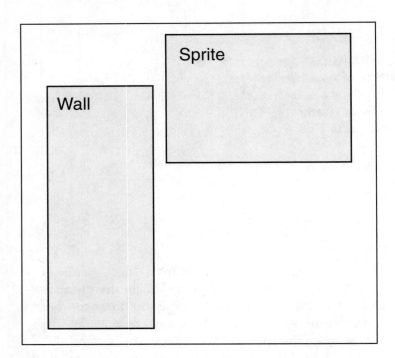

Figure 6-6

A situation in which the top half of the sprite can move left, but the bottom half cannot. In this case, the sprite cannot move left.

The following function checks whether or not the sprite can move left:

```
Boolean PhysicsController::CanMoveLeft(short distance, GameLevelPtr currentLevel,
                       GameTileListPtr theTileList)
{
        // Distance is the number of pixels we want to move.

        short tileNum;
        GameTileTypetileAttribute;
        short theLevelWidth = currentLevel->GetLevelWidth();
        UInt32 mapIndex;

        // Test if the tile distance pixels to the left is a wall
        short rowToTest = modelToControl->GetWorldY() / kTileHeight;
        short columnToTest = (modelToControl->GetWorldX() - distance) /
                                kTileWidth;
        mapIndex = (rowToTest * theLevelWidth) + columnToTest;
        tileNum = currentLevel->levelMap[mapIndex].GetValue();
        tileAttribute = theTileList->tileTable[tileNum].GetTileType();
        if (tileAttribute == kWallTile)
                return false;
```

```
        // We've just tested the top edge of the sprite.
        // Now test the bottom edge;
        short bottomEdge = modelToControl->GetWorldY() + modelToControl-
                              >GetSpriteHeight();
        rowToTest = bottomEdge / kTileHeight;
        mapIndex = (rowToTest * theLevelWidth) + columnToTest;
        tileNum = currentLevel->levelMap[mapIndex].GetValue();
        tileAttribute = theTileList->tileTable[tileNum].GetTileType();
        if (tileAttribute == kWallTile)
               return false;

        // At this point, there are no walls blocking us
        return true;
}
```

If the `CanMoveLeft()` function returns `false`, we may still be able to move. For example, we might want to move 12 pixels, but the wall is 4 pixels away. In this case, we'd want to move three pixels instead of 12. The following function calculates how far the sprite can move left:

```
short PhysicsController::HowFarLeft(void)
{
        // This function is called after CanMoveLeft() fails. So we can assume
        // that the adjacent tile is a wall. We just check how many pixels
        // x is from the next tile.

        short result;
        short pixelsToNextTile;

        pixelsToNextTile = modelToControl->GetWorldX() % kTileWidth;

        if (pixelsToNextTile == 0)
               result = pixelsToNextTile;
        else
               // Make sure the sprite doesn't go through the wall
               result = pixelsToNextTile - 1;

        return result;
}
```

Moving Right

To determine whether a sprite can move right x pixels, we take the upper-right corner of the sprite's boundary rectangle and move it right x pixels. Then we check the tile at that location. If the tile is a wall tile, we can't move. If the upper-right corner of the sprite has not encountered a wall tile,, then we check the lower-right corner of the sprite. Figure 6-7 shows a situation in which part of the sprite is blocked. In this case, the sprite cannot move right. If both corners are clear, then the sprite can move right.

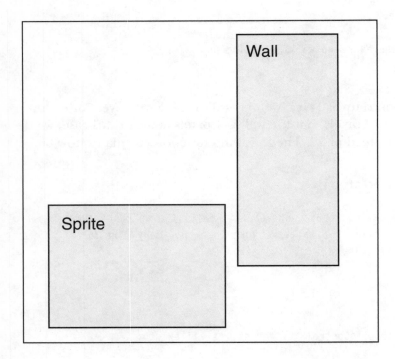

Figure 6-7

A situation in which the bottom half of the sprite can move right, but the top half cannot. In this case, the sprite cannot move right.

The following function checks whether or not the sprite can move right:

```
Boolean PhysicsController::CanMoveRight(short distance, GameLevelPtr currentLevel,
                        GameTileListPtr theTileList)
{
        // Distance is the number of pixels we want to move.

        short tileNum;
        GameTileType tileAttribute;
        short theLevelWidth = currentLevel->GetLevelWidth();
```

```
    UInt32 mapIndex;

    // Test if the tile distance pixels to the right is a wall
    short rowToTest = modelToControl->GetWorldY() / kTileHeight;
    short columnToTest = (modelToControl->GetWorldX() +
            modelToControl->GetSpriteWidth() + distance) / kTileWidth;

    mapIndex = (rowToTest * theLevelWidth) + columnToTest;
    tileNum = currentLevel->levelMap[mapIndex].GetValue();
    tileAttribute = theTileList->tileTable[tileNum].GetTileType();
    if (tileAttribute == kWallTile)
            return false;

    // We've just tested the top edge of the sprite.
    // Now test the bottom edge;
    short bottomEdge = modelToControl->GetWorldY() +
                    modelToControl->GetSpriteHeight();
    rowToTest = bottomEdge / kTileHeight;
    mapIndex = (rowToTest * theLevelWidth) + columnToTest;
    tileNum = currentLevel->levelMap[mapIndex].GetValue();
    tileAttribute = theTileList->tileTable[tileNum].GetTileType();
    if (tileAttribute == kWallTile)
            return false;

    // At this point, there are no walls blocking us
    return true;
}
```

If the `CanMoveRight()` function returns `false`, we may still be able to move. For example, we might want to move 8 pixels, but the wall is 6 pixels away. In this case, we'd want to move 5 pixels instead of 8. The following function calculates how far the sprite can move right:

```
short PhysicsController::HowFarRight(void)
{
    // This function is called after CanMoveRight fails. So we can assume
    // that the adjacent tile is a wall. We just check how many pixels
    // x is from the next tile.

    short result;
    short pixelsToNextTile;
```

```
short rightEdge = modelToControl->GetWorldX() +
            modelToControl->GetSpriteWidth();
pixelsToNextTile = kTileWidth - (rightEdge % kTileWidth);
if (pixelsToNextTile == kTileWidth)
        // There's nowhere to move
        result = 0;
else
        // Make sure the sprite doesn't go through the wall
        result = pixelsToNextTile - 1;
        return result;
}
```

Moving Diagonally

Checking for diagonal movement differs from checking for movement up, down, left, and right. Instead of checking two edges of the sprite to see whether the whole sprite can pass, we must check three tiles to determine whether the sprite can move diagonally. Figure 6-8 shows the tiles you must check for the four diagonal directions.

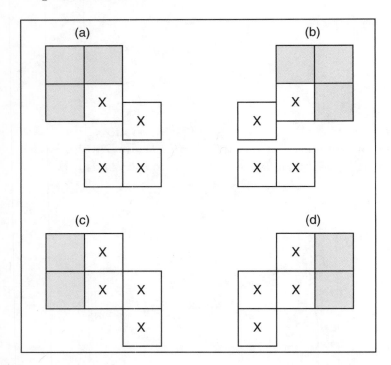

Figure 6-8

The tiles you must check when moving up and left (a), up and right (b), down and left (c), and down and right (d).

X represents the tiles the sprite currently occupies. The shaded tiles are the tiles to check.

CAUTION

Figure 6-8 and my code assume that the sprite is no more than two tiles tall and two tiles wide. If you have very large sprites, you must check more tiles. For example, if the sprite in Figure 6-8 (a) were five tiles tall and five tiles wide, you must check the three tiles to the right of the shaded tiles and the three tiles below the shaded tiles.

Let's look at the case of movement up and left. First, we look at the tile above the upper-left corner of the sprite. If it's not a wall, move one tile to the left and check the new tile. If that tile is not a wall, move one tile down and make a third test. If there's no wall there, then the sprite can move up and left. I could have chosen to move one tile left, one tile up, and then one tile right; going up, left, and then down was just a personal preference. Testing the other diagonal directions works similarly. The following function tests whether the sprite can move up and left:

```
Boolean PhysicsController::CanMoveUpAndLeft(short distance,
                        GameLevelPtr currentLevel, GameTileListPtr
theTileList)
{
        // Distance is the number of pixels we want to move.

        short tileNum;
        GameTileType tileAttribute;
        short theLevelWidth = currentLevel->GetLevelWidth();
        UInt32 mapIndex;

        // Test if the tile distance pixels above the sprite is a wall
        short rowToTest = (modelToControl->GetWorldY() - distance) / kTileHeight;
        short columnToTest = modelToControl->GetWorldX() / kTileWidth;
        mapIndex = (rowToTest * theLevelWidth) + columnToTest;
        tileNum = currentLevel->levelMap[mapIndex].GetValue();
        tileAttribute = theTileList->tileTable[tileNum].GetTileType();
        if (tileAttribute == kWallTile)
                return false;

        // Now move one column to the left to see if the tile above
        // and to the left is a wall
        columnToTest--;
```

```
        mapIndex = (rowToTest * theLevelWidth) + columnToTest;
        tileNum = currentLevel->levelMap[mapIndex].GetValue();
        tileAttribute = theTileList->tileTable[tileNum].GetTileType();
        if (tileAttribute == kWallTile)
                return false;

        // Now move one row down and test if it is a wall
        rowToTest++;
        mapIndex = (rowToTest * theLevelWidth) + columnToTest;
        tileNum = currentLevel->levelMap[mapIndex].GetValue();
        tileAttribute = theTileList->tileTable[tileNum].GetTileType();
        if (tileAttribute == kWallTile)
                return false;

        // At this point, none of the three tiles we tested is a wall.
        // We can move up and left because the 4th tile to test is part
        // of the current sprite position and we know that's not a wall.
        return true;
}
```

NOTE

You might be curious about my comment at the end of the CanMoveUpAndLeft() function. When moving up and left, the lower-right corner of the sprite will end up where the upper left corner of the sprite currently is, which you can visualize in Figure 6-8. That tile cannot be a wall or the sprite would have never been able to move to its current position. That's why we need to test only three tiles for diagonal movement instead of four.

Dirty Rectangle Animation

So far, we've been drawing the entire screen each frame. Usually, most of the screen does not change from one frame to the next. If we could find a way to draw only the parts of the screen that change from one frame to the next, our drawing would move much faster. Miraculously, there *is* a way to draw only what must be updated on the screen. The method is *dirty rectangle animation*.

In dirty rectangle animation, you place an imaginary grid across the screen. The grid is initially "clean." When an area of the screen must be redrawn, you mark that area of the grid as "dirty." When you're ready to draw the frame, you check the grid. If a piece of the grid is dirty, you draw that piece. If that piece of the grid is not dirty, you do nothing. Figure 6-9 shows an example of a dirty rectangle grid. In the figure, the grid has 300 entries (20 columns and 15 rows). The figure has 17 grid entries marked as dirty. Drawing only those 17 tiles (assuming that each grid entry corresponds to a tile) is much faster than drawing the whole screen with 300 tiles.

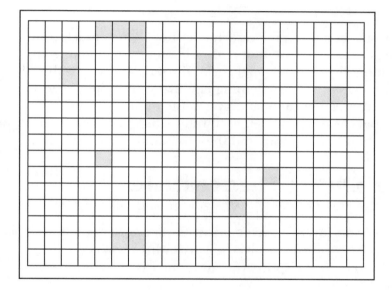

Figure 6-9

A dirty rectangle animation grid. Only the gray squares are dirty and must be redrawn.

You may be wondering what causes a rectangle to become dirty. Sprite movement is the usual culprit. The sprites appear in front of the background, and when they move, the background tiles must be redrawn to reflect the fact that the sprite is no longer in front of the tiles. Figure 6-10 shows an example of this. In the first picture, the box appears on the floor. In the second picture, the player grabbed the box, so the box is no longer on the floor. We must restore the floor tiles that were obscured by the box.

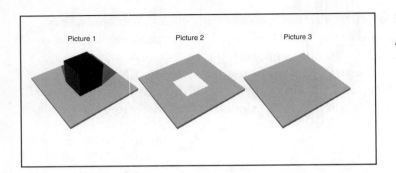

Figure 6-10

A dirty rectangle example

Dirty rectangle animation works best when the screen does not change much from frame to frame. In this case, the reduced amount of drawing more than makes up for the overhead of maintaining the dirty rectangle grid. If your game scrolls the screen whenever the player moves or does something else that causes the screen's contents to change often, dirty rectangle animation is a waste of time. In such a situation, it's easier to just redraw the entire screen each frame than first determining that 90 percent of the screen must be redrawn and then redrawing that 90 percent.

QuickDraw's Dirty Rectangle Support

QuickDraw provides some support for dirty rectangles in Carbon. After you draw a sprite, call the function QDSetDirtyRegion() to mark the area where you drew as dirty. After calling CopyBits() to draw the sprite, you make the call to QDSetDirtyRegion(), like this:

```
CopyBits(GetPortBitMapForCopyBits(theSource),
            GetPortBitMapForCopyBits(theDestination),
&sourceRect, &destinationRect, drawingMode, nil);
OSStatus error;
RgnHandle dirtyRgn;
(**dirtyRgn).RgnBBox = destinationRect;
error = QDSetDirtyRegion(theDestination, dirtyRgn);
```

For animation, the offscreen buffer containing the background has all the dirty rectangles. When you are ready to draw to the screen, you do the following:

1. Call the function QDGetDirtyRegion() to find the portions of the screen that must be redrawn.

2. QuickDraw needs a rectangle for drawing. The dirty region is probably an

arbitrary area inside the QuickDraw coordinate plane, as shown in Figure 6-11. Calling the function `RectRgn()` converts the region to a rectangle.

3. Draw to the screen with `CopyBits()`, using the dirty rectangle you received from the `RectRgn()` as the source and destination rectangles.

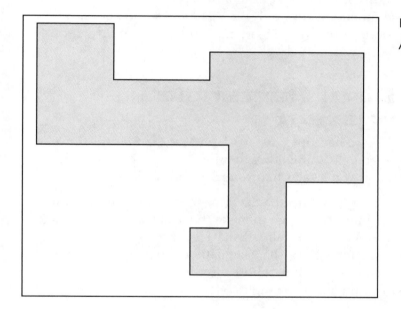

Figure 6-11

A sample region

The following code snippet draws to the screen using dirty rectangles:

```
OSStatus error;
RgnHandle dirtyRgn;
Rect dirtyRect;

if (QDIsPortBufferDirty(background)) {
        error = QDGetDirtyRegion(background, dirtyRgn);
        if (error != noErr)
                return;

        // Convert the dirty region to a rectangle
        RectRgn(dirtyRgn, &dirtyRect);

        // Draw from the background to the screen, using the
        // variable dirtyRect as both the source and destination
        // rectangle to CopyBits().
```

```
CopyBits(GetPortBitMapForCopyBits(background),
              GetPortBitMapForCopyBits(theScreen),
              &dirtyRect, &dirtyRect, drawingMode, nil);
}
```

Apple introduced the functions QDGetDirtyRegion() and QDSetDirtyRegion() in version 1.1 of Carbon, so these functions work only on Mac OS 8.6 and above. If we want to support earlier versions of the Mac OS, we must roll our own dirty rectangle animation system.

Creating a Dirty Rectangle Animation System

As part of my ongoing crusade to have my code work on Mac OS 8.1 and above, we will develop our own dirty rectangle animation system. It sounds like a daunting task, but it's not too difficult, as you'll see when you read this section.

To develop a dirty rectangle system, we need a 2D array to store the areas of the screen that are dirty. To determine how large to make the array, we must decide on the size of the dirty rectangles. Because we already have functions to draw one tile on the screen (we wrote these functions in the last chapter), making the dirty rectangles the size of one tile makes sense. If we chose another size, we'd have to write new drawing functions to draw the dirty rectangles. Here's how large our dirty rectangle table has to be:

Number Of Rows = Screen Height / Tile Height

Number Of Columns = Screen Width / Tile Width

The dirty rectangle grid will be part of the GameContext class we created in the last chapter. This is how the grid will be declared:

```
char* dirtyRectGrid;
```

The dirty rectangle grid will be a 2D array of characters. I chose characters because characters take up just one byte of space, with values ranging from -128 to 127. The following function allocates the dirty rectangle grid:

```
void GameContext::AllocateDirtyRectGrid(void)
{
    // Assumes we have already determined the screen width and screen height.
    short rowCount = screenHeight / kTileHeight;
    short columnCount = screenWidth / kTileWidth;
```

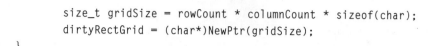

```
        size_t gridSize = rowCount * columnCount * sizeof(char);
        dirtyRectGrid = (char*)NewPtr(gridSize);
}
```

The `AllocateDirtyRectGrid()` function assumes that we have already calculated the screen width and height. Refer to the section "Graphics Devices" in Chapter 4, "Introduction to Macintosh Graphics," to learn how to determine the screen size.

Now that we have our dirty rectangle table, we must write some functions to support dirty rectangle animation. At a minimum, these functions accomplish the following tasks:

- Clean the table
- Set an entry in the table to dirty
- Determine whether a rectangle on the screen is dirty

Cleaning the table just involves going through the table and marking each entry as clean. I defined the following constants for dirty rectangles:

```
const char kRectangleIsClean = 0;
const char kRectangleIsDirty = 1;
```

The following function cleans the dirty rectangle grid by setting all the grid's values to kRectangleIsClean:

```
void GameContext::CleanDirtyRectangleTable(void)
{
        short rowCount = screenHeight / kTileHeight;
        short columnCount = screenWidth / kTileWidth;
        char gridIndex;

        for (short row = 0; row < kNumberOfRows; row++) {
                for (short column = 0; column < kNumberOfColumns; column++) {
                        gridIndex = (row * columnCount) + column;
                        dirtyRectGrid[gridIndex] = kRectangleIsClean;
                }
        }
}
```

Setting an entry in the table to dirty is pretty easy. You find the location in the grid and set it to the value `kRectangleIsDirty`. The following function marks a rectangle as dirty:

```
void GameContext::MarkRectangleDirty(short row, short column)
```

```
{
        short rowCount = screenHeight / kTileHeight;
        short columnCount = screenWidth / kTileWidth;
        char gridIndex;

        gridIndex = (row * columnCount) + column;
        dirtyRectGrid[gridIndex] = kRectangleIsDirty;
}
```

Determining whether a rectangle is dirty is also pretty easy. You find the location in the grid and check its value. If the grid has a value of kRectangleIsDirty, the rectangle is dirty. The following function checks whether or not a particular rectangle is dirty:

```
Boolean IsRectangleDirty(short row, short column)
{
        short rowCount = screenHeight / kTileHeight;
        short columnCount = screenWidth / kTileWidth;
        char gridIndex;

        gridIndex = (row * columnCount) + column;

        if (dirtyRectGrid[gridIndex] == kRectangleIsDirty)
                return true;
        else
                return false;
}
```

In your drawing code, you would go through the table and see whether a particular rectangle is dirty. If so, you would draw the tile. If not, you would do nothing. Here's how the code might look:

```
void GameContext::DrawBackground(GameLevelPtr theLevel)
{
        short rowCount = screenHeight / kTileHeight;
        short columnCount = screenWidth / kTileWidth;

        for (short row = 0; row < rowCount; row++) {
                for (short column = 0; column < columnCount; column++) {
                        if (IsRectangleDirty(row, column))
                                DrawTileFromLevelMap(theLevel, row, column);
                }
```

```
        }
}
```

The `DrawTileFromLevelMap()` function takes care of all the dirty details of drawing the tile, such as determining the tile to draw, calculating the tile's rectangle in tile space, and determiningthe destination for the tile in the game world. Refer to the section "Drawing Tiles" in Chapter 5, "Tiles and Scrolling" for the source code to the `DrawTileFromLevelMap()` function.

Summary

Consider how far we've come in just three chapters! We now know how to draw to the screen, create game worlds, scroll backgrounds, create characters to inhabit our game world, and animate these characters. Congratulations! If you've made it this far, you have enough knowledge of graphics to create a computer game.

This chapter covered the wonderful world of animation. We began by learning about sprites, and introduced some techniques for drawing them. There are two techniques to draw sprites transparently so that the sprites look like recognizable object instead of rectangles. The first technique reserves one color as a transparent color and uses the `CopyBits()` transparent transfer mode to avoid drawing pixels containing the transparent color. The second technique uses a mask, which is a pixel map the size of the sprite. Only the pixels that have a value of 1 in the corresponding position in the mask appear on the screen.

After covering sprite transparency, we discussed some techniques to organize the sprites. The best solution is to store a related collection of sprites, such as one character's sprites, in its own picture. Then we moved on to cover the techniques to organize the sprites in the picture. Any way you choose to organize them will work, but grouping related sprites together makes animation support easier.

From sprite organization, we moved to the actual animation process. We covered topics such as determining the sprite to draw, drawing the sprite, performing multi-frame animations, and looping animations. We also learned how to make our sprites move through the game worlds we made in the last chapter without walking through walls.

Finally, we covered the topic of dirty rectangle animation, which is a method of drawing in which you draw only the parts of the screen that must be redrawn each frame. We learned to use QuickDraw for dirty rectangle animation and also developed our own dirty rectangle animation system.

The sample program for this chapter adds a sprite to the game world; you can maneuver this sprite using the arrow keys on the keyboard. You can find the program and its source code on the CD-ROM that accompanies this book.

CHAPTER 7

InputSprocket

After working through the examples in Chapter 6, "Animation," we have a cartoon—and a beautiful one at that. To transform our cartoon into a game, we have to add interactivity; that is, we have to read input from the player. Because the game we are developing is an action game, the player should be able to use any joystick or gamepad he owns. If the player does not own a game controller, our game should let the player use the keyboard or mouse to play the game. With InputSprocket, we can easily support any game controller the user owns. This chapter delves into InputSprocket and shows how you can use it in your games.

Introduction to InputSprocket

InputSprocket is a software development kit that makes it easy for game developers to support game controllers, such as joysticks, gamepads, steering wheels, and multi-button mice. By using InputSprocket, you make it simple to read data from game controllers, and you allow players to easily configure their controllers for your game. What makes InputSprocket nice is that with one set of code, players can play your game with the keyboard, the mouse, or any game controller they happen to own.

The type of game you develop determines whether InputSprocket is right for you. If your game has any fast action that requires a real-time response (such as shooters, sports games, driving games, or flight simulators) you should use InputSprocket. You can better support other game genres (such as strategy games, board games, card games, point-and-click adventures, and role-playing games) by just using the keyboard and mouse (see Chapter 9, "Reading the Keyboard and Mouse Plus Event Handling").

To the player, InputSprocket is an extension in his System folder. Mac OS versions 8.6 through 9.1 include InputSprocket as part of the standard operating system installation. Because Mac OS X uses Mac OS 9.1 when running in Classic mode, you can be pretty sure that all the Mac OS X users out there have InputSprocket installed on their machines. You can't be 100 percent sure because the user can always remove the InputSprocket extension. If you want to support earlier versions of the Mac OS than 8.6, you can license InputSprocket from Apple for free and allow the user to install InputSprocket when he installs your game.

There is one major problem with InputSprocket. Apple decided to replace InputSprocket with the HID Manager (as described in Chapter 8, "HID Manager") in OS X. If you write your game using InputSprocket, an OS X user can play your game only from the Classic environment. He will not be able to take advantage of OS X features, such as the Aqua interface, protected memory, and preemptive multitasking, which he would be able to use if your game ran natively in OS X. Because the HID Manager runs only on OS X, there's no way for your game to support game controllers *and* run natively on both Mac OS 8/9 and OS X with one set of code. Table 7-1 lists your options along with the advantages and disadvantages of each.

Table 7-1   Options for Reading User Input

Option	Benefits	Drawbacks
Use InputSprocket only	Only one set of code to write Game will run on Mac OS 8/9/X. Game will support all controllers.	Game will not run natively in OS X.
Use HID Manager only	Only one set of code to write Game will run natively in OS X. Game will support all controllers.	Game will not run on Mac OS 8/9.
Use both InputSprocket and HID Manager	Game will run on Mac OS 8/9. Game will run natively in OS X. Game will support all controllers.	Two sets of code to write and support.
Use keyboard and mouse only	Only one set of code to write. Game will run on Mac OS 8/9. Game will run natively in OS X.	No support for game controllers.

As you can see from Table 7-1, there's no easy solution. I know that none of the options are ideal, but imagine how difficult it would be if games were not Apple's number one priority! The option you use depends on what input devices and which OS versions you want to support. Assuming that you are writing an action game, I recommend that you write your game to use both InputSprocket and the HID Manager. By doing this, you maximize the number of people who can play your game, and you give your players the best possible playing experience on their machines. I know you'll have to write two versions of your game, but the two versions will be very similar. You have to create two versions of an input controller class. The Mac OS 8/9 version will use InputSprocket, and the Mac OS X version will use the HID Manager. Other than the input controller class, the two versions will be identical. Because our game will use both the HID Manager and InputSprocket, you will learn how to support both with relative ease. I will write the InputSprocket version of an input controller class in this chapter and the HID Manager version in the next chapter.

Setting Up Your Game to Use InputSprocket

The most difficult part of using InputSprocket is setting up your program properly. If you do not properly set up your game, it will either generate a ton of compiler errors or crash. The following sections describe some things you must know to avoid pain when using InputSprocket.

What to Place in Your System Extensions Folder

As part of the InputSprocket SDK (Software Development Kit), Apple includes both debug (named `InputSprocket Debug Extension`) and non-debug (`InputSprocket Extension`)versions of the InputSprocket extension. Place one of these versions in the Extensions folder inside the System folder. Do not place both versions of the InputSprocket extension in your System Extensions folder. If the computer finds multiple versions of the InputSprocket extension in the System Extensions folder, the machine will crash.

For development purposes, you should use the debug version of the InputSprocket extension. If you use the non-debug version, and your game breaks into the debugger, you will be unable to move the mouse or use your keyboard. I had this happen to me when I accidentally set a breakpoint in my program. I thought I was using the debug version, but I wasn't. I played my game, and the program reached the breakpoint, switching me to the debugger. I could not move the mouse or use the keyboard, and I had to restart the machine.

What Is a Debugger?

A *debugger* is a program that lets you examine your code while you're running it. With a debugger, you can step through your code, line by line, and examine all your program's variables. A debugger is a powerful tool that can help you discover what's going wrong in your program and where it's going wrong. CodeWarrior contains a debugger you can use with the code in this book.

Because games are long programs containing thousands of lines of code, you normally don't want to step through the program line by line from the very beginning. Usually there's one area of the code that is causing problems, and you want to use the debugger on only that area of code. By setting a breakpoint on a line of code, you tell the compiler to run the program normally at first. When the compiler reaches the line of code where you set the breakpoint, it switches you to the debugger. Once in the debugger, you can step through the code line by line from the breakpoint. The process of switching to the debugger when reaching a breakpoint is called *breaking into the debugger*.

NOTE

In InputSprocket version 1.7, which I've included on the accompanying CD-ROM, Apple streamlined the number of InputSprocket extensions. Older versions had extensions for the keyboard, mouse, speech recognition, and every game controller company in addition to the InputSprocket extension. If you happen to be using an older version, you must add these extensions to your system extensions folder. For example, I have a Gravis Mousestick joystick in addition to the mouse and keyboard. I would have to add the debug versions of the InputSprocket Extension, InputSprocket Gravis, InputSprocket Mouse, and InputSprocket Keyboard extensions.

What to Place in Your Compiler

When developing your game with InputSprocket, you must do some things in your compiler for it to compile your code without errors:

- Add either `InputSprocketStubLib` or `InputSprocketLib` to your project. If you are using CodeWarrior, add one of these libraries to the Mac Libraries section of your CodeWarrior project (see Figure 7-1). `InputSprocketLib` contains the `InputSprocket` library. `InputSprocketStubLib` is a minimal version of the `InputSprocket` library that you use for linking. I urge you to use `InputSprocketStubLib`.

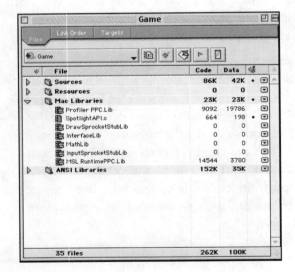

Figure 7-1

The CodeWarrior project window

- Add the location of your InputSprocket libraries to the compiler's list of access paths if the compiler has not already done it for you.
- Include the header file `InputSprocket.h` in the appropriate source code files.

InputSprocket Resources

When you compile and run your game for the first time, you must supply three resources to InputSprocket for the game to run properly:

- An InputSprocket application resource (resource type `isap`), which tells InputSprocket to use either high-level or low-level InputSprocket. We will be using high-level InputSprocket. Low-level InputSprocket is a royal pain in the butt. With low-level InputSprocket, you have to write your own configuration dialog box and write code for every game controller you plan to support. In addition, low-level InputSprocket has very little documentation. Other than these issues, working with low-level InputSprocket is pure pleasure.

- A set list resource (resource type `setl`), which contains a list of saved control sets. For example, your game could contain multiple keyboard, mouse, and joystick control layouts. The set list resource holds a list of all these layouts. Figure 7-2 gives a high-level overview of the contents of a set list resource and saved set resources.

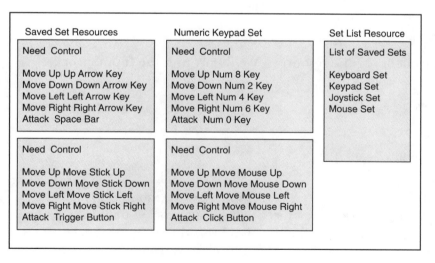

Figure 7-2

An example of set list resources and saved set resources

- A saved set resource (resource type `tset`) containing a control layout for your game. Although your game can have many saved sets, you can just provide a default keyboard layout during development. When your InputSprocket code is working properly, you create additional sets by playing your game and configuring the controls inside your game.

To make it easier for you to create the necessary InputSprocket resources, Apple supplies a file with the InputSprocket SDK called InputSprocket.r. This file contains a template for the application, set list, and saved set resources, plus a list of keyboard constants. Use this template to create a resource file containing the actual application, set list, and saved resources. You add this resource file to your CodeWarrior project.

When making your resource file, here is the first line you need:

```
#include "InputSprocket.r"
```

This line tells Rez, the resource compiler included with CodeWarrior, to include the InputSprocket.r file. If you don't include InputSprocket.r, Rez will not know about the constants that are part of the InputSprocket.r file and your resource file will not compile.

Next, you have to define the resource IDs for the InputSprocket resources, as shown in the following code:

```
#define kResourceID_isap        128
#define kResourceID_setl        129
#define kResourceID_tset_KeyboardDefaultSet    129
```

Now it's time to start defining the resources. We'll start with the InputSprocket application resource:

```
resource 'isap' (kResourceID_isap)
{
        callsISpInit,
        usesInputSprocket
};
```

The first line says that we're creating an isap resource with resource ID kResourceID_isap. The code inside the braces tells InputSprocket that this resource calls the function ISpInit() and uses the high-level version of InputSprocket. This is all there is to the InputSprocket application resource. You should not have to make any changes to this resource.

Now let's move on to the set list resource:

```
resource 'setl' (kResourceID_setl, "InputSprocket sets")
{
        currentVersion,
        {
```

```
                "Default", 0, kISpDeviceClass_Keyboard, kISpKeyboardID_Apple,
                notApplSet, isDefaultSet, kResourceID_tset_KeyboardDefaultSet,

        };
};
```

The first line says that we're making a set1 resource with resource ID
kResourceID_set1 and resource name "InputSprocket sets". Inside the braces, the
first line tells InputSprocket to use the current version of the set list resource,
which is version 2. After that is an array of set list entries. Because all we want is a
default keyboard set, the array has only one element. Table 7-2 explains what each
part of the set list entry means. You should not have to make any changes to this
resource.

Table 7-2   Set List Entries

Field	Description
pstring	A string describing the entry.
length	The length of the set. InputSprocket allows you to specify 0, which is a lot easier than trying to calculate the number of bytes in the set.
deviceClass	The physical device class, such as keyboard, mouse, or joystick. Table 7-10, later in this chapter, lists all the device classes.
deviceIdentifier	An identifier for the device. The value I used, kISpKeyboardID_Apple, tells InputSprocket that this device is an Apple keyboard.
notApplSet	Tells InputSprocket that the set is not defined by the application. If a set is defined by the application, use the value isApplSet.
isDefaultSet	Tells InputSprocket that the set is a default set. If you add other sets that are not default sets, use the value notDefaultSet.
resourceID	The resource ID of the set.

Finally, let's define the default keyboard set:

```
resource 'tset' (kResourceID_tset_KeyboardDefaultSet, "Default (Keyboard)")
{
        supportedVersion,
        {

                /* Movement needs. Use the arrow keys for movement */
                upKey,                          /* up */
                 rControlOff, rOptionOff, rShiftOff, controlOff, optionOff, shiftOff,
                        commandOff,

                downKey,                        /* down */
                 rControlOff, rOptionOff, rShiftOff, controlOff, optionOff, shiftOff,
                        commandOff,

                leftKey,                        /* left */
                 rControlOff, rOptionOff, rShiftOff, controlOff, optionOff, shiftOff,
                        commandOff,

                rightKey,                       /* right */
                 rControlOff, rOptionOff, rShiftOff, controlOff, optionOff, shiftOff,
                        commandOff,

                /* Fire (button) need */
                spaceKey,
                 rControlOff, rOptionOff, rShiftOff, controlOff, optionOff, shiftOff,
                        commandOff,

                /* Change weapon need */
                optionKey,
                 rControlOff, rOptionOff, rShiftOff, controlOff, optionOff, shiftOff,
                        commandOff,


                /* Pause (button) need */
                escKey,
                 rControlOff, rOptionOff, rShiftOff, controlOff, optionOff, shiftOff,
                        commandOff,
                /* You would put your other needs here. See
                        InputSprocket.r for a list of the keyboard constants. */
```

```
    };
};
```

The first line says that we're making a `tset` resource with resource ID `kResourceID_tset_KeyboardDefaultSet` and name `"Default (Keyboard)"`. The first line inside the braces tells InputSprocket to use the supported version of the `tset` resource, which is 1. What follows is an array of keys, one for each need in your game. For each element in the array, you provide the key and whether modifier keys (Ctrl, Option, Shift, Cmd) should be held down with the key. As you can see from the source, you normally do not want to have the modifier keys held down. This example contains a keyboard default set for movement, fire, and pause game needs. If your game has additional needs, which it probably will, add them to the array.

When your InputSprocket code is working, you will want to add other saved sets to your game so that the players can jump in and play right away. If you ship your game with only the default keyboard layout you used during development, the players will have to configure their joysticks and gamepads before they can use them in your game. Here's what you need to do to add other saved sets to your game:

- Run your game, making sure that your game lets the user configure the controls. If you don't have a menu option to let the user configure the controls, add one. Players get angry when the developer does not let them customize the game's controls.

- In your game, make all the saved sets you want to supply with your game by configuring the controls. At a minimum, you should provide saved sets for the keyboard, mouse, and joystick.

- Go to your System Preferences folder and find the InputSprocket preferences file (the file called `InputSprocket Preferences`). This file contains all the saved sets you made. Copy the saved sets from the preferences file to your game's resource file.

> **CAUTION**
>
> If your game's control needs change during development, you will have to trash your InputSprocket preferences file. You will also have to rerun your game and re-create your saved sets.

InputSprocket Programming

Now that we've moved past the difficult stuff, we're ready to tackle the more interesting challenge of programming with InputSprocket.

InputSprocket Terminology

To fully understand InputSprocket, you first must know some InputSprocket terms. Following are some important terms and definitions:

Needs—Needs are the control needs your game has. Examples of needs in a first-person shooter are fire, change weapon, jump, duck, and strafe. In a basketball game, some needs are shoot, pass, jump, and change the defender. A common game need is movement. You can express this need as either a direction pad need or as two axis needs (X and Y axes). To determine which way to express movement, ask yourself this question: "If the player uses a joystick, do I want the player to move faster if he moves the joystick all the way than if he moves it just a little?" If the answer is yes, use axis needs. Otherwise, use a direction pad need. See the "Reading Player Movement" section, later in this chapter, for examples of using direction pad and axis needs.

> **NOTE**
>
> You can use axis needs even if the player uses the keyboard to play your game. InputSprocket will treat a key press as if the player moved a joystick all the way in the direction the particular key press represented. Although the player will not get the full effect he would get with a joystick, he will still be able to play the game.

Elements—Elements are the physical components of an input device. For example, the individual keys are the elements of the keyboard. The elements of a joystick are the stick and buttons.

Virtual elements—A virtual element is a bridge between needs and elements. InputSprocket uses virtual elements to map your game's needs to the player's input device.

Figure 7-3 shows the relationship between needs, elements, and virtual elements. As you can see, it doesn't matter whether the player presses the spacebar on the keyboard, pushes the trigger button on his joystick, or clicks the mouse button. With virtual elements, InputSprocket knows the player fired a weapon, and it tells your game that he fired.

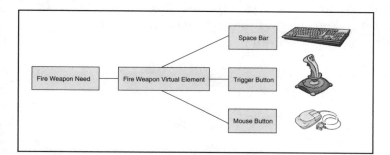

Figure 7-3

The relationship between needs, elements, and virtual elements.

TIP

When working with InputSprocket, think in terms of your game's control needs instead of physical devices, such as joysticks and keyboards. Your InputSprocket code will work the same no matter what game controller the player has. That's the beauty of virtual elements.

The InputController Class

When I introduced InputSprocket earlier in this chapter, I said I was going to create two versions of an input controller class, one for InputSprocket and one for the HID Manager. Now I'm ready to define that class, InputController. To make the sample code in the rest of the chapter easier to understand, I'll list the data members of our InputController class here:

```
class InputController
{
    protected:
        ISpElementReference virtualElements[kNumberOfNeeds];
        ISpElementListReference eventList;
        SInt32 xAxisValue;
        SInt32 yAxisValue;
};
```

The variable `virtualElements` is just an array of our game's virtual elements. We use the `eventList` variable to read input from the player. The `xAxisValue` and `yAxisValue` variables store how far the player moved the joystick.

Starting InputSprocket

Before you can use InputSprocket in your game, you must start InputSprocket by calling the function `ISpStartup()`. You should call this function at the start of your game as part of your game's initialization routine.

```
OSStatus InputController::Startup(void)
{
        return ISpStartup();
}
```

Determining the Version of InputSprocket the Player Has

If you want to see what version of InputSprocket the player has installed on his machine, call the function `ISpGetVersion()`. The main purpose of calling `ISpGetVersion()` is to make sure that the player has a version of InputSprocket that will run with your game. If he doesn't, your game can tell him the problem and let him exit the game, which beats the alternative of crashing his computer.

```
NumVersion InputController::GetInputSprocketVersion(void)
{
        return ISpGetVersion ();
}
```

If you use the resource file I created earlier in this chapter to make the required InputSprocket resources, you must check to make sure that the player has InputSprocket version 1.3 or later. Version 1.3 introduced the `InputSprocket.r` file, which earlier versions of InputSprocket won't be able to recognize. Because the resource file I made uses the `InputSprocket.r` file, earlier InputSprocket versions won't be able to recognize it either. To check whether the version is greater than 1.3, compare the value returned by `ISpGetVersion()` with the hexadecimal number `0x01300000`. If you require a higher version of InputSprocket, either version 1.4 or version 1.7, replace the 3 in the hexadecimal number with either 4 or 7.

InputSprocket Versions

InputSprocket has versions ranging from 1.0 to 1.7. Each new version fixed bugs and added controllers to the list of supported devices. Following is a list of InputSprocket versions and the changes each version means for the game programmer.

- Version 1.0 is the original InputSprocket and contains most of the current API (Application Programming Interface).

- Version 1.1 added the functions `ISpStartup()`, `ISpShutdown()`, `ISpTickle()`, `ISpDevices_ActivateClass()`, and `ISpDevices_DeactivateClass()` to the InputSprocket API. Version 1.1 also introduced speech recognition to InputSprocket.

- Version 1.2 added the `delta` need type to the list of need types. It also added the fields `playerNum` and `group` to the `ISpNeed` structure. Version 1.2 introduced the InputSprocket application resource (`isap`) and was the first version in which speech recognition worked properly. Version 1.2 added the function `ISpTimeToMicroseconds()` to the InputSprocket API.

- Version 1.3 added the `InputSprocket.r` resource file to make it easier to create the resources your game needs to run with InputSprocket. Version 1.3 also made it possible to use the keyboard and mouse when debugging with InputSprocket. Version 1.3 was the first version to support 68K Macs.

- Version 1.4 added the ability to have separate needs to pause and quit your game. This allows the player to quit your game without having to pause it first. Version 1.4 is the last version that supports 68K Macs.

- Version 1.7 streamlined the number of extensions in InputSprocket. It also made it possible for all USB game controllers to work properly right out of the box. Version 1.7 runs only on Power Macs with Mac OS version 8.1 and above. The latest version of InputSprocket is version 1.7.3.

As you can see from this list, 99 percent of the InputSprocket functions will run on versions 1.1 and above. The needs and resources changed the most in version 1.2 and later updates to InputSprocket.

The code I write in this chapter will run on InputSprocket versions 1.4 and above. To support version 1.3, design your game so that the player must pause your game before quitting. There's no reason to support InputSprocket versions before version 1.3. The only reason to worry about versions earlier than version 1.7 is to support 68K Macs, and 68K Macs can't run any version of InputSprocket before version 1.3. To learn more about the different versions of InputSprocket, read the Release Notes that come with the InputSprocket SDK.

Initializing InputSprocket

To initialize InputSprocket, we must perform the following steps:

- Make a list of our game's needs.
- Create virtual elements from the needs by calling `ISpElement_NewVirtualFromNeeds()`.
- Create an element list for event handling by calling `ISpElementList_New()`.
- Fill in the element list from the game's virtual elements by calling `ISpElementList_AddElements()`.
- Call `ISpInit()` to initialize InputSprocket.
- Turn on the keyboard and mouse handlers so that the keyboard and mouse work in our game.

The InputSprocket Need Structure

To create a list of our game's needs, we must learn about `ISpNeed`, InputSprocket's need structure. Table 7-3 describes the fields of `ISpNeed`. Table 7-4 describes the types of needs you can have.

> **TIP**
>
> When creating a list of needs, place your game's most important needs first. The input devices go through the list of needs in order and try to fulfill them. You don't want the player to be unable to fire a weapon with his gamepad because InputSprocket filled the gamepad's buttons with less-pressing needs.

Table 7-3   `ISpNeed` Fields

Field	Description
`name`	A string naming the need. Examples include `"Jump"`, `"Duck"`, and `"Change Weapon"`.
`iconSuiteResourceID`	The resource ID for the icon that will represent this need in the InputSprocket configuration dialog box. To create your icons, use a resource editor such as ResEdit or Resorcerer.
`playerNum`	The player for whom the need applies. If the need does not affect a particular player, but affects the game as a whole (as is the case with a pause game need), use the value 0. Otherwise, use 1 for player 1, 2 for player 2, and so on.
`group`	In InputSprocket you can create your own groups to better organize controller configuration. If you are writing a first-person shooter game with 12 weapons, you will want a change-weapon need. You will also want needs to change to each weapon in the game so that the player can change to a particular weapon quickly. By creating a group for the 12 change-to-weapon needs, you isolate those needs from the other game needs. Use 0 if you have no groups. Otherwise, supply a group number in the range 1 to 255.
`theKind`	This field defines the element type that will produce the data for the need in the game. See Table 7-4 for a list and description of each.
`theLabel`	This field defines an element label representing what you will be using the data for. In the InputSprocket documentation, I counted 72 labels. If none of these 72 labels fits your needs, use the value `kISpElementLabel_None`.
`flags`	If your game has special control needs, InputSprocket includes some flags you can set. If you don't want to use any flags, use the value 0. See Table 7-5 for a list and description of each flag.
`reserved1`	Use the value 0 for this reserved field.
`reserved2`	Use the value 0 for this reserved field.
`reserved3`	Use the value 0 for this reserved field.

Table 7-4   InputSprocket Element Types

Type*	Description
Button	The Button type returns two values: up and down. Most of the needs in your games will be Button needs. Examples of button needs are fire, jump, and pause.
DPad	The DPad type returns directional data. There are nine possible values: up, down, left, right, up-left, up-right, down-left, down-right, and center.
Axis	The Axis type returns a 32-bit unsigned number that tells how far a joystick moved along a particular axis. If the player uses a keyboard instead of a joystick, any key press is recorded as full movement along that axis.
Delta	The Delta type tells you how far you moved in inches. You use delta needs if your game has a cursor that the player can control with the mouse.
Movement	Do not use this type. It does not work properly, and Apple has no plans to ever fix it.
Virtual	Calling ISpElement_NewVirtual() gives you an element of type Virtual. I know of no reason why you would need one of these elements in your game.

* All the element types have the prefix kISpElementKind_.

Table 7-5   InputSprocket Need Flags

Flag*	Description
NoMultiConfig	Only one physical device will bind to the need during autoconfiguration.
Utility	The Utility flag tells InputSprocket that the need is a utility function, such as changing the volume of the sound in the game. Utility functions are the types of functions you assign to the keyboard instead of to the joystick if you are using a joystick to play the game.
PolledOnly	You can get information about the need only by polling it as opposed to by receiving events about the need. In polling, InputSprocket periodically (about 30 times per second) checks the physical device to see whether the need was activated.

Flag*	Description
EventsOnly	You can get information about the need only by checking for events rather than by polling. The EventsOnly flag is the opposite of the PolledOnly flag.
NoAutoConfig	The need will not appear in the default configuration of the physical device.
NoConfig	The player cannot change the configuration of the need.
Invisible	The need is invisible to the user.
Button_AlreadyAxis	An axis version of this button need also exists. This flag lets you use the same need as an axis need, and a button need, which is something that InputSprocket does not normally allow. Applies only to button needs.
Button_ClickToggles	Pressing the button toggles between two states, such as music being on or off. Applies only to button needs.
Button_ActiveWhenDown	The need is active only when the player presses the button. Applies only to button needs.
Button_AlreadyDelta	A delta version of this button need also exists. This flag lets you use the same need as a delta need, and a button need, which is something that InputSprocket does not normally allow. Applies only to button needs.
Axis_AlreadyButton	A button version of this axis need also exists. This flag lets you use the same need as an axis need, and a button need, which is something that InputSprocket does not normally allow. Applies only to axis needs.
Axis_Asymetric	The axis has no logical center.
Axis_AlreadyDelta	A delta version of this axis need also exists. This flag lets you use the same need as an axis need, and a delta need, which is something that InputSprocket does not normally allow. Applies only to axis needs.
Delta_AlreadyAxis	An axis version of this delta need also exists. This flag lets you use the same need as an axis need, and a delta need, which is something that InputSprocket does not normally allow. Applies only to delta needs.
Delta_AlreadyButton	A button version of this delta need also exists. This flag lets you use the same need as a delta need, and a button need, which is something that InputSprocket does not normally allow. Applies only to delta needs.

* All the need flags have the prefix kISpNeedFlag_.

Creating Virtual Elements

The simplest way to create the virtual elements for a game is to call
`ISpElement_NewVirtualFromNeeds()`. The `ISpElement_NewVirtualFromNeeds()` function
creates a list of virtual elements from a list of needs. The function takes four parameters, which are shown in Table 7-6.

Table 7-6   `ISpElement_NewVirtualFromNeeds()` Parameters

Parameter	Description
count	The number of virtual elements to create.
needs	The list of our game's needs.
outElements	The array of virtual elements that `ISpElement_NewVirtualFromNeeds()` creates.
flags	If you want to allocate the virtual elements in temporary memory, use the value `kISpVirtualElementFlag_UseTempMem`. Otherwise, use 0.

Creating and Filling an Element List

So that InputSprocket will properly handle events in our game, we create an element list and fill it with our virtual elements. We call `ISpElementList_New()` to create
the list. This function takes four parameters, as listed in Table 7-7.

Table 7-7   `ISpElementList_New()` Parameters

Parameter	Description
count	The number of elements in the element list.
inElements	The array of virtual elements to place in the element list.
outElements	The element list that `ISpElementList_New()` creates.
flags	If you want to allocate the element list in temporary memory, use the value `kISpElementListFlag_UseTempMem`. Otherwise, use 0.

To fill the element list, we call `ISpElementList_AddElements()`. This function also takes four parameters, as shown in Table 7-8.

Table 7-8 `ISpElementList_AddElements()` Parameters

Parameter	Description
`inElementList`	The element list to which we will add the elements.
`refCon`	An identifier for the element we are adding to the list.
`count`	The number of elements to add.
`newElements`	The virtual elements we want to add to the element list.

TIP

Because each element in the element list must have a unique identifier in the `refCon` **field, we must add the elements to the list one at a time. The easiest way to do this is with a** `for` **loop that you go through once for each need in the game. You pass the loop index as the** `refCon` **parameter to** `ISpElementList_AddElements()`.

Performing the Actual Initialization

To actually initialize InputSprocket, we call the function `ISpInit()`. Table 7-9 lists all the parameters for the `ISpInit()` function.

Table 7-9   ISpInit() Parameters

Parameter	Description
count	The number of needs our game has.
needs	The list of needs, which is an array of ISpNeed structures.
inReferences	The list of virtual elements we created by calling the function ISpElement_NewVirtualFromNeeds().
appCreatorCode	A four-character identifier for our game.
subCreatorCode	Another four-character identifier. InputSprocket uses a combination of the appCreatorCode and subCreatorCode values to save and restore user preferences.
flags	Set the flags parameter to 0.
setListResourceID	The resource ID of our game's set list resource. See "InputSprocket Resources," earlier in this chapter for more information about set list resources.
reserved	Set this reserved field to 0.

Activating the Mouse and Keyboard

By default, InputSprocket does not activate the mouse and keyboard. To let the user play our game using his mouse and keyboard, we must explicitly activate these devices in InputSprocket. We do this with two calls to ISpDevices_ActivateClass(), once for the mouse and once for the keyboard. If your game supports speech recognition, you must call ISpDevices_ActivateClass() one more time to activate the microphone for speech recognition. Table 7-10 lists the device classes you can pass to the ISpDevices_ActivateClass() function. InputSprocket activates joysticks, gamepads, wheels, pedals, and levers by default so you don't have to call ISpDevices_ActivateClass() for joysticks and keypads.

Table 7-10   InputSprocket Device Classes

Class*	Description
SpeechRecognition	A speech recognition device, such as a microphone.
Mouse	A one-button mouse.
Keyboard	A keyboard.
Joystick	A joystick.
Gamepad	A gamepad.
Wheel	A steering wheel.
Pedals	Gas and brake pedals.
Levers	The device is built around a thrust lever.
Tickle	The device requires calls to ISpTickle() to operate.
Unknown	The device (such as a multibutton mouse) does not fit any of the other device classes.

* All the element types have the prefix kISpDeviceClass_.

The Initialization Sample Code

Enough long-winded explanations. The following code shows how to initialize InputSprocket by creating virtual elements, creating an element list, filling the element list with the virtual elements, calling ISpInit(), and activating the keyboard and the mouse.

```
void InputController::Initialize(void)
{
      // Define the game needs
      ISpNeed theNeeds[kNumberOfNeeds] = {
            // The list of needs won't fit here.
            // Check out the sample code on the CD to see them.
      };

      OSStatus error;
      short index;

      // Create the virtual elements from the game's needs
```

```
        error = ISpElement_NewVirtualFromNeeds(kNumberOfNeeds, theNeeds,
virtualElements, 0);
        if (error != noErr)
            ExitToShell();

        // Create the element list
        ISpElementList_New(0, nil, &eventList, 0);

        // Fill in the element list using the virtual elements
         for(index= 0; index< kNumberOfNeeds; index++)
            ISpElementList_AddElements(eventList, index, 1,
&virtualElements[index]);

         // Initialize InputSprocket
        error = ISpInit(kNumberOfNeeds, theNeeds, virtualElements, kAppCreatorCode,
            kSubCreatorCode, 0, kSetListResourceID, 0);

        if (error != noErr)
            ExitToShell();

}

void InputController::ActivateMouseAndKeyboard(void)
{
        // Turn on the keyboard and mouse handlers so we
        // can use the keyboard and mouse in the game.
        // Call this function when you are ready to play the game.
        ISpDevices_ActivateClass (kISpDeviceClass_Keyboard);
        ISpDevices_ActivateClass (kISpDeviceClass_Mouse);
}
```

Letting the User Configure the Controls

You will ship your game with control sets so that the user can start playing right
away. No matter how many sets you include, some users will want to control the
game in a way you didn't imagine. For example, someone may want to use the
right-arrow key to move left and vice versa, so it's always a good idea to let the user
configure the game controls. Configuring the controls is very easy in

InputSprocket. One call to `ISpConfigure()`, and you're finished. `ISpConfigure()` displays a dialog box that allows the game player to configure the game controls. Figure 7-4 shows a sample configuration dialog box for my Gravis Mousestick 2 joystick. Your configuration dialog box may look slightly different depending on what game controllers you have connected to your computer. If you need to, you can supply an event handler as a parameter to `ISpConfigure()`. Otherwise just pass `nil` as the parameter. The optional event handler handles update events. The event handler does not provide much benefit because the configuration dialog is modal, which means the player cannot move the dialog. Because the player cannot move the dialog, there is not much of a chance of an update event happening.

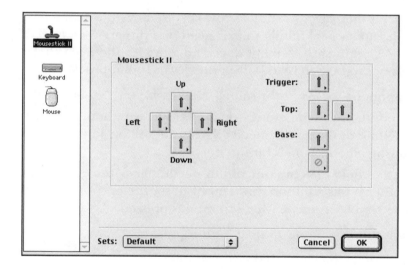

Figure 7-4

The InputSprocket configuration dialog box for a Gravis Mousestick 2 device.

Here's the code to show the InputSprocket configuration dialog box and let the user customize the controls:

```
void InputController::Configure(void)
{
        OSStatus error;

        // Activate the mouse and keyboard so
        // InputSprocket can configure them
        ActivateMouseAndKeyboard();
        error = ISpConfigure(nil);
        if (error != noErr)
                ExitToShell();
```

```
        // Deactivate the mouse and keyboard
        // so the user can do normal OS things.
        DeactivateMouseAndKeyboard();
}
```

Reading Button Presses

By the phrase "reading button presses," I mean determining whether a button
need was fulfilled and whether it occurred through a key press or a joystick button
press. If the player uses the keyboard to play your game, obviously every key he
presses is a physical button press, but it may not show up as an InputSprocket button press. For example, if the player uses the arrow keys to move the character in
your game, pressing the arrow keys fulfills an axis need or a direction pad need,
but not a button need. The physical element doesn't matter. It's the need that
counts. Here are the steps to take to read button presses in InputSprocket:

1. Check the event queue for events by calling `ISpElementList_GetNextEvent()`.

2. If there was an event, check the event's `refCon` field to see whether the event
    corresponded to one of the game's needs. This code will be a massive `switch`
    statement involving all our game's button needs.

3. If the event's `refCon` field matches one of our needs, check the event's data
    field to see whether it was a button down event. If so, the user pressed a but-
    ton, and we have to tell the game what button was pressed.

The following function shows you how to read button presses:

```
InputControllerAction InputController::DetermineAction(void)
{
        OSStatus error;

        // Give time to the InputSprocket drivers
        error = ISpTickle();

        // Check for button presses.
        Boolean wasEvent;
        ISpElementEvent theEvent;

        do {
                error = ISpElementList_GetNextEvent(eventList,
sizeof(ISpElementEvent),
```

```
                        &theEvent, &wasEvent);

        switch (theEvent.refCon) {
            case kAttackNeed:
                if (theEvent.data == kISpButtonDown)
                        return kAttack;
                break;

            case kChangeWeaponNeed:
                if (theEvent.data == kISpButtonDown)
                        return kChangeWeapon;
                break;

            case kPauseGameNeed:
                if (theEvent.data == kISpButtonDown)
                        return kPauseGame;
                break;

            // You would put your additional needs here

            default:
                return kNoButtonsPressed;
                break;
        }
    } while (wasEvent && !error);

    // At this point, nothing occurred
    return kNoButtonsPressed;
}
```

As you can see from the code, the function will tell you one of four things: the player attacked, the player changed weapons, the player paused the game, or the player did not press any buttons. The code does not tell you what physical button was pressed. For example, many games use the Esc key to pause the game. If the player configured the game this way, the DetermineAction() function will tell you that the player paused the game when he pressed the Esc key. It's impossible for InputSprocket to tell you that the player pressed the Esc key because InputSprocket has no way of knowing what key the user will choose to pause the game. The player can use any key on the keyboard, the mouse button, or a joystick button to pause the game, and the player can change that physical element at any time.

Reading Player Movement

There are three ways you can read player movement in InputSprocket: using direction pad needs, using axis needs, and using delta needs. The following sections describe these three ways to read player movement.

Reading Direction Pad Movement

Using a direction pad need (a DPad need) is the simplest way to read player movement in a game. You call ISpElement_GetSimpleState() and then do a switch statement on all the possible directions. Here's a sample function that reads movement with a direction pad need:

```
InputControllerAction InputController::DetermineDigitalMovement(void)
{
      UInt32 theInput;
      OSStatus error =
ISpElement_GetSimpleState(virtualElements[kDirectionPadNeed],
            &theInput);
      if (error != noErr)
            return kNoMovement;

      switch (theInput) {
            case kISpPadLeft:
                  return kMoveLeft;
                  break;

            case kISpPadUpLeft:
                  return kMoveUpAndLeft;
                  break;

            case kISpPadUp:
                  return kMoveUp;
                  break;

            case kISpPadUpRight:
                  return kMoveUpAndRight;
                  break;

            case kISpPadRight:
                  return kMoveRight;
```

```
                    break;

            case kISpPadDownRight:
                    return kMoveDownAndRight;
                    break;

            case kISpPadDown:
                    return kMoveDown;
                    break;

            case kISpPadDownLeft:
                    return kMoveDownAndLeft;
                    break;

            default:
                    return kNoMovement;
                    break;
        }
}
```

Reading Axis Movement

The actual reading of movement with axis needs is the same as for a direction pad
need: You call ISpElement_GetSimpleState() once for each axis. What complicates
matters for axis needs is that you must do more after reading the movement.
Although a direction pad need converts the movement into one of nine possible
directions, all you get with an axis need is a 32-bit integer. It's up to you to make
sense of the data.

To interpret the integer returned by ISpElement_GetSimpleState() for an axis need,
we will create our own axis system and write a function to convert the axis data that
InputSprocket gives us to our axis system. We will store the results in the xAxisValue
and yAxisValue data members of our InputController class. As a start, let's create
some constants that will define the axis system:

```
const SInt32 kAxisMinimumValue = -5;
const SInt32 kAxisCenterValue = 0;
const Sint32 kAxisMaximumValue = 5;
```

For the X-axis, the kAxisMinimumValue constant represents the joystick being pulled
all the way to the left. The kAxisMaximumValue constant represents the joystick being
pulled all the way to the right, and the kAxisCenterValue represents the joystick
being centered horizontally.

Here's the code to convert the X-axis data:

```
SInt32 InputController::ConvertXAxisData(ISpAxisData axisValue, SInt32 minValue,
SInt32 maxValue)
{
        SInt32 divisor = kISpAxisMaximum / (maxValue - minValue);
        SInt32 result = (axisValue / divisor) + minValue;
        return result;
}
```

InputSprocket uses a 32-bit integer to store the axis data, which gives us a range of values from 0 to approximately 4 billion (2 raised to the power of 32). We want to convert this data into a number in the range of the minValue and maxValue parameters we supply to ConvertXAxisData() (kAxisMinimumValue and kAxisMaximumValue in our case). The first step is to come up with a number we can divide into the InputSprocket axis value. This number is the maximum possible InputSprocket axis value divided by the difference of the maxValue and minValue parameters we supplied to ConvertXAxisData(). For our system, the value of (maxValue − minValue) is 10 (5 − (−5)), and the number is approximately 400 million (4 billion divided by 10).

After calculating the number to divide into the InputSprocket axis value, we perform the division. The division gives us a number between 0 and the value of (maxValue − minValue). In our axis system, the division gives us a number ranging from 0 and 10. The final step is to add the minimum axis value (the minValue parameter to ConvertXAxisData()) to the quotient. For our axis system, we would add the value −5 to the quotient, giving us a number ranging from −5 to 5, which are our axis system's minimum and maximum axis values respectively.

For the Y-axis there's a problem. We want the kAxisMinimumValue constant to represent the joystick being pulled all the way up, and the kAxisMaximumValue constant to represent the joystick being pulled all the way down. This arrangement makes the control line up with the graphic coordinate system, where the top of the screen has a vertical coordinate of 0, and the vertical coordinate increases as you move down the screen. Unfortunately, in InputSprocket, the axis data value *decreases* as you move the joystick downward (see Figure 7-5). So we have to create a function to convert the Y-axis data that reverses what we do in the ConvertXAxisData() function. Reversing things will give us what we want: the kAxisMinimumValue representing the joystick being moved all the way up.

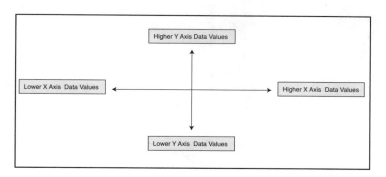

Figure 7-5

The axis values when the player moves the joystick up, down, left, and right.

Here's the code to convert the Y-axis data:

```
SInt32 InputController::ConvertYAxisData(ISpAxisData axisValue, SInt32 minValue,
        SInt32 maxValue)
{
        SInt32 divisor = kISpAxisMaximum / (maxValue - minValue);
        SInt32 result = (axisValue / divisor) + minValue;

        // Change the sign.
        // Because InputSprocket returns higher values for moving the joystick
        // up, we have to reverse what we do in the ConvertXAxis() function.
        // This will make our axis system work the way we want, with lower values
        // for moving the joystick up.

        result = result * -1;
        return result;
}
```

Now here's the code to read the player movement:

```
InputControllerAction InputController::DetermineAnalogMovement(void)
{
        // Determine if there was horizontal movement.
        UInt32 theInput;
        OSStatus error;
        error = ISpElement_GetSimpleState(virtualElements[kXAxisNeed] , &theInput);

        if (error != noErr)
                return kNoMovement;

        xAxisValue = ConvertXAxisData(theInput, kAxisMinimumValue,
                        kAxisMaximumValue);
```

```
        // Determine if there was vertical movement
        error = ISpElement_GetSimpleState(virtualElements[kYAxisNeed] , &theInput);

        if (error != noErr)
                return kNoMovement;

        yAxisValue = ConvertYAxisData(theInput, kAxisMinimumValue,
                        kAxisMaximumValue);


        // Determine the direction the player moved.
        if ((yAxisValue < kAxisCenterValue) && (xAxisValue == kAxisCenterValue))
                return kMoveUp;
        else if ((yAxisValue < kAxisCenterValue) && (xAxisValue < kAxisCenterValue))
                return kMoveUpAndLeft;
        else if ((yAxisValue < kAxisCenterValue) && (xAxisValue > kAxisCenterValue))
                return kMoveUpAndRight;
        else if ((yAxisValue > kAxisCenterValue) && (xAxisValue < kAxisCenterValue))
                return kMoveDownAndLeft;
        else if ((yAxisValue > kAxisCenterValue) && (xAxisValue > kAxisCenterValue))
                return kMoveDownAndRight;
        else if ((yAxisValue > kAxisCenterValue) && (xAxisValue == kAxisCenterValue))
                return kMoveDown;
        else if ((yAxisValue == kAxisCenterValue) && (xAxisValue < kAxisCenterValue))
                return kMoveLeft;
        else if ((yAxisValue == kAxisCenterValue) && (xAxisValue > kAxisCenterValue))
                return kMoveRight;
        else
                return kNoMovement;
}
```

Reading Delta Movement

Here are the steps to take to read movement using delta needs in InputSprocket:

1. Check the event queue for delta movement events by calling
   ISpElement_GetNextEvent().
2. If there was a delta movement event, check the event's data field to determine the amount of movement.

NOTE

You may be wondering why we call ISpElement_GetNextEvent() to check for delta movement, but we called ISpElementList_GetNextEvent() to check for button presses. Most games have many button needs, and we want to see which of these buttons was pressed with a single function call. ISpElementList_GetNextEvent() does this for us. When checking for delta movement, we are interested in only one need—the delta need—so ISpElement_GetNextEvent() works for us in this case.

Here are a couple of things to keep in mind when working with delta movement:

- InputSprocket returns delta movement as a 32-bit fixed-point number. When checking the event's data field, you must typecast to data type Fixed.
- InputSprocket returns negative values for upward movement and positive values for downward movement, just as it does for axis data. If you want to reverse the delta value, you must multiply the delta value by –1.

The game we're developing in this book has no use for delta needs, but here's a sample function that would read delta movement if you needed that functionality:

```
InputControllerAction InputController::DetermineDeltaMovement(void)
{
        // Assume that we have deltaX and deltaY movement needs.

        // For your game, you would want to make these data members
        // of the InputController class.
        Fixed xDeltaValue;
        Fixed yDeltaValue;
        const Fixed kDeltaCenterValue = 0;

        OSStatus error;

        // Check for button presses.
        Boolean wasEvent;
        ISpElementEvent theEvent;

        do {
                // Check if the player moved horizontally
                error = ISpElement_GetNextEvent(virtualElements[kDeltaXNeed},
```

```
                       sizeof(ISpElementEvent), &theEvent, &wasEvent);

     if ((wasEvent) && (!error)) {
             // We have to typecast to the Fixed data type.
             xDeltaValue = (Fixed) theEvent.data;
     }

     // Check if the player moved vertically
     error = ISpElement_GetNextEvent(virtualElements[kDeltaYNeed},
                  sizeof(ISpElementEvent), &theEvent, &wasEvent);

     if (wasEvent && !error) {
             // We have to typecast to the Fixed data type.
             yDeltaValue = (Fixed) theEvent.data;

             // Change the sign of the delta y data to
             // match our needs
             yDeltaValue = yDeltaVelue * -1;
     }
} while (wasEvent && !error);

// Determine the direction the player moved.
if ((yAxisValue < kDeltaCenterValue) && (xAxisValue == kDeltaCenterValue))
     return kMoveUp;
     else if ((yAxisValue < kDeltaCenterValue) && (xAxisValue <
     kDeltaCenterValue))
     return kMoveUpAndLeft;
     else if ((yAxisValue < kDeltaCenterValue) && (xAxisValue >
     kDeltaCenterValue))
     return kMoveUpAndRight;
     else if ((yAxisValue > kDeltaCenterValue) && (xAxisValue <
     kDeltaCenterValue))
     return kMoveDownAndLeft;
     else if ((yAxisValue > kDeltaCenterValue) && (xAxisValue >
     kDeltaCenterValue))
     return kMoveDownAndRight;
     else if ((yAxisValue > kDeltaCenterValue) && (xAxisValue ==
     kDeltaCenterValue))
     return kMoveDown;
     else if ((yAxisValue == kDeltaCenterValue) && (xAxisValue <
     kDeltaCenterValue))
```

```
                return kMoveLeft;
        else if ((yAxisValue == kDeltaCenterValue) && (xAxisValue >
kDeltaCenterValue))
                return kMoveRight;
        else
                return kNoMovement;
}
```

Pausing and Resuming InputSprocket

When the user pauses the game, we must suspend InputSprocket temporarily so that the user can use the keyboard and mouse as he normally does when using the Mac OS. If we do not suspend InputSprocket, the player will be unable to move the mouse cursor, forcing him to restart his computer. I doubt this player would ever play your game again—or play any other game you develop—if he has to restart his computer every time he wants to pause a game. The function to pause InputSprocket is ISpSuspend(), shown in the following code:

```
OSStatus InputController::Suspend(void)
{
        return ISpSuspend();
}
```

When the user is ready to resume the game, we call ISpResume() to have the keyboard and mouse work the way we want it to in our game:

```
OSStatus InputController::Resume(void)
{
        return ISpResume();
}
```

Quitting InputSprocket

When it's time to quit the game, we stop InputSprocket and then dispose of the event list and virtual elements. If we did not dispose of the event list and virtual elements, we would create a memory leak in our game. A memory leak occurs when you allocate memory and forget to dispose of the memory you allocated. The memory leak will eventually crash the computer.

The following code works to close down InputSprocket neatly, freeing up the memory we used and stopping any potential memory leaks:

```
void InputController::Cleanup(void)
{
        ISpStop();

        if (eventList != nil) {
                ISpElementList_Dispose(eventList);
                eventList = nil;
        }

        ISpElement_DisposeVirtual(kNumberOfNeeds, virtualElements);
}
```

Summary

We've covered a lot of material in this chapter. We learned what InputSprocket does and how to make it work properly with our games. We learned how to initialize, pause, resume, and quit InputSprocket as well as how to use it to read user input from a number of physical devices.

For more information on InputSprocket, check out the InputSprocket reference included with the InputSprocket SDK. The reference guide contains descriptions of all the InputSprocket functions, data structures, and constants. Conveniently, you can find the InputSprocket documentation on the CD-ROM included with this book.

I wrote a sample program, which you can also find on the CD-ROM. It builds on the programs I wrote in the previous three chapters. As you might guess, the program for this chapter uses InputSprocket to move the sprite around the screen. As always, I have included the full source code, which you can modify to suit your own needs.

CHAPTER 8

HID Manager

In the previous chapter, we discussed InputSprocket, the Mac technology used to read input from game controllers for Mac OS 8 and 9. In this chapter, we'll cover the HID (Human Interface Devices) Manager, the new technology used to support game controllers on Mac OS X. After reading this chapter, you will be able to add support for joysticks and gamepads to your Mac OS X games.

Introduction to the HID Manager

Apple created the I/O Kit for the use of peripheral vendors who are writing OS X drivers for their products; the I/O Kit also provides application developers with low-level access to peripherals. The I/O Kit is enormous, with families for different classes of peripherals. For example, there's a PCI family for PCI cards such as 3D graphics accelerators that you install inside your Mac; there's a FireWire family for products that plug into one of the Mac's FireWire ports; and there's a Graphics family for monitors.

One of the I/O Kit's families is the HID family. (If the HID family did not exist, the previous paragraph would have been pointless.) The HID family of peripherals consists of devices people use to control a computer: joysticks, gamepads, steering wheels, mice, and keyboards. HID is part of the USB specification so the peripheral must be a USB peripheral to be a HID device. The HID Manager gives you, the game programmer, low-level access to these gaming devices. This low-level access gives you more power than InputSprocket provides, but it also means that programming with the HID Manager is more difficult than programming with InputSprocket.

Currently, the HID Manager supports only joysticks, gamepads, audio devices, and non-Apple monitors. For the purposes of game development, what matters is the support for the joystick and gamepad. Because the HID Manager does not yet support the keyboard and mouse, the use of the HID Manager in Mac games has not flourished. Every Mac has a keyboard and mouse, so game developers must support the keyboard and mouse. Game developers are doing just that: supporting the keyboard and mouse instead of using the HID Manager. Apple is working to add keyboard and mouse support to the HID Manager. Hopefully this support will come by the time you read this and make this paragraph obsolete.

NOTE

To check if your version of Mac OS X has keyboard and mouse support in the HID Manager, run the program for this chapter with no game controllers connected to your Mac. If it runs, you have HID support for the keyboard and mouse.

If Apple has not added keyboard and mouse support to the HID Manager when you are reading this note, I cannot tell you when the support will appear. Be on the lookout for updates to Mac OS X. The improved HID Manager will appear in an operating system update. It will not be available as a separate download. Check Apple's Web site or your favorite Mac news site for announcements on new updates to Mac OS X.

Another problem with the HID Manager is that you can directly call the HID Manager functions only from Mach-O Carbon programs that do not run on Mac OS 8 and 9. Using the HID Manager in a CFM Carbon program that runs on Mac OS 8, 9, and X is a pain in the butt. You must create a Mach-O bundle for the HID Manager framework (see Chapter 15, "Files," for an explanation of bundles), include the bundle with your game, and write code to extract function pointers from the bundle. This means that you cannot easily write a CFM Carbon application that uses InputSprocket on Mac OS 8 and 9 and that also uses the HID Manager on Mac OS X.

The alternatives to writing a hack so that you can use the HID Manager in a CFM Carbon program are having two versions of your game and limiting support to the keyboard and mouse. The path you choose depends on your needs. I prefer having two versions of the game: a Mac OS 8/9 version and a Mac OS X version. This is the path I chose for the code in this book. Because the two versions differ only in reading player input, keeping these two versions of the source code in sync is easier than using the HID Manager in a CFM Carbon program. If having one version of the game is your top priority, then you should add the code to call the HID Manager in a CFM Carbon program. The Carbon SDK includes a sample program for calling a Mach-O framework from a CFM Carbon program, which will help you use the HID Manager in your CFM Carbon game. The *easiest* solution is to limit your support to the keyboard and mouse; whether or not it is the *best* solution depends on the type of game you're writing. If you are developing a strategy game, board game, puzzle game, or role-playing game, keyboard and mouse support is sufficient. Action games should allow the player to use a joystick or gamepad.

Setting Up Your Game to Use the HID Manager

Every Mac running Mac OS X has the I/O Kit framework, which contains the HID Manager header files and libraries, so you do not have to worry about the player not having a HID Manager extension. This makes life easy for us because there are no extensions to install.

To use the HID Manager in your game, add the I/O Kit framework, `IOKit.framework`, to your game's project. Refer to Chapter 2, "Project Builder," for information about adding frameworks to Project Builder programs.

At a minimum, you need to include the following header files in your project:

```
#include <IOKit/hid/IOHIDLib.h>
#include <IOKit/hid/IOHIDKeys.h>
#include <IOKit/IOKitLib.h>
#include <IOKit/IOCFPlugin.h>
```

The `IOHIDLib.h` and `IOHIDKeys.h` header files contain the majority of the HID Manager's data types and function calls. The `IOKitLib.h` file contains most of the I/O Kit functions you have to call to use the HID Manager in your games. The `IOCFPlugin.h` file contains the remaining I/O Kit functions you must call to add HID Manager support to your game.

Programming with the HID Manager

Now we can proceed to writing HID Manager code, which is going to be one heck of a ride. Before we begin, I should warn you that the HID Manager data structures include functions as well as data. This approach differs from InputSprocket, which keeps the data structures and functions separate. It's something to keep in mind when reading this chapter.

HID Manager Terminology

Before we begin programming with the HID Manager, there are some terms to learn that will make the rest of the chapter easier to understand. The next several sections cover these important concepts.

Device Lists

When using the HID Manager, your game has the responsibility to create a list of all input devices connected to the player's computer so that the player can choose the input device he wants to use to play the game. Device lists contain a list of all connected HID input devices. The HID Manager uses the data type io_iterator_t to store device lists. The data type io_iterator_t is an I/O Kit data type that contains a list of I/O Kit devices. We have the responsibility to ensure that our device lists contain only HID devices; I will show you how to do this later in the chapter.

Devices

Devices are physical input devices, such as joysticks, gamepads, keyboards, and mice. I created a class, InputDevice, that stores all the HID Manager data for an input device. You can see the InputDevice class's data members in the following listing:

```
class InputDevice
{
        protected:
                Str255 transportKey;
                long vendorID;
                long productID;
                long version;
                Str255 manufacturer;
                Str255 productName;
                Str255 serialNumber;
                long USBLocationID;
                long usagePage;
                long usage;
};
```

Table 8-1 provides a description of each of the fields that make up a HID input device. The field of greatest interest to you should be the productName field. When the player selects a controller to play the game, you provide the names of all connected devices so that he can determine which one to use.

Table 8-1   HID Device Data

Field	HID Manager Name	Description
transportKey	kIOHIDTransportKey	You should not have to worry about the device's transport key. Currently, the only transport key is USB.
vendorID	kIOHIDVendorKey	A number identifying the manufacturer of the device.
productID	kIOHIDProductIDKey	A number identifying the device, the specific product of the manufacturer identified in the vendorID field.
version	kIOHIDVersionNumberKey	A number identifying the version of the device.
manufacturer	kIOHIDManufacturerKey	The name of the device's manufacturer.
productName	kIOHIDProductKey	The name of the device.
serialNumber	kIOHIDSerialNumberKey	The device's serial number.
USBLocationID	kIOHIDLocationIDKey	A number identifying the location of the device on the USB chain. Macs with USB connections have a chain of USB devices connected to the computer.
usagePage	kIOHIDPrimaryUsagePageKey	A number identifying the HID usage page for the device. HID devices generally have a usage page of 1, which is the Generic Desktop page.
usage	kIOHIDPrimaryUsageKey	A number identifying the general usage for the device, such as whether the device is a joystick, gamepad, keyboard, or mouse. Table 8-2 lists usage values on the Generic Desktop page for common input devices.

Table 8-2   Usage Values for Common Input Devices

Value*	Description
0x02	Mouse
0x04	Joystick
0x05	Gamepad
0x06	Keyboard

* All these usage values reside in the Generic Desktop page, which has a usage page value of 1. All HID usage page and usage values are hexadecimal (digits 0–9 and A–F), not decimal (0–9) numbers.

Elements

Each input device has one or more elements, which represent individual controls on the physical device. For example, a keyboard has one element for each key. HID elements can nest inside other elements. If you have a gamepad with an analog stick (such as the controllers for the GameCube, PlayStation 2, and XBox consoles), the HID Manager reports the stick as a pointer element. Inside the pointer element are two more elements: one for x-axis movement and one for y-axis movement.

To simplify working with elements, I created an `InputDeviceElement` class that contains all the data associated with an element. You can see all the data the HID Manager stores on an element in the following declaration:

```
class InputDeviceElement
{
        protected:
                IOHIDElementCookie cookie;
                IOHIDElementType type;

                long usagePage;
                long usage;

                long rawMin;
                long rawMax;
```

```
            long scaledMin;
            long scaledMax;

            long size;

            Boolean isRelative;
            Boolean isWrapping;
            Boolean isNonLinear;
            Boolean hasPreferredState;
            Boolean hasNullState;

            long units;
            long unitExponent;
            Str255 elementName;
};
```

I describe each of the fields in the InputDeviceElement class in Table 8-3. You can see
from Table 8-3 that device elements have usage pages and usage values, just as
input devices do. Button elements have a usage page value of 9 while their usage
values depend on the number of buttons on the device. For example, a joystick
with five buttons would have usage values from 1 to 5, where the first button has
the value 1, the second button has the value 2, and so on.

Table 8-3   HID Element Data

Field	HID Manager Name	Description
cookie	kIOHIDElementCookieKey	A value, stored as a 32-bit integer, which uniquely identifies the element.
type	kIOHIDElementTypeKey	The type of element. Table 8-4 lists the HID element types.
usagePage	kIOHIDElementUsagePageKey	The HID usage page for the element. Most HID device elements have a usage page of 1, which is the Generic Desktop page.

Field	HID Manager Name	Description
usage	kIOHIDElementUsageKey	The general usage for the element, such as a button, x-axis movement, or y-axis movement.
rawMin	kIOHIDElementMinKey	The minimum value the element returns. For buttons, this value will be 0; axis values depend on the individual device.
rawMax	kIOHIDElementMaxKey	The maximum value the element returns. For buttons, this value is 1; axis values depend on the device.
scaledMin	kIOHIDElementScaledMinKey	The scaled minimum value.
scaledMax	kIOHIDElementScaledMaxKey	The scaled maximum value.
size	kIOHIDElementSizeKey	The size of the data (in bits) the element returns.
isRelative	kIOHIDElementIsRelativeKey	Is the reading relative to the last reading? For example, when reading mouse movement, this field reports the movement relative to the last location of the mouse.
isWrapping	kIOHIDElementIsWrappingKey	Does the element's data wrap around? Think of the escape passages in PacMan. When you go into the passage at the right edge of the screen, you come out at the left edge. The element's data does the same thing if isWrapping is true. When you exceed the element's maximum value, the data wraps to the element's minimum value.

(continues)

Table 8-3   HID Element Data (continued)

Field	HID Manager Name	Description
isNonLinear	kIOHIDElementIs NonLinearKey	Does the element have nonlinear data? An example of an element with nonlinear data is an element that measures the tip pressure on a drawing tablet.
hasPreferredState	kIOHIDElementHas PreferredStateKey	Does the element have a preferred state? For example, the buttons on a joystick have a preferred state of being up.
hasNullState	kIOHIDElementHas NullStateKey	Does the element have a zero state? The buttons on a gamepad have a *zero state*, which means that the player has not pressed the button.
units	kIOHIDElementUnitKey	The unit of measurement for the rawMin, rawMax, scaledMin, and scaledMax fields. For example, the hat switch of a joystick could measure the angular position of the switch. Buttons do not use the units field.
unitExponent	kIOHIDElementUnit ExponentKey	An exponent for the unit of measure-ment in the units field. Normally, the exponent is 0.
elementName	kIOHIDElementNameKey	The name of the element.

Table 8-4   HID Element Types

Type*	Description
Input_Misc	Any input-only elements that do not fall into the Input_Button, Input_Axis, or Input_ScanCodes category.
Input_Button	Button elements, such as the buttons on a joystick or the keys on a keyboard.
Input_Axis	Axis elements, such as the stick portion of a joystick.
Input_ScanCodes	Keyboards may have scan codes for the individual keys on the keyboard.
Output	Force feedback devices have output elements, which output data to the player instead of reading data from the player. An example of a force feedback device is the Playstation 2's controller.
Feature	The capabilities of a universal power supply may have feature elements. Game controllers do not have feature elements. Obviously you should not have to worry about feature elements in your game.
Collection	A collection of additional elements. For example, the stick of a joystick would be a collection element-containing elements for x-axis and y-axis movement.

* All the element types have the prefix kIOHIDElementType.

The common game controller elements reside in the Generic Desktop usage page, which means they have a usage page value of 1. Table 8-5 lists the usage values for common game elements.

Table 8-5   Usage Values for Common Game Elements

Value*	Description
0x 01	Pointer; the pointer element contains axis elements inside it
0x 30	X-axis movement
0x 31	Y-axis movement
0x 32	Z-axis movement
0x 33	Rotate around x-axis
0x 34	Rotate around y-axis
0x 35	Rotate around z-axis
0x 36	Slider
0x 37	Dial
0x 38	Wheel
0x 39	Hat switch
0x 90	Direction pad up
0x 91	Direction pad down
0x 92	Direction pad left
0x 93	Direction pad right

* All HID usage page and usage values are hexadecimal numbers (digits 0–9 and A–F), not decimal (0–9) numbers.

Device Interfaces

The HID Manager uses device interfaces to read data from an input device's elements. Device elements are handles to data of type IOHIDDeviceInterface.

Queues

When your game reads the player's input, it reads the most recent value of the input device's element. This works well when reading player movement, but not so well when reading button presses for actions, such as firing weapons, jumping, and

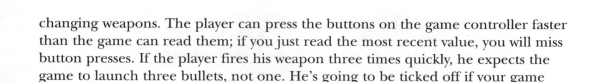

changing weapons. The player can press the buttons on the game controller faster than the game can read them; if you just read the most recent value, you will miss button presses. If the player fires his weapon three times quickly, he expects the game to launch three bullets, not one. He's going to be ticked off if your game doesn't launch the correct number of bullets.

The solution is to use the HID Manager's *queues.* You place the device elements whose button presses you don't want to miss into the queue. When an event involving one of the elements in the queue occurs, the event goes into the queue. Your game reads events from the queue until the queue is empty so that you don't miss any important events.

Cookies

HID Manager *cookies* serve two purposes. First, they are identifiers for elements of an input device. You read data from the element by using its cookie.

Second, cookies give you the ability to use InputSprocket-style needs in your HID Manager game. Create an array of type IOHIDElementCookie, the data type for HID Manager cookies, with one entry for each control need your game has. In your game's configure controller dialog box (which we will write later in this chapter), the player tells your game what controls he wants to use to perform each action in the game. Read the player's selection, get the cookie for the element the player selects, and place that cookie in the array.

HID Manager Version of the InputController Class

The HID Manager is a whole new ball game compared to InputSprocket, so our InputController class looks different from a data standpoint. The following declaration shows the data members of the InputController class that uses the HID Manager:

```
class InputController
{
        public:
                IOHIDElementCookie gameNeeds[kNumberOfNeeds];
        protected:
                mach_port_t masterPort;
                LinkedList elementList;
                LinkedList controllerList;
```

```
        InputDevicePtr controllerDevice;

        IOHIDDeviceInterfaceHandle controllerDeviceInterface;
        IOHIDQueueInterfaceHandle eventList;

        short xAxisValue;
        short yAxisValue;
};
```

The gameNeeds array contains a list of our game's needs and the element on the input device corresponding to that need (for example, which button on the gamepad is the button used to fire a weapon). This array is my attempt to re-create InputSprocket functionality with the HID Manager, using game needs instead of device elements.

To connect to the I/O Kit Registry (the list of input and output devices connected to the player's machine) to assemble a list of HID devices on the player's computer, we need a Mach (Mac OS X has a Mach kernel, a byproduct of OS X having Unix as the base for the operating system) port. We use the masterPort data member to store the Mach port.

The elementList data member holds the list of elements of the device the player uses to play the game. The controllerList data member contains the list of HID devices connected to the player's machine. The controllerDevice data member contains the HID device the player is using to play the game. I wrote the classes LinkedList and InputDevice; they are not Apple-supplied data types. I covered the internals of the InputDevice class earlier in this chapter. You should be able to figure out the purpose of the LinkedList class.

To read input from the player using the HID Manager, we need a device interface so that our game can communicate with the HID Manager. The controllerDeviceInterface data member is our device interface.

When reading button presses, we use a HID Manager queue to store an accumulation of button presses so that we don't miss any events. The eventList data member stores this queue.

The xAxisValue and yAxisValue data members store how far the player moved the joystick in the x-axis and y-axis, respectively. We must store these values because the functions we use to read input return only the direction of movement, not the amount of movement. By storing the x-and y-axis values, we can use the amount of movement to move the player appropriately.

Finding the Player's HID-Capable Devices

The first thing you must do when programming with the HID Manager is to make a list of the HID devices connected to the player's computer so that the player can choose which device to use to play the game. Creating this list requires three function calls. First, you must get a Mach port so that you can communicate with the I/O Kit. At its lowest level, Mac OS X contains a Mach kernel, which runs the operating system behind the Aqua interface. Mach ports are the way a programmer accesses the Mach kernel, which is what we need to do to find the HID devices on the player's machine. To retrieve a Mach port, call IOMasterPort(), as shown in the following function:

```
void InputController::CreateMasterPort(void)
{
        IOReturn result;
        result = IOMasterPort(MACH_PORT_NULL, &masterPort);
}
```

Second, call the function IOServiceMatching() to create a matching dictionary so that you can search the I/O Registry for HID devices. Pass the value kIOHIDDeviceKey to limit the dictionary to HID devices. A Mac OS X dictionary works similarly to a real dictionary, but instead of storing a list of words, a Mac OS X dictionary stores a list of anything you choose—in this case, HID devices.

Finally, you retrieve the list of HID devices by calling IOServiceGetMatchingServices(). This function takes three parameters. The first parameter is the Mach port you retrieved in the call to IOMasterPort(). The second parameter is the matching dictionary you created by calling IOServiceMatching(). The final parameter is the list of HID devices that IOServiceGetMatchingServices() returns. The following function gives us a list of connected HID devices:

```
void InputController::CreateControllerList(void)
{
        IOReturn result;
        CFMutableDictionaryRef matchingDictionary;
        Boolean noMatchingDevices;
io_iterator_t deviceList;

        // Dispose of any previously created controller list
        DisposeControllerList();
```

```
        // Create matching dictionary of HID devices
        matchingDictionary = IOServiceMatching(kIOHIDDeviceKey);

        // Look for any HID controllers connected
        // to the player's machine
        result = IOServiceGetMatchingServices(masterPort, matchingDictionary,
                    &deviceList);
        if ((controllerList == nil) || result != kIOReturnSuccess)
                noMatchingDevices = true;
        else
                noMatchingDevices = false;

        if (noMatchingDevices) {
                // Stop using the HID Manager because there are no HID Manager
devices
                return;
        }
        else {
                FillControllerList(deviceList);
        }


        // We're finished with the matching dictionary.
        // IOServiceGetMatchingServices() released it for us.
        matchingDictionary = nil;

        IOObjectRelease(deviceList);
}
void InputController::FillControllerList(io_iterator_t deviceList)
{
        io_object_t currentDevice;
        kern_return_t result;
        CFMutableDictionaryRef deviceProperties;
        InputDevicePtr deviceToAdd = new InputDevice;

     currentDevice = IOIteratorNext(deviceList);

        while (currentDevice != nil) {
                // Retrieve the name of the current controller
                result = IORegistryEntryCreateCFProperties(currentDevice,
```

```
                          &deviceProperties, kCFAllocatorDefault, kNilOptions);

        // Fill our InputDevice object with its data
        // and add it to the controller list.
        deviceToAdd->SetDeviceObject(currentDevice);
        deviceToAdd->StoreDeviceData(deviceProperties);
        controllerList.AddItem(deviceToAdd);

        // Get next controller
        deviceToAdd = new InputDevice;
        currentDevice = IOIteratorNext(deviceList);
        }

    }
```

Creating Device Interfaces

After compiling a list of HID devices, you must create a device interface for each
device. Creating a device interface involves three HID Manager function calls. First,
call IOCreatePlugInInterfaceForService(). This function creates a plug-in interface
you will use to create the device interface. Plug-in interfaces let your program
access the computer hardware. The device interface is a special kind of plug-in that
lets you access a particular class of devices. We will create a HID device interface,
which allows our game to access HID devices like joysticks. The
IOCreatePlugInInterfaceForService() function takes five parameters, which Table
8-6 describes.

Table 8-6   IOCreatePlugInInterfaceForService() Parameters

Parameter	Description
service	The service for which we create the plug-in interface. When working with the HID Manager, you pass the device for which you want to create a device interface.
pluginType	The type of plug-in you want to create. When creating HID device interfaces, use the value kIOHIDDeviceUserClientTypeID.
interfaceType	The type of interface you want to create. Use the value kIOCFPlugInInterfaceID to create a plug-in interface.
theInterface	The plug-in interface that IOCreatePlugInInterfaceForService() creates.
theScore	IOCreatePlugInInterfaceForService() returns a 32-bit signed integer in the theScore parameter. You shouldn't have to use this parameter in your game.

To create the device interface, you then call the member function QueryInterface() for the plug-in interface you created by calling IOCreatePlugInInterfaceForService(). The QueryInterface() function takes three parameters. In the first parameter, pass the plug-in interface you created by calling IOCreatePlugInInterfaceForService(). Pass the device interface you want to create in the third parameter. The QueryInterface() function expects a void handle in the third parameter, so you must typecast the device interface to be of data type LPVOID.

The second parameter is a bit tricky (which is why I am explaining it in a separate paragraph). It requires a Core Foundation Universally Unique Identifier (CFU-UID), which is a 128-bit number. To retrieve the CFUUID, call the function CFUUIDGetUUIDBytes(). (That function name just rolls right off the tongue, doesn't it?) You pass an object of type CFUUIDRef to the CFUUIDGetUUIDBytes() function. For the purposes of creating a HID device interface, you should pass the constant kIOHIDDeviceInterfaceID, which is the unique identifier for a HID Manager device interface, to CFUUIDGetUUIDBytes().

After creating the device interface, you can dispose of the plug-in interface by calling the plug-in interface's Release() member function.

The following code creates a device interface:

```
void InputController::CreateDeviceInterface(void)
{
        IOReturn result;
        io_name_t deviceClassName;

        result = IOObjectGetClass(controllerDevice ->GetDeviceObject(),
                        deviceClassName);

        IOCFPlugInInterfaceHandle plugInInterface;
        HRESULT plugInResult;
        SInt32 score;

        // Create the plugin so we can create the device interface.
        result = IOCreatePlugInInterfaceForService (
                controllerDevice ->GetDeviceObject(),
                kIOHIDDeviceUserClientTypeID, kIOCFPlugInInterfaceID,
                &plugInInterface, &score);

        // Create the device interface
        plugInResult = (*plugInInterface)->QueryInterface(
                (IOCFPlugInInterface*)plugInInterface,
                CFUUIDGetUUIDBytes(kIOHIDDeviceInterfaceID),
                (LPVOID*) &controllerDeviceInterface);

        (*plugInInterface)->Release(plugInInterface);
}
```

Calling the HID Manager data structures' member functions results in some funky-looking code. The HID Manager functions use handles to the HID Manager data structures, but the structures' member functions require pointers or the data structure itself. That's why the plug-in interface's Release() function look like this:

```
(*plugInInterface)->Release(plugInInterface);
```

The term (*plugInInterface) treats the plugInInterface variable as a pointer so that we can call the member functions for the plug-in. Alternatively, I could have treated the plugInInterface variable as a structure of type IOCFPlugInInterface by calling the plug-in interface's Release() function as in the following statement:

```
(**plugInInterface).Release(plugInInterface);
```

Opening a Connection to the Input Device

To open a connection so that you can read data from a HID device, you call the device interface's open() member function. The device interface's open() member function takes two parameters. The first parameter is the device interface, and the second parameter contains flags. The HID Manager currently does not use the second parameter, so you can pass the value 0. The following function opens a connection so that the HID Manager can read data from the game controller:

```
void InputController::OpenDevice(void)
{
      IOReturn result;

      if (controllerDeviceInterface == nil)
            return;

      result = (*controllerDeviceInterface)->open(controllerDeviceInterface, 0);
}
```

Reading Button Presses

There are two ways you can read button presses: with or without queues (just like the famous U2 song). If you read button presses without queues, you can read only the most recent button press. If you want to read all button presses that have occurred since the last check, you should create a queue to read the presses.

Reading without Queues

If all you are interested in is the most recent button press, call the device interface's getElementValue() member function, whose parameters are listed in Table 8-7. This function fills a HID event structure called IOHIDEventStruct. Table 8-8 lists the fields of the HID event structure. Read the value field of this structure to determine whether or not there was a button press.

Table 8-7 `getElementValue()` Parameters

Parameter	Description
self	The device interface whose elements you read with the call to `getElementValue()`.
elementCookie	The specific input device element that `getElementValue()` checks for events.
valueEvent	The event structure that `getElementValue()` fills.

Table 8-8 `IOHIDEventStruct` Fields

Field	Description
type	The type of element that generated the event.
elementCookie	The element that generated the event. For button presses, it would be the button on the game controller that the player pressed.
value	The value of the event. Button presses have a value of 1.
timestamp	A timestamp detailing when the event occurred.
longValueSize	The size of the data in the `longValue` field. You should not have to worry about this field.
longValue	Additional data about the event. You should not have to worry about this field.

The following function demonstrates how you would read button presses if you chose not to create a queue:

```
InputControllerAction InputController::DetermineAction(void)
{
    HRESULT error;
    IOHIDEventStruct event;

    if (controllerDeviceInterface == nil)
        return kNoButtonsPressed;
```

```
// Check for attack
error = (*controllerDeviceInterface)->
        getElementValue(controllerDeviceInterface, gameNeeds[kAttackNeed],
        &theEvent);



if (event.value == kButtonDown)
        return kAttack;

// Check for change weapon
error = (*controllerDeviceInterface)->
        getElementValue(controllerDeviceInterface,
        gameNeeds[kChangeWeaponNeed], &event);



if (event.value == kButtonDown)
        return kChangeWeapon;

// Check for pause game

error = (*controllerDeviceInterface)->
        getElementValue(controllerDeviceInterface,
        gameNeeds[kPauseGameNeed], &event);

if (event.value == kButtonDown)
        return kPauseGame;
// Your game would check for additional button presses here

// At this point, no buttons were pressed
return kNoButtonsPressed;
}
```

Creating Queues

Alternatively, you can read button presses by creating a queue. The queue stores a
list of events—in this case, button presses. To create a queue, declare a variable that
is a handle to data type IOHIDQueueInterface, then call the device interface's
allocQueue() member function to allocate memory for the queue.

After allocating the queue, call the queue's `create()` member function to create the queue. The `create()` member function takes three parameters, which are listed in Table 8-9.

Table 8-9 `create()` Parameters

Parameter	Description
self	The queue we are creating.
flags	Pass the value 0. The HID Manager does not currently use the `flags` parameter.
depth	The size of the queue that `create()` makes. I cannot imagine you needing to hold more than 10 events in the queue, but if you find you need more space, you can increase the value of the depth parameter.

Now that you have created a queue, you must add elements to the queue (or there's no point in having the queue). The elements are the buttons or other controls you want to store in the queue. To add an element to the queue, call the queue's `addElement()` member function. Table 8-10 lists the parameters the `addElement()` member function takes.

Table 8-10 `addElement()` Parameters

Parameter	Description
self	The queue to which we want to add the element.
elementCookie	The element to add to the queue.
flags	Pass the value 0. The HID Manager does not currently use the `flags` parameter.

The following function creates a queue and adds all our game's button needs to the queue:

```
void InputController::CreateEventList(void)
{
        if (controllerDeviceInterface == nil)
                return;

        // Allocate space for the event list.
        eventList = (*controllerDeviceInterface)->
                allocQueue(controllerDeviceInterface);

         if (eventList == nil)
                return;

        IOReturn result;

        // Create the event list.
        result = (*eventList)->create(eventList, 0, kEventListSize);

        // Keep the event list from reading events until the game starts.
        Pause();
        // Add button elements to the queue
        result = (*eventList)->addElement(eventList,
                        gameNeeds[kAttackNeed], 0);
        if (result != kIOReturnSuccess)
                return;

        result = (*eventList)->addElement(eventList,
                        gameNeeds[kChangeWeaponNeed], 0);


}
```

To determine whether or not an element is in the queue, call the queue's hasElement() member function. The hasElement() function takes two parameters. The first parameter contains the queue, and the second parameter contains the element to search for.

If the player changes the input device element to perform an action in the game—say that he decides to use button 4 on his gamepad to fire the weapon instead of button 1—you must remove the old element from the queue and replace it with the new element. To remove an element from the queue, call the queue's removeElement() member function. The removeElement() function takes two parameters. The first parameter is the queue, and the second parameter contains the element to remove from the queue. The following code snippet removes the element the player used to attack from the eventList queue:

```
IOReturn result;
result = (*eventList)->removeElement(eventList, gameNeeds[kAttackNeed]);
```

Reading from the Queue

At this stage we have the elements we want in the queue, but the queue has no events in it yet. Now we must tell the queue to start receiving events or else the queue will never be able to read any button presses. To begin reading button presses or other events from the queue, call the queue's start() member function. This function tells the HID Manager to begin delivering events into the queue, as you can see in the following code:

```
IOReturn result;
result = (*eventList)->start(eventList);
```

Once you tell the HID Manager to start sending events to the queue, any button presses whose elements are part of the queue move into the queue. The events enter the queue automatically; there's no need for you to explicitly check the input device for events; just check the queue. When an event moves into the queue, it starts at the end of the queue. If the queue is full, the new event bumps all the other events up one spot in the queue. The event at the head of the queue (the oldest event in the queue) disappears from the queue, its contents lost forever.

To read events from the queue, call the queue's getNextEvent() member function. Table 8-11 lists the four parameters used by the getNextEvent() function. The getNextEvent() function reads the event at the head of the queue. After calling getNextEvent(), you should check the event's elementCookie field to see whether it matches one of the game's control needs. If it does match, check the event's value field to see whether it was a button press.

Table 8-11 getNextEvent() Parameters

Parameter	Description
self	The queue we check for events.
event	The event that getNextEvent() finds. You supply a pointer to a HID event structure, and getNextEvent() fills it with the event data.
maxTime	The latest moment in time that getNextEvent() will check for events. In most cases, you should pass the value 0. If you use a non-zero value for maxTime, getNextEvent() limits the reading to events that occurred before maxTime.
timeoutMS	The timeout value, specified in milliseconds. If you specify a timeout value of 0, getNextEvent() will return the empty queue result code if there are no events in the queue. If you specify a value other than 0, the application will stop for the amount of time in the timeoutMS field or until an event arrives in the queue. You should use 0 as the timeout value for an action game.

The following function uses a queue to read button presses:

```
InputControllerAction InputController::DetermineAction(void)
{
        HRESULT error;

        // Check for button presses.
        IOHIDEventStruct theEvent;

        if (eventList == nil)
                return kNoButtonsPressed;

        // Read next event in the list
        error = (*eventList)->getNextEvent(eventList, &theEvent,
                        kZeroTime, 0);

        // Does the event list have no events in it?
        if (error == kIOReturnUnderrun)
                return kNoButtonsPressed;
```

```
        // Check each of the needs in the queue.
        if (theEvent.elementCookie == gameNeeds[kAttackNeed]) {
                if (theEvent.value == kButtonDown) {
                        return kAttack;
                }
        }
        else if (theEvent.elementCookie == gameNeeds[kChangeWeaponNeed]) {
                if (theEvent.value == kButtonDown) {
                        return kChangeWeapon;
                }
        }
        // Insert additional needs here

        // At this point, nothing occurred
        return kNoButtonsPressed;


}
```

Reading Digital Movement

Reading digital movement with the HID Manager requires more work than the
same task does with InputSprocket. You must check for presses in all four directions on the direction pad (up, down, left, and right) by calling the device interface's getElementValue() member function. Then you can determine the direction
the player moved from the four getElementValue() calls. For example, if the player
pressed the direction pad diagonally northeast, the calls to getElementValue() would
record that the button was down for the up and the right elements of the direction
pad. The following function reads digital movement from a direction pad:

```
InputControllerAction InputController::DetermineDigitalMovement(void)
{
        HRESULT result;
        IOHIDEventStruct event;

        Boolean movedUp;
        Boolean movedDown;
        Boolean movedLeft;
        Boolean movedRight;

        if (controllerDeviceInterface == nil)
```

```
            return kNoMovement;

    // Check for movement in the four directions
    // Up
    result = (*controllerDeviceInterface)->
            getElementValue(controllerDeviceInterface,
            gameNeeds[kDirectionPadUpNeed], &event);
    if (event.value == kButtonDown)
            movedUp = true;
    else
            movedUp = false;


    // Down
result = (*controllerDeviceInterface)->
            getElementValue(controllerDeviceInterface,
            gameNeeds[kDirectionPadDownNeed], &event);
    if (event.value == kButtonDown)
            movedDown = true;
    else
            movedDown = false;


    // Left
    result = (*controllerDeviceInterface)->
            getElementValue(controllerDeviceInterface,
            gameNeeds[kDirectionPadLeftNeed], &event);
    if (event.value == kButtonDown)
            movedLeft = true;
    else
            movedLeft = false;


    // Right
    result = (*controllerDeviceInterface)->
            getElementValue(controllerDeviceInterface,
            gameNeeds[kDirectionPadRightNeed], &event);
    if (event.value == kButtonDown)
            movedRight = true;
    else
            movedRight = false;


    // Determine direction of movement
    if ((movedUp) && (movedLeft))
```

```
                return kMoveUpAndLeft;
        else if ((movedUp) && (movedRight))
                return kMoveUpAndRight;
        else if ((movedDown) && (movedLeft))
                return kMoveDownAndLeft;
        else if ((movedDown) && (movedRight))
                return kMoveDownAndRight;

        // At this point, we know the movement is not diagonal
        else if (movedUp)
                return kMoveUp;
        else if (movedDown)
                return kMoveDown;
        else if (movedLeft)
                return kMoveLeft;
        else if (movedRight)
                return kMoveRight;
        else
                return kNoMovement;
}
```

Looking at the DetermineDigitalMovement() function, you can see that I check for
diagonal movement before non-diagonal movement. Checking for diagonal movement first simplifies the logic of the code. If I checked for upward movement first
with the following code:

```
if (movedUp)
        return kMoveUp;
```

I would miss upward diagonal movement. For example, if the player moved up and
left, the variable movedUp would be true, and DetermineDigitalMovement() would
return the value kMoveUp, not kMoveUpAndLeft. To fix the code, I would have to check
that the variables movedLeft and movedRight were both false, as in the following code:

```
if ((movedUp) && (!movedLeft) && (!movedRight) )
        return kMoveUp;
```

Checking for movement in the other three non-diagonal directions would also have
three conditions to test. Testing for diagonal movement first makes the code easier
to follow.

Reading Analog Movement

Reading analog movement is identical to reading button presses without a queue. Call the device interface's getElement() member function and read the value field in the IOHIDEventStruct structure. You can use a queue to read analog movement, but you shouldn't have to employ queues for movement. When reading movement, all you care about is the most recent direction the player moved. If you had the analog movement in a queue, the player character may continue to move after the player stopped moving the character, which would be strange behavior. The following function reads analog movement:

```
InputControllerAction InputController::DetermineAnalogMovement(void)
{
        // Determine whether there was horizontal movement.
        UInt32 xAxisInput;
        UInt32 yAxisInput;
        HRESULT result;
        IOHIDEventStruct event;

        // Check for horizontal movement
        result = (*controllerDeviceInterface)->
                getElementValue(controllerDeviceInterface,
                gameNeeds[kXAxisNeed], &event);

        if (result != noErr)
                return kNoMovement;

        xAxisInput = event.value;
        xAxisValue = ConvertXAxisData(xAxisInput, kAxisMinimumValue,
                        kAxisMaximumValue);

        // Check for vertical movement
        result = (*controllerDeviceInterface)->
                getElementValue(controllerDeviceInterface,
                gameNeeds[kYAxisNeed], &event);

        if (result != noErr)
                return kNoMovement;

        yAxisInput = event.value;
        yAxisValue = ConvertYAxisData(yAxisInput, kAxisMinimumValue,
```

```
kAxisMaximumValue);    // Return the direction the player moved
        if ((yAxisValue < kAxisCenterValue) && (xAxisValue == kAxisCenterValue))
                return kMoveUp;
        else if ((yAxisValue < kAxisCenterValue) && (xAxisValue < kAxisCenterValue))
                return kMoveUpAndLeft;
        else if ((yAxisValue < kAxisCenterValue) && (xAxisValue > kAxisCenterValue))
                return kMoveUpAndRight;
        else if ((yAxisValue > kAxisCenterValue) && (xAxisValue < kAxisCenterValue))
                return kMoveDownAndLeft;
        else if ((yAxisValue > kAxisCenterValue) && (xAxisValue > kAxisCenterValue))
                return kMoveDownAndRight;
        else if ((yAxisValue > kAxisCenterValue) && (xAxisValue == kAxisCenterValue))
                return kMoveDown;
        else if ((yAxisValue == kAxisCenterValue) && (xAxisValue < kAxisCenterValue))
                return kMoveLeft;
        else if ((yAxisValue == kAxisCenterValue) && (xAxisValue > kAxisCenterValue))
                return kMoveRight;
        else
                return kNoMovement;

}
```

Configuring Controllers

Configuring input devices is where the HID Manager differs most from
InputSprocket. While InputSprocket supplies a configuration dialog box that
requires only a call to ISpConfigure(), we must create a dialog box and write code
to handle the dialog box to configure controllers with the HID Manager. The game
developers Apple talked to hated the fact that they had to use Apple's dialog box to
configure InputSprocket games. These developers preferred to create their own
custom configuration dialog boxes, and Apple listened to them, forcing every
developer to write configuration code with the HID Manager.

The Configuration Dialog Box

I'm going to keep the configuration dialog box simple, so I will use standard Mac
OS controls and make the dialog box look like a typical Mac OS X dialog box
rather than create a custom dialog box that matches the look and feel of the game.
By using the same type of dialog box that non-game applications use, we can use
the Dialog Manager instead of writing custom dialog handling code. Figure 8-1
shows the configuration dialog box we will create in this section.

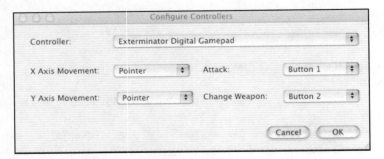

Figure 8-1

The dialog box that allows the player to configure the game's controls.

Pop-up menus dominate the configuration dialog box. The player uses one pop-up menu to select the controller and other pop-up menus to choose the control for each control need (movement, attack, and change weapon) in the game. The items inside the menu depend on the controllers connected to the computer. Every joystick and gamepad (and eventually the mouse and keyboard) plugged into the computer will appear in the Controller menu. Every control on the selected device appears in the other, related pop-up menus. My Gravis Exterminator gamepad reports 11 buttons, a joystick, a hat switch, and a dial; what appears in your menus depends on your game controller.

The ConfigurationDialog Class

We need a new class to handle the dialog box we'll use to configure the game controllers. Here are the data elements of the new ConfigurationDialog class:

```
class ConfigurationDialog: public MovableModalDialog
{
        protected:
                InputControllerPtr currentController;
}
class MovableModalDialog
{
        protected:
                DialogRef dialog;
}
```

The ConfigurationDialog class inherits from a MovableModalDialog class I also developed. The MovableModalDialog class handles the generic dialog box functions while the ConfigurationDialog class handles the functions specific to the configure controls dialog box. The currentController data member stores the controller the player is configuring with the dialog box. The currentController data member lets us move information about the controller into the dialog box, and lets us move information from the dialog box (the player's selections) to the controller.

Creating the Dialog Box

I created the dialog box and its elements in Resorcerer. If you don't have Resorcerer, you can use either ResEdit or Interface Builder to build the dialog box. To load the dialog box into memory, I call the Dialog Manager function `GetNewDialog()`, which loads a dialog box resource from disk into memory. `GetNewDialog()` also loads the dialog item list, which is the list of controls for the dialog box (the text and the pop-up menus in this case), and draws them in the dialog. If you use Interface Builder to create your dialog box, call `CreateWindowFromNib()` to move the dialog box into RAM. The following function loads a dialog box into memory:

```
void MovableModalDialog::Create(short resourceID)
{
        //WindowPtr(-1) will bring the dialog box to the front
        dialog = GetNewDialog(resourceID, nil, WindowPtr(-1));
}
```

Filling the Controller Menu

Creating the dialog box displays the pop-up menus for our dialog box, but the menus are initially empty because we do not know what controllers the player has until he runs the game. To fill the Controller menu, we must begin by compiling a list of the controllers connected to the player's computer. Even if you have done this already in your code when you initialized the game, it's a good idea to do it again. USB game controllers are hot-swappable, meaning that the player can connect or disconnect them at any time. The player may have plugged in his gamepad right before choosing to configure it. If you use the `controllerList` variable you created earlier, the recently connected gamepad will not appear in the Controller list.

Before appending controllers to the Controller menu, you should call the Dialog Manager function `GetDialogItem()` to retrieve the menu, then call the Menu Manager function `DeleteMenuItems()` to delete any existing menu items. Deleting any existing menu entries ensures that the Controller menu won't show duplicate menu items for an input device.

Now we can fill the menu. To do this, we first call the function `CreateControllerList()` that we wrote earlier in the chapter. At this point we have a linked list of InputDevice objects. We take the first device in the list and get its product name data member, which contains the device name we want to add to the menu. After getting the input device's name, we call `GetDialogItem()` to retrieve the Controller menu. Then we call `AppendMenuItemText()` to add the input device's name to the menu. We repeat this cycle for all the HID devices connected to the computer. The following function fills the Controller menu:

```
void ConfigurationDialog::FillChooseControllerMenu(
                    InputControllerPtr controller)
{
    controller->CreateControllerList();

    LinkedList deviceList = controller->GetControllerList();



    MenuRef chooseControllerMenu;
    ControlRef chooseControllerMenuControl;
    Rect chooseControllerMenuControlRect;
    DialogItemTypeitemType;

     // Clear the menu of any items it has
    GetDialogItem(dialog, kChooseControllerMenu, &itemType,
                    (Handle *)&chooseControllerMenuControl,
                    &chooseControllerMenuControlRect);

    // The value (ctrlItem + resCtrl) is the item type of
    // a popup menu.
    if ((itemType == (ctrlItem + resCtrl)) &&
            (chooseControllerMenu != nil)) {
            chooseControllerMenu =
                    GetControlPopupMenuHandle(chooseControllerMenuControl);
            DeleteMenuItems(chooseControllerMenu, kFirstItem,
                    CountMenuItems(chooseControllerMenu));


    }

    // Fill the menu with all the controllers connected
    // to the player's machine.
    InputDevicePtr currentDevice;
```

```
        Iterator deviceListIterator(&deviceList);
        OSStatus result;
        ConstStr255Param deviceString;

        currentDevice = (InputDevicePtr)deviceListIterator.Next();

        while (currentDevice != nil) {
                deviceString = currentDevice->productName;

                // Add the name to the configuration menu
                GetDialogItem(dialog, kChooseControllerMenu, &itemType,
                        (Handle *)&chooseControllerMenuControl,
                        &chooseControllerMenuControlRect);
                if ((itemType == (ctrlItem + resCtrl)) &&
                        (chooseControllerMenuControl != nil)) {
                        chooseControllerMenu =
                                GetControlPopupMenuHandle(chooseControllerMenuControl);
                        result = AppendMenuItemText(chooseControllerMenu,
deviceString);

            }

                // Get next device in list
                currentDevice = (InputDevicePtr)deviceListIterator.Next();
        }

        SetControlMaximum(chooseControllerMenuControl, deviceList.GetNumberOfItems());

        // Set the selected menu item
        InputDevicePtr chosenDevice = controller->GetControllerDevice();
        Str255 chosenDeviceName;
        chosenDeviceName = chosenDevice->productName;
        Str255 menuText;
        short menuItemCount = CountMenuItems(chooseControllerMenu);
        short stringsMatchResult;

        // Go through each item in the menu.  If its device
        // name matches the chosen device name, set the menu
        // to that item.
        for (short index = 1; index <= menuItemCount; index++) {
                GetMenuItemText(chooseControllerMenu, index, menuText);
```

```
            // PLstrcmp() is a Toolbox function that compares two Pascal strings
            stringsMatchResult = PLstrcmp(menuText, chosenDeviceName);
            if (stringsMatchResult == kStringsMatch)
                    SetControlValue(chooseControllerMenuControl, index);
    }


    ShowControl(chooseControllerMenuControl);


}
```

Compiling the Element List

After the player has selected the controller device, we must compile a list of the elements for that input device so that he can assign the elements to different actions in the game. Assembling the list requires the following steps:

1. Get the first element in the device's list of elements.
2. Retrieve the element's data.
3. Add the element to the element list.
4. Retrieve the next element in the list.
5. Repeat steps 2 through 4 until you reach the end of the element list.

To find the first element for an input device, call IORegistryCreateCFProperties() to get the device's properties. Table 8-12 lists the parameters that IORegistryCreateCFProperties() takes. Call CFDictionaryGetValue(), passing the value CFSTR(kIOHIDElementKey) in the second parameter to get the first element.

Table 8-12   IORegistryEntryCreateCFProperties() Parameters

Parameter	Description
entry	The I/O Registry entry whose properties we want to retrieve. In the HID Manager, the entry parameter contains an input device.
properties	IORegistryEntryCreateCFProperties() returns the properties of the input device in the properties parameter.
allocator	Currently, the only valid value for the allocator parameter is kCFAllocatorDefault.
options	There currently are no options so use the value kNilOptions for this parameter.

The first element in the input device's collection of elements is a Core Foundation array containing all the elements for the input device. This array may contain other arrays. The stick of a joystick contains an array with separate elements for the x-axis and y-axis of the stick. Core Foundation has a nice feature where you can tell Core Foundation to call a function that you supply for each element in a Core Foundation array by calling the function CFArrayApplyFunction(). What we must do is write a function to add one element to the list, then supply that function as an argument to CFArrayApplyFunction(). The computer will call the function we write once for each element, building the list for us.

What we must do in our function to add an element to the element list is look at the type of element this particular element is (Table 8-4 lists the possible element types). If the element type is a collection, that means it contains an array of additional elements. In this case, we process the additional elements by calling CFArrayApplyFunction() for the collection. Otherwise, we add the element to the element list.

Getting the element's data into a form we can use is a pain because it involves converting every piece of data about the element from Core Foundation data types to the data types in our InputDeviceElement structure: long, Str255, IOHIDElementType, IOHIDElementCookie, and Boolean. Call CFDictionaryGetValue() to find the value you want out of the element. Then call a Core Foundation conversion function such as CFNumberGetValue() to convert the data into a form we can use.

The following code creates a list of elements for an input device (There's a lot of code here):

```
void InputController::CreateElementList(io_object_t device)
{
        // Gets a list of elements (controls)
        // for an input device.

        // Dispose of any previously created element list
        DisposeElementList();

        kern_return_t result;
        CFMutableDictionaryRef deviceProperties;

        result = IORegistryEntryCreateCFProperties(device, &deviceProperties,
                kCFAllocatorDefault, kNilOptions);

        if (result != KERN_SUCCESS)
```

```
              return;

        // Get first element
        CFTypeRef firstElement = CFDictionaryGetValue(deviceProperties,
              CFSTR(kIOHIDElementKey));

        CFTypeID elementType = CFGetTypeID(firstElement);
        if (elementType == CFArrayGetTypeID()) {
              FillElementList(firstElement);
        }

void InputController::FillElementList(CFTypeRef currentElement)
{
        // Lists of HID elements are stored in nested arrays.
        // Mac OS X's Core Foundation arrays let you apply a function
        // to each element of an array by calling CFApplyFunction().
        // This is what I do to fill the element list.

        CFTypeID currentElementType = CFGetTypeID(currentElement);
        CFTypeID arrayType = CFArrayGetTypeID();

        if (currentElementType == arrayType) {
                              CFIndex elementCount =
              CFArrayGetCount((CFArrayRef)currentElement);
              CFRange elementRange = {0, elementCount};

              // Call the AddElementToList() function
              // for each element of the input device.
              CFArrayApplyFunction((CFArrayRef)currentElement, elementRange,
                    InputController::AddElementToList, (void *)this);
        }
}

void InputController::AddElementToList(const void* value, void* parameter)
{
        // The value parameter contains the Core Foundation element data.
        // The parameter parameter contains our InputController object.

        CFTypeRef elementData = (CFTypeRef) value;
        InputControllerPtr currentController = (InputControllerPtr) parameter;
        LinkedList theElementList = currentController->GetElementList();
```

```
        // Store the element's data.
        InputDeviceElementPtr elementToAdd = new InputDeviceElement;
        elementToAdd->StoreElementData(elementData);

        // If the element is a collection of other elements, call
        // FillElementList() to fill the elements in the collection.
        // Otherwise, add the element to the list.
        if (elementToAdd->GetType() == kIOHIDElementTypeCollection) {
                CFTypeRef collectionElement =
                        CFDictionaryGetValue((CFDictionaryRef)elementData,
                                CFSTR(kIOHIDElementKey));
                currentController->FillElementList(collectionElement);
        }
        else {
                theElementList.AddItem(elementToAdd);
                currentController->SetElementList(theElementList);
        }

}
```

The StoreElementData() function hides the implementation details of getting the data into our InputDeviceElement class. You can see from the following source code listing that this function calls a bunch of other functions, each of which reads a data member into an object of type InputDeviceElement.

```
void InputDeviceElement::StoreElementData(CFTypeRef theElement)
{
        // Getting the information about an element
        // out of the HID Manager is a royal pain in the butt.
        // This function calls a ton of small functions to
        // fill the element data structure in a relatively
        // simple matter.

        StoreCookieData(theElement);
        StoreTypeData(theElement);
        StoreUsagePageData(theElement);
        StoreUsageData(theElement);
        StoreRawMinData(theElement);
```

```
            StoreRawMaxData(theElement);
            StoreScaledMinData(theElement);
            StoreScaledMaxData(theElement);
            StoreSizeData(theElement);
            StoreIsRelativeData(theElement);
            StoreIsWrappingData(theElement);
            StoreIsNonLinearData(theElement);
            StoreHasPreferredStateData(theElement);
            StoreHasNullStateData(theElement);
            StoreUnitsData(theElement);
            StoreUnitExponentData(theElement);
            StoreElementNameData(theElement);
}
```

I'm not going to list all the Store*Xxxxx*Data() functions here because there are too many of them. However, I will show the StoreCookieData() function as an example of storing a numerical value, the StoreElementNameData() function as an example of storing a string value, and the StoreIsRelativeData() function as an example of storing a Boolean value. The other functions are similar to these three functions:

```
void InputDeviceElement::StoreCookieData(CFTypeRef theElement)
{
        CFTypeRef elementProperty;
        elementProperty = CFDictionaryGetValue(theElement,
                    CFSTR(kIOHIDElementCookieKey));

        if (elementProperty == nil)
              return;

        long cookieValue;
        CFNumberGetValue((CFNumberRef)elementProperty, kCFNumberLongType,
              &cookieValue);

        SetCookie((IOHIDElementCookie)cookieValue);
}


void InputDeviceElement::StoreElementNameData(CFTypeRef theElement)
{
        CFTypeRef elementProperty;
        elementProperty = CFDictionaryGetValue(theElement,
                    CFSTR(kIOHIDElementElementNameKey));
```

```
        if (elementProperty == nil)
                StoreElementNameFromResource();
                return;


        long elementNameValue;
        // Convert the name into a Str255 value
        CFStringEncoding systemEncoding = CFStringGetSystemEncoding();
        CFIndex stringLength = 256;
        Boolean conversionSuccess =
                CFStringGetPascalString((CFStringRef)elementProperty,
                (StringPtr)&elementNameValue, stringLength, systemEncoding);
        if (!conversionSuccess)
                return;


        elementName = elementNameValue;

}
void InputDeviceElement::StoreIsRelativeData(CFTypeRef theElement)
{
        CFTypeRef elementProperty;
        elementProperty = CFDictionaryGetValue(theElement,
                    CFSTR(kIOHIDElementIsRelativeKey));

        if (elementProperty == nil)
                return;

        Boolean isRelativeValue;
        isRelativeValue = CFBooleanGetValue((CFBooleanRef)elementProperty);

        SetRelative(isRelativeValue);
}
```

Filling the Control Menus

After building the list of elements, we can fill the remaining menus in the configuration dialog box with the element list. The following code fills the control menus:

```
void ConfigurationDialog::FillControlMenus(InputControllerPtr controller)
{
        // Get element list so we can fill the control menus
```

```
        InputDevicePtr selectedDevice = controller->GetControllerDevice();
        controller->CreateElementList(selectedDevice->GetDeviceObject());

        FillXAxisMenu(controller);
        FillYAxisMenu(controller);
        FillAttackMenu(controller);
        FillChangeWeaponMenu(controller);
}
```

Filling the individual control pop-up menus works similarly to filling the Controller menu earlier in this chapter. We take the list of elements and add each element to the menu by calling the Menu Manager function AppendMenuItemText(). The following function fills the X-Axis Movement menu with all of the selected input device's elements:

```
void ConfigurationDialog::FillXAxisMenu(LinkedList elementList)
{
        MenuRef xAxisMenu;
        ControlRef xAxisMenuControl;
        Rect xAxisMenuControlRect;
        DialogItemType itemType;

        // Clear the menu of any items it has
        GetDialogItem(dialog, kXAxisMenu, &itemType,
                (Handle *)&xAxisMenuControl, &xAxisMenuControlRect);
        // The value (ctrlItem + resCtrl) is the item type of
        // a popup menu.
        if ((itemType == (ctrlItem + resCtrl)) && (xAxisMenuControl != nil)) {
                xAxisMenu = GetControlPopupMenuHandle(xAxisMenuControl);
                DeleteMenuItems(xAxisMenu, kFirstItem, CountMenuItems(xAxisMenu));
        }



        // Fill the menu with the elements of the selected input device.
        LinkedList elementList = controller->GetElementList();

        Iterator elementListIterator(&elementList);
        InputDeviceElementPtr currentInputElement;
        int elementsToFill = elementList.GetNumberOfItems();
```

```
        OSStatus result;
        ConstStr255Param currentElementName;
        short menuItemToSelect;

        while(elementsToFill > 0) {
                // Get element name
                currentInputElement =
(InputDeviceElementPtr)elementListIterator.Next();
                        currentElementName = currentInputElement->elementName;

                // If you wanted to limit the elements that appear in the menu,
                // you would do so here.

                // Add the element name to the menu
                GetDialogItem(dialog, kXAxisMenu, &itemType,
                        (Handle *)&xAxisMenuControl, &xAxisMenuControlRect);
                if ((itemType == (ctrlItem + resCtrl)) && (xAxisMenuControl != nil))
{

                        xAxisMenu = GetControlPopupMenuHandle(xAxisMenuControl);
                        result = InsertMenuItemText(xAxisMenu, currentElementName,
                                kInsertAtStartOfMenu);

                        // This code assumes we insert the menu items
                        // at the start of the menu.
                        if (currentInputElement->GetCookie() ==
                                controller->gameNeeds[kXAxisNeed]) {
                                menuItemToSelect = elementsToFill;
                        }
                }

        elementsToFill--;
        }

        SetControlMaximum(xAxisMenuControl, elementList.GetNumberOfItems());
        SetControlValue(xAxisMenuControl, menuItemToSelect);
        ShowControl(xAxisMenuControl);

}
```

The FillXAxisMenuItem() function fills the pop-up menu with all of the input
device's elements. There are some situations where you may want to limit the ele-

ments that appear in the pop-up menu. For example, if you have a control need
that would best be handled by a button element (such as firing a weapon or jumping), you might want to limit the menu to display only button elements so that the
player doesn't accidentally use the joystick for jumping instead of a joystick button.
To limit the elements that appear in the pop-up menu, check each element's element type before adding the element to the menu. The following version of the
FillAttackMenu() function adds only button elements to the Attack menu:

```
void ConfigurationDialog::FillAttackMenu(InputControllerPtr controller)
{
        MenuRef attackMenu;
        ControlRef attackMenuControl;
        Rect attackMenuControlRect;
        DialogItemType itemType;

        // Clear the menu of any items it has
        GetDialogItem(dialog, kAttackMenu, &itemType,
        (Handle *)&attackMenuControl, &attackMenuControlRect);
        // The value (ctrlItem + resCtrl) is the item type of
        // a popup menu.
        if ((itemType == (ctrlItem + resCtrl)) && (attackMenuControl != nil)) {
                attackMenu = GetControlPopupMenuHandle(attackMenuControl);
                DeleteMenuItems(attackMenu, kFirstItem, CountMenuItems(attackMenu));
    }

        // Fill the menu with the selected device's elements.
        LinkedList elementList = controller->GetElementList();

        Iterator elementListIterator(&elementList);
        InputDeviceElementPtr currentInputElement;
        int elementsToFill = elementList.GetNumberOfItems();

        OSStatus result;
        ConstStr255Param currentElementName;
        short menuItemToSelect;
        IOHIDElementType currentElementType;

        while(elementsToFill > 0) {
                // Get element name
                currentInputElement =
(InputDeviceElementPtr)elementListIterator.Next();
```

```
currentElementName = currentInputElement->elementName;
// See whether the current element is a button element.
// If so, add it to the menu.
currentElementType = currentElement->GetType();
if (currentElementType == kIOHIDElementTypeInput_Button) {
        // Add the element name to the menu
        GetDialogItem(dialog, kAttackMenu, &itemType,
                (Handle *)&attackMenuControl, &attackMenuControlRect);

        if ((itemType == (ctrlItem + resCtrl)) && (attackMenu != nil))
{
                attackMenu =
                        GetControlPopupMenuHandle(attackMenuControl);
                result = InsertMenuItemText(attackMenu,
                        currentElementName, kInsertAtStartOfMenu);

                // This code assumes we insert the menu items
                // at the start of the menu.
                if (currentInputElement->GetCookie() ==
                        controller->gameNeeds[kAttackNeed]) {
                        menuItemToSelect = elementsToFill;
                 }

        }
}

elementsToFill--;
}

SetControlMaximum(attackMenuControl, elementList.GetNumberOfItems());
SetControlValue(attackMenuControl, menuItemToSelect);
ShowControl(attackMenuControl);

}
```

Our menu filling code depends on the game controller manufacturer supplying a meaningful name for each element in the low-level driver for the game controller. Unfortunately, this is a risky dependency. Every game controller I tested had no element name, which means that the pop-up menus in the configuration dialog would contain blank strings. My solution to the problem was to compose an array of strings that corresponded to the recommended usage of the element. In the code, I looked at the element's usage page and usage information, and used that information to display the proper string in the menus, as you can see in the following function:

```
void InputDeviceElement::StoreElementNameFromResource(void)
{
        // If the game controller's drivers do not include element
        // names, we must generate an element name from the
        // element's usage page and usage.  I stored strings for
        // the element names in an STR# resource.  This function
        // reads the element's usage page and usage and sets the
        // element name accordingly.

        // This function assumes that the usage page and usage for
        // the element have already been set.
        short resourceID;

        if (GetUsagePage() == kGenericDesktopPage)
                resourceID = kGenericDesktopStringListID;
        else if (GetUsagePage() == kButtonPage)
                resourceID = kButtonStringListID;
        else
                return;

        GetIndString(elementName, resourceID, GetUsage());
}
```

My approach works pretty well for all elements except buttons. With buttons all my solution can do is assign button numbers so the button elements in the menus have names like Button 1 and Button 2, which makes configuration difficult for the player. If the player has a joystick with eight buttons, he has no way of easily knowing which button is Button 1, which is Button 2, and so on. He must experiment with the game to learn the way the buttons are numbered.

There is no easy solution to the problem of meaningful button names if the manufacturer does not supply a meaningful name in the driver. You would have to compile a database of every game controller on the market and a list of every button for each controller along with a meaningful name for each button. At best, this would be only a temporary solution. When new game controllers came on the market, you would have to release a patch of your game to support the new controllers.

Handling Events

When an event occurs in the configuration dialog box, such as a mouse click or a
key press, we call the Dialog Manager function IsDialogEvent() to make sure that it
is an event for the dialog box. If IsDialogEvent() returns true, we call the Dialog
Manager function DialogSelect() to handle the event. DialogSelect() handles most
of the events that occur within a movable modal or a modeless dialog box. The following function handles the events that occur in our configuration dialog box:

```
void MovableModalDialog::DoDialogEvent(EventRecord* event)
{
        short itemHit;

        // The Dialog Manager DialogSelect() does most
        // of the work for us when handling dialog events.
        if (IsDialogEvent(event)) {
                if (DialogSelect(event, &dialog, &itemHit))
                        DoItemHit(itemHit);
        }
}
```

We must take care of three special cases. We treat the player pressing the Esc key as
if the player had clicked the Cancel button in the dialog box. An alternative
method of canceling the dialog box is when the player presses the
Command+period key combination. The player pressing the Return key is treated
as the equivalent of clicking the OK button in the dialog box. The following function handles these three special cases:

```
void ConfigurationDialog::HandleKeyDown(EventRecord* event)
{
        char keyPressed;

        keyPressed = (char)(event->message & charCodeMask);

        // Check for Command-period, which is another method of
        // canceling on the Mac.
        if (event->modifiers & cmdKey) {
                if (keyPressed == '.')
                        DoItemHit(cancel);
        }
        else {
                // check for return key
```

```
                if (keyPressed == kReturnKeyCharCode || keyPressed ==
kEnterKeyCharCode)
                        DoItemHit(ok);
                // check for Esc key
                else if (keyPressed == kEscapeKeyCharCode)
                        DoItemHit(cancel);
        }
}
```

The DoItemHit() function checks which item in the dialog box the player hit. Our
dialog box has seven items to check: the OK button, the Cancel button, and the
five pop-up menus.

```
void ConfigurationDialog::DoItemHit(short theItem)
{
        switch (theItem) {
                case ok:
                        HandleOKSelection();
                        break;

                case cancel:
                        HandleCancelSelection();
                        break;

                case kChooseControllerMenu:
                        HandleControllerMenuSelection();
                        break;

                case kXAxisMenu:
                        HandleXAxisMenuSelection();
                        break;

                case kYAxisMenu:
                        HandleYAxisMenuSelection();
                        break;

                case kAttackMenu:
                        HandleAttackMenuSelection();
                        break;

                case kChangeWeaponMenu:
                        HandleChangeWeaponMenuSelection();
```

```
                break;

        default:
                break;

    }
}
```

Handling Item Hits

When the player makes a selection in the dialog box, we must handle the selection appropriately. Our game is responsible for the following actions the player may take in the dialog box:

- Pressing the Cancel button.
- Pressing the OK button.
- Selecting an input device from the Controller menu.
- Selecting elements from the four control menus.

Cancel Button

The player clicking the Cancel button in the dialog box is the easiest item to handle. When the player chooses Cancel, the game ignores any selections the player might have made in the dialog box. The one problem area is that the player may have selected another controller, then cancelled the selection. In this case, we rebuilt the element list. What we must do is restore the input device the player was using before configuring the controls and rebuild the element list, as you can see here:

```
void ConfigurationDialog::HandleCancelSelection(void)
{
        // Restore the selected controller.  If the player chose
        // a different controller, then cancelled, the
        // controllerDevice data member of the InputController class
        // changes so we need to restore the selected device.
        InputDevicePtr theDevice = GetStoredDevice();
        currentController->SetControllerDevice(theDevice);

        // We must recreate the element list in case the player
        // chose a different controller.  If the player chose a new
        // input device before cancelling, the old element list got
```

```
        // erased so we could fill the control menus with the new
        // device's events.  Rebuilding the element list ensures
        // we have the current device's elements.
        currentController->CreateElementList(
                theDevice->GetDeviceObject());
        Close();
}
```

To close the dialog box, we call the Dialog Manager function `DisposeDialog()`, as you can see in the following code:

```
void MovableModalDialog::Close(void)
{
        if (dialog != nil) {
                DisposeDialog(dialog);
                dialog = nil;
        }
}
```

OK Button

When the player clicks the OK button, we must transfer the player's control choices from the menus in the dialog box to the game. We must set the `controllerDevice` and `gameNeeds` data members of the `InputController` class before closing the dialog box. The following code handles the player pressing the OK button in the configuration dialog box:

```
void ConfigurationDialog::HandleOKSelection(void)
{
        UpdateControllerDevice();
        SetControlNeeds();

        // Set up the newly selected controller so we can
        // read data from it
        currentController->CloseDevice();
        currentController->Setup();

        Close();
}
```

The Menu Manager tells us the item number of the item the player selected in the Controller menu. We must retrieve the name of the controller the player selected from this menu, and then find the input device in the controller list whose name matches the name of the player's selection. The Menu Manager function GetMenuItemText() performs the first step for us. The second step requires a lot more work, as you can see in the following code:

```
void ConfigurationDialog::UpdateControllerDevice(void)
{
        // Set the controller to play the game to the
        // device the player selected in the configuration dialog.

        MenuRef controllerMenu;
        ControlRef controllerMenuControl;
        Rect controllerMenuControlRect;
        DialogItemType itemType;
        int menuItemSelected;
        Str255 selectedDeviceName;

        // Find the name of the device the player selected
        GetDialogItem(dialog, kChooseControllerMenu, &itemType,
                (Handle *)&controllerMenuControl, &controllerMenuControlRect);
        // The value (ctrlItem + resCtrl) is the item type of
        // a popup menu.
        if ((itemType == (ctrlItem + resCtrl)) && (controllerMenuControl != nil)) {
                menuItemSelected = GetControlValue(controllerMenuControl);
                controllerMenu = GetControlPopupMenuHandle(controllerMenuControl);
                GetMenuItemText(controllerMenu, menuItemSelected, selectedDeviceName);
        }
        else {
                return;
        }

        LinkedList deviceList = currentController->GetControllerList();

        InputDevicePtr currentDevice;
        Iterator deviceListIterator(&deviceList);

        currentDevice = (InputDevicePtr)deviceListIterator.Next();
        short stringsMatchResult;

        // Go through the device list looking for the matching device
        // If we find it set the controller to use to that device.
        while (currentDevice != nil) {
```

```
        // PLstrcmp() is a Toolbox function that compares two Pascal strings
        stringsMatchResult = PLstrcmp(currentDevice->productName,
                selectedDeviceName);
        if (stringsMatchResult == kStringsMatch) {
                currentController->SetControllerDevice(currentDevice);
                return;
        }


    // Retrieve the next device if there is one.
    currentDevice = (InputDevicePtr)deviceListIterator.Next();
    }


}
```

The following function sets the control needs for our game:

```
void ConfigurationDialog::SetControlNeeds(void)
{
      SetXAxisControlNeed();
      SetYAxisControlNeed();
      SetAttackControlNeed();
      SetChangeWeaponControlNeed();
}
```

Obviously, all the work involved in setting the game's needs does not reside entirely within the SetControlNeeds() function. To set an individual need, we read the player's choice of input element from the particular menu. Next, we call the Menu Manager function GetMenuItemText() to retrieve the element name. Then we go through the list of elements for the input device and compare the element's name with the menu item's text. If they match, we copy the element's cookie field to the InputController class's gameNeeds[] array. The following routine sets up the attacking control need:

```
void ConfigurationDialog::SetAttackControlNeed(void)
{
      MenuRef attackMenu;
      ControlRef attackMenuControl;
      Rect attackMenuControlRect;
      DialogItemType itemType;
      int menuItemSelected;
      Str255 selectedElementName;

      // Find the name of the element the player selected
```

```
GetDialogItem(dialog, kAttackMenu, &itemType, (Handle *)&attackMenuControl,
        &attackMenuControlRect);
// The value (ctrlItem + resCtrl) is the item type of
// a popup menu.
if ((itemType == (ctrlItem + resCtrl)) && (attackMenuControl != nil)) {
        menuItemSelected = GetControlValue(attackMenuControl);
        attackMenu = GetControlPopupMenuHandle(attackMenuControl);
        GetMenuItemText(attackMenu, menuItemSelected, selectedElementName);
}
else {
        return;
}


LinkedList elementList = currentController->GetElementList();

InputDeviceElementPtr currentElement;
Iterator elementListIterator(&elementList);

currentElement = (InputDeviceElementPtr)elementListIterator.Next();
short stringsMatchResult;

// Go through the element list looking for the matching element
// If we find it set the controller object's gameNeeds array entry.
while (currentElement != nil) {
        // PLstrcmp() is a Toolbox function that compares two Pascal strings
        stringsMatchResult = PLstrcmp(currentElement->elementName,
                selectedElementName);
        if (stringsMatchResult == kStringsMatch) {
                currentController->gameNeeds[kAttackNeed] =
                        currentElement->GetCookie();
                return;
        }

                // Retrieve the next element if there is one.
        currentElement = (InputDeviceElementPtr)elementListIterator.Next();
}
}
```

Controller Menu

When the player selects a controller to use for the game, we must fill the remaining menus with the elements for the input device the player just selected. Fortunately, the FillControlMenus() function we wrote earlier in this chapter does this for us.

The tricky part is getting the input device from the player's menu selection. The Menu Manager tells us the menu item the player chose. We have to go from the menu item, which is an integer, to an input device with type io_object_t. Calling the function GetMenuItemText() gives us the name of the input device the user selected. Then we go through the list of controllers connected to the player's computer. We compare the name of each input device to the name of the player's chosen device. If they match, we call FillControlMenus(), and we're finished. The following code handles the player's selection of a controller:

```
void ConfigurationDialog::HandleControllerMenuSelection(void)
{
        // Fill the other menus with the selected
        // menu's elements
        MenuRef chooseControllerMenu;
        ControlRef chooseControllerMenuControl;
        Rect chooseControllerMenuControlRect;
        DialogItemType itemType;
        int menuItemSelected;
        Str255 selectedDeviceName;

        // Find the name of the input device the player chose.
        GetDialogItem(dialog, kChooseControllerMenu, &itemType,
                (Handle *)&chooseControllerMenuControl,
                &chooseControllerMenuControlRect);
        // The value (ctrlItem + resCtrl) is the item type of
        // a popup menu.
        if ((itemType == (ctrlItem + resCtrl)) &&
                (chooseControllerMenuControl != nil)) {
                menuItemSelected = GetControlValue(chooseControllerMenuControl);
                chooseControllerMenu =
                        GetControlPopupMenuHandle(chooseControllerMenuControl);
                GetMenuItemText(chooseControllerMenu, menuItemSelected,
                        selectedDeviceName);
        }
        else {
                return;
```

```
        }

        // Find the input device the player chose from
        // the controller list.
        LinkedList deviceList = currentController->GetControllerList();

        InputDevicePtr currentDevice;
        Iterator deviceListIterator(&deviceList);
        Str255 currentDeviceString;

        currentDevice = (InputDevicePtr)deviceListIterator.Next();
        short stringsMatchResult;

        while (currentDevice != nil) {
                // Get the name of the input device.
                currentDeviceString = currentDevice->productName;

                // PLStrcmp() is a Toolbox function that compares two Pascal strings
                stringsMatchResult = PLstrcmp(currentDeviceString,
                selectedDeviceName);
                if(stringsMatchResult == kStringsMatch) {
                        // This is the device we want
                        currentController->SetControllerDevice(currentDevice);
                        FillControlMenus(currentController);
                        return;
                }

                // Get next device in list
                currentDevice = (InputDevicePtr)deviceListIterator.Next();
        }

}
```

Control Menus

When the player selects any of the four control pop-up menus—X-Axis Movement, Y-Axis Movement, Attack, or Change Weapon—there's no mandatory work to perform; we could leave the functions blank. However, you probably want to disable the selected menu item in the other pop-up menus so that the player does not accidentally assign two control functions to the same element. To support menu item disabling, we must add the following data members to the ConfigurationDialog class:

```
int oldXAxisSelectedItem;
int oldYAxisSelectedItem;
int oldAttackSelectedItem;
int oldChangeWeaponItem;
```

These data members store the menu item the player had chosen before he made his selection. We need them to enable the old menu item when the player makes a new selection in one of the menus.

If each of the control menus has the same elements in it, enabling and disabling the menu items is simple. Call the Control Manager function GetControlValue() to find the newly selected item and *dis*able that item in the other menus. Use the new data members of the ConfigurationDialog class to *en*able the particular item in the other menus. If the four control menu's items do not match (as they might if you limited the items you added to the menus based on appropriateness—for example, only buttons for the Attack menu), there's a lot more work to do. You must compare the *text* of the menu items instead of the number of the menu item. The following function handles the player selecting an element from the Attack menu:

```
void ConfigurationDialog::HandleAttackMenuSelection(void)
{
        MenuRef attackMenu;
        ControlRef attackMenuControl;
        Rect attackMenuControlRect;
        DialogItemType itemType;
        int menuItemSelected;
        Str255 selectedDeviceName;

        // Find the item the player selected
        GetDialogItem(dialog, kAttackMenu, &itemType, (Handle *)&attackMenuControl,
                      &attackMenuControlRect);
        if ((itemType == (ctrlItem + resCtrl)) && (attackMenuControl != nil)) {
                menuItemSelected = GetControlValue(attackMenuControl);
                chooseControllerMenu = GetControlPopupMenuHandle(attackMenuControl);
                GetMenuItemText(attackMenu, menuItemSelected, selectedDeviceName);
         }
        else {
                return;
        }

        // Disable the newly selected item in the other menus
        DisableMenuItem(kXAxisMenu, menuItemSelected);
```

```
      DisableMenuItem(kYAxisMenu, menuItemSelected);
      DisableMenuItem(kChangeWeaponMenu, menuItemSelected);

      // Enable the previously selected item in the other menus
      EnableMenuItem(kXAxisMenu, oldAttackSelectedItem);
      EnableMenuItem(kYAxisMenu, oldAttackSelectedItem);
      EnableMenuItem(kChangeWeaponMenu, oldAttackSelectedItem);

      // Update the previously selected item to handle future selections
      SetOldAttackSelectedItem(menuItemSelected);
}
```

Setting Default Controls

When players get their hands on a new game, they want to start playing immediately.
Little details like reading the manual and configuring the game's controls can wait.
To let the player jump into the game right away, we should provide a set of reasonable default controls. As we learned from the last chapter, you provide a set of
default controls in InputSprocket by running your game, configuring the controls,
and creating a list of control sets that you ship with the game. The HID Manager
does not come with the capability to supply a series of control sets with your game.
If you do not provide a method for supplying default controls in your game, the
player will not be able to use his game controllers without configuring the controls
first. Our best friends in setting default controls are the usage page and usage fields
of input devices and their elements. For an input device, the combination of usage
page and usage tells us what kind of device this particular device is (such as joystick
or gamepad). For an input device element, the combination of usage page and
usage tells us what kind of element it is (examples include button, axis, and hat
switch). By reading the usage page and usage information we can provide an intu-
itive set of default controls that let the player begin playing immediately.

As we develop a set of default controls for the game we're making, we must select a
default game controller, then set default controls for that controller. To choose a
default controller, we begin by assembling a list of HID devices connected to the
player's computer. We go through that list, examine a device and check to see if it
is a joystick or gamepad. If it is, we make that device the default controller. Right
now, the chances of a device being a joystick or gamepad is high because of the
lack of keyboard and mouse support in the HID Manager, but our code is ready for
that support when it comes. One problem with our method is that it could pick an
input device different from the one the player wants to use if he has multiple

joysticks hooked up to his Mac. It is a problem that will not occur often because it's rare for someone to have more than one game controller connected. If a player does have multiple joysticks, we have to select one as the default; it might as well be the first one. The player can go to the configuration dialog and choose a different controller to use if he needs to. The following function selects a default controller to use in the game:

```
void InputController::SetDefaultController(void)
{
        // This function finds the first joystick or gamepad
        // connected to the player's machine and uses that as
        // the default controller.  This function allows the
        // player to play the game without having to configure
        // the controllers first.

        CreateControllerList();
        Iterator controllerListIterator(&controllerList);
        InputDevicePtr currentInputDevice;

        long primaryUsage;
        long primaryUsagePage;

        currentInputDevice = (InputDevicePtr)controllerListIterator.Next();

        while(currentInputDevice != nil) {
                // Find primary usage of this controller
                primaryUsagePage = currentInputDevice->GetUsagePage();
                primaryUsage = currentInputDevice->GetUsage();

                // If it's a joystick or gamepad, make it the default controller
                if(primaryUsagePage == kGenericDesktopPage) {
                        if (primaryUsage == kJoystickUsage) {
                                SetControllerDevice(currentInputDevice);
                                return;
                        }
                        else if (primaryUsage == kGamepadUsage) {
                                SetControllerDevice(currentInputDevice);
                                return;
                        }
                }
```

```
                    // Get next controller in list
                    currentInputDevice = (InputDevicePtr)controllerListIterator.Next();
            }

    }
```

After selecting a default controller, we must assign elements of that controller to fill our game's control needs. Recall that our game has four control needs: horizontal movement (x-axis), vertical movement (y-axis), attack, and change weapon. We begin by creating a list of our default input device's elements, then navigate the list. If the element has a primary usage of x-axis movement (such as the x-axis of a joystick or the left and right buttons of a direction pad), we assign that element to our horizontal movement control need. If the element has a primary usage of y-axis movement (the y-axis of a joystick, for example), we assign that element to our vertical movement control needs. If the element is a button element, things change slightly. We assign the first button we find to the attack control need and the second button we find to the change weapon control need. The attack control need has the higher priority so we assign it first. Should the player's joystick have only one button (Suppose a player found a way to hook up an Atari 2600 joystick to a USB port, for example), he will at least be able to attack his enemies. The code below assigns default controls for the game:

```
void InputController::SetDefaultControls(void)
{
        // This function assigns default controls so the player
        // can play without configuring the controls.  It will use
        // the x-axis and y-axis elements for movement, the first button
        // for attacking, and the second button for changing weapons.

        if (controllerDevice == nil)
                return;

        io_object_t deviceObj = controllerDevice->GetDeviceObject();
        CreateElementList(deviceObj);

        Iterator elementListIterator(&elementList);
        InputDeviceElementPtr currentInputElement;
        long primaryUsage;
        long primaryUsagePage;
```

```
int elementCount = elementList.GetNumberOfItems();

while(elementCount > 0) {
        currentInputElement =
        (InputDeviceElementPtr)elementListIterator.Next();
        // Find primary usage of this controller
        primaryUsagePage = currentInputElement->GetUsagePage();
        primaryUsage = currentInputElement->GetUsage();

        if (primaryUsagePage == kGenericDesktopPage) {
                // If the element is primarily used for axis movement
                // assign it to axis movement by default.
                if (primaryUsage == kXAxisUsage) {
                        gameNeeds[kXAxisNeed] = currentInputElement-
                        >GetCookie();
                }
                else if (primaryUsage == kYAxisUsage) {
                        gameNeeds[kYAxisNeed] = currentInputElement-
                        >GetCookie();
                }
        }
        // Make button 1 the default attack button
        // and button 2 the default change weapon button
        else if (primaryUsagePage == kButtonPage) {
                if (primaryUsage == kButton1Usage) {
                        gameNeeds[kAttackNeed] =
                        currentInputElement>GetCookie();
                }
                else if (primaryUsage == kButton2Usage) {
                        gameNeeds[kChangeWeaponNeed] =
                                currentInputElement>GetCookie();
                }
        }

        // Get next element
        elementCount--;
    }
}
```

Pausing and Resuming

The players pausing and resuming games doesn't have much effect on the HID Manager unless you use queues to read the player's input. If you use queues, you should stop the delivery of events to the queue by calling the queue's stop() member function when the player pauses the game. This action prevents your game from receiving events from a game controller when the game is paused. When the player resumes the game, call the queue's start() member function to resume the delivery of events to the queue. The following functions pause and resume the controller:

```
void InputController::Pause(void)
{
      IOReturn result;
      result = (*eventList)->stop(eventList);
}

void InputController::Resume(void)
{
      IOReturn result;
      result = (*eventList)->start(eventList);
}
```

Cleaning Up

At the end of the game, you must perform the following clean-up functions to keep the player's system running smoothly:

- Dispose of any queues you created to read events.
- Dispose of the device interfaces.
- Dispose of the controller list.
- Dispose of the master port.

To clean the queues, you call two functions. You must call the queue's dispose() member function to dispose of the queue and then call the queue's Release() member function to free the memory the HID Manager allocated to create the queue.

Disposing of the device interfaces also requires two function calls. First call the device interface's close() function to close the device interface. Then call the device interface's Release() function to release the memory allocated for the device interface.

We must also call IOObjectRelease() to release the object iterator we created to compile the list of HID devices. Finally, we call mach_port_dellocate() to release the Mach port we created. The following source code performs the clean-up duties for our game:

```
void InputController::CleanUp(void)
{
        DisposeEventList();
        CloseDevice()
        DisposeDeviceInterface();
        DisposeElementList();
        DisposeControllerList();
        DisposeMasterPort();
}
void InputController::DisposeEventList(void)
{
        IOReturn result;

        if (eventList != nil) {
                result = (*eventList)->dispose(eventList);
                (*eventList)->Release(eventList);
                eventList = nil;
        }
}
void InputController::CloseDevice(void)
{
        IOReturn result;

        if (controllerDeviceInterface != nil) {
                result = (*controllerDeviceInterface)->close
                        (controllerDeviceInterface);
}
}
void InputController::DisposeDeviceInterface(void)
{
        if (controllerDeviceInterface != nil) {
                (*controllerDeviceInterface)->Release(controllerDeviceInterface);
        controllerDeviceInterface = nil;
        }
}
void InputController::DisposeElementList(void)
```

```
{
    Iterator elementListIterator(&elementList);
    InputDevicePtr currentInputDevice;

    int itemsToDispose = elementList.GetNumberOfItems();

    while(itemsToDispose > 0) {
        currentInputDevice = (InputDevicePtr)elementListIterator.Next();
        elementList.RemoveItem(currentInputDevice);
        itemsToDispose--;
    }

}

void InputController::DisposeControllerList(void)
{
    Iterator controllerListIterator(&controllerList);
    InputDevicePtr currentInputDevice;

    int itemsToDispose = controllerList.GetNumberOfItems();

    while(itemsToDispose > 0) {
        currentInputDevice = (InputDevicePtr)controllerListIterator.Next();
        controllerList.RemoveItem(currentInputDevice);
        itemsToDispose--;
    }

}
void InputController::DisposeMasterPort()
{
    if (masterPort != nil) {
        mach_port_deallocate(mach_task_self(), masterPort);
    }
}
```

Summary

This chapter covered the HID Manager so that your game can support joysticks and gamepads in Mac OS X. To read data from a joystick with the HID Manager, you must perform the following steps:

- Create a list of input devices the player has connected to his computer.
- Create a device interface to read data from the input device.
- Open a connection to the input device.
- Read data from the input device.

To read data from an input device, you call the device interface's `getElementValue()` member function. The `getElementValue()` function fills a HID Manager event structure, `IOHIDEventStruct`. Read the event structure's `elementCookie` field to discover which element generated the event and then read the `value` field to determine the type of event that occurred.

Using the device interface's `getElementValue()` function allows us to retrieve the last value of an element. HID Manager queues let you store a queue of events for important input device elements so that you don't miss any events. To create a queue, call the function `allocQueue()` to allocate memory for the queue, then call the `create()` function to create the queue. To add elements to the queue, call the function `addElement()`. The `start()` function initiates the delivery to the queue. Call the `getNextEvent()` function to read events residing in the queue.

The HID Manager forces you to write your own dialog boxes to let the player configure the game's controls. I used the Macintosh Dialog Manager to implement a configuration dialog box. To learn more about user-interface programming with Carbon, go to Apple's developer site or refer to the documentation that comes with Apple's developer tools for Mac OS X.

The sample program for this chapter adds HID Manager support to the work we have done so far in the book. Because the HID Manager runs only on Mac OS X, only Mac OS X users can run the program. Sorry, Mac OS 8 and 9 users. It's out of my hands.

CHAPTER 9

Reading the Keyboard and Mouse Plus Event Handling

The previous two chapters covered joystick support in games. However, many games do not have to support joysticks. I, for one, have never needed a joystick to enjoy *Civilization 2* and *Starcraft*. Even if your game would benefit from joystick support, you may not want the hassle of writing two sets of code to support joysticks in both Mac OS 8/9 and Mac OS X. In this case, your game should support just the keyboard and mouse. This chapter shows you how to read keyboard and mouse input. In addition, this chapter demonstrates event handling using both traditional Mac OS events and Carbon events.

Reading the Keyboard Directly

To read the keyboard directly (as opposed to using events to indirectly read the keyboard), use the function GetKeys(). This function returns an array containing all the keys on the keyboard and whether or not each of the keys was pressed.

Apple uses a KeyMap structure to return the state of the keyboard when you call GetKeys(). Apple originally wrote the Toolbox, from which Carbon inherits, in Pascal, and they made the KeyMap structure a packed array containing 128 elements of one bit each. A Pascal-packed array packs all the array elements together to save space. In the case of the KeyMap structure, a packed array makes the 128-element array take up just one bit of memory per element for a total of 16 bytes of memory. To check whether the player pressed a certain key, you look at the appropriate element in the KeyMap structure. If the element has a value of 1, the player pressed the key.

Apple uses virtual key codes as the indexes in the KeyMap structure. A *virtual key code* is a way to separate the physical key from the character on the key. Different countries have different keyboard layouts. United States keyboards have the QWERTY layout, but French keyboards have an AZERTY layout. By using virtual key codes, pressing the W key on the U.S. keyboard will generate the same code, 13, as pressing the Z key on a French keyboard. Virtual key codes range from 0 to 127.

Unfortunately, the C language does not support packed arrays. In C, the KeyMap structure is an array of 16 8-bit integers, which equals the Pascal 128-element packed array. To determine whether the user pressed a particular key, you must do the following:

1. Determine which of the 16 integers in the array contains the key. You do this by dividing the key code by the integer 8 (the number of bits in each array entry). When you use integer division, the computer eliminates everything after the decimal point, yielding a value between 0 and 15. For example, in integer division, 4/8 = 0, not 0.5.

2. Determine which of the 8 bits in the integer contains the key. To do this, you perform the modulus operator on the key code with the value 8. The modulus operator returns the remainder of the key code divided by 8. This gives you a value between 0 and 7, which is the bit of the desired key.

3. Determine whether the bit is 1. If it is, the user pressed the key. The bit is 0 if the user did not press the key.

Let's work through an example. For the example, we'll see whether the player pressed the W key on the U.S. keyboard.

1. The W key has virtual key code 13. Performing an integer division, 13/8, yields a result of 1. This means that the virtual key code is in the second element, element 1, of the array.

2. Now we have to find which bit in the second element has the virtual key code 13. Dividing 13 by 8 yields a remainder of 5, so the virtual key code for the W key is the fifth bit in the second element of the array.

3. Finally we check whether the fifth bit of the second element is 1. We do this by performing a bitwise AND between the second element of the array and the fifth bit as you can see in the following code.

```
Boolean WasKeyPressed(short keyCode, KeyMap theKeyboard)
{
        short keymapIndex;
        short bitInIndex;
        short keymapEntrySize = 8;

        // The keymap consists of 16 8-bit numbers.
        // Find which of the 16 numbers to check.
        keymapIndex = keyCode / keymapEntrySize;

        // Find which bit to check in the keymap index.
        bitInIndex = keyCode % keymapEntrySize;

        // Raise the number 2 by the power of
        // the value of bitInIndex to determine
```

```
            // the number we should test in the keymap
            // to see if the key was pressed.  The left
            // shift operator (<<) performs a multiply by 2.
            short keyTestValue;
            keyTestValue = 1 << bitInIndex;

            // Get the value of the keymap entry
            // we want to test
            char* startOfKeymap =  (char *) &theKeyboard[0];
            char keymapEntryValue = * (startOfKeymap + keymapIndex);

            // Compare the keymap entry with the value
            // of the key we want to test to determine
            // if the player pressed the key.
            return ((keymapEntryValue & keyTestValue) != 0);
}
```

Reading the Mouse Directly

Reading the mouse directly is less complicated than reading the keyboard directly
because you can read only two items from the mouse—the mouse cursor location
and the mouse button—as opposed to more than 100 keys to read from the keyboard. You can buy mice for the Mac with multiple buttons and a scroll wheel, but
the Mac OS does not provide functions to directly read the extra buttons and scroll
wheel. To support multibutton mice and scroll wheels, you have three options:
InputSprocket (which I covered in Chapter 7, "InputSprocket"), the HID Manager
(which I covered in Chapter 8, " HID Manager"), and Carbon events. I will cover
Carbon events later in this chapter.

Reading the Mouse Location

You read the location of the mouse cursor by calling the function GetMouse().
GetMouse() returns the mouse location in the local coordinates of the current
graphics port. Chapter 4, "Introduction to Macintosh Graphics," explains the difference between local and global coordinates. The following code snippet demonstrates the use of the GetMouse() function:

```
Point mouseLocation;
mouseLocation = GetMouse();
MovePlayer(mouseLocation.h, mouseLocation.v);
```

Notice that the Macintosh `Point` structure uses the data members h and v to designate the horizontal and vertical components of a point instead of x and y. Reading the current location of the mouse is fine for certain situations, such as determining the mouse location when the player clicks the mouse button. However, if you want to know which direction the player moved the mouse and how much he moved it, you must read the current mouse location and compare it to the mouse location the last time you checked. The following function determines the direction the player moved the mouse:

```
InputControllerAction DetermineMouseMovement(Point previousLocation)
{
        Point currentLocation;

        // Read current mouse location
        currentLocation = GetMouse();

        Boolean movedUp;
        Boolean movedDown;
        Boolean movedLeft;
        Boolean movedRight;

        // Check for movement in the four directions
        // Up
        if (currentLocation.v < previousLocation.v)
                movedUp = true;
        else
                movedUp = false;

        // Down
        if (currentLocation.v. > previousLocation.v)
                movedDown = true;
        else
                movedDown = false;

        // Left
        if (currentLocation.h < previousLocation.h)
                movedLeft = true;
        else
                movedLeft = false;

        // Right
```

```
        if (currentLocation.h > previousLocation.h)
                movedRight = true;
        else
                movedRight = false;

        // Determine direction of movement
        if ((movedUp) && (movedLeft))
                return kMoveUpAndLeft;
        else if ((movedUp) && (movedRight))
                return kMoveUpAndRight;
        else if ((movedDown) && (movedLeft))
                return kMoveDownAndLeft;
        else if ((movedDown) && (movedRight))
                return kMoveDownAndRight;

        // At this point, we know the movement is not diagonal
        else if (movedUp)
                return kMoveUp;
        else if (movedDown)
                return kMoveDown;
        else if (movedLeft)
                return kMoveLeft;
        else if (movedRight)
                return kMoveRight;
        else
                return kNoMovement;
}
```

We could use the DetermineMouseMovement() function in our game to let the player move his character around the game world with the mouse. However, for the type of game we are making, it is more natural to play the game with the keyboard or a game controller. Besides, InputSprocket lets the player use the mouse if he wishes, and InputSprocket supports mice with multiple buttons so InputSprocket is a better solution for reading the mouse for action games than calling GetMouse().

Reading the Mouse Button

You determine whether the mouse button is down (that is, whether the user pressed the mouse button) by calling the function Button(). The function returns true if the button is down and returns false if the button is up. If you then want to check whether the mouse button is still down, call the function StillDown().

`StillDown()` returns `true` if the mouse button is still down and `false` if the button is up. The following code snippet fires a missile when the player presses and releases the mouse button:

```
if (Button()) {
        while (StillDown()) {
                // Do nothing in the loop.
                // Wait for the mouse button to be released.
        }
        FireMissile();
}
```

Using the Classic Event Manager

Most Macintosh programs—such as Internet browsers, word processors, and spreadsheets—use events to read the keyboard and mouse. To handle events, the operating system spends most of its time waiting for events. When the player generates input in your game by pressing a key or clicking the mouse button, the operating system tells your program that an event has occurred and passes along information about the event. If you are writing a slower-paced game, such as a turn-based strategy game or a board game, you can use events to read keyboard and mouse input.

The Macintosh programmer has two ways to handle events in Carbon: the Classic Event Manager and the Carbon Event Manager. We'll begin by discussing the Classic Event Manager.

Events

There are ten types of events in the Classic Event Manager in Carbon, as described in Table 9-1. The most important events for game developers are mouse down (event type `mouseDown`), key down (event type `keyDown`), update (event type `updateEvt`), and high-level (event type `kHighLevelEvent`) events.

Table 9-1   Types of Events

Event	Description
nullEvent	There are no other pending events.
mouseDown	The user pressed the mouse button.
mouseUp	The user released the mouse button.
keyDown	The user pressed a key on the keyboard.
keyUp	The user released a key on the keyboard.
autoKey	The user is holding down a key on the keyboard.
updateEvt	Part of the screen must be redrawn.
activateEvt	A window has been activated or deactivated. This event occurs when you have multiple windows, and you switch from one window to another.
osEvt	An operating system event. Operating system events occur when the user moves the mouse and for suspend and resume events. Suspend and resume events occur when you switch from one application to another.
kHighLevelEvent	A high-level Apple event. Apple events let you do things such as allow the user to double-click a saved-game icon to launch the game and open the saved game.

The Macintosh Classic Event Manager uses the EventRecord data structure to store information about events. Table 9-2 lists the fields in the EventRecord structure. Not all events use every field of the EventRecord structure. For example, mouse events do not use the message field, and update events do not use the modifiers field.

Table 9-2   EventRecord Fields

Field	Description
what	The event type as listed in Table 9-1.
message	Additional information about the event. For example, a key down event (event type keyDown) would contain the virtual key code of the pressed key in the message field.
when	When the event happened. This value is recorded as the number of clock ticks since the user turned on the computer. A clock tick is 1/60 of a second.
where	The location of the mouse cursor (in global coordinates) when the event occurred.
modifiers	For a key down event, this field tells you what modifier keys the user pressed. Modifier keys are the Shift, Option, Ctrl, Alt, Cmd (Apple), and Caps Lock keys. For an activate event (event type activateEvt), this field determines whether it's an activate or deactivate event.

Looking for Events

You check for events by calling WaitNextEvent(). WaitNextEvent() takes the four parameters shown in Table 9-3.

Table 9-3   WaitNextEvent() Parameters

Parameter	Description
eventMask	The types of events to look for. To look for all events, pass the value everyEvent.
theEvent	The first event, WaitNextEvent(), is part of the event mask you supplied in the eventMask parameter.
sleep	The number of clock ticks to give other programs when there are no events pending.
mouseRgn	If the mouse moves outside of mouseRgn, a mouse moved event will occur. If you pass nil, no mouse moved events will be generated. Remember from Table 9-1 that moused moved events are operating system events (event type osEvt), not their own unique event type.

The value you provide in the sleep parameter to WaitNextEvent() depends on whether your game is running on Mac OS X or an earlier version of Mac OS. On pre-OS X systems, you want to provide a small value in the sleep parameter, such as 0 or 1. Passing a small sleep value on pre-OS X computers allows your game to take over the CPU so that your game can run at maximum speed. Versions of the Mac OS before OS X have cooperative multitasking to allow multiple applications to run at once. With cooperative multitasking, the application chooses how much time to give to other applications. As a game programmer, you have the option to be a bad neighbor and give no time to other applications on a cooperative multi-tasking system. Providing a small sleep value makes you a bad neighbor, but provides maximum performance when calling WaitNextEvent().

Mac OS X changed the multitasking model from cooperative multitasking to preemptive multitasking. With preemptive multitasking, the operating system decides how much time to give to each application. If your game does not yield time to other programs, the operating system puts your game at the end of the line for processor time. In Mac OS X, you should pass a larger sleep value (Apple recommends using the hexadecimal value 0x7FFFFFFF) to WaitNextEvent() to ensure that your game gets enough processor time. As a game programmer, you have four options for the sleep parameter to WaitNextEvent():

- Use a large sleep parameter. The number of OS X users is growing every day while the number of OS 8 and 9 user is falling. Using a large sleep parameter in OS 9 will have a lower performance hit than using a small sleep parameter in OS X.

- Use a small sleep parameter. This option will tick off your OS X users, but they can always run your game in Classic mode.

- Have two versions of your program with the OS 8/9 version using a small sleep parameter and the OS X version having a large sleep parameter. If you're supporting joysticks on both OS 8/9 and OS X, you already have two versions of your game, so this option won't be a problem for you.

- Determine at run time which operating system version the user is running and use the appropriate sleep value for the player's machine. Chapter 16, "Putting It All Together," shows you how to determine which version of Mac OS the user is running.

I recommend using one of the last two options for your game. You should give the player the best playing experience on his particular system, which may not happen if you use one of the first two options.

For game programming, you can generally get away with using nil as the value for the mouseRgn parameter to WaitNextEvent(). The hardware driver for the mouse moves the mouse cursor, not mouse moved events, so the player will be able to move the mouse cursor if you provide a nil mouse region to WaitNextEvent(). The main use of mouse moved events is to change the cursor when the mouse moves to different areas of the screen. As a test, run CodeWarrior and open a source code window. Now move the mouse over the window. The mouse cursor should change from an arrow to an I-beam cursor so that you can type text in the source code window. When you move the mouse outside of the window, the mouse cursor should change back to an arrow. You've just witnessed mouse moved events at work. Unless your game changes the cursor when the player moves the mouse over different areas of the screen, you won't need to deal with mouse moved events.

The following code shows a sample event loop that calls WaitNextEvent():

```
void GameApp::EventLoop(void)
{
RgnHandle        cursorRgn = nil;
      Boolean           haveEvent;
      EventRecord      event;

      do{
            haveEvent = WaitNextEvent(everyEvent, &event, kSleepValue, cursorRgn);

            if (haveEvent)
                  HandleEvent(&event);
            else
                  HandleIdleEvent(&event);
      } while (! done);
}
```

Handling Events

Figure 9-1 shows the functions a typical Mac application must provide when handling events. Fortunately, our game is going to be easier from an event-handling point of view than a word processor or CodeWarrior would be. Our game has only one window, so it won't be receiving any activate events. Our game's window contains only a content region so the player won't be closing, resizing, or moving any windows. Our game doesn't have the player drag units across the game screen, so we won't have to worry about mouse up events. Our game doesn't change the mouse cursor, so we don't have to worry about mouse moved events. This event handling stuff is easy when you don't have to handle the events.

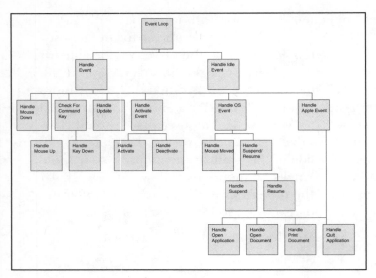

Figure 9-1

A general-purpose event handling function hierarchy

Although our game doesn't have to handle all the events listed in Figure 9-1, I'm going to include functions for all these events. If your game needs to handle events the game in this book doesn't handle, you can fill in the functions that I leave blank. The following code shows a typical Macintosh event handler:

```
void GameApp::HandleEvent (EventRecord* event)
{
        switch (event->what) {

                case mouseDown:
                        HandleMouseDown(event);
                        break;

                case mouseUp:
                        HandleMouseUp(event);
                        break;

                case keyDown:
        case autoKey:
                        // This code is for both keyDown and autoKey events
                        CheckForCommandKey(event);
                        break;

                case activateEvt:
```

```
                        HandleActivate(event);
                        break;

                case updateEvt:
                        HandleUpdate(event);
                        break;

                case osEvt:
                        HandleOSEvent(event);
                        break;

                case kHighLevelEvent:
                        HandleHighLevelEvent(event);
                        break;
        }
}
```

As you can see from the source code, all the event handler does is check the event's what field to determine the type of event that occurred. Then it performs a massive switch statement on the what field, with one case for each of the possible event types. Null events are not handled in the HandleEvent() function. When a null event occurs in the event loop, WaitNextEvent() returns false and calls the HandleIdleEvent() function. You should not have to change this code at all for your game. The only code you might have to change is the individual functions for handling each particular type of event.

Handling Null Events

Null events (events of type nullEvt) occur when no events are in the event queue and the call to WaitNextEvent() in the event loop returns false. You can use null events, also known as *idle events,* to do background processing while no events are happening. A game such as *Sim City* might use null events to process the simulation. Another use of the null event is to blink the cursor when it's in an edit box. Most games do nothing with a null event.

```
void GameApp::HandleIdleEvent(EventRecord* event)
{
        // do nothing
}
```

Handling Mouse Events

To handle mouse down (events of type `mouseDown`) events, you must determine where the mouse was when the user pressed the button. You determine the location of the mouse with a call to `FindWindow()`. `FindWindow()` tells you whether the mouse cursor was in a menu, in a window, or in another place. If the mouse was in a menu, you can then handle the menu selection. If the mouse was in a window, you must establish where in the window the mouse click occurred to determine what to do next. Figure 9-2 shows the areas of a window you may have to check. If the mouse was in the close box when the user clicked the mouse button, your game should close the window. If you have a full-screen game like the one we're making in this book, your window will be composed entirely of the content region, which simplifies the task of handling mouse down events. If you don't have a full-screen game, you may have to worry about responding to the player closing, dragging, growing, and zooming the window (depending on the type of windows you use in your game).

The square in the upper-left corner of the window is the close box, which closes the window.

The name of the window (Sample Window in the screenshot) and the 5 horizontal gray bars along the top of the menu constitute the title bar. The user uses the title bar to move the window.

The leftmost square in the upper-right corner of the window (the square with the square inside it) is the zoom box. It zooms the window between the size the user had it, and full screen.

The right square in the upper-right corner of the window is the collapse box. It hides everything below the title bar when clicked (or restores everything below the menu bar if the window was already collapsed).

The square in the bottom-right corner of the screen is the grow box. The user drags the grow box to resize the window.

The large white area inside the window is the content region.

(a)

The red button in the upper-left corner of the window closes the window.

The yellow button minimizes the window and places it in the Dock.

The green button works like the zoom box does in a Mac OS 9.1 window.

The title bar is in the same location as a Mac OS 9.1 window.

The grow box is in the same location as a Mac OS 9.1 window.

The large white area inside the window is the content region.

(b)

Figure 9-2

The areas of a Mac OS window in Mac OS 9.1 (a) and in Mac OS X (b).

Here's some sample code that handles the mouse down event:

```
void GameApp::HandleMouseDown(EventRecord* event)
{
        int            partOfScreen;
        WindowPtr      thisWindow;

        //Map cursor location at time of mouse down event
        partOfScreen = FindWindow(event->where, &thisWindow);

        switch(partOfScreen){
                case inMenuBar:
                        AdjustMenus();
                        HandleMenuCommand(MenuSelect(event->where));
                        break;

                case inContent:
                        if (thisWindow != FrontWindow()) {
                                SelectWindow(thisWindow);
                        }
                        else {
                                // Have the window handle a content click
                        }
                        break;

                case inDrag:
                        // Drag the window
                        break;

                case inGrow:
                        // Grow the window
                        break;

                case inGoAway:
                        if (TrackGoAway(thisWindow, event->where))
                                CloseWindow(thisWindow);
                        break;

                case inCollapseBox:
                        if (isWindowCollapsed(thisWindow))
                                // Restore the collapsed window
```

```
                              CollapseWindow(thisWindow, false);
                      else
                              // Collapse the window
                              CollapseWindow(thisWindow, true);
                      break;

              case inZoomIn:
              case inZoomOut:
                      // This code is for both ZoomIn and ZoomOut areas
                      if (TrackBox(thisWindow, event->where, partOfScreen) &&
                          (thisWindow!= nil))
                              // Zoom the window
                      break;
      }
}
```

Many games don't have to deal with mouse up events; usually games care more about mouse down events. Strategy games and board games may have to take advantage of mouse up events to drag units from one area of the map to another. In this case, your main concern will be finding the location of the mouse cursor when the mouse up event occurs. You check the event's where field to determine the location of the mouse cursor when the mouse up event happens. Your game then moves the unit to where the mouse up event occurred.

> **NOTE**
>
> The where field of a mouse up event tells you the location of the mouse cursor in global coordinates, not in the local coordinates the function GetMouse() returns. If you need the location of the mouse cursor in local coordinates, call the function GlobalToLocal(), which converts a point in global coordinates to local coordinates.

The following code sample shows you how to handle mouse up events:

```
void GameApp::HandleMouseUp(EventRecord* event)
{
      Point mouseLocation = event->where;

      // Do what you need with the mouse location here.
      // If the player drags a unit in a strategy game from one location
```

```
// to another, move the unit to the area on the screen where the
// player dragged it.
}
```

Handling Keyboard Events

When your game gets a key down event (an event of type keyDown), you have to first check if the Cmd key (the Apple key) was held down when the user pressed the other key. If the Cmd key was held down, you should do a menu selection, such as quitting the program if Cmd+Q was pressed.

Here's some code that checks whether the user held down the Cmd key when he pressed a key on the keyboard:

```
void GameApp::CheckForCommandKey (EventRecord* event)
{
        // Checks if Command Key was pressed. If so, handle menu selection.
        // If not, your game will have to handle the key press appropriately.

        WindowPtr activeWindow = nil;

        char key;

        // Get the key pressed
        key = (char)(event->message & charCodeMask);

        // Was command key hit
        if (event->modifiers & cmdKey) {
                AdjustMenus();
                HandleMenuCommand(MenuKey(key));

        }
        else {
                // Handle the key down event.
                // This will be game specific. You would have to
                // write a function to handle the event.

        }

}
```

Handling Activate Events

If your game has just one window, you won't have to worry about activate events (events of type activateEvt). If you have multiple windows, however, you must handle activate events. An activate event occurs when you have multiple windows open and you switch from one window to another. The event's message field tells you what window must be activated. The event's modifiers field will tell you whether it's an activate or a deactivate event. You have to do a bitwise AND operation between the modifiers field and the activeFlag modifier to determine whether the event is an activate event or a deactivate event. Here's a sample function that handles the activate event:

```
void GameApp::HandleActivate (EventRecord* event)
{
        WindowPtr        theWindow;
        theWindow = (WindowPtr) event->message;

        Boolean activating = (event->modifiers & activeFlag);

        if (activating)
                // Activate the window here
                ActivateWindow(theWindow);
        else
                // Deactivate the window here
                DeactivateWindow(theWindow);
}
```

To activate a window, call the function SelectWindow(). If your window has scrollbars, call the function ShowControl() for each scrollbar so that the scrollbars will function properly. You don't call a function to explicitly deactivate a window; SelectWindow() automatically does it for you. If the window you're deactivating has any scrollbars, you must call the function HideControl() to deactivate the scrollbars. The following functions activate and deactivate a window:

```
void ActivateWindow(WindowPtr theWindow)
{
        SelectWindow(theWindow);

        // If you have any scrollbars, call ShowControl()
        // to activate them.
}
```

```
void DeactivateWindow(WindowPtr theWindow)
{
        // If you have any scrollbars, call HideControl()
        // to deactivate them.
}
```

To learn more about activating windows, download a copy of *Inside Macintosh: Macintosh Toolbox Essentials* from Apple's Developer Web site at **http://www. apple.com/developer**. The chapters of interest are the ones on the Window Manager and the Control Manager.

F I N D I T

ONLINE

Apple's Developer Web site:
http://www.apple.com/developer

Handling Update Events

Update events (events of type updateEvt) tell your program that part of the screen must be redrawn. Update events occur when you do something that changes what appears on the screen. Examples include resizing windows, moving windows, and closing dialog boxes. To handle update events, you first check which window must be updated by checking the event's message field. After you know which window to update, you can proceed to updating the window. To update the window, call BeginUpdate(), redraw the window, and then call EndUpdate(). The following sample code handles updates:

```
void GameApp::HandleUpdate (EventRecord* event)
{
        WindowPtr theWindow;

        // Determine the window that needs to be updated.
        theWindow = (WindowPtr) event->message;

        BeginUpdate(theWindow);
        // Redraw the window here

        EndUpdate(theWindow);
}
```

I covered how to draw into a window in Chapter 4, "Introduction to Macintosh Graphics." Refer to the section "Drawing to the Screen" for details about drawing into a window.

Handling Operating System Events

An operating system event (events of type osEvt) can be a mouse moved event, a suspend application event, or a resume application event. Suspend application and resume application events occur when you switch from one application to another. For example, if I'm programming in CodeWarrior and I switch to *Deus Ex* to take a little break, CodeWarrior would receive a suspend application event and *Deus Ex* would receive a resume application event.

When handling operating system events, you must first determine which of the three types of events it is. You check the high byte of the event's message field to see whether the action was a mouse moved event or a suspend/resume event. If it's a suspend/resume event, you must figure out whether the event is a suspend application or a resume application event. Here's some sample code to handle operating system events:

```
void GameApp::HandleOSEvent(EventRecord* event)
{
        char    eventType;

        // Get high byte of message field
        eventType = event->message >> 24;

        if (eventType & mouseMovedMessage) {   // mouse moved event
              HandleMouseMoved(event);
        }
        else if (eventType & suspendResumeMessage) { // suspend/resume event
              HandleSuspendResume(event);
        }
}


void GameApp::HandleMouseMoved(EventRecord* event)
{
        // Treat mouse moved like an idle event
        HandleIdleEvent(event);
}
```

```
void GameApp::HandleSuspendResume(EventRecord* event)
{
      if (event->message & resumeFlag) {     // resume event
            // Activate front window
      }
      else {  // suspend event
            // Put application in background
      }
}
```

Handling Apple Events

The Mac OS uses Apple events (events of type kHighLevelEvent) to allow an application to send events to other applications. Suppose that we have a PDF file. If we double-click the file's icon, Adobe Acrobat Reader loads and opens the file we double-clicked. The double-clicking of the PDF file generated two Apple events: an Open Application event and an Open Documents event.

Before Mac OS X came along, games could get away with not supporting Apple events. Games on pre-Mac OS X systems placed a Quit menu item in the File menu and handled the Quit menu selection to quit the game. Mac OS X uses the Quit Application Apple event rather than an item in the File menu to quit programs. Figure 9-3 shows the menu you would use to quit OS X's Mail program. When the user chooses to quit, the operating system sends a Quit Application Apple event to the application (the Mail program in the case of Figure 9-3). If your game does not support Apple events, when the user chooses the Quit menu item, nothing will happen and he will be unable to quit your game. There are tons of Apple events, and there's no way I could cover them all in this chapter, but you have to worry about supporting only four of them: Open Application, Open Documents, Print Documents, and Quit Application. These four events are called the *required Apple events.* If you want to know more about the other Apple events, download a copy of the book *Inside Macintosh: Interapplication Communication* from Apple's Developer Web site at **http://www. apple.com/developer**.

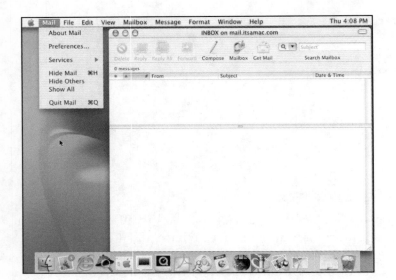

Figure 9-3

The menu command used to quit an OS X application.

To handle an Apple event, just call the function `AEProcessAppleEvent()`. `AEProcessAppleEvent()` determines what Apple event occurred and calls the appropriate Apple event handler function. We will have to write the specific Apple event handlers ourselves, one function for each Apple event we want to support. The following code handles an Apple event simply by passing the Apple event to the specific Apple event handler:

```
void GameApp::HandleHighLevelEvent(EventRecord* event)
{
        OSErr err;

        // Just process the required Apple Events
        err = AEProcessAppleEvent(event);
}
```

Installing Apple Event Handlers

Before we can handle Apple events, we first must install the Apple event handlers. For the game we're developing, we must install four handlers, one for each of the Apple events we're going to support: Open Application, Open Documents, Print Documents, and Quit Application. To install the Apple event handlers, we call the function `AEInstallEventHandler()` once for each handler we want to install. The `AEInstallEventHandler()` takes five parameters, as shown in Table 9-4.

Table 9-4 `AEInstallEventHandler()` **Parameters**

Parameter	Description
theAEEventClass	The type of Apple events the handler will handle. Pass the value `kCoreEventClass` to handle the four required Apple events.
theAEEventID	The specific Apple event the handler will handle.
handler	A pointer to an Apple event handler. I use the function `NewAEEventHandlerUPP()` to create the handler.
handlerRefcon	A reference constant that the Apple Event Manager passes to the handler each time it calls the handler. If you have any data you want to pass to the handler, place it in this parameter. Use 0 if your handler does not have any data to pass to the handler.
isSysHandler	Do you want the handler added to the system or to your application's Apple event dispatch table? If you add it to the system dispatch table, all other applications can use your handler. Pass `false` to add the handler to your application's Apple event dispatch table.

The following code installs the Apple event handlers for the four required Apple events:

```
void GameApp::InitAppleEventHandlers (void)
{
    OSErr error;

    // Install the required Apple Event Handlers
    // (Open Application, Open Documents, Print Documents and
    //     Quit Application)
    error = AEInstallEventHandler(kCoreEventClass, kAEOpenApplication,
        NewAEEventHandlerUPP(HandleOpenApplication),
        (unsignedlong)this, false);

    if (error == noErr)
        error = AEInstallEventHandler(kCoreEventClass, kAEOpenDocuments,
            NewAEEventHandlerProc(HandleOpenDocument),
            (unsigned long)this, false);
```

```
if (error == noErr)
        error = AEInstallEventHandler(kCoreEventClass, kAEPrintDocuments,
            NewAEEventHandlerProc(HandlePrintDocument),
            (unsigned long)this, false);

if (error == noErr)
        error = AEInstallEventHandler(kCoreEventClass, kAEQuitApplication,
            NewAEEventHandlerProc(HandleQuitApplication),
            (unsigned long)this, false);
}
```

I can hear you saying right now "What the <bleep> does (unsigned long)this
mean?" In the handlerRefCon parameter, you pass any data you need to pass to the
Apple event handler, and the data must be in the form of an unsigned long. I want
to pass a pointer to my GameApp class. For example, I have a Quit() function in the
GameApp class that performs some cleanup duties. I want the HandleQuitApplication()
event handler to call my Quit() function, but the event handler needs a pointer to
a GameApp object so it can call my Quit() function. In C++, the keyword this is a
pointer to the current object of a class. By passing this to the
AEInstallEventHandler() function, I ensure that the event handler has access to my
GameApp object. Because the event handler needs its user data in the form of an
unsigned long, I must typecast my GameApp pointer to an unsigned long so that the
event handler can use the pointer. Typecasting results in some nasty-looking code,
and should be avoided unless it's absolutely necessary, but it's absolutely necessary
in this case.

Passing Apple Event Parameters

Each Apple event has its own set of required parameters. For example, the Open
Application and Quit Application Apple events have no parameters, but the Open
Documents and Print Documents Apple events take a list of document files as their
required parameters. When handling an Apple event, the event handler needs the
right number of parameters. If an Open Documents Apple event contains no documents to open, then we have a problem. The operating system sends the Apple
events to our game, so we have no direct control over what parameters will be
passed to our Apple event handlers. We will have to write a function to check
whether our Apple event handler functions have the correct number of parameters.

Call the function AEGetAttributePtr() to check whether the handler function has
received the correct number of parameters. This function takes seven parameters,
as listed in Table 9-5.

Table 9-5   AEGetAttributePtr() Parameters

Parameter	Description
theAppleEvent	The Apple event whose attribute we want to know.
theAEKeyword	The desired attribute.
desiredType	The desired descriptor type for the returned data. The Apple Event Manager will try to convert the returned data to the desired type unless you specify typeWildCard as the desired type.
typeCode	The descriptor of the returned data.
dataPtr	A pointer to the returned data.
maximumSize	The maximum size of the returned data.
actualSize	The actual size of the returned data.

The AEGetAttributePtr() function is unusual in that you do not want it to return noErr. A return value of noErr means that there's an extra parameter sitting around, which means that the event handler did not receive the proper number of parameters. The result code we want here is errAEDescNotFound, which means that there are no extra parameters sitting around. The following function checks an Apple event's parameters. The Apple event handler functions we write later in this chapter will call this function.

```
OSErr GameApp::GotRequiredAEParameters(const AppleEvent* theAppleEvent)
{
      DescType returnedType;
      Size actualSize;
      OSErr error;

      error = AEGetAttributePtr(theAppleEvent, keyMissedKeywordAttr,
                  typeWildCard, &returnedType, nil, 0, &actualSize);

      if (error == errAEDescNotFound)
            // We got all the required parameters
            return noErr;
      else
```

```
        // We missed a parameter
        return errAEParamMissed;

}
```

Handling the Open Application Event

When our game receives an Open Application event, the operating system will open the game for us. If there's anything additional we want to do when the game starts, we put it in the Open Application event handler. For example, a word processor would want to create a new document when it starts, so the word processing program would have a function to create a new document in its Open Application event handler. In general, all you want to do in a game at the beginning is to load the game; normally you don't have to write any special code to handle Open Application events. Here's some code to handle the Open Application event:

```
pascal OSErr GameApp::HandleOpenApplication(constAppleEvent* theAppleEvent,
            AppleEvent* theReply, unsigned long userData)
{
        // Do whatever you want to do at startup here.

        // GotRequiredAEParameters is written in the Apple
        // Event Parameters section earlier in this chapter.
        return GotRequiredAEParameters(theAppleEvent);
}
```

I'm sure that you are wondering why the HandleOpenApplication() function needed the parameters theReply and userData because the function doesn't use them. The reason is that an Apple event handler must take this form whether the event handler uses all the parameters or not:

```
pascal OSErr HandlerFunctionName(const AppleEvent* theAppleEvent,
        AppleEvent* theReply, unsigned long handlerRefCon)
```

The pascal at the front of the function tells the compiler to use Pascal function-calling conventions. The Event Manager expects Apple event handling functions to use Pascal function-calling conventions.

Handling the Open Documents Event

Let me begin by explaining what Open Documents Apple events are. Open Documents Apple events occur when the user opens one or more documents in the Finder, either by double-clicking the document file's icon or by dragging and dropping document files into the application. For example, if you drag and drop three word processing documents into Microsoft Word, Word would receive an Open Documents Apple event with a list of the three files to open. Word would then open the three documents. For a game, you use Open Documents Apple events to let the player open saved games in the Finder. Games normally don't have more than one saved game open at one time, but using Apple events gives your game the capability to open more than one saved game if you so desire.

Handling the Open Documents Apple event takes most of the work out of all the required Apple events. It requires the following steps:

1. Get the list of documents to open. For a game, this is a list of one or more saved game files. You do this by calling the function `AEGetParamDesc()`. This function takes four parameters, as shown in Table 9-6.

2. Get the number of documents in the document list by calling the function `AECountItems()`. The `AECountItems()` function takes two parameters, described in Table 9-7. Most games have only one saved game, so `AECountItems()` will probably return the value 1.

3. Open each document in the list. For each document you must do the following:

   3A. Call the function `AEGetNthDesc()` to find the file containing the document. The `AEGetNthDesc()` returns a variable of type `AEDesc`. Table 9-8 lists the parameters you must provide to the `AEGetNthDesc()` function.

   3B. Get the file specification record (`FSSpec`) for the file by using the `dataHandle` field of the `AEDesc` variable you got from the call to `AEGetNthDesc()`. The file's file specification record contains the file's name and location on disk. As a programmer, you need the file specification record to work with the file.

   3C. Open the document. Chapter 15, "Files," covers files and explains how to open a document file.

Table 9-6   AEGetParamDesc() Parameters

Parameter	Description
theAppleEvent	The Apple event containing the desired parameter.
theAEKeyword	The desired parameter.
desiredType	The desired descriptor type for the returned data. The Apple Event Manager will try to convert the returned data to the desired type unless you specify typeWildCard as the desired type.
result	The Apple event descriptor for the desired parameter.

Table 9-7   AECountItems() Parameters

Parameter	Description
theAEDescList	The descriptor list to count.
theCount	The number of items in the descriptor list.

Table 9-8   AEGetNthDesc() Parameters

Parameter	Description
theAEDescList	The descriptor list that contains the desired descriptor.
index	The location of the descriptor in the descriptor list.
desiredType	The desired descriptor type for the returned data. The Apple Event Manager will try to convert the returned data to the desired type unless you specify typeWildCard as the desired type.
theAEKeyword	The keyword of the descriptor record.
result	The desired descriptor record.

The following code handles an Open Documents Apple event:

```
pascal OSErr GameApp::HandleOpenDocument(const AppleEvent* theAppleEvent,
                  AppleEvent* theReply, unsigned long userData)
{
      OSErr error;
      long    numberOfFilesInList, fileCount;
      AEDescList       theFileList;
      // We passed a pointer to a GameApp object in the userData field.
      // Convert back to a GameApp object
      GameAppPtr currentApp = (GameAppPtr)userData;

      // Get the list of files to open
      error = AEGetParamDesc(theAppleEvent, keyDirectObject, typeAEList,
                  &theFileList);
      if (error != noErr)
            return error;

      // Get the number of files in the list
      error = AECountItems(&theFileList, &numberOfFilesInList);
      if (error != noErr)
            return error;

      // Open each file in the list
      for (fileCount = 1; fileCount < numberOfFilesInList; fileCount++){
            AEDesc  fileToOpen;
            AEKeyword        dummyKeyword;

            error = AEGetNthDesc(&theFileList, fileCount, typeFSS,
                              &dummyKeyword, &fileToOpen);
            if (error == noErr) {
                  // Get fileToOpen into a format that OpenDocument can use
                  FSSpec* fileName = (FSSpec*)fileToOpen.dataHandle;

                  // You must write your own OpenDocument function.
                  // See Chapter 15 to learn how to do this.
                  currentApp.OpenDocument(fileName);
            }
            else {
                  return error;
            }
```

```
      }
      return GotRequiredAEParameters(theAppleEvent);
}
```

Handling the Print Documents Event

A Print Documents Apple event is generated when a user tries to print one or more documents in the Finder. For your game to receive a Print Documents event, the player would have to select one of your game's document files, such as a saved game file, and try to print it while he's in the Finder. Most games don't need to print, so we'll just tell the operating system that we won't handle the event. It might sound as if I'm wimping out on providing coverage of this event, but this is a game programming book, not a printing book. In the rare case that the player really does have to print one of your game's files, the operating system will look for another application that can print the contents of the file. If the operating system cannot find another application to print the file, an error message will come up saying that the operating system could not find an application capable of printing the document. Here's the code to handle the Print Documents event:

```
pascal OSErr GameApp::HandlePrintDocument(const AppleEvent* theAppleEvent,
            AppleEvent* theReply, unsigned long userData)
{
      // Tell the OS we didn't handle the event.
      return errAEEventNotHandled;
}
```

Handling the Quit Application Event

Your application receives a Quit Application Apple event when the user shuts down his computer while your application is still in memory. The operating system sends a Quit Application Apple event to all open programs so that the computer can shut down properly. In addition, Mac OS X generates a Quit Application event when the user selects the Quit menu item in the Applications menu (refer back to Figure 9-3). Handling the Quit Application event is easy: We just quit our application. Here's the code to handle the Quit Application Apple event:

```
pascal OSErr GameApp::HandleQuitApplication(const AppleEvent* theAppleEvent,
            AppleEvent* theReply, unsigned long userData)
{
      // Just quit as if the user selected Quit from the menu
      // We passed a pointer to our game when we installed the event handler.
      GameAppPtr currentApp = (GameAppPtr)userData;
```

```
        currentApp->Quit();

        return GotRequiredAEParameters(theAppleEvent);
}
```

Removing Apple Event Handlers

When the player quits our game, we must remove the Apple event handlers we installed. To remove the handlers, we call AERemoveEventHandler() once for each Apple event handler we installed. The AERemoveEventHandler() function takes four parameters—the same parameters used by the AEInstallEventHandler() function earlier—except for the handlerRefcon parameter. When calling AERemoveEventHandler(), you use the same values you used to install the event handler.

Here's some sample code that removes the Apple event handlers we installed earlier:

```
void GameApp::RemoveAppleEventHandlers(void)
{
        OSErr error;

        // Remove the required Apple Event Handlers
        // (Open Application, Open Documents, Print Documents and
                Quit Application)
        error = AERemoveEventHandler(kCoreEventClass, kAEOpenApplication,
                    NewAEEventHandlerProc(HandleOpenApplication), false);

        if (error == noErr)
                error = AERemoveEventHandler(kCoreEventClass, kAEOpenDocuments,
                    NewAEEventHandlerProc(HandleOpenDocument), false);

        if (error == noErr)
                error = AERemoveEventHandler(kCoreEventClass, kAEPrintDocuments,
                    NewAEEventHandlerProc(HandlePrintDocument), false);

        if (error == noErr)
                error = AERemoveEventHandler(kCoreEventClass, kAEQuitApplication,
                    NewAEEventHandlerProc(HandleQuitApplication), false);
}
```

Using Carbon Events

In version 1.1 of Carbon, Apple introduced the Carbon Event Manager as an alternative to the Classic Event Manager. Where the two event models differ is in their focus. The traditional event model that the Classic Event Manager uses focuses on the event itself. You end up writing a function to handle each type of event. Most event handling functions try to determine where an event occurred and then handle the event appropriately.

The event model used by the Carbon Event Manager changes the focus from the event to the recipient of the event. In this model, an application event handler handles application-level events and window event handlers handle window events. You might even choose to give other things, such as window controls, their own event handlers. Figure 9-4 shows how the Carbon Event Manager handles events.

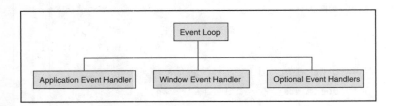

Figure 9-4

The Carbon Event Manager

What makes the Carbon Event Manager shine is that Apple has already written standard application and window event handlers that take care of most of the work for you. All you have to do to use the standard event handlers is to install them. If you're starting from scratch, you will find it much easier to use Carbon events than traditional Mac OS events. The only reason to use the Classic Event Manager is to support older versions of the Mac OS.

NOTE

Carbon events run only on Mac OS 8.6 and above. If you want your game to run on earlier versions of Mac OS, you must use the Classic Event Manager.

Installing the Standard Window Event Handler

After creating a window, you call the function `InstallStandardEventHandler()` to install the standard event handler for that window. You call `InstallStandardEventHandler()` once for each window you create. The call to `InstallStandardEventHandler()` looks something like this:

```
InstallStandardEventHandler(GetWindowEventTarger(newWindow));
```

After you install it, the standard window event handler will take care of the standard window events, including the following:

- Closing the window if the user clicks the close box (the red button in Mac OS X).
- Moving the window if the user drags the title bar at the top of the window.
- Resizing the window if the user drags the grow box at the bottom of the window.
- Zooming the window if the user clicks the zoom box (the green button in Mac OS X).
- Collapsing the window (or restoring it if the window was collapsed) if the user clicks the collapse box.
- Minimizing the window and placing it in the dock at the bottom of the screen if the user clicks the yellow button in Mac OS X.
- Activating and deactivating windows.
- Providing standard responses for controls in windows, such as scrollbars.

Because our game's windows consist of only the content area, the game does not benefit much from the standard window event handler. If your game uses standard Macintosh windows, the standard window event handler will simplify your window event handling.

Installing the Standard Application Event Handler

All you have to do to use the standard application event handler is to call the function `RunApplicationEventLoop()`. The `RunApplicationEventLoop()` automatically installs the standard application event handler. The following function shows an event loop using Carbon events:

```
void GameApp::EventLoop(void)
{
        RunApplicationEventLoop();
}
```

Compare this EventLoop() function to the one I wrote earlier in this chapter that used the Classic Event Manager. I'm sure that you found the Carbon event version easier to follow.

After you call the RunApplicationEventLoop() function, the Carbon Event Manager waits for an event, doing nothing if there are no events to process. When an event occurs, the Carbon Event Manager wakes up and routes the event to the appropriate event handler. The Carbon Event Manager will keep waiting for events and then routing them until you break out of the event loop.

When you install the standard application event handler, it will handle the standard events for an application, including the following:

- Handling the user switching applications and quitting your application.
- Telling your application when the user chooses a menu item, saving you from writing code that checks whether the user held the Cmd key while pressing another key.
- Opening and closing menus. For example, if the user clicks the File menu, the list of menu items in the File menu (New, Open, Save, and so on) will appear.

Defining Menu Commands

The standard event handlers contain most of the standard menu commands (such as New, Save, Open, Cut, and Paste) in an application. However, there is one standard menu command you will have to define yourself: the Quit command. In addition, you must define menu commands for any game-specific menu items, such as a menu item to configure your game's controls. It is possible to define menu commands and use the Classic Event Manager. However, defining menu commands is mandatory when using Carbon events, which is why I placed this section with the Carbon events material.

Defining the Quit Command

On every version of Mac OS up through Mac OS 9, the File menu contained the Quit menu item, which was used to quit the application. In Mac OS X, Apple moved the Quit menu item out of the File menu and into the Application menu. If your program runs on a machine running Mac OS 8 or 9 (the only versions of Mac OS earlier than OS X that can use Carbon events), you must register the Quit menu command so that the operating system quits the application when the user selects Quit from the File menu. The Apple-supplied event handlers will tell you when the user selects Quit from the Applications menu in Mac OS X.

To register the Quit menu command, call the function SetMenuItemCommandID(). Here's the code to register the Quit menu command:

```
// kFileMenu stands for the resource ID of the File menu.
// kQuitMenuItem stands for the number of the Quit menu item.
SetMenuItemCommandID(GetMenuRef(kFileMenu), kQuitMenuItem, kHICommandQuit);
```

Defining Game-Specific Menu Commands

To define a menu command for one of your game's menu items, you must first create a menu command. Your menu command is a four-character code. Apple reserves all the codes with all-capital and all-small letters; you can use any other codes. Here's how a menu command code to configure the controls might look:

```
Const MenuCommand kCommandConfigureControls = FOUR_CHAR_CODE ('Cnfg');
```

After you have a menu command code, you call SetMenuItemCommandID() to register your menu command with the standard event handlers. The SetMenuItemCommandID() takes three parameters, as shown in Table 9-9.

Table 9-9 SetMenuCommandID( ) Parameters

Parameter	Description
inMenu	The menu containing the menu item whose command we want to set.
inItem	The item number of the menu item whose command we want to set.
inCommandID	The menu command code we want to set.

Defining a command to configure the controls in an Options menu for your game would look like this:

```
SetMenuItemCommandID(GetMenuRef(kOptionsMenu), kConfigureControlsMenuItem,
                     kCommandConfigureControls);
```

Breaking Out of the Carbon Event Loop

When the player quits your game, you break out of the Carbon event loop by calling the function `QuitApplicationEventLoop()`.

Creating Your Own Carbon Event Handlers

Although the standard Carbon event handlers will satisfy most game programmers' needs, you may have to handle some events in a nonstandard way. If so, you will have to write your own Carbon event handlers.

Determining Which Events to Handle

It's impossible for me to predict what events your game will have to handle in such a way as to require a special event handler. I suggest that you start with the standard Carbon event handlers. When an event in your game is handled in an unsatisfactory way, you can add that event to the list of events your event handler will handle.

When you have assembled the final list of events you must handle, you have to decide what type of event handler to write. Your decision will most likely be between an application and a window event handler. The question to ask is whether the window or application is more appropriate for handling the events you need to handle. Mouse clicks and key presses inside a window's content region are good candidates for a window event handler. Application event handlers are best for handling menu selections. If you're not sure, make the event handler an application event handler.

> **NOTE**
>
> The event handlers you write work in conjunction with the standard event handlers; they do not replace the standard event handlers. Your event handlers should contain only the events you have to handle. Any events your handler doesn't handle will filter to the standard event handler.

After you've decided what events your handler will handle, you create an array of type `EventTypeSpec`, which contains the events to handle. The `EventTypeSpec` type has two fields: an event class and an event kind. Table 9-10 lists the event classes. You use the mouse, keyboard, window, and command classes most often.

Table 9-10   Carbon Event Classes

Class*	Description
Mouse	Mouse events.
Keyboard	Low-level keyboard events.
TextInput	Text input events.
Application	Application-related events, such as launching, quitting, suspending, and resuming applications.
EPPC	Apple events.
Menu	Menu-related events, such as enabling and disabling menu items.
Window	Window-related events, such as moving, resizing, and closing windows.
Control	Events for user interfaces controls such as scrollbars, buttons, and check boxes.
Command	Command events. The actions you perform when the user selects a menu item—such as quitting when the user selects Quit—are `Command` events.
Tablet	Events generated by drawing tablets.
Volume	Events involved with file volumes, such as inserting and ejecting a CD-ROM.

* All the event classes have the prefix `kEventClass`.

> **NOTE**
>
> An event handler class is not limited to the events of its class; for example, a window event handler can handle more than window events. You can write an application event handler that handles mouse events and a window event handler that handles keyboard events. You can even write an application event handler that handles window events. Just because a particular class of event handler (application or window, for example) can handle any type of event does not mean that class should handle any type of event. The advice I gave earlier about which events a particular class of event handler should handle still applies.

The event kind is the specific event. There are too many event kinds to list here, but examples are `kEventMouseMoved` for a mouse moved event and `kEventWindowClickContentRgn` for a mouse click in a window's content region. The header file `CarbonEvents.h`, included with the Carbon SDK, contains a list of all the Carbon events.

> **NOTE**
>
> There are no update Carbon events. Instead, there is a draw content event, `kEventWindowDrawContent`. Because the draw content event tells your program to redraw the contents of the window, it works similarly to an update event in the Classic Event Manager.

Here's an example of an event list for a window event handler that will handle mouse down and mouse scroll-wheel movement events:

```
EventTypeSpec windowEventList[ ] = { {kEventClassMouse, kEventMouseDown},
                    {kEventClassMouse, kEventMouseWheelMoved}};
```

Installing the Handlers

To install an application event handler, call the function `InstallApplicationEventHandler()`. The `InstallApplicationEventHandler()` function takes five parameters, as shown in Table 9-11.

Table 9-11	InstallApplicationEventHandler() Parameters
Parameter	**Description**
handlerUPP	The event handler you are installing.
numTypes	The number of event types the handler will handle.
typeList	The list of event types the event handler will handle.
userData	Data you want to pass to the event handler goes here.
handlerRef	A data reference to the event handler. You need this reference to add events to or remove events from the event handler. You also need this reference to uninstall the event handler.

To install a window event handler, call, you guessed it, `InstallWindowEventHandler()`. The `InstallWindowEventHandler()` takes six parameters, as shown in Table 9-12.

Table 9-12 `InstallWindowEventHandler()` Parameters

Parameter	Description
theWindow	The window for which you are installing the event handler.
handlerUPP	The event handler you are installing.
numTypes	The number of event types the handler will handle.
typeList	The list of event types the event handler will handle.
userData	Data you want to pass to the event handler goes here.
handlerRef	A data reference to the event handler. You need this reference to add events to or remove events from the event handler. You also need this reference to uninstall the event handler.

Writing the Handler

If you are going to write your own Carbon event handler, it must take the following form:

```
static pascal OSStatus MyEventHandler (EventHandlerCallRef myHandlerChain,
                    EventRef event, void* userData)
```

Carbon event handlers must be static functions that use Pascal calling conventions and return a variable of type `OSStatus`. A Carbon event handler takes three parameters, as shown in Table 9-13.

Table 9-13   Event Handler Parameters

Parameter	Data Type	Description
myHandlerChain	EventHandlerCallRef	The hierarchy of event handlers that could handle this event. This parameter is useful if you want to call another event handler in your event handler.
event	eventRef	The event.
userData	void *	Holds any user data you specified when you installed the event handler.

In the event handler, you would call the function GetEventKind() to determine what event occurred. Then you would have a switch statement with cases for all the events the handler will handle. Here's what an event handler that supports multi-button mice and mouse scroll-wheel movement might look like:

```
static pascal OSStatus GameApp::WindowEventHandler(EventHandlerCallRef
                                    myHandlerChain, EventRef event,
                                    void* userData)
{
      UInt32 whatHappened;
      OSStatus result;

      whatHappened = GetEventKind(event);

      switch (whatHappened) {
             case kEventMouseDown:
                    result = HandleMouseDown(event);
                    break;

             case kEventMouseWheelMoved:
                    result = HandleMouseWheelMoved(event);
                    break;

             // Place any other events you want to handle here.
```

```
        default:
            // If nobody handled the event, it gets handled
            // by the application event handler.
            result = eventNotHandledErr;
            break;
    }
    return result;
}
```

Supporting Multibutton Mice

The event handler function we wrote in the previous section tells us that a mouse button was pressed. To support multibutton mice, we must find out which button the player pressed. Call the function GetEventParameter() to determine which mouse button the player pressed. The GetEventParameter() function has seven parameters, as shown in Table 9-14.

Table 9-14   GetEventParameter() Parameters

Parameter	Description
inEvent	The event containing the parameter we want.
inName	The name of the parameter we want.
inDesiredType	The type of parameter we want GetEventParameter() to give us.
outActualType	The actual parameter type GetEventParameter() gives us. Use nil if you don't care about the parameter type GetEventParameter() returns.
inBufferSize	The desired size of the data GetEventParameter() returns to us.
outActualSize	The actual size of the data GetEventParameter() returns to us. Use nil if you don't care about the actual size.
ioBuffer	GetEventParameter() will return the parameter here.

For a mouse down event, use the value kEventParamMouseButton for the inName parameter. Use the value typeMouseButton for the inDesiredType parameter. Use the value sizeof(EventMouseButton) for the inBufferSize parameter, and use a pointer to a variable of type EventMouseButton for the ioBuffer parameter. The ioBuffer parameter tells you which mouse button the user pressed. The following function shows you how to determine which mouse button the player pressed:

```
OSStatus GameApp::HandleMouseDown(EventRef event)
{
      OSStatus result;
      EventMouseButton buttonPressed;

      // Find out which button was pressed.
            result = GetEventParameter (event, kEventParamMouseButton,
                        typeMouseButton, NULL, sizeof(EventMouseButton),
                        NULL, &buttonPressed);

      switch (buttonPressed) {
            case kEventMouseButtonPrimary:
            // The button on a one button mouse or
            // the left button on a multi-button mouse was pressed.
            // The HandleLeftMouseButtonClick() function is game specific.
                  result = HandleLeftMouseButtonClick(event);
                  break;

            case kEventMouseButtonSecondary:
            // The right button on a two or three button mouse was pressed.
            // The HandleRightMouseButtonClick() function is game specific.
                  result = HandleRightMouseButtonClick(event);
                  break;

            case kEventMouseButtonTertiary:
            // The center button on a three button mouse was pressed.
            // The HandleCenterMouseButtonClick() function is game specific.
                  result = HandleCenterMouseButtonClick(event);
                  break;

            // Handle any additional mouse buttons you want to check.

            default:
                  result = eventNotHandledErr;
```

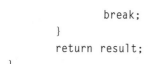

```
        break;
    }
    return result;
}
```

Supporting Scroll Wheels

To support scroll wheels, you must call GetEventParameter() to determine the axis along which the scroll wheel moved. For axis determination, use the value kEventParamMouseWheelAxis for the inName parameter. Use the value typeMouseWheelAxis for the inDesiredType parameter. Use the value sizeof(MouseWheelAxis) for the inBufferSize parameter, and use a pointer to a variable of type EventMouseWheelAxis for the ioBuffer parameter. The ioBuffer parameter tells you the axis along which the wheel moved. The following function shows you how to determine the axis along which the scroll wheel moved:

```
OSStatus GameApp::HandleMouseWheelMoved (EventRef event)
{
    OSStatus result;
    EventMouseWheelAxis axisOfMovement;

    // Find out along which axis the scroll wheel moved.
        result = GetEventParameter (event, kEventParamMouseWheelAxis,
                    typeMouseWheelAxis, NULL, sizeof(MouseWheelAxis),
                    NULL, &buttonPressed);

    switch (axisOfMovement) {
        case kEventMouseWheelAxisX:
            result = HandleMouseWheelMovedXAxis(event);
            break;

        case kEventMouseWheelAxisY:
            result = HandleMouseWheelMovedYAxis (event);
            break;

        // Handle any additional axes you want to check.

        default:
            result = eventNotHandledErr;
        break;
    }
```

```
        return result;
}
```

After you have determined the axis of movement, you must find how much the user moved the scroll wheel. Doing this involves yet another call to `GetEventParameter()`. To read delta movement, use the value `kEventParamMouseWheelDelta` for the `inName` parameter. Use the value `typeLongInteger` for the `inDesiredType` parameter. Use the value `sizeof(long)` for the `inBufferSize` parameter, and use a pointer to a variable of type `long` for the `ioBuffer` parameter. The `ioBuffer` parameter tells you how far the user moved the scroll wheel. The following example demonstrates how to calculate the amount of wheel movement:

```
OSStatus GameApp::HandleMouseWheelMovedYAxis (EventRef event)
{
        OSStatus result;
        long amountOfMovement;

        result = GetEventParameter (event, kEventParamMouseWheelDelta,
                            typeLongInteger, NULL, sizeof(long), NULL,
                            &amountOfMovement);

// At this point, your game does what it needs to do with the wheel movement.
}
```

Handling Menu Selections

The standard application event handler tells your game when the user selects a menu item, but your game is responsible for handling the event. For example, if the player chooses to open a saved game file, your game is responsible for bringing up the dialog box to let the user choose the file to open and for opening the file.

You must write an event handler function to handle menu selections. Normally, you write an application event handler for menu selections, but you can write a window event handler if the menu selection affects the window. To determine what menu item the user chose, call the function `GetEventParameter()`. For menu selection, use the value `kEventParamDirectObject` for the `inName` parameter. Use the value `typeHICommand` for the `inDesiredType` parameter. Use the value `sizeof(HICommand)` for the `inBufferSize` parameter, and use a pointer to a variable of type `HICommand` for the `ioBuffer` parameter. The `ioBuffer` parameter tells you which menu item the user selected.

After calling `GetEventParameter()`, you perform a `switch` statement on the menu selections (plus any other events) the event handler supports, as you can see in the following code:

```
static pascal OSStatus GameApp::MenuEventHandler(EventHandlerCallRef
                                myHandlerChain, EventRef event,
                                void* userData)
{
    HICommand menuCommand;
    OSStatus result;

    GetEventParameter(event, kEventParamDirectObject, typeHICommand, nil,
                    sizeof(HICommand), nil, &menuCommand);

    // The commandID field of the HICommand structure tells you
    // the menu command.
    switch (menuCommand.commandID) {
        case kHICommandAbout:
            result = DisplayAboutBox();
            break;

        case kCommandConfigureControls:
            result = ConfigureControls();
            break;

        case kHICommandQuit:
            result = Quit();
            break;

        // Place any other menu items you want to handle here.

        default:
            // If nobody handled the event, it gets handled
            // by the standard application event handler.
            result = eventNotHandledErr;
            break;
    }
    return result;
}
```

Event Loop Timers

An event loop timer is a trigger that tells the Carbon Event Manager to call a function that you supply. As the programmer, you get to specify how often the event loop timer fires, which makes event loop timers a powerful tool for games. A hockey game might create an event loop timer that fires once per second to take one second off the game clock. Your game could run at a constant frame rate on all computers by creating an event loop timer that calls your game's main loop. You tell the event loop timer to fire at the frame rate you desire.

As the programmer, you must do two things to use event loop timers in your games. First, you must install the event loop timer. Second, you must write the routine that the Carbon Event Manager calls each time the timer fires.

Installing an Event Loop Timer

For the Carbon Event Manager to call your event loop timer, you must install it by calling the function InstallEventLoopTimer(). The InstallEventLoopTimer() function takes six parameters described in Table 9-15. You can specify the inFireDelay and inInterval parameters in seconds, minutes, hours, days, milliseconds, microseconds, and nanoseconds. To specify the parameters in seconds, use the constant kEventDurationSecond; substitute the appropriate time unit for Second if you choose a different time unit.

Table 9-15   InstallEventLoopTimer() Parameters

Parameter	Description
inEventLoopf	The event loop where we're installing the timer.
inFireDelay	The delay before the timer begins calling the timer procedure you specify in the inTimerProc parameter. A value of 0 (Apple supplies the constant kEventDurationNoWait) will cause the timer to fire immediately.
inInterval	The interval between calls to the timer procedure. If you use a value of 0, the timer will fire one time only.
inTimerProc	The function you wrote that the timer calls.
inTimerData	Data, if any, that you want to pass to the timer procedure.
outTimer	The timer that InstallEventLoopTimer() installs.

One thing to remember about the `InstallEventLoopTimer()` function is that the interval you specify in the `inInterval` parameter does not begin until the timer procedure finishes. If you tell a timer to fire every second, but the timer procedure takes 10 seconds to complete, the timer will end up firing every 11 seconds: 10 seconds to run the procedure plus a one-second delay. The following function installs an event loop timer that fires 20 times a second:

```
void GameApp::InstallTimer(void)
{
        EventLoopRef mainLoop;
        EventLoopTimerRef timer;

        mainLoop = GetMainEventLoop();

        // timerFunction is a data member of the GameApp class and has
        // data type EventLoopTimerUPP.
        // Your timer function must have the same name as the
        // function you supply toNewEventLoopTimerUPP().
        timerFunction = NewEventLoopTimerUPP(GameLoopTimerFunction);

        // Install the timer. The nil says we're not supplying any user
        // data to the timer function.
        InstallEventLoopTimer(mainLoop, kEventDurationNoWait,
                    (kEventDurationSecond / 20), timerFunction, nil, timer);
}
```

Writing an Event Loop Timer Function

Your event loop timer function must take the following form:

```
pascal void TimerAction(EventLoopTimerRef theTimer, void* userData)
```

The `pascal` at the front of the function tells the compiler to use Pascal function-calling conventions. The Carbon Event Manager routines use Pascal calling conventions, and the Carbon Event Manager expects your timer function to do the same.

You can choose your own function name instead of `TimerAction()`, but remember that your function name must match the function name you supplied to `NewEventLoopTimerUPP()` when you installed the timer.

As long as you follow the proper form of a timer function, you're free to do what you want in the timer function. The following timer function runs a game's main loop:

```
pascal void GameApp::GameLoopTimerFunction(EventLoopTimerRef theTimer,
                            void* userData)
{
        GameLoop();
}
```

Removing an Event Loop Timer

When the player quits your game—or whenever you want to stop using your event loop timer—you must remove the timer. Removing an event loop timer is easy; just call RemoveEventLoopTimer(), which you can see in the following example:

```
void GameApp::RemoveTimer(void)
{
        // timerFunction is a data member of the GameApp class and has
        // data type EventLoopTimerUPP.
        RemoveEventLoopTimer(timerFunction);
}
```

Summary

This chapter covered a variety of topics that, on first glance, seem unrelated. On further review, you can see that all the topics in this chapter are related to reading the keyboard and mouse. I began the chapter by covering the low-level functions you use to read the keyboard and mouse. Then I moved on to reading the keyboard and mouse using the Classic Event Manager, which forced me to cover general event handling. From there, I covered the use of Carbon events to read multibutton mice and scroll wheels. In the discussion of Carbon events, I covered the use of Carbon event timers, which let you specify how often the Carbon Event Manager calls one of your routines.

Most of the chapter discussed event handling. You have two ways of doing your event handling: using traditional Mac OS events and using Carbon events. Carbon events are much easier to use than the old-school Mac OS events, but they require Mac OS 8.6 or higher. If you don't plan on supporting older Mac OS versions, I highly recommend using Carbon events.

The main sample program I wrote for this chapter uses the keyboard to move the character around the screen. I also wrote two event shell programs, one for traditional Mac events and one for Carbon events. You can use these programs (which you'll find on the CD-ROM that accompanies this book) as templates for handling events in your games, saving yourself a lot of typing in the process.

CHAPTER 10

Sound

Up to this point, we've spent most of our time covering graphics. Although graphics are an undeniably important part of the game-playing experience, audio is also important. Movie directors use sound to heighten the tension and suspense in a horror movie. As a game developer, you can use sound in a similar way to enhance the atmosphere of your game and make your game more immersive. In this chapter, I will teach you the basics of Macintosh sound so that you can excite your players' ears as well as their eyes.

A Sound Introduction

Apple provides the game programmer with two options for working with sound. The Sound Manager gives the programmer low-level control over the audio in his programs. It allows you to do high-level actions such as play, pause, resume, and stop sounds, but the Sound Manager also lets you do lower-level actions with your sound. With the Sound Manager, you can do things such as schedule sounds to play at a later time, delay sounds, change the sample rate of sounds, and stream sounds from a CD-ROM.

If you want to work with audio at a higher level, then QuickTime is for you. Built on the Sound Manager, QuickTime is Apple's multimedia technology. QuickTime provides you with an easy way to play, pause, resume, and stop sounds. Many games don't need to do more with sound than this; if your game has only these basic audio needs, QuickTime is perfect for you. QuickTime also provides file conversion capabilities so that your game can work with more sound formats than it can if you use the Sound Manager.

Sound Formats

The next sections detail some of the more popular ways of storing sound and music for Macintosh games.

Sound Resources

Sound resources contain sound commands and sound data. In your game, you can have one sound resource for each sound effect and a musical track. The advantages of sound resources are that you can store them inside your application file and that they are easy to play through the Sound Manager. By having the sounds inside the application file, you don't have to worry about the user/player moving or deleting external sound files. The disadvantage of sound resources is that they are limited to 16MB each. Because sound resources are so easy to play, they are an excellent choice to store your sound effects. Most sound effects last only a few seconds so the 16MB limit won't be a problem. Refer to Chapter 15, "Files," for more information about resources.

AIFF Files

AIFF stands for Audio Interchange File Format. AIFF files are Apple's standard file format for external sound files, and they are not subject to the 16MB limit of sound resources. This makes AIFF files a good choice for longer sound sequences. AIFF files are the only external sound files the Sound Manager supports. If you need to use the Sound Manager's low-level functions in your game, you're stuck with AIFF files.

AIFF files provide high-quality sound, but the file sizes are large, up to 10MB for a minute of sound. You can compress the files by a factor of 3 to 1 or by a factor of 6 to 1, but the sound quality goes way down when you compress the files. It's also possible to write your own compression algorithm, but that subject is beyond the scope of this book.

MP3 Files

I'm sure that most of you have heard of MP3 files, but for those of you who haven't, MP3 files are the most popular way of storing music for online distribution. If you trade music with your friends online, you're probably trading MP3 files.

Now it's time for a little information you may not have known about MP3 files. MP3 is short for MPEG Audio Layer 3 (MPEG stands for Moving Pictures Experts Group, which is a standards committee for audio and video—but I'm sure you knew that already); MP3 is a standard for audio file compression. MP3 files store audio at a sample rate ranging from 1 to 16 kilobytes per second. The highest quality sample rate, 16 kilobytes per second, provides a sound quality nearly equal to an audio compact disc but takes 12 times *less* storage space than a compact disc. A person with a 56K modem can download an MP3 file containing a three-minute song in less than 10 minutes at the highest sample rate. Musicians realized the power of MP3 and used MP3 files to get their music out to potential listeners worldwide, starting the MP3 boom.

The advantages of MP3 files are the high compression of data and the MP3 file format's popularity. Because MP3 files are so popular, your game can allow players to substitute their favorite MP3 files for the MP3 files you use for the music in your game. The technical disadvantage of MP3 files is that MP3 files take a lot of CPU time to process compared to other formats. This isn't much of a problem for the person who wants to listen to music while surfing the Internet, but it *is* a problem for games. Games like to use the CPU to do bizarre things such as draw backgrounds, animate characters, detect collisions, and make computer-controlled characters act intelligently. If you want your game to run on older Power Macs (pre-G3 systems), you shouldn't use MP3 files, but MP3 files are fine for systems built in 1998 or later.

A disadvantage of MP3 files for Mac programmers is that the Sound Manager does not support MP3 files. To play MP3 files in your game, you must use QuickTime. If all you have to do with sounds and music is play, pause, resume, and stop them, using QuickTime will work for you. If you have to manipulate sounds at a lower level, you'll have to use the Sound Manager and AIFF files or sound resources.

MIDI Files

A MIDI (Musical Instrument Digital Interface) file stores music created by a musical synthesizer or other MIDI device. Rather than storing the actual sound, a MIDI file stores a list of instruments and notes. The sound hardware (or a piece of software if the sound hardware does not contain a synthesizer) takes the contents of the MIDI file and creates the sound.

Because a MIDI file contains no actual sound, the file size is small, which is the main advantage of using MIDI files. The disadvantage of using MIDI files is that the sound quality depends on the user's sound hardware, which is a big problem for Macintosh computers. The built-in sound on Windows computers is so bad that every computer comes with a sound card. The sound cards usually contain a built-in synthesizer so it's easy to get high-quality sound from MIDI files on Windows computers. Macintosh computers have better built-in sound, so most users don't purchase a sound card. However, the Macintosh's standard audio hardware does not possess a synthesizer, so most Macs cannot play MIDI files in hardware. Instead, most Macs have to use QuickTime, which is a software-only solution, to play MIDI files.

MOD Files

MOD(ule) files originated on the Amiga computer and were a popular way to store background music in computer games in the early 1990s. MOD files contain sequences of notes inside pattern lists. These sequences can be played repeatedly and can be played in different orders. Because the sequences can be played in different orders, you can play a high variety of music with a low number of sequences. Having a low number of sequences means that MOD files take up little space compared to other sound file formats. The problem with MOD files is that the Mac OS does not directly support them. You must use an external MOD-playing library to play MOD files in your games.

Sampled Sounds

Unless you happen to possess the ability to compose music, you will most likely use sampled sounds for your game's music and sound effects. When you use sampled sound, you're playing a previously recorded sound. The alternative to using sampled sound is playing individual notes, which requires knowledge of music that few game programmers possess.

An example of sampling sound is copying a portion of your favorite Backstreet Boys CD, transferring it to your computer, and using it in your game. To avoid getting sued by the record company—and to maintain your self-respect—you are better off creating your game's sound with a music composition program (such as Cubase, Logic Audio Platinum, or Mixman Studio Pro) or finding a musician to record the audio samples for your game. When using sampled sounds, you have some decisions to make:

- What sample rate should I use?
- Should I use 8-bit or 16-bit sound?
- Should I use monophonic or stereo sound?

NOTE

This section assumes that you're using AIFF files or sound resources for your sounds. MIDI and MOD files store notes, so they don't use sampled sounds. MP3 files have their own sampling rates ranging from 1 to 16 kilobytes per second.

Sample Rates

Do you remember graphing equations in algebra class? Given an equation, you had to figure out y when x is 0, figure out x when y is 0, and then plot some other points. Then you would draw a line that connected the points, graphing the equation in the process. Figure 10-1 shows the graph of the equation x + y = 5.

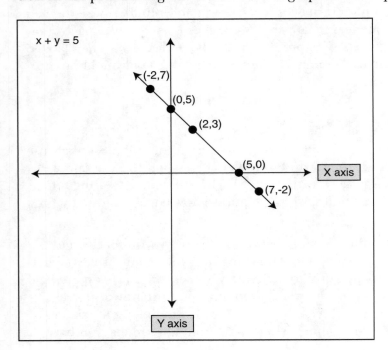

Figure 10-1

A graph of the equation
x + y = 5

Digitally sampling sound works in a way similar to graphing an equation. The analog sound corresponds to the equation. The digital sound sampler plots points of the sound and puts them together to re-create the sound. Figure 10-2 shows a digitally sampled sound wave.

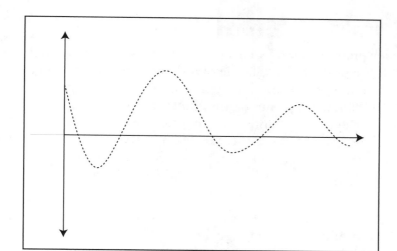

Figure 10-2

A digitally sampled sound wave

Just as plotting more points produces a more accurate graph of an algebraic equation, taking more samples produces a more accurate digital sample of the analog sound. On the Macintosh, you can sample sounds at 44,100, 22,050, or 11,025 samples per second. Compact discs sample music at the 44,100 samples per second rate, and this sample rate produces the highest quality sound. The 22,050 and 11,025 sample rates exist to save space at the expense of lower-quality sound.

The sample rate also affects the sound frequency you can record. When digitally sampling a sound, you can record frequencies up to half the sample rate. If you use a sampling rate of 44,100 samples per second, you can record frequencies up to 22,050 hertz. Sounds with frequencies above 22,050 hertz are clipped to 22,050 hertz. Because the range of human hearing is 20 to 20,000 hertz, clipping sounds to 22,050 hertz won't impact the listener's audio experience.

Lower sampling rates can affect the listening experience, however. A 22,050 samples per second sampling rate records frequencies up to 11,025 hertz, which means that the listener won't get the full impact of the high notes. If you're going to include opera music with your game, you should sample it at 44,100 samples per second. An 11,025 samples per second sampling rate records frequencies up to 5,512 hertz. Any sound above 5,512 hertz is clipped to 5,512, which means that the 11,025 samples per second sampling rate cannot accurately record more than 70 percent of the range of sounds people can hear.

8-Bit versus 16-Bit Sound

When a digital sound sampler plots the points of a sound, it stores an integer representing the amplitude of the sound. The amplitude of a sound is its relative loudness. For example, shouting has a higher amplitude than whispering. Heavy metal music has a higher amplitude than new age music. Amplitude does not measure the actual loudness of a sound; the volume control of the listening device (stereo, TV, or computer) determines the actual loudness. If I listen to heavy metal music at the lowest volume level and listen to new age music at the highest volume level, the new age music is going to sound louder even though the heavy metal music has a higher amplitude.

Eight-bit sound allows for 256 different amplitude values ranging from −128 to 127. 16-bit sound allows for 65,536 amplitude values ranging from −32768 to 32767. An amplitude of 0 means silence; higher absolute values denote higher amplitudes. Positive values represent outward speaker motion, negative values represent inward speaker motion, and 0 represents the speaker at rest. If you've been to a party or concert where loud music was playing, you may have seen the speakers vibrate. The vibrating visually demonstrates inward and outward speaker motion.

Figure 10-3 shows a sample sound wave at 8 bits and at 16 bits. As you can see, an 8-bit sound with amplitude 127 has the same amplitude as a 16-bit sound with amplitude 32,767. An 8-bit sound with amplitude 100 will have much higher amplitude than a 16-bit sound with amplitude 100. Moving from amplitude value 100 to value 101 produces a much higher amplitude change in 8-bit sound than the same shift does in 16-bit sound. Eight-bit and 16-bit sound cover the same spectrum of amplitudes, but 16-bit sound covers the spectrum with a larger number of degrees: 65,536 with 16-bit sound versus 256 with 8-bit sound. Sixteen-bit sound data gives you finer control of a sound's amplitude, producing higher-quality sound than 8-bit sound, but it takes up twice the space.

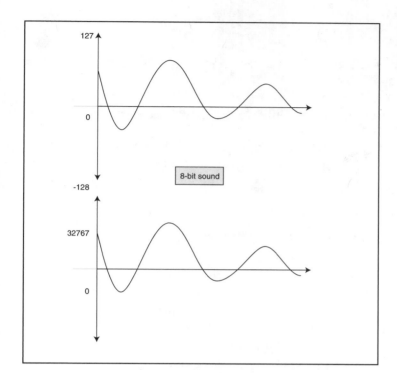

Figure 10-3

A sample sound wave shown at 8 bits and 16 bits

Monophonic versus Stereo Sound

Monophonic sound has one channel of sound while stereo sound has two channels. If you have a stereo with two speakers, monophonic sound comes out of only
one of the speakers. Stereo sound comes out of both speakers. The Macintosh
takes a monophonic sound and splits it between the speakers if the user/player has
two speakers on his computer. In that case, a sound with volume level 6 has a volume level 3 coming out of both speakers. Stereo sound takes up twice the space of
monophonic sound because it has twice the number of channels.

What Options Are Right for Me?

When choosing your sample rate, sound data size, and number of channels, you
must choose between sound quality and storage space. Stereo sound sounds better
than monophonic sound, but it takes up twice the space. Sampling at 44,100 times
per second produces a better sound than a sample rate of 11,025 samples per second, but the higher sample rate takes up four times as much space. Table 10-1
shows how much space one minute of sound takes up at the highest, middle, and
lowest quality of sound.

Table 10-1   Storage Requirements for One Minute of Audio

Variable	Highest Quality	Middle Quality	Lowest Quality
Samples per second	44,100	22,050	11,025
Bytes per sample	2 (16-bit sound)	1 (8-bit sound)	1 (8-bit sound)
Channels	2 (stereo)	2 (stereo)	1 (mono)
Seconds per minute	60	60	60
Needed Storage	10,584,000 bytes	2,646,000 bytes	661,500 bytes

As you can see from the table, one minute of CD-quality sound takes up approximately 10MB of space. If you're going to have people download your game from the Internet, you're going to either have to limit the amount of music in your game or use lower-quality sound in your game. The choice is yours.

To save space, many games use looping sounds to play background music. With *looping sound*, you take a short musical sequence, 15 to 30 seconds long, and play it repeatedly. By using short sequences, you can create a lot of musical variety without taking up much space. In the space of one 3-minute song, you can store six 30-second musical loops.

If looping sounds doesn't save you enough space, you'll have to make the difficult decision of reducing the sound's quality. Here's what I would recommend you do to save space:

1. Reduce the sample rate to 22,050 samples per second.
2. If reducing the sample rate isn't enough, switch to monophonic sound. Switching to monophonic sound reduces your sound quality in half, but going from 16-bit to 8-bit sound will reduce your sound quality by a factor of up to 256.
3. If you have to save even more space, then switch to 8-bit sound.
4. As a last resort, reduce the sample rate to 11,025 samples per second.

No matter what choices you make regarding the sample rate, 8-bit versus 16-bit sound and stereo versus monophonic sound for your game, record the sounds at the highest quality rate, 44,100 samples per second of 16-bit stereo sound. Then use a sound conversion program, such as SoundApp, to convert the sound to suit your needs. Taking a lower-quality sound and converting it to a higher-quality one sounds worse than recording it at higher quality in the first place.

Programming Sound with the Sound Manager

As mentioned earlier in this chapter, there are two ways to program audio on the Macintosh: the Sound Manager and QuickTime. The headline for this section should give you a clue as to which technology I will cover first.

The GameSound Class

Throughout this book, I create C++ classes to illustrate concepts in code. In this chapter, I'm making a GameSound class for our game's audio needs. To make the code in the rest of the chapter easier to read, here are the data members for our GameSound class:

```
class GameSound
{
        protected:
                SndChannelPtr channel;
                SndListHandle soundData;
};
```

We will have one GameSound object for each sound in our game. A GameSound object consists of a sound channel and the sound to play. As you read through this chapter, you will notice that most of the Sound Manager routines take a sound channel as a parameter. We will be passing the channel variable to those routines. The soundData variable contains the sound we will be playing. The GameSound class wouldn't be much of a class if there were no sound to play.

Playing a Sound

Playing a sound resource with the Sound Manager is quite simple. One call to the function SndPlay(), and you're finished. The SndPlay() function takes three parameters, which are described in Table 10-2.

Table 10-2   SndPlay() Parameters

Parameter	Description
chan	The sound channel from which we play the sound
sndHndl	The sound to play
async	Do we play the sound asynchronously? For games, pass the value true. If we pass false, everything else stops when a sound plays. Because we want the game to continue playing while the sound plays, we want the sound to play asynchronously.

Because we want our sounds to play asynchronously, we have to do one thing before calling SndPlay(): manually create a sound channel. If we don't, the Sound Manager will create one for us and play the sound synchronously. Playing the sound synchronously is bad for games because nothing can happen in the game until the synchronous sound stops playing. A sound channel contains a queue of sound commands plus other information the Sound Manager needs to play sounds.

To create the sound channel to play our sound, we have to call the function SndNewChannel(). For our game, we will have one sound channel for the background music plus one channel per sound effect. Each channel can play only one sound at a time, so it's easier to give each sound its own channel rather than shuttling sounds in and out of a single channel. When the player kills an enemy, he wants to hear the sound effect immediately. He doesn't want to wait for your game to load the enemy-dying sound effect from disk. Having all the sound effects in RAM gives the player the instant gratification he desires. If we were to have hundreds of sounds in our game, we wouldn't be able to have one sound channel per sound effect, but we won't have too many sound effects so there won't be a problem. The number of channels you can have open at one time depend on the CPU and the amount of RAM on your computer, but you can assume a minimum of eight channels. The SndNewChannel() function takes four parameters, which are shown in Table 10-3.

Table 10-3   SndNewChannel() Parameters

Parameter	Description
chan	The sound channel that SndNewChannel() creates
synth	The type of sound data to play in the channel. Pass the value sampledSynth for sampled sound data, which is the only option available in Carbon.
init	The desired initialization parameters for the channel. Pass the value initStereo to create a stereo channel. Pass the value initMono to create a monophonic channel.
userRoutine	A callback routine for the channel to call when a sound finishes playing. If you do not have a callback routine, pass nil as the parameter. We will discuss callback routines later in this chapter.

The following sample code creates a sound channel:

```
void GameSound::Create(void)
{
      OSErr error;

      // Create a sound channel with a queue
      // length of 128 commands.
      channel = (SndChannelPtr)NewPtr(sizeof(SndChannel));
      channel->qLength = stdQLength;

      error = SndNewChannel(&channel, sampledSynth, initStereo, nil);
}
```

As you can see from the source code, I created a sound channel with the standard queue length of 128 commands. I can't imagine that you would need a larger command queue (the queue normally contains only a handful of sound commands at one time), but if you do, you can substitute your own queue length for stdQLength.

To retrieve our sound data, we have to read it from disk. If you have one sound per sound channel, then you must read the sound data once. If you want to use a single channel to play more than one sound, you must read the sound data each time you change the sound in the channel. Here's the code to read our sound data:

```
void GameSound::ReadSoundData(short soundID)
{
        if (soundData != nil)
                DisposeSoundData();

        soundData = (SndListHandle)Get1Resource('snd ', soundID);
}
```

Finally, here's the code to play the sound:

```
void GameSound::Play(void)
{
        OSErr error;

        if ((channel == nil) || (soundData == nil))
                return;

        // Make sure the sound data doesn't move while
        // the sound plays.
        HLock((Handle)soundData);
        error = SndPlay(channel, soundData, kPlayAsynchronously);

}
```

While the sound is playing, your game may be doing things that allocate and deallocate memory, such as creating enemies and then disposing of them when the player kills them. To make the most efficient use of memory, the Macintosh Memory Manager may move memory around when these memory allocations and deallocations occur. The Sound Manager needs the sound data to stay in the same memory location while the sound is playing. The HLock() function tells the Memory Manager not to move the memory containing the sound data.

Sound Commands

If you want to do anything with a sound other than play it, you'll have to learn about sound commands. As a programmer, you give the Sound Manager sound commands to manipulate sounds. With sound commands, you can do things such as play, pause, resume, and stop sounds. To execute a sound command, you must do the following:

1. Fill the sound command structure.
2. Place the command in the sound channel's command queue.

The sound channel executes the commands in its queue one at a time, starting with the head of the queue.

The Sound Command Structure

The sound command structure, SndCommand, contains three fields, described in Table 10-4.

Table 10-4   SndCommand Fields

Field	Description
cmd	The command to perform
param1	First parameter
param2	Second parameter

Table 10-5 lists all the commands you can send to the Carbon Sound Manager. It's a fairly long list—21 commands—but don't be intimidated. Remember that programs other than games, such as music composition and sound editing programs, use the Sound Manager. Those other programs have different audio needs than games do, and they need the Sound Manager to support their needs. Chances are you won't need to call all the sound commands in your game.

Table 10-5   Carbon Sound Manager Commands

Command	Description
nullCmd	Do nothing.
quietCmd	Stops a sound that is currently playing
flushCmd	Flushes all sound commands in the sound channel
reInitCmd	Reinitializes a sound channel
waitCmd	Suspends processing commands in a sound channel
pauseCmd	Pauses processing commands in a sound channel. The pauseCmd command does not pause any sounds that are currently playing.
resumeCmd	Resumes processing commands in a sound channel. The resumeCmd command does not resume playing any paused sounds.
callBackCmd	Executes a callback routine
syncCmd	Synchronizes multiple channels of sound
availableCmd	Tells you whether the Sound Manager supports the initialization options specified in the command.
versionCmd	Determines which version of a sound data format is available
volumeCmd	Sets the volume of a sound channel
getVolumeCmd	Gets the current volume of a sound channel
clockComponentCmd	Turns the sound clock on or off. You normally execute this command before executing a scheduledSoundCmd.
getClockComponentCmd	Returns the current status of the sound clock
scheduledSoundCmd	Schedules a sound or a callBackCmd command to play at a later time
linkSoundComponentsCmd	Preconfigures a sound channel's components. You use this command when you create your own sound components.
soundCmd	Installs a sample sound in a sound channel
bufferCmd	Plays a buffer of sampled sound
rateMultiplierCmd	Provides a multiplier to the current playback rate, such as playing a sound at double the current rate. You use this command to pause and resume sounds.
getRateMultiplierCmd	Gets the current rate multiplier

As you look through Table 10-4 and Table 10-5, you're probably wondering what to place in the `param1` and `param2` fields of the `SndCommand` structure for each of the commands in Table 10-5. What you place in the `param1` and `param2` fields depends on the command, and the explanation for each is too long to fit in a table. In later sections of this chapter, I will show you how to execute the commands that game developers use the most.

Placing a Command in the Command Queue

After we fill the sound command data structure, we have to place the command in our sound channel's command queue so that the Sound Manager can execute the command. There are two ways to place the sound command: by calling the `SndDoCommand()` function and by calling the `SndDoImmediate()` function. `SndDoCommand()` places the command at the end of the queue, and `SndDoImmediate()` places the command at the head of the queue. In the unlikely event that the sound channel's command queue is full, `SndDoCommand()` cannot place the command in the command queue. If the command queue is full, `SndDoImmediate()` bumps the last command off the queue. Figure 10-4 shows the difference between the two functions.

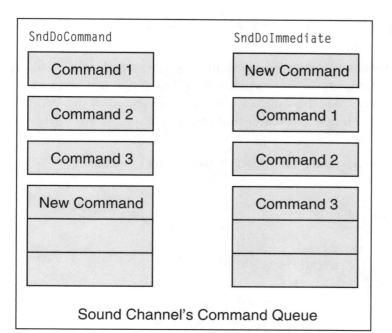

Figure 10-4

The difference between the `SndDoCommand()` *and* `SndDoImmediate()` *functions*

The decision to call SndDoCommand() or SndDoImmediate() depends on the urgency of your command. Suppose that somebody is playing your game at the office and sees the boss coming. He'll want to pause your game and switch to another program so that it looks as if he's working. If he pauses the game and your music continues playing, he'll get fired and blame you for ruining his life. To keep this from happening, you must pause the sound when the player pauses the game. Because you want the pause sound command to execute immediately, you'll call SndDoImmediate(). Less-urgent commands, such as a nullCmd, would call SndDoCommand().

Callback Functions

The Sound Manager uses callback functions to perform a specified action after a sound finishes playing. If you need the Sound Manager to do something at the end of a sound, you must write a callback function that does what you need to be done.

Using callback functions takes three steps:

1. Allocating space for the callback function when creating the sound channel.
2. Installing the callback function when playing the sound.
3. Writing the callback function itself.

Allocating Space for the Callback Function

Allocating space for the callback function is fairly simple. You just declare a variable of type SndCallBackUPP and then call the function NewSndCallBackProc(). When you create your sound channel, you pass the callback variable you created as the last parameter to SndNewChannel(). Here's a function that creates a game sound using a callback function:

```
void GameSound::CreateWithCallback(SndCallBackProcPtr theCallback)
{
        OSErr error;
        SndCallBackUPP callbackUPP;

        // Allocate space for the channel
        channel = (SndChannelPtr)NewPtr(sizeof(SndChannel));
        channel->qLength = stdQLength;

        // Create the callback function
```

```
        callbackUPP = NewSndCallBackProc(theCallback);
        error = SndNewChannel(&channel, sampledSynth, initStereo, callbackUPP);

}
```

Installing the Callback Function

Installing the callback involves creating a callback sound command (a command of type `callBackCmd`) and adding it to the channel's command queue. For the first parameter in the command, pass any non-zero value. There's a bug in the Sound Manager: If you use 0 for the first parameter, the Sound Manager calls your callback function too soon. We're going to place a pointer to the sound data in the second parameter. Because we're using C++, we will make the second parameter a pointer to a `GameSound` object that contains the sound data. If you were using C, you would either pass a pointer to the sound data (the equivalent of the `soundData` data member of the `GameSound` class) or a pointer to a programmer-defined structure containing the sound data.

As long as you have a non-zero value as the first parameter to the callback command, you can use the two parameters to pass anything you want to the callback command. For example, I can place a pointer to the sound data as the first parameter and make the second parameter 0. I can pass two dummy variables to the callback command if I want. If I have any more data I want the callback command to act on, I can pass that data as the first parameter. Just remember that you have the freedom to pass whatever you want to a callback command.

After we fill the `SndCommand` structure, we call the function `SndDoCommand()` to add the callback function to the sound channel's command queue. We use `SndDoCommand()` because we don't want the callback function to execute until the sound finishes playing. If we called `SndDoImmediate()`, the callback routine would execute immediately, and the player would never hear the sound. Here's the code to install a callback function:

```
OSErr GameSound::InstallCallback(void)
{
        OSErr error;
        SndCommand commandToPerform;

        commandToPerform.cmd = callBackCmd;
        commandToPerform.param1 = kSoundManagerID;
        commandToPerform.param2 = (long) this;
```

```
        // True means to return a result queueFull if the queue is full.
        error = SndDoCommand(channel, &commandToPerform, true);
}
```

You install the callback function
when you play the sound. Here's a
function that installs a callback function when a sound starts to play:

> **NOTE**
> In C++, the variable this is a pointer to
> the current object in a class. We use the
> value this as the second parameter so
> that the callback function will refer to
> the GameSound object that created it.

```
void GameSound::PlayRepeatedly(void)
{
        OSErr error;

        if ((channel == nil) || (soundData == nil))
                return;

        HLock((Handle)soundData);
        error = SndPlay(channel, soundData, kPlayAsynchronously);

        if (error == noErr) {
                soundPlaying = true;
                error = InstallCallback();
        }
}
```

Writing the Callback Function

A callback function must be of this form:

```
pascal void SoundCallback(SndChannelPtr theChannel, SndCommand* theCommand)
```

The pascal at the front of the function tells the compiler to use Pascal function-
calling conventions. All the Sound Manager routines have Pascal function-calling
conventions, and the Sound Manager expects your callback routine to use the same
conventions.

As long as you follow the proper form of a callback function, you're free to do
almost anything you want in the callback function. If you want to play a sound over
and over again, you use a callback function to play the sound again, like in the following function:

```
pascal void GameSound::LoopSoundCallback(SndChannelPtr theChannel,
            SndCommand* theCommand)
{
```

```
        GameSoundPtr theSound;

        // We put a pointer to a GameSound object in param2
        // when we installed the callback function.
        theSound = (GameSoundPtr)theCommand->param2;
        theSound->PlayRepeatedly();
}
```

On Mac OS 8 and 9, executing the callback generates an interrupt, which is a signal to the operating system that tells the operating system to handle the signal
immediately This means you can call only functions that are interrupt-safe (safe to
call during an interrupt) inside the callback function. Inside the callback routine,
you cannot allocate, move, or deallocate memory, and you cannot call any
Resource Manager routines because these are not interrupt-safe actions. If you use
sound resources, you cannot dispose of the resource in the callback function. Be
aware of these limitations when writing your callback routine.

Looping a Sound

When playing background music, it is common to have a segment of music loop
continuously. Sound data takes up a lot of space, and you can save space by playing
a 1-to-2–minute segment of sound repeatedly rather than having a 20-minute musical sequence. The Sound Manager gives us the capability to loop sounds.

To loop sounds, we must keep track of when a sound finishes playing. When it finishes, we replay the sound. One way to determine when a sound finishes playing is
to use a callback function, as discussed in the preceding section. When we installed
the callback routine, remember that we used the param2 field of the callBackCmd to
store a pointer to a GameSound object. To play the sound again, we have to get the
pointer to the object.

If you find using callback routines to be a major hassle, there is another way to
determine when a sound finishes playing. You can check the sound channel's status
by calling SndChannelStatus(). You check the status to see whether the channel is
busy. If the channel is not busy, there are no commands in the queue, and you
know that the sound has finished playing. Here's some code that checks whether a
sound is playing:

```
Boolean GameSound::IsSoundPlaying(void)
{
        SCStatus theStatus;
        OSErr error;
```

```
        error = SndChannelStatus(channel, sizeof(SCStatus), &theStatus);
        if (error == noErr) {
                return(theStatus.scChannelBusy);
        }
        return(false);
}
```

In your game's event loop, you would call the function IsSoundPlaying(). If the
function returns false, call the Play() function to play the sound again. Using the
IsSoundPlaying() function is a little slower than using a callback routine because
you have to constantly check the sound's status with the IsSoundPlaying() function.
That's the price you have to pay if you don't want to deal with callback functions.

Setting a Sound's Volume

To set a sound's volume, you use (surprise) a volume command (a command of
type volumeCmd). You put 0 in the param1 field because the Sound Manager ignores
the param1 field of a volume command. In the param2 field, you put the volume.
What complicates matters is that there are two channels of sound—left and right—
for you to assign volume, but the param2 field is one value, not two. What you have
to do is combine the left and right channel's volume into one value, as you can see
in the following code:

```
void GameSound::SetVolume(short leftVolume, short rightVolume)
{
        // Sets the sound's volume. You pass the volume for the left
        // and right channels. The value for the left and right channel
        // volume can range from 0 to 256.

        SndCommand commandToExecute;

        // Combine left and right channel values in the param2 field
        // The high 16 bits are the right channel's volume, and
        // the low 16 bits are the left channel's volume.
        commandToExecute.cmd = volumeCmd;
        commandToExecute.param1 = 0;
        commandToExecute.param2 = (rightVolume << 16) | leftVolume;

        SndDoImmediate(channel, &commandToExecute);
}
```

The volumes for the left and right channels are 16-bit numbers with values ranging from 0 to 256. The two 16-bit numbers must be combined into a single 32-bit number that makes up the param2 field. The right channel's volume takes up the high 16 bits of the param2 field while the left channel's volume takes up the low 16 bits. The following line of code does this for us:

```
commandToExecute.param2 = (rightVolume << 16) | leftVolume;
```

The rightVolume << 16 shifts the rightVolume 16 bits to the left so that the right channel's volume is in the high 16 bits of the param2 field. The | leftVolume performs a bitwise OR with the rightVolume variable, merging the two values into one.

Normally, you want the volume from the left and right channels to be identical, but you can create some interesting effects by giving the channels different volumes. For example, you might have an enemy coming toward you from the right, and you would want the sound from his footsteps to come from the right. By setting the left channel's volume to 0 and the right channel's volume to a non-zero value, the sound will come from the right speaker only.

Pausing a Sound

If you skim through the list of sound commands in Table 10-5, you might think you'd need a pause command (a command of type pauseCmd) to pause a sound. It sounds logical, but you'd be wrong. A pause command pauses the *command processing* in a sound channel. To actually pause the *sound*, you set the sound's sample rate to zero. You set the sample rate with a rate multiplier command (a command of type rateMultiplierCmd), placing the desired sample rate—0 for pausing a sound—in the param2 field. The Sound Manager ignores the param1 field for the rate multiplier command, so you can use 0 for that parameter. Here's the code to pause a sound:

```
void GameSound::Pause(void)
{
        OSErr error;
        SndCommand commandToExecute;

        // Pause by setting the sample rate to 0
        commandToExecute.cmd = rateMultiplierCmd;
        commandToExecute.param1 = 0;
        commandToExecute.param2 = kPauseSampleRate;
        error = SndDoImmediate(channel, &commandToExecute);
}
```

Resuming a Sound

To resume a sound, you use a rate multiplier command (a command of type rateMultiplierCmd), passing the standard sample rate (the fixed-point number 0x00010000) in the param2 field. Here's the code to resume a paused sound:

```
void GameSound::Resume(void)
{
        OSErr error;
        SndCommand commandToExecute;

        commandToExecute.cmd = rateMultiplierCmd;
        commandToExecute.param1 = 0;
        commandToExecute.param2 = kNormalSampleRate;
        error = SndDoImmediate(channel, &commandToExecute);
}
```

Stopping a Sound

To stop a sound, you first use a quiet command (a command of type quietCmd) to stop the sound. Then you flush all the commands out of the sound channel's queue with a flush command (a command of type flushCmd) to ensure the silence. Both the quiet and flush commands ignore the param1 and param2 fields of the SndCommand structure. Here's the code to stop a sound:

```
void GameSound::Stop(void)
{
        OSErr error;
        SndCommand commandToExecute;

        // Stop the sound
        commandToExecute.cmd = quietCmd;
        error = SndDoImmediate(channel, &commandToExecute);

        // Flush the queue
        commandToExecute.cmd = flushCmd;
        error = SndDoImmediate(channel, &commandToExecute);

}
```

Cleaning Up

When we're finished with our sound, we must dispose of the memory we allocated for the sound. For our GameSound class, we have to dispose of the sound channel and the sound data. We dispose of the sound channel by calling SndDisposeChannel(). We dispose of the sound data by calling ReleaseResource(). Here's the clean-up code:

```
void GameSound::Dispose(void)
{
        OSErr error;

        DisposeSoundData();

        if (channel != nil) {
                error = SndDisposeChannel(channel, kDisposeNow);
                DisposePtr((Ptr)channel);
                channel = nil;
        }
}
void GameSound::DisposeSoundData(void)
{
        if (soundData != nil) {
                HUnlock((Handle)soundData);
                ReleaseResource((Handle)soundData);
                soundData = nil;
        }
}
```

Low-Level Sound Playing

When you call SndPlay() to play a sound, it plays a sound resource from beginning to end. Normally, this is all you want to do with a sound, but sometimes you want to do more. You may want to play only a portion of a sound. You may want to start playing in the middle. You may want to play a large sound file from disk rather than loading it all into memory. If you want to do any of these things with your sound, you need to work with the sound at a lower level.

In the next few sections, I'll show you how to play an AIFF file with multiple buffers. Figure 10-5 demonstrates what will happen. We will have two buffers to hold a portion of the audio from the external file. When buffer 1 is playing a portion of the sound, buffer 2 is reading data from disk. When buffer 1 finishes playing, buffer 2 starts playing and buffer 1 reads data from the file. This cycle continues until the sound has finished playing. If you want to play the sound repeatedly, the cycle goes on indefinitely. By using buffers to play the sound, we can play a large file without using a large amount of memory.

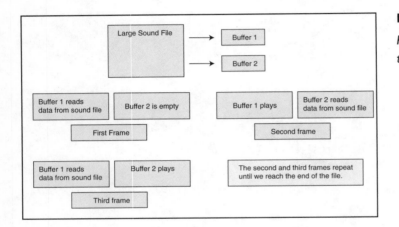

Figure 10-5

Playing a large sound file with two buffers

Additional Data Members for the GameSound Class

To play a sound from an external file using buffers, we're going to need to store a little more data than just a sound channel and the sound data. Here is a list of the additional data members of the GameSound class:

```
class GameSound
{
        protected:
                Ptr buffer1;
                Ptr buffer2;
                ExtSoundHeader soundHeader;
                short soundFileRefNum;
                long startOfSoundData;
};
```

The buffer1 and buffer2 data members contain the two buffers we're going to use to play the sound. If necessary, you can add more buffers, but two buffers will work for now. The Sound Manager cannot directly play the two buffers because the

buffers contain only the sound data, and the Sound Manager needs additional information to play the sound. That's where the `soundHeader` data member comes in; it contains the extra information the Sound Manager needs.

To read data from Macintosh files, we need the file's reference number so that's why we have the `soundFileRefNum` data member. To learn more about files, read Chapter 15, "Files."

The `startOfSoundData` data member stores where the sound data begins in the AIFF file. AIFF files contain a variable amount of header information so it's impossible to tell where the sound data begins in the file without going through the file first. Having the `startOfSoundData` data member tells us where the sound data starts so that we can quickly go back to the beginning of the sound if we want to loop the playback of the sound.

Allocating the Buffers

One of the first things we have to do is to allocate space for the buffers so that we can read data into them. The following function allocates space for the two buffers:

```
void AllocateBuffers(long bufferSize)
{
        // When allocating buffers, make sure the buffer size
        // does not exceed the size of the sound you want to play.
        // If you make the buffer larger than the sound, static
        // will play when you reach the end of the sound.
        buffer1 = NewPtr(bufferSize);
        buffer2 = NewPtr(bufferSize);
}
```

The `AllocateBuffers()` function lets you specify the size of the two buffers. You should make your buffer size a multiple of 512 because the Sound Manager allocates memory in 512-byte increments. This sounds complicated, but remember that one kilobyte (KB) equals 512 times 2, making it a multiple of 512. If you allocate a number of kilobytes that is a power of 2—such as 16K, 32K, 64K, or 128K—you'll be fine.

Opening the Sound File

To open a file, you need its file specification record (`FSSpec`), which contains the file's volume (hard disks, CD-ROM drives, and Zip drives are examples), directory (folder), and file name. Usually you get a file's file specification record by bringing up a dialog box and letting the user choose the file. In game development, we already know the files we want to play so we won't let the user choose the file. The question becomes, "How do we get the file's file specification record?"

The answer to this question is to use the function FSMakeFSSpec(). This function creates a file specification record. We supply a volume, directory, and file name, and FSMakeFSSpec() gives us a file specification record. We will use the value 0 for the file's volume and directory, which means that the file is located in our game's directory. It's very important that your game's sound files reside in the same directory as your game so that the FSMakeFSSpec() function works properly.

After we have the file specification record, we can open the file by calling the function FSpOpenDF(). We supply a file specification and file permission, and FSpOpenDF() opens the file and returns a file reference number so that we can work with the file. In our case, we only want to read the file so we will use the file permission fsRdPerm to provide read-only access to the file. The following function opens the sound file:

```
void OpenSoundFile (Str255 filename)
{
        FSSpec fileSpec;
        OSErr error;

        // The two zeroes tell the File Manager to
        // look in our application's directory for the file.
        error = FSMakeFSSpec(0, 0, filename, &fileSpec);
        if (error != noErr)
                return;

        // Now open the file
        error = FSpOpenDF(&fileSpec, fsRdPerm, &soundFileRefNum);
}
```

Finding the Sound Data in the File

To find where the sound data begins in the sound file, call the function ParseAIFFHeader(). The ParseAIFFHeader() function takes four parameters, as shown in Table 10-6.

Table 10-6 `ParseAIFFHeader()` Parameters

Parameter	Description
fRefNum	The AIFF file that `ParseAIFFHeader()` is to parse.
sndInfo	The `ParseAIFFHeader()` function returns information about the file in the `sndInfo` parameter. Refer to Table 10-7 for the information returned in the `sndInfo` parameter.
numFrames	The `ParseAIFFHeader()` function returns the number of frames of sound data in the `numFrames` parameter.
dataOffset	The `ParseAIFFHeader()` function returns the position in the file where the sound data begins in the `dataOffset` parameter.

Table 10-7 `SoundComponentData` Fields

Field	Description
flags	Bit flags that are of interest only if you're making your own sound components
format	The format of the sound data. This field tells you the type of compression the sound has, if it has any.
numChannels	The number of channels of sound. This value will be 1 for monophonic sound and 2 for stereo sound.
sampleSize	The number of bits in each sample. This value is normally either 8 for 8-bit sound or 16 for 16-bit sound.
sampleRate	The sampling rate for the sound. This value is normally 44100, 22050, or 11025.
sampleCount	The number of samples in the `buffer` field
buffer	The location of the buffer that contains the sound data
reserved	The `reserved` field is 0.

If all you want to do is find the
beginning of the file and start playing from there, all you have to worry
about is the dataOffset parameter
returned by ParseAIFFHeader(). This
is what the following function does:

NOTE

If you want to parse a sound resource
instead of an AIFF file, you call the function ParseSndHeader(). This function
returns the same information as
ParseAIFFHeader(); you supply a sound
resource handle instead of an AIFF file.

```
void
GameSound::FindStartOfSoundData(void)
{
        SoundComponentData soundInfo;
        long numberOfSoundFrames;
        OSErr error;

        // startOfSoundData is a data member of the GameSound class.
        error = ParseAIFFHeader(soundFileRefNum, &soundInfo,
                            &numberOfSoundFrames, &startOfSoundData);

        // Set file position to the beginning of the sound data.
        SetFPos(soundFileRefNum, startOfSoundData);

        // Initialize our sound header using the information
        // we got from ParseAIFFHeader().
        InitializeSoundHeader(&soundInfo, numberOfSoundFrames);
}
```

If you want to start playing a sound somewhere other than the beginning of the
file, you must add a little more code to the FindStartOfSoundData() function. First,
you have to find the total number of seconds of sound in the file, which involves
code that looks like this:

```
long secondsOfSound = (numberOfSoundFrames * soundInfo.numChannels) /
        soundInfo.SampleRate;
```

In English, this code snippet says that the number of seconds of sound equals the
number of sound frames times the number of channels divided by the sample rate.
Next, you must calculate the total amount of sound data, like this:

```
long totalSoundSize = numberOfSoundFrames * soundInfo.numChannels * numChannels*
        soundInfo.sampleSize;
```

This code snippet says that the total sound size equals the number of sound frames
times the number of channels times the sample size. Next, you must calculate

where in the file your desired starting position is and then finally position the file at your desired starting position, as you can see in the following code sample:

```
// Move 10 seconds into the file, then start playing.
long desiredStartTime = 10;

// Make sure we're in the range of the file. We
// don't want to start playing past the end of file.
if (desiredStartTime >= secondsOfSound)
        desiredStartTime = secondsOfSound - 1;

// Compute where in file to begin playing.
long desiredStartFilePosition = totalSoundSize *
                    (desiredStartTime / secondsOfSound);

// Move file position to where we want to begin playing.
SetFPos(soundFileRefNum, startOfSoundData + desiiredStartFilePosition);
```

Initializing the Sound Header

Now we're going to initialize our sound header so that we can play our buffers from it. The Sound Manager has three types of sound headers, as listed in Table 10-8. We're going to use the extended sound header format because our sounds are uncompressed, and we'd like the capability to play both16-bit and stereo sounds.

Table 10-8 Types of Sound Headers

Header	Description
SoundHeader	The original sound header format. You can use this header to play 8-bit monophonic sounds only.
ExtSoundHeader	The extended sound header format. You can use this header to play any uncompressed sound.
CmpSoundHeader	This header format allows you to play compressed sounds.

To initialize the sound header, we must fill the ExtSoundHeader data structure. Table 10-9 lists the fields in the ExtSoundHeader structure. There are a lot of fields in the structure, but do not be alarmed. Many of the fields will be 0, and the ParseAIFFHeader() function gives us the information to fill most of the remaining fields.

Table 10-9   ExtSoundHeader Fields

Field	Description
samplePtr	The audio data resides here or in the sampleArea field. If the data resides in the sampleArea field, the samplePtr field will be nil.
numChannels	The number of channels of sound. This value is 1 for monophonic sound and 2 for stereo sound.
sampleRate	The sampling rate for the sound. This value is normally 44100, 22050, or 11025.
loopStart	Set the loopStart field to 0 in Carbon. The Carbon version of the Sound Manager does not use this field.
loopEnd	Set the loopEnd field to 0 in Carbon. The Carbon version of the Sound Manager does not use thisfield.
encode	The encoding method used to sample the sound. Use the value extSH for an extended sound header.
baseFrequency	The base frequency for the original sound sample. Use the constant kMiddleC to specify the middle C note.
numFrames	The number of frames of sound data
AIFFSampleRate	The sample rate at which the frames were sampled before compression. Use the value 0 because the sound data is not compressed in an extended sound header.
markerChunk	Set the markerChunk field to 0. The Sound Manager does not currently use this field.
instrumentChunks	Instrument information. You can set this field to 0.
AESRecording	Audio recording device information. You can set this field to 0.
sampleSize	The number of bits in each sample. This value is normally either 8 for 8-bit sound or 16 for 16-bit sound.

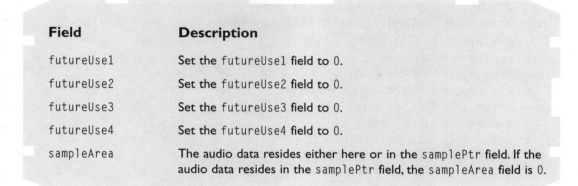

Field	Description
futureUse1	Set the futureUse1 field to 0.
futureUse2	Set the futureUse2 field to 0.
futureUse3	Set the futureUse3 field to 0.
futureUse4	Set the futureUse4 field to 0.
sampleArea	The audio data resides either here or in the samplePtr field. If the audio data resides in the samplePtr field, the sampleArea field is 0.

One field we must calculate ourselves is the numFrames field. The number of frames that ParseAIFFHeader() returns is for the whole file, not for the buffer we're going to play. If we don't recalculate the number of frames, the Sound Manager will keep playing the sound past the end of the buffer, which will have disastrous results. We must compute the number of frames of sound that fit in one of our sound buffers. The size of a frame of sound is the number of channels of sound multiplied by the size of a sample. Dividing the buffer size by the size of a sound frame yields the number of frames that will fit into the buffer.

The following function initializes our sound header:

```
void InitializeSoundHeader(SoundComponentDataPtr soundInfo,
      unsigned long numberOfFrames)
{
      // Need this value to set the AIFFSampleRate properly.
      // A Float80 is an 80 bit fixed point number so using
      // dummyValue = 0.0;
      // generates a compiler error
      Float80 dummyValue;
      dummyValue.exp = 0;
      dummyValue.man[0] = 0;
      dummyValue.man = 0;
      dummyValue.man = 0;
      dummyValue.man = 0;

      // Have the header point to buffer 1 initially
      soundHeader.samplePtr = buffer1;
```

```
           soundHeader.numChannels = soundInfo->numChannels;
           soundHeader.sampleRate = soundInfo->sampleRate;
           soundHeader.loopStart = 0;
           soundHeader.loopEnd = 0;
           soundHeader.encode = extSH;
           soundHeader.baseFrequency = kMiddleC;
           soundHeader.AIFFSampleRate = dummyValue;
           soundHeader.markerChunk = 0;
           soundHeader.instrumentChunks = 0;
           soundHeader.AESRecording = 0;
           soundHeader.sampleSize = soundInfo->sampleSize;
           soundHeader.futureUse1 = 0;
           soundHeader.futureUse2 = 0;
           soundHeader.futureUse3 = 0;
           soundHeader.futureUse4 = 0;
           soundHeader.sampleArea = 0;

           // Now calculate the number of frames that our buffer can hold.

           // Find the size of the buffer. I assume that
           // both buffers are the same size.
           long bufferSize = GetPtrSize(buffer1);
           long bytesPerSample = soundInfo->sampleSize / 8;
           long sizeOfFrame = soundInfo->numChannels * bytesPerSample;
           long framesInBuffer = bufferSize / sizeOfFrame;

           soundHeader.numFrames = framesInBuffer;
}
```

Reading the Data into the Buffer

To read the sound data from the file to the buffer, we must call the function
FSRead(). We must pass the file reference number, the number of bytes to read, and
the buffer to FSRead(). In our case, this is very easy because we have data members
in the GameSound class representing the file reference number and the buffer.

Before we call FSRead(), we must make sure that we don't read past the end of the
file. If we have a 16K buffer size, but there's only 10K of data left in the file, we
want to read only 10K, not 16K. The following function reads the data from the
sound file to the buffer:

```
void GameSound::ReadSoundData(Ptr soundBuffer)
```

```
{
        // soundBuffer will be either buffer1 or buffer2

        long currentFilePosition;
        long endOfFilePosition;
        long bytesToRead;
        OSErr error;

        error = GetFPos(soundFileRefNum, &currentFilePosition);
        if (error != noErr)
                return;

        error = GetEOF(soundFileRefNum, &endOfFilePosition);
        if (error != noErr)
                return;

        // If we reach the end of file, go back to the start of the file.
        if (currentFilePosition >= endOfFilePosition) {
                SetFPos(soundFileRefNum, fsFromStart, startOfSoundData);
        }

        bytesToRead = GetPtrSize(soundBuffer);
        long spaceLeftInFile = endOfFilePosition - currentFilePosition;

        // Check if there's enough room left on the file to read a whole buffer
        // of data.  If not, read what's left on the file
        if (spaceLeftInFile < bytesToRead)
                bytesToRead = spaceLeftInFile;


        // Calculate the number of frames of sound data to read.
        // Most of the time, it will use the buffer size, but if we
        // hit the end of the file, it will use the space remaining in the file.
        long bufferSize = bytesToRead;
        long bytesPerSample = soundHeader->sampleSize / 8;
        long sizeOfFrame = soundHeader->numChannels * bytesPerSample;
        long framesInBuffer = bufferSize / sizeOfFrame;

        soundHeader->numFrames = framesInBuffer;

        // Now read the file
```

```
        error = FSRead(soundFileRefNum, bufferSize, soundBuffer);
}
```

Queuing the Sound

To ensure that the sound plays without interruption, we must queue the sound so that when one buffer finishes playing, the other one begins. Queuing the sound requires a buffer command (a command of type bufferCmd) followed by a callback command (a command of type callBackCmd). The buffer command plays the sound, and the callback command does everything else.

When calling a buffer command, you pass 0 in the param1 field. In the param2 field, you pass the sound to play. Here's the code to queue a sound:

```
void QueueSoundFrame(void)
{
        SndCommand commandToExecute;
        OSErr error;

        // Queue the buffer command
        commandToExecute.cmd = bufferCmd;
        commandToExecute.param1 = 0;
        commandToExecute.param2 = (long) soundHeader;
        error = SndDoCommand(channel, &commandToExecute, true);

        // Queue the callback command
        commandToPerform.cmd = callBackCmd;
        commandToPerform.param1 = kSoundManagerID;
        commandToPerform.param2 = (long) this;
        error = SndDoCommand(channel, &commandToPerform, true);
}
```

Writing the Callback Function

In the callback function, we must queue a buffer and then swap the buffers. Swapping the buffers makes the buffer that just finished playing read more data from the file while the other buffer starts playing. Here's the callback routine to accomplish this goal:

```
pascal void GameSound::MultiBufferSoundCallback(SndChannelPtr theChannel,
        SndCommand* theCommand)
{
```

```
            GameSoundPtr theSound;

            theSound = (GameSoundPtr)theCommand->param2;
            theSound->SwapBuffers();
            theSound->QueueSoundFrame();
}
void GameSound::SwapBuffers(void)
{
            // Were we currently playing sound in buffer 1?
            if (soundHeader.samplePtr == buffer1) {
                    // Play buffer 2 and read more data into buffer 1.
                    soundHeader.samplePtr = buffer2;
                    ReadSoundData(buffer1);
            }
            else {
                    // Play buffer 1 and read more data into buffer 2.
                    soundHeader.samplePtr = buffer1;
                    ReadSoundData(buffer2);
            }

}
```

Programming Sound with QuickTime

You can do a lot with sound resources, but resources have one potential problem. The maximum size of the resource fork of a file (read Chapter 15, "Files," for more information about the forks of a file) is 16MB; 16MB is the largest potential sound resource you can create. If you sample the sound at the highest possible quality, you can fill the 16MB limit with just two minutes of sound. If you have a long music sequence you want to play, you'll have to store the sequence in an external file. Even if sound resources had no size limit, you wouldn't want to have a five-minute sequence of CD-quality sound reside totally in memory anyway. That sequence would take 50MB of RAM to store. Assuming that your game will contain artwork, sound effects, and artificial intelligence, the memory requirements for your game would be so high that most people couldn't play it.

The Sound Manager has functions to play a sound from an external file, but they did not survive the transition to Carbon. The only way to play a sound from an external file with the Sound Manager is to use a low-level technique such as the one described in the section "Low-Level Sound Playing," earlier in this chapter. If you want an easy way to play a sound from an external file and maintain Carbon compatibility, you should use QuickTime to play the sound.

In case you weren't aware, QuickTime is Apple's technology to support video and audio. If you've ever downloaded a film or music file from the Internet and played it on your Macintosh, you most likely used QuickTime to view the film or listen to the music. Using QuickTime for your game's audio provides several advantages over the Sound Manager:

- QuickTime is important to Apple, so you don't have to worry about Apple dropping support for it the way the company dropped support for Game Sprockets and QuickDraw 3D.
- QuickTime can play many more sound file formats than the Sound Manager can, including MP3 and Windows .wav files.
- QuickTime runs on both Macintosh and Windows computers. If you have hopes of your game being ported to Windows, QuickTime is the audio solution for you.
- With QuickTime, you can play multiple sounds simultaneously. For example, you can have music playing in the background while somebody speaks dialogue in your game.

QuickTime works at a higher level than the Sound Manager; playing sounds with QuickTime takes more CPU time than playing them with the Sound Manager. QuickTime doesn't give the programmer the low-level control of sound that the Sound Manager does. Whether this is an advantage or disadvantage depends on how much control you want over your game's audio.

QuickTime Movies

QuickTime plays multimedia data through the use of movies. A movie can contain multiple tracks of video and audio. Although QuickTime has functions you can use in your game to create a movie from another type of file, it's best to convert the files to movies yourself using QuickTime Player. By converting the files to QuickTime movies during development and storing them as movies in the game, you have all the movies ready to load in your game. The player of your game is not going to want to wait for your game to convert music files at the start of the game.

Converting a file to a QuickTime movie isn't as difficult as it sounds. You run the QuickTime Player program, which comes with QuickTime so you already have it on your computer unless you have manually removed it. Inside QuickTime Player, you open the file you want to convert and then save the file. When saving the file, you should save the file as a self-contained movie. A *self-contained movie* has all the data in the movie and is roughly the same size as the original file. If you don't save the file as a self-contained movie, you end up with a minimal movie that references the original file. This means you have to ship two files—the minimal movie and the original file—with your game instead of one self-contained movie. If you rename, move, or edit the original file, QuickTime will not be able to load the minimal movie. Maintain your sanity by saving your movies as self-contained movies.

Because this chapter covers audio, all the movies we use in the code examples in this chapter contain only audio. You can use most of the code presented in the following sections to play movies containing video. To do so, you must first create a window to show the video portion of the movie.

The GameSong Class

For the QuickTime code in this chapter, I'm creating another class, the GameSong class. As you can see in the following code, the GameSong class has just one data member, soundToPlay, which is a QuickTime movie.

```
class GameSong
{
      protected:
              Movie soundToPlay;
};
```

Starting QuickTime

Starting QuickTime is simple. Just call the function EnterMovies(), and you're finished.

```
void GameSong::StartQuickTime(void)
{
      EnterMovies();
}
```

Reading a Movie from Disk

Reading a movie from disk into memory is the most difficult part of using QuickTime for audio. Reading a movie into memory takes two steps. First you must open the file containing the movie by calling OpenMovieFile(). The OpenMovieFile() function takes three parameters, shown in Table 10-10.

Table 10-10   `OpenMovieFile()` Parameters

Parameter	Description
pFile	The file containing the movie
resRefNum	The reference number `OpenMovieFile()` creates. You take this reference number and pass it as a parameter to the function `NewMovieFromFile()`.
permission	The read/write permission for the file. Because we're only playing movies (not creating or editing them), pass the value `fsRdPerm` to grant read-only permission.

After opening the movie file with the function `OpenMovieFile()`, you move the movie into memory by calling `NewMovieFromFile()`. The `NewMovieFromFile()` function takes six parameters, listed in Table 10-11. If you read through the flags you can pass to `NewMovieFromFile()`, you will see several mentions of *data references*. QuickTime uses data references to find the data (audio data in our case) it's supposed to handle. A data reference can be a file, a Web page, or a location in memory. Because we're using self-contained movie files, we won't have to worry about resolving data references; the data is in the movie file.

Table 10-11   `NewMovieFromFile()` Parameters

Parameter	Description
theMovie	The movie that `NewMovieFromFile()` creates
resRefNum	The reference number of the file `OpenMovieFile()` created for us
resID	The resource ID of the movie to open from the file. If we have multiple movies in a file, pass the resource ID here. If not, pass 0, and QuickTime will load the first movie it finds in the file.
resName	`NewMovieFromFile()` returns the title of the movie here. Pass `nil` if you don't care about the title.
newMovieFlags	Flags you can pass to `NewMovieFromFile()`, listed in Table 10-12. You should pass the flag `newMovieActive`, which makes the movie active so that you can play it.
dataRefWasChanged	Returns `true` if QuickTime had to change any data as it moved the data from the file to memory. Pass `nil` if you don't care about this.

Table 10-12 `NewMovieFromFile()` Flags

Flag	Description
`newMovieActive`	Makes the newly created movie active
`newMovieDontResolveDataRefs`	If you pass this flag, QuickTime looks only in the specified file for the data references. Otherwise, QuickTime searches all disks for the data reference.
`newMovieDontAskUnresolvedDataRefs`	If you pass this flag, QuickTime does not ask the user to locate the file containing the data reference. Otherwise, QuickTime asks the user to locate the file if it cannot find the data reference.
`newMovieDontAutoAlternate`	If you pass this flag, you must manually enable tracks in the movie. Otherwise, QuickTime enables the tracks for you.

After reading the movie into memory, you call `CloseMovie()` to close the file. The following code demonstrates how to read a file into memory:

```
void GameSong::ReadSoundToPlay(Str255 filename, short soundID)
{
        // Takes a file and converts it to a QuickTime
        // movie in memory. The soundID is the resource ID for
        // the QuickTime movie. If you use a soundID of 0, QuickTime
        // will load the first movie in the file.

        OSErr error;
        FSSpec soundFile;

        // The two zeroes tell the File Manager to
        // look in our application's directory for the file.
        error = FSMakeFSSpec(0, 0, filename, &soundFile);
        if (error != noErr)
                return;

        short soundFileRefNum;
```

```
// Read the file from disk
error = OpenMovieFile(&soundFile, &soundFileRefNum, fsRdPerm);

if (error != noErr)
        return;

// Now put it in memory.
// The first nil says we don't care what the title of the movie is.
// The second nil says we don't care if QuickTime
// changed any data references.
// The newMovieActive parameter tells QuickTime to make
// the movie active.
error = NewMovieFromFile(&soundToPlay, soundFileRefNum, &soundID, nil,
                                    newMovieActive, nil);

// Now that we've loaded the movie into memory,
// we can close the movie file.
error = CloseMovieFile(soundFileRefNum);
}
```

Playing a Movie

After you load a QuickTime movie into memory, the rest of what you need to do is pretty easy. To play a movie, just call the function StartMovie(), as you can see in the following code:

```
void GameSong::Play(void)
{
        // Plays a sound one time
        StartMovie(soundToPlay);
}
```

To play a sound repeatedly, check whether the movie has finished by calling the function IsMovieDone(). If the movie has finished, call the function GoToBeginningOfMovie() to—you guessed it—go back to the beginning of the movie. Finally, you make another call to StartMovie() to play the movie again.

```
void GameSong::PlayRepeatedly(void)
{
        // Loops a sound repeatedly
```

```
        if (IsMovieDone(soundToPlay)) {
                GoToBeginningOfMovie(soundToPlay);
                StartMovie(soundToPlay);
        }
        // Give QuickTime the time it needs.
        // The value 0 tells QuickTime to determine
        // the amount of time it needs.
        MoviesTask(soundToPlay, 0);

}
```

Setting a Movie's Volume

To set a QuickTime movie's volume, call the function `SetMovieVolume()`, which takes a QuickTime movie and volume as parameters. QuickTime volume has a range between −1.0 and 1.0. QuickTime stores the floating-point value as a 16-bit fixed-point number, where the highest eight bits represent the integer portion of the volume (either 0 or 1) and the lowest eight bits represent the fractional portion of the volume. This type of number is known as an *8:8 fixed-point number.* It sounds complicated, but you can just use a `short` variable and use values ranging from −256 to 256 for your volumes. A `short` with the value 256 is equivalent to an 8:8 fixed-point number with value 1.0. Just remember to use integers between −256 and 256 when setting the volume for your movie.

Volumes less than or equal to 0 produce silence. Negative volumes act as a mute button. You can take the current volume and multiply it by −1 to temporarily silence the movie and multiply again by −1 to restore the original volume. The following code sets a movie's volume and mutes a playing sound:

```
void QTSound::SetVolume(short volume)
{
        // Valid volume ranges for this function are
        // -256 to 256, but the practical range is
        // 0 to 256 since negative volumes create silence.

        SetMovieVolume(soundToPlay, volume);
}


void QTSound::Mute(void)
{
        // Mutes a sound by taking its current volume
```

```
            // and changing the sign. If the sound is already
            // muted, the Mute() function will unmute the sound.

            short currentVolume = GetMovieVolume(soundToPlay);
            SetVolume (currentVolume * -1);
}
```

Pausing and Resuming Movies

To pause a movie, all you have to do is call StopMovie(). This function stops the movie at its current point, pausing the movie. You resume the movie by calling StartMovie(). StartMovie() starts playing the movie at the point at which you paused it.

```
void GameSong::Pause(void)
{
        StopMovie(soundToPlay);
}
void GameSong::Resume(void)
{
        StartMovie(soundToPlay);
}
```

Stopping a Movie

To stop a movie from playing, call the function StopMovie(). As you learned in the previous section, just calling StopMovie() acts like pausing the movie. If you're through with the movie, you should call the function GoToBeginningOfMovie() to reset the movie. If you don't call GoToBeginningOfMovie(), the movie will resume playing wherever it was when you called StopMovie().

```
void GameSong::Stop(void)
{
        StopMovie(soundToPlay);

        // Go back to start of movie so the movie
        // plays properly when the player plays
        // the game again
        GoToBeginningOfMovie(soundToPlay);
}
```

Giving Your Movie a Chance to Play

QuickTime needs CPU time to play movies. To give QuickTime the time it needs, call the function `MoviesTask()` inside your game's event loop. The `MoviesTask()` function takes two parameters, described in Table 10-13.

Table 10-13 MoviesTask() Parameters

Parameter	Description
theMovie	The movie QuickTime is currently servicing
maxMilliSecToUse	How much time you want to give QuickTime to service the movie, in milliseconds (1000 milliseconds equals one second). If you pass 0, QuickTime determines how much time to give itself.

The following code shows how to call `MoviesTask()`:

```
void QTSound::GiveTimeToQuickTime(long timeToGive)
{
        MoviesTask(soundToPlay, timeToGive);
}
```

In your game, you would have an object of class `QTSound`:

```
QTSound backgroundMusic;
```

In your game's event loop, you would have a statement like this one to give QuickTime the time it needs:

```
backgroundMusic.GiveTimeToQuickTime(0);
```

Passing a value of 0 to `MoviesTask()` tells QuickTime to take the time it needs to service every movie. If you have just one movie playing, passing 0 works well. QuickTime services the movie once and then returns; in our case, the playing time won't be long because our movies don't contain video. If you have many movies playing at once, you should specify your own `maxMilliSecToUse` parameter so that your game doesn't get bogged down servicing movies. In this case, I wouldn't use a value greater than 50. A value of 50 means that QuickTime will spend 1/20 of a second servicing the movie. A value higher than 50 will slow your game's frame rate to an unacceptable level.

Quitting QuickTime

When the player wants to quit our game, we must take the following steps to shut down QuickTime:

- Stop the movie by calling `StopMovie()`.
- Set the movie to the beginning by calling `GoToBeginningOfMovie()`. When the player plays the game again, the movie will start playing at the beginning rather than where it was when the player quit.
- Dispose of the movie's memory by calling `DisposeMovie()`.
- Call `ExitMovies()` to exit QuickTime.

The following bit of code properly quits QuickTime and ties up all the loose ends:

```
void GameSong::Dispose(void)
{
        Stop();
        DisposeMovie(soundToPlay);
}

void GameSong::ExitQuickTime(void)
{
        ExitMovies();
}
```

Summary

In this chapter, you learned how to play, loop, pause, resume, and stop sounds as well as how to set a sound's volume. You learned how to do these things using both the Sound Manager and QuickTime. In addition, you learned how to play an external file with multiple buffers to conserve memory. QuickTime is a massive subject—the reference manual alone is over 1,100 pages—and the Sound Manager is pretty big, too, so I couldn't cover all there is to know about them in this single chapter. To learn more about Macintosh audio, check out the book list in Appendix B.

You can find the complete program for this chapter on the CD-ROM that accompanies this book. Our evolving game now includes audio in addition to the other features we've been adding to it in the previous chapters. The sample game now features both looping background music and sound effects.

CHAPTER 11

PHYSICS

It may be sacrilegious to say this, but a computer game's graphics consist of a bunch of colored dots on the screen. To the player, it appears as if there are living, breathing objects, such as aliens, aircraft, tanks and fireballs on the screen, but in reality, those objects are colored dots. It's up to us as game developers to make the objects in the game behave in a believable manner so that the player doesn't realize that the game's objects are merely colored dots.

Physics allows us to move from colored dots onscreen to the illusion of actual objects, such as people, spacecraft, and cars. Physics makes the objects in games walk, run, jump, and fly. Physics keeps characters in the game from running through each other and detects when a bullet hits the player character. In this chapter, we will add physics to the game we're making.

You can make your game's physics as simple or complicated as you like. This chapter wouldn't be very interesting if I used a simple physics model so I'm going with a moderately complex physics model. When adding physics to your game, remember that you are programming a game, which is supposed to be a fun experience. You can have the most realistic physics in the history of video games, but if the realistic physics makes the game difficult to play, players will quickly tire of your game. Use physics to make your game more fun to play.

Up to this point, the chapters in this book have covered little theory and have dealt mainly with practical things, such as algorithms and code. Physics is a complicated subject, and pumping out some code samples won't cover physics sufficiently. We must delve into physics theory and even work out some mathematical formulas. Don't worry. I'll lead you step by step through the more complicated mathematical portions of the chapter. If you have taken an algebra course, you have enough mathematical knowledge to understand the math in this chapter.

Vectors

This chapter is the most mathematically challenging one in the whole book, so I must begin with some mathematical explanations. Many of the topics in this chapter deal with vectors, so I will start things off by introducing you to vectors. I'm going to warn you right now that this section deals with theoretical math. I will make it practical later in the chapter. You might want to bookmark this section so that you can easily come back to it.

A *vector quantity* has both magnitude and direction; in contrast, a *scalar quantity* has magnitude only. If you're traveling 50 miles per hour (80 kilometers an hour for those of you using the metric system) in your car, the 50 miles per hour is a scalar quantity. However, if you're traveling 50 miles per hour westward, you have a vector quantity because you have both a magnitude (the 50 miles per hour), and a direction (west).

For the purposes of this chapter, we will be using two-dimensional vectors. A vector v, is shown in Equation 11-1.

Definition of a 2D Vector: $v = <x,y>$

Equation 11-1

The two-dimensional vector v has two components: x and y. A three-dimensional vector has a z component as well. The x component tells us how far to draw the vector along the x-axis, and the y component tells us how far to draw the vector along the y-axis. How the vector looks depends on the starting point of the vector, as you can see in Figure 11-1. The vector in the figure travels four units horizontally and two units vertically no matter where the vector begins.

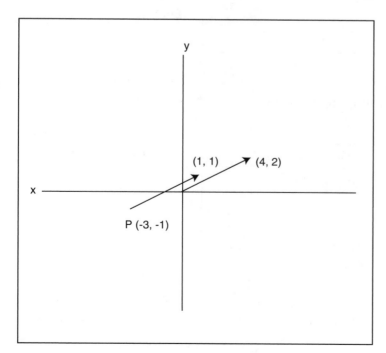

Figure 11-1

How the vector v = <4, 2> *looks when based at the origin (0,0) and when based at the point P (−3, −1).*

The vector's sign reflects the vector's direction; it has nothing to do with the magnitude of the vector. For example, these two vectors are the same vector with opposite directions:

v1 = <4, 0>   and   v2 = <-4, 0>

Vector v1 moves four units right, and v2 moves four units left.

To work with vectors in our game, we will create a vector class, Vector2D, whose data members you can see here:

```
class Vector2D
{
        double x;
        double y;
};
```

It's a fairly simple class from a data standpoint; it just has the x and y components that constitute a two-dimensional vector.

To compute the length of a vector (also called the *magnitude* or the *norm* of a vector), you square the components, sum them, and take the square root of the sum as you can see in the Equation 11-2.

Equation 11-2

$$\text{Magnitude of a Vector:} \quad \|v\| = \sqrt{x^2 + x^2}$$

The vector <–5, 3> has the following magnitude:

Example 11-1

$$\text{Magnitude Example:} \quad \|v\| = \sqrt{(-5)^2 + 3^2}$$
$$= \sqrt{25 + 9}$$
$$= \sqrt{34}$$

The following function computes the magnitude of a vector:

```
double Vector2D::GetLength(void)
{
        double result;
        double xSquared = x * x;
        double ySquared = y * y;

        result = sqrt(xSquared + ySquared);
        return result;
}
```

Vector Sums and Differences

You can add and subtract vectors the same way you add and subtract integers. To add two vectors, you just add their components, as shown in Equation 11-3.

Vector Sums: $u = <x_1, y_1>$ $v = <x_2, y_2>$
$u + v = <x_1 + x_2, y_1 + y_2>$

Equation 11-3

To subtract two vectors, you subtract their components, as shown in Equation 11-4.

Vector Differences: $u = <x_1, y_1>$ $v = <x_2, y_2>$
$u - v = <x_1 - x_2, y_1 - y_2>$

Equation 11-4

Example 11.2 shows some vector sums and differences.

Vector Sum Example: $u = <5, 2>$ $v = <3, 4>$
$u + v = <5 + 3, 2 + 4> = <8, 6>$
$u - v = <5 - 3, 2 - 4> = <2, -2>$

Example 11-2

Figure 11.2 provides a picture of the vectors we added and subtracted in Example 11-2. For Figures 11-1 and 11-2, I'm using the traditional mathematical view of the world, in which the point (0, 0) is the center of the world and points above the origin are positive and points below the origin are negative. Remember from Chapter 4, "Introduction to Macintosh Graphics," that in QuickDraw's coordinate system, the point (0, 0) is the upper-left corner of the screen; the game we're developing uses the point (0, 0) as the upper-left corner of the game world. In our game's world, the y component increases as you move down and decreases as you move up, the opposite of the mathematical world.

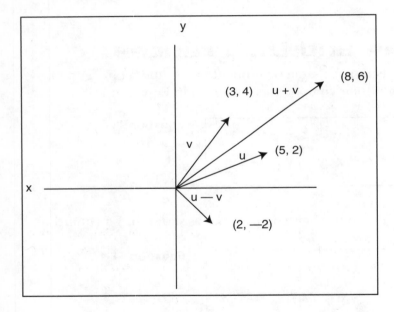

Figure 11-2

Adding and subtracting the vectors u = ⟨5, 2⟩ and v = ⟨3, 4⟩, which are based at the origin.

If the vector's sign changes as a result of adding or subtracting vectors, the vector's direction changes. In Figure 11-2, subtracting the vector v from the vector u results in a negative y component so the vector difference points downward instead of upward as the vectors u and v do.

The following code computes the sum and difference of two vectors:

```
Vector2D VectorSum(Vector2DPtr u, Vector2DPtr v)
{
        double newXComponent;
        double newYComponent;
        Vector2D result;
```

```
        newXComponent = u->GetXComponent() + v->GetXComponent();
        newYComponent= u->GetYComponent() + v->GetYComponent();

        result.SetXComponent(newXComponent);
        result.SetYComponent(newYComponent);
        return result;
}
Vector2D VectorDifference(Vector2DPtr u, Vector2DPtr v)
{
        double newXComponent;
        double newYComponent;
        Vector2D result;

        newXComponent= u->GetXComponenent() - v->GetXComponent();
        newYComponent= u->GetYComponent() - v->GetYComponent();

        result.SetXComponent(newXComponent);
        result.SetYComponent(newYComponent);
        return result;
}
```

Multiplication by a Scalar

You can multiply a vector by a scalar, in much the same way you would multiply two integers. You multiply both components of the vector by the scalar quantity, resulting in a vector quantity. Equation 11-5 shows how it looks mathematically.

Scalar Multiplication: $cv = <cx, cy>$

Equation 11-5

Example 11-3 shows a scalar multiplication example.

Scalar Multiplication Example: $v = <1, -2>$ $4v = <4, -8>$

Example 11-3

Figure 11-3 draws a picture of the scalar multiplication example in Example 11-3.

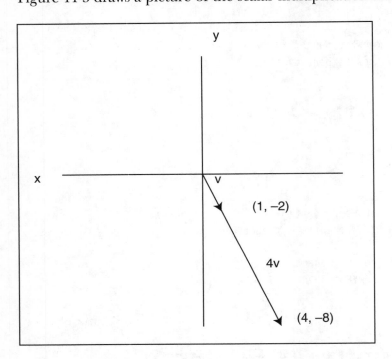

Figure 11-3

The vector 4v *based at the origin, where* v = <1, -2>.

The following function performs a scalar multiplication on a vector:

```
Vector2D ScalarProduct(Vector2DPtr v, double scalar)
{
        // This function multiplies a vector by a scalar quantity
        // Many books refer to the dot product of two vectors as a
        // scalar product, but I can't think of a better function name
        // for multiplying a vector by a scalar than ScalarProduct.
        double newXComponent;
        double newYComponent;
        Vector2D result;

        newXComponent= v->GetXComponent() * scalar;
        newYComponent= v->GetYComponent() * scalar;

        result.SetXComponent(newXComponent);
        result.SetYComponent(newYComponent);
        return result;

}
```

Dot Product

The *dot product* is the result you get when you multiply two vectors. There are two ways to compute the dot product; Equation 11-6 shows the first approach.

Equation 11-6

Dot Product: $u = <x_1, y_1>$ $v = <x_2, y_2>$

$u \cdot v = \qquad x_1 x_2 + y_1 y_2$

Example 11-4 calculates the dot product of two vectors.

Example 11-4

Dot Product Example: $u = <2, 7>$ $v = <4, 0>$

$u \cdot v = (2)(4) + (7)(0)$

$= 8 + 0 = 8$

As you can see from Example 11-4, the dot product is a scalar quantity, not a vector.

The second method of computing the dot product depends on theta, the angle between the two vectors. Figure 11-4 shows some examples of theta. To compute the dot product, you multiply the magnitudes of the two vectors, then multiply that product by the cosine of theta, as shown in Equation 11-7.

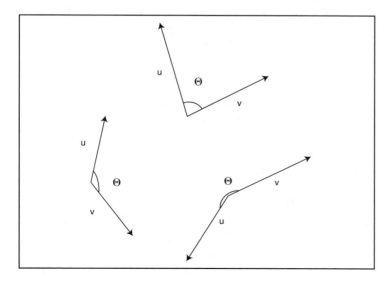

Figure 11-4

Examples of the angle between two vectors.

Dot Product Example: $u = <2, 7>$ $v = <4, 0>$ **Equation 11-7**

$$u \cdot v = (2)(4) + (7)(0)$$

$$= 8 + 0 = 8$$

The following function computes the dot product between two vectors:

```
double DotProduct(Vector2DPtr u, Vector2DPtr v)
{
        double x1 = u->GetXComponent();
        double y1 = u->GetYComponent();
        double x2 = v->GetXComponent ();
        double y2 = v->GetYComponent ();

        double result = (x1 * x2) + (y1 * y2);
        return result;
}
```

If you wanted to use the alternative method of computing the dot product, the DotProduct() function would look like this:

```
double DotProduct(Vector2DPtr u, Vector2DPtr v, double theta)
{
        double uLength = u->GetLength();
        double vLength = v->GetLength();

        double result = uLength * vLength * cosine(theta);
        return result;
}
```

You will prefer using the first DotProduct() function. Computing square roots and cosines of angles is time-consuming, so the second DotProduct() function will be slower than the first. Plus, you must measure the angle theta in the second version, and you will notice I didn't show you how to measure theta. Measuring theta requires even more computational work, slowing the second DotProduct() function even more.

Unit Vectors

A *unit vector* is a vector where one of the vector's components has the value of 1, and the other components (It may be a 3D vector) have the value 0. For two-dimensional vectors, there are two unit vectors, as shown in Equation 11-8.

Equation 11-8

Unit Vectors: $i = <1, 0>$ $j = <0, 1>$

You can use unit vectors to describe a vector instead of using the $<x, y>$ notation. For example, the two vectors shown in Example 11-5 are equivalent.

Example 11-5

$$
\begin{aligned}
\text{Unit Vector Example:} \quad & V_1 = <4, 6> \quad V_2 = 4i + 6j \\
& 4i = 4<1, 0> = <4, 0> \\
& 6j = 6<0, 1> = <0, 6> \\
& 4i + 6j = <4, 0> + <0, 6> \\
& \qquad\quad = <4, 6> = V_1
\end{aligned}
$$

Parallel and Orthogonal Vectors

Two vectors are *parallel* if one of the vectors is a scalar multiple of the other. For example, the two vectors shown in Example 11-6 are parallel.

Example 11-6

$$
\begin{aligned}
\text{Parallel Vector Example:} \quad & V_1 = <3, 1> \quad V_2 = <6, 2> \\
& V_2 = 2\,V_1 \\
& 2\,V_1 = 2<3, 1> = <6, 2> = V_2
\end{aligned}
$$

If you look at Figure 11-5, you can tell visually that the two vectors, v1 and v2, are parallel.

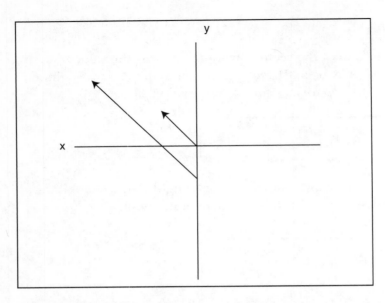

Figure 11-5

Parallel vectors.

Now you may be wondering what *orthogonal* means. No, it has nothing to do with putting braces on your teeth. Orthogonal is a synonym for perpendicular, and if you're not familiar with the term perpendicular, Figure 11-6 will give you an idea of the term. Orthogonal vectors form either a T shape or an upside down T shape.

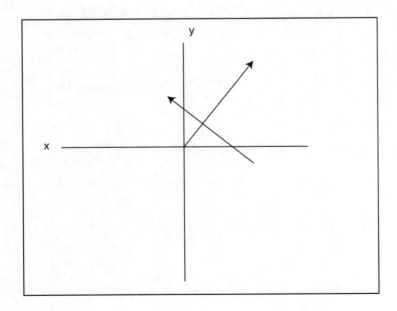

Figure 11-6

Orthogonal (perpendicular) vectors.

Two vectors are orthogonal if their dot product is zero. Two orthogonal vectors will have either a 90-degree angle or a 270-degree angle between them. The cosine of both 90-degree and 270-degree angles is zero, which will give you a dot product of zero.

The following function computes the vector perpendicular to a given vector:

```
Vector2D GetPerpendicularVector(Vector2DPtr v)
{
        // The perpendicular vector of v = <x, y> can be either
        // <-y, x> or <y, -x>
        // I chose to use <-y, x> for this function
        Vector2D result;
        double newXComponent;
        double newYComponent;

         newXComponent= v->GetYComponent() * -1.0;
         newYComponent= v->GetXComponent();

        result.SetXComponent(newXComponent);
        result.SetYComponent(newYComponent);
        return result;
}
```

Linear Motion

Now that the unpleasant vector math is out of the way, we can move on to the unpleasant math of rigid body dynamics. Physics is a huge subject with many fields covering topics such as astronomy, electricity, magnetism, heat, and subatomic particles. For game development purposes, the physics field of greatest interest is dynamics, which is the study of forces and how they affect movement. Rigid body dynamics deal with forces acting on rigid bodies, which are bodies where each point in the body remains the same in relation to the other points in the body. In English, a rigid body is a body that cannot bend. There are no completely rigid bodies in the physical world, but we can consider objects such as a block of wood, a brick, or a metal pole to be rigid bodies. Rigid body dynamics provides a reasonable approximation of moving people and animals, and the math is a lot easier than the math behind the dynamics of human motion.

I will begin the discussion of rigid body dynamics by explaining *linear motion,* which is motion in a straight line without any angular or rotational effects. Bodies spinning and rotating complicate the math, so I decided to start with the simpler linear motion.

Position

Position is the location of the rigid body in the world. For a game, the position is the location of the player, an enemy, a vehicle, or a missile in the game's world. Remember from Chapter 6, "Animation," that the GameSprite class had the worldX and worldY data members. Those data members represent the sprite's position in the game world. Physics is where the position of the sprite comes into play. Now that we know about vectors, we can change the GameSprite's positional data members from:

```
short worldX;
short worldY;
```

to:

```
Vector2D position;
```

Velocity

Velocity measures a body's change in position over time. Mathematically, the formula for velocity looks like the one shown in Equation 11-9.

$$\text{Velocity:} \quad v = \frac{dr}{dt}$$

Equation 11-9

This is a piece of calculus, which states that velocity is the derivative of position (r) with respect to time (t). dr is the change in position. (Don't ask me why the physics books use r instead of p to denote position.) dt is the change in time.

Don't freak out. You do not have to know calculus to compute the velocity in your game. Computers aren't very good at doing calculus, and you purchased a game programming book not a calculus textbook, so I'm not going to spend dozens of pages teaching you how to calculate derivatives and integrals. We'll use a method to calculate the velocity that we can do on the computer.

You normally compute position from the velocity rather than the other way around. That would involve calculating an integral using calculus, but we will approximate the position using the following formula:

```
newPosition = oldPosition + (velocity * timeStep)
```

Assuming that the velocity stays constant throughout the duration of the time step, the value (velocity * timeStep) is the amount we moved during the time step. For example, if the old position is 32 miles east, and we're traveling 60 miles per hour east, and we're measuring our position every minute, we calculate the new position like this:

```
32 + (60 * (1/60)) = 32 + 1 = 33 miles east
```

We've just done real physics without having to resort to calculus. The new position equals the old position (32) plus the velocity (60 miles per hour) times the time step (one minute, which equals 1/60 of an hour). In a game, the time step will be much shorter than one minute. The time step depends on how quickly we want our game's physics engine to run. If we want the physics engine to run at a rate of 60 times per second, the time step will be 1/60 of a second.

Remember that velocity is a vector quantity so it has direction as well as magnitude. The magnitude of velocity is its speed. Most people use the terms speed and velocity interchangeably, but it's not technically accurate: velocity has direction; speed doesn't. Bring that fact up when somebody uses the term velocity when they mean speed. I'm sure they will get a huge kick out of it. If we were traveling 60 miles per hour west in the preceding example, the new position would have been calculated like this:

```
32 + (-60 * (1/60)) = 32 - 1 = 31 miles east
```

With the change in position from east to west, the velocity changes from 60 miles per hour to –60 miles per hour, so the new position is one mile west of the old position—31 miles east.

When we created the GameSprite class in Chapter 6, "Animation," to store game objects, we had xSpeed and ySpeed data members to store the object's speed in the horizontal and vertical directions. With our newfound knowledge of vectors, we can change the GameSprite's data members from:

```
float xSpeed;
float ySpeed;
```

to:

```
Vector2D velocity;
```

Acceleration

Acceleration measures a body's change in velocity over time. Mathematically the formula for acceleration is shown in Equation 11-10.

$$\text{Acceleration:} \quad a = \frac{dv}{dt}$$

Equation 11-10

This equations shows that acceleration is the derivative of velocity (v) with respect to time (t). dv is the change in velocity, and dt is the change in time.

We will compute our game object's velocity from its acceleration in much the same way that we computed our object's position from its velocity in the last section. We know that we don't want to use calculus, so let's see what our approximation will be:

```
newVelocity = oldVelocity + (acceleration * timeStep)
```

If the acceleration stays constant throughout the duration of the time step, the value (acceleration * timeStep) measures the change in velocity during the time step. If we're traveling 50 miles per hour east, accelerating 300 miles per hour squared east, and measuring the velocity every minute, the new velocity will be calculated like this:

```
50 + (300 * (1/ 60)) = 50 + 5 = 55 miles per hour east
```

You can see that automobiles accelerate and decelerate at a rate greater than 300 miles per hour squared. If it took one minute to increase your speed by five miles per hour, city driving would be unbearable. Just like velocity, acceleration has direction as well as magnitude. If we were accelerating 600 miles per hour squared west instead of 300 miles per hour squared east, the new velocity would have been calculated like this:

```
50 + (-600 * (1 / 60)) = 50 - 10 = 40 miles per hour east
```

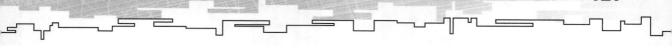

Force

The *force* I'm discussing in this chapter has nothing to do with Jedi Knights or the Dark Side. In the realm of physics, force influences an object's acceleration the same way acceleration influences the velocity, and velocity influences the position. When you walk, jump, or push something, you are generating a force. Jumping, for example, creates a force that allows you to briefly (.49 seconds for me—I measured my hang time at the Basketball Hall of Fame) accelerate upward faster than gravity, making you airborne.

Gravity is a downward force that makes your acceleration 9.8 meters per second squared down. The amount of force gravity applies to you depends on your mass; the heavier you are, the greater the gravitational force keeping you on the ground. When you jump, the force of jumping gives you an upward acceleration greater than 9.8 meters per second squared, and you leave the ground. The upward force does not last very long, and you decelerate quickly. When your upward acceleration reaches 9.8 meters per second squared, you've reached the peak of your jump, and you're about to go down. The force of gravity pushes you down, and your feet land on the ground.

In a computer game, when the player moves the joystick or presses a key on the keyboard, it generates a force on the player character. This force changes the player's acceleration, which then changes the player's velocity, which changes the player's position, and the player character moves.

Force measures a body's change in linear momentum over time. *Linear momentum* is an object's mass multiplied by its velocity, as you can see in Equation 11-11.

$$\text{Linear Momentum:} \quad p = mv$$

Equation 11-11

Mathematically, the formula for force is shown in Equation 11-12(a).

$$\text{Force:} \quad F = \frac{dp}{dt}$$

Equation 11-12(a)

This formula is the derivative of linear momentum (p) with respect to time (t). dp is the change in linear momentum, and dt is the change in time. Remember that linear momentum is mass times velocity, so we can rewrite the formula for force as shown in Equation 11-12(b).

$$= \frac{d(mv)}{dt}$$

Equation 11-12(b)

The mass is going to stay constant as we apply the force. This makes sense if you think about it. When you run or jump, your mass stays the same. If you have a mass of 170 pounds, your mass will remain 170 pounds during the duration of the run or jump. Your mass is not going to balloon to 180 pounds during the middle of a jump. Because the mass stays constant for the duration of the force, the formula can be simplified as shown in Equation 11-12(c).

$$= m \frac{dv}{dt}$$

Equation 11-12(c)

From the last section, you know that dv/dt is the acceleration of the object, which gives us Equation 11-12(d).

$$= ma$$

Equation 11-12(d)

If you've taken a high school physics course, that's the equation with which you're familiar for calculating the force.

This equation looks very easy to implement in a game. You calculate the object's acceleration by dividing the mass by the force, as shown in Equation 11-13, and move on from there.

Equation 11-13

$$\text{Acceleration From Force:} \quad a = \frac{F}{m}$$

Unfortunately, the F = ma equation measures the force at only a single point. We need to know the *total* force acting on the body to move the entire body. Our game's objects have mass distributed over an area, resulting in an infinite number of points to test using the F = ma equation. Mathematically, the total force is the change in total linear momentum over time, resulting in the formula shown as Equation 11-14.

Equation 11-14

$$\text{Total Force:} \quad F^T = \frac{d\,(p^T)}{dt}$$

Equation 11-14 is the derivative of linear momentum (p) with regard to time (t). I bet you wish they had used r to measure linear momentum and used p to measure position, but there's not much we can do about it now. The total linear momentum is the sum of all the linear momentums for the points in the object, as shown in Equation 11-15.

Equation 11-15

$$\text{Total Momentum:} \quad p^T = \sum_i m^i v^i$$

The problem is that there's an infinite number of points to add together to compute the total linear momentum. Surely, there must be an easier way to determine the total linear momentum.

Center of Mass

Our calculations would be much easier if we could measure only one point instead of an infinite number of points to determine the total linear momentum. Fortunately, we can introduce a point in the body called the *center of mass*. The center of mass is a point containing the sum of all the points in the body multiplied by their masses divided by the total mass of the object. Equation 11-16 shows how this looks mathematically.

Equation 11-16

Center of Mass: $r^{cm} = \dfrac{\sum\limits_{i} m^i r^i}{M}$

If you have a body in which every point has the same mass, the center of mass will be in the center of the body, as you can see in Figure 11-7 (a). For some bodies, the center of mass might not be inside the body itself, as you can see in Figure 11-7 (b). If there are differing masses inside the body, the center of mass tilts in the direction of the highest mass, as you can see in Figure 11-7 (c).

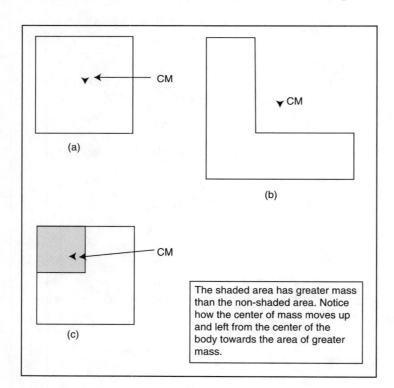

(a)

CM

(b)

▼ CM

(c)

CM

The shaded area has greater mass than the non-shaded area. Notice how the center of mass moves up and left from the center of the body towards the area of greater mass.

Figure 11-7

The centers of mass of three objects. In (a), every point has an equal mass. In (b), the center of mass isn't inside the body. In (c), a body has points of differing masses.

The center of mass simplifies the calculation of the total linear momentum and the total force. Instead of sampling an infinite number of points, we compute the linear momentum at the center of mass to determine the total linear momentum and compute the force at the center of mass to determine the total force.

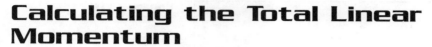

Calculating the Total Linear Momentum

Now that we have defined the center of mass, how can we use it to help us calculate the total linear momentum? Let's begin with the equation for the center of mass (Equation 11-16) and multiply both sides by the total mass, M. The result is shown in Equation 11-17 (a).

Equation 11-17 (a)

> Calculating Total Momentum
> $$Mr^{cm} = \sum_i m^i r^i$$

Now take the derivative of both sides of the equation, as shown in Equation 11-17 (b).

Equation 11-17 (b)

$$\frac{d\,(Mr^{cm})}{dt} = \sum_i \frac{d(m^i r^i)}{dt}$$

Because the mass will stay constant, we can rewrite Equation 11-17 (b) as shown in Equation 11-17 (c).

Equation 11-17 (c)

$$= \sum_i m^i \frac{d(r^i)}{dt}$$

The derivative dr/dt is the definition of velocity; we can recast the equation as shown in Equation 11-17 (d).

Equation 11-17 (d)

$$= \sum_i m^i \, v^i$$

The right side of the equation is the definition for total
linear momentum, so the equation can be simplified as shown in Equation
11-17 (e).

Equation 11-17 (e)

$$= p^T$$

Because the total mass remains constant, the equation can be shown as in Equation
11-18 (a).

Equation 11-18 (a)

$$p^T = M \, \frac{dr^{cm}}{dt}$$

Because we know that dr/dt is the definition of velocity, the equation for total
momentum looks like the one in Equation 11-18 (b).

Equation 11-18 (b)

$$= Mv^{cm}$$

Equation 11-18 (b) tells us that the total linear momentum equals the total mass of
the object multiplied by the velocity of the object at the center of mass.

Calculating the Total Force

The *total force* is the derivative of the total linear momentum, giving us Equation 11-
19 (a).

Equation 11-19 (a)

> Calculating Total Force
>
> $$F^T = \frac{d(p^T)}{dt}$$

Substituting the equation for the total linear momentum that we derived in the last section, we get Equation 11-19 (b).

Equation 11-19 (b)

> $$= \frac{d(MV^{cm})}{dt}$$

Because the total mass remains constant, we can recast this formula as shown in Equation 11-19 (c).

Equation 11-19 (c)

> $$= M\frac{dv^{cm}}{dt}$$

Because dv/dt is the acceleration of the center of mass, we can simplify the formula again, as shown in Equation 11-19 (d).

Equation 11-19 (d)

> $$= M\,a^{cm}$$

To summarize, the total force equals the total mass times the acceleration at the center of mass.

To calculate the acceleration, we take the total force and divide it by the total mass, which is expressed by Equation 11-20.

> **Calculating Acceleration From Total Force**
>
> $$a^{cm} = \frac{F^T}{M}$$

Equation 11-20

We can use this acceleration equation to compute the velocity and then compute the new position.

Going from Math to Code

I can tell you've reached a breaking point on mathematical equations, so I'm going to show you how to make the equations work in your game. Here are the steps you must take to implement the physics we've done so far into your game:

1. Calculate the initial position, velocity, and acceleration for each object in the game.
2. Calculate the center of mass.
3. Determine the force.
4. Use the force to compute the acceleration.
5. Use the acceleration to calculate the velocity.
6. Use the velocity to determine the position.
7. Draw the object at the new position.

None of the objects in the game will be moving initially, so their initial velocity and acceleration will be 0. The level contains the starting position of all the level's objects, so we can read the initial positions from disk when we load the level.

Calculating the center of mass can be tricky. We'll keep things simple and assume that each point in the body has the same mass. If we center our sprites inside the sprite rectangle, we can use the center of the sprite rectangle as the center of mass. If points in the body have differing masses, the calculation becomes more difficult. You would have to write a game-specific function to calculate the center of mass for that particular body. This function calculates the center of mass based on the specific distribution of mass throughout the body.

The forces you must deal with in your game will depend on the game itself. A billiards game, a flight simulator, and a side-scrolling platform game all have forces, but they are all different kinds of forces. A billiards game has to handle the force of the pool cue hitting the ball. A flight simulator must deal with aerodynamic forces. A side-scroller with jumping must deal with gravity.

The game we are creating in this book has three types of forces to handle: the player character moving, enemies moving, and launching missiles. I go into greater detail about these forces in the next three sections of the chapter.

After calculating the force, the rest of the math is pretty easy. It requires only a few lines of code, which you can see here:

```
acceleration = force / mass;
velocity = velocity + (acceleration * timeStep);
position = position + (velocity * timeStep);
```

Calculating the Player Force

Computing the force for the player character in our game is going to be relatively easy because the player character can do only thing: run. If he could jump, kick, or fly, we would have to compute forces for the multiple actions the player could perform. The player's input determines the force for the player character's movement. Here's where using axis values to read player input can come in handy. We can calculate the force based on how far the player moves the joystick; the farther he moves the stick, the greater the force.

We have to place a limit on how fast the player can move in the game. When people run, their bodies generate a lot of force to accelerate. The human body can generate only so much force, so people can run full-tilt for only a short time. You can try this yourself. After warming up (to prevent injuries), go into a full sprint. I doubt you will be able to keep it up for more than ten seconds.

In a game, all the player is doing to move the character is pressing a key on the keyboard or holding a joystick in a certain position. Obviously, this does not require a great deal of energy and stamina; if it did, avid video game players would be the most physically fit people on the planet. If the player character continues to accelerate as long as the player keeps pressing a key on the keyboard, the player character will move like The Flash. This characteristic would work if you were making a superhero game, but for most games, the movement will be unbelievable. Placing a limit on how fast the player can move will keep the movement somewhat realistic. The following lines of code keep the player from moving too quickly:

```
velocity = velocity + (acceleration * timeStep);
if (velocity > kMaximumVelocity)
        velocity = kMaximumVelocity;
```

Calculating the Enemy Force

When calculating the force for the non-player characters in the game, you have no player input to go on. You must directly calculate the force for each enemy. Computing the force for enemies requires some experimentation. You'll have to play around with the force values to get the kind of enemy movement you want.

Just as you do with player characters, you will want to place a limit on how fast each non-player character can move. Enemies that move too fast will frustrate the player.

Calculating Missile Force

For the purposes of this section, a missile is what discharges from the player's weapon when he fires his weapon, whether it be an arrow from a bow, a bullet from a shotgun, or a torpedo from a submarine. When we move a character in the game, we assume that the character is initially at rest. We apply a force over a period of time, and the character accelerates and moves. Launching a missile is different; we apply one large force, and the missile flies toward its target. Gravity slows the missile down until it either hits the target or drops to the ground.

In a 3D world, the missile would travel on its path (north, south, east, or west), and gravity would pull the missile down to the ground. Our game's world is a 2D world, which means that south and down are the same direction. Because of this, we must apply gravity differently than we would in a 3D world. Instead of gravity pulling the missile down, gravity will pull the missile in the opposite direction of the direction the player fired the missile. If the missile travels west, gravity will point east, slowing the missile down. With this scheme, it's important to kill the missile when the velocity reaches 0. Otherwise, the missile will change direction and move infinitely in the new direction, which is slightly unrealistic behavior.

The following function provides an example of how gravity slows down a missile in a 2D game world:

```
void GameWeapon::CalculateCurrentForce(double timeStep)
{
        // Apply gravity to the current force

        Vector2D gravityForce;

        double oldXComponent;
        double oldYComponent;
```

```
// currentForce is a data member of the GameWeapon class.
oldXComponent = currentForce.GetXComponent();
oldYComponent = currentForce.GetYComponent();

double gravityMagnitude = kGravityAcceleration * GetMass() * timeStep;
SpriteDirection missileDirection = GetSpriteDirection();

// Pick the direction to apply the gravitational force.
// Gravity moves in the opposite direction that the
// missile is traveling.
switch (missileDirection) {
        case kSpriteFacingUp:
                gravityForce.SetXComponent(kStandingSpeed);
                gravityForce.SetYComponent(gravityMagnitude * -1.0);
                        break;

        case kSpriteFacingDown:
                gravityForce.SetXComponent(kStandingSpeed);
                gravityForce.SetYComponent(gravityMagnitude);
                        break;

        case kSpriteFacingLeft:
                gravityForce.SetXComponent(gravityMagnitude * -1.0);
                gravityForce.SetYComponent(kStandingSpeed);
                break;

        case kSpriteFacingRight:
                gravityForce.SetXComponent(gravityMagnitude);
                gravityForce.SetYComponent(kStandingSpeed);
                break;

        default:
                gravityForce.SetXComponent(kStandingSpeed);
                gravityForce.SetYComponent(kStandingSpeed);
                break;
}

double newXComponent;
double newYComponent;

newXComponent = oldXComponent + gravityForce.GetXComponent();
```

```
      newYComponent = oldYComponent + gravityForce.GetYComponent();

      currentForce.SetXComponent(newXComponent);
      currentForce.SetYComponent(newYComponent);
}
```

Angular Motion

The linear motion we covered in the last section dealt with objects moving forward, backward, upward, and downward. For many games, linear motion is enough, but you might find that your game benefits from angular motion as well. In *angular motion*, the object may rotate, either at rest or while moving forward, backward, upward, or downward. Angular motion works in addition to, not as a substitute for, linear motion, so don't forget your linear motion knowledge.

Orientation

The angular equivalent to position is orientation, which we denote with the Greek letter capital omega, which you can see in Equation 11-21.

Equation 11-21

$$\text{Orientation: } \Omega$$

When a body rotates, the body's x and y axes rotate as well, as you can see in Figure 11-8. The body's *orientation* is the angle between the world's x and y axes and the body's x and y axes, which is a measure of how much the body has rotated. To add angular motion to our game, we must add a data member to the GameSprite class for the sprite's orientation. You can either measure the orientation in degrees (0 to 360) or in radians (0 to 2 pi). If you choose to measure the orientation in degrees, the data member will look like this:

```
short orientation;    // in degrees
```

If you choose to measure in radians, the data member will be a floating point value, looking like this:

```
double orientation;    // in radians
```

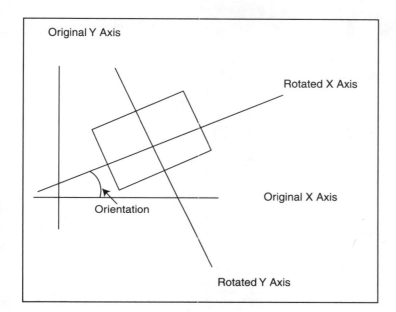

Original Y Axis

Rotated X Axis

Original X Axis

Orientation

Rotated Y Axis

Figure 11-8

Measuring orientation.

Angular Velocity

The *angular velocity* measures how quickly the body is rotating, making it the angular equivalent of linear velocity. The equation for angular velocity is shown in Equation 11-22.

$$\text{Angular Velocity:} \quad W = \frac{d\,\Omega}{dt}$$

Equation 11-22

This equation states that the angular velocity (lowercase omega) is the derivative of orientation (uppercase omega) with respect to time. Angular velocity measures the change in orientation over time.

Calculating Linear Velocity from Angular Velocity

We can use the angular velocity to compute a body's linear velocity at point A. If the body is not translating (that is, it is not moving to new x and y coordinates while it is rotating), we can calculate the linear velocity by taking the perpendicular vector from the origin to point A and multiplying this vector by the angular velocity, as you can see in Figure 11-9, giving us the formula in Equation 11-23.

Linear Velocity (No Translation): $V^A = Wr_\perp^{DA}$

Equation 11-23

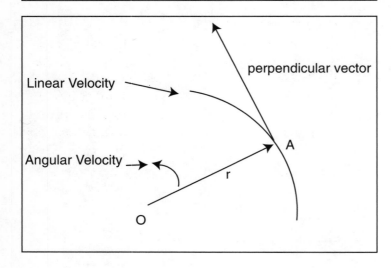

Linear Velocity

perpendicular vector

Angular Velocity

r

A

O

Figure 11-9

Computing linear velocity from angular velocity.

A vector perpendicular to a vector with the components ⟨x, y⟩ will have the components ⟨-y, x⟩, so you can calculate the components of the linear velocity as shown in Equation 11-24 (a) and (b).

$$V_x^A = Wy$$

$$V_y^A = -Wx$$

Equation 11-24 (a) and (b)

Now let's work through some math to see that it actually works. (If you take my word for it that the equations are correct, and you don't want to deal with the math, feel free to move on to the next section.) There are three things we have to test to see whether the equation for computing the linear velocity from the angular velocity is correct:

- Is the vector for the linear velocity perpendicular to the vector from point 0 to point A?
- Is the magnitude of the linear velocity correct?
- Is the direction of the linear velocity vector in Figure 11-9 correct?

Let's begin by showing that the linear velocity vector is perpendicular to the vector from point 0 to point A. If the object is only rotating, the point A moves in a circle around the origin (see Figure 11-10). The vector r, which goes from point 0 to point A, is the position vector. Remember from our discussion about linear motion that the linear velocity is the derivative of the position. This means that the linear velocity has the derivative of the vector r in it. There's a theorem from calculus that helps us:

> If V is a differentiable vector-valued function on a time interval and ||V(t)|| is constant for all t in the interval, then the vectors V(t) and DtV(t) are orthogonal.

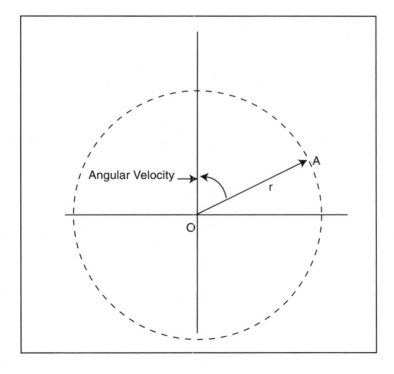

Figure 11-10

The path the point A can take rotating around the origin 0 if the object is only rotating.

What the theorem says in English is that if the magnitude of a vector V's magnitude stays constant, then the derivative of vector V is a vector that is perpendicular to V. This theorem tells us that the velocity vector must be perpendicular to the position vector. The point A is moving in a circle around the origin, as Figure 11-10 shows, which means that the distance from point A to point O always has the length of the vector r. Because the vector r always has the same length, the derivative of r—the linear velocity—is orthogonal (perpendicular) to r. If we weren't taking angular effects into account, the linear velocity would just be the vector perpendicular to r. However, we are covering angular motion here, and we must take the angular velocity into account. That's why we multiply the perpendicular vector by the angular velocity.

Now that we know that the linear velocity vector is perpendicular to the vector from the origin to point A, we can check whether or not Equation 11-23 calculates the magnitude of the linear velocity correctly. Figure 11-11 shows the body rotating from point A to point B. The body has moved (omega * r) radians in the rotation from point A to point B. We can measure the magnitude of the velocity vector, its speed, by differentiating the equation for its movement as shown in Equation 11-25 (a).

Equation 11-25 (a)

$$\text{Proving Magnitude of Linear Velocity:} \qquad \|v^A\| = \frac{d\,(\Omega r)}{dt}$$

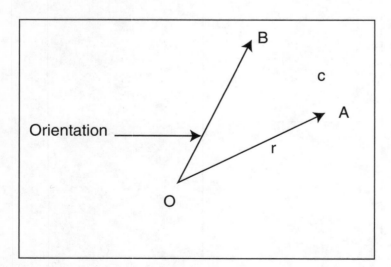

Figure 11-11

Rotating from point A to point B.

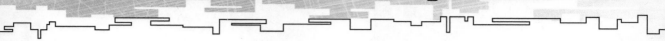

Because point A is rotating only, r drops out of the derivative, giving us Equation 11-25 (b).

$$= r \frac{d\Omega}{dt}$$

Equation 11-25 (b)

Because the value d(uppercase omega)/dt is the angular velocity, we can rewrite the formula.

The magnitude of the vector perpendicular to r will be the same as the magnitude of r, so the linear velocity's magnitude will be correct using the vector perpendicular to r, as you can see in Example 11-7.

$$\|r\| = \sqrt{x^2 + y^2}$$

$$\|r_\perp\| = \sqrt{(-y)^2 + x^2} = \sqrt{x^2 + y^2}$$

Example 11-7

Now we know that our equation for computing linear velocity from angular velocity computes the linear velocity's magnitude correctly. Let's see whether it gets the direction right. There are two possible vectors perpendicular to r (see Figure 11-12). The vector v points counterclockwise, and the vector -v points clockwise.

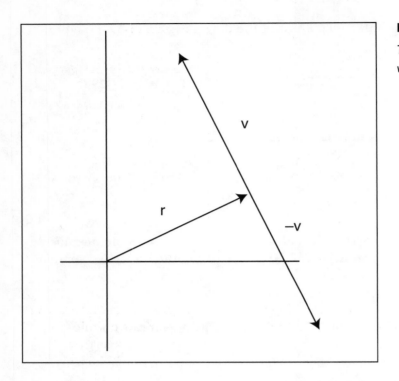

Figure 11-12

The two vectors, v and -v, which are perpendicular to r.

Most physics books measure the orientation counterclockwise. Figure 11-13 shows the difference between clockwise and counterclockwise rotation. We will measure the orientation counterclockwise as most physics books do so that the angular velocity is positive when we move counterclockwise. In this case, we want the perpendicular vector that is counterclockwise to r, and that vector is v, not -v. If we measured the orientation clockwise, the velocity vector would have been -v, not v. Now we've shown that our equation for computing linear velocity is correct. *Woo hoo!*

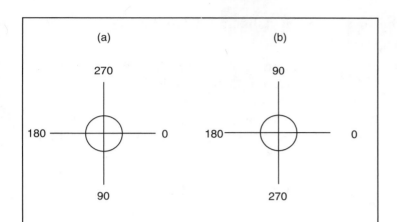

Figure 11-13

Clockwise (a) and counterclockwise (b) rotation.

Translating and Rotating Simultaneously

The equations we derived to calculate the linear velocity from the angular velocity assumed that the object was only rotating. Obviously, objects can move while they're rotating in the physical world. To calculate the body's linear velocity at point A when the body is also translating at point 0, we use Equation 11-26.

Equation 11-26

Linear Velocity (Translation): $V^A = V^O + Wr_\perp{}^{OA}$

This equation states that we take the linear velocity we computed for a body that was not rotating and add to that computed velocity the linear velocity of the body at the translating point.

Angular Acceleration

The *angular acceleration* measures how quickly the body's angular velocity is changing, making it the angular equivalent of linear acceleration. The equation for angular acceleration is shown in Equation 11-27.

Equation 11-27

Angular Acceleration: $\alpha = \dfrac{dW}{dt}$

This equation states that the angular velocity (alpha) is the derivative of orientation (lowercase omega) with respect to time.

We can use the angular acceleration to compute a body's linear acceleration at point A in much the same way that we calculated the linear velocity from the angular velocity earlier in the chapter. If the body is not translating (that is, it is not moving to new x and y coordinates while rotating), we can calculate the linear acceleration by taking the perpendicular vector from the origin to point A and multiplying this vector by the angular acceleration, as shown in Equation 11-28.

Equation 11-28

Linear Acceleration (No Translation): $a^A = \alpha r_\perp^{OA}$

A vector perpendicular to a vector with the components $\langle x,\ y \rangle$ will have the components $\langle -y,\ x \rangle$, so you can calculate the components of the linear acceleration as shown in Equation 11-29 (a) and (b).

Equation 11-29 (a) and (b)

$$a_X^A = \alpha y$$

$$a_Y^A = -\alpha x$$

If the body is translating while it's rotating, you add the angular acceleration at the translation point to the acceleration we calculated in the previous paragraph, resulting in Equation 11-30.

Equation 11-30

Linear Acceleration (Translation): $a^A = a^O + \alpha r_\perp^{OA}$

The math for proving the equations for calculating linear acceleration from angular acceleration is exactly the same as the math for proving the linear velocity equations, so I will not rehash it here. Instead, I will pull the old textbook cop-out and leave the proofs as an exercise for the reader.

Angular Momentum

To begin, we'll define the angular momentum of one point B, around another point A, using Equation 11-31 (a).

$$L^{AB} = r_\perp^{AB} \cdot p^B$$

Angular Momentum:

Equation 11-31 (a)

This equation says that the angular momentum of point B around point A is equal to the dot product of the vector perpendicular to the vector from point A to B and the linear momentum at point B. The angular momentum measures how much of point B's linear momentum is rotating around point A. Figure 11-14 provides an illustration of angular momentum.

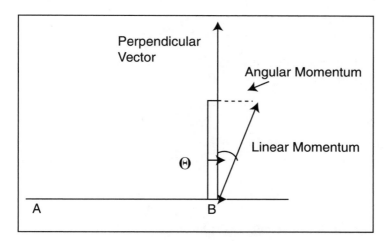

Figure 11-14

Angular momentum.

A vector perpendicular to a vector with the components $\langle x, y \rangle$ will have the components $\langle -y, x \rangle$, so you can calculate the components of the angular momentum as shown in Equation 11-31 (b).

$$L^{AB} = xp_y - yp_x$$

Equation 11-31 (b)

This equation says that we can calculate the angular momentum by taking the y component of the vector AB and multiplying it by the x component of the linear momentum and subtracting that value from the x component of the vector AB multiplied by the y component of the linear momentum.

Torque

Torque is the angular equivalent of force. It measures the change in angular momentum over time. Torque is a kind of twisting force. When you open a lid on a jar, you're applying torque on the jar. The equation for the torque applied at point B rotating around point A is given in Equation 11-32 (a).

$$\text{Torque:}\quad T^{AB} = \frac{d\,(L^{AB})}{dt}$$

Equation 11-32 (a)

What we'd like to know is how torque relates to force. We begin by using the equation for angular momentum, as shown in Equation 11-32 (b).

$$= \frac{d\,(r_{\perp}{}^{AB} \cdot p^{B})}{dt}$$

Equation 11-32 (b)

There's a theorem in calculus that says the derivative of the dot product of two vectors, u and v, equals the dot product of the derivative of u and the vector v plus the dot product of the vector u and the derivative of v. Equation 11-32 (c) shows the result of that theorem.

$$= \frac{d\,(r_{\perp}{}^{AB})}{dt} \cdot p^{B} + r_{\perp}{}^{AB} \cdot \frac{d\,(p^{B})}{dt}$$

Equation 11-32 (c)

We take the definitions of linear velocity and linear momentum to simplify the first dot product and the definition of linear momentum to simplify the second dot product, giving us Equation 11-32 (d).

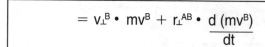

Equation 11-32 (d)

$$= v_{\perp}^{B} \bullet mv^{B} + r_{\perp}^{AB} \bullet \frac{d\,(mv^{B})}{dt}$$

The first dot product is 0 because we're taking the dot product of two orthogonal vectors. Let's say that the linear velocity vector has the components $\langle x,\ y \rangle$. Multiplying that vector by the mass gives us $\langle mx,\ my \rangle$. The perpendicular vector has components $\langle -y,\ x \rangle$. The first dot product becomes:

`-ymx + xmy`

The result of this equation is 0. The mass stays constant during the time interval of the derivative. Our equation now looks like Equation 11-32 (e).

Equation 11-32 (e)

$$= r_{\perp}^{AB} \bullet m\,\frac{d(v^{B})}{dt}$$

The derivative we have left is the definition of linear acceleration, as shown by Equation 11-32 (f).

Equation 11-32 (f)

$$= r_{\perp}^{AB} \bullet ma^{B}$$

We take the definition of a force at a point to give us Equation 11-32 (g).

Equation 11-32 (g)

$$= r_{\perp}^{AB} \bullet F^{B}$$

This equation says that the torque is the dot product of the vector perpendicular from the vector from point A to point B and the force at point B. A vector perpendicular to a vector with components $\langle x,\ y \rangle$ will have components $\langle -y,\ x \rangle$, so you can calculate the components of the angular momentum as shown by Equation 11-33.

$$T = xF_y - yF_x$$

Equation 11-33

This equation says that to calculate the torque, you take the y component of the vector AB and multiply it by the x component of the force. You take this product and subtract it from the product of the x component of the vector AB and the y component of the force.

Much as we did with linear motion, we would like to be able to easily calculate the total torque rather than calculating the torque for an infinite number of points. We need an angular equivalent of the center of mass.

Moment of Inertia

The angular equivalent of the center of mass is the *moment of inertia*. Equation 11-34 defines the moment of inertia at a point A.

$$\text{Moment of Inertia:} \quad I^A = \sum_i m^i \, (r_\perp^{Ai})^2$$

Equation 11-34

The moment of inertia is the sum of the masses multiplied by the square of the distance of each mass from the axis. For the work we're doing, we want the moment of inertia at the center of mass. With the newly discovered moment of inertia, we can more easily determine an object's total angular momentum and total torque.

Calculating the Total Angular Momentum

Let's use the moment of inertia we computed in the previous section to calculate the total angular momentum. We begin by defining the total angular momentum as shown in Equation 11-35 (a):

$$\text{Total Angular Momentum:} \quad L^{AT} = \sum_i r_\perp^{Ai} \cdot p^i$$

Equation 11-35 (a)

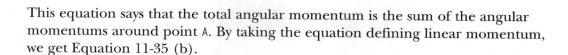

This equation says that the total angular momentum is the sum of the angular momentums around point A. By taking the equation defining linear momentum, we get Equation 11-35 (b).

$$= \sum_i r_\perp^{Ai} \cdot m^i v^i$$

Equation 11-35 (b)

Converting our linear velocity to an angular velocity gives us Equation 11-35 (c).

$$= \sum_i r_\perp^{Ai} \cdot m^i W r_\perp^{Ai}$$

Equation 11-35 (c)

The angular velocity is the same for all points in the body, making the equation look like Equation 11-35 (d).

$$= W \sum_i r_\perp^{Ai} \cdot m^i r_\perp^{Ai}$$

Equation 11-35 (d)

Taking the dot product inside the sum gives us Equation 11-35 (e).

$$= W \sum_i m^i (r_\perp^{Ai})^2$$

Equation 11-35 (e)

That sum is the moment of inertia so we can write the total angular momentum as shown in Equation 11-35 (f).

$$= W I^A$$

Equation 11-35 (f)

The total angular momentum equals the momentum of inertia multiplied by the angular velocity.

Calculating the Total Torque

Now that we have the total angular momentum, we can calculate the total torque. The total torque is the derivative of the total angular momentum, as shown in Equation 11-36 (a).

$$\text{Total Torque:} \quad T^{AT} = \frac{d\,(L^{AT})}{dt}$$

Equation 11-36 (a)

Substituting the calculation for the total angular momentum we computed in the last section gives us Equation 11-36 (b).

$$= \frac{d\,(WI^{A})}{dt}$$

Equation 11-36 (b)

The moment of inertia is constant, so it drops out of the derivative, giving us Equation 11-36 (c).

$$= I^{A}\,\frac{dW}{dt}$$

Equation 11-36 (c)

The derivative we have is the definition for angular acceleration, so we can write the equation for total torque as shown in Equation 11-36 (d).

$$= I^{A}\alpha$$

Equation 11-36 (d)

The total torque equals the moment of inertia multiplied by the angular acceleration.

Going from Math to Code

Obviously, calculating angular motion will add more work to the work we've done in calculating linear motion. Here are the extra steps to perform:

1. Calculate the initial orientation, angular velocity, and angular acceleration.
2. Calculate the moment of inertia at the center of mass.
3. Calculate the total torque.
4. Calculate the angular acceleration from the total torque.
5. Calculate the angular velocity and linear acceleration from the angular acceleration.
6. Calculate the orientation and linear velocity from the angular velocity.

Step 1 requires little work. Because the objects do not rotate at the start, the orientation, angular velocity, and angular acceleration will be 0.

Calculating the moment of inertia requires some calculus. Fortunately, most physics books contain formulas for the moments of inertia of common objects. For a rectangular object, the moment of inertia is as follows:

```
Total Mass * (height squared + width squared) / 12
```

After calculating the moment of inertia, it's just a matter of plugging in the formulas we derived to calculate the total torque, angular and linear acceleration, angular and linear velocity, and orientation, which you can see in the following code:

```
angularAcceleration = totalTorque / momentOfInertia;
perpVector = GetPerpendicularVector(theVector);
linearAcceleration = angularAcceleration * perpVector;
angularVelocity = angularVelocity + (angularAcceleration * timeStep);
linearVelocity = angularVelocity * perpVector;
orientation = orientation + (angularVelocity * timeStep);
position = position + (linearVelocity * timeStep);
```

Collision Detection

Collision detection can make or break an action game. The player's going to be ticked off if it looks like he hits an enemy with a bullet, but the enemy doesn't get hit. The player will also be upset if he takes a phantom hit from a monster. To keep the players of your game from becoming frustrated and dragging your game to the trash, you should implement an accurate collision detection system. Coincidentally, I do just that in the next two sections.

Bounding Boxes

Bounding boxes are a quick way to detect collisions. What you do with bounding boxes is measure rectangles around the perimeter of both objects. If the rectangles do not intersect, there's no collision. If they do intersect, there may or may not be a collision. Figure 11-15 shows a situation in which the bounding boxes intersect, but there's no collision between the two objects.

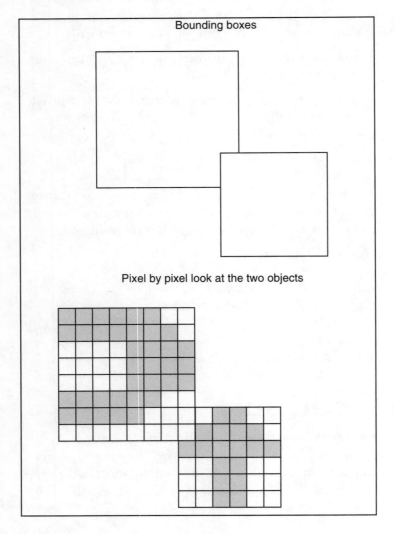

Bounding boxes

Pixel by pixel look at the two objects

Figure 11-15

Two objects whose bounding boxes intersect, but are not colliding.

The following function detects collisions using bounding boxes:

```
Boolean PhysicsController::DetectCollision(GameSpritePtr collidingModel
        // Calculate the bounding boxes
        short topEdge = modelToControl->GetWorldY();
        short bottomEdge = topEdge + modelToControl->GetSpriteHeight();
        short leftEdge = modelToControl->GetWorldX();
        short rightEdge = leftEdge + modelToControl->GetSpriteWidth();

        short colliderTopEdge = collidingModel->GetWorldY();
        short colliderBottomEdge = colliderTopEdge
                                + collidingModel->GetSpriteHeight();
        short colliderLeftEdge = collidingModel->GetWorldX();
        short colliderRightEdge = colliderLeftEdge
                                + collidingModel->GetSpriteWidth();

        if (topEdge > colliderBottomEdge)
            return false;

        if (bottomEdge < colliderTopEdge)
            return false;

        if (leftEdge > colliderRightEdge)
            return false;

        if (rightEdge < colliderLeftEdge)
            return false;
        // At this point, the two sprite bounding boxes intersect.
        // Check to see if there actually is a collision
        return (DetectExactCollision(collidingSprite));
}
```

The DetectCollision() function begins by calculating the bounding boxes of the two objects we want to check for a collision. Then the function checks if the two bounding boxes intersect, which requires up to four steps:

1. If the top of object A is below the bottom of object B, then object A is below object B, and there is no collision.

2. If the bottom of object A is above the top of object B, then object A is above object B, and there is no collision.

3. If the left edge of object A is to the right of object B, then object A is to the right of object B, and there is no collision.

4. If the right edge of object A is to the left of object B, then object A is to the left of object B, and there is no collision.

If all four tests fail, then the bounding boxes intersect, and there may be a collision. Some games can get away with just using bounding boxes, but if you want 100% accurate collision detection, you must perform another test, which is explained in the next section.

Pixel-Perfect Collision Detection

In the last section, we discussed using bounding boxes for collision detection. Bounding boxes are a quick method for determining that two pixels did not collide. However, all bounding boxes can tell us is whether or not two rectangles intersect. If they do intersect, we must go further to determine whether a collision actually occurred.

To determine whether or not we have a collision, we must take the intersection of the two bounding boxes and do a pixel test. Remember that sprites have a transparent color to allow them to appear as non-rectangular shapes. We must check the pixels in both objects for non-transparent pixels. If a pixel is non-transparent in both objects, we have a collision, so we can stop testing. If we go through the bounding box intersection without finding a place where both objects have a non-transparent color, then there was no collision. The following code detects an exact collision between two objects:

```
Boolean PhysicsController::DetectExactCollision(GameSpritePtr
                                                collidingModel)
{

        Rect spriteRect;
        Rect collidingSpriteRect;
        Rect overlapRect;

        spriteRect.top = modelToControl->GetWorldY();
        spriteRect.bottom = spriteRect.top + modelToControl->GetSpriteHeight();
        spriteRect.left = modelToControl->GetWorldX();
        spriteRect.right = spriteRect.left + modelToControl->GetSpriteWidth();

        collidingSpriteRect.top = collidingModel->GetWorldY();
```

```
collidingSpriteRect.bottom = collidingSpriteRect.top
                            + collidingModel->GetSpriteHeight();
collidingSpriteRect.left = collidingModel->GetWorldX();
collidingSpriteRect.right = collidingSpriteRect.left
                            + collidingModel->GetSpriteWidth();

Boolean haveOverlap;

haveOverlap = SectRect(&spriteRect, &collidingSpriteRect, &overlapRect);
if (haveOverlap == false)
        return false;

// Go through all the pixels in the rectangle that overlap
// the two sprites. If one of the pixels in both sprites is not
// transparent then there is a collision.

short spritePixelRow;
short spritePixelColumn;
short spriteTestRow;
short spriteTestColumn;
short spritePixelValue;
SpriteBuffer theSpriteStorage;

short collidingSpritePixelRow;
short collidingSpritePixelColumn;
short collidingSpriteTestRow;
short collidingSpriteTestColumn;
short collidingSpritePixelValue;
SpriteBuffer collidingSpriteStorage;

for (short row = overlapRect.top; row < overlapRect.bottom; row++) {
        for (short column = overlapRect.left; column < overlapRect.right;
                column++) {
                // Get the sprite's local pixel.
                spritePixelRow = overlapRect.top - spriteRect.top + row;
                spritePixelColumn = overlapRect.left - spriteRect.left
                                    + column;

                // Get the pixel to test in the sprite buffer
                spriteTestRow = (modelToControl->GetSpriteRow() *
                        modelToControl->GetSpriteHeight()) + spritePixelRow;
```

```
                    spriteTestColumn = (modelToControl->GetSpriteColumn() *
                          modelToControl->GetSpriteWidth())
                          + spritePixelColumn;

                    theSpriteStorage = modelToControl->GetSpriteStorage();
                    spritePixelValue =
                                  theSpriteStorage.GetPixelValue(spriteTestRow,
                                  spriteTestColumn);

                    // Repeat the process for the colliding sprite
                    collidingSpritePixelRow = overlapRect.top
                                         - collidingSpriteRect.top + row;
                    collidingSpritePixelColumn = overlapRect.left
                                         - collidingSpriteRect.left + column;

                    collidingSpriteTestRow = (collidingModel->GetSpriteRow() *
                          collidingModel->GetSpriteHeight())
                             + collidingSpritePixelRow;
                    collidingSpriteTestColumn =
                          (collidingModel->GetSpriteColumn() *
                          collidingModel->GetSpriteWidth())
                             + collidingSpritePixelColumn;

                    collidingSpriteStorage = collidingModel->GetSpriteStorage();
                    collidingSpritePixelValue = collidingSpriteStorage.
                                  GetPixelValue(collidingSpriteTestRow,
                                  collidingSpriteTestColumn);

                    // Check if the two sprites have transparent values
                    // at their current pixels.
                    if ((spritePixelValue != kSpriteTransparencyValue) &&
                          (collidingSpritePixelValue !=
                                  kSpriteTransparencyValue))
                                  return true;


              }
         }

    // At this point, there was no collision
    return false;

}
```

Performing a pixel-by-pixel test can be time consuming, especially if the bounding box test detected a false collision. That's the reason why we perform the bounding box test first. The bounding box test quickly determines whether there definitely was no collision, eliminating the need for many pixel tests. If there was a possible collision, the intersecting rectangle will be much smaller than the sprite rectangles for both objects, minimizing the number of pixels to test. The fewer pixel tests we perform, the faster our collision detection will be.

Collision Response

When we detect a collision, we must resolve it. If we don't resolve it, the colliding objects will continue on their current paths, and the objects will go through each other. Imagine a baseball game where the pitched ball goes through the bat and keeps on moving, and you'll see the problems that can occur with improper collision response.

Figure 11-16 shows a sample collision between two objects, A and B, at point P. Each object has its own velocity at the point of collision. To resolve the collision, we want to apply a force to each object to keep the objects from penetrating into each other. The problem is that a force takes some time to apply. In this short time it takes to apply the force, the two objects will be inside each other. What we need is an instantaneous force that changes the objects' velocities before they penetrate. Fortunately, there is such an instantaneous force; it's called an *impulse*. An impulse instantaneously changes an object's momentum, making it an instantaneous force.

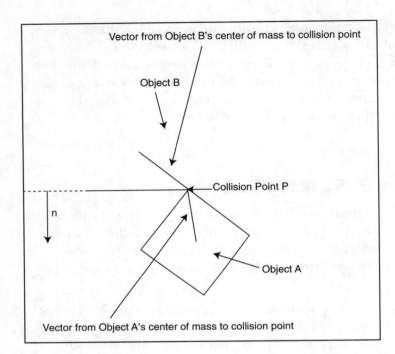

Vector from Object B's center of mass to collision point

Object B

Collision Point P

n

Object A

Vector from Object A's center of mass to collision point

Figure 11-16

A collision between two objects.

An impulse is a vector quantity, so it has both magnitude and direction. We use the scalar quantity j to signify the magnitude, and we use the normal vector for the collision (the vector n in Figure 11-16) for the impulse's direction. If we have an impulse, jn, for object A, then the impulse for object B is -jn because of Newton's Third Law of Motion. Newton's Third Law states that for every action, there is an equal and opposite reaction. When we apply an impulse jn to object A, object B feels an impulse of -jn.

Computing the Linear Velocities

Because the impulse is a force, we can write the equation for the impulse for object A as shown in Equation 11-37.

$$\text{Impulse:} \quad jn = Ma$$

Equation 11-37

So we can compute the acceleration at point A as shown in Equation 11-38.

$$\text{Acceleration:} \quad a = \frac{jn}{M}$$

Equation 11-38

We can use this acceleration to compute the linear velocity of point A after the collision, giving us Equation 11-39 (a).

$$\text{Outgoing Linear Velocities:} \quad V_2{}^A = V_1{}^B + \frac{jn}{M}$$

Equation 11-39 (a)

This equation states that the linear velocity of object A after the collision equals the linear velocity of object A before the collision plus the acceleration of object A, which is the impulse divided by object A's mass. The equation works similarly for object B except that the impulse on object B is -jn so the linear velocity of object B after the collision is shown by Equation 11-39 (b).

$$V_2{}^B = V_1{}^B - \frac{jn}{M^B}$$

Equation 11-39 (b)

These equations don't sound too bad. At the time of collision, we know the velocity at collision time, the normal vector for the collision, and the total mass of the object. There's just one problem. What value do we use for j? That's going to require some more math.

Relative Velocities

To compute the magnitude of the impulse, j, for the collision, we need to know the relative velocity between the colliding objects. The *relative velocity* is the difference between the two objects' velocities at the collision point, as shown by Equation 11-40.

$$\text{Relative Velocity:} \quad V^{AB} = V^{AP} - V^{BP}$$

Equation 11-40

We can take the relative velocity and the normal vector (vector n in Figure 11-16) for the collision to compute the relative normal velocity between the colliding objects. The relative normal velocity is the dot product of the normal velocity and the normal vector, as shown by Equation 11-41.

> Relative Normal Velocity: $V^{AB} \bullet n = (V^{AP} - V^{PB}) \bullet n$

Equation 11-41

We can compute the relative normal velocity after the collision using the Equation 11-42.

> Relative Normal Velocity After Collision: $V_2^{AB} \bullet n = -ev_1^{AB} \bullet n$

Equation 11-42

This formula states that the relative normal velocity after the collision equals the dot product of the negative of the product of the coefficient of restitution and the relative normal velocity at the time of the collision and the normal vector. What is the *coefficient of restitution?* It's a value between 0 and 1 that measures how much of the object's kinetic energy remains after the collision. In other words, it measures the "bounciness" of the collision. The higher the coefficient of restitution, the more the object bounces after the collision. Basketballs and tennis balls hitting the ground will have a higher coefficient of restitution than will a brick or a bowling ball dropping on the ground.

Computing the Impulse's Magnitude

Now that we know the relative normal velocities before and after the collision, we can use those quantities to calculate the magnitude of the impulse for nonrotating bodies. Equation 11-43 shows this formula (trumpet blast).

> Impulse Magnitude (No Rotation): $j = \dfrac{-(1te)\,V_1^{AB} \bullet n}{n \bullet n \left(\dfrac{\perp}{M^A} + \dfrac{\perp}{M^B}\right)}$

Equation 11-43

The numerator of the magnitude j is simply the relative normal velocity at the time of collision multiplied by the quantity $-(1 + e)$, where e is the coefficient of restitution. The denominator is the dot product of the normal vector and the product of the normal vector and the sum of 1 over the mass of both objects.

How did I come up with this equation? (Feel free to move to the next section if you don't care.) I began by taking the equation for the relative normal velocity after the collision (Equation 11-42) and substituting the definition of relative normal velocity (Equation 11-41) into the left side of the equation, giving me Equation 11-43 (a).

$$(V_2{}^A - V_2{}^B) \bullet n = -e \, (V_1{}^A - V_1{}^B) \bullet n$$

Equation 11.43 (a)

Then I substituted the equations for the outgoing linear velocities (Equations 11.39 (a) and (b)), resulting in the Equation 11-43 (b).

$$\left[\left(V_1{}^A + \frac{jn}{M^A}\right) - \left(V_1{}^B + \frac{jn}{M^B}\right) \right] \bullet n = -e \, (V_1{}^{AB}) \bullet n$$

Equation 11-43 (b)

I added the terms on the left side so that the equation simplifies to Equation 11-43 (c).

$$\left(V_1{}^A + \frac{jn}{M^A}\right) - V_1{}^B + \frac{jn}{M^B} \bullet n = -e \, (V_1{}^{AB}) \bullet n$$

Equation 11-43 (c)

Next I used the definition of relative velocity (Equation 11-40) to calculate the relative velocity before the collision, resulting in the Equation 11-43 (d).

$$\left(V_1{}^{AB} + \frac{jn}{M^A} + \frac{jn}{M^B}\right) \bullet n = -e \, (V_1{}^{AB}) \bullet n$$

Equation 11-43 (d)

Then I applied the dot product to the left side of the equation, which results in Equation 11-43 (e).

Equation 11-43 (e)

$$(V_1{}^{AB} \bullet n) + \frac{(jn \bullet n)}{M^A} + \frac{(jn \bullet n)}{M^B} = -e\,(V_1{}^{AB}) \bullet n$$

I moved the relative normal velocity to the right side of the equation, so the equation looks like Equation 11-43 (f).

Equation 11-43 (f)

$$\frac{(jn \bullet n)}{M^A} + \frac{(jn \bullet n)}{M^B} = (-V_1{}^{AB} - eV_1{}^{AB}) \bullet n$$

I isolated the impulse (jn) on the left side, giving me Equation 11-43 (g).

Equation 11-43 (g)

$$jn \left(\frac{\perp}{M^A} + \frac{\perp}{M^B} \right) \bullet n = (-Ite)\,V_1{}^{AB}) \bullet n$$

I divided both sides by the dot product of 1 over the masses and the normal vector, giving me Equation 11-43 (h).

Equation 11-43 (h)

$$jn = \frac{(-Ite)\,V_1{}^{AB} \bullet n}{n \bullet \left(\dfrac{\perp}{M^A} + \dfrac{\perp}{M^B} \right)}$$

Dividing both sides of Equation 11-43 (h) by the normal vector gives us the value of j, which you can see back up in Equation 11-43. Isn't math fun?

Computing the Angular Velocities for Rotating Bodies

Should an off-center collision occur, we would like the objects to rotate, so we have to compute angular velocities as well as linear ones. Because the impulse is the equivalent of torque for a rotating body, we can write the equation for the impulse for object A as shown in Equation 11-44 (a).

Equation 11-44 (a)

$$\text{Angular Acceleration:} \quad r_\perp^{AP} \bullet jn = I^A d$$

From our discussion about torque earlier in this chapter, remember that the torque of object A at point P is the dot product of the perpendicular vector and the torque. In this case, we want an angular impulse instead of a torque, so we substitute the value of the impulse, jn, for the torque. That explains the left side of the equation. Solving for angular acceleration gives us Equation 11-44 (b).

Equation 11-44 (b)

$$d = \frac{r_\perp^{AP} \bullet jn}{I^A}$$

We can use the angular acceleration to compute the angular velocity of point A after the collision, giving us Equation 11-45 (a).

Equation 11-45 (a)

$$W_2^A = W_1^A + \frac{r_\perp^{AP} \bullet jn}{I^A}$$

This equation states that the angular velocity of object A after the collision equals the angular velocity of object A before the collision plus the angular acceleration of object A, which is the impulse divided by object A's moment of inertia. The equation works similarly for object B except that the impulse on object B is -jn, so the linear velocity of object B after the collision is shown in Equation 11-45 (b).

Equation 11-45 (b)

$$W_2^B = W_1^B + \frac{r_\perp^{BP} \bullet jn}{I^B}$$

Of course, the value of j we calculated earlier for nonrotating bodies does not apply to rotating bodies, so we must calculate a new value of j.

Computing the Impulse's Magnitude for Rotating Bodies

Equation 11-46 is what we need to find the magnitude of an impulse for rotating bodies.

Impulse Magnitude (Rotation):

$$j = \frac{-(1+e)\, V_1^{AB} \bullet n}{n \bullet n \left(\dfrac{1}{M^A} + \dfrac{1}{M^B}\right) + \dfrac{(r_\perp^{AP} \bullet n)^2}{I^A} + \dfrac{(r_\perp^{BP} \bullet n)^2}{I^B}}$$

Equation 11-46

The numerator of the magnitude j is the same as the numerator for the equation of j on a nonrotating body. It's equal to the relative normal velocity at the time of collision multiplied by the quantity -(1 + e), where e is the coefficient of restitution.

The denominator is a lot more complicated for a rotating body than it is for a nonrotating one. It begins with the denominator for nonrotating bodies, which is the dot product of the normal vector and the product of the normal vector and the sum of 1 over the mass of both objects. To this denominator, we add the square of the dot product of the perpendicular vector and the normal vector, and divide that square by the moment of inertia. We do this for both colliding bodies.

How do we come up with Equation 11-46? We begin with the equation for the relative normal velocity after the collision, giving us Equation 11-46 (a).

$$V_2^{AB} \bullet n = -e\, (V_1^{AB}) \bullet n$$

Equation 11-46 (a)

Then we use the definition of relative normal velocity, making the formula look like Equation 11-46 (b).

$$(V_2^{AP} - V_2^{BP}) \bullet n = -e\, (V_1^{AB}) \bullet n$$

Equation 11-46 (b)

Next, we use the equation for computing the linear velocity from the angular velocity (Equation 11-23) to give us Equation 11-46 (c).

$$[(V_2^A + W_2^A \, r_\perp^{AP}) - (V_2^B + W_2^B \, r_\perp^{BP})] \bullet n =$$

Equation 11-46 (c)

Adding the quantities inside the brackets changes the appearance of the equation as shown in Equation 11-46 (d).

$$(V_2^A + W_2^A \, r_\perp^{AP} - V_2^B - W_2^B \, r_\perp^{BP}) \bullet n = -e \, (V_1^{AB}) \bullet n$$

Equation 11-46 (d)

Plugging in the equations that define the linear and angular velocities after the collision (Equations 11-39 (a), 11-39 (b), 11-45 (a), and 11-45 (b)) makes the equation look like Equation 11-46 (e).

$$\left[\left(V_1^A + \frac{jn}{M^A}\right) - \left(V_1^B - \frac{jn}{M^B}\right) + \left(W_1^A + \frac{r_\perp^{AP} \bullet jn}{I^A}\right) r_\perp^{AP} - \left(W_1^B - \frac{r_\perp^{BP} \bullet jn}{I^B}\right) r_\perp^{BP}\right] \bullet n = -e \, (V_1^{AB}) \bullet n$$

Equation 11-46 (e)

Multiplying the angular velocities by the perpendicular vectors gives us Equation 11-46 (f).

$$\left[\left(V_1^A + \frac{jn}{M^A} - V_1^B + \frac{jn}{M^B}\right) + W_1^A \, r_\perp^{AP} + \frac{r_\perp^{AP} (r_\perp^{AP} \bullet jn)}{I^A} - W_1^B \, r_\perp^{BP} + \frac{r_\perp^{BP} (r_\perp^{BP} \bullet jn)}{I^B}\right] \bullet n = -e \, (V_1^{AB}) \bullet n$$

Equation 11-46 (f)

A little rearranging makes the equation look like Equation 11-46 (g).

$$\left[(V_1^A + W_1^A \, r_\perp^{AP}) - (V_1^B + W_1^B \, r_\perp^{BP}) + \frac{jn}{M^A} + \frac{jn}{M^B} + \frac{r_\perp^{AP} (r_\perp^{AP} \bullet jn)}{I^A} + \frac{r_\perp^{BP} (r_\perp^{BP} \bullet jn)}{I^B}\right] \bullet n = -e \, (V_1^{AB}) \bullet n$$

Equation 11-46 (g)

The first two values in parentheses at the left end of Equation 11-46 (g) are the linear velocities before the collision of objects A and B respectively. We can therefore rewrite the equation as shown in Equation 11-46 (h).

$$\left[V_1^{AP} - V_1^{BP} + \frac{jn}{M^A} + \frac{jn}{M^B} + \frac{r_\perp^{AP} (r_\perp^{AP} \bullet jn)}{I^A} + \frac{r_\perp^{BP} (r_\perp^{BP} \bullet jn)}{I^B}\right] \bullet n = -e \, (V_1^{AB}) \bullet n$$

Equation 11-46 (h)

The difference between the linear velocities before the collision of objects A and B is the definition of relative velocity (Equation 11-40); substituting that equation results in Equation 11-46 (i).

$$[V_1^{AB} + \frac{jn}{M^A} + \frac{jn}{M^B} + r_{\perp}^{AP} \frac{(r_{\perp}^{AP} \bullet jn)}{I^A} + r_{\perp}^{BP} \frac{(r_{\perp}^{BP} \bullet jn)}{I^B}] \bullet n = -e(V_1^{AB}) \bullet n$$

Equation 11-46 (i)

Now we multiply the relative velocity by the normal vector so that we can move the resulting relative normal velocity to the right side of the equation, as shown in Equation 11-46 (j).

$$V_1^{AB} \bullet n + [\frac{jn}{M^A} + \frac{jn}{M^B} + r_{\perp}^{AP} \frac{(r_{\perp}^{AP} \bullet jn)}{I^A} + r_{\perp}^{BP} \frac{(r_{\perp}^{BP} \bullet jn)}{I^B}] \bullet n = -e(V_1^{AB}) \bullet n$$

Equation 11-46 (j)

Moving the relative normal velocity to the right side of the equation makes the formula look like Equation 11-46 (k).

$$[\frac{jn}{M^A} + \frac{jn}{M^B} + r_{\perp}^{AP} \frac{(r_{\perp}^{AP} \bullet jn)}{I^A} + r_{\perp}^{BP} \frac{(r_{\perp}^{BP} \bullet jn)}{I^B}] \bullet n = -(V_1^{AB} - e V_1^{AB}) \bullet n$$

Equation 11-46 (k)

Isolating j in the left side of the equation gives us Equation 11-46 (l).

$$j[n(\frac{\perp}{M^A} + \frac{\perp}{M^B}) + r_{\perp}^{AP} \frac{(r_{\perp}^{AP} \bullet jn)}{I^A} + r_{\perp}^{BP} \frac{(r_{\perp}^{BP} \bullet jn)}{I^B}] \bullet n = (-1te) V_1^{AB} \bullet n$$

Equation 11-46 (l)

Performing a dot product with the bracketed quantity on the left and the normal vector makes the formula look like Equation 11.46 (m).

$$j[n(\frac{\perp}{M^A} + \frac{\perp}{M^B}) + \frac{(r_{\perp}^{AP} \bullet n)^2}{I^A} + \frac{(r_{\perp}^{BP} \bullet n)^2}{I^B}] = (-1te) V_1^{AB} \bullet n$$

Equation 11-46 (m)

We divide both sides of the equation by the bracketed quantity on the left side of the equation to solve for j. Doing this gives us Equation 11-46, which is the magnitude of the impulse for rotating bodies.

Going from Math to Code

To resolve a collision, we must perform the following steps:

1. Compute the normal vector.
2. Compute the coefficient of restitution.
3. Compute the impulse.
4. Calculate the linear velocity after the collision.
5. Calculate the angular velocity after the collision.

Computing the normal vector depends on the type of collision. If the collision is a vertex-edge collision (as was the collision shown earlier in Figure 11-16), the normal vector should be perpendicular to the edge, as the vector n is in Figure 11-16. For an edge-edge collision (imagine if one of the sides of object A collided with object B in Figure 11-16 instead of just one point), the normal vector should be perpendicular to one of the edges.

For a vertex-vertex collision, which is a collision in which one vertex of object A collides with one vertex of object B, things get more complicated. To keep things consistent with what we've been doing in this chapter, we will have the normal vector point away from object B. We can make the normal vector perpendicular to the edge of object B that contains the collision point, as is shown by the horizontal dotted line coming off object B in Figure 11-17. The other alternative is to imagine that object B has been extended in a plane, as is shown in the diagonal dotted line in Figure 11-17. The normal vector is perpendicular to the extension of object B. Which normal vector you decide to use is up to you.

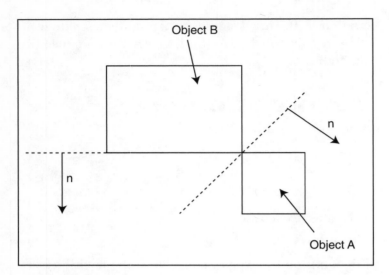

Figure 11-17

Vertex-vertex collision.

Object B

Object A

n

n

Choosing a coefficient of restitution depends on what you want to happen in the collision. If you want the two objects to bounce off each other, use a high value (a value close to 1) for the coefficient of restitution. If you want the two objects to stick together, use a low value (a value close to 0) for the coefficient of restitution. Experiment with different coefficients of restitution to find the value that works for your game.

Calculating the impulse involves plugging in the formulas we derived earlier in this chapter. For nonrotating bodies, the code will look like this:

```
double impulseNumerator = (-1.0 * coefficientOfRestitution) *
                          DotProduct(linearVelocity, collisionNormal);
double oneOverMass = (1.0 / massA) + (1.0 / massB);
Vector2D normalTimesOneOverMass = ScalarProduct(collisionNormal, oneOverMass);
double impulseDenominator = DotProduct(collisionNormal, normalTimesOneOverMass);
double impulse = impulseNumerator / impulseDenominator;
```

For rotating bodies, the numerator of the impulse stays the same, and the first part of the impulse's denominator stays the same. We must add rotational effects to the denominator. Here's what the rotational code looks like:

```
Vector2D normalTimesOneOverMass = ScalarProduct(collisionNormal, oneOverMass);
double linearImpulseDenominator = DotProduct(collisionNormal,
                                  normalTimesOneOverMass);

double perpDotA = DotProduct (CMToCornerPerpA,CollisionNormal);
double angularA = perpDotA * perpDotA / momentOfInertiaA;
```

```
double perpDotB = DotProduct (CMToCornerPerpB,CollisionNormal);
double angularB = perpDotB * perpDotB / momentOfInertiaB;
double angularImpulseDenominator = angularA + angularB;
double impulseDenominator = linearImpulseDenominator + angularImpulseDenominator;
double impulse = impulseNumerator / impulseDenominator;
```

After we've computed the impulse, the rest of the calculations become relatively easy. For object A, the outgoing linear velocity will look like this:

```
linearVelocity = linearVelocity + ((impulse/mass) * collisionNormal);
```

For object B, we use the negative of the impulse's magnitude because Newton's Third Law states that every action has an equal and opposite reaction. The linear velocity after the collision will look like this:

```
linearVelocity = linearVelocity + (((impulse * -1.0)/mass) * collisionNormal);
```

Object A's angular velocity will look like this:

```
Vector2D jn = ScalarProduct(collisionNormal, impulse);
double angularNumerator = DotProduct(perpDotA, jn);
angularVelocity = angularvelocity + (angularNumerator / momentOfInertia);
```

Just as we did with linear velocity, we use the negative of the impulse's magnitude for object B, so the code looks like this:

```
Vector2D jn = ScalarProduct(collisionNormal, (impulse * -1.0));
double angularNumerator = DotProduct(perpDotB, jn);
angularVelocity = angularvelocity + (angularNumerator / momentOfInertia);
```

Summary

Hooray! We covered some difficult material in this chapter; making it through the entire chapter is an accomplishment. We began the chapter by discussing vectors, which are quantities that have both magnitude and direction. The sign of the vector indicates the vector's direction.

You can perform many operations on vectors. You can add and subtract vectors by adding and subtracting the vectors' components. You can multiply a vector by a scalar. The dot product of two two-dimensional vectors is the product of the x components plus the product of the y components. If two vectors have a dot product of 0, the vectors are orthogonal, which means that the two vectors are perpendicular to each other.

We then moved from vectors to linear motion, which is motion in a straight line. An object's position represents its location in the world. Velocity measures the object's change in position, and acceleration measures the object's change in velocity. A body's linear momentum is its mass multiplied by its velocity. A force measures the body's change in linear momentum, which ends up equaling the object's mass multiplied by its acceleration.

Unfortunately, the famous $F = ma$ equation applies only to the force at a single point. To compute the force of the entire body, we introduced the center of mass, which is a point containing the sum of all the points in the body multiplied by the mass of each point divided by the body's total mass. The center of mass allows us to calculate the object's total linear momentum and total force. The total linear momentum is the object's mass multiplied by the velocity at the center of mass. The total force is the object's mass multiplied by the acceleration at the center of mass.

From linear motion, we moved to angular motion, which involves an object rotating in addition to moving in a straight line. To add angular motion to our game's physics engine, we must introduce angular equivalents to an object's position, velocity, acceleration, linear momentum, force, and center of mass. Orientation is the angular equivalent of position, and it measures the angle of rotation. Angular velocity measures the change in orientation, and angular acceleration measures the change in angular velocity. The angular momentum of a point B around a point A is the dot product of the vector perpendicular to the vector AB and the object's linear momentum at point B. The torque measures the amount of force applied at point B that rotates around point A, and it is the dot product of the vector perpendicular to the vector AB and the force applied at point B.

To calculate the total angular momentum and the total torque, we introduced the angular equivalent of the center of mass, the moment of inertia. The moment of inertia is the sum of the masses multiplied by the square of the distance of each mass from the axis. The total angular momentum is the moment of inertia multiplied by the angular velocity. The total torque is the moment of inertia multiplied by the angular acceleration.

We moved from angular motion to collision detection. Our collision detection system has two phases. In the first phase, we take the bounding rectangles of the two objects we're testing and check whether or not the two rectangles intersect. If they do not intersect, there is no collision. If they intersect, we move to the second phase, where we perform a pixel test on the intersecting rectangle. If a particular pixel is not transparent in both objects, we have detected a collision. If not, we move to the next pixel. If we go through all the pixels in the intersecting rectangle without finding a pixel that is not transparent in both objects, there is no collision.

If we detect a collision, we must resolve the collision so that the two colliding objects do not penetrate. To keep the objects from penetrating, we apply an instantaneous force called an impulse to the two colliding objects. The impulse will change the objects' acceleration and velocity, moving the objects away from each other.

If you didn't understand everything the first time through this chapter, don't get discouraged. This is difficult material; I had to read a bunch of articles dozens of times to get a handle on game physics. You may have to read this chapter several times to absorb everything.

As you can tell from reading this chapter, physics is a complicated subject. The complexity of physics makes it difficult to write a standalone physics program, so I decided to add physics support to the work we've been doing. The program in this chapter replaces the simple physics model I was using for the programs in previous chapters with the more complex physics model I covered in this chapter. You can find the program and its source code on the CD-ROM that comes with this book.

CHAPTER 12

Beginning Artificial Intelligence

We have covered quite a bit of material in this book so far. We have created a game world and made it appear on the screen. We have made a player character and allowed the user to navigate the player through the game world. In addition, we have added audio to the game. Now we must give the player something to do. For our project to be considered a game, we must create some challenges for the player. Although it's possible to create a challenge without artificial intelligence—*Tetris* consists entirely of falling blocks—most games need some form of artificial intelligence to challenge the player. For the game we're making, the challenge will be computer-controlled monsters looking to kill the player. This chapter introduces you to artificial intelligence so that we can make our monsters act intelligently and provide a fun experience for the player.

Introduction to Game AI

Games use artificial intelligence to run the game's computer-controlled entities. Most of the time, the computer takes the role of the player's opponent when you're playing a board game or a strategy game; in an action game, the computer controls the enemies. Sometimes the entity helps the player, such as units in a strategy game or non-player characters in a role-playing game.

If you are an avid game player, you have noticed that the AI in most games is the weak link. This is because game AI is difficult to craft. There are two general approaches to generating AI: deterministic approaches and non-deterministic approaches. In *deterministic* AI, the game developer programs all of the creatures' behaviors. Deterministic approaches to AI normally employ a series of rules that govern a creature's behavior. Programmers usually code the rules with `if-then-else` statements, which are easy to program. Here are some sample rules in a first-person shooter:

```
if (player in range)
        fire weapon

if (out of ammo)
        change weapon
```

```
if (severely wounded)
      run away

if (player tries to escape)
      block exit
```

Deterministic approaches run fast, but they place a great burden on the game programmer. He must program every entity's behavior in advance, which forces the programmer to consider every possible situation a computer-controlled character may face in the game and write code to deal with each situation. Inevitably, something happens during the game that the programmer did not write code to handle, and the computer-controlled character does something stupid.

Because deterministic behavior uses a scripted set of rules, the behavior is predictable. If a certain condition is true, the computer performs the same action every time, which makes players tire of playing against the computer. For example, in the rules listed earlier in this section, if the enemy is close enough to attack, he will attack. If the enemy has the chance to get closer and improve his chances of hitting the player, he won't do it because that behavior is not one of the rules. Think of an enemy with deterministic behavior as if he's a member of the Brady Bunch: He lives by exact words—the rules the game developer programmed for him.

Non-deterministic approaches to AI shift the burden of controlling the agent's behavior from the programmer to the computer. The programmer specifies some basic behavior for the agent, then the computer evolves that behavior to deal with situations the programmer did not take into account. Non-deterministic behavior is less predictable and more interesting, but these more interesting agents come with a price. It takes a lot of CPU time to create non-deterministic behavior, something most games do not have.

Game programmers face a dilemma. They can use fast, deterministic behavior that results in predictable opponents, or they can use slow, non-deterministic behavior that results in interesting opponents. To this puzzle, add the fact that practical information on advanced game AI is scarce—most academic research on AI involves turn-based games that don't have to be fast. Now you can see why many commercial game developers focus on multiplayer *online* play. It's easier to write networking code to develop an interesting opponent—another real person—than it is to create an interesting computer opponent.

This chapter focuses on deterministic behavior because it's easier to understand. In addition, we need the speed of deterministic behavior for the action game we are creating.

Our AI System

In our game, the AI is to the enemies what the game controller is to the player. Our game's AI must be able to perform the equivalent of the player moving the joystick or pressing a button on a gamepad. Remember from Chapters 7 through 9 that when we read player input, all we are doing is determining the direction the player moved. The physics engine actually moves the player. Similarly, our AI system simply returns the direction the enemy should move, and the physics engine handles the details of moving the enemy. Our AI system has three components, which you can see in Figure 12-1. The action functions perform maneuvers during the game, such as chasing the player. The lowest level function is the MoveModel() function, which chooses the direction in which the enemy will move. The Chase() and Flee() functions tell the MoveModel() function where to move. The Patrol() function tells the creature to patrol an area of the game world, looking for the player.

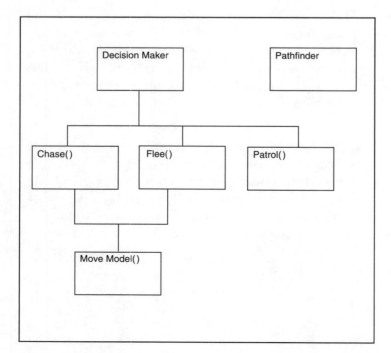

Figure 12-1

Components of the AI system.

Above the action functions in the hierarchy shown in Figure 12-1 is the Decision Maker that decides which of the action functions to perform. The final component of the AI system is the Pathfinder, which lets the enemy navigate its way around obstacles. Pathfinding is a large subject; I devote the next chapter to it.

To handle the AI in our game, I created an AIController class, whose data members you can see in the following code listing:

```
Class AIController
{
        protected:
                GameEnemyPtr modelToControl;
                FiniteStateMachine decisionMaker;
                Pathfinder pathMaker;
};
```

The modelToControl data member contains the enemy the AIController class is going to move. The decisonMaker data member determines which action function to perform. The pathMaker data member calculates paths for the enemy to follow to reach its targets.

Action Functions

As Figure 12-1 in the previous section shows, our game has four action functions. The MoveModel() function moves a creature from its current location to a location you pass to it. The Chase() and Flee() functions provide the goal location for the MoveModel() function. The Chase() function tells the MoveModel() function to move toward the player; the Flee() function tells the MoveModel() function to avoid the player. The Patrol() function has the creature patrol an area of the game world, keeping its eye out for the player.

Moving an Opponent

At the lowest level, our game's enemies have to move from one location to another. The following function moves an opponent:

```
InputControllerAction AIController::MoveModel(short goalX, short goalY)
{
        // This function assumes that there are no obstacles
        // in the way from the model's current position to
        // the goal position.
```

```
            short centerX = modelToControl->GetWorldX() +
                        (modelToControl->GetSpriteWidth() / 2);
            short centerY = modelToControl->GetWorldY() +
                        (modelToControl->GetSpriteHeight() / 2);

            // Compare monster's position to the goal's and act accordingly.
            if ((goalX < centerX) && (goalY < centerY))
                    return kMoveUpAndLeft;
            else if ((goalX > centerX) && (goalY < centerY))
                    return kMoveUpAndRight;
            else if ((goalX < centerX) && (goalY > centerY))
                    return kMoveDownAndLeft;
            else if ((goalX > centerX) && (goalY > centerY))
                    return kMoveDownAndRight;

            // At this point, we know that either the goalX or goalY
            // is within our monster sprite's boundaries.
            else if (goalY < centerY)
                    return kMoveUp;
            else if (goalY > centerY)
                    return kMoveDown;
            else if (goalX < centerX)
                    return kMoveLeft;
            else if (goalX > centerX)
                    return kMoveRight;
            else
                    return kNoAction;
}
```

Looking at the code, you can see that even though the MoveModel() function has many lines of code, it does not actually do a whole lot. It compares the opponent's position to the goalX and goalY parameters you pass to the function and chooses the appropriate direction to move. For example, if the opponent's position is below the position of the goal, the opponent will choose to move up. There are eight directions to test, which accounts for the high code-line count. The work of choosing a goal and actually moving the enemy fall to other functions.

Chasing

One maneuver that enemies in every action game must perform is chasing the player. Imagine how boring a fantasy role-playing game would be if the player went through the dungeons and the inhabitants of the dungeon ignored him. In our initial version of the Chase() routine, the enemy moves closer to the player by calling the MoveModel() function as you can see in the following code:

```
InputControllerAction AIController::Chase(short preyX, short preyY,
                  GameLevelPtr theLevel, GameTileListPtr theTiles)
{
        if (modelToControl == nil)
                return kNoAction;

        if (CanAttack(preyX, preyY))
                return kAttack;


        InputControllerAction result = MoveModel(preyX, preyY);
        return result;
}
```

If there are no obstacles between the enemy and the player, the Chase() function above works beautifully. The enemy moves toward the player, and when it gets close enough to the player it attacks. Problems arise if an obstacle blocks the enemy's path to the player; the enemy will get stuck and be unable to maneuver around the obstacle. You can verify this by running the program for this chapter that comes on the CD-ROM. To fix the problem, we must calculate a path for the enemy to follow so it can move around the obstacle. The next chapter covers the subject of pathfinding, which is why the code to build paths does not appear in this chapter.

Evading

When the battle turns against the computer enemy—say he's fighting a killer rabbit—it would be nice if he bravely ran away. Evading the player requires the exact opposite behavior that chasing the player does: The creature should move away from the player. To make the evading behavior realistic, however, you have to compute an escape path for the creature. Figure 12-2 shows an example where moving away from the player will not provide much relief for the monster. The player (P) is northeast of the creature (X). However, if the enemy moves southwest to move away from the player, the creature will trap himself in the southwest corner of the room, where the player will kill him. What the enemy has to do is find a path to the exit at the northeast corner of the room while simultaneously avoiding the player, which is a difficult balancing act.

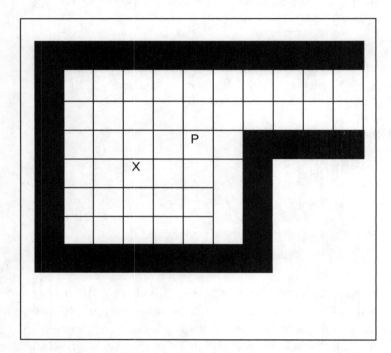

Figure 12-2

A sample situation in which the enemy (X) has to escape from the player (P) while keeping away from the player.

The following function tells a computer-controlled agent to run away:

```
InputControllerAction AIController::Flee(short predatorX, short predatorY,
                LevelPtr theLevel, TileListPtr theTiles)
{
        if (modelToControl == nil)
            return kNoAction;

        if (NoEscapePathCreated())
            Pathfinder.CreateEscapePath();

        InputControllerAction result = FollowEscapePath();
        return result;
}
```

The Flee() function pushes the hard work of finding a route out of trouble to the pathfinder. Moving the work to another function provides flexibility. If you want to use a different algorithm to plan an escape route, you don't have to change the Flee() function. All you must change is the CreateEscapePath() function. I cover pathfinding next chapter. In the program for this chapter that appears on the CD-ROM, the enemies flee by blindly running away from the player, which causes them to trap themselves in the corner of the room.

Patrolling

In a lot of games, it is nice to have the opponents patrolling areas, looking for action, instead of just sitting around waiting for the player to come and attack.

There are several ways to implement patrolling behavior for our game's enemies. A straightforward way is to have the enemy move in one direction until he hits an obstacle. He then turns either left or right, but once you pick a direction to turn, you must turn in that direction every time. After turning, the creature moves in the new direction until it can't move anymore, at which point the creature turns again. This move-and-turn cycle executes over and over again to create the patrolling behavior—assuming that the area isn't too large. In the wide-open areas of a wilderness, the enemy might "patrol" in one direction for miles and miles if there's nothing to force the creature to turn.

Another way to make our enemies patrol is to calculate a patrol rectangle for each creature. The creature walks around this rectangle, patrolling the area specified by the patrol rectangle. The following Patrol() function shows how this technique can be coded:

```
InputControllerAction AIController::Patrol(void)
{
        if (modelToControl == nil)
                return kNoMovement;

        switch (modelToControl->GetSpriteDirection()) {
                case kSpriteFacingUp:
                        return (PatrolUp());
                        break;

                case kSpriteFacingDown:
                        return (PatrolDown());
```

```
                        break;

                case kSpriteFacingLeft:
                        return (PatrolLeft());
                        break;

                case kSpriteFacingRight:
                        return (PatrolRight());
                        break;

                default:
                        return kNoMovement;
                        break;
        }
        return kNoMovement;
}
```

The code for patrolling in a particular direction is similar for all directions. The discussion that follows explains the process of patrolling up. Examine the source code on the CD-ROM that accompanies this book to learn about patrolling in the other directions. To patrol up, we compare the top of the creature's sprite rectangle to the top of the patrol area. If the sprite is below the top of the patrol area, the creature moves up. If not (that is, if the creature is already at the top of the patrol area), the creature turns. The following code demonstrates the action of patrolling up:

```
InputControllerAction AIController::PatrolUp(void)
{
        if (modelToControl == nil)
                return kNoMovement;

        short topEdgeOfSprite = modelToControl->GetWorldY();

        Rect patrolRect = modelToControl->GetViewRect ();

        // Is enemy below the top edge of the patrol area?
        // If so, move up. If not, turn left.
        if (centerX > patrolRect.top)
                return kMoveUp;
        else
                return (TurnLeft());
}
```

As you can see in the PatrolUp() function, I chose to turn left like a NASCAR stock car racer. If you prefer to turn right, feel free to do so; the patrolling behavior is the same either way. Here's what the TurnLeft() function looks like:

```
ControllerAction AIController::TurnLeft(void)
{
        if (modelToControl == nil)
                return kNoMovement;

        switch (modelToControl->GetSpriteDirection()) {
                case kSpriteFacingUp:
                        return kMoveLeft;
                        break;

                case kSpriteFacingDown:
                        return kMoveRight;
                        break;

                case kSpriteFacingLeft:
                        return kMoveDown;
                        break;

                case kSpriteFacingRight:
                        return kMoveUp;
                        break;

                default:
                        return kNoMovement;
                        break;

        }
        return kNoMovement;
}
```

One question remains; how do we calculate the patrol rectangle? One method is to take the creature's position and find the nearest solid tile above, below, left, and right of the creature to create the patrol rectangle. Figure 12-3 shows a sample rectangle that this method computes. The gray tiles make up the patrol rectangle. This method works well with indoor settings that have mostly rectangular areas and don't have much open space.

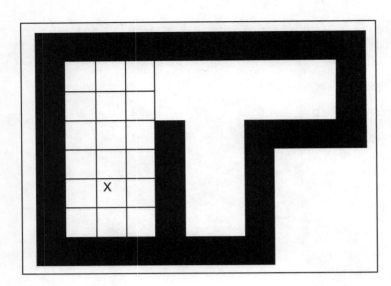

Figure 12-3

A sample patrol rectangle.

Obviously, using rectangles to patrol non-rectangular areas will not give you perfect patrolling behavior. Outdoor settings can be a problem; the enemy could patrol for miles and miles. In this case, you would set an arbitrary limit to how far the creature patrols. The following function computes a patrol rectangle that works best in an indoor setting:

```
void GameEnemy::DeterminePatrolRect(GameLevelPtr theLevel,
                      GameTileListPtr theTiles)
{
      Rect newPatrolRect;

      newPatrolRect.top = ComputePatrolRectTop(theLevel, theTiles);
      newPatrolRect.bottom = ComputePatrolRectBottom(theLevel, theTiles);
      newPatrolRect.left = ComputePatrolRectLeft(theLevel, theTiles);
      newPatrolRect.right = ComputePatrolRectRight(theLevel, theTiles);

      SetPatrolRect(newPatrolRect);
}
```

The DeterminePatrolRect() function does little work. It calls four functions that compute the four corners of the patrol rectangle. In the discussion that follows, I will explain the process of calculating the top of the patrol rectangle; calculating the other "sides" of the patrol rectangle is similar.

Begin by taking the tile above the creature's current position and testing to see whether or not that tile is solid. If it is not, move up one tile and test again. The process continues until we hit a solid tile, which gives us the top boundary of the patrol rectangle. The following code calculates the top of the patrol rectangle:

```
short GameEnemy::ComputePatrolRectTop(GameLevelPtr theLevel,
                    GameTileListPtr theTiles)
{
        short tileNum;
        GameTileType tileAttribute;
        short theLevelWidth = theLevel->GetLevelWidth();
        UInt32 mapIndex;

        short rowToTest = (worldY - 1)/ kTileHeight;
        short columnToTest = worldX / kTileWidth;
        mapIndex = (rowToTest * theLevelWidth) + columnToTest;
        tileNum = theLevel->levelMap[mapIndex].GetValue();
        tileAttribute = theTiles->tileTable[tileNum].GetTileType();

        // We start at the tile one pixel above us. We move up one tile at a
        // time until we hit a wall or door tile.
        while ((tileAttribute != kWallTile) && (tileAttribute != kDoorTile)) {
                rowToTest--;
                mapIndex = (rowToTest * theLevelWidth) + columnToTest;
                tileNum = theLevel->levelMap[mapIndex].GetValue();
                tileAttribute = theTiles->tileTable[tileNum].GetTileType();
        }
        return (rowToTest * kTileHeight);
}
```

Finite State Machines

In our game, we use a finite state machine to decide which of the action functions that we created earlier in this chapter we want our creature to perform. Finite state machines are one of the most popular methods of implementing artificial intelligence in games. They are relatively simple to program, easy to test for correctness, and can achieve complex behavior.

The term *finite state machine* implies a complex piece of machinery, but state machines are actually simple to understand. Finite state machines consist of a list of states—one of which is the active state—and the conditions that can trigger state changes to modify the active state. A simple example of a finite state machine is a light switch. It has two states: On and Off. Flipping the switch makes the transition from Off to On and vice versa.

In an action or role-playing game, the states in a state machine can reflect a creature's mood (happy, angry, hungry, frightened). The player's actions trigger a mood change. For example, if the player attacks the creature, the enemy's mood would change from happy to angry. If the player injures the enemy, that action could then change the creature's mood from angry to frightened, and the enemy would run away. As you can see in this example, a finite state machine does not have to be a physical machine.

You can use finite state machines for aspects of your game other than artificial intelligence. Consider a door in a dungeon-digging game. It can have the states Open, Closed, Locked, and Unlocked, which you can see in Figure 12-4. Suppose the player comes to a locked door. If he has a key to unlock the door, he can use it, which changes the door's state to Unlocked. Then the player can turn the doorknob to change the door's state to Open so that he can enter the room. If the player does not have a key to unlock the door, he may choose to break down the door, which changes the door's state directly to Open. I'm sure that you can come up with many more uses of finite state machines in your games.

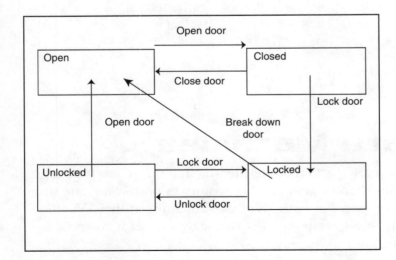

Figure 12-4

The finite state machine for a door in a dungeon.

Our State Machine

Figure 12-5 provides a picture of the finite state machine the enemies in our game will use to make decisions about which action to take. This is not the most complex state machine ever developed; I know you can build on it to create better AI. I'm keeping things simple so that you can figure out what I'm talking about.

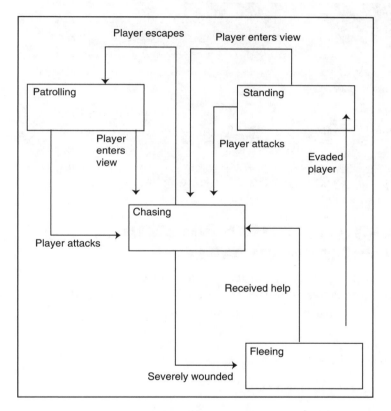

Figure 12-5

The finite state machine for the enemies in the game we are creating.

The enemy begins in either the Patrolling or Standing states and stays in one of those states as long as the player is nowhere near it. From the player's point of view, the enemy is either standing or patrolling as long as it is off the screen. When the player either attacks or comes near the enemy, things become interesting. The enemy's state changes to the Chasing state, and it begins to hunt the player. The hunt continues until the player dies, the player evades the enemy, or the player severely wounds the enemy. If the player dies, the game ends. If the enemy cannot find the player, it resumes patrolling, keeping its eyes open for any trace of the player. If the enemy takes some punishment from the player, it retreats.

Although this particular state machine is pretty simple, intelligent behavior does result from the machine. The enemies are smart enough to run away when the player injures them, which is something the enemies in many games do not do. The opponents don't wander around, oblivious to the player, so they at least appear intelligent.

> **NOTE**
>
> The behaviors you can add to the state machine are endless, but I will give some examples here. You could give an enemy the ability to sound an alarm, which would bring in reinforcements to aid in the fight against the player. You could give the enemy the ability to heal itself with healing potions that appear in the level, reducing the player's ability to heal himself in the process. You could give the enemy the ability to take bribes of food or money from the player. This particular behavior would give the player alternatives to fighting as well as provide interesting enemy behavior. Use your imagination to make compelling enemy behavior.

Programming a State Machine with `switch` Statements

The two most popular ways of programming finite state machines are `switch` statements and Finite State Machine classes. The `switch` statement approach is the easiest way to do it; you have one `case` for each state, as shown in the following code:

```
switch (state) {
    case (kPatrollingState):
        if (PlayerInView()) {
            ChangeState(kChasingState);
        }
        Patrol();
        break;

    case (kStandingState):
        if (PlayerAttacks()) {
            ChangeState(kChasingState);
        }
        Stand();
        break;
```

```
case (kChasingState):
        if (Wounded()) {
                ChangeState(kFleeingState);
        }
        ChasePlayer(playerX, playerY, theLevel, theTiles);
        break;

case (kFleeingState):
        if (PlayerNotInView()) {
                ChangeState(kStandingState);
        }
        Flee(playerX, playerY, theLevel, theTiles);
        break;
}
```

The switch statement works pretty well, but the code can become a mess. The state-transition conditions to test and the state transitions themselves mix with the function for the state machine to perform while in the current state. For example, in the patrolling state, the code is checking whether or not to change the state to chasing as well as telling the enemy to patrol its area. If you had to check ten conditions for state changes in each state in the machine, the code would become difficult to read. To separate the state transitions from the actions to perform, you can have two functions with switch statements: a DidStateChange() function that checks whether a condition occurred that results in a state change, and a PerformManeuver() function that determines the action to perform depending on the enemy's state.

Creating Finite State Machine Classes

For simple state machines, switch statements work best because they are the quickest and easiest to develop. If you want to use more complex state machines or have many different state machines in your game, developing a state machine data structure is the way to go because this structure gives you more flexibility. By creating state machine data structures, you trade ease of development for flexibility. I'm going to create a C++ class for our game's state machines, but you can use a structure if you're programming in C. Actually, I'm going to make three classes: a StateTransition class that stores information about moving from one state to another, a FiniteState class that stores information about one state in the machine, and a FiniteStateMachine class that contains the machine itself.

The Machine's States

To make life easier, I made an enumerated data type for all the states an enemy can be in during the game. Here's what the code for that looks like:

```
enum StateType
{
        kStandingState = 0,
        kPatrollingState,
        kChasingState,
        kFleeingState,
        kStatesInGame
};
```

Our state machine is pretty simple, having just four states; the kStatesInGame value exists solely for the purpose of creating arrays. I chose the states based on the actions the enemies can perform in the game: stand, patrol, chase, and flee. You could create states based on the monster's state of mind instead: happy, hungry, neutral, angry, afraid. Most likely, you will want many states in your game so that you can create more complex behavior in your computer-controlled characters. If your game's AI needs require different states than those listed here, feel free to add, delete, and change the states in the StateType data type. Just make sure you keep the value kStatesInGame at the end of the list of states. If you add new states after kStatesInGame, you will have problems if you declare an array of all the states in the machine like this:

```
StateType stateList[kStatesInGame];
```

The Machine's Transitions

In addition to listing the states in the state machine, we must also list the events that cause state transitions. Without state transitions, the machine will stay in its current state for the duration of the game—which is dull from an artificial intelligence standpoint. For our fairly simple state machine, this code lists the transitions:

```
enum StateTransitionType
{
        kEmptyTransition = -1;
        kPlayerEntersView = 0,
        kPlayerAttacks,
        kPlayerEscapes,
        kSeverelyWounded,
```

```
        kEvadedPlayer,
        kReceivedHelp,
        kTransitionsInGame
};
```

Our state machine has six real transitions. A transition occurs when the player comes into view of a patrolling enemy, when the player attacks an enemy, when the player escapes (that is, when the creature can't find the player), when the enemy becomes wounded, when a fleeing enemy escapes from the player, or when the enemy receives help. The enemy can receive help either by healing itself or by enlisting other creatures to come to its aid.

I use the transition value kEmptyTransition for errors; if I have a problem creating a transition, I return the value kEmptyTransition. The value kTransitionsInGame becomes helpful if you want to declare an array of state transitions; just declare the array to be size kTransitionsInGame, and the array will contain one entry for each type of state transition.

The StateTransition Class

Now it's time for some class declarations. Let's begin by looking at the data members of the StateTransition class:

```
class StateTransition
{
    protected:
            StateTransitionType transitionTrigger;
            StateType newState;
};
```

As you can see, the StateTransition class is simple. The transitionTrigger data member stores the condition that triggers the state change. The newState data member stores the new state.

The FiniteState Class

The following code lists the data members of our FiniteState class, which represents one of the states in the finite state machine:

```
class FiniteState
{
    protected:
            short transitionTotal;
```

```
            StateTransitionPtr transitionTable;
            StateType state;
};
```

The `transitionTotal` data member stores how many transitions this state has. The `transitionTable` lists all the transitions this state contains. The `state` data member identifies which state this `FiniteState` object represents. I will show you how to fill the transition table later in the chapter.

The FiniteStateMachine Class

Last, but not least, we come to the `FiniteStateMachine` class. You can see its data members in the following declaration:

```
class FiniteStateMachine
{
        protected:
                short stateTotal;
                FiniteStatePtr stateTable;
                short currentState;
};
```

The `stateTotal` data member stores the number of states that this particular state machine has. If you have only one state machine in the game, `stateTotal` will equal `kStatesInGame`. Having a `stateTotal` data member lets you have multiple state machines, where each machine contains fewer states than the total number of states in the game. The `stateTable` data member contains the states in the state machine, and the `currentState` data member tells us which state in the state table the machine is in at the moment.

Using the State Machine Classes

My declarations of class data members aren't enough for you? You'd like to know how to *use* these state machines in the game? Your demands are insatiable, but I cannot resist them. Let's move on to using our state machine classes.

Adding Transitions

An empty transition table makes for a useless state machine; we must fill our `FiniteState` class's transition table. The following function adds a transition to the table:

```
void FiniteState::AddTransition(StateTransitionPtr transitionToAdd, short index)
{
        // The index parameter tells us where to add the
        // transition in the table

        // Make sure we don't go past the array bounds
        if (index < 0)
                return;
        else if (index >= transitionTotal)
                return

        transitionTable[index] = *transitionToAdd;
}
```

Filling the entire table involves calling the AddTransition() function multiple times, once for each transition in the state. The following function fills the transition table:

```
void FiniteState::FillTransitionTable(StateTransitionPtr tableToAdd)
{
        for (short index = 0; index < transitionTotal; index++)
                AddTransition(tableToAdd[index], index);
}
```

Now the question becomes "Where do the state transitions come from?". You can store the transitions on disk and load them when you initialize the game. Alternatively, you can hard code the transitions. The following code shows how I hard coded the transitions:

```
// It would be better to store the states
// and transitions on disk and read them in, but
// I'm hard coding it for now.

// Transitions from the patrolling state
StateTransitionPtr patrollingTransitions = new
        StateTransition[kNumberOfPatrollingTransitions];

patrollingTransitions[0].SetTransitionTrigger(kPlayerEntersView);
patrollingTransitions[0].SetNewState(kChasingState);
patrollingTransitions.SetTransitionTrigger(kPlayerAttacks);
patrollingTransitions.SetNewState(kChasingState);
```

```
// Transitions from the standing state
StateTransitionPtr standingTransitions = new
        StateTransition[kNumberOfStandingTransitions];

standingTransitions[0].SetTransitionTrigger(kPlayerEntersView);
standingTransitions[0].SetNewState(kChasingState);
standingTransitions.SetTransitionTrigger(kPlayerAttacks);
standingTransitions.SetNewState(kChasingState);

// Transitions from the chasing state
StateTransitionPtr chasingTransitions = new
        StateTransition[kNumberOfChasingTransitions];

chasingTransitions[0].SetTransitionTrigger(kPlayerEntersView);
chasingTransitions[0].SetNewState(kChasingState);
chasingTransitions.SetTransitionTrigger(kPlayerAttacks);
chasingTransitions.SetNewState(kChasingState);

// Transitions from the fleeing state
StateTransitionPtr fleeingTransitions = new
        StateTransition[kNumberOfStandingTransitions];

fleeingTransitions[0].SetTransitionTrigger(kPlayerEntersView);
fleeingTransitions[0].SetNewState(kChasingState);
fleeingTransitions.SetTransitionTrigger(kPlayerAttacks);
fleeingTransitions.SetNewState(kChasingState);

FiniteStatePtr gameStates = new FiniteState[kStatesInGame];

// Fill each state's transition table
gameStates[kPatrollingState].SetState(kPatrollingState);
gameStates[kPatrollingState].SetTransitionTotal(kNumberOfPatrollingTransitions);
gameStates[kPatrollingState].FillTransitionTable(patrollingTransitions);

gameStates[kStandingState].SetState(kStandingState);
gameStates[kStandingState].SetTransitionTotal(kNumberOfStandingTransitions);
gameStates[kStandingState].FillTransitionTable(standingTransitions);

gameStates[kChasingState].SetState(kChasingState);
gameStates[kChasingState].SetTransitionTotal(kNumberOfChasingTransitions);
gameStates[kChasingState].FillTransitionTable(chasingTransitions);
```

```
gameStates[kFleeingState].SetState(kFleeingState);
gameStates[kFleeingState].SetTransitionTotal(kNumberOfFleeingTransitions);
gameStates[kFleeingState].FillTransitionTable(fleeingTransitions);
```

Adding States to the Machine

After we fill the data for one of our game's finite states, we must add the state to the state machine. Here's a function that adds a state to the finite state machine:

```
void FiniteStateMachine::AddState(FiniteStatePtr stateToAdd, short index)
{
        // The index parameter tells us where to add the
        // state in the table

        // Make sure we don't go past the array bounds
        if (index < 0)
                return;
        else if (index >= stateTotal)
                return

        stateTable[index] = *stateToAdd;
}
```

We call AddState() repeatedly to fill the stateTable, which is similar to what we did to fill a state's transitionTable. The following function fills a finite state machine's state table:

```
void FiniteStateMachine::FillStateTable(FiniteStatePtr tableToAdd)
{
        for (short index = 0; index < stateTotal; index++)
                AddState(tableToAdd[index], index);
}
```

Making a Transition

When an event occurs in the game that causes a state transition, we send the transition to the state machine. For example, if the player fires his weapon, our game sends a kPlayerAttacks message to the state machine. The state machine decides what the enemy's new state should be, and returns that. The following code makes a state transition:

```
void FiniteStateMachine::HandleStateTransition(StateTransitionType
                              theTransition)
{
      StateType theNewState;

      // Have the state handle the transition
      theNewState = stateTable[currentState].HandleTransition(theTransition);

      // Find the new state in the state table and
      // set current state to the index of the new state
      StateType currentStateType;
      for (short index = 0; index < stateTotal; index++) {
            currentStateType = stateTable[index].GetState();
            if (currentStateType == theNewState) {
                  SetCurrentStateIndex(index);
                  return;
            }
      }
      // We should never get here, but if we do, we'll do nothing,
      // which means the state remains unchanged
}


StateType FiniteState::HandleTransition(StateTransitionType theTransition)
{
      StateTransitionType currentTransition;
      StateType result;

      for (short index = 0; index < transitionTotal; index++) {
            currentTransition = transitionTable[index].GetTransitionTrigger();
            if (currentTransition == theTransition) {
                  result = transitionTable[index].GetNewState();
                  return result;
            }
      }

      // At this point, we found no matching transition
      return kStandingState;
}
```

If you look at the code to handle the transitions, you will notice that there is no mention of any of our state machine's states and transitions. This separation of the state machine's data and code makes the code difficult to follow (It makes the code abstract.), but it provides one big advantage. The code to handle the transition stays the same, no matter how many states and transitions your game handles. If you want to rip out my state machine and substitute your own state machine with 20 states and 10 transitions per state, you can do that without having to change the code to handle the transitions.

Making a Decision

Earlier in this chapter, we discussed how the top level of our game's AI system decided which action the creature should perform. That "decision maker" is a finite state machine, so let's see how a finite state machine makes decisions. The following code determines which action function our enemy should perform:

```
InputControllerAction AIController::PerformManeuver(short playerX,
                    short playerY, GameLevelPtr theLevel, GameTileListPtr
theTiles)
{
        InputControllerAction result;

        if (modelToControl == nil)
                return kNoMovement;

        decisionMaker.SetCurrentStateIndex(modelToControl->GetMood());

        short currentStateIndex = decisionMaker.GetCurrentStateIndex();
        StateType theCurrentState = stateTable[currentStateIndex].GetState();

        switch (theCurrentState) {
                case kStandingState:
                        result = kNoMovement;
                        break;

                case kPatrollingState:
                        result = Patrol();
                        break;

                case kChasingState:
                        result = Chase(playerX, playerY, theLevel, theTiles);
                        break;
```

```
        case kFleeingState:
                result = Flee(playerX, playerY, theLevel, theTiles);
                break;

        default:
                result = kNoMovement;
                break;
    }

    return result;
}
```

The PerformManeuver() function begins by finding the current state of the state machine and then uses the current state to decide which action to take. The code to decide which action to take is straightforward because each state in the state machine corresponds to an action. For example, when the creature is in the patrolling state, the decision maker tells it to patrol.

State Machine Enhancements

Although the state machine we developed provides some interesting enemy behavior, there are things we can do to improve that behavior. The following sections list enhancements you can make to finite state machines.

Probability

A state machine's behavior becomes predictable after a while. If a patrolling enemy charges every time the player appears, the player can use that information to ambush the enemy. Using probability in programming your state machine can result in more unpredictable behavior for the computer-controlled enemy. A patrolling enemy that spots the player could charge 60% of the time, sound an alarm 30% of the time, and run away 10% of the time. When the player enters the enemy's area, he can't be entirely sure what the enemy will do.

Adding probability to our state machine classes would require some minor changes. We would have to add a data member to the StateTransition class that stores the chances of this transition occurring. We can store it either as an integer between 0 and 100 (representing the percent chance of the transition happening), or we can store it as a floating-point number between 0 and 1. Here's what the StateTransition class's data members look like when we store the transition's chances of happening as an integer between 0 and 100:

```
class StateTransition
{
        protected:
                StateTransitionType transitionTrigger;
                MachineStatePtr newState;
                short transitionChances;                // Between 0 and 100
};
```

Performing the state transition becomes more difficult when we add probability to the state machine. Before, when a state transition occurred, there was only one possible output. In the state machine shown back in Figure 12-5, if the enemy is patrolling an area and the player comes into its view, the enemy chases the player. With probability, two or more different outputs are possible. For the example earlier in this section, there would be three possible outputs: the enemy could chase the player, flee the player, or sound the alarm.

Because each state transition has multiple results, we must search the FiniteState object's transition table for every transition that matches the condition that triggers the transition. Then we must generate a random number and use it to determine which transition to perform.

Using Multiple State Machines

Having only one finite state machine to model every behavior of every creature in your game will cause problems. Every enemy will behave the same, and the state machine will be difficult to manage. A solution to this problem is to create multiple state machines. If your game has seven types of enemies, for example, you can make seven state machines, one for each enemy. This way, each type of enemy can have its own unique behavior.

You don't have to limit yourself to one finite state machine per creature. You can make multiple state machines for each type of creature to provide some individuality to each creature. We know that all people are not identical. Some people are more intelligent than others. Some people frighten more easily than others. Having multiple state machines can make the computer-controlled agents seem more human. Suppose that we have trolls in a game set in a fantasy world. We can make one state machine for typical trolls and add state machines for different types of trolls we want in the game. If we want a cowardly troll in the game, we make a state machine where the troll runs away when the player approaches and we can use that state machine to control the troll's behavior.

If the behavior of a computer-controlled opponent is particularly complex, you can divide its behavior into multiple finite state machines. Let's take the example of a computer player in a real-time strategy game. The computer player must make high-level strategic decisions, give orders to units in the game, and have those units behave intelligently. In this example, you would have three state machines: one for the high-level decisions, one for the low-level decisions, and one for the units themselves.

Remember that the `FiniteStateMachine` class is a data type in the same way that integers, floating-point numbers, and characters are data types. You can create arrays, lists, stacks, queues, and trees of state machines—or any other data structure you want. To have an agent patrol an area, you could create a queue of state machines. The queue would contain four state machines, one for moving to each corner of the patrol area. When the player reaches a corner of the patrol area, the current state machine would go to the back of the queue. I'm not telling you to use state machines to have your enemies patrol; use whatever patrolling method you want. I am just using patrolling as an example of using multiple state machines.

Hierarchical Finite State Machines

If you use hierarchical finite state machines, some of the top-level machine's states may, in fact, be finite state machines themselves. Hierarchical finite state machines simplify organization. Instead of having one massive state machine, you have several smaller ones.

From a data standpoint, adding hierarchy to our `FiniteStateMachine` class is simple, involving one extra data member as shown here:

```
FiniteStateMachinePtr stateMachineList;
```

The `stateMachineList` data member contains the state machines below it in the state machine hierarchy. Because the `stateMachineList` data member is an array of type `FiniteStateMachine`, each entry in the list can contain its own array of `FiniteStateMachine` objects. This arrangement achieves the hierarchy; each `FiniteStateMachine` object can have its own array of `FiniteStateMachine` objects, and the hierarchy can continue indefinitely.

Other AI Methods

Games can use many methods to implement artificial intelligence. There are more methods available than I can put into a single game. The following sections cover some AI techniques that games use, but that we don't use in the game we are making.

Scripting

In *scripting*, a computer-controlled character executes a script that you write. Movies and television shows use scripts to tell the actors what to say, what to do, and where to move. Game scripts work the same way, except that the characters in video games do less talking than do movie or television characters. You wouldn't think that scripted behavior would be intelligent, but well-written scripts can produce surprising behavior.

The classic arcade game *Space Invaders* uses a simple form of scripting. The aliens move right until they hit the edge of the screen; then they move down and to the left. When the aliens hit the edge of the screen again, they move down and to the right. This script continues running until the player dies or the player kills all the aliens—when a new level loads, the aliens execute the script again.

First-person shooting games such as the *Quake* and *Unreal* series make extensive use of scripts. The scripts control the behavior of the enemies and trigger traps and puzzles. The scripts are separate from the game code so that players can modify existing scripts or write new scripts, allowing players to change the behavior of the creatures in the game. Letting playing change the enemies' behaviors keeps the game interesting for the player, extending the shelf life of the title.

To use scripting in your game, you have three options:

- Put your scripts in the game's code
- Use an existing scripting language
- Develop your own scripting language

To place scripts in your game's code, you would write each script as a subroutine. If you use C or C++ to program your code, each script would be a function. The advantage of this approach is that you can use the same language you use to write the game to write the script. The disadvantage is that you embed the scripts in the game code. If you want to change a script, you must recompile the entire game.

If you choose to use an existing scripting language to write your game's scripts, you have many choices. Here are some popular scripting languages:

- Python, an object-oriented scripting language.
- Perl, popular in developing Web pages.
- Apple Script, a popular Mac scripting language.
- Tcl, a scripting language that is popular in the Unix world that also happens to have a Mac version.
- JavaScript, the leading cause of Internet browser crashes.
- Lisp, an AI language that also has scripting capabilities. Lisp is the most popular language for writing artificial intelligence programs.

In addition, many games use Java as a scripting language, even though it is technically not a scripting language. The major advantage of using an existing scripting language is that you don't have to go through the effort of creating a language and writing a compiler for the language. In addition, thousands of other programmers write scripts in the languages listed above, and they can help you use these languages. Scripting languages are easier to use than languages such as C or C++, so you can write your scripts faster with a scripting language than you can if you write scripts in C. There are several things to keep in mind when using scripting languages. First, it takes time to learn the syntax and nuances of the particular language. You're not going to download a Python development kit on Monday and have intelligent enemy behavior on Tuesday. Second, scripts written in a scripting language execute slower than C or C++ programs. Scripting languages trade execution speed for development speed. Third, scripting languages were not specifically designed for games. Of course, C and C++ were not designed specifically for games either. Writing games for the Mac in C++ would be difficult without Apple supplying technologies like QuickDraw, the Sound Manager, and InputSprocket. Scripting languages do not come with special libraries to simplify the process of writing scripts to control the behavior of game characters.

If you want a scripting language that is totally in sync with your game's needs, you must create the language. I can think of two good reasons to develop your own scripting language. The first reason is to give your scripts greater execution speed than existing scripting languages. The second reason, and the more compelling reason, is to create a language simple enough for non-programmers to write scripts. Scripting languages are easier to use than languages like C++, but they are too difficult for people with no programming background. Many large game companies create their own scripting languages and integrate them with their level

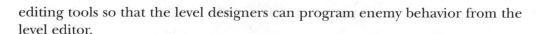

editing tools so that the level designers can program enemy behavior from the level editor.

Developing a new scripting language involves creating the syntax for the language and writing the compiler for the language so that your game can execute the scripts. As you can imagine, developing an entire language from scratch requires a lot of work. I wouldn't recommend creating a scripting language for your first game project.

Should you decide to develop a scripting language, there are tools available to help you. Unix has the programs flex and bison that can help with compiler writing. Because Mac OS X has Unix at its core, you have access to these tools if your computer runs OS X. The Internet is teeming with information about flex and bison, so you should be able to learn them easily. You should also pick up a book on compiler writing; I can't imagine writing a compiler without such a book. Do a search at an online bookstore with the word *compiler* to find a list of books on writing a compiler.

When creating a scripting language, don't lose sight of the reasons why you decided to write the new language. The scripting language is supposed to provide an easy way to script behavior in your game. Keep your language simple. The more complicated the language becomes, the more work you must do to write the compiler. Sometimes people go overboard with language features and end up with a language that closely resembles the C language. Don't waste your time reinventing C. Other people have already written perfectly good C compilers; you're probably using one to program your game right now.

Random Movement

You wouldn't think that moving in a random direction could result in anything resembling intelligent behavior, but random movement has its place in some games. The enemies in a game may be unintelligent by design. Take the game *Asteroids*. The challenge for the player in the game is to shoot asteroids. Asteroids, being chunks of rock, do not have any intelligence, and they just float through space. Having the asteroids move in random directions is acceptable behavior.

Random actions result in unpredictable behavior, which can be very helpful in a game. For example, in a shooting game, if an enemy is running away from the player, it would be easy to kill if it just ran in a straight line. However, if the enemy zigzags while it's trying to escape from the player, it becomes more difficult for the player to kill, which makes the enemy appear intelligent.

Programming random movement for an enemy is easy. Calling the standard C function `rand()` generates a random number. Take the number that `rand()` generates and perform the modulus operator on it by the number of directions the opponent can move (generally four or eight). This will give you a number between 0 and 3 (or 0 and 7, if you have eight directions). The following code generates random movement in one of four directions:

```c
enum {
        kUp = 0,
        kDown,
        kLeft,
        kRight
};

InputControllerAction MoveRandomly(void)
{
        int randomValue;

        // Get random number between 0 and 3
        randomValue = rand() % 4;

        switch (randomValue) {
                case kUp:
                        return kMoveUp;
                        break;

                case kDown:
                        return kMoveDown;
                        break;

                case kLeft:
                        return kMoveLeft;
                        break;

                case kRight:
                        return kMoveRight;
                        break;
        }
}
```

You would not want to call the `MoveRandomly()` function in every frame. In the animation system we developed in Chapter 6, "Animation," when a sprite changes direction, it does not move in the first frame. For random movement in four directions, there's only a 25 percent chance of the direction being the same as the current direction. This means that the sprite will spend most of its time changing direction and not moving. Instead of calling `MoveRandomly()` every frame, you are better off calling it every second or two to give you the random movement you desire.

Expert Systems

An *expert system* models a human expert in a field. The developers of the expert system pick the expert's brain about how he makes decisions, and the developers then write a program in which the computer makes decisions the way the expert does.

To create an expert system for a game, you find a person who plays the game well and examine the strategies he uses to play the game. This is easiest to do if you're making a computer version of an existing game. If you were making a poker game, for example, you would find an expert poker player and learn his strategies of playing poker. If you're creating an original game, you will play the role of the expert. You will have to compile a list of winning strategies for your game.

After you get your knowledge from the expert, it's time to put the knowledge in the computer. In an expert system, the knowledge base contains the information the expert knows. Normally, the knowledge follows a series of rules, which you can code as a series of `if-then-else` statements. A simple expert system for the game checkers would look similar to the following:

```
if (can jump other player)
        jump him
else if (in danger of being jumped)
        move out of danger
else if (can be kinged)
        move to be kinged
else if (can set up a jump next move)
        make that move
else
        move one of the remaining pieces
```

This set of rules works in general, but what move should the expert system make if it can make one of multiple jumps? We must develop more rules. If the expert system has multiple opportunities to jump its opponent, it should first look for double-jump chances, then look for jumps that won't cause it to lose a checker, then look for jumps that involve each player losing a checker. The new rules for choosing which jump to make would look like the following:

```
if (can double jump)
        perform that jump
else if (can jump without being jumped by opponent)
        perform that jump
else
        pick a random jump
```

An expert system for a game can have hundreds and even thousands of rules in its knowledge base. Board and strategy games benefit the most from using expert systems. The computer plays the role of a player in these types of games, so emulating a human expert results in a challenging computer-controlled player. Monsters in action and role-playing games do not exist to be like the player, so teaching them to act like a good player does not make sense. You wouldn't want a role-playing game where a fire-breathing dragon behaved like a human being. Avoid expert systems if you are creating an action or role-playing game.

Cheating

It sounds sacrilegious to be writing a section about cheating, but cheating can be an effective way to make a challenging computer opponent for a game. Strategy games employ cheating the most. Many strategy games have complex rules, and it can be difficult to program a computer to play the game as well as a human player can play it. Even with good AI, the computer is no match for an outstanding human player. To balance the game, the computer player enjoys advantages the human player does not have. The computer player may start the game with more units, and it may be able to build new units faster than the human player can. The breaks the computer player receives compensate for the human player's intellectual superiority. By subtly cheating for the computer player, the programmer gives the computer a fighting chance against the human player.

Action games use explicit cheating less often than strategy games. In action games, game designers balance the game by throwing more enemies at the player or by making the enemies more powerful. If an action game cheats, it normally does so by giving a creature information it would have no way of knowing. For example, in a dungeon digging game, the game has to track the player's location. The game could give a monster in a room five rooms away the player's location so that the monster can go hunt the player. The monster has no other way of knowing where anybody outside its room is; giving it the player's location is cheating.

I don't recommend cheating as your main strategy for creating your game's artificial intelligence. Start with the techniques I covered in this chapter, and go on with some of the strategies discussed in the next chapter. If the AI approaches I cover in this book don't suit your needs, do some research on the Internet for alternative techniques, such as neural networks, genetic algorithms, and machine learning. If that fails, and the only way you can create a playable computer opponent is to cheat, then cheat. It's better to make a fun game that cheats than a dull game that doesn't cheat.

Summary

This chapter introduced artificial intelligence and the AI system used in the game we're developing. Games use artificial intelligence for the creatures the computer controls. The computer may play the role of one of the players in a board or strategy game, the enemies in an action game, or the nonplayer characters in a role-playing game.

Our game's AI system has three major components. The first component is the action functions that let the enemies perform maneuvers in the game. We have `Chase()`, `Flee()`, and `Patrol()` functions to hunt, evade, and patrol, respectively. To simplify hunting and evading, I wrote a `MoveModel()` function that moves a creature from where it is to a specified location in the game world. The `MoveModel()` function assumes that there are no obstacles blocking the creature from reaching its goal location. If there are obstacles, we must use the second component, the pathfinder, to create a path to the goal. You will learn all about pathfinding in the next chapter.

The final component of our AI system is the decision maker that determines which action function the enemy will perform. I used a finite state machine to develop the decision maker.

I finished the chapter by discussing popular methods for creating game AI that were not used in the game we are making in this book. Scripting involves writing scripts to create the opponents' behaviors. You can embed these scripts in your game's code, use an existing scripting language, or create your own scripting language.

Expert systems attempt to transfer an expert's knowledge to a computer program. Expert systems work best for board and strategy games: You create a list of strategies to use to play the game well, and then you create a series of rules for the expert system to follow. If all else fails in your artificial intelligence attempts, you can resort to cheating. By subtly tilting the balance of the game toward the computer player, you create a challenging computer opponent for the player so that he will continue to play the game.

The sample program for this chapter, which you can find on the accompanying CD-ROM, builds on our previous work by adding enemies to the game. When you play with the program, you will notice that the enemies often get stuck. The reason this happens is that we have not added pathfinding to keep the creatures from getting stuck. I will add pathfinding capabilities for the game's enemies in the next chapter.

CHAPTER 13

PATHFINDING

Many types of computer games need intelligent pathfinding. A strategy game such as *Starcraft* isn't much fun to play if you give a unit an order to go somewhere, and the unit gets stuck on its way to the destination. Computer enemies in an action game that cannot make their way out of a room don't provide much of a challenge. This chapter shows you techniques you can use to make the computer-controlled characters in your game move intelligently from point A to point B.

Introduction to Pathfinding

Pathfinding focuses on planning routes from one location to another. For any game that has characters that can move, pathfinding is a fundamental concept. If a computer-controlled character cannot move from one place to another in the game world, the player will not believe that the character has intelligence. Academic research in the field of robotics has placed a great deal of emphasis on pathfinding to improve the navigation of mobile robots in the physical world. We game programmers can use this research to improve the navigation of our games' characters within the game worlds.

Pathfinding algorithms fall into two categories: *Offline pathfinding* algorithms calculate the complete path before moving along the path. *Real-time pathfinding* algorithms calculate enough of the path for the computer-controlled character to move. The character makes its move, then the algorithm makes more computations. This cycle continues until the character reaches the goal location.

Offline pathfinding algorithms find better paths because they take the time to compute the entire path before making a move. Real-time algorithms perform faster pathfinding because they compute only a portion of the path, but the paths are not as good. Faster-paced games use real-time pathfinders, while slower-paced ones use the higher quality offline pathfinders.

Fast, Stupid Pathfinding

If your game's world consists of a lot of open spaces with few obstacles, you can get away with not using a special pathfinding algorithm. The `Move()`, `Chase()`, and `Flee()` functions we wrote in the last chapter are enough to move the characters in the game. If the creature hits an obstacle, he can pick a direction, left or right, and turn in that direction until he makes his way around the obstacle. The creature won't look particularly intelligent while he's navigating the obstacle, but he will find a way out—and the code is simple to write. Look at your game and decide whether or not you need a fancy pathfinder. Your game will be simpler to write without it, but if you do need a pathfinder, read the rest of this chapter and decide which algorithm is best for you.

The A* Algorithm

By far the most popular pathfinding algorithm is the A* (A-Star) algorithm. If you set up A* properly, it will find the best path between two points, and it will find the path quickly, relative to other searching algorithms. A* computes the total cost of the path using the following formula:

```
f(n) = g(n) + h(n)
```

In the formula, `f(n)` represents an estimate of the total cost of the path, `g(n)` represents the total cost of moving from the start area to the point n, and `h(n)` (also known as the *heuristic function*) represents the estimated cost of moving from point n to the goal. Using this algorithm, you can decide the cost of moving from one area to an adjacent area. Cost can represent anything you want, such as distance, time, or expense (such as tolls being the cost of traveling along a given road). I use distance as the measure of cost in our game, and I chose to give each non-diagonal move a cost of 1 and each diagonal move a cost of 1.5. To provide more realistic movement, you should make diagonal moves cost more. If diagonal moves have the same cost as non-diagonal ones, the diagonal moves look attractive to A*, and A* will construct a path consisting of mostly diagonal moves. You can substitute your own costs for diagonal and non-diagonal moves if you wish. For example, if you do not want to deal with floating-point numbers, you could give each non-diagonal move a cost of 2 and each diagonal move a cost of 3. If you were making a game such as *Age of Empires*, you would give each terrain type a unit cost. In a strategy game, moving through the mountains would cost more than moving along a road, and A* can take the terrain into account when formulating the path.

To ensure that the pathfinder finds an optimal path, the estimated cost from the current location to the goal, $h(n)$, must be less than or equal to the actual cost. When selecting a path estimate, remember the rule on guessing the cost of a prize from the TV game show *The Price is Right*: Come as close as possible to the actual cost without going over.

Before the search begins, A* has a start location, a goal location, an empty list of examined locations (also called the *closed list*), and an empty list of unexamined locations (also called the *open list*). We begin by creating initial values for $f(n)$, $g(n)$, and $h(n)$. Because we are at the start location, $g(n)$ equals 0, and the total cost equals the estimate of the cost of moving from the start location to the goal location. Finally, we place the start location in the open list.

A* begins finding the path by taking the first entry in the open list and examining its neighbors. If any neighbors are not in the open or closed lists, A* places them in the open list and sorts the open list so that the least expensive estimated cost appears at the top of the list. If the neighbor resides in the open or closed lists, A* compares the newly calculated estimated path cost with the neighbor's stored estimated path cost. If the newly calculated path cost is lower, we update the neighbor's estimated path cost to reflect the lower cost and place the neighbor on the open list if it is not already there. Then the current entry moves from the open list to the closed list. This cycle repeats until A* finds the goal or the open list becomes empty, in which case A* could not find a path. In pseudocode, the A* algorithm looks like this:

```
Initialize start location
Put start location on open list

While (open list is not empty)
        Retrieve best entry from open list

        if (at the goal)
                Construct path
                Exit

        for (each neighbor of best entry)
                cost = (cost from start to best entry) +
                        (cost from best entry to neighbor)
                if (neighbor is not on open or closed list)
```

```
                    Initialize neighbor location
                    Compute f(n), g(n), h(n) for neighbor
                    Add neighbor to open list
            else if (cost < existing cost)
                    // New cost is less than old one so update the
                    // entry's path cost
                    if (existing location is on open list)
                            update path costs

                    if (existing location is on closed list)
                            update path costs
                            move location to open list

            Sort open list
        Move best entry to closed list
No path found if we get here
```

A* Example

A* is a pretty complicated algorithm, which makes it worthy of an in-depth example. We're going to step through the A* algorithm to find a path in the 6-by-6 tile grid shown in Figure 13-1. The gray square represents the goal, the black squares mark impassable barriers, and the * character shows the start location. When I work through the example, I will use the character **X** in the figures to represent the current position.

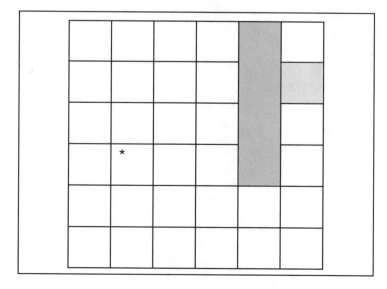

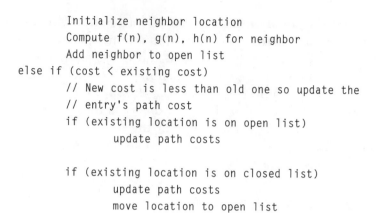

Figure 13-1

The starting location in the A* algorithm example.

In this example, non-diagonal moves (up, down, left, right) have a cost of 1; diagonal moves have a cost of 1.5. For the heuristic function, $h(n)$, which estimates the path cost, I calculate the number of diagonal and non-diagonal moves it takes to reach the goal and multiply by the cost of each move—assuming that there are no obstacles to the goal. For example, getting from the start location to the goal with no obstacles in Figure 13-1 would require two diagonal moves and two horizontal moves. The value for $h(n)$ in this case is 5: 3 for the two diagonal moves and 2 for the two horizontal moves — assuming that diagonal moves have a cost of 1.5 and non-diagonal moves have a cost of 1.

Initiating the Search

At the start, the open and closed lists have no entries. We must initiate the search by placing the start location onto the open list. Now, we go through the open list, grab the top entry from the open list (which will be the start location because the open list has only one entry right now), and examine its neighbors. The world in the example uses tiles, so each location has eight neighbors. For each neighbor, we estimate the cost of reaching the goal by applying the $f(n) = g(n) + h(n)$ formula. Figure 13-2 lists the estimated cost of reaching the goal from each of the start location's eight neighbors.

Let's walk through the process of calculating the estimated path from the tile northeast of the start location. The value of $g(n)$ is 1.5 because the diagonal move from the start to the northeast tile costs 1.5. Reaching the goal from the northeast tile would require one more diagonal move and two horizontal moves if the obstacle were not in the way. This makes the value of $h(n)$ 3.5: 1.5 for the diagonal move plus 2 for the horizontal moves. The total estimated cost is 5 (1.5 + 3.5).

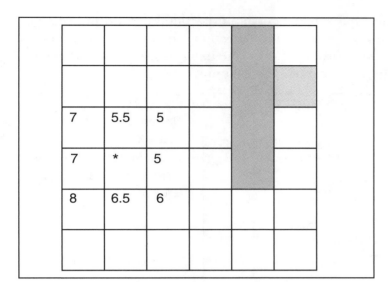

Figure 13-2

The estimated costs of reaching the goal for the start location's neighbors.

Because none of the neighbors appear in the open list, we add all of them to the list, sorted by cost. The neighbor northeast of the start location and the neighbor east of the start location have the lowest cost, 5, so we place them at the top of the list. I chose to put the northeast neighbor first, but most A* algorithm implementations break ties randomly. Finally, we move the start location to the closed list.

Step 2

Now we go through the open list, find the first entry—the one with the lowest cost—and examine its neighbors. We calculate the estimated cost of reaching the goal from each of the neighbors if we got to the neighbor from the entry location (the tile marked with an **X**). If the neighbors don't currently appear in the open list, we add them to the open list. If the neighbor does appear on the open list, we check whether the newly calculated estimated path cost for that location is lower than the entry's current estimated path cost. If the new cost is lower, we update the entry with the new, lower path cost.

If you look at Figure 13-3, you can see that the current location has five new neighbors, whose estimated cost paths appear in the figure. It also has three old neighbors—the neighbors to the west, south, and southwest—that currently reside in the open list. The costs for those old neighbors are not going to improve because reaching those neighbors from the current location (the **X**) results in backtracking, which does not yield an optimal path. For example, moving south from the current location in Figure 13-3 takes you to the tile east of the start location. The $g(n)$ cost for the east tile becomes 2.5: 1.5 for the diagonal move from the start location to the current location, and 1 for the move south. Moving to the east tile from the start location costs only 1. The h(n) value is the same in each case, so backtracking to the east tile increases the cost of the path by 1.5 units.

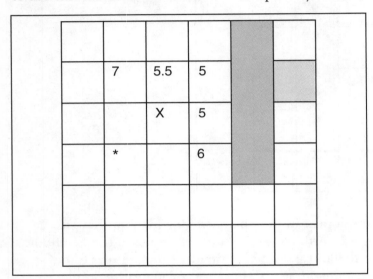

Figure 13-3

The cost of the current location's neighbors. The west, south, and southwest neighbors keep the same cost they had before.

Once again, the northeast and east neighbors have the lowest estimated cost to the goal. We add the five new neighbors to the open list, making sure that the lowest-cost goal appears at the top of the list, and move the current location to the closed list. At this point, we have three locations with an estimated cost of 5: the two neighbors we calculated in this section, and the location one tile east of the start location, which we computed in the previous section. I'm going to break the tie by choosing to move northeast again.

Step 3

Now the situation looks like what is shown in Figure 13-4. It's time to find more neighbors and calculate estimated path costs. We've hit the obstacle so, there are only five potential neighbors here. The neighbors west, south, and southwest result in backtracking, so they don't improve the path cost. This leaves us two neighbors to add to the open list: the neighbors north and northwest.

The new neighbors don't result in promising paths, as you can see in Figure 13-4, so we must go back to one of the other locations that have an estimated path cost of 5. I'm choosing the location south of the current location.

NOTE

You may be confused about the places A* acknowledges the obstacles and the places A* ignores the obstacles. A* ignores the obstacles only when estimating the path to the goal from a particular location. To estimate the cost to the goal, I just use the number of diagonal and non-diagonal moves from that location to the goal, ignoring the obstacles in the process. In all other cases, A* must deal with the obstacles. When checking for neighbors, we do not consider the obstacle tiles to be valid neighbors because obstacle tiles cannot be part of the final path. It would not be much of a path if the character using it tried to run through walls.

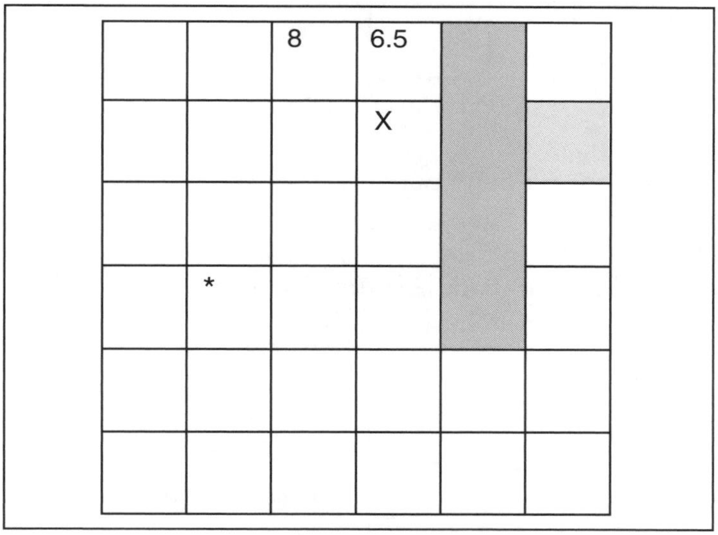

Figure 13-4

The cost of the current location's neighbors. The obstacle east of the current location reduces the number of potential neighbors to five.

Step 4

Looking at Figure 13-5, you can see that the current location (row 4, column 3) has nothing new to add. Obstacles block any eastward movement, and none of the other five neighbors improves the path cost. We must go to the final location that had a cost of 5: the tile to the east of the start location.

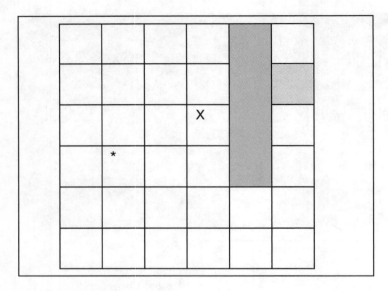

Figure 13-5

The cost of the current location's neighbors. There are no promising neighbors, which is why no costs appear in the figure.

Steps 5 and 6

Figure 13-6 shows the current situation. Six potential neighbors result in backtracking, but one old neighbor's path improves. The east neighbor had a previous cost of 6, which you can see in Figure 13-3, but following this path improves its cost to 5. The neighbor to the southeast is new, but its path cost of 7 doesn't make it as attractive as the born-again east neighbor, which vaults to the top of the open list.

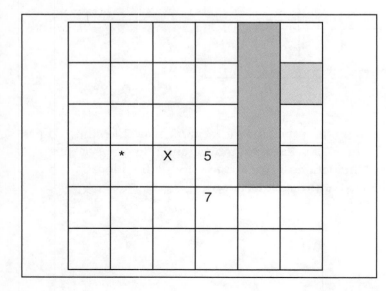

Figure 13-6

The cost of the current location's neighbors. The tile east of the start location became the current location because it had the lowest estimated cost.

Examining the east neighbor presents us with the situation shown in Figure 13-7. The obstacle eliminates two potential neighbors, and four other neighbors involve backtracking. The south and southeast neighbors are new, both with a cost of 7.

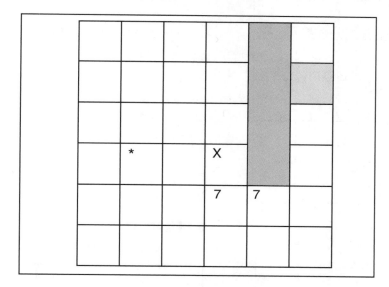

Figure 13-7

The cost of the east neighbor's neighbors.

Even though it's obvious to us that taking the southeast neighbor will lead us to the goal, A* can't move to it just yet. There are two entries in the open list with a cost of 5.5 to examine (see Figures 13-2 and 13-3), one entry with a cost of 6 (see Figure 13-2), and two entries with a cost of 6.5 (see Figures 13-2 and 13-4) that are ahead of the obvious solution in the queue. Bear with me as A* examines these locations.

Examining the Locations with a Cost of 5.5

Now it's time to examine the two entries that have an estimated path cost of 5.5. Figures 13-8 and 13-9 show the potential neighbors. The tile north of the current location in Figure 13-9 has a cost of 6, which propels it to the top of the list.

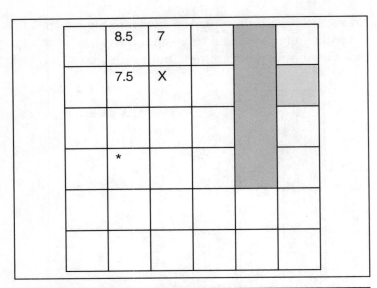

Figure 13-8

The cost of the neighbors of the first location with a cost of 5.5.

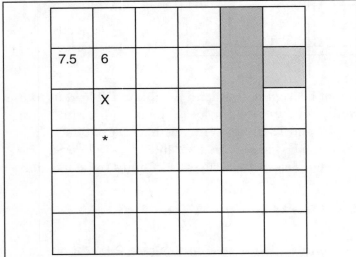

Figure 13-9

The cost of the neighbors of the second location with a cost of 5.5.

Examining the Locations with a Cost of 6

Now there are two locations that have an estimated path cost of 6, and Figures 13-10 and 13-11 show their neighbors. The location shown in Figure 13-10 yielded no interesting neighbors, but the location in Figure 13-11 produced one interesting neighbor. The tile east of the current location in Figure 13-11 improved from 7 (as shown in Figure 13.7) to 6.5, which elevates it to the head of the open list.

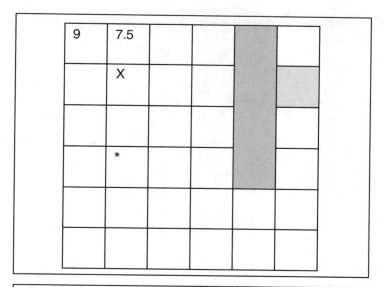

Figure 13-10

The cost of the neighbors of the first location with a cost of 6.

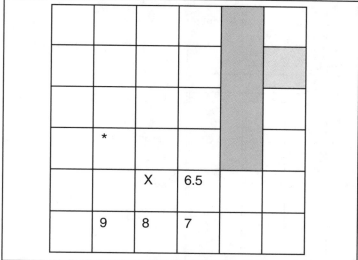

Figure 13-11

The cost of the neighbors of the second location with a cost of 6.

Examining the Locations with a Cost of 6.5

We're going to continue by examining the location whose estimated cost improved from 7 to 6.5 in the previous section. Figure 13-12 shows its neighbors. The tile east of the current location also has a cost of 6.5, so we'll move there as you can see in Figure 13-13. The tile northeast of the current location looks good; it has a cost of

7 and leads us toward the goal. Unfortunately, there are two other locations with an estimated path cost of 6.5 to check first.

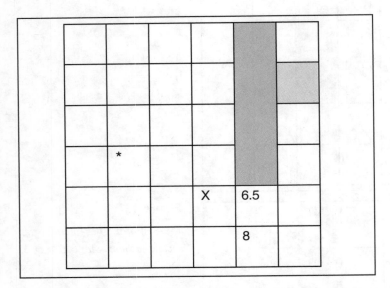

Figure 13-12

The cost of the neighbors of the first location with a cost of 6.5.

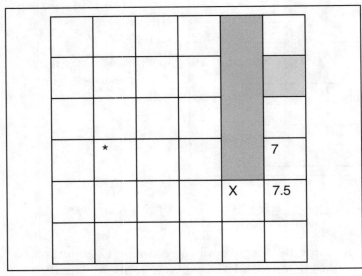

Figure 13-13

The cost of the neighbors of the second location with a cost of 6.5.

Figures 13-14 and 13-15 show the neighbors of the two locations left on the open list that have an estimated path cost of 6.5. As you can see from the figures, there are only two new neighbors for those locations, and those neighbors have costs of 8.5 and 9. Let's return to the location shown in Figure 13-13 and its neighbor with a cost of 7 that moves toward the goal.

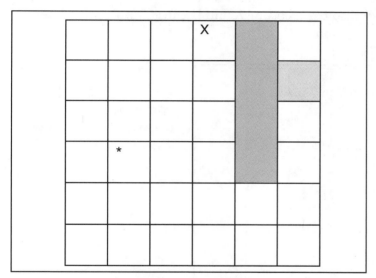

Figure 13-14

The cost of the neighbors of the third location with a cost of 6.5.

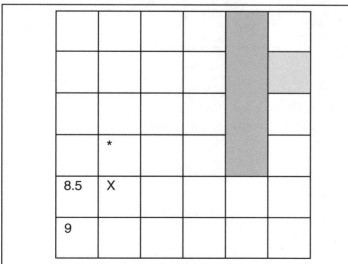

Figure 13-15

The cost of the neighbors of the fourth location with a cost of 6.5.

Closing in on the Goal

Now that we have examined the locations with a path cost of 6.5, we can examine the locations with a path cost of 7. To finally finish this example, I chose to examine the location that moved us around the obstacle in the last section. Figure 13-16 lists its potential neighbors. With an obstacle to the west and no neighbors to the east, there are only three neighbors to examine, two of which involve backtracking. The one remaining neighbor also has a cost of 7, and because it brings us closer to the goal, we'll examine that location.

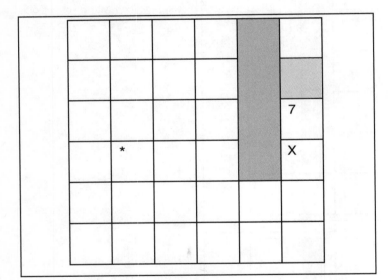

Figure 13-16

The cost of the current location's neighbors. The pathfinder is making its way toward the goal now.

Figure 13-17 shows how close we are to the goal. The only neighbor to examine is the goal location, and it has an estimated cost of 7. We move to the goal location, and we're finished searching.

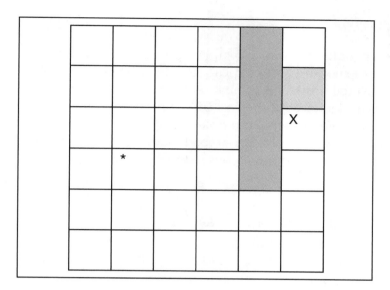

Figure 13-17

The cost of the current location's neighbors. The obstacle to the west limits the number of possible neighbors.

Creating the Path

After we reach the goal, we backtrack from the goal to the start location. Figure 13-18 shows the path we found in this example. Starting from the goal, we moved south two tiles, southwest one tile, west two tiles, and northwest one tile to reach the start location. You will find that there are no other paths with a lower cost than the one A* found in this example.

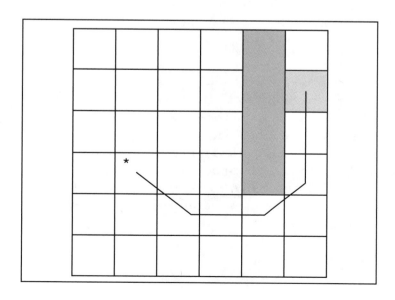

Figure 13-18

The path that the A algorithm computes in this example.*

Analysis

To find the goal quickly, two conditions must be met. First, the open list must be sorted by cost so that the least expensive paths appear at the top of the list. In this example, sorting the list prevented wasteful examination of the locations southwest of the start location. Second, the estimate of the cost from a location to the goal must be reasonable. I used the distance between the two points if there were no barriers in the way as my estimate. In the example, it made moving north and east less expensive than moving south and west, which pushed the navigator in the proper direction.

Estimating the Path Cost

The key to getting good performance out of the A* algorithm is wisely choosing the h(n) function that estimates the cost to the goal. Ideally, we want the estimate to equal the actual cost to the goal for each location in the game world; if that were the case, A* would head straight for the goal. Unfortunately, it's rarely possible to make the estimate equal the actual cost to the goal. If we could quickly calculate the actual cost to the goal, we wouldn't have to use the A* algorithm in the first place.

If you want to be sure that A* selects one of the best paths (there may be multiple paths that share the same total cost), do not overestimate the cost to the goal. To put it another way, make sure that your h(n) function does not exceed the actual cost to the goal. A* examines the location with the lowest estimated path cost. If you overestimate a path cost of a location that is part of the best path, A* may not examine it because the estimated cost is too high, and may create a path that does not include this location.

You might be wondering, "Why don't you just use a low value such as 0 or 1 as the estimate? Then you will never overestimate the goal." Using a low value as your heuristic function *will* result in the best path, but A* will have to do a lot more work. Figure 13-19 shows what A* does when the value of h(n) equals 0: From the start location **X**, A* examines all the locations marked with a 1. Then it examines all the locations marked with a 2, and then the locations marked with a 3. A* continues to search like this until it finds the goal. In the example from the last section, A* would waste its time searching the locations northwest and southwest of the goal if the estimated cost to the goal were 0.

3	3	3	3	3	3	3
3	2	2	2	2	2	3
3	2	1	1	1	2	3
3	2	1	X	1	2	3
3	2	1	1	1	2	3
3	2	2	2	2	2	3
3	3	3	3	3	3	3

Figure 13-19

The order in which A* examines paths when h(n) equals 0.

A good starting estimate for the cost of the path is to multiply the Manhattan distance from a location to the goal by the average cost of the terrain. The Manhattan distance between a start location (x1, x2) and (y1, y2) is:

|x1 – x2| + |y1 – y2|

In English, the Manhattan distance is the sum of the absolute value of the distance between x1 and x2 and the absolute value of the distance between y1 and y2. The actual cost to the goal will be at least as much as the Manhattan distance (unless there are ways to teleport in the game), so we will get one of the best paths. If there are few obstacles between the start location and the goal, using the Manhattan distance ensures that the A* algorithm will find its way to the goal quickly. The calculation I used in the A* example worked similarly to calculating the Manhattan distance, even though it was technically not the Manhattan distance.

Coding the A* Algorithm

I have talked long enough about A* theory. It's time to start writing some code—and believe me, there's a lot of code to write. A* balloons in size when going from algorithm to working code.

The PathLocation Class

To perform our pathfinding, I am going to create two classes. The first class, PathLocation, stores information about a location in the game world for the purposes of pathfinding, such as its coordinates and its costs to the goal location. You can see the data members for the PathLocation class in the following declaration:

```
class PathLocation
{
      short row;
      short column;

      double totalCost;
      double costFromStart;
      double estimatedCostToGoal;

      PathLocationPtr parent;
}
```

The row and column data members store where the PathLocation object resides in the game world. The totalCost, costFromStart, and estimatedCostToGoal data members measure $f(n)$, $g(n)$, and $h(n)$ respectively. The parent data member stores the location that led us to this point. We use it to build the path when we find the goal.

The Pathfinder Class

The second class for pathfinding is the Pathfinder class, which implements the A* algorithm in this case. The following declaration lists the data members of the Pathfinder class:

```
class Pathfinder
{
      LinkedList openList;
      LinkedList closedList;
      LinkedList completePath;
};
```

The openList and closedList data members store the open and closed lists that the A* algorithm requires to find the path. The completedPath data member stores the path that the A* algorithm builds.

Implementing the Open and Closed Lists

How should we store the open and closed lists? We can implement the closed list any way we choose because we do not have to sort it. The most common ways to implement it are with arrays and linked lists. I'm going to use a linked list so that I can dynamically allocate entries to the closed lists.

The common data structure to implement the open list is a priority queue. A *queue* is a last-in/first-out (LIFO) data structure. An example of a queue is waiting in line for tickets to a concert, movie, or sporting event. When you enter the line, you begin at the end of the line. When the people ahead of you in line get their tickets, you move up in the queue. Eventually you reach the head

> **NOTE**
>
> A *linked list* is a data structure that lets you dynamically add and remove links from the list. The linked list works like a chain. Each link in the list contains data and a pointer to the next link in the list. The advantage linked lists have over arrays is that you can easily add items to the list. When you declare an array, you must supply the array size. If you need to store more data in the array than the array holds, you must declare a new array. With a linked list, if you need to hold more data in the list, you just add a new link. Linked lists are especially useful when you need to store a group of data, but you do not know how many members are in the group.

of the line, you buy your tickets, and you exit the queue. The *priority queue* differs from a normal queue in that it orders the elements according to their priority rather than according to the time they entered the queue. An example of a priority queue is the starting position of cars in an auto race. All the cars can't be in the front row, so the cars begin in rows. The cars with the fastest qualifying times (the highest priority) appear in the front row.

Now how do we implement the priority queue? Most implementations of priority queues use a *binary heap*, which is a tree structure where the value of the root is higher than the value of its leaf nodes. I'm going to keep things simple and use a linked list to store the open list. To retrieve the highest priority item, I go through the linked list and pull out the entry with the highest priority (in this case, the lowest path cost). If the open list is large, my method will be slow because I must go through every entry in the list. However, not having to sort the list makes my programming task easy.

If your game has a large open list, you will benefit from creating a real priority queue. The C++ language has a priority queue class in the Standard Template Library (STL) you can use; I didn't want to explain the Standard Template Library in a game programming book, which is why I did not use the priority queue class in the code for this book. If you use the C programming language, you can create your own priority queue structure and write functions to implement it. Any decent book on data structures covers priority queues and how to program them.

Implementing the A* Algorithm

Finally we come to the point we have all been waiting for. The function that implements A* is shown here:

```
Boolean Pathfinder::CalculatePathAStar(short startRow, short startColumn,
          short goalRow, short goalColumn,
          GameLevelPtr currentLevel, GameTileListPtr theTileList)
{
      ClearOpenList();
      ClearClosedList();

      // Fill the start location's data
      PathLocation startLocation;
      startLocation.SetRow(startRow);
      startLocation.SetColumn(startColumn);
      startLocation.SetCostFromStart(0.0);

      double estimatedCost;
      estimatedCost = startLocation. EstimatePathCost(goalRow, goalColumn);

      startLocation.SetEstimatedCostToGoal(estimatedCost);
      startLocation.SetTotalCost(estimatedCost);
      startLocation.SetParent(nil);
      openList.AddItem(&startLocation);

      // Go through the open list, looking for the goal
      while(openList.GetNumberOfItems() > 0) {
            cheapestLocation = FindCheapestLocation(openList);

            if (cheapestLocation.AtGoal(goalRow, goalColumn)) {
                  BuildPath(cheapestLocation);
```

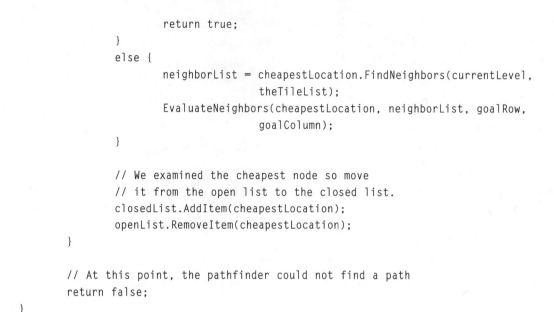

```
                            return true;
                    }
                    else {
                            neighborList = cheapestLocation.FindNeighbors(currentLevel,
                                    theTileList);
                            EvaluateNeighbors(cheapestLocation, neighborList, goalRow,
                                    goalColumn);
                    }

                    // We examined the cheapest node so move
                    // it from the open list to the closed list.
                    closedList.AddItem(cheapestLocation);
                    openList.RemoveItem(cheapestLocation);
            }

            // At this point, the pathfinder could not find a path
            return false;
}
```

The pathfinder has to know the game world so that it can plan its way around obstacles. That's the reason for the currentLevel and theTileList parameters appearing in the CalculatePath() function.

As you can see, the CalculatePath() function delegates a lot of the work to other functions. Dividing the work into multiple functions was the only way I could make the code show any semblance of clarity; A* is a more complicated algorithm than it looks when you read an article about it. The next several sections cover the functions that bear the brunt of the pathfinding work.

Clearing the Open and Closed Lists

When we start a new search, we want the open and closed lists to be empty. To make sure that there aren't any entries from a previous search sitting around in those lists, we explicitly clear both lists. The following code clears the open list; the code to clear the closed list is similar.

```
void Pathfinder::ClearOpenList(void)
{
        Iterator openListIterator(openList);
        PathLocationPtr currentLocation;
        int locationsToDelete = openList->GetNumberOfItems();
```

```
        while (locationsToDelete > 0) {
                currentLocation = (PathLocationPtr)openListIterator.Next();
                openList.RemoveItem(currentLocation);
                locationsToDelete--;
        }
}
```

Finding the Cheapest Unexamined Location

My decision to use a linked list instead of writing a priority queue class means that finding the location on the open list with the lowest cost takes more work. To find the lowest cost location on the open list, we must go through the entire open list and compare each entry's cost to the current lowest cost location. The following code finds the lowest cost location on the open list:

```
PathLocationPtr Pathfinder::FindCheapestLocation(LinkedList listToSearch)
{
        PathLocationPtr cheapestLocation;
        PathLocationPtr currentLocation;
        double cheapestLocationCost;
        double currentLocationCost;

        Iterator listIterator(listToSearch);

        // Read first location in open list and mark it
        // as the cheapest location
        currentLocation = (PathLocationPtr)openListIterator.Next();
        cheapestLocation = currentLocation;
        cheapestLocationCost = cheapestLocation->GetTotalCost();

        // Traverse the open list looking for the cheapest location
        while (currentLocation != nil) {
                currentLocation = (PathLocationPtr)listIterator.Next();
                if (currentLocation != nil) {
                        currentLocationCost = currentLocation->GetTotalCost();
                        if (currentLocationCost < cheapestLocationCost) {
                                // We have a new lowest cost location
                                cheapestLocation = currentLocation;
                                cheapestLocationCost = currentLocationCost;
                        }
```

```
        }
        return cheapestLocation;
}
```

Are We at the Goal?

One of the simple, yet important, functions we must perform when implementing the A* algorithm is determining whether or not we have reached the goal. All we do is compare the current location's row and column to the goal's row and column. If they match, we have reached the goal, as you can see in the following code:

```
Boolean PathLocation::AtGoal(short goalRow, goalColumn)
{
        if ((goalRow == GetRow()) && (goalColumn == GetColumn()))
                return true;
        else
                return false;
}
```

Finding Neighbors

Finding the neighbors of a path location is one portion of the A* algorithm that most pathfinding articles gloss over. Calculating neighbors depends on the organization of your game world. In the tile-based world of the game we are creating, the "neighbors" are the locations one tile away from the current location, giving us a maximum of eight neighbors. In addition to finding the neighbors, we must set each neighbor's data, which consists of the data members of the PathLocation class. The following function finds all the neighbors of a given path location:

```
LinkedList PathLocation::FindNeighbors(GameLevelPtr currentLevel,
            GameTileListPtr theTileList,
            short goalRow, short goalColumn)
{
        LinkedList neighborList;
        // Define the boundaries of the neighbor search.
        short topEdge = GetRow() -1;
        short bottomEdge = GetRow() + 1;
        short leftEdge = GetColumn() -1;
        short rightEdge = GetColumn() + 1;

        UInt32 mapIndex;
        short tileNum;
```

```
GameTileType tileAttribute;
short theLevelWidth = currentLevel->GetLevelWidth();
PathLocation newNeighbor;

double startingCost;
double estimatedCost;
double overallCost;

for(short currentRow = topEdge; currentRow <= bottomEdge; currentRow++) {
        for(short currentColumn = leftEdge; currentColumn <= rightEdge;
                currentColumn++) {
                // Make sure that we're looking at a neighbor of the
                // location and not the location itself.
                if ((currentRow != GetRow()) || (currentColumn !=
                        GetColumn())) {
                        // Find the type of tile at the neighbor's location
                        mapIndex = (currentRow * theLevelWidth) +
                                        currentColumn;
                        tileNum =
                                currentLevel->levelMap[mapIndex].GetValue();
                        tileAttribute =
                                theTileList->tileTable[tileNum].GetTileType();
                        if (tileAttribute != kWallTile) {
                        // Create a PathLocation object for the new neighbor
                        // and add it to the neighbor list
                                newNeighbor = new PathLocation;
                                newNeighbor.SetRow(currentRow);
                                newNeighbor.SetColumn(currentColumn);
                                startingCost = GetCostFromStart() +
                                        newNeighbor->GetMovementCost(this);
                                newNeighbor.SetCostFromStart(startingCost);

                                estimatedCost =
                                        newNeighbor->EstimatePathCost(goalRow,
                                                goalColumn)
                                newNeighbor.SetEstimatedCostToGoal(estimatedCos
        t);

                                overallCost = newNeighbor->GetCostFromStart() +
                                        newNeighbor->GetEstimatedCostToGoal();
                                newNeighbor.SetTotalCost(overallCost);
```

```
                              newNeighbor.SetParent(this);
                              neighborList.AddItem(&newNeighbor);
                       } // end if
                       // If the tile was a wall, do nothing. Walls cannot
                       // be part of the path so there's no point in making
                       // a wall a valid neighbor.

                } // end outer if
           } // end inner for
      } // end outer for
      return neighborList;
}
```

Evaluating Neighbors

The EvaluateNeighbors() function performs the bulk of the pathfinding effort. It
goes through all the neighbors for the current location and calculates each neighbor's estimated path cost. It then checks to see whether or not the neighbor is new.
If it is, EvaluateNeighbors() adds the new neighbor to the open list. If the new
neighbor already exists in either the open or closed list, EvaluateNeighbors() compares the new estimated path cost with the cost stored in either the open or closed
list. If the new path cost is less, we update the location to the new path cost. If the
location resides in the closed list, we move it to the open list so that we can reexam-
ine it. Here is the source code for the EvaluateNeighbors() function:

```
void Pathfinder::EvaluateNeighbors(PathLocationPtr parent,
          LinkedList neighborList, short goalRow, short goalColumn)
{
      PathLocationPtr currentNeighbor;
      Iterator neighborListIterator(neighborList);

      currentNeighbor = (PathLocationPtr)neighborList.Next();

      double newCost;
      double estimatedCost;
      double overallCost;

      while (currentNeighbor != nil) {
            newCost = currentNeighbor->GetCostFromStart() +
                  currentNeighbor->GetMovementCost(parent);
```

```
                    if ((!AlreadyInOpenList(currentNeighbor)) ||
                            (!AlreadyInClosedList(currentNeighbor))) {
                            // This neighbor is new.
                            currentNeighbor->SetParent(parent);
                            currentNeighbor->SetCostFromStart(newCost);
                            estimatedCost = currentNeighbor->EstimatePathCost(goalRow,
                                        goalColumn);
                            currentNeighbor->SetEstimatedCostToGoal(estimatedCost);
                            overallCost = currentNeighbor->GetCostFromStart() +
                                        estimatedCost;
                            currentNeighbor->SetTotalCost(overallCost);
                            openList.AddItem(currentNeighbor);
                    }
                    else if (currentNeighbor->GetCostFromStart() > newCost)) {
                            // This neighbor is improved.
                            if (AlreadyInClosedList(currentNeighbor)) {
                                    closedList.RemoveItem(currentNeighbor);
                            }

                            if (AlreadyInOpenList(currentNeighbor)) {
                                    // This entry is improved. Update its cost.
                                    UpdateEntryInOpenList(currentNeighbor);
                            }
                            else (
                                    // Move improved entry from the closed list
                                    // to the open list.
                                    openList.AddItem(currentNeighbor);
                            }
                    } // end else if

                    // Read next neighbor
                    currentNeighbor = (PathLocationPtr)neighborList.Next();
            } // end while
    }
```

Calculating the Cost to Move to a Neighbor

When calculating the cost from the start location, g(n), for a neighbor, we add the cost from the start for the neighbor's parent —the parent's g(n) value— to the cost of moving from the parent to the neighbor. Mathematically, the formula looks like the following:

```
Neighbor g(n) = Parent g(n) + (Cost of moving from parent to neighbor)
```

In our case, determining the cost of moving from a given location to one of its neighbors is easy. If the move is diagonal, the cost is 1.5; otherwise the cost is 1. In your game, you may want to multiply the cost by the average terrain cost. The following function computes the cost of moving to a neighbor:

```
double PathLocation::GetMovementCost(PathLocationPtr parent)
{
        //This function assumes that the start and destination locations
        // are neighbors. The function determines whether or not
        // the move from source to destination is diagonal and
        // assigns a cost based on whether or not the move is diagonal.
        short startRow = parent->GetRow();
        short destinationRow = GetRow();

        Boolean diagonalMove;
        if (startRow != destinationRow)
                diagonalMove = true;
        else
                diagonalMove = false;

        if (diagonalMove)
                return kDiagonalMoveCost;
        else
                return kStraightMoveCost;
}
```

Estimating the Cost to the Goal

The key to fast and accurate pathfinding is providing a good estimate of the cost of reaching the goal from a given location. The EstimatePathCost() function provides such an estimate by calculating the number of diagonal and non-diagonal moves between the given location and the goal, as you can see in the following code:

```
double PathLocation::EstimatePathCost (short goalRow, short goalColumn)
{
        // Calculates the number of horizontal and vertical
        // moves between the current
```

```
// location and the goal location

short rowDistance;
short columnDistance;

rowDistance = GetRow() - goalRow;

// Get absolute value. There shouldn't
// be any negative path costs
if (rowDistance < 0)
        rowDistance = rowDistance * -1;


columnDistance = GetColumn() - goalColumn;

// Get absolute value. There shouldn't
// be any negative path costs
if (columnDistance < 0)
        columnDistance = columnDistance * -1;


double cost;
short straightMoves;
short diagonalMoves;

// Calculate the number of diagonal and straight moves the
// creature must make to reach the goal.
if (rowDistance == columnDistance) {
        // All moves are diagonal. No straight moves.
        diagonalMoves = rowDistance;
        straightMoves = 0;
}
else if (rowDistance > columnDistance) {
        // The number of diagonal moves is equal to the smaller
        // of the two distances, and the number of straight moves
        // is equal to the difference between the two distances.
        diagonalMoves = columnDistance;
        straightMoves = rowDistance - columnDistance;
}
else {
        // The number of diagonal moves is equal to the smaller
        // of the two distances, and the number of straight moves
        // is equal to the difference between the two distances.
```

```
                diagonalMoves = rowDistance;
                straightMoves = columnDistance - rowDistance;
        }


        // Calculate the path cost
        cost = (diagonalMoves * kDiagonalMoveCost) +
                        (straightMoves * kStraightMoveCost);
        return cost;
}
```

Determining Whether or Not a Location Resides in the Open List

Testing whether or not a given location already exists in the open list is fairly simple: We go through the list and compare each item in the list with the given location. If both the rows and columns match, the location resides in the open list. Determining whether or not a given location resides in the closed list is similar, and its source code is nearly identical to the following code, which tests whether a given location is in the open list:

```
Boolean PathFinder::AlreadyInOpenList(PathLocationPtr locationToTest)
{
        PathLocationPtr currentLocation;
        short currentLocationRow;
        short currentLocationColumn;
        Iterator openListIterator(openList);

        currentLocation = (PathLocationPtr)openListIterator.Next();
        while (currentLocation != nil) {
                currentLocationRow = currentLocation->GetRow();
                currentLocationColumn = currentLocation->GetColumn();
                if ((locationToTest->GetRow() == currentLocationRow) &&
                        (locationToTest->GetColumn() == currentLocationColumn))
                                return true;

                currentLocation = (PathLocationPtr)openListIterator.Next();
        }

        // At this point, we know that the location is not in the open list
        return false;
}
```

Updating the Open List

When a path location's cost improves, and the location already resides in the open list, we must update the location's cost in the open list. The procedure is exactly the same as determining whether or not a path location exists in the open list: We go through the list and compare each item's row and column. In this case, we will eventually find the item because we know that it already appears in the open list. When we find the item, we change the appropriate fields to the updated values, as you can see in the following routine:

```
void Pathfinder::UpdateOpenList(PathLocationPtr locationToUpdate)
{
        PathLocationPtr currentLocation;
        short currentLocationRow;
        short currentLocationColumn;
        Iterator openListIterator(openList);

        currentLocation = (PathLocationPtr)openListIterator.Next();
        Boolean performedUpdate = false;

        while ((!performedUpdate) && (currentLocation != nil)) {
                currentLocationRow = currentLocation->GetRow();
                currentLocationColumn = currentLocation->GetColumn();
                if ((locationToTest->GetRow() == currentLocationRow) &&
                        (locationToTest->GetColumn() == currentLocationColumn)) {
                        // Perform the update
                        currentLocation->SetTotalCost(locationToUpdate-
                        >GetTotalCost());
                        currentLocation->SetCostFromStart(
                                locationToUpdate->GetCostFromStart());
                        currentLocation->SetEstimatedCostToGoal(
                                locationToUpdate->GetEstimatedCostToGoal());
                        performedUpdate = true;
                }
                currentLocation = (PathLocationPtr)openListIterator.Next();
        }
}
```

Building the Path

Last, but not least, we must reconstruct the path that the A* algorithm has calculated for us. We start at the goal location and examine its parent field. We move to the location specified in the parent field and examine its parent. This examination of parent fields continues until we find a nil parent field, which means that we have reached the start location. Building a list for the PathLocation objects we examined stores the path for us, as you can see in the following code:

```
void Pathfinder::BuildPath(PathLocationPtr goalLocation)
{
        ClearDiscoveredPath();
        discoveredPath.AddItem(goalLocation);

        // Start with the goal location's parent
        PathLocationPtr currentPathLocation;
        PathLocationPtr nextPathLocation;
        currentPathLocation = goalLocation->GetParent();

        while(currentPathLocation != nil)
                // Add location to the found path
                discoveredPath.AddItem(currentPathLocation);

                // Find next location in the path
                nextPathLocation = currentPathLocation->GetParent();
                currentPathLocation = nextPathLocation;
        }
}
```

Weaknesses of the A* Algorithm

Although A* is a fine pathfinding algorithm, it does have some potential weaknesses that can make it unsuitable for some games. A* can require a ton of memory if the game world is large. A game world 1000 units tall and 1000 units wide would result in a potential search space of one million units. An open list with thousands of entries requires a good deal of RAM, something your game may not have because of the memory it needs to store graphics, sound, and other game data. You can work around this problem in several ways.

In the next section, I discuss the Iterative Deepening A* algorithm, which uses less memory than does the A* algorithm. Another solution is to use hierarchical pathfinding to reduce the space of a single search. I cover hierarchical pathfinding later in this chapter.

Large game worlds also make the open list more difficult to sort, which slows down the search. Finding a path to a far-off location is slow because the pathfinder has to perform thousands of steps instead of the 16 it performed in the example earlier in this chapter. The A* algorithm computes the entire path, which may take too long in a real-time game. A solution to this problem is to use a real-time pathfinding algorithm that computes only part of the path at a time. Later in this chapter, I discuss the Learning Real-Time A* algorithm, which is a real-time version of the A* algorithm.

The A* algorithm assumes that the goal and the terrain do not move or change in any way. If the target (the goal location) can move, the A* algorithm has to compute an entire new path to the target's new location. In the time it takes to calculate the new target, the target may have moved again, meaning that the creature may never reach its goal.

The Iterative Deepening A* Algorithm

One of the problems with using the A* algorithm is the amount of memory it requires to store all the locations in the open and closed lists. Large game worlds can result in hundreds or thousands of entries in the open list, consuming precious memory. A solution to this problem is to use the Iterative Deepening A* (IDA*) algorithm.

Rather than using an open list to store unexamined locations, the IDA* algorithm uses a depth-first search to create the path. The depth-first search begins with the start location, chooses one of its neighbors, and examines the neighbor. Then the algorithm chooses one of that location's neighbors and examines it. The depth-first search continues on a path until it reaches a dead end or finds the goal. If it reaches a dead end, it backtracks and examines a new path.

Consider performing a depth-first search on Figure 13-20. The algorithm begins by moving from the start position to location A. Next, it moves from location A to location A1, and then to location A11. A11 is a dead end, so the depth-first search then moves to location A12. A12 has two neighbors, so the depth-first search examines location A121 and then A122. Finding dead ends there, the depth-first search backtracks and examines location A13. After examining A13, the search then examines locations A14, A2, A3, A4, B, C, and finally D.

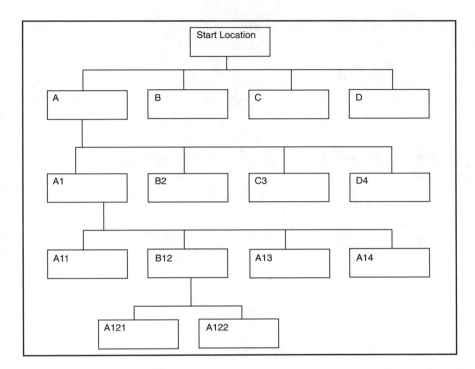

Figure 13-20

*A depth-first
search example*

The search tree for a game world is going to be much larger than the example in the previous paragraph. A location in a tile-based world like the one we are using can have up to eight neighbors. The tree can have dozens of levels instead of the five levels in the example, so a depth-first search can take a long time. For depth-first search to be useful, we need a way to keep the search from continuing too long.

That's where the "iterative deepening" part of the IDA* algorithm comes in. We begin by using the estimated cost from the start location to the goal—the heuristic function h(n) in the A* algorithm—as the initial cutoff value. Then we perform the depth-first search. If the cost of a path exceeds the cutoff value, we quit searching that path and examine another path. If the computer finds no path, it increases the cutoff value to the lowest cost value that exceeds the cutoff value (you can just increment the cutoff value by 1 if you want). Then the computer searches again. The cycle of searching and increasing the cutoff value continues until the computer finds the goal or until the entire game world has been examined. In the latter case, there is no path.

The major advantage of the IDA* algorithm is that it uses less memory than the A* algorithm. The memory requirements of IDA* grow linearly while the memory requirements of A* grow exponentially. If the depth of the tree to the goal doubles in the IDA* algorithm, the memory requirements also double. In A*, if the depth to the goal doubles, the memory requirements quadruple. The Iterative Deepening A* algorithm is also easier to code because we don't have to worry about creating open and closed lists and sorting the open list. The disadvantage of IDA* is that it examines more locations than A*, which means that it takes more time to calculate the path than A* does.

Coding the Iterative Deepening A* Algorithm

When coding the IDA* algorithm, we begin by taking the start location and filling the fields of the PathLocation structure. Then we set the initial cutoff value. After setting the initial cutoff value, we perform a depth-first search. If we reach the goal, we build the path and leave. If not, we increase the cutoff value and try again.

```
Boolean Pathfinder::CalculatePathIDAStar (short startRow, short startColumn,
            short goalRow, short goalColumn,
            GameLevelPtr currentLevel, GameTileListPtr theTileList)
{
        // Use the iterative deepening A* algorithm
        PathLocation startLocation;
        startLocation.SetRow(startRow);
        startLocation.SetColumn(startColumn);
        startLocation.SetCostFromStart(0.0);

        double estimatedCost;
        estimatedCost = startLocation. EstimatePathCost(goalRow, goalColumn);

        startLocation.SetEstimatedCostToGoal(estimatedCost);
        startLocation.SetTotalCost(estimatedCost);
        startLocation.SetParent(nil);

        double cutoffValue = estimatedCost;
        Boolean goalFound;
        while(cutoffValue < kMaximumCutoffValue) {
                goalFound = DepthFirstSearch(&startLocation, cutoffValue,
                        currentLevel, theTileList, goalRow, goalColumn);

                if (goalFound) {
                        return true;
```

```
            }
            else {
                    cutoffValue = cutoffValue + kCutoffIncrement;
            }
      }
      // At this point, the pathfinder could not find a path
      return false;
}
```

The EstimatePathCost() function is the same function we wrote earlier in this chapter when we coded the A* algorithm.

Coding the Depth-First Search

The depth-first search begins by testing the start location's total cost to the cutoff value. If the total cost exceeds the cutoff value, it stops this search. Otherwise, it finds the start location's neighbors. Then, for each neighbor, it performs another depth-first search. This process of repeatedly performing depth-first searches is called *recursion*. We continue the depth-first searches until we reach the goal, exceed the cutoff value, or exhaust all the possible locations in the game world. You can see the code for the depth-first search in the following function:

```
Boolean Pathfinder::DepthFirstSearch(PathLocationPtr startLocation,
            double cutoffValue, GameLevelPtr currentLevel,
            GameTileListPtr theTileList, short goalRow, short goalColumn)
{
      // If we exceeded the cutoff value, stop going down this path.
      if(startLocation->GetTotalCost() > cutoffValue)
            return false;

      LinkedList neighborList;
      neighborList = startLocation->FindNeighbors(currentLevel, theTileList,
                                      goalRow, goalColumn);

      Iterator neighborListIterator(neighborList);
      PathLocationPtr currentLocation;
      currentLocation = (PathLocationPtr)neighborListIterator.Next();

      Boolean goalFound;

      while (currentLocation != nil) {
```

```
            // Make a recursive call to DepthFirstSearch().
            goalFound = DepthFirstSearch(currentLocation, cutoffValue,
                    currentLevel, theTileList, goalRow, goalColumn);

            if (currentLocation->AtGoal(goalRow, goalColumn)) {
                    BuildPath(currentLocation);
                    return true;
            }
            currentLocation = (PathLocationPtr)closedListIterator.Next();
        }
        return false;
    }
}
```

The `FindNeighbors()`, `AtGoal()`, and `BuildPath()` functions are the same ones we wrote to implement the A* algorithm.

The Learning Real-Time A* Algorithm

The A* algorithm computes the entire path before embarking on it. Although the A* algorithm does construct the best path to the goal location, calculating the entire path may take too long to be useful. For example, if you used the A* algorithm to compute a path to the player so that an enemy could kill him, the player will probably move by the time the computer creates the path, forcing the computer to make another path.

There is hope if you want to use the A* algorithm to create partial paths so that you can create paths fast enough. The solution is the Learning Real-Time A* algorithm (LRTA*). Instead of calculating the entire path, the Learning Real-Time A* algorithm calculates the next move to make. The algorithm takes the current location, x, examines each neighbor, y, and performs the following calculation:

$$f(y) = k(x, y) + h(y)$$

The value $f(y)$ represents the total estimated cost to the goal from position y; the value $k(x, y)$ represents the cost of moving from x to y; and $h(y)$ represents the estimated cost to the goal from y. LRTA* calculates only one move at a time, so the current location is always the start location. Because of this, the $k(x, y)$ value measures the cost from the start, making it the LRTA* equivalent of the A* algorithm's $g(x)$ value.

The calculations LRTA* performs are similar to the ones you make in the A* algorithm. The LRTA* algorithm chooses the neighbor with the cheapest total estimated cost and moves there. Then it repeats the cycle until it finds the goal. LRTA* eventually reaches the goal. It may not reach the goal as quickly as the A* algorithm because LRTA* calculates only one move at a time, but it does generate a decent path. The faster path calculation compensates for the weaker path plan; it's a tradeoff between speed and quality.

My explanation has clarified the "real-time" portion of the acronym LRTA*, but where does the "learning" come into it? There's one more step to add to the algorithm. When we pick the lowest cost neighbor y as the place to move, we adjust the current position's estimated path cost to the goal, h(x) to the f(y) function we calculated. By doing this, the h(x) function more accurately reflects the true cost to the goal; it "learns" the cost to the goal.

To store the h(x) values so that the learning sticks, we need a two-dimensional array. In the case of our tile-based world, the array is the size of the level. The problem is that you need a level-sized array for each active creature in the game. In an action game, you would not want an opponent to start using LRTA* until the player enters that opponent's area of the level. By doing this, you limit the number of arrays you need. Having a level-sized 2D array for every enemy in a level would drive your game's memory requirements through the roof.

LRTA* Example

In this section, I'll use LRTA* to solve the same problem we solved using the A* algorithm earlier in the chapter. By working through this example, you should be able to better understand the workings of the LRTA* algorithm. Figure 13-21 shows the estimated cost from each location in the grid to the goal location. The estimated cost from the start location to the goal location is 5 (2 diagonal moves and 2 non-diagonal moves. Remember that we do not take the obstacles into account when estimating the path cost).

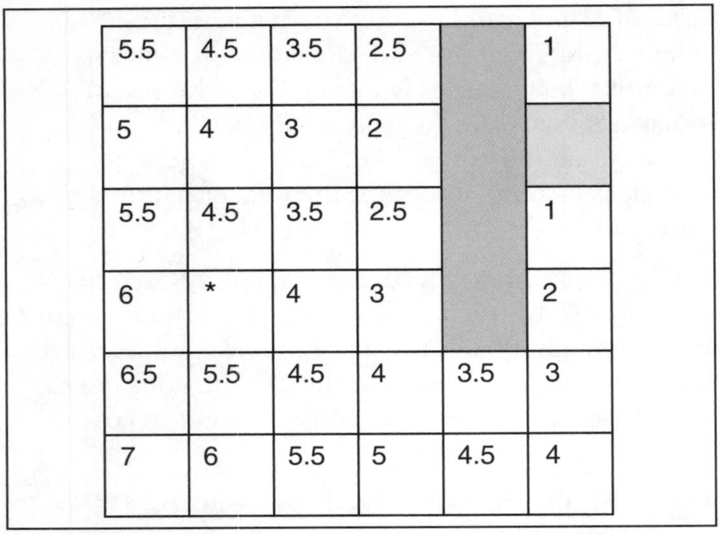

5.5	4.5	3.5	2.5		1
5	4	3	2		
5.5	4.5	3.5	2.5		1
6	*	4	3		2
6.5	5.5	4.5	4	3.5	3
7	6	5.5	5	4.5	4

Figure 13-21

The initial heuristic values to the goal location. The start location has a heuristic value of 5.

From the start location (the tile marked with an asterisk in Figure 13-21), LRTA* has eight possible directions it can go. The pathfinder decides to travel northeast because it has the lowest estimated cost, 3.5. The start location's heuristic value remains 5: 3.5 for the estimated cost from the northeast neighbor to the goal plus the cost of 1.5 from the start location to the northeast tile. Remember that diagonal moves have a cost of 1.5 and nondiagonal moves have a cost of 1.

The pathfinder makes another northeast move for its second move because the northeast neighbor has an estimated cost of 2, the lowest among the possible moves the pathfinder can make. The northeast neighbor's estimated cost of 2 plus the cost of 1.5 for the diagonal move makes the original location's heuristic value 3.5, which is the same as it was before.

At this point, the pathfinder has two places it can go. It can move north or south because each of those locations has an estimated cost of 2.5. For the sake of simplicity, I will have the pathfinder turn south. The move south changes the original location's heuristic value from 2 to 3.5: 1 for the move south plus the estimated cost of 2.5 to reach the goal from the southern neighbor.

Because of the obstacle to the east of the creature, the pathfinder has five possible directions it can move. The southern and northwest neighbors have the lowest estimated cost, 3. To make life easier, the pathfinder will move south. Remember that the northern neighbor's estimated cost increased to 3.5. The move south changes the original location's heuristic value from 3 to 4: 1 for the move south plus the estimated cost of 3 to reach the goal from the southern neighbor.

At this moment, the creature is west of the southernmost obstacle tile. The pathfinder has six directions it can choose from to make its next move. The southeast and northwest neighbors have the lowest estimated cost, 3.5. I don't feel like backtracking, and I doubt you want me to cover areas that obviously are not part of the optimal path, so I will have the pathfinder move southeast. The southeast move increases the original location's heuristic value from 3 to 5: 1.5 for the diagonal move southeast plus the southeast neighbor's estimated path cost of 3.5.

LRTA* is working its way around the obstacle and heading toward the goal. For its next move, the pathfinder moves northeast because the northeast neighbor's cost of 2 is the lowest among the current location's neighbors. The current location's heuristic costs remains 3.5: 1.5 for the diagonal move northeast plus the estimated cost of 2 to reach the goal from the northeast neighbor.

The pathfinder makes two more moves north to reach the goal. Neither of the two moves changes any heuristic values. Figure 13-22 charts the entire path from the start location to the goal. For an initial trial, the path is pretty good, but there's room for improvement.

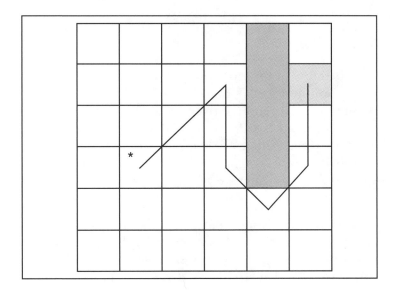

Figure 13-22

The initial path the LRTA* algorithm follows to the goal.

Trial 2

To improve the path that the LRTA* algorithm calculates, we must run the algorithm again so that LRTA* can learn the best path to the goal. Figure 13-23 lists the estimated costs to the goal from each location in the grid at the start of the second trial. The tiles in rows 2 through 4 located one tile west of the obstacle changed from the first trial. Just as we did in the first trial, the best move to make now is to move northeast. The move northeast does not change the start location's heuristic cost.

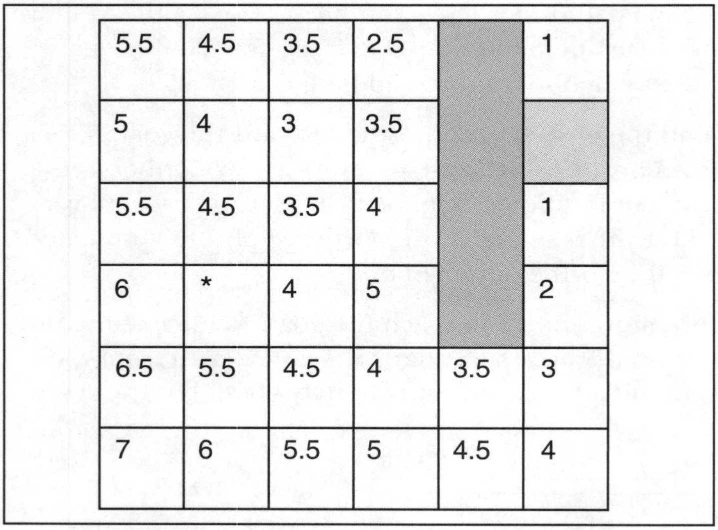

5.5	4.5	3.5	2.5		1
5	4	3	3.5		
5.5	4.5	3.5	4		1
6	*	4	5		2
6.5	5.5	4.5	4	3.5	3
7	6	5.5	5	4.5	4

Figure 13-23

The heuristic values to the goal location at the start of the second trial. The heuristic value for the start location is 5.

The lowest heuristic cost among the current location's neighbors is the northern neighbor with a cost of 3. As its second move, LRTA* moves north. The move north increases the current location's heuristic value from 3.5 to 4: 1 for the move north plus the northern neighbor's estimated path cost of 3. The pathfinder's third move is northeast because the northeast neighbor's cost of 2.5 is the lowest. The northeast move increases the heuristic cost of the new current location from 3 to 4: 1.5 for the diagonal move northeast plus 2.5 for the estimated cost from the northeast neighbor to the goal.

LRTA* finds itself trapped in the corner at the moment. From its current location, it has three directions it can move. The southern and western neighbors tie for the lowest cost with 3.5; the southwest neighbor's cost increased from 3 to 4 with LRTA*'s last move. I'm going to move west, which does not sound right, but trust me. The move west increases the original location's heuristic value from 2.5 to 4.5: 1 for the move west and 3.5 for the cost to the goal from the western neighbor.

From its current location, the pathfinder has only five directions to move because we're at the northern boundary of the example world. The pathfinder will move southeast because the southeast neighbor has an estimated cost of 3.5, which is the lowest of all the current location's neighbors. We're where we would have been if we had moved south instead of west in the last turn. The southeast move raises the current location's heuristic value from 3.5 to 5: 1.5 for the diagonal move southeast plus the southeast neighbor's estimated cost of 3.5.

At this point, the pathfinder has three identical best locations for its next move. The western, southwestern, and southern neighbors all have an estimated cost of 4. I'm going to have the pathfinder move south because I've already examined the western and southwestern neighbors in this trial. The move south changes the original location's heuristic value from 3.5 to 5: 1 for the move south plus the southern neighbor's estimated cost of 4.

Just as it did in the last turn, the pathfinder has three best locations for the next move. The northwestern, western, and southwestern neighbors have an estimated path cost of 4. To avoid going to locations I've already been in this trial, the pathfinder will move southwest. The move southwest increases the original location's heuristic cost from 4 to 5.5. For its next move, LRTA* will go southeast because the southeast neighbor has an estimated cost of 4. The northern neighbor also has an estimated cost of 4, but I've already been there. The move southeast raises the current location's heuristic value from 4 to 5.5.

From this point, LRTA* will work just as it did in the first trial, moving around the obstacle and then traveling north to the goal. This path involves four moves: east, northeast, north, and north. The move east increases the current location's heuristic cost from 4 to 4.5. No other heuristic values change.

Figure 13-24 shows the entire path LRTA* traversed to reach the goal in the second trial. This path looks worse than the first one; it doesn't appear that LRTA* learned anything. The first trial increased the heuristic values of the stronger locations to better reflect the true cost to the goal, which makes those locations look worse compared to the other locations that have not had their true cost reflected. From the pathfinder's point of view, the unexamined locations northeast of the start location looked superior. LRTA* had to examine them and determine that they didn't lead anywhere. By building a comparatively stupid path, the pathfinder knows a lot more about the world now than it did at the start.

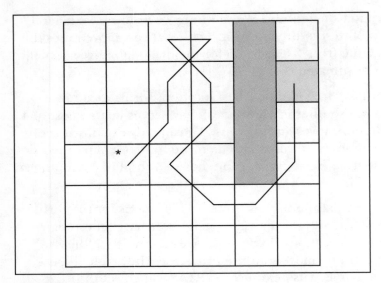

Figure 13-24

The path LRTA* follows to the goal during the second trial.

Trial 3

It should be obvious from running the second trial that LRTA* has more learning to do, so we must run another trial. Figure 13-25 lists the estimated costs to the goal at the start of the third trial. The costs of the first four rows in the third column changed from the start of the second trial as did rows 1, 2, 3, and 5 of the fourth column For the third time, the northeast neighbor has the lowest estimated path cost. This time, however, moving northeast increases the start location's heuristic value from 5 to 5.5 because the previous trial raised the northeast neighbor's heuristic cost from 3.5 to 4.

5.5	4.5	5	4.5		1
5	4	4	5		
5.5	4.5	4	5.5		1
6	*	5.5	5		2
6.5	5.5	4.5	4.5	3.5	3
7	6	5.5	5	4.5	4

Figure 13-25

The heuristic values to the goal location at the start of the third trial. The heuristic value for the start location is 5.

The pathfinder has two choices for its second move: moving north and moving northwest. In this case, the pathfinder will go north. The move north increases the current location's heuristic cost from 4 to 5. For its third move, the pathfinder will move west because the western neighbor has the lowest estimated path cost, 4. The move west increases the new current location's heuristic value from 4 to 5.

At this point, the pathfinder can choose to move north or south because both of these neighbors have an estimated path cost of 4.5. Obviously, moving north leads nowhere, so the pathfinder will move south, which changes the current location's heuristic cost from 4 to 5.5. Now the pathfinder can move east, northeast or northwest because each of these neighbors share the lowest estimated cost of 5. For the sake of simplicity, the pathfinder will move east. The move east raises the new current location's heuristic value from 4.5 to 5.5.

We're back to the tile northeast of the start location. The pathfinder can choose to move north, northeast, or southeast because all three of these neighbors have an estimated path cost of 5. For this example, the pathfinder will move southeast, which raises the current location's heuristic value from 5 to 6.5. Now the path works like it did in the first two trials. The pathfinder moves southeast and northeast to maneuver around the obstacle, and then moves north twice to reach the goal. None of these moves changes any of the heuristic values.

Figure 13-26 shows the entire path LRTA* traversed to reach the goal in the third trial. This path looks like the worst one yet. This trial wasted a lot of time examining the tiles north of the start location. However, this trial run raised the estimated path cost for the tiles to the north so LRTA* shouldn't look at them in future trials. Although it doesn't look like it from the final path, this trial taught the pathfinder a great deal about the world. The path from the next trial is going to look much better.

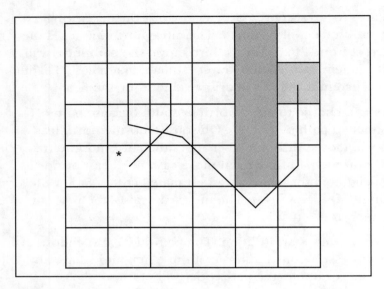

Figure 13-26

The path LRTA* follows to the goal in the third trial.

Trial 4

It's time to run another trial to see whether LRTA* learned anything from the first three trials. Figure 13-27 shows the initial estimated costs to the goal at the start of this trial. In this trial, the pathfinder makes a radical change and moves southeast because the southeast neighbor's estimated path cost of 4.5 is the lowest. The move southeast raises the starting location's heuristic value from 5.5 to 6.

5.5	4.5	5	4.5		1
5	5.5	5	5		
5.5	5.5	6.5	5.5		1
6	*	5.5	5		2
6.5	5.5	4.5	4.5	3.5	3
7	6	5.5	5	4.5	4

Figure 13-27

The heuristic values to the goal location at the start of the fourth trial. The heuristic value for the start location is 5.5.

For its second move, the pathfinder moves east because the eastern neighbor's estimated path cost of 4.5 is the lowest among the current location's neighbors. The move east increases the current location's heuristic value from 4.5 to 5.5. The pathfinder then moves east again because the east neighbor's path cost of 3.5 is the lowest. The move east has no effect on the new current location's heuristic cost.

At this point, the pathfinder moves northeast to move around the obstacle and moves north twice to reach the goal. None of these moves affects any of the heuristic values. Figure 13-28 shows the path to the goal that LRTA* took in this fourth trial, and it looks excellent.

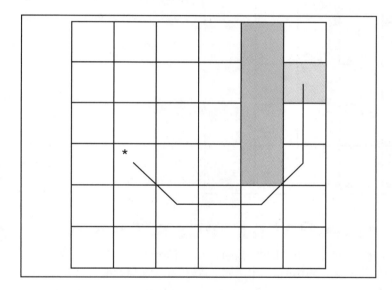

Figure 13-28

The path LRTA* follows to the goal in the fourth trial.

For future trials, the initial heuristic values look like they do in Figure 13-29. Five neighbors share the lowest estimated path cost of 5.5. If the pathfinder chooses to move southeast, the path will look like it did in Figure 13-28. If the pathfinder chooses a different direction for its initial move, that path will look different than Figure 13-28, but future paths will be more likely to look like Figure 13-28. The performance of the LRTA* algorithm is impressive; it found an optimal path in four trials without having to plan the entire path in advance. It seems that LRTA* did learn something from the previous trials.

Because LRTA* requires multiple trials to build an optimal path, it is not an algorithm you drop into your game and have intelligent behavior instantly appear. To use LRTA* in your game, you have two options. You can play your game repeatedly, giving LRTA* time to build solid paths, then include this data with your game. Alternatively, the computer characters can build stupid paths when the player first starts playing the game, then the paths improve the more the player plays. Learning requires time and space for the computer to remember what it learned, which is why learning is not a component in many video games.

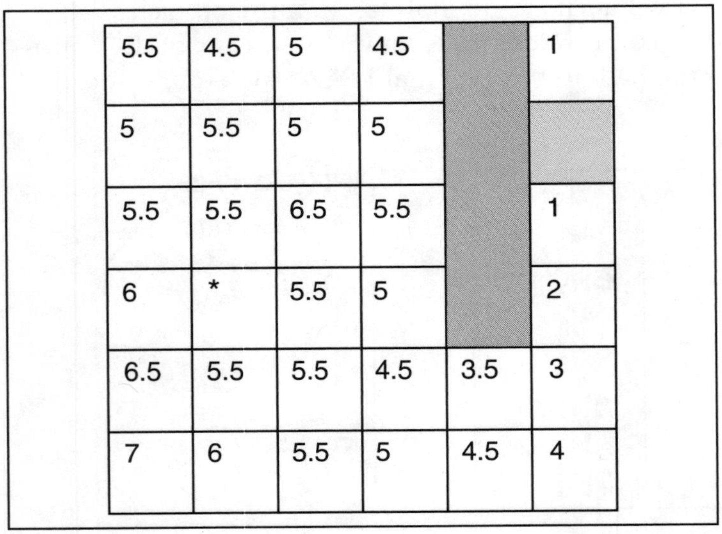

5.5	4.5	5	4.5		1
5	5.5	5	5		
5.5	5.5	6.5	5.5		1
6	*	5.5	5		2
6.5	5.5	5.5	4.5	3.5	3
7	6	5.5	5	4.5	4

Figure 13-29

The heuristic values to the goal location at the start of future trials. The heuristic value for the start location is 6.

Changes to the Pathfinder Class

Changing from the A* algorithm to the LRTA* algorithm changes the Pathfinder class from a data standpoint. We can eliminate the openList and closedList data members because LRTA* does not use lists of examined and unexamined locations. Because LRTA* calculates the next move to make instead of the entire path, the pathfinder's solution consists of just one PathLocation object instead of a list of PathLocation objects. When you use LRTA* as the pathfinding algorithm, the Pathfinder class changes to look like the following:

```
class Pathfinder
{
        protected:
                PathLocationPtr destination;

        public:
                double* estimatedCostTable;
}
```

The `destination` data member stores the next location on the path to the goal; it tells the creature where to go next. The `estimatedCostTable` data member stores the list of estimated path costs to the goal for each location in the game level. I made the `estimatedCostTable` a `public` data member so that I could access it easier; using accessor functions to return arrays is awkward.

Coding LRTA*

The code for the LRTA* algorithm starts out identically to the code for the A* algorithm. We fill the start location's data, find its neighbors, and determine which neighbor has the best path cost. From this point on, however, the code changes. LRTA* takes the best neighbor's data and uses it to update the start location and the table of estimated path costs to the goal. Because LRTA* makes only one move at a time, it moves to the best neighbor and returns it in the `destination` data member of the `Pathfinder` class. The following function implements the LRTA* algorithm:

```
Boolean Pathfinder::CalculatePathLRTAStar(short startRow, short startColumn,
      short goalRow, short goalColumn, GameLevelPtr currentLevel,
      GameTileListPtr theTileList)
{
      // Use the Learning Real-Time A* algorithm

      PathLocation startLocation;
      startLocation.SetRow(startRow);
      startLocation.SetColumn(startColumn);
      startLocation.SetCostFromStart(0.0);

      double estimatedCost;
      estimatedCost = startLocation.EstimatePathCost(goalRow, goalColumn);

      startLocation.SetEstimatedCostToGoal(estimatedCost);
      startLocation.SetTotalCost(estimatedCost);
      startLocation.SetParent(nil);

      LinkedList neighborList;
      PathLocationPtr bestNeighbor;
      neighborList = startLocation->FindNeighbors(currentLevel, theTileList,
                  goalRow, goalColumn);
      bestNeighbor = FindCheapestLocation(neighborList);
```

```
startLocation.SetEstimatedCostToGoal(bestNeighbor->GetTotalCost());

// Update the estimated cost table
UInt32 mapIndex;
short theLevelWidth = currentLevel->GetLevelWidth();
mapIndex = (startLocation.GetRow() * theLevelWidth) +
                      (startLocation.GetColumn());
estimatedCostTable[mapIndex] = bestNeighbor->GetTotalCost();

// Return the one entry path
discoveredPath = bestNeighbor;

return true;
}
```

The EstimatePathCost(), FindNeighbors(), and FindCheapestLocation() functions are
the identical functions we wrote for the A* algorithm. Isn't it nice not to have to
rewrite major sections of code when using a different algorithm to solve a problem?

Hierarchical Pathfinding

You can use *hierarchical pathfinding* with any of the pathfinding algorithms in this
chapter to simplify the search. Look at the situation in Figure 13-30. Computing a
path from the start location to the goal location using the A* algorithm requires
the examination of a lot of locations. The computer will spend time exploring the
eastern half of the hallway (location B) even though there's no way to reach room
E from the hallway. The pathfinder may even examine room C, which would also
be a waste of time.

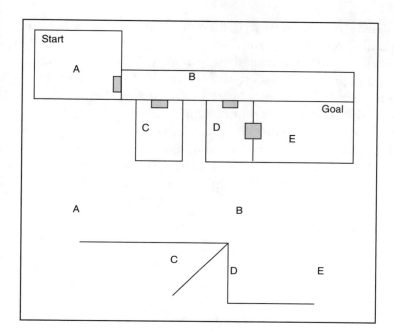

Figure 13-30

A sample dungeon with four rooms and a hallway; the bottom portion of the figure shows the dungeon's connectivity graph.

Hierarchical pathfinding breaks up the pathfinding into smaller chunks. First, it uses a connectivity graph to determine the high-level path. Using the connectivity graph in Figure 13-30, the pathfinder would determine that it should go from room A to the hallway (location B) to room D to room E to reach the goal.

From this high-level path, the hierarchical pathfinder computes the individual high-level paths. In our example, the pathfinder would begin by creating a path from the start location to the start of the hallway. When the enemy reaches the hallway, the pathfinder then finds the path to room D. After arriving in room D, the pathfinder makes a path to room E, and then it creates the final path from the entrance to room E to the goal.

The beauty of hierarchical pathfinding is that instead of computing the entire path to the goal, we compute the path room by room until we reach the goal. By finding only the path out of the room, we reduce the search size to one room, which reduces the amount of time and memory needed to find the path. The difficult part is creating the connectivity graph for the level. You will have to create a connectivity graph when you make each of your game's levels. You can use hierarchical pathfinding with any of the pathfinding algorithms in this chapter or any other algorithms you discover.

At the heart of the connectivity graph is a data structure that represents one area of the level (areas A through E in Figure 13-30). In this data structure, you would need to store a minimum of three pieces of data. First, you would need a rectangle that tells you how much space the room or hallway encompasses. This data would let you know which area of a game level a particular point in the level belongs. Second, you would need a list of the area's neighbors. Finally, for each neighbor, you would need a connection point where the two areas meet. These connection points correspond to the doors in Figure 13-30. You would pass the connection point as the goal to the pathfinder to calculate the low-level path from one area to the next. The following declarations show how a sample connectivity graph might look:

```
struct GameArea
{
        short areaID;
        Rect areaRect;
        GameNeighborPtr neighborList;
}

struct GameNeighbor
{
        GameAreaneighborArea;
        short connectionPointX;
        short connectionPointY;
}
```

To perform hierarchical pathfinding from a starting location to a goal location, you would perform the following steps:

1. Determine which areas of the connectivity graph the start and goal locations belong in by checking to see whether or not the two locations intersect an area's areaRect data member.

2. Navigate the connectivity graph from the start area to the goal area by following the neighborList data member of the game level's areas. This step creates a high-level path to follow.

3. For each area of the high-level path, create a low-level path from one area to the next. Plug in the connectionPointX, and connectionPointY data members into the low-level pathfinder as the goal location to find paths from one area to the next.

Summary

Pathfinders calculate paths from one location to another, which is something games have to do to make the computer-controlled characters appear intelligent. Pathfinding algorithms fall into two general categories. Offline algorithms compute the entire path before making a move while real-time algorithms compute enough of the path for the creature to make any move. Real-time pathfinding algorithms find paths quicker, but the paths have lower quality than the paths found by offline algorithms.

The most popular pathfinding algorithm is the A* algorithm, which uses heuristic searches to aid in pathfinding. The key to the A* algorithm is the heuristic function, which estimates the cost of moving from a given location to the goal. The closer the heuristic function is to the actual cost of reaching the goal from the given location, the less time the search takes. To ensure that the A* algorithm finds an optimal path, the value of the heuristic function must be less than the actual cost of reaching the goal. A good starting heuristic value is the Manhattan distance between the start location and the goal location.

At the beginning, A* has an open list of unexamined locations that includes the start location; it also has an empty closed list of examined locations. A* examines the best location in the open list, finds the location with the lowest estimated cost to the path, and identifies its neighbors. If a neighbor does not appear in the open or closed list, A* adds it to the open list. If a neighbor does appear in the open or closed list, A* checks to see whether or not the neighbor's new estimated cost is less than the location's current estimated cost. If it is, A* updates the location and moves the location to the open list. After examining the neighbors, A* moves the current location to the closed list. A* then selects the best location remaining in the open list and repeats the cycle until it finds the goal or until no items remain in the open list. If A* goes through the entire open list, that means it could not find a path to the goal.

The downside to using A* is the amount of memory it requires to store the list of examined and unexamined locations. The Iterative Deepening A* (IDA*) algorithm uses less memory to compute the path. IDA* uses a series of depth-first searches to find the goal and uses a cutoff value to prevent infinite searches.

The initial cutoff value is the estimated cost of reaching the goal from the start location. If the depth-first search does not find the goal, you raise the cutoff value and perform another depth-first search. Keep raising the cutoff value until you reach the goal.

To increase the speed of your searches, you can use the Learning Real-Time A* (LRTA*) algorithm. LRTA* examines the neighbors of the current location and moves to the neighbor with the lowest estimated cost to the goal. It then updates the estimated cost of the original location to the sum of the estimated cost from the neighbor to the goal and the cost of the move from the original location to the neighbor. By maintaining a list of estimated costs to the goal, LRTA* learns the best path to the goal without calculating the entire path in advance.

No matter which algorithm you use for your game's pathfinding, you can benefit from hierarchical pathfinding. Hierarchical pathfinding first calculates a high-level path, such as the rooms a character would have to go through to move from one location to another in the dungeon. You would then use your game's pathfinding algorithm to find the path from one room to another in the high-level path. Instead of performing one large search with your pathfinding algorithm, you perform a series of smaller searches. Hierarchical pathfinding limits the area you have to search to find the path, saving you time and memory.

CHAPTER 14

DrawSprocket

Numerous games have the need to change the resolution of the player's display. Artists design 2D graphics for a specific screen resolution, and the game should be in that resolution to look its best. If the player's screen resolution is too high, the game's characters will look microscopic; if the player's screen resolution is too low, the graphics will look blocky. In addition, many games use a lower-than-normal screen resolution to improve the game's speed. Lower screen resolutions mean there are fewer pixels to draw, which results in faster drawing.

I am sure that, as a Mac user, you have noticed that virtually every application that is not a game (Internet browsers, word processors, compilers, and the Finder are examples) keeps the menu bar visible at all times. I'm also sure that you have seen many games hide the menu bar to further immerse the player in the game world. How do these games hide the menu bar, and what does hiding the menu bar have to do with changing the screen resolution?

The answer to both questions involves DrawSprocket (as you could probably tell from the chapter title). DrawSprocket is the technology that makes it easy for games to change the resolution and the color depth of the screen. DrawSprocket also provides game developers with a way to hide the menu bar and go into full-screen mode.

Introduction to DrawSprocket

The DrawSprocket technology simplifies the process of working with displays in games. Some of DrawSprocket's capabilities include

- The ability to hide the menu bar so that your game can take over the entire screen.
- The ability to change the screen resolution and the screen's color depth.
- Simplified double buffering.
- The ability to quickly set entries in a color lookup table.
- Performing gamma fades for smooth transitions in and out of full-screen mode.

A sizable chunk of DrawSprocket did not survive the transition to Mac OS X. The functions that did not make it into OS X simplified 2D graphics (including a dirty animation system) and gave your game the ability to set a maximum frame rate so that the game did not run too fast. In this chapter, I will cover the portions of DrawSprocket that did make it into OS X. The DrawSprocket SDK, which you can download from Apple's developer Web site (refer to Appendix B, "Game Development Resources" or the numerous other places I mentioned it in this book for the URL to the site) has a reference guide that details all the DrawSprocket functions, including the functions that are not in OS X. If you are interested in these obsolete DrawSprocket functions, read the DrawSprocket reference.

One thing to keep in mind when working with DrawSprocket is that Apple designed DrawSprocket for full-screen games that hide the menu bar during the playing of the game. You can show the menu bar, but you must pause the game to display the menu bar. If the menu bar must be visible during your game's action, then DrawSprocket is not for you.

DrawSprocket versus QuickTime

If you looked through the sample programs I wrote for previous chapters in this book, you probably noticed that I used the QuickTime functions `BeginFullScreen()` and `EndFullScreen()` to go into full-screen mode. QuickTime and DrawSprocket are two equally valid ways to hide the menu bar and take over the screen. If all you want to do is hide the menu bar, the choice is yours. If you want more control over the monitor's resolution and color depth, however, DrawSprocket is for you. DrawSprocket's advantages over QuickTime include

- DrawSprocket's ability to easily change the color depth. QuickTime's full-screen functions do not allow you to change the color depth; if you use QuickTime, you must perform additional work to change the color depth.
- DrawSprocket can automatically create a back buffer and a front buffer for your game. With QuickTime, you must explicitly create a window to display your game and explicitly create an offscreen buffer to do your drawing.
- DrawSprocket lets you create a list of all possible screen resolutions and color depths to allow the player to choose the screen resolution.
- DrawSprocket works with multiple monitors better than QuickTime's full-screen functions.

QuickTime's advantages over DrawSprocket include

- QuickTime's cross-platform capability. QuickTime runs on both Macintosh and Windows computers; DrawSprocket runs only on Macintosh computers.

- QuickTime lets you keep the menu bar visible while the game runs. If resolution switching is all that interests you, use QuickTime.

- QuickTime's ease in keeping the current screen resolution. Keeping the same resolution with DrawSprocket requires additional work, as you will see in this chapter.

For the game we're making, DrawSprocket is the better choice. Our game uses 8-bit color, so DrawSprocket's capability to change the color depth of the screen to 8-bit color and DrawSprocket's color table capabilities make DrawSprocket perfect for us. If your situation fits one of the situations where QuickTime has the advantage over DrawSprocket, use QuickTime.

Draw Contexts

A *draw context* is a drawing area for your game. It consists of one, two, or three video pages. You specify the number of video pages you want along with the width, height, and color depths of the pages.

When we drew to the screen previously, we had to manually create a window so that our graphics appeared on the screen, and we manually created an offscreen buffer. We drew into the offscreen buffer and then copied the graphics from the offscreen buffer to the window. DrawSprocket automatically creates a window so we don't have to make one. If you specify a draw context with two or three pages, DrawSprocket will create one or two offscreen buffers so that you don't have to manually create an offscreen buffer to store the game's background. Now you should be able to see why we're using DrawSprocket for our game.

Setting Up DrawSprocket

Before you can begin programming with DrawSprocket, you must perform a few setup duties to avoid compiler errors and crashes when running your game. The following two sections explain what you must place in your System folder and compiler to make your DrawSprocket programming go smoothly.

What to Place in Your System Folder

If you are running Mac OS 8 or 9, you must place the DrawSprocket library in the Extensions folder inside your System folder. There are debug (DrawSprocketDebugLib) and release (DrawSprocketLib) versions of the DrawSprocket library that come with the DrawSprocket SDK. Place one—but not both—versions of the DrawSprocket library in your Extensions folder. Having both versions in your Extensions folder will cause the computer to crash when your game starts. I recommend using the debug version of the DrawSprocket library during development.

DrawSprocket comes as part of the standard install on Mac OS X, so you don't have to worry about placing any libraries in your System folder. If you're curious, you can find the DrawSprocket framework on your hard disk at the location /System/Library/Frameworks.

What to Place in Your Compiler

For your DrawSprocket programs to compile, you must do the following in your compiler:

- On Mac OS 8 and 9, add either the library DrawSprocketLib or DrawSprocketStubLib to your game's project. DrawSprocketStubLib is a minimal version of the DrawSprocket used for linking purposes. Use DrawSprocketStubLib if it comes as part of the DrawSprocket SDK you're using. If it's not there, use DrawSprocketLib instead.
- On Mac OS 8 and 9, add the location of the folder containing the DrawSprocket libraries to the compiler's list of access paths.
- On Mac OS X, include the DrawSprocket framework, DrawSprocket.framework, to your game's project. The DrawSprocket framework contains all the header files and libraries to write DrawSprocket programs in Mac OS X.
- Include the header file DrawSprocket.h in the appropriate source code files.

Programming with DrawSprocket

At last, we're ready to start programming with DrawSprocket. The amount of work you will have to do with DrawSprocket depends on whether you want to specify the screen resolution and color depth or you want to let the player decide. If you specify the screen resolution, things are a lot easier. All you have to do is supply your desired screen resolution and color depth to DrawSprocket, and DrawSprocket will give you a draw context.

To allow the player to choose the screen resolution, you must compile a list of all possible draw contexts on the player's machine, and then provide a way to let the player decide. The most common ways are to bring up a dialog box or have a menu with the possible draw contexts from which the player can choose.

Your first instinct is most likely to let the player choose the screen resolution. On the surface, it sounds good; let the player make the choice. The problem for a 2D game is that the game's graphics look best at one resolution: the resolution at which the artist created them. If the player chooses a resolution that does not match the graphics' ideal resolution, the game's visual quality could suffer. Because you know the best resolution for your game's graphics, you should be the one to select the game's resolution, which is the argument for you choosing your game's screen resolution. Ultimately, it's your decision over who should choose the game's resolution.

If you decide to pick the game's resolution, the question becomes, "What resolution should I pick?" This is an important question, and one you should answer early in the development process. Your artist must know the target screen resolution so that he can create the best possible backgrounds and sprites.

To reach the widest possible audience, use a screen resolution of 640-by-480 pixels. Virtually every Mac supports this resolution, making it a good lowest common denominator. 800-by-600 pixels is another good resolution choice. Every desktop Mac with a 15-inch or larger monitor can handle the 800-by-600-pixel resolution. At resolutions higher than 800-by-600 pixels, you risk an unplayable game on older Macs. Many older Macs lack the video memory or the horsepower to play games at high resolutions. A 1024-by-768–pixel screen, which is generally the next highest screen resolution, has nearly 800,000 pixels. Each of those pixels requires one to four bytes of data. That's a lot of data to move, especially when you have to move it 30 times a second, as you do in a game.

The DrawContext Class

To add DrawSprocket support to the game we are making, we must create some new classes. Our first class is the `DrawContext` class, whose data members you can see here:

```
class DrawContext
{
    protected:
        DSpContextAttributesPtr contextData;
        DSpContextReference contextRef;
};
```

The `contextData` data member stores data about the draw context, such as the screen resolution, color depth, and number of buffers. We use the `contextRef` data member as a parameter to DrawSprocket functions. The `contextRef` data member stores a pointer to the DrawSprocket context.

The `DrawContext` class handles monitor resolution switching. We derive a class from the `DrawContext` class, called `GameContext`, which handles drawing with Draw-Sprocket. If you want to use DrawSprocket for resolution switching only, you can just stick with the `DrawContext` class. If you want to use DrawSprocket for drawing, the `GameContext` class is there for your use. Here are the data members of the `GameContext` class:

```
class GameContext : public DrawContext
{
    protected:
        GameOffscreenBuffer background;
        GameOffscreenBuffer tileStorage;
        GameOffscreenBuffer playerSpriteStorage;
        GameOffscreenBuffer enemySpriteStorage;

        short hOffset;          // In tiles
        short vOffset;          // In tiles
        Blitter tileBlitter;
};
```

The `background` data member stores the game's background. The `tileStorage`, `playerSpriteStorage`, and `enemySpriteStorage` data members store the game's tiles, player sprites, and enemy sprites, respectively. The `hOffset` and `vOffset` data members measure how much we have scrolled from the upper-left portion of the game world. The `tileBlitter` data member draws tiles to the background.

Starting DrawSprocket

To start DrawSprocket, call the function DSpStartup(), as shown in the following function:

```
void DrawContext::Startup(void)
{
      OSStatus error;

      error = DSpStartup();

      // Get rid of this when the game is ready for release
      if (error == noErr)
            error = DSpSetDebugMode(true);
}
```

In the Startup() function, notice that I call the function DSpSetDebugMode() after calling DSpStartup(). By calling DSpSetDebugMode() and passing it the value true, DrawSprocket goes into debug mode. In debug mode, DrawSprocket does not display the blanking window and does not fully fade the screen in and out. This is very helpful when you're developing your game because the debug mode allows you to see the debugger window when your DrawSprocket-based game drops into the debugger. To summarize: The debug mode allows you to debug your game. When your game is ready for release, you won't need to go into debug mode, so you can comment out the call to DSpSetDebugMode() at that time.

Setting a Draw Context's Needs

After we start DrawSprocket, we must tell it our game's display needs, such as the screen resolution and color depth we want to use. To do this, we fill the GameContext class's contextData data member. The contextData data member is a structure of type DSpContextAttributes, whose fields you can see in Table 14-1. The DSpContextAttributes structure also contains several reserved and filler fields that I do not list in Table 14-1. You would set those fields to 0.

Table 14-1   `DSpContextAttributes` Fields

Field	Description
frequency	The rate at which the monitor refreshes. This field does not apply to LCD monitors because LCD monitors do not refresh. DrawSprocket ignores this field if you try to specify a frequency for your game.
displayWidth	The width of the screen
displayHeight	The height of the screen
colorNeeds	This field says whether or not your game needs to be in color. There are three possible values: kDSpColorNeeds_DontCare says that your game doesn't care if it plays in color or grayscale. kDSpColorNeedsRequest says that your game prefers color, but can go grayscale if necessary. kDSpColorNeeds_Require says that your game must be in color.
colorTable	If your game uses 8-bit color, you pass the color table you want to use in this parameter. 16-bit and 32-bit color games do not use color tables, so they ignore the colorTable field.
contextOptions	Display features you want to use in the draw context. The only one you might use is kDSpContextOption_DontSyncVBL, which tells DrawSprocket not to synchronize the updating of the draw context with the vertical retrace of the screen.
backBufferDepthMask	The acceptable color depths for the back buffer. This value should match the value of displayDepthMask. To allow all color depths, use the value kDSpDepthMask_All.
displayDepthMask	The acceptable color depths for the screen. To allow all color depths, use the value kDSpDepthMask_All.
backBufferBestDepth	The preferred color depth for the back buffer in your game. This value should match the value of displayBestDepth.
displayBestDepth	The preferred color depth for the screen in your game
pageCount	The number of buffers you want. Passing a value of 1 gives you one buffer, the front buffer for the screen. Passing a value of 2 gives you two buffers, a front and a back buffer.
gameMustConfirmSwitch	You do not specify a value here. If DrawSprocket outputs the value true in this field, your game should check if the context is visible by bringing up a dialog box asking the user if he can see the display.

Every DrawSprocket game should set the `displayWidth`, `displayHeight`, `displayDepthMask`, `displayBestDepth`, and `pageCount` fields of the `DSpContextAttributes` structure before choosing a draw context. The `displayWidth` and `displayHeight` fields contain the screen resolution at which you want your game to play. For example, an 800-by-600–pixel screen resolution would have the value 800 in the `displayWidth` field and the value 600 in the `displayHeight` field.

The `displayDepthMask` field contains the possible color depths at which your game can run. Most games will use the value `kDSpDepthMask_All`, which means that the game can use any color depth (1-bit, 2-bit, 4-bit, 8-bit, 16-bit, and 32-bit color). However, if you use direct color (16-bit or 32-bit color) for your game's artwork, you would want to limit your game to monitors that can display 16-bit and 32-bit color. The following statement restricts context selection to 16-bit and 32-bit color draw contexts:

```
contextData->displayDepthMask = kDSpDepthMask_16 | kDSpDepthMask_32;
```

The `displayBestDepth` field contains the color depth you want for your game. Possible values are 1, 2, 4, 8, 16, and 32. DrawSprocket first looks for a context that matches the value of `displayBestDepth` for the screen resolution you specify. If DrawSprocket cannot find a suitable context for the color depth you want, it will look for other color depths from the `displayDepthMask` field. For example, if your game looks best with a monitor resolution of 800-by–600–pixels in 32-bit color, but the player's computer does not have enough video memory for an 800-by-600-pixel display with 32-bit color, DrawSprocket looks for a 16-bit color draw context and uses that if it finds one. This is why most games should use the value `kDSpDepthMask_All` in the `displayDepthMask` field: The more color depths you allow, the greater the chances of the player's monitor being suitable to play your game.

The `pageCount` field tells DrawSprocket how many video pages to use for your game. If you specify a page count of 1, DrawSprocket allocates one buffer, the front buffer, which holds what appears on the screen. By using DrawSprocket, you don't have to explicitly create a window for your drawing; DrawSprocket does it for you. If you specify a page count of 2, DrawSprocket allocates two buffers, a front buffer and a back buffer. Your game will do its drawing in the back buffer and transfer the contents from the back buffer to the front buffer. It's possible to have a page count of 3, which gives you two back buffers, but one back buffer is generally sufficient.

Your game might have to set the `colorNeeds`, `colorTable`, `contextOptions`, `backBufferDepthMask`, and `backBufferBestDepth` fields of the `DSpContextAttributes` structure. The `colorNeeds` field determines whether or not your game can run in grayscale instead of in color. If your game requires color, use the value

kDSpColorNeeds_Require. Otherwise, use either kDSpColorNeeds_Request or
kDSpColorNeeds_DontCare. You must supply a value for the colorTable field if your
game uses 8-bit color. If your game uses two or three video pages (the pageCount
field is set to a value of 2 or 3), you must set the backBufferDepthMask and
backBufferBestDepth fields. The backBufferDepthMask field's value should be identical
to the value for displayDepthMask; the backBufferBestDepth field should equal the
displayBestDepth field.

If you look through the DrawSprocket documentation, you will notice the context
option kDSpContextOption_PageFlip, which is intended to use a draw context that
supports hardware page flipping. In *hardware page flipping*, the operating system can
change the base address of the screen in video memory. This means that any part
of the video memory can appear on the screen. Figure 14-1 shows a sample layout
of video memory. At the start, Page 1 contains the screen, and Page 2 contains the
back buffer. The game does its drawing into Page 2, and then the page flips. In the
page flip, we move the video memory pointer to point to Page 2. This makes Page
2 appear on the screen, and we proceed to draw into Page 1. After drawing into
Page 1, we perform another page flip. Page 1 appears on the screen, and Page 2
becomes the back buffer. This cycle continues for the duration of the game.
Changing one pointer in video memory is much faster than copying thousands of
pixels from the back buffer to the screen.

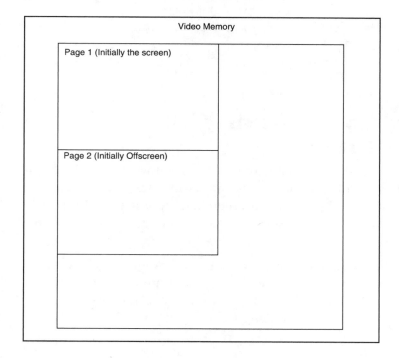

Figure 14-1

*A sample layout of video
memory. Page flipping involves
moving the base address of the
screen from Page 1 to Page 2
and then back to Page 1.*

The previous paragraph persuaded you to use hardware page flipping in your DrawSprocket game, but don't do it. Although most Mac video cards support hardware page flipping, few Macs support DrawSprocket's page flipping, and those Macs were built in the mid-1990s, before the advent of the iMac. If you request hardware page flipping, DrawSprocket will most likely not be able to find a suitable draw context because most Macs don't support DrawSprocket's page flipping. Not being able to find a suitable draw context means that DrawSprocket won't be able to do its thing, and the player will not be able to play your game. You most likely will have no need for the DSpContextAttributes structure's contextOptions field. Using dirty rectangle animation reduces the need for hardware page flipping so not having hardware page flipping with DrawSprocket doesn't hurt much.

The following function sets our game's display needs:

```
void DrawContext::SetContextNeeds(UInt32 width, UInt32 height,
                    UInt32 colorDepth, UInt32 bufferCount)
{
        contextData -> displayWidth = width;
        contextData -> displayHeight = height;
        contextData -> colorNeeds = kDSpColorNeeds_DontCare;
        contextData -> colorTable = kStandardCLUT;
        contextData -> backBufferDepthMask = kDSpDepthMask_All;
        contextData -> displayDepthMask = kDSpDepthMask_All;
        contextData -> backBufferBestDepth = colorDepth;
        contextData -> displayBestDepth = colorDepth;
        contextData -> pageCount = bufferCount;
}
```

Maintaining the Current Screen Resolution

Changing the screen resolution for your game and then switching back to the original resolution can wreak havoc with the user's desktop. Windows and icons can be messed up so that some windows are partially offscreen and icons are on the other side of the screen. To avoid altering the player's desktop, you might want to use the current screen resolution as your game's screen resolution.

You learned to determine the current screen resolution in "Graphics Devices" in Chapter 4, "Introduction to Macintosh Graphics," but I will summarize the process here. Call the function GetMainDevice() and find the boundary rectangle of the graphics device. The following function calculates the current screen resolution:

```
Rect DrawContext::GetCurrentScreenResolution(void)
{
        // Get the main screen
        GDHandle        mainDevice = nil;
        mainDevice = GetMainDevice();

        // The gdRect field of the main device contains the screen resolution.
        Rect screenRect = (**mainDevice).gdRect;
        return screenRect;
}
```

To have your draw context match the current screen resolution, call
GetCurrentScreenResolution(), extract the screen width and height from the rectangle that GetCurrentScreenResolution() returns, and pass the screen width and height to our function SetContextNeeds(). The following function keeps the player's screen resolution as your game's resolution:

```
void DrawContext::UseCurrentScreenResolution(UInt32 colorDepth,
                    UInt32 bufferCount)
{
        short screenWidth;
        short screenHeight;

        Rect screenRect = GetCurrentScreenResolution();

        screenWidth = screenRect.right - screenRect.left;
        screenHeight = screenRect.bottom - screenRect.top;

        SetContextNeeds(screenWidth, screenHeight, colorDepth, bufferCount);
}
```

Selecting a Draw Context

After setting your game's display needs, you must tell DrawSprocket to select a draw context that matches your needs. The easiest way to do this is by calling the function DSpFindBestContext(). This function finds the draw context that best matches your game's display needs. To the function, you pass your game's display needs (the contextData data member of the DrawContext class); and DrawSprocket returns a draw context. The following function selects a draw context:

```
void DrawContext::Choose(void)
{
```

```
OSStatus error;

SetContextNeeds();

// contextData and contextRef are data members of the DrawContext class.
error = DSpFindBestContext(contextData, &contextRef);
}
```

The draw context your game receives depends on your game's display needs, the player's monitor, and the amount of video memory the user has. If the user's monitor supports the resolution and color depth you request, the draw context will match your request. If not, DSpFindBestContext() will return a draw context that best matches your game's display needs. Suppose that your game requests a resolution of 1600-by-1024 pixels (the maximum screen resolution of an Apple 22-inch Cinema Display). In this scenario, only players who own Apple 22-inch Cinema Displays can play the game at your requested resolution. If the player does not have an Apple 22-inch Cinema Display, DrawSprocket will find a screen resolution on the player's monitor that comes closest to 1600-by-1024 pixels. On my 15-inch Apple Studio Display monitor, DrawSprocket would choose a 1024-by-768–pixel context, which is the highest resolution for my monitor.

Many games choose to run in a 640-by-480–pixel screen resolution to reach the widest audience. A 640-by-480–pixel screen resolution requires fewer pixels to draw, resulting in faster drawing performance so that players with older Macs can enjoy the game also. Larger monitors do not support a 640-by-480–pixel screen resolution because they were meant to display graphics at higher resolutions. When a player with a large monitor wants to play a 640-by-480–pixel game, DrawSprocket chooses the smallest screen resolution that the monitor supports. The 640-by-480–pixel portion of the screen displaying the game resides in the center of the screen; DrawSprocket blacks out the edges of the screen, as shown in Figure 14-2.

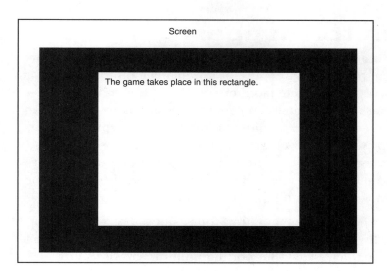

Screen

The game takes place in this rectangle.

Figure 14-2

How a low-resolution DrawSprocket game appears on large monitors

DrawSprocket can adjust the color depth and screen resolution from your game's requests so that the player can play your game on his monitor. However, if your game requests a specific feature, such as hardware page flipping, DrawSprocket limits the context search to draw contexts that support the requested feature. If the player's monitor does not support the feature, DrawSprocket cannot find a suitable context, and DSpFindBestContext() returns a null draw context. This is why you shouldn't bother requesting hardware page flipping. Most Macs do not support DrawSprocket's page flipping; if you request it, DSpFindBestContext() will return a null draw context.

To see what features the draw context actually has, call the function DSpContext_GetAttributes(). The following function retrieves a draw context's attributes:

```
DSpContextAttributesPtr DrawContext::GetAttributes(void)
{
        DSpContextAttributesPtr result;
        OSStatus error;

        error = DSpContext_GetAttributes(contextRef, result);
        return result;
}
```

Multiple Monitor Support

The code presented in the last section assumed that the player has only one monitor attached to his computer, but we can't be sure of how many monitors the player has. Although most Mac users have just one monitor connected to their computer— I barely have room on my desk for a 15-inch flat panel monitor—many people who use their Macs for work connect multiple monitors. Professional Mac programmers like to have two monitors for software development; the debugger runs on one monitor and the program they're developing runs on the second monitor. As you can imagine, debugging a game is a lot easier with two monitors. Artists like having multiple monitors so that they can view multiple pieces of artwork at once.

Even though most Mac users have just one monitor, your game should provide support for multiple monitors. If your game does not properly support multiple monitors, you'll get some nasty e-mail messages. Supporting multiple monitors with DrawSprocket does not entail too much work (at least on Mac OS 8 and 9), as you will see in the sections that follow. The effort it takes to support multiple monitors will pay off with fewer angry e-mails from customers.

The Old Way

For pre–Mac OS X systems, the easiest way to support multiple monitors is to use the function DSpUserSelectContext(). If the player has one monitor, DSpUserSelectContext() works identically to the function DSpFindBestContext(). If the player has multiple monitors and more than one of these monitors meets your game's display needs, DrawSprocket will display a dialog box to let the player choose the screen on which he wants to play the game. Table 14-2 lists the parameters for the DSpUserSelectContext() function.

Table 14-2   DSpUserSelectContext() Parameters

Parameter	Description
inDesiredAttributes	Your game's display needs
inDialogDisplayLocation	The screen where the dialog box to choose the screen appears. If you use a value of 0, the dialog box appears on the screen containing the menu bar.
inEventProc	An event handling function your game supplies.
outContext	The context that DSpUserSelectContext() selects

The following function uses DSpUserSelectContext() to select a draw context:

```
void DrawContext::ChooseOS9(void)
{
      // Assumes the player's system is not running Mac OS X because
      // the DSpUserSelectContext() function is not available in OS X.
      OSStatus error;

      SetContextNeeds();
      error = DSpUserSelectContext(contextData, 0, nil, &contextRef);
}
```

The New Way

Unfortunately, the function DSpUserSelectContext() did not make it into Mac OS X's version of DrawSprocket. To support multiple monitors on Mac OS X, we must first compile a list of all the screens on the player's machine before letting him select the context. Cycling through the list of screens requires two calls to the Display Manager (the portion of Mac OS that supports monitors): DMGetFirstScreenDevice() and DMGetNextScreenDevice(). If you do not care about letting the player choose the screen to play the game on, all you do is call DSpFindBestContext(), and you are finished, as the following code demonstrates:

```
void DrawContext::Choose(UInt32 width, UInt32 height, UInt32 colorDepth, UInt32
bufferCount)
{
```

```
OSStatus error;

// Go through the list of all screens on the player's machine
GDHandle currentGDevice;

// Using true means to find the first screen that is turned on.
currentGDevice = DMGetFirstScreenDevice (true);

do {
        // Using true means to find the next screen that is turned on.
        currentGDevice = DMGetNextScreenDevice (currentGDevice, true);
} while (currentGDevice != nil);

SetContextNeeds(width, height, colorDepth, bufferCount);
error = DSpFindBestContext(contextData, &contextRef);
}
```

As you can see, it's not much more work to support multiple monitors. Keep in mind that the Choose() function used in the preceding code runs on Mac OS 8, 9, and X. The advantage that DSpUserSelectContext() provides is the ability to let the player choose the screen on which to play the game. You may want to check the player's operating system at run time and use the ChooseOS9() function that calls DSpUserSelectContext() on pre-OS X systems; on OS X systems, use the Choose() function.

Giving the player the power to select the screen on which to play the game complicates matters on Mac OS X. To let the player choose the screen he wants to play the game on, you must display a dialog box to let the user choose the screen after compiling the screen list. This step is the most difficult step in the process of multiple monitor support and is the reason you would choose not to do so. What makes things difficult is that the Display Manager tells you the GDevice and the ID of the screen, but it doesn't give you the name of the screen so you have no direct way to show the screen information in a way that the player can understand it.

When the player chooses the screen he wants, you must find the ID of that particular screen. The function DMGetDisplayIDByGDevice() returns the display ID of a graphics device you supply to the function. After finding the ID of the screen you want to use for the game, call the function DSpFindBestContextOnDisplayID(), which chooses the context on a particular screen that best matches your game's display needs. You supply the ID that DMGetDisplayIDByGDevice() gives you to DSpFindBestContextOnDisplayID(). Here's how the Choose() function would look with multiple monitor support that allows the player to choose the screen:

```
void DrawContext::Choose(UInt32 width, UInt32 height, UInt32 colorDepth,
        UInt32 bufferCount)
{
        OSStatus error;

        // Get a list of all screens on the player's machine
        LinkedList screenList
        GDHandle currentGDevice;

        // Using true means to find the first screen that is turned on.
        currentGDevice = DMGetFirstScreenDevice (true);
        do {
                screenList.AddItem(currentGDevice);
                // Using true means to find the next screen that is turned on.
                currentGDevice = DMGetNextScreenDevice (currentGDevice, true);
        } while (currentGDevice);


        // UserSelectDisplay is a function you would write that brings up
        // a dialog box that contains a list of the monitors hooked up to
        // the player's computer and prompts him to select a display..
        currentGDevice = UserSelectDisplay (screenList );

        // Get ID of screen the player chose
        DisplayIDType screenID;

        // Passing true means to return the ID of the main screen
        // if currentGDevice is invalid.
        error = DMGetDisplayIDByGDevice(currentGDevice, &screenID, true)
        SetContextNeeds(width, height, colorDepth, bufferCount);


        // contextData and contextRef are data members of the DrawContext class.
        error = DSpFindBestContextOnDisplayID(contextData, &contextRef, screenID);
}
```

Making a List of All Draw Contexts

If you want to allow the player to choose the screen resolution for your game, you must compile a list of the available draw contexts on the player's computer so that he can choose one. To compile a list of draw contexts, you must perform the following steps:

1. Call the function `DMGetFirstScreenDevice()` to retrieve the first screen.
2. Call the function `DMGetDisplayIDByGDevice()` to get the display ID of the screen. DrawSprocket needs the display ID to find all the draw contexts for a monitor.
3. Call the function `DSpGetFirstContext()` to find the first draw context for the display.
4. Call the function `DSpGetNextContext()` to find the next draw context. Continue calling `DSpGetNextContext()` until it returns a value of `kDSpContextNotFoundErr`, which means that there are no more draw contexts to find.
5. Call the function `DMGetNextScreenDevice()` to retrieve any additional screens the player has. If there are no more screens, you are finished.
6. Repeat steps 2 through 5 for each monitor the player has. Most players have only one monitor, and some will have two monitors. Not many players will have more than two monitors, but we're ready to support those who do.

What you do with a draw context that you retrieve is up to you. You might want to create a menu of context choices for the player. In this case, you would take each context you find, create a menu item for that context, and add that item to the menu of resolution choices. The following function compiles a list of all draw contexts:

```
void DrawContext:IterateContexts(void)
{
        DisplayIDType currentDisplayID;
        GDHandle currentGDevice;
        OSStatus error;
        UInt32 contextIndex = 0;

        currentGDevice = DMGetFirstScreenDevice(true);

        while (currentGDevice != nil) {
                error = DMGetDisplayIDByGDevice(currentGDevice, currentDisplayID,
```

```
                                                   true);

            // Go through the list of draw contexts for this display
            error = DSpGetFirstContext(currentDisplayID, &contextRef);
            while (error != noErr) {
                    // Do whatever you want with the first context here.
                    // We'll just get the context attributes here.
                    contextData = GetAttributes();

                    contextIndex++;

                    // Get the next draw context
                    error = DSpGetNextContext(contextRef, &contextRef);
            } // End first while

            // Get the next display, if the player has multiple monitors
            currentGDevice = DMGetNextScreenDevice(true);
    } // End second while
}
```

Activating a Draw Context

To go into full-screen mode, it's not enough to select a draw context. You must also
activate the draw context. Activating a draw context requires two function calls.
First, call the function DSpContext_Reserve() to reserve the draw context. Then call
the function DSpContext_SetState() to set the state to active,
kDSpContextState_Active. In the active state, DrawSprocket is in full-screen mode.
The blanking window covers the screen, hiding the menu bar, and your game cannot make calls to the Window Manager or Dialog Manager. If your game must
access the menu bar or use the Dialog Manager to display a dialog box, you must
pause the draw context, which I detail in the next section. The following function
activates a draw context:

```
void DrawContext::Activate(void)
{
        HideCursor();
        OSStatus error;

        error = DSpContext_Reserve(contextRef, contextData);
        error = DSpContext_FadeGammaOut(kDSpEveryContext, nil);
        error = DSpContext_SetState(contextRef, kDSpContextState_Active);
```

```
     // Video mode could be unstable. If so,
     // confirm that the video mode is visible to the user
     if (error == kDSpConfirmSwitchWarning) {
             error = DSpContext_FadeGammaIn(contextRef, nil);
             ConfirmContext();
             error = DSpContext_FadeGammaOut(contextRef, nil);
     }

     error = DSpContext_FadeGammaIn(kDSpEveryContext, nil);
}
```

Although the actual draw context activation requires only the calls to `DSpContext_Reserve()` and `DSpContext_SetState()`, there's a little bit more work we have to do, as you can see in the `Activate()` function. The game we are creating has no need for the mouse cursor, so we hide it while the game is in progress. The `HideCursor()` function hides the mouse cursor, as you could probably guess. If your game must access the mouse cursor during the game's action, you remove the `HideCursor()` function call.

CAUTION

If your game calls the `HideCursor()` function, it had better call `ShowCursor()` to bring back the mouse cursor when the player finishes the game. If you do not call `ShowCursor()`, the player will be not be able to do anything with the mouse and will have to restart his computer.

Activating a draw context brings up the blanking window and might cause a change in monitor resolution. If the screen resolution for the game differs from the current screen resolution, then DrawSprocket must perform a monitor resolution switch. The monitor resolution switch causes the screen to flicker. To make the resolution switch easier on the eyes, you should perform a gamma fade when activating the context. That's what the `DSpContext_FadeGammaOut()` and `DSpContext_FadeGammaIn()` functions do. I will go into more detail about those functions in the "Gamma Fades" section, later in this chapter.

Dealing with Questionable Resolutions

The draw context DrawSprocket selects might not work on the player's monitor. There are two ways to determine whether the draw context is questionable. In the first method, you check the `gameMustConfirmSwitch` field of the draw context's

DSpContextAttributes structure. If the gameMustConfirmSwitch field is true, the draw context is questionable. In the DrawSprocket code we've been developing in this chapter, the following statement would check for a questionable draw context:

```
if (contextData->gameMustConfirmSwitch == true)
```

The second way to look for a questionable draw context is to check the result of the DSpContext_SetState() function call when activating the draw context. If DSpContext_SetState() returns an error code of kDSpConfirmSwitchWarning, the draw context is questionable. The Activate() function used in the previous section looks for a questionable draw context. Two questions come to mind: Why would a draw context be questionable, and how do we deal with questionable draw contexts?

A draw context is questionable if its screen resolution does not match the list of the monitor's safe resolutions. A computer's graphics system consists of a video card and a monitor. On modern Macs, the video card is a 3D graphics accelerator, such as the ATI Rage 128, ATI Radeon, or the nVidia GeForce 3. It would be bad for both the video card maker and the consumer if the video card worked on only one model of monitor. A video card supports many screen resolutions; one card can work with many monitors. Each monitor supports only a subset of these many resolutions. What happens with a questionable draw context is that the video card supports the draw context's screen resolution and changes the screen resolution. If the new screen resolution is not one of the monitor's safe resolutions, the monitor might not be able to support the new resolution, making the draw context questionable.

To deal with a questionable draw context, you must ask the player if he can see the draw context. You do this by fading in the screen (a gamma fade) and displaying a timed dialog box like the one in Figure 14-3. If the draw context is unsuitable, the player will be unable to see the dialog box; the dialog box will therefore time out after the period of time you specify (usually between five and ten seconds). If the player clicks the OK button in the confirmation dialog box, you know that the draw context works on the player's monitor, and you can use the questionable draw context. If the player clicks the Cancel button or the dialog box times out, you must discard the questionable draw context and find another draw context. To find another draw context, you must cycle through the draw contexts as we did in "Making a List of All Draw Contexts," earlier in the chapter, and looking for a context where the gameMustConfirmSwitch field is false.

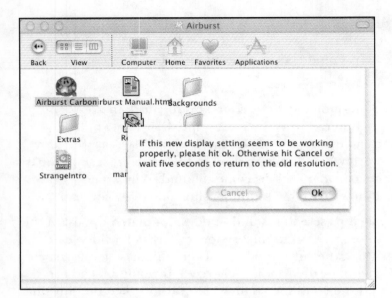

The following code provides an example of how you can handle questionable draw contexts:

```
void DrawContext::ConfirmContext(void)
{
        // Display a timed dialog box.
        // If the player presses OK, use this context.
        // If the player presses Cancel or the dialog times out,
        // find another context.

        DialogRef confirmationDialog;

        // Retrieve the confirmation dialog from disk. The WindowPtr (-1)
        // tells the operating system to bring the dialog to the front.
        confirmationDialog = GetNewDialog(kConfirmationDialogResourceID, nil,
                                            WindowPtr(-1));
        DrawDialog(confirmationDialog);
        ShowWindow((WindowRef)confirmationDialog);

        // Set the timeout for 10 seconds.
        OSStatus error;
        error = SetDialogTimeout(confirmationDialog, cancel, 10);

        // Wait for the player to press either OK or Cancel.
```

```
        // If the dialog times out, it generates a Cancel button press.
        //  The nil in the first parameter means to use
        // the standard dialog event handler
        DialogItemIndex itemHit;
        ModalDialog(nil, &itemHit);

        // See if the player hit the OK button or the Cancel button
        if (itemHit == ok) {
                // Dispose of the dialog box and move on.
                DisposeDialog(confirmationDialog);
        }
        else {
                // Discard the current context and look for another draw context.
                Release()
                FindFirstAcceptableContext();
                DisposeDialog(confirmationDialog);
        }
}


void DrawContext:FindFirstAcceptableContext(void)
{
        DisplayIDType currentDisplayID;
        GDHandle currentGDevice;
        OSStatus error;

        currentGDevice = DMGetFirstScreenDevice(true);

        while (currentGDevice != nil) {
                error = DMGetDisplayIDByGDevice(currentGDevice, currentDisplayID,
                                                        true);

                // Go through the list of draw contexts for this display
                error = DSpGetFirstContext(currentDisplayID, &contextRef);
                while (error != noErr) {
                        // Is this context acceptable?
                        // If so, we use the context.
                        contextData = GetAttributes();
                        if (contextData-> gameMustConfirmSwitch == false) {
                                // Use the current values of contextData
                                // and contextRef, so we just have to return.
                                return;
```

```
            }

            // Get the next draw context
            error = DSpGetNextContext(contextRef, &contextRef);
      } // End first while

      // Get the next display, if the player has multiple monitors
      currentGDevice = DMGetNextScreenDevice(true);
   } // End second while
}
```

Because this is a game development book and not a user-interface programming book, I'm going to briefly summarize the code for confirming the draw context. The two major components of the confirmation dialog box are the SetDialogTimeout() and ModalDialog() functions. The SetDialogTimeout() function selects a dialog box item (that is, it performs the equivalent of a mouse click) after a specified amount of time elapses without the player clicking the OK or Cancel button. I set the SetDialogTimeout() function to click the Cancel button after 10 seconds. The ModalDialog() call notifies your game when the player clicks an item in the dialog box. For our ConfirmContext() function, everything in the game stops until the player clicks the OK button, clicks the Cancel button, or 10 seconds elapse (in which case the computer "clicks" the Cancel button). If the player clicks the OK button, we just dispose of the dialog box because we know that the questionable draw context is acceptable. Otherwise, we must discard the current draw context and search for another draw context before discarding the dialog box. To learn more about dialog boxes, go to Apple's developer Web site (refer to Appendix B for the URL). There you'll find documentation you can download about Dialog Manager, the Apple technology to support dialog boxes.

An alternative method of finding a substitute draw context is to use the player's current screen resolution, as discussed in "Maintaining the Current Screen Resolution," earlier in this chapter. We know that the player can use the current screen resolution, or he wouldn't be able to see anything on his Mac.

Pausing and Resuming Draw Contexts

When the player wants access to the menu bar—to switch applications, save a game, or quit the game—your game should pause the draw context. To pause the draw context, use the function DSpContext_SetState() and set the context to the paused state, `kDSpContextState_Paused`. In the paused state, the menu bar becomes visible, and your game can make calls to the Dialog Manager and Window Manager. The following function pauses a draw context:

```
void DrawContext::Pause(void)
{
        OSStatus error;

        error = DSpContext_FadeGammaOut(contextRef, nil);
        error = DSpContext_SetState(contextRef, kDSpContextState_Paused);
        error = DSpContext_FadeGammaIn(contextRef, nil);
        ShowCursor();
        DrawMenuBar();
}
```

Just as we did when we activated a draw context, we perform a gamma fade when we change the context's state. Because we hid the mouse cursor when we activated the draw context, we must show the mouse cursor when pausing the draw context. Finally, we draw the menu bar so that the player can access the menu bar.

When the player is ready to move back to the game, we call `DSpContext_SetState()` to set the draw context state back to active, as you can see in the following code:

```
void DrawContext::Resume(void)
{
        HideCursor();
        OSStatus error;

        error = DSpContext_FadeGammaOut(contextRef, nil);
        error = DSpContext_SetState(contextRef, kDSpContextState_Active);
        error = DSpContext_FadeGammaIn(contextRef, nil);
}
```

Gamma Fades

I'm sure that you have noticed that every time we changed the draw context's state, we performed a gamma fade. *Gamma fades* change the screen's color intensity from 100 percent to 0 percent and then back to 100 percent. These are the steps involved in performing a gamma fade:

1. Fade out, which means going from 100 percent to 0 percent color intensity.

2. Do what you want when the color is faded, such as change the draw context's state.

3. Fade in, which means going from 0 percent to 100 percent color intensity.

Call the function `DSpContext_FadeGammaOut()` to perform a full fade out; call the function `DSpContext_FadeGammaIn()` to perform a full fade in. If you look at the functions `Activate()`, `Pause()`, and `Resume()` that I wrote earlier in the chapter, you will notice that I used `nil` as the second parameter for the gamma fade functions. Passing `nil` means that black is the fade color. If you want to use a different color for gamma fades, pass that color as the second parameter to the gamma fade functions. To pass a different color, declare a variable of type `RGBColor`, fill the `RGBColor` structure's red, green, and blue components, and pass a pointer to the variable to the gamma fade functions.

If you want to perform partial gamma fades, use the function `DSpContext_FadeGamma()`. Table 14-3 lists the three parameters that the function `DSpContext_FadeGamma()` takes.

Table 14-3   DSpContext_FadeGamma() Parameters

Parameter	Description
inContext	The context whose display we're fading. To fade all the monitors, use the value kDSpEveryContext.
inPercentOfOriginalIntensity	The percentage of color intensity to which you want to fade. This value should range from 0 to 100.
inZeroIntensityColor	The fade color. If you pass nil, black is the fade color.

When performing a gamma fade with DrawSprocket's gamma fade functions, you have the option of fading one monitor or fading all monitors. To fade one monitor, you pass the draw context you want to fade (the `contextRef` data member of the `DrawContext` class for the examples in this chapter) as the first parameter to DrawSprocket's gamma fade functions. To fade all the monitors, pass the value `kDSpEveryContext` as the first parameter to the gamma fade functions. Generally, you fade all the monitors when activating a draw context, and fade only the current draw context (the screen on which the player is playing the game) when pausing and resuming a draw context. Of course, if the player has only one monitor, fading all the monitors is equivalent to fading one monitor, but it's nice to be prepared for a multiple-monitor setup.

Event Handling

When your game's context is in the paused or inactive state, you must pass all events through DrawSprocket. You do this by calling the function `DSpProcessEvent()` in your event loop, either after calling `WaitNextEvent()` or `RunApplicationEventLoop()`. DrawSprocket will handle suspend and resume events (switching to another application) and update events in the blanking window. For all other events, DrawSprocket will tell your game it did not handle the event. It's up to your game to then handle the event. The following event loop demonstrates the use of `DSpProcessEvent()`:

```
void GameApp::EventLoop(void)
{
        RgnHandle       cursorRgn = nil;
        Boolean         haveEvent;
        Boolean         eventHandled;
        EventRecord     event;

        do{
                // If game is not paused, run our game loop.
                if (gameInProgress) {
                        GameLoop();
                }
                else {
                        // Game is paused. Handle system events.
                        haveEvent = WaitNextEvent(everyEvent, &event, kSleepValue,
                                                        cursorRgn);

                        if (haveEvent) {
                                // See if DrawSprocket will handle the event
                                DSpProcessEvent(&event, &eventHandled);

                                // Handle any event DrawSprocket can't
                                if (eventHandled == false) {
                                        HandleEvent(&event);
```

```
                    }
               }
               else {
                    HandleIdleEvent();
               }
          }
     } while (! done);
}
```

Manipulating Color Tables

DrawSprocket provides functions to simplify the process of working with color tables. Remember from Chapter 4, "Introduction to Macintosh Graphics," that a color table is an array of colors. Each entry in the table contains an entry number and the color that corresponds to that entry. If your game uses 8-bit color, you will be dealing with color tables; 16-bit and 32-bit color games do not use color tables.

To set entries in a color table, use the function DSpContext_SetCLUTEntries(). This function takes four parameters, which you can see in Table 14-4. Make sure that the sum of inStartingEntry and inEntryCount does not exceed 255. If it does, you will write past the end of the color table, and your game will crash.

Table 14-4   DSpContext_SetCLUTEntries() Parameters

Parameter	Description
inContext	The draw context containing the color table
inEntries	The colors to add to the color table
inStartingEntry	The first entry in the color table to set
inEntryCount	The number of entries to set in the color table

The following code snippet sets the entries for an entire color table:

```
ColorSpec newColors;
OSStatus error;

error = DSpContext_SetCLUTEntries(contextRef, &newColors, 0, 255);
```

To retrieve the values of a set of entries in a color table, use the function DSpContext_GetCLUTEntries(). This function also takes four parameters, which you can see in Table 14-5.

Table 14-5 DSpContext_GetCLUTEntries() Parameters

Parameter	Description
inContext	The draw context containing the color table
outEntries	The colors retrieved from the color table
inStartingEntry	The first entry in the color table to retrieve
inEntryCount	The number of entries to retrieve from the color table

The following code snippet retrieves every entry in a color table:

```
ColorSpec currentColorTable;
OSStatus error;

error = DSpContext_GetCLUTEntries(contextRef, &currentColorTable, 0, 255);
```

DrawSprocket Buffering

To draw using DrawSprocket's buffers, follow these steps:

1. Retrieve the back buffer by calling the function DSpContext_GetBackBuffer(), whose parameters you can see in Table 14-6. You should retrieve the back buffer once per frame because calling DSpContext_GetBackBuffer() clears all the changes made to the back buffer. This assumes the draw context contains at least two buffers. If your draw context has only one buffer, there will be no back buffer.

   The first time I wrote animation code using DrawSprocket, I retrieved the back buffer each time I drew a sprite. To my horror, only one sprite appeared on the screen. I didn't realize it at the time, but each call to retrieve the back buffer erased the sprite I drew previously so that only the last sprite I drew made it to the screen. Call DSpContext_GetBackBuffer() once per frame, and you will avoid the mistake I made.

2. Draw the background and the sprites in the back buffer.

3. Call the function DSpContext_SwapBuffers() to copy the graphics from the back buffer to the screen. Table 14-7 lists the three parameters DSpContext_SwapBuffers() takes.

Table 14-6   DSpContext_GetBackBuffer() Parameters

Parameter	Description
inContext	The draw context containing the back buffer
inBufferKind	The buffer kind. DrawSprocket has only one buffer kind at this time: kDSpBufferKind_Normal.
outBackBuffer	The back buffer that DSpContext_GetBackBuffer() returns

Table 14-7   DSpContext_SwapBuffers() Parameters

Parameter	Description
inContext	The draw context containing the buffers to swap
inBusyProc	A function your game supplies that performs any tasks that must be done before swapping buffers.
inUserRefCon	A piece of data DrawSprocket sends to your game after it calls the function you specify in the inBusyProc parameter.

The function DSpContext_SwapBuffers() returns immediately, even if the actual buffer swap has not yet occurred. Before calling DSpContext_SwapBuffers(), you should call the function DSpContext_IsBusy() to determine whether the back buffer is available. The following function waits for the back buffer:

```
void GameContext::WaitForBackBuffer(void)
{
        OSStatus error;
        Boolean backBufferBusy = true;

        while (backBufferBusy) {
                error = DSpContext_IsBusy(contextRef, &backBufferBusy);
        }

}
```

The following function retrieves the back buffer:

```
CGrafPtr GameContext::GetBackBuffer(void)
{
        CGrafPtr backBuffer;
        OSStatus error;

        error = DSpContext_GetBackBuffer(contextRef, kDSpBufferKind_Normal,
                                         &backBuffer);
        return backBuffer;
}
```

The following function swaps the buffers:

```
void GameContext::PageFlip(void)
{
        OSStatus error;

        error = DSpContext_SwapBuffers(contextRef, nil, nil);
}
```

In the game itself, you would call the GetBackBuffer() and PageFlip() functions
when rendering the frame. A RenderFrame() function is a function you call repeatedly as part of your game's main loop; it looks something like this:

```
void GameApp::RenderFrame(void)
{
        // Prepare for drawing
        CGrafPtr backBuffer = theDrawContext->GetBackBuffer();

        if (backBuffer == nil)
                return;
```

```
        // Draw the sprites here.      // Have the drawing we've done show on the
screen.
        if (theDrawContext != nil) {
                theDrawContext->PageFlip();
        }
}
```

Double-buffered drawing with DrawSprocket sounds nice, but it has one major flaw. If you look at the DrawSprocket documentation, you will see that the function `DSpContext_SwapBuffers()` draws the entire screen unless you call the function `DSpContext_InvalBackBufferRect()`. `DSpContext_InvalBackBufferRect()` marks an area of the back buffer as dirty; DrawSprocket draws only the dirty areas of the back buffer to the screen when it swaps the buffers. Unfortunately, `DSpContext_InvalBackBufferRect()` did not make it into the Mac OS X version of DrawSprocket. This means that when you call `DSpContext_SwapBuffers()` on Mac OS X, DrawSprocket draws the entire screen, which can be slow. To use dirty rectangle animation with DrawSprocket on Mac OS X, you must use a single-buffered draw context and use your own dirty animation system like the one we made in Chapter 6, "Animation."

Working with the Mouse

The game we are developing in this book does not use the mouse in the traditional sense (in which moving the mouse moves the mouse cursor). The player may decide to use the mouse to move the player in the game or use the mouse button to fire a weapon, but our game plays better using a joystick, gamepad, or keyboard than using the mouse. In our game, the Mac OS mouse cursor gets in the way, and the player wouldn't be able to use the mouse to play the game if the mouse cursor stayed visible. That is why our game hides the mouse cursor when it goes into full-screen mode.

However, your game might need the mouse cursor on the screen to play the game, especially if you're making a strategy game or a role-playing game. If you use DrawSprocket and the mouse cursor, you must use the DrawSprocket routines to read the mouse. DrawSprocket draw contexts might have different coordinates than the regular QuickDraw coordinate system, so the Mac OS routines that read the mouse location could provide incorrect coordinates. The DrawSprocket routines to read the mouse location will read the proper coordinates; that's why you must use them.

To read the location of the mouse cursor, call the function `DSpGetMouse()`. This function returns the location of the mouse cursor in global coordinates. To determine which context belongs to that point, use the function `DSpFindContextFromPoint()`. To convert the mouse cursor location that `DSpGetMouse()` returns from global coordinates to the local coordinates of the draw context, use the function `DSpContext_GlobalToLocal()`. To convert from local to global coordinates, call the function `DSpContext_LocalToGlobal()`. The following code reads the location of the mouse cursor in the draw context's local coordinates:

```
Point DrawContext::ReadMouseLocation(void)
{
        OSStatus error;
        Point mouseLocation;

        error = DSpGetMouse(&mouseLocation);
        error = DSpContext_GlobalToLocal(contextRef, &mouseLocation);

        return mouseLocation;
}
```

Cleaning Up

When the player quits the game, we must take the following steps to shut down DrawSprocket properly:

1. Set the draw context's state to inactive, `kDSpContextState_Active`, by calling `DSpContext_SetState()`.

2. Release the draw context by calling `DSpContext_Release()`.

3. Shut down DrawSprocket with a call to `DSpShutdown()`.

The following code performs the necessary clean-up duties:

```
void Context::Release(void)
{
        OSStatus error;

        if (contextRef != nil) {
                error = DSpContext_FadeGammaOut(kDSpEveryContext, nil);
                error = DSpContext_SetState(contextRef,
                                                kDSpContextState_Inactive);
                ShowCursor();
                error = DSpContext_FadeGammaIn(kDSpEveryContext, nil);
```

```
                error = DSpContext_Release(contextRef);
                delete contextData;
        }
}


void Context::Shutdown(void)
{
        OSStatus error;

        error = DSpShutdown();
}
```

Notice that I split the clean-up duties into Release() and Shutdown() functions. The reason for this is that you might decide to change draw contexts; to do that, you must release the old draw contexts. You don't want to shut down DrawSprocket every time you change a draw context, so that's why I have separate Release() and Shutdown() functions.

When would you want to change draw contexts? Your game could allow the player to choose the screen resolution for the game. If the player selects a screen resolution, plays for a while, and then chooses a new screen resolution, your game must release the draw context at the old resolution and create a new draw context with the new screen resolution.

Utility Functions

DrawSprocket contains some functions you may find useful, but don't neatly fall into a category. The following sections cover these utility functions.

Getting the DrawSprocket Version

To retrieve the version of DrawSprocket the user has on his computer, call the function DSpGetVersion(). The following function returns the DrawSprocket version:

```
NumVersion DrawContext::GetDrawSprocketVersion(void)
{
        return DSpGetVersion ();
}
```

Because Apple did not introduce the DSpGetVersion() function until DrawSprocket version 1.7, getting the DrawSprocket version is less useful than getting the versions of InputSprocket and NetSprocket. Apple has not added any new functionality to

DrawSprocket since version 1.7, so version 1.7 would be the latest version of DrawSprocket to have as a requirement to play your game. The problem is that if the player has a version of DrawSprocket below version 1.7, you won't be able to call DSpGetVersion(). The only purpose DSpGetVersion() serves is to determine whether the player is using the Mac OS X version of DrawSprocket. If the DrawSprocket version is 1.9 or above, the player has the Mac OS X version of DrawSprocket; otherwise, the player has the Mac OS 8/9 version of DrawSprocket.

Setting the Color of the Blanking Window

By default, DrawSprocket sets the blanking window to black. If you want a different color, call the function DSpSetBlankingColor(). You supply a pointer to an RGBColor structure that specifies the color you want for the blanking window, and DSpSetBlankingColor() sets the blanking window to the color you specify. An RGBColor structure contains the red, green, and blue components of a color. The following code shows an example of setting the blanking window's color:

```
void DrawContext::SetBlankingWindowColor(short red, short green, short blue)
{
        OSStatus error;
        RGBColor blankingColor;

        blankingColor.red = red;
        blankingColor.green = green;
        blankingColor.blue = blue;

        error = DSpSetBlankingColor(&blankingColor);
}
```

Finding the Monitor's Frequency

A monitor's *frequency* measures the number of times the monitor refreshes per second. CRT monitors (the big bulky ones) refresh at least 60 times per second; LCD monitors (the flat-screen ones) do not constantly refresh. Some games may want to synchronize their drawing with the monitor's frequency (draw when the monitor refreshes) to make the animation smoother. To measure the refresh rate of the player's monitor, call the function DSpContext_GetMonitorFrequency(), as you can see in the following code:

```
Fixed DrawContext::GetMonitorRefreshRate(void)
{
        Fixed result;
        OSStatus error;

        error = DSpContext_GetMonitorFrequency(contextRef, &result);
        return result;
}
```

Summary

In this chapter, we learned about DrawSprocket, a technology that simplifies the process of hiding the menu bar and changing the monitor's resolution and color depth. At the heart of DrawSprocket is the draw context, a place for games to draw. The draw context consists of one to three video pages, each with a given height, width, and color depth. The programmer can specify how many video pages—and the height, width, and color depth of these pages.

To use a draw context in a game, we begin by filling a DSpContextAttributes data structure that tells DrawSprocket such things as how many video pages we want, the screen resolution we want, and the color depth we want in our game. Then we call the function DSpFindBestContext(), and DrawSprocket finds the draw context on the user's monitor that best matches the game's display request. After finding the context, we reserve the context with a call to DSpContext_Reserve(), and activate it by calling DSpContext_SetState().

DrawSprocket also provides some functions to help draw to the screen. Each frame, we call the function DSpContext_GetBackBuffer() to retrieve the back buffer, draw into the back buffer, then call DSpContext_SwapBuffers() to copy the graphics from the back buffer to the screen.

If your game uses 8-bit colors, DrawSprocket has two functions to simplify color table management. The function DSpContext_SetCLUTEntries() fills part or all of a color table with new colors. The function DSpContext_GetCLUTEntries() retrieves part or all of a color table.

DrawSprocket games that use the mouse cursor must use DrawSprocket's functions for retrieving the location of the mouse cursor. The function DSpGetMouse() gets the mouse cursor in global coordinates. To convert the mouse cursor location to local coordinates, call DSpContext_GlobalToLocal(). The function DSpContext_LocalToGlobal() converts local coordinates back to global ones.

As mentioned earlier in the chapter, I chose to cover the parts of DrawSprocket that made it into Mac OS X. DrawSprocket has some very useful functions for 2D graphics that did not survive the transition to Mac OS X. If you don't mind your game running in Classic mode on Mac OS X, you can read the DrawSprocket reference that comes with the DrawSprocket SDK to learn more about the obsolete DrawSprocket functions.

CHAPTER 15

FILES

The game we're creating has quite a bit of data: graphics, music, sound effects, levels, and enemies to name a few. The game data does not magically appear in the computer's memory when the player launches the game. The data resides in files on a hard disk, CD-ROM, or DVD-ROM. This chapter demonstrates the techniques you'll need to read game data from files into memory.

Many types of games are too long to be played in a single session. The game *Baldur's Gate 2* has approximately 100 hours of gameplay. Not many people would want to stay up for four straight days to play *Baldur's Gate 2* from beginning to end. Games that are too long to finish in one session allow the player to save the game he's playing and resume the game at another time. As part of this chapter, I will teach you to save and open games.

Introduction to Navigation Services

Navigation Services provide a Carbon-compliant way to bring up the dialog boxes to let the user open and save files. Every Mac capable of running Carbon has the ability to use Navigation Services. Figure 15-1 shows the look of the Navigation Services dialog boxes.

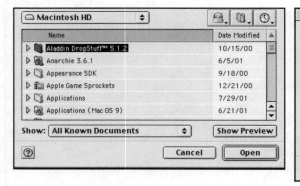
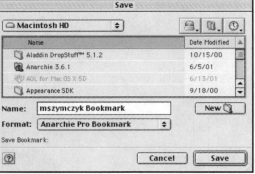

Figure 15-1

The standard Open and Save File dialog boxes from Navigation Services.

The following components make up a Navigation Services dialog box:

- The Location pop-up menu, which tells the user where he is in the file system hierarchy.
- The Shortcuts button, which provides a quick way to access desktop items and any mounted volumes (hard disks, CD-ROMs, DVD-ROMs, and Zip disks are examples of mounted drives).
- The Favorites button, which contains a list of file locations the user has saved so that he can reach them easily.
- The Recent button, which contains a list of recently opened files and folders.
- The browser list, which lets the user navigate the file system to find a file to open or a location to which to save a file.
- The Show pop-up menu, which allows the user to choose the types of files to show in the Browser List when opening a file. When saving a file, the Show menu becomes the Format pop-up menu that allows the user to choose the file format for saving.
- A Cancel button to allow the user to go back to what he was doing without opening or saving the file. Pressing the Esc key is the keyboard equivalent of pressing the Cancel button.
- A default button, usually titled Open for opening a file and Save for saving a file. Pressing the Return key is the keyboard equivalent of pressing the default button.

The Navigation Services code I write in this book uses Navigation Services 2.0, which runs on Mac OS 8.1 and above. Apple introduced Navigation Services 3.0 as part of Carbon version 1.1. Navigation Services 3.0 provides new functions that display Open File and Save File dialog boxes. These new functions allow OS X users to use filenames longer than 31 characters, but they also run on Mac OS 8.6 and higher. I used Navigation Services 2.0 to have greater backward compatibility instead of using Navigation Services 3.0 to get long filenames. To learn more about Navigation Services 3.0 and any subsequent releases of Navigation Services, check out Apple's developer Web page (http://www.apple.com/developer).

Opening Files

To open a file using Navigation Services, you must display an Open File dialog box to let the player choose the file he wants to open. To bring up the Open File dialog box, you call the function NavGetFile(). This function takes eight parameters, which Table 15-1 lists and describes.

Table 15-1   NavGetFile() Parameters

Parameter	Description
defaultLocation	When the dialog box opens, this is the folder where the player will start looking for a file to open. You should use your game's folder as the default location. If you pass the value nil here, Navigation Services will use the last location the player opened when calling NavGetFile().
reply	The player's file selection is returned to your game in the reply parameter.
dialogOptions	Options for displaying the dialog box. Refer to Table 15-4 for a list of options.
eventProc	An event handler for the dialog box. If you want the player to be able to move or resize the dialog box, you must supply an event handler.
previewProc	A function you can write to draw a preview of a file.
filterProc	A function you can write to filter the types of files that show up in the dialog box. For example, in a game, you would want the user to be able to open only saved game files. In this case, you would write a filter procedure to filter all files that are not saved game files.
openList	As an alternative to a filter procedure, you can use the openList parameter to tell Navigation Services to display only the types of files that are in the open list. Using a list of file types to open is much easier than using a filter procedure.
callBackUD	User data that Navigation Services passes back to your program after calling your event handler.

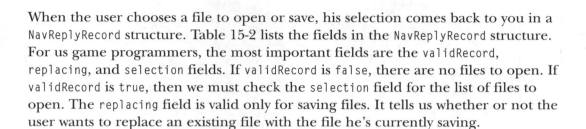

When the user chooses a file to open or save, his selection comes back to you in a NavReplyRecord structure. Table 15-2 lists the fields in the NavReplyRecord structure. For us game programmers, the most important fields are the validRecord, replacing, and selection fields. If validRecord is false, there are no files to open. If validRecord is true, then we must check the selection field for the list of files to open. The replacing field is valid only for saving files. It tells us whether or not the user wants to replace an existing file with the file he's currently saving.

Table 15-2   NavReplyRecord Fields

Field	Description
version	The version of the data structure. You don't need to worry about this parameter.
validRecord	If the user pressed the Return key or the default button, validRecord is true. If the user pressed the Esc key or the Cancel button, validRecord is false. If validRecord is false, the rest of the fields do not contain valid data.
replacing	Tells us whether or not the user is replacing an existing file.
isStationery	Tells us whether or not the file should be saved as a stationery document. For games, isStationery is normally false.
translationNeeded	Does the file have to be translated to a valid type? You will probably not need to translate files in your game.
selection	The list of files the user wants to open or save.
keyScript	The keyboard script system the filename uses. You should not have to worry about this parameter for your game.
fileTranslation	An array of translations. For each file in the selection parameter, there is a fileTranslation array entry containing the file type to which to convert the file. Generally, Navigation Services automatically translates files, so you won't be concerned with the contents of the fileTranslation structure.

The following code reads a filename to open:

```
Boolean SavedGame::OpenGameFile(void)
{
        OSErr error;
        Boolean fileOpened;
        NavReplyRecord userSelection;
        NavDialogOptions dialogOptions;
        NavTypeListHandle validFileTypes;
        NavEventUPP eventHandler;

        eventHandler = NewNavEventUPP (FileDialogEventHandler);

        // Allow the user to open only one file.
        // For games, the default dialog box options work except for two options.
        // The default options allow multiple file selections, and most games
        // allow only one game to be played at a time.  The saved game files don't
        // show up in the dialog unless we add the option kNavNoTypePopup.
        error = NavGetDefaultOptions(&dialogOptions);
        if (error != noErr) {
                return false;
        }
        dialogOptions.dialogOptionFlags =kNavDefaultNavDlogOptions + kNavNoTypePopup -
                        kNavAllowMultipleFiles;

        // Read our list of valid file types
        validFileTypes = (NavTypeListHandle)GetResource(kNavTypeListResource,
                                kNavTypeListResourceID);

        // Bring up the Open File dialog box
        // The NULL means to use start at the last
        // spot the player used Navigation Services.
        // Our event handling function needs a pointer
        // to the object to do its work, which is why
        // we pass this as the last parameter.
        error = NavGetFile(NULL, &userSelection, &dialogOptions,
                                eventHandler, kDontPreview, kNoFilterProcedure,
                                validFileTypes, this);

        // If the user didn't cancel, open the file
```

```
        if ((userSelection.validRecord == true) && error == noErr) {
                fileOpened = OpenFile(userSelection);
        }
        else {
                fileOpened = false;
        }


        // Clean up
        error = NavDisposeReply(userSelection);
        DisposeNavEventUPP (eventHandler);
        if (validFileTypes != nil) {
                ReleaseResource((Handle)validFileTypes);
        }
        return fileOpened;
}
```

Look at the call to `NavGetFile()` in the `OpenGameFile()` function and notice that I used a navigation type list to filter unwanted file types instead of a filtering procedure. Navigation type lists are easier to use than filtering procedures. The advantage a filtering procedure provides is that it allows you to filter objects from the Shortcuts, Favorites, and Recent lists as well as the browser list; a navigation type list filters objects from only the browser list. Because the game in this book only has to filter files from the browser list, I chose to use navigation type lists instead of a filtering procedure.

Navigation Services Dialog Box Options

Navigation Services provides multiple ways you can customize the Open File and Save File dialog boxes, which you can see in Table 15-3. The options seem overwhelming, but the default options will satisfy most game programmers' needs. To use the default options, call the function `NavGetDefaultDialogOptions()`. To add or remove an option from the default options list, add or subtract the appropriate flag in Table 15-4 from the flag `kNavDefaultNavDlogOptions`.

Table 15-3   NavDialogOptions Fields

Field	Description
version	The version of the data structure. You don't need to worry about this parameter.
dialogOptionFlags	Configuration options for the dialog box. Table 15-4 lists the options.
location	The location of the dialog box on the screen. If you pass the point (-1, -1), the dialog box will appear at the last location the user had the dialog box when he was either opening or saving a file.
clientName	The name of your program.
windowTitle	If you want to override the default window title, put your window title here.
actionButtonLabel	The text that appears in the action (default) button. For an Open File dialog box, this parameter will most likely be "Open".
cancelButtonLabel	The text that appears in the Cancel button, most likely "Cancel".
savedFileName	For a Save File dialog box, this field would contain the default filename. Open File dialog boxes do not use this field.
message	The text for the prompt that appears below the browser list.
preferenceKey	An application-defined value that identifies which set of dialog box preferences Navigation Services should use. If your game lets the user open multiple file types, you can have a set of preferences for each file type and use the appropriate preference when a certain file type is open. You most likely will not worry about this parameter in your game; if that's the case, use the value 0 here.
popupExtension	Any items your game adds to the Show pop-up menu in the dialog box.

Table 15-4   Dialog Box Configuration Options

Option	Description
kNavDefaultNavDlog	Use the default features. The defaults are: ■ No custom control titles ■ No banner or prompt message ■ Automatic ally resolve aliases ■ Allow file previews ■ Don't display invisible files ■ Allow multiple file selection ■ Allow stationery
kNavNoTypePopup	If you use this option in an Open File dialog box, the Show pop-up menu will not be displayed. In a Save File dialog box, the Format pop-up menu will not be displayed.
kNavDontAutoTranslate	Tells Navigation Services not to automatically translate the file. If you choose this option, you will have to translate the file yourself using the function NavTranslateFile().
kNavDontAddTranslateItems	Tells Navigation Services not to display file translation options in the Show pop-up menu.
kNavAllFilesInPopup	Adds the option "All Documents" to the File Type pop-up menu.
kNavAllowStationery	Adds the Stationery menu option to the File Type pop-up menu so that the user can save the file as stationery instead of as a document.
kNavAllowPreviews	Lets Navigation Services display a preview of a selected file.
kNavAllowMultipleFiles	Allows the user to select multiple files. You probably want the user to open only one saved game at a time. If this is the case, disable this option.
kNavAllowInvisibleFiles	Lets the user choose invisible files in the dialog box.

(continues)

Table 15-4   Dialog Box Configuration Options (continued)

Option	Description
kNavDontResolveAliases	If the user selects an alias file to open, Navigation Services will not open the original file.
kNavSelectDefaultLocation	Tells Navigation Services to select the default location in the browser list. If you disable this option, Navigation Services will use the System Folder as the default location.
kNavSelectAllReadableItem	Selects All Readable Documents from the Show pop-up menu when displaying an Open File dialog box.

In the game we're developing, there are two default options we don't want to use. The first option is the ability to open multiple files at once. We limit the player to playing one game at a game; letting him open multiple games will mess us up.

By default, Navigation Services displays a pop-up menu listing possible file types. For an Open File dialog box, the pop-up menu lists the possible file types the program can open. For a Save File dialog box, the pop-up menu lists the possible file types the user can save the file as. This option is useful only for programs that can save multiple file types. For example, a word processing program might give the user the ability to save a document in the program's native file type, in plain text, and in HTML. Our game works only with saved game files so we do not need to display a file type pop-up menu. To avoid displaying the file type pop-up menu, we add the option kNavNoTypePopup to the default options. The following code snippet from the OpenGameFile() function demonstrates how to open only one file at a time while not displaying the file type pop-up menu:

```
error = NavGetDefaultOptions(&dialogOptions);
if (error != noErr) {
        return false;
}
dialogOptions.dialogOptionFlags = kNavDefaultNavDlogOptions + kNavNoTypePopup -
            kNavAllowMutlipleFiles;
```

Event Handlers

If you want the user to be able to move and resize the Navigation Services dialog boxes, you must supply an event handler. The event handler function must take the following form:

```
pascal void MyEventProc ( NavEventCallbackMessage callBackSelector,
                          NavCBRecPtr callBackParms,
                          NavCallBackUserData callBackUD );
```

Table 15-5 describes the parameters you must supply in your event handler.

Table 15-5   Event Handler Parameters

Parameter	Description
callBackSelector	The type of call Navigation Services will make to your event handler. Table 15-6 lists the possible options.
callBackParms	Data describing the event the function will handle.
callBackUD	A value Navigation Services passes to your program after completing the event handler.

Table 15-6   Event Message Constants

Value	Description
kNavCBEvent	An event happened. This is the constant you will use most often.
kNavCBCustomize	Negotiate customization space.
kNavCBStart	The dialog box is starting.
kNavCBTerminate	The dialog box is closing.
kNavCBAdjustRect	The user resized the dialog box.
kNavCBNewLocation	The user chose a new location in the browser.

(continues)

Table 15-6   Event Message Constants (continued)

kNavCBShowDesktop	The user navigated to the desktop.
kNavCBSelectEntry	The user made a selection in the browser.
kNavCBPopupMenuSelect	The user made a selection in a pop-up menu.
KNavCBAccept	The user accepted a navigation dialog box. For example, the user chose Open in an Open File dialog box.
kNavCBCancel	The user cancelled a navigation dialog box.
kNavCBAdjustPreview	The user either toggled the preview option or resized the preview area

At a minimum, your game must handle update events to allow the user to move and resize the dialog box. The following function handles update events:

```
pascal void SavedGame::FileDialogEventHandler(NavEventCallbackMessage
                        callBackSelector, NavCBRecPtr callBackParms,
                        NavCallBackUserData callBackUD )
{
      EventRecordPtr theEvent = callBackParms->eventData.event;
      SavedGamePtr currentGame = (SavedGamePtr) callBackUD;

      switch (callBackSelector) {
            case kNavCBEvent:
                  switch (theEvent) {
                        case updateEvt:
                              currentGame->Update(theEvent);
                              break;

                        // Handle other events here
                  }

                  break;
            // Handle other Navigation Services events here
}
```

Navigation Type Lists

You use navigation type lists to restrict the files that appear in the browser list when the player wants to open or save a file. For example, most games allow the player to save a game to continue playing at another time. When you bring up a dialog box to let the player open a saved game, you want only saved game files to show up in the browser. You don't want the player to be able to open a word processing document or a spreadsheet in your game. Navigation type lists allow you to restrict the browser list so that it shows only saved game files.

You create a navigation type list by using a navigation type list (a resource of type open) resource. To create the navigation type list resource, you go into a resource editor such as Resorcerer and fill it with all the file types you want to show in the browser. For a game, the only file type you would place in the navigation type list is your saved game file type. Figure 15-2 shows the navigation type list I used for the program I wrote for this chapter. As you can see from the figure, I have only one file type in the list, 'Svgm', which is the file type I used for saved games. All the navigation type list contains is a list of four-character codes. The codes only mean something to the person who created the file type; they look like gibberish to anyone else.

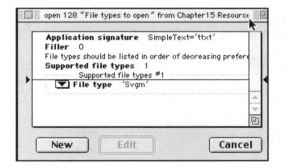

Figure 15-2

The navigation type list for the program in this chapter

After You Get the File to Open

When the player selects the file or files he wants to open and presses the Open button in the Open File dialog box, Navigation Services sends your program a list of Apple event descriptors containing the files to open. Opening the files is very similar to handling the Open Document Apple event, described in Chapter 9, "Reading the Keyboard and Mouse Plus Event Handling." Here are the steps you must take to open the file:

1. Retrieve the number of files in the file list by calling the function
   `AECountItems()`. Refer to Chapter 9, "Reading the Keyboard and Mouse Plus
   Event Handling," for more information about the `AECountItems()` function.

2. Open each document in the list. For each document you must do the following:

   2A. Call the function `AEGetNthDesc()` to find the file containing the docu-
       ment. The `AEGetNthDesc()` function returns a variable of type `AEDesc`.

   2B. Get the `FSSpec` for the file by using the `dataHandle` field of the `AEDesc`
       variable you got from the call to `AEGetNthDesc()`.

   2C. Open the file.

After you've opened the file or files, you must do some memory clean up:

1. Call `NavDisposeReply()` to dispose of the list of files to open.

2. Call `DisposeNavEventUPP ()` to dispose of our event handler and filtering functions.

3. Call `ReleaseResource()` to dispose of our list of file types to display.

The following function opens the file or group of files the user requested from a
Navigation Services dialog box:

```
Boolean SavedGame::OpenFile(NavReplyRecord userSelection)
{
        OSErr error;
        long numberOfFilesInList;
        long fileCount;

        // Get the number of files in the list
        error = AECountItems(&(userSelection.selection), &numberOfFilesInList);
        if (error != noErr)
                return false;

        FSSpec* fileName;

        // Open each file in the list
        for (fileCount = 1; fileCount < numberOfFilesInList; fileCount++){
                AEDesc fileToOpen;
                AEKeyword       dummyKeyword;

                error = AEGetNthDesc(&(userSelection.selection), fileCount,
```

```
                              typeFSS, &dummyKeyword, &fileToOpen);

        if (error == noErr) {
            // Get fileToOpen into a format that ReadSavedGame can use

            BlockMoveData(*fileToOpen.dataHandle, fileName,
sizeof(FSSpec));

            ReadGameData(fileName);
        }
        else {
            return false;
        } // end if-then-else
    } // end for

    return true;
}
```

Saving Files

To bring up a Save File dialog box, call the function NavPutFile(). The NavPutFile() function takes seven parameters, as shown in Table 15-7. Most of the parameters work the same way they do when you call NavGetFile() to open a file. The parameters of special interest are fileType and fileCreator. The fileType parameter is a four-character code describing the type of file. The fileCreator parameter is a four-character code identifying the application that created those files. A saved game file for the game *Doom* might have a file type of Save, and a file creator of Doom. Apple maintains a list of file types and creator codes that other applications use to prevent your game from conflicting with another program. You can find the list at the following URL: **http://developer.apple.com/dev/cftype**

Table 15-7   NavPutFile() Parameters

Parameter	Description
defaultLocation	When the dialog box opens, this is the folder where the player will start looking for a file to open. You should use your game's folder as the default location. If you pass the value nil here, Navigation Services uses the last location the player opened when calling NavPutFile().
reply	The player's file selection will be returned to your game in the reply parameter.
dialogOptions	Options for displaying the dialog box. Table 15-4 lists the options.
eventProc	An event handler for the dialog box. If you want the player to be able to move or resize the dialog box, you must supply an event handler.
fileType	The file type of the saved file.
fileCreator	The application that created the file.
callBackUD	User data that Navigation Services passes back to your program after calling your event handler.

When choosing a file type and file creator for your saved game files, remember that Apple reserves the codes containing all uppercase and all lowercase characters. Possible file types for a saved game file include Game, Save, and SvGm. For our game in the book, we'll define a couple of constants for the saved game file's type and creator, as you can see in this code:

```
const OSType kSavedGameFileType = 'Game';
const OSType kSavedGameFileCreator = 'MyGm';
```

The following function saves a file to disk:

```
Boolean SavedGame::SaveGameFile(void)
{
        OSErr error;
        Boolean fileSaved;
        NavReplyRecord userSelection;
        NavDialogOptions dialogOptions;
```

```
            NavTypeListHandle validFileTypes;
            NavEventUPP eventHandler;


            eventHandler = NewNavEventUPP (FileDialogEventHandler);

            // Use the default options for saving
            error = NavGetDefaultOptions(&dialogOptions);
            if (error != noErr) {
                    return false;
            }


            // We only want to save games so we use the
            // kNavNoTypePopup constant.  If you wanted to save
            // multiple file types, you would remove the kNavNoTypePopup
            // constant.  You would also have to supply
            // a list of strings specifying the types of files
            // your program could save.
            dialogOptions.dialogOptionFlags = kNavDefaultNavDlogOptions +
kNavNoTypePopup;


            // Bring up the Save File dialog box
            // The NULL means to use start at the last
            // spot the player used Navigation services.
            // Our event handling function needs a pointer
            // to the object to do its work, which is why
            // we pass this as the last parameter
            error = NavGetFile(NULL, &userSelection, &dialogOptions,
                                eventHandler, kSavedGameFileType,
                                kSavedGameFileCreator, this);


            // If the user didn't cancel, save the file
            if ((userSelection.validRecord == true) && (error == noErr)) {
                    fileSaved = SaveFile(userSelection);
            }
            // Clean up
            error = NavDisposeReply(userSelection);
            DisposeNavEventUPP (eventHandler);


            return fileSaved;
    }
```

After you have the filename to save, you must do the following to save the file:

1. Call the function AEGetNthDesc() to find the file containing the document. The AEGetNthDesc() function returns a variable of type AEDesc.

2. Get the FSSpec for the file by using the dataHandle field of the AEDesc variable you got from the call to AEGetNthDesc().

3. Check to see whether the filename already exists by checking the reply's replacing field.

4. Create the new file, either the actual file if the reply record's replacing field is false or a temporary file if the replacing field is true.

5. Write the data to the file.

6. Call the function NavCompleteSave() to complete the save.

The following code saves a file using the filename the user supplied in a Navigation Services dialog box:

```
Boolean SavedGame::SaveFile(NavReplyRecord userSelection)
{
        OSErr error;
        AEDesc fileToSave;
        AEKeyword dummyKeyword;
        Boolean success;
        FSSpec* fileName;

        // The list has only one file because you can save
        // only one file at a time.
        error = AEGetNthDesc(&(userSelection.selection), kOneFile, typeFSS,
                          &dummyKeyword, &fileToSave);


        // Save the file
        if (error == noErr) {
                // Get fileToSave into a format that WriteSavedGame can use

                BlockMoveData(*fileToSave.dataHandle, fileName, sizeof(FSSpec));
                WriteGameData(fileName);
                error = NavCompleteSave(&userSelection, kNavTranslateInPlace);
        }
        else {
```

```
            return false;
    }
    return true;
}
```

Data and Resource Forks of a File

Each file on a Macintosh computer has two forks: a data fork and a resource fork, as Figure 15-3 shows. The *data fork* contains the file's data as a series of consecutive bytes. The data fork corresponds to files on file systems such as Windows and Linux that have only one fork. An example of the use of the data fork is a word processing document; the text of the document resides in the document's data fork.

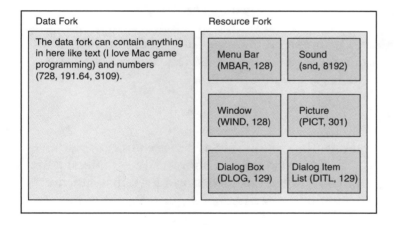

Figure 15-3

The data fork and the resource fork of a file.

The *resource fork* of a file contains the file's resources. For a game, you use resources to store pregenerated data, such as graphics, sound effects, windows, menus, and dialog boxes.

It sounds pretty simple, right? Place your resources in the resource fork and other data in the data fork. In Carbon, however, things get a little hazy. You can continue to put your resources in the resource fork, but Apple recommends that you place your resources in the data fork of a separate file. Mac OS X has two file systems: Hierarchical File System Plus (HFS+) and Unix File System (UFS). HFS+ is the default file system. UFS does not support multiple forks in a file, so by placing your resources in the data fork of a file, Mac OS X users will be able to read the file no matter which file system they use. In addition, most file systems, including Windows, Unix, and the Internet, do not recognize the resource forks of files. Placing your resources in the data fork makes it easier to transfer your data from the Mac to other systems.

Carbon routines can handle resources stored in either the data or the resource fork of a file, so your code will be the same no matter which fork you choose to store your resources.

Now you're thinking, "You've convinced me. I'll place my resources in the data fork." There is another problem, however. Versions of Mac OS before 9.1 do not support resources stored in the data fork of a file. You're damned if you put your resources in the resource fork (the code is hard to convert to other operating systems) and damned if you put them in the data fork (the code works only on Mac OS 9.1 and above). It's a paradox. Because this is a Mac game programming book, I chose to store my resources in the resource fork. Project Builder will take the resources you store in the resource fork of a file and place them in the data fork of a separate file when you compile your code so storing the resources in the resource fork isn't that big of a problem. I recommend that you do the same for your Mac games. If you choose to port your game to other systems, you can create new files and copy your resources to the data fork of the new files.

Resources

A *resource* is a piece of structured data that is stored in a file's resource fork or in the data fork (on computers running Mac OS 9.1 and above). Apple defined a ton of resource types to cover user interface elements such as windows, dialog boxes, menus, icons, and scrollbars. In addition, Apple defined resource types to handle graphics and sound.

You can create your own resource types to augment the Apple defined ones. For game development, you will create your own resources to store levels and saved games. Any data you store in C++ classes or C structures are perfect candidates to save as resources.

Table 15-8 shows the fields the Resource Manager (the portion of the Mac Toolbox that deals with resources) uses to find a resource in a file's resource map (the list of resources in the resource fork of the file). The maximum size of a file's resource map is 16MB. If your resources exceed this size, you must create separate files and move the resources there. Sound data is likely to be the main reason your resources will exceed the 16MB limit.

Table 15-8   Fields to Identify a Resource

Field	Description
ID	A numerical ID used to identify a particular resource among a group of resources of the same type. Valid resource ID values for your resources range from 128 to 32,767. The exception is sound resources, which have values ranging from 8,192 to 32,767. Apple reserves the values 0 through 127 (0 through 8,191 for sound resources) for its own resources.
Resource Type	A four-character string uniquely identifying the type of resource. If you use an Apple-supplied resource, all you need to know is the string. If you are creating your own resource type, you need to know that Apple reserves all resource types that contain all capital and all lowercase letters. For a saved game resource, the values 'GAME' and 'game' are invalid resource types; instead, use 'Game', 'gAmE', or 'GAmE'.

The Resource Manager has one more limitation. A file's resource map can store no more than 2,727 resources. Each picture you have for your game's graphics is one resource. This is why I stored a group of game tiles in one picture. If I stored each tile in its own picture, the number of resources would skyrocket. Every sound you play as a sound resource is one resource. Each menu in your game is one resource, and the menu bar itself constitutes one resource. As you can see, the number of resources in a file can grow pretty quickly. When searching the resource map for a particular resource, the Resource Manager searches sequentially, starting at the beginning of the map. If you plan to support older Macs (computers built in 1997 or earlier), make your resource limit smaller than 2,727. The sequential search can be pretty slow on older machines, so 500 resources is usually a practical limit for one file on older Macs.

Common Apple-Defined Resource Types

A complete list of the resource types Apple defines is too large to fit in this book, but Table 15-9 lists the Apple-defined resources game developers use the most.

Table 15-9   Popular Apple-Defined Resources

Resource	Description
PICT	A picture resource, which contains a set of QuickDraw commands. For your games, you will use pictures to store the pixel maps containing your game's sprites and backgrounds.
snd	A sound resource, which contains a sampled sound. You use sound resources to store your game's background music and sound effects.
clut	A color lookup table, which contains a list of colors. You use color lookup tables if your game runs in 8-bit color.
MBAR	A menu bar resource. Every Macintosh program contains one of these resources.
MENU	A menu resource. You have one menu resource for every menu in your game.
DLOG	A dialog box resource.
ALRT	An alert box resource. You use an alert box to display error messages or ask the player whether he wants to save the game.
DITL	A dialog item list resource. This resource contains all the controls that appear in a dialog box, such as buttons, check boxes, radio buttons, and pop-up menus. Each dialog box resource has its own dialog item list resource.
WIND	A window resource.
STR#	A string list resource. You can use this resource to store a list of error messages or a list of phrases that characters in the game can say to the player.
BNDL	A bundle resource. Your game can have a bundle resource to show the icons your game and the saved games use. In addition, a bundle resource lets users start your game by double-clicking on a saved game file. Do not confuse the bundle resource with bundles, discussed later in this chapter.
carb	Your Carbon-based game needs a carb resource with an ID of 0 containing four bytes of zero data. Without this resource, your Carbon-based game will not run on Mac OS 8 and 9.
plst	A property list resource. A Carbon game needs this resource to run natively on Mac OS X.

Creating Resources

To create user interface resources such as menus, windows, and dialog boxes, using a tool to visually create them is the easiest way to go. For the Macintosh, you have three choices: ResEdit, Resorcerer, and Interface Builder. ResEdit is a free but ancient visual resource editor. It hasn't been updated since 1994. Resorcerer is an up-to-date resource editor, but it's not free. Interface Builder comes as part of the Developer Tools package included with Mac OS X. Interface Builder lets you create user interfaces visually as you can in Real Basic, Delphi, and Visual Basic. Interface Builder stores the user interface as one or more nib files, which you can add to your game's project. You can use Interface Builder for user interface elements only. You cannot use Interface Builder to make other types of resources.

You can paste your game's graphics and sounds from their external files into a resource editor such as Resorcerer. The other option is to use a conversion program such as Graphic Converter or Sound App to convert the graphics and sound files into resources.

Another tool for creating resources is Rez, an Apple-supplied resource compiler that comes with CodeWarrior and Apple's OS X Developer Tools. With Rez, you lay out resources the way you would lay out a class in C++. In Chapter 7, "InputSprocket," I used Rez to create the resources InputSprocket needs.

To create game-specific resources such as levels, traps, and puzzles, you can use Rez, use resource templates, or you can write tools to speed up the process of making these resources. Rez works best for smaller resources. For example, if you made a navigation type list resource containing the file types your game opens, it is easier to create the resource using Rez than to write a tool for the purpose. Your game will have only one navigation type list resource, and it probably contains one entry—saved game files—so writing a tool provides little benefit. Resource templates (resources of type TMPL) let you make custom resources visually in a resource editor like Resorcerer instead of by typing in the data like you must with Rez. For larger resources such as level maps, writing a tool to create the resource works best. If you had a level that was 200 tiles tall and 200 tiles wide, you would have to type in 40,000 tile values if you used Rez to make your levels. Writing a level editing tool can save you from typing in tens of thousands of numbers, speeding up the level-creation process and eliminating the possibility of typing erroneous tile values. Tool creation goes beyond the scope of this book; pick up a book on Mac GUI programming to learn the techniques to create your own tools.

Writing Resources

Writing resources to disk is something that's difficult to do the first time, but after you write one resource, it gets easier. After you write code to write one resource, you can use most of the same source code to write other types of resources.

Before you write a resource, you need a handle to the data you're writing to the resource. For example, if you are writing a picture to disk, you need a `PicHandle`, which is a handle to a QuickDraw picture.

Writing a resource takes many steps, but don't be intimidated. Let me take you by the hand and lead you down the path to resource-writing Nirvana. Figure 15-4 shows a high-level flowchart of resource writing.

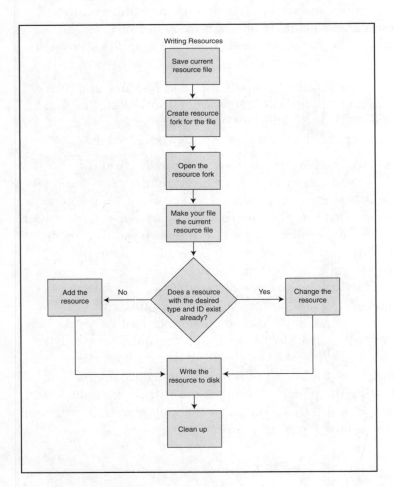

Figure 15-4

Writing a resource to disk.

You must take the following steps to write a resource to disk:

1. Save the number of the resource file (The operating system assigns numbers to files when you open them.) that's currently in use. When you're finished writing the resource, you will restore the resource file you saved here. Call the function CurResFile() to save the current resource file number.

2. Create a resource fork for the file so that you can write resources to the file. Call the function FSpCreateResFile() to create the resource fork. If the file already has a resource fork, calling FSpCreateResFile() does nothing.

3. After calling FSpCreateResFile(), call the function ResError() to see whether an error occurred when creating the resource fork of the file. If ResError() returns a value other than noErr, an error occurred when creating the resource file.

4. Open the newly created resource fork by calling the function FSpOpenResFile(). After calling FSpOpenResFile(), check for errors by calling ResError(). You're going to be calling ResError() often when working with resources.

5. After opening your resource file, tell the Resource Manager to use your file as the current resource file. You do this by calling the function UseResFile(). Then you make the obligatory call to ResError().

6. At this point, you have the file all set to write the resource. Before writing the resource, you must see whether a resource exists in the file's resource fork that matches the resource type and ID you want to write. A resource will exist unless you are saving the file for the first time. There are two functions you can call to see whether such a resource exists: Get1Resource() and GetResource(). Get1Resource() searches the current resource file only. GetResource() searches the current resource file first and, if it doesn't find a match, it searches the application's resource fork and the system's resource fork. Don't forget to call ResError() for error checking.

7. If the Resource Manager did not find a resource that had your resource's type and ID, you must create a handle for the data you want to write to disk. Then you must move the data to the handle. Then call AddResource() to add the resource to the file's resource map. Finally, call ResError() to make sure that everything went well.

8. If the Resource Manager found a resource that matched your resource's type and ID, you must change the data stored in the resource to the data you want to save. Then you call `ChangedResource()` to change the resource followed by the good old `ResError()` check.

9. At this point, all you've done is write your resource in RAM. To write the resource to disk, you must call the function `UpdateResFile()`. Call `ResError()` to be safe.

10. Now that you've written your resource to disk, you must clean up. First call `ReleaseResource()` to free up the memory your data handle was using. If you don't call `ReleaseResource()`, you'll get a memory leak. Call `ResError()` to check for errors on the `ReleaseResource()` call. Second, call `UseResFile()` to restore the old resource file. Finally, call `CloseResFile()` to close the resource file.

Looking at the list of steps, you will see that after most Resource Manager function calls, you should call the function `ResError()` to see if a problem occurred. If `ResError()` returns a value other than `noErr`, you have a potential problem. If you have an error, you must check to see whether it is serious enough to stop writing the resource. In most cases, it will be, and you stop the resource writing. A case where an error is not serious occurs when you call the function `FSpOpenResFile()`. If the resource file is already open, `ResError()` will return an error code telling you that this is the case. Opening a file that is already open is not much of a problem; you just do what you want with the file because it's already open.

Reading Resources

Reading a resource from disk is much easier than writing one to disk, requiring fewer steps. Figure 15-5 shows a high-level flowchart of reading a resource.

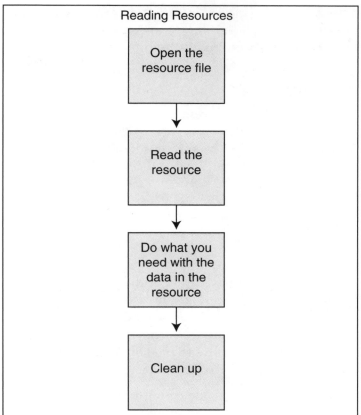

Reading Resources

Open the
resource file

Read the
resource

Do what you
need with the
data in the
resource

Clean up

Figure 15-5

Reading a resource from disk.

To read a resource from disk, you must do the following:

1. If you are reading a resource from an external file, you must open the resource file by calling `FSpOpenResFile()`. Then call `ResError()` to see whether there was an error. If you are reading a resource from your application's resource fork, you can skip this step.

2. After you have opened the resource file, you read the resource by calling either `Get1Resource()` or `GetResource()`. `Get1Resource()` checks the current resource file only. `GetResource()` checks the current resource, then the application's resource fork, and then the system's resource fork. As you probably know by now, you must call `ResError()` afterwards.

3. At this point, you do what you need to do with the resource. For example, if you are reading a picture, you would want to draw it into an offscreen buffer.

4. All that's left is to clean up. You call ReleaseResource() to free up the memory used by the data you read from disk. Call ResError() to check for errors. Then call CloseResFile() to close the resource. You're finished!

A Resource Example

To demonstrate the concept of reading and writing resources, we will save and open games. The first thing we need to do is create a SavedGame class, which contains the information we will save to disk. This is how the class looks:

```
class SavedGame
{
        protected:
                GamePlayer playerInfo;
                GameLevel levelInfo;
};
```

The playerInfo data member stores the player information at the time of the save, such as his location in the game world, his hit points, and his score. The levelInfo data member stores the state of the level when the player saved the game, such as the location of the monsters and goodies for the level. You can substitute your own data in this SavedGame class and still use the same code to read and write saved games. The code works the same no matter what data the SavedGame class contains.

First, here are some constants to make the source code easier to digest:

```
const short kGameResourceID = 200;
const OSType kGameFileType = 'Svgm';
const ResType kGameResourceType = 'Game';
const Str255 kGameName = "\pSaved Game Resource";
```

To write a resource, the Resource Manager has to know the resource ID, file type, resource type, and resource name. We will supply the constants listed earlier to the Resource Manager so that the Resource Manager can write the resource.

And now here's the code to write a resource:

```
Boolean SavedGame::WriteGameData(FSSpec fileSpec, OSType fileCreator)
{
        // Returns true if the write is successful
        // and false if it's unsuccessful

        short savedResourceFileNumber;
        short error;
```

```
short fileRefNum;
Handle gameToSave;
SavedGame currentGame;

// Code to fill the data of the currentGame variable omitted

// Save current resource file number
 savedResourceFileNumber = CurResFile();

 // Create resource fork
FSpCreateResFile(&fileSpec, fileCreator, kGameFileType, smSystemScript);
error = ResError();
if (SeriousError(error))
        return false;

 // Open the resource fork so we can write
 // the saved game to it.
fileRefNum = FSpOpenResFile(&fileSpec, fsRdWrPerm);
if (fileRefNum < 0) {
        error = ResError();
        return false;
}


// Set current resource file to our file
UseResFile(fileRefNum);
error = ResError();
if (SeriousError(error))
        return false;

// See if a saved game resource exists
// for the current file.
// Because we just called UseResFile, we can call
// Get1Resource instead of GetResource.
gameToSave = Get1Resource(kGameResourceType, kGameResourceID);

if (gameToSave == nil) {
        // Write our newly created saved game resource to disk
        Size handleSize = sizeof(SavedGame);
        gameToSave = NewHandle(handleSize);
        BlockMoveData(&currentGame, *gameToSave, sizeof(SavedGame));
        error = MemError();
```

```
            if (SeriousError(error))
                    return false;


            AddResource(gameToSave, kGameResourceType, kGameResourceID,
                        kGameName);
            error = ResError();
            if (SeriousError(error))
                    return false;
     }

   else {
            // Change the contents of the saved game
            // that's on disk
            BlockMoveData(&currentGame, *gameToSave, sizeof(SavedGame));
            ChangedResource(gameToSave);
            error = ResError();
            if (SeriousError(error))
                    return false;
   }


    // Write the resource to disk
   if (gameToSave != nil) {
            UpdateResFile(fileRefNum);
            error = ResError();
            if (SeriousError(error))
                    return false;


            // Free the memory
            ReleaseResource(gameToSave);
            error = ResError();
            if (SeriousError(error))
                    return false;
   }


   // Restore the resource file we saved earlier
   UseResFile(savedResourceFileNumber);
   // Close the resource file
   CloseResFile(fileRefNum);

   return true;
}
```

The following function reads a resource:

```
Boolean SavedGame::ReadGameData(FSSpec fileSpec)
{
        // Returns true if the read is successful
        // and false if it's unsuccessful

        short error;
        short fileRefNum;
        Handle savedGame;
        SavedGame newGame;

        // Open resource file
        fileRefNum = FSpOpenResFile(&fileSpec, fsRdWrPerm);
        error = ResError();
        if (SeriousError(error))
                return false;

        // Retrieve the resource
        savedGame = Get1Resource(kGameResourceType, kGameResourceID);
        error = ResError();
        if ((error != noErr) || (savedGame == nil))
                return false;

        // Now let's read the data from disk
        // to the SavedGame structure.

        BlockMoveData(*savedGame, &newGame, sizeof(SavedGame));
        error = MemError();
        if (SeriousError(error))
                return false;

        // Code to transfer the data from the newGame variable
        // to the game itself omitted.

         // Clean up
        ReleaseResource(savedGame);
        error = ResError();
        if (SeriousError(error))
                return false;
         CloseResFile(fileRefNum);
```

```
        return true;
}
```

SeriousError() is just a utility function to determine whether the error is serious enough to stop reading or writing the resource. The only errors that are not serious enough to stop whatever we are doing are no error, and the file already existing when you try to open it. The Resource Manager has separate errors for the file existing when you try to read from it (dupFNErr) and write to it (opWrErr). The SeriousError() function makes the code easier to read rather than having an if statement with four conditions to test every error check.

```
Boolean SeriousError(OSErr errorCode)
{
        switch (errorCode) {
                case noErr:
                case dupFNErr:
                case opWrErr:
                        return false;

                default:
                        return true;

        }
}
```

Writing to the Data Fork

If you prefer to store your game's data in the data fork instead of in resources, you must take the following steps to write data to a file:

1. Create a temporary file to store the data initially if you are replacing a file that already exists. If you overwrite an existing file directly, you risk losing the old data if an error occurs while writing the data. You first use the function FindFolder() to see whether a temporary file already exists. If it doesn't, call the function FSMakeFSSpec() to create a file specification record for the temporary file.

2. Call FSpCreate() to create the file (or the temporary file).

3. Call FSpOpenDF() to open the data fork of the file (or the temporary file).

4. At this point, you're ready to write data to the file. Now you must set the file position to where you want to start writing. Because the file we are writing—either the actual file or the temporary file—is brand new, you set the file to the beginning with a call to SetFPos(). Table 15-10 lists the three parameters the SetFPos() function takes.

5. Call the function FSWrite() to write the data to the file. Table 15-12 lists the three parameters the FSWrite() function takes.

6. To write any more data, call SetFPos() to move the file position to the end of the file so that you can continue to write data without erasing what you've already written. Then call FSWrite() to write the additional data.

7. When you're finished writing data, call the function SetEOF() to place the end-of-file marker.

8. Call GetVRefNum() to find the volume where the file resides. Then call the function FlushVol() to flush the volume.

9. If you used a temporary file, call FSpExchangeFiles() to exchange the temporary file with the file the user told you to use. Now the user file contains the saved data.

10. If you used a temporary file, call FSpDelete() to delete the temporary file.

Table 15-10 SetFPos() Parameters

Parameter	Description
refNum	The reference number of the file whose position you want to set.
posMode	Tells the File Manager how to position the file mark. Table 15-11 lists the possible positioning modes.
posOff	The number of bytes to move the file position pointer from the positioning mode specified in the posMode parameter. If the positioning mode is fsAtMark, the File Manager ignores the posOff parameter.

Table 15-11   File-Positioning Modes

Mode	Description
fsAtMark	Keep the file mark at its current position.
fsFromStart	Move the file mark relative to the start of the file.
fsFromLEOF	Move the file mark relative to the logical end of file.
fsFromMark	Move the file mark relative to its current position.

Table 15-12   FSWrite() Parameters

Parameter	Description
refNum	The reference number of the file where we will write the data.
count	The number of bytes to write. On output, the File Manager will use this parameter to return the number of bytes that were actually written.
buffPtr	A data buffer containing the data we're writing to the file.

The following function writes a saved game to the data fork:

```
Boolean WriteGameData(FSSpec fileSpec, OSType fileCreator, Boolean replacing)
{
        // Returns true if the write is successful
        // and false if it's unsuccessful

        OSErr error;
        short fileRefNum;
        Ptr gameToSave;
        SavedGame currentGame;

        // Code to read the saved game omitted

        // Make a temporary file if we're replacing the file
```

```
FSSpec tempFile;
short tempVolumeRefNum;
long tempDirectoryID;
Str255 tempFilename = "\pTempFile";

if (replacing) {
      // Create a file specification record for the
      // temporary file.
      error = FindFolder(fileSpec.vRefNum, kTemporaryFolderType,
                             kCreateFolder, tempVolumeRefNum,
                             tempDirectoryID);
      if (SeriousError(error))
            return false;

      error = FSMakeFSSpec(tempVolumeRefNum, tempDirectoryID,
                                 tempFilename, &tempFile);
      if (SeriousError(error))
            return false;

}


// Create the file
if (replacing) {
      // Create a temporary file
      error = FSpCreate(&tempFile, kTempFileType, kTempFileType,
                           smSystemScript);
}
else {
      // Create the actual file
      error = FSpCreate(&fileSpec, fileCreator, kGameFileType,
                           smSystemScript);
}
if (SeriousError(error))
      return false;

// Open the data fork so we can write
// the saved game to it.
if (replacing) {
      error = FSpOpenDF (&tempFile, fsRdWrPerm, &fileRefNum);
}
else {
```

```
                error = FSpOpenDF (&fileSpec, fsRdWrPerm, & fileRefNum);
        }

        if (SeriousError(error))
                return false;

        // Set the file position to the start of the file
        error = SetFPos(fileRefNum, fsFromStart, 0);
         if (SeriousError(error))
                return false;

        // Allocate enough space to hold the saved game
        long fileSize;
        error = FSpGetEOF(fileRefNum, &fileSize);
        if (SeriousError(error))
                return false;

        savedGame = NewPtr(fileSize);
        BlockMoveData(*savedGame, &currentGame, sizeof(SavedGame));

        // Write the data to disk
        error = FSWrite(fileRefNum, &fileSize, savedGame);
        if (SeriousError(error))
                return false;

        // Set the End of File
        error = SetEOF(fileRefNum, fileSize);
        if (SeriousError(error))
                return false;

        // Flush the volume
        short volumeRefNum;
        error = GetVRefNum(fileRefNum, &volumeRefNum);
        if (SeriousError(error))
                return false;

        // If we're replacing, exchange the files
        if (replacing) {
                error = FSpExchangeFiles(&tempFile, &fileSpec)
                if (SeriousError(error))
                        return false;
```

```
}

// Write was successful
DisposePtr(gameToSave);
return true;
}
```

Why Don't I Have to Create a Temporary File for Resources?

As you read about writing data to a temporary file first and then exchanging files with the actual file, you may be wondering why you need to do this when writing to the data fork, but not when writing resources. The answer is because the data fork is just one continuous sequence of bytes, as shown in Figure 15-3 earlier in this chapter. When you set the file position to the start of the file and begin writing data, you erase any previously saved data. If an error occurs during the middle of the write, the entire file becomes corrupted. When writing to the data fork, using a temporary file is the safe thing to do.

On the other hand, the resource fork can contain many types of resources, not just a single resource. Suppose that you have a file with five resources, and you want to update one of the resources. If you created a temporary file, wrote the resource, and exchanged the files, you would end up with a file with only one resource. The other four resources would be lost forever. In the case of resources, not using a temporary file is the safe way to go. The worst that can happen if an error occurs is that one resource becomes corrupted. The rest of the file will be fine.

Reading from the Data Fork

Just as is true with resources, reading from the data fork is easier than writing data. Here's what you have to do to read data:

1. Call SetFPos() to set the file position to the start of the file.
2. Determine how much data you want to read. To read the whole file, use GetEOF() to determine the file's length. Then allocate a buffer large enough to hold the data.
3. Call FSRead() to read the data. Table 15-13 describes the three parameters FSRead() takes.
4. To do any additional reading, move the file position, calculate how much data to read, then call FSRead() to read again.

Table 15-13   FSRead() Parameters

Parameter	Description
refNum	The reference number of the file where we will read the data.
count	The number of bytes to read. On output, the File Manager uses this parameter to return the number of bytes that were actually read.
buffPtr	A data buffer containing the destination for the data we're reading from disk.

The following function reads a saved game from the data fork:

```
Boolean ReadGameData(FSSpec fileSpec)
{
        // Returns true if the read is successful
        // and false if it's unsuccessful

        OSErr error;
        short fileRefNum;
        Ptr savedGame;
        SavedGame newGame;

        // Open the file
        error = FSpOpenDF (&fileSpec, fsRdWrPerm, & fileRefNum);
        if (SeriousError(error))
                return false;
```

```
        // Set the file position to the start of the file
        error = SetFPos(fileRefNum, fsFromStart, 0);
        if (SeriousError(error))
                return false;


        // Allocate enough space to hold the saved game
        long fileSize;
        error = FSpGetEOF(fileRefNum, &fileSize);
        if (SeriousError(error))
                return false;


        savedGame = NewPtr(fileSize);


        // Now let's read the data from disk
        // to the SavedGame structure.
        // A real game would then copy the data
        // from the variable newGame
        // to a game-related data structure.
        error = FSRead(fileRefNum, &fileSize, savedGame);
        if (SeriousError(error))
                return false;


        BlockMoveData(&newGame, *savedGame, sizeof(SavedGame));
        error = MemError();
        if (SeriousError(error))
                return false;


        // Do whatever you need to with the data you read from disk


        // Read was successful
        return true;
}
```

Bundles

Back in my day (before Mac OS X), small games crammed all their data in the resource fork of their application's file. Larger games had to use external files because of the Resource Manager's limit of 16MB of resources per file. At a minimum, there were external files for graphics, sounds, and levels. At a maximum, there were files for each sound, graphic, and level in the game. The problem with having external files is that the player can intentionally or unintentionally wreak havoc with them. He can accidentally delete a file, or he can rename a file. If your game had a file titled `Explosion Sounds` that contained sound effects for explosions, and the player removed this file from his hard drive, problems will occur when you want to play an explosion sound. At best, your game won't play the sound, or it will exit the game with an error message. At worst, your game will crash.

Bundles solve the problem of using external files in games and other applications. A *bundle* is a directory that contains an application and the external files the application uses. To the player, the bundle appears as one file—your game—so he cannot accidentally delete or rename any of your game's external files. You can put foreign-language versions of your game's resources in the same bundle, giving you the ability to have multiple language versions of your game in one bundle. Throw in the fact that one bundle will run on Mac OS 8, 9, and X, and you'll want to be using bundles to package your game.

A Bundle's Contents

At a bare minimum, the contents of a game's bundle will look like Figure 15-6. As you can see from the figure, a minimal game bundle contains six elements:

- The bundle itself with the title `GameTitle.app`, where `GameTitle` is your game's title. The `.app` extension tells the operating system that the file is an application bundle; you must have the `.app` extension at the end of your bundle name. The `.app` extension is not visible to the player; the bundle appears to him as a file with the name `GameTitle`.

- A `Contents` directory that contains the bundle's files.

- Your game's application file with the name `GameTitle`.

- A resource file containing your game's data resources. You can use a file in which you store the data in the data fork, but you will have a file containing data for your game such as graphics, sounds, and game levels. If you use a resource file, you can give it a different name than `GameTitle.rsrc`, but giving it that name allows Core Foundation's Bundle Services (the part of Carbon that supports bundles) to automatically open the resource file when it opens the bundle.

- The `PkgInfo` file, which contains the bundle's file type and creator code.

- The `Info.plist` file, which contains information about the bundle.

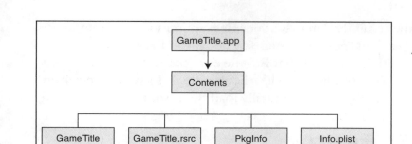

Figure 15-6

A minimal bundle for a game

The bundles for most games will be a little more complicated than what we've just described. Figure 15-7 shows a sample bundle for a game that has separate executable files for Mac OS 8/9 and Mac OS X, that has English and Spanish versions of text, and that has spoken messages. Following are the interesting additions to the minimal bundle for the game bundle shown in Figure 15-7:

- The Mac OS Classic directory, which contains files that are specific to Mac OS 8 and 9.
- The Mac OS directory, which contains files specific to Mac OS X.
- The Resources directory, which contains the resource files in the bundle.
- The English.lproj directory, which contains English language resources. Resources specific to a language must be in their own directory, which has the .lproj extension.
- The Spanish.lproj directory, which contains Spanish language resources. If you want to support other languages, just add directories for the additional languages.

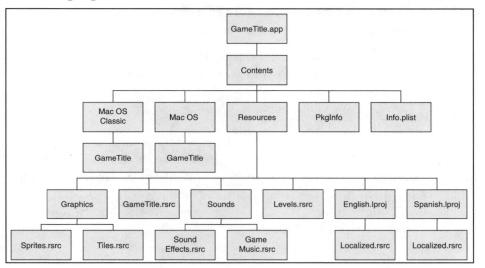

Figure 15-7

A slightly more complicated game bundle

The file `Localized.rsrc` contains all the language-specific resources such as menus, dialog box text, text messages, and spoken messages. The reason I used the name `Localized.rsrc` for the localized resources is that Bundle Services automatically opens a resource file named `Localized.rsrc` when it loads the bundle. If I gave the localized resources a different name, I would have to manually load the resource files.

Creating a Bundle

I'm sure your mind is swimming with questions after reading the previous section. How do I make a bundle? How do I make the `PkgInfo` file? How do I make the `Contents` directory? How do I make the `info.plist` file? If your compiler is capable of making bundles (CodeWarrior Pro 6 and later versions of CodeWarrior and Project Builder have the capability), all you have to do is choose a Carbon bundle when you create a project. The compiler will take care of most of the details for you. You still must create the actual resource files (the files with the `.rsrc` extensions in Figures 15-6 and 15-7), but the compiler takes care of everything else. The compiler will take all your resource files and create a resource file with the same name as your application so you don't even have to worry about giving a resource file the same name as your game.

If you choose to use an older version of CodeWarrior instead of using of the version included on the CD that accompanies this book, then creating a bundle involves a lot more work. In fact, if you don't use Project Builder or CodeWarrior Pro 6 or later, I recommend that you don't use bundles.

Finding the Application's Main Bundle

To find the application's main bundle, call the function `CFBundleGetMainBundle()`. This function takes no parameters. Here's how you find the main bundle:

```
CFBundleRef gameBundle;
gameBundle = CFBundleGetMainBundle();
```

The functions that locate a resource file inside a bundle take a variable of type `CFBundleRef` as a parameter, so we must find the main bundle to pass to those functions. More complex applications may have bundles embedded in the main bundle. Most games have only one bundle: the main bundle. Normally, you call `CFBundleGetMainBundle()` once and use the `CFBundleRef` variable that the function returns to retrieve resources from the bundle.

Extracting Resources from a Bundle

The easiest way to read resources from a bundle is to let the computer do most of the work for you. By default, Project Builder takes the resource files you have in the ResourceManager Resources section of your project (refer to the Files and Build Phases section of Chapter 2, "Project Builder," for more details.) and creates a file named GameTitle.rsrc, where GameTitle is the name of your game. The GameTitle.rsrc file loads automatically when your game loads, giving you access to your game's resources. You make the appropriate function calls to load the resources. If you look at the Project Builder code from previous chapters, you will notice that I could load all of the program's resources (pictures of the tiles and sprites, sound effects, the menu bar, and the game's menu) without making any special bundle function calls.

If you have resource files that the operating system cannot load, one method to extract the resources is to call the function CFBundleOpenBundleResourceMap(). This function takes a variable of type CFBundleRef as its lone parameter, and it returns a reference number to the bundle's resource map. This reference number is the same number that the Resource Manager function FSpOpenResFile() returns. You use this file reference number to read resources from disk like we covered earlier in the chapter. Here's how the code might look to read a resource file from a bundle:

```
CFBundleRef gameBundle;
short refNum;

gameBundle = CFBundleGetMainBundle();
refNum = CFBundleOpenResourceMap(gameBundle);

// Use the refNum variable to read the resource
// using the techniques we covered earlier in the chapter.
```

There are two things to be aware of when using the function CFBundleOpenBundleResourceMap(). First, CFBundleOpenBundleResourceMap() is available only on systems running Mac OS 8.6 and above. Second, all your resources of a particular type should have unique resource IDs. For example, if you have three different music files, each with a resource ID of 8192, the Resource Manager uses the first sound resource it finds with ID 8192; you can't be sure which one the Resource Manager will choose.

If you have multiple language versions of your game in one bundle, call the function CFBundleOpenResourceFiles() to open the resource file. The CFBundleOpenResourceFiles() function returns separate file reference numbers for your localized and nonlocalized resources—which is good if you have resources in multiple languages. For example, if you have menus in multiple languages, you want each menu to have the same resource ID so that the same code works for all languages. If you call CFBundleOpenResourceMap() to open the resource file, the Resource Manager uses the first menu it finds with the correct menu resource ID, which may not be in the language you want. Using CFBundleOpenResourceFiles() instead ensures that the Resource Manager uses the proper menu. CFBundleOpenResourceFiles() takes three parameters, which you can see in Table 15-14. CFBundleOpenResourceFiles() runs on Mac OS 8.6 and above.

Table 15-14   CFBundleOpenResourceFiles() Parameters

Parameter	Description
bundle	The bundle containing the resource file to open.
refNum	The reference number for the non-localized resources that CFBundleOpenResourceFiles() returns.
localizedRefNum	The reference number of the localized resources that CFBundleOpenResourceFiles() returns.

If you need access to a specific resource file in the bundle, call the function CFBundleCopyResourceURL(). Table 15-15 lists the four parameters that CFBundleCopyResourceURL() takes.

Table 15-15   CFBundleCopyResourceURL() Parameters

Parameter	Description
bundle	The bundle containing the resource file to open.
resourceName	The resource filename. It must be a variable of type CFStringRef.
resourceType	The resource file type.
subDirName	The subdirectory in the resource to search. Use the value nil to search the standard locations for the resource.

In the Project Builder code I wrote to play a QuickTime movie in Chapter 10, "Sound," I stored the movie inside the bundle and used CFBundleCopyResourceURL() to find the movie file. CFBundleCopyResourceURL() returns a variable of type CFURLRef, which is a path to the resource file, and QuickTime requires a file specification record (FSSpec) to load the movie from disk. Unfortunately, there is no single function to convert the CFURLRef variable that CFBundleCopyResourceURL() returns to the FSSpec variable that QuickTime requires. What I had to do was call the Core Foundation function CFURLGetFSRef() to convert the CFURLRef variable to a file system reference (FSRef). Apple introduced file system references in Mac OS 9. File system references are similar to file specification records (they identify a file without having to know the file's path), but they allow file names longer than 31 characters. After getting the file system reference, I had to convert it to a file specification record by calling the function FSGetCatalogInfo(). The following code retrieves a QuickTime movie file from a bundle:

```
// filename is a parameter to the function to read the file.
OSErr error;
FSSpec soundFile;

CFBundleRef gameBundle = CFBundleGetMainBundle();
CFURLRef resourceFileLocation;

// Get the movie file name into a Core Foundation string so Bundle
// Services can find it.
CFStringRef resourceFileToFind;
resourceFileToFind = CFStringCreateWithPascalString(nil, filename,
     CFStringGetSystemEncoding());
```

```
// Find the movie file in the bundle
CFStringRef resourceFileType = nil;
resourceFileLocation = CFBundleCopyResourceURL(gameBundle, resourceFileToFind,
        resourceFileType, nil);

if (resourceFileLocation == nil)
        return;

// Get the file system reference
FSRef fileRef;
Boolean success = CFURLGetFSRef(resourceFileLocation, &fileRef);

if (!success)
        return;

// Convert the FSRef to an FSSpec so we can call OpenMovieFile().
// The first nil says we don't care about catalog info.
// The second nil says we don't care about the file's name.
// The third nil says we don't care about the parent directory.
error = FSGetCatalogInfo(&fileRef, kFSCatInfoGettableInfo, nil, nil,
        &soundFile, nil);
if (error != noErr)
        return;

// Call the QuickTime functions to read the movie into memory
```

The code above works well, but the problem with this approach is that FSRef variables work only with Mac OS 9 and above. This is the reason why I used bundles in the Mac OS X version of the code only. There's not much point in writing code to run on Mac OS 9 and X that does not run on Mac OS 9. Things would be a lot easier if there were a function to convert a variable of type CFURLRef to a file specification record. I believe that Apple did not supply such a function to encourage developers to use file system references instead of file specification records.

Preference Files

Most Macintosh programs use preference files to store user settings. For games, you use a preference file to store things such as control configurations, the desired screen resolution, the desired pixel depth, and the volume for the sounds in the game. Some programs, such as Internet browsers, have multiple preference files, but most games can get away with one preference file.

On pre-Mac OS X systems, you place the game's preference file in the Preferences folder inside the user's System folder. Things get a little more complicated with Mac OS X. Mac OS X allows a computer to have multiple users, each with his own set of preferences. Each user has a Library folder, and the Library folder contains a Preferences folder. You place your game's preference file inside the user's Preferences folder.

Apple recommends that you use the following naming scheme for your game's preference file:

```
com.<Company>.<Program Name>.plist
```

As an example, AOL Instant Messenger's preference file would look like this:

```
com.aol.aim.plist
```

If your compiler has built-in bundle support (Project Builder and CodeWarrior Pro 6 and later versions have bundle support), you give your application a bundle identifier in the project settings with the following naming convention:

```
com.<Company>.<Program Name>
```

Figure 15-8 shows where you would place your game's bundle identifier in Project Builder. When creating the preference file, the computer will take your bundle identifier and attach the extension .plist to make the preference file. If you use Core Foundation's Preference Services, which I discuss next section, the computer will write all your game's preferences to the preference file.

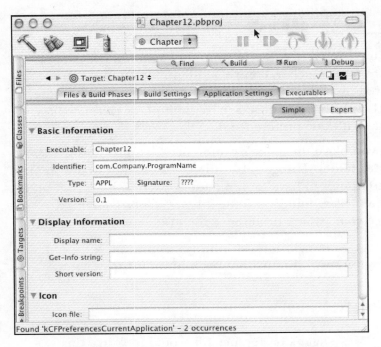

Figure 15-8

Setting your game's bundle identifier in Project Builder.

If your compiler does not have built-in bundle support, I recommend not going with Apple's naming terminology and not using Core Foundation's Preference Services. Instead you should give your preference file the name "Program Name Preferences", where Program Name is the name of your game. Write your preferences to the data fork or the resource fork of the preference file using the techniques I covered previously in this chapter.

Core Foundation's Preference Services

In the old days of Mac programming, games and other applications stored their preferences in the data fork or in resources in the resource fork of the preference file. You can still do this using the techniques covered earlier in this chapter to write resources and write to the data fork of a file. There is an easier way, however.

Mac OS X has Preference Services as part of its Core Foundation technology. These services make it easy to read, write, and update preferences. As a bonus, these services made it into Carbon so Mac OS 8 and 9 programs can use them as well.

When using Preference Services, preferences are stored as key/value pairs, as shown in Figure 15-9. The *key* identifies the given preference. Examples of keys for a game include color depth, screen resolution, volume, and high scores. The *value* is the value for that particular preference (for example, a value of 16 for a color depth key). The three main data types for your preference values are CFStringRef, CFNumberRef, and CFArrayRef. I'm sure you can figure out what each of those types represents.

Key	Value
Screen Width	800
Screen Height	600
Color Depth	16
High Scores	[45000, 37500, 31600, 25000, 20500]
Volume	6
Move Left	123 (Left Arrow Key)
Move Right	124 (Right Arrow Key)
Fire	49 (Spacebar)

Figure 15-9

A sample preference file for a Space Invaders clone using Core Foundation's Preference Services.

Writing Preferences

To create an individual preference inside your game's reference file, call the function CFPreferencesSetAppValue(). This function takes the three parameters listed in Table 15-16.

Table 15-16 `CFPreferencesSetAppValue()` Parameters

Parameter	Description
key	The preference.
value	The value to give the preference. Passing nil deletes the preference.
appName	The application containing the preference to write. The usual value to pass is kCFPreferencesCurrentApplication, which will write the preference to your game's preference file.

After calling `CFPreferencesSetAppValue()` to create preferences, call the function `CFPreferencesAppSynchronize()` to write the preferences to disk. The `CFPreferencesAppSynchronize()` function takes one parameter: the appName parameter you supplied to `CFPreferencesSetAppValue()`. Call `CFPreferencesAppSynchronize()` after you set all your game's preferences.

Here's a simple example that writes the volume to the preference file:

```
CFStringRef volumeKey = CFSTR("Volume");
int desiredVolume;

// Your game should read the user selection instead of going with the value 5.
desiredVolume = 5;

// Convert the desired volume from an int to a CFNumberRef
volume = CFNumberCreate(NULL, kCFNumberIntType, &desiredVolume);

// Set the preference value
CFPreferencesSetAppValue(volumeKey,volume, kCFPreferencesCurrentApplication);

// Write the preference to disk
CFPreferencesAppSynchronize(kCFPreferencesCurrentApplication);

// Release the temporary variable volume
CFRelease(volume);
```

Start writing a preference by creating the key. The key must be of type `CFStringRef`. What you name the key is up to you. Next, get the value to write to the reference. Because Core Foundation cannot write integers, we must create a variable of type `CFNumberRef` and place the integer value there. That's what the `CFNumberCreate()` call does. Then we call the `CFPreferencesSetAppValue()` function to create the preference in memory; we call `CFPreferencesAppSynchronize()` to write the preference to disk. Finally, we release the memory we allocated to create the `CFNumberRef` to temporarily store the volume.

Reading Preferences

To read a preference from disk, call the function `CFPreferencesCopyAppValue()`. Table 15-17 describes the two parameters this function takes.

Table 15-17   `CFPreferencesCopyAppValue()` Parameters

Parameter	Description
key	The preference to read.
appName	The application containing the preference to write. The usual value to pass is `kCFPreferencesCurrentApplication`, which will read the preference from your game's preference file.

Here's how we would read the preference we created in the preceding section:

```
CFStringRef volumeKey = CFSTR("Volume");
CFNumberRef preferredVolume;
int volume;
Boolean conversionSuccessful;

preferredVolume = CFPreferencesCopyAppValue(volumeKey,
                                 kCFPreferencesCurrentApplication);
```

```
// Convert the read volume from a CFNumberRef to an integer
conversionSuccessful = CFNumberGetValue(preferredVolume, kCFNumberIntType,
                                        &volume);
if (conversionSuccessful) {
        // Set the system volume here
}
```

As you can see, reading a preference is easier than writing one. For numerical values, CFPreferencesCopyAppValue() returns a variable of type CFNumberRef. If you want an integer returned so that you do not have to manually convert the preference to an integer, call the function CFPreferencesGetAppIntegerValue(). The following code snippet reads the volume directly into an integer:

```
CFStringRef volumeKey = CFSTR("Volume");
int preferredVolume;
Boolean preferenceExists

preferredVolume = CFPreferencesGetAppIntegerValue(volumeKey,
                          kCFPreferencesCurrentApplication, &preferenceExists);
if (preferenceExists) {
        // Set the system volume here
}
```

> **NOTE**
>
> The CFPreferencesGetAppIntegerValue() runs on Mac OS 8.6 and above. If you want to support Mac OS 8.1 and 8.5, you must call CFPreferencesCopyAppValue() and convert the CFNumberRef to an integer.

Updating Preferences

In most cases, updating a preference works exactly the same as writing a preference; you write the preference, replacing the old value with the new one. An exception would be high scores in an arcade game. In this case, you should read the high score and check whether the current score is higher. If it is higher, you update the preference to reflect the new high score, as shown in the following code snippet:

```
CFStringRef highScoreKey = CFSTR("High Score");
int currentScore;
int previousHighScore;
Boolean preferenceExists;

// You would read the current score here

// Read the previous high score
previousHighScore = CFPreferencesGetAppIntegerValue(volumeKey,
                            kCFPreferencesCurrentApplication, &preferenceExists);

// Check to see if we need to update the high score list
if ((!preferenceExists) || (currentScore > previousHighScore)) {
        // Write the new high score to disk
        tempScore = CFNumberCreate(NULL, kCFNumberIntType, &currentScore);
        CFPreferencesSetAppValue(highScoreKey,tempScore,
                                kCFPreferencesCurrentApplication);
        CFPreferencesAppSynchronize(kCFPreferencesCurrentApplication);
        CFRelease(tempScore);
}
```

Summary

This chapter covered the world of files. It's not a glamorous topic in the world of game programming, but a knowledge of files is essential if you want to read your game's data from disk to memory. The chapter began with Navigation Services, the Mac technology that displays dialog boxes that allow the user to open and save files.

After covering Navigation Services, I discussed the two forks of Mac files: the data fork and resource fork. I showed you what you need to know to read and write to both forks of a file. Next, I covered bundles, which are collections of directories and files that appear to the user as a single file. I showed how you can retrieve files and data from a bundle. Finally, I discussed preference files, which store the user's settings for your game.

To learn more about files, go to Apple's developer Web site (refer to Appendix B, "Game Development Resources" for the Web address). The site contains documentation on Navigation Services, the Resource Manager Core Foundation's Bundle Services, and Core Foundation's Preference Services.

If you ask, "Are we there yet?" with regard to our game programming journey, the answer is, "Just a little farther." In the next chapter, we fill in the gaps to make a complete game. I bet the anticipation is killing you.

CHAPTER 16

Putting It All Together

At this point in our efforts in creating a game, we have all the major components of the game in place. We have the graphics, the sound, the artificial intelligence, and the physics. We can read input from the player, load game assets from disk, save games, and open saved game files. To make the game complete, we must assemble all these components and then put in some finishing touches, which I cover in this chapter.

Checking the Player's Runtime Environment

When your game begins, it's a good idea to examine the player's system to make sure that it can run the game. If the player's system lacks something your game requires, it's much better to bring up a dialog box that tells the player what's missing and then exit the game rather than to crash. For a player running Mac OS 8 or 9, crashing the game adds insult to injury by forcing him to restart his computer.

The function `Gestalt()` returns details about the player's system. `Gestalt()` takes two parameters. The first parameter contains the aspect of the player's system you want to examine, such as the amount of memory or the version of Mac OS that's running. You supply a pointer to a 32-bit signed integer in the second parameter, and `Gestalt()` fills this integer with the information requested in the first parameter. On an operating system the size of Mac OS, there are an enormous number of items you can check, so I can't provide an exhaustive list here. Refer to the Gestalt Manager section of the Carbon Developer Documentation area of Apple's developer Web site (**www.apple.com/developer**) for such a list. The next few sections show you how to use the `Gestalt()` function to check for runtime elements a typical game should check.

Finding the Operating System Version

To find which version of Mac OS the player's system is running, supply the constant `gestaltSystemVersion` as the first parameter to `Gestalt()`. `Gestalt()` returns the operating system version as a four-digit hexadecimal number. If the player were running

Mac OS 9.2.1, `Gestalt()` would return the hexadecimal number 0921. If the player were running Mac OS X 10.1.3, `Gestalt()` would return 1013. The following function determines whether or not the player is running Mac OS X:

```
Boolean GameApp::RunningOSX(void)
{
        SInt32 OSVersion;
        OSErr error;

        error = Gestalt(gestaltSystemVersion, &OSVersion);
        if (error != noErr)
                return;

        if (OSVersion >= 0x01000)
                return true;
        else
                return false;
}
```

Finding the `CarbonLib` Version

If you want to use Carbon events in your game, it's not enough to check whether or not the player is running Mac OS 8.6 or higher. You must check whether the player has `CarbonLib` (the Carbon library) version 1.1 or above. You also need `CarbonLib` version 1.1 or higher to make many Carbon function calls.

To check the `CarbonLib` function on the player's computer, pass the value `gestaltCarbonVersion` as the first parameter to `Gestalt()`. `Gestalt()` returns the Carbon library version as a four-digit hexadecimal number, just as it does with the operating system version. If the player has `CarbonLib` version 1.4 installed on his Mac, `Gestalt()` returns the hexadecimal number 0140. The following function determines whether or not you can use Carbon events on the player's machine:

```
Boolean GameApp::CanUseCarbonEvents(void)
{
        SInt32 carbonVersion;
        OSErr error;

        error = Gestalt(gestaltCarbonVersion, &carbonVersion);
```

```
        if (error != noErr)
                return;

        if (carbonVersion >= 0x0110)
                return true;
        else
                return false;
}
```

Determining the Amount of Memory

Every game requires a minimum amount of memory, no matter how low that value might be. It's a good idea to be safe and check that the player's machine has enough memory to play your game.

Gestalt() lets you test both the physical and logical memory the player has on his Mac. The *physical memory* is the amount of RAM installed on the player's computer. The *logical memory* is the physical memory plus the virtual memory. *Virtual memory* uses the computer's hard disk as additional RAM. Checking the logical memory is useful only on pre–Mac OS X systems because those systems let the user set the amount of virtual memory. Virtual memory on Mac OS X is limited only by the size of the hard disk, which most likely will exceed the limits of a 32-bit signed integer, which is what Gestalt() uses.

To determine the amount of physical memory on the player's pre–Mac OS X machine, pass the constant gestaltPhysicalRAM to Gestalt(); Gestalt() returns the number of bytes of physical memory. To determine the amount of logical memory, pass the constant gestaltLogicalRAM. Remember that Gestalt() just calculates the amount of memory on the player's computer. Gestalt() does not know how much memory your game requires; you must determine that yourself. Chapter 19, "Game Development Tips," covers some tools you can use on Mac OS X to figure out how much memory your game needs. The following code determines whether or not the player has enough memory to play the game:

```
Boolean GameApp::PlayerHasEnoughRAM(SInt32 requiredRAM)
{
        SInt32 physicalRAMSize;
        OSErr error;
```

```
      error = Gestalt(gestaltPhysicalRAM, &physicalRAMSize);
      if (error != noErr)
              return;

      if (physicalRAMSize >= requiredRAM)
              return true;
      else
              return false;
}
```

Finding the CPU Type

Games sometimes like to know the
CPU that is powering the player's
Mac so that they can use special
code that takes advantage of that
particular processor. To determine
the CPU on the player's computer,
supply the constant
gestaltNativeCPUType to Gestalt().
Gestalt() returns the processor the
player's computer has using the
value gestaltCPUXXX, where the XXX
represents the particular processor. If
the player has a G4 processor, for example, Gestalt() returns the value
gestaltCPUG4.

NOTE

The gestaltNativeCPUType value does
not take into account any processor
upgrade cards the player might have on
his computer. For example, if the player
has a computer with a Power PC 601
chip and has installed a G3 upgrade
card, Gestalt() tells you that the player
has a Power PC 601 processor, not a G3.

If all you are interested in is making sure that the player has a Power PC processor
(a minimum requirement for Carbon programs), pass the value
gestaltSysArchitecture to Gestalt(). If the player has a Power PC Mac, Gestalt()
returns the value gestaltPowerPC.

Determining Whether or Not
QuickTime Is Installed

Games can use the QuickTime application to play music, play video, and go into
full-screen mode. If you're going to use QuickTime, you should make sure that the
player's machine has QuickTime installed. To check whether or not QuickTime is

installed, pass the value `gestaltQuickTime` as the first parameter to `Gestalt()`. If `Gestalt()` returns the result `noErr`, QuickTime exists on the player's machine, as you can see in the following function:

```
Boolean GameApp::IsQuickTimeInstalled(void)
{
        SInt32 result;
        OSErr error;

        error = Gestalt(gestaltQuickTime, &result);
        if (error == noErr)
                return true;
        else
                return false;

}
```

To check the version of QuickTime installed on the player's machine, pass the value `gestaltQuickTimeVersion` to `Gestalt()` and `Gestalt()` will tell you the version. `Gestalt()` returns the QuickTime version as a hexadecimal number, just like it does when determining the operating system and `CarbonLib` versions the player has. If the player is using QuickTime 5, `Gestalt()` returns the hexadecimal number `0500`. The QuickTime functions we use in the book do not require the latest and greatest version of QuickTime. As long as the player has QuickTime installed, the code will run fine.

Loading a Level's Enemies and Items

In Chapter 5, "Tiles and Scrolling," we learned how to load a level's background. Game levels also consist of enemies for the player to fight and items for him to acquire; without enemies and items, the game would be dull. To store this additional information, I created a level population resource for each game level, which consists of the following information:

- The version number
- The player's starting position in the level
- The combined total of enemies and items in the level
- The list of enemies and items in the level

The version number is useful if you want to make changes to the resource, such as storing additional information in the level population resource. When you make a change to the resource, update the version number. When reading the level population resource, you check the version number to make sure the resource matches the current version before reading the data.

If you have run the programs from earlier chapters in this book, you noticed that the player always starts at the upper left corner of the level. Storing the player's starting position lets you place the player anywhere in the level.

Storing the combined total of enemies and items in the level tells us how many entities (enemies and items) we will be reading from the level population resource. Following the total is the entity list; each entry in the entity list tells us what the entity is (such as an enemy, additional ammo, or a healing potion) and its starting position in the level.

To load the level's enemies and items, we read the combined total of enemies and items in the level. Next, we read each entity in the list. If the entity is an enemy, we add it to the game's enemy list; otherwise, we add it to the item list. The following code loads the level's enemies and items from disk:

```
Boolean GameApp::ReadLevelPopulation(short populationID)
{
        short error;
        short refNum;
        Handle savedPopulation;

        // Clear out anything that's remaining in the monster and item lists
        DeleteEnemyList();
        DeleteItemList();

        savedPopulation = Get1Resource(kLevelPopulationResourceType,
                populationID);
        error = ResError();
        if ((error != noErr) || (savedPopulation == nil))
                return false;

        // Now let's set the level data
        short version;
        short startX;
        short startY;
        short populationCount;
```

```
Size offset = 0;

BlockMoveData(*savedPopulation + offset, &version, sizeof(short));
offset = offset + sizeof(short);

// If resource is obsolete, don't load it.
if (version != kCurrentLevelPopulationVersion) {
        ReleaseResource(Handle(savedPopulation));
        CloseResFile(refNum);
        return false;
}

// At the start of the level population resource is the
// player's starting position in the level.  We read this
// data, but don't do anything with it here.
BlockMoveData(*savedPopulation + offset, &startX, sizeof(short));
offset = offset + sizeof(short);
BlockMoveData(*savedPopulation + offset, &startY, sizeof(short));
offset = offset + sizeof(short);

// Read the number of enemies and items in the level.
BlockMoveData(*savedPopulation + offset, &populationCount, sizeof(short));
        offset = offset + sizeof(short);

LevelResident currentResident;

// Read the enemies and items from disk
for (short i = 0; i < populationCount; i++) {
        currentResident = new LevelResident;
        BlockMoveData(*savedPopulation + offset, currentResident,
                sizeof(LevelResident));
        AddEnemyToList(currentResident, weaponList, context);

        if (IsResidentAnEnemy(&currentResident)) {
                AddEnemyToList(&currentResident, weaponList, context);
        }
        else {
                AddItemToList(&currentResident, context);
        }

        offset = offset + sizeof(LevelResident);
```

```
        }

        // Clean up
        ReleaseResource(Handle(savedPopulation));
        error = ResError();
        if (SeriousError(error))
                return false;

        return true;

}
```

The Game Loop

The heart of the game is the game loop. When the game is in progress, we spend 100 percent of the time in the game loop. The only way to leave the loop is to pause the game. Figure 16-1 shows the game loop in action. The loop begins by computing how much time has elapsed since the last frame, where a "frame" is one time through the game loop. We use the elapsed time to move the objects in the game properly. Next, we read any input the player gives to the game.

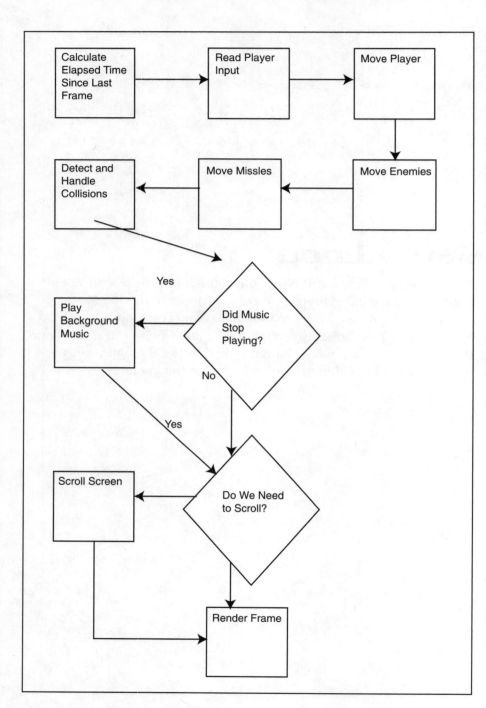

Figure 16-1

The action that takes place in one iteration of our game loop. When the Render Frame step completes, we go back to the start of the loop.

After reading the player input, we move the game objects, which in the case of our game are the player character, the enemies, and the missiles the player fires. I chose to move the player first, then the enemies, then the missiles. You could choose to move the enemies before the player, but it's important to move the player before you move the missiles. This is because the player's move in this frame might have been to fire a weapon (launch a missile). But if you've already moved the missiles for this frame, the newly launched missile would not move until the next frame. After moving the game objects, we check for any collisions between the objects. If there are collisions, we handle them.

Now the game loop checks whether or not the background music stopped playing. If it did, we play the music again. This test can occur anywhere in the game loop. I can't remember why I decided to place it in the middle of the game loop; you can move it to the end of the loop if you want.

At this stage, we must check whether the player's movement forces us to scroll the screen. If it does, we scroll the screen. If not, we move on to rendering the frame on the screen. Then we go back to the beginning of the loop.

Calculating the Elapsed Time

The range of Macs capable of running Carbon games is vast. At the low end, we have Macs with 60MHz Power PC 601 chips. The high end continues to evolve each time Steve Jobs gives a MacWorld keynote address. As game programmers, we have the challenge of making the action move at the same speed on all Power PC Macs as well as on Macs that will come out five or ten years from now. To meet the challenge, we calculate the game's frame rate and use it to move the characters in the game. Suppose that we want to move the player at a rate of 300 pixels per second. Also suppose that our game runs at 100 frames per second on player A's Mac and at 30 frames per second on player B's Mac. On player A's machine, we have to move the character three pixels per frame; on player B's computer, we have to move the character 10 pixels per frame. To both players, the character appears to move at the same speed even though the game runs approximately three times faster on player A's computer.

To make sure that the game runs at the same speed on all computers, we must calculate how much time has elapsed since the last frame and use that value to move the characters in the game. In Carbon, we have three routines for timing: `TickCount()`, `Microseconds()`, and `UpTime()`.

The TickCount() Routine

TickCount() is the easiest Carbon routine to use for timing, but gives you the least precision. TickCount() returns the number of clock ticks that have occurred since the player turned on his Mac. A clock tick is approximately 1/60 of a second. To calculate the elapsed time, you take the most recent result you got from TickCount() and subtract the previous result from TickCount(). The major problem with TickCount() is that it is only accurate to 1/60 of a second. If your game's frame rate is faster than 60 frames per second, using TickCount() can give you an elapsed time of 0, which will mess up your physics engine.

The Microseconds() Routine

The Microseconds() routine returns the number of microseconds that have elapsed since the player booted his machine. A *microsecond* is one millionth of a second. Microseconds() returns its result in a 64-bit integer, which makes it hard to calculate the amount of time elapsed since the start of the previous frame (64-bit arithmetic is difficult to do on most Macs). If you use Microseconds() to do your timing, the easiest thing to do is to convert the 64-bit integer into a value of type double, then subtract the double values. Microseconds() uses an UnsignedWide data structure, which contains two 32-bit integers—one to represent the high end of the 64-bit value and one to represent the low end of the value. To convert the 64-bit integer to a double, take the high end, multiply it by the number 2 raised to the power of 32, then add that value to the low end, as was done in the following function:

```
double GameApp::ConvertMicrosecondsToDouble(UnsignedWidePtr microsecondsValue)
{
        double twoPower32 = 4294967296.0;
        double result;

        double upperHalf = (double) microsecondsValue->hi;
        double lowerHalf = (double) microsecondsValue->lo;
        result = (upperHalf * twoPower32) + lowerHalf;
        return result;
}
```

After you convert the integer to a double, calculating the elapsed time is easy. Just take the current value that Microseconds() returned and subtract from it the previous value you stored from Microseconds(). This gives you the number of microseconds that have elapsed since the previous frame. In my game, however, I want to see the elapsed time in terms of seconds, so I multiply the number of microseconds by the definition of a microsecond—one millionth of a second—as you can see in the following code:

```
double GameApp::CalculateTimeStep(void)
{
        UnsignedWide currentTime;
        double currentTimeAsDouble;

        // Find current time and convert it to a double.
        // The UnsignedWide data type that Microseconds() uses
        // makes it difficult to perform mathematical operations.
        // Converting to a double makes it easier to calculate the elapsed time.
        Microseconds(&currentTime);
        currentTimeAsDouble = ConvertMicrosecondsToDouble(&currentTime);

        // Find elapsed time
        double elapsedTime = currentTimeAsDouble - previousTime;

        // Calculate time step in terms of seconds
        double oneMicrosecond = .000001;
        double result = oneMicrosecond * elapsedTime;

        // Update previousTime for next timestep calculation.
        previousTime = currentTimeAsDouble;
        return result;
}
```

The UpTime() Routine

If you need more accuracy than Microseconds() supplies, then use UpTime(). The UpTime() routine gives you the most accuracy of these three options, but it is hard to extract the data into something your game can use. UpTime() returns its result in an AbsoluteTime() structure, which is a 64-bit integer. You can convert the AbsoluteTime() type into either type Nanoseconds or type Duration.

The function AbsoluteToNanoseconds() converts the AbsoluteTime() value UpTime() gives us into the Nanoseconds data type. Converting into Nanoseconds tells you how many nanoseconds have elapsed since the player turned on the computer. A nanosecond equals one billionth of a second. Then you can convert from type Nanoseconds to type double as we did earlier with the Microseconds() call. The following function shows how we would convert from Nanoseconds to double:

```
double GameApp::ConvertNanosecondsToDouble(Nanoseconds* nanosecondsValue)
{
        double twoPower32 = 4294967296.0;
        double result;

        double upperHalf = (double) nanosecondsValue->hi;
        double lowerHalf = (double) nanosecondsValue->lo;
        result = (upperHalf * twoPower32) + lowerHalf;
        return result;
}
```

I used `Microseconds()` to compute the time step for our game, but if you were to use `UpTime()` and wanted nanosecond accuracy, the code would look like the following:

```
double GameApp::CalculateTimeStep(void)
{
        AbsoluteTime currentTime;
        Nanoseconds currentTimeAsNanoseconds;
        double currentTimeAsDouble;

        currentTime = UpTime();
        currentTimeAsNanoseconds = AbsoluteToNanoseconds(currentTime);
        currentTimeAsDouble = ConvertNanosecondsToDouble(&currentTimeAsNanoseconds);

        // Find elapsed time
        double elapsedTime = currentTimeAsDouble - previousTime;

        // Calculate time step in terms of seconds
        double oneNanosecond = .000000001;
        double result = oneNanosecond * elapsedTime;

        // Update previousTime for next timestep calculation.
        previousTime = currentTimeAsDouble;
        return result;
}
```

Converting the `AbsoluteTime` value that `UpTime()` gives us to type `Duration` tells us the number of milliseconds that have elapsed since the player booted his computer. The `Duration` data type is a signed 32-bit integer, so we don't have to convert the value to a `double`. The following codes show how to compute the elapsed time using the `UpTime()` routine and millisecond accuracy:

```
double GameApp::CalculateTimeStep(void)
{
        AbsoluteTime currentTime;
        Duration currentTimeAsDuration;

        currentTime = UpTime();
        currentTimeAsDuration = AbsoluteToDuration(currentTime);

        // Find elapsed time
        Duration elapsedTime = currentTimeAsDuration - previousTime;

        // Calculate time stamp in terms of seconds
        double oneMillisecond = .001;
        double result = oneMillisecond * elapsedTime;

        // Update previousTime for next timestep calculation.
        previousTime = currentTimeAsDuration;
        return result;
}
```

Moving the Player

Moving the player involves three steps:

1. Read the player's input.
2. Update the player's physics.
3. Update the player's animation.

On Mac OS 8 and 9, reading the player input is easy. We use the InputController class we developed in Chapter 7, " InputSprocket," and call two functions. We call DetermineAction() to check whether the player fired a missile, and then we call DetermineAnalogMovement() to check for any player movement. I separated the reading of movement from other types of player input to let the player perform other actions such as shooting and jumping while moving. The following code snippet reads the player input on Mac OS 8 and 9:

```
InputControllerAction playerAction;
InputControllerAction playerMovement;

playerAction = player1InputController->DetermineAction();
playerMovement = player1InputController->DetermineAnalogMovement();
```

The HID Manager's current lack of support for keyboards complicates matters on Mac OS X. When the HID Manager adds keyboard support, we can use the same code in the game loop on Mac OS X that we do in Mac OS 8 and 9. Until that happens, we need two sets of code, one that uses the HID Manager, and one that reads the keyboard.

The first thing to discover is whether or not the player has any HID Manager devices connected to his computer. We accomplish this with the following function:

```
Boolean InputController::AnyConnectedHIDDevices(void)
{
        IOReturn result;
        CFMutableDictionaryRef matchingDictionary;
        io_iterator_t deviceList;
        mach_port_t theMachPort;

        // Create the mach port
        result = IOMasterPort(bootstrap_port, &theMachPort);
        if (result != kIOReturnSuccess)
                return false;

        // Create matching dictionary of HID devices
        matchingDictionary = IOServiceMatching(kIOHIDDeviceKey);

        // Look for any HID controllers connected
        // to the player's machine
        result = IOServiceGetMatchingServices(theMachPort, matchingDictionary,
&deviceList);

        Boolean matchingDevices;

        if ((deviceList == nil) || (result != kIOReturnSuccess))
                matchingDevices = false;
        else
                matchingDevices = true;

        // We're finished with the matching dictionary.
        // IOServiceGetMatchingServices() released it for us.
        matchingDictionary = nil;

        IOObjectRelease(deviceList);
        mach_port_deallocate(mach_task_self(), theMachPort);
```

```
        return matchingDevices;
}
```

For more information on the details of finding HID devices on the player's computer, refer to the section, "Finding the Player's HID-Capable Devices," in Chapter 8, "HID Manager." When initializing the game, we make the following call to determine whether or not the player is using a joystick:

```
usingHID = player1InputController->AnyConnectedHIDDevices();
```

To read the player input, we use the following code:

```
Boolean escapeKeyPressed;

if (usingHID) {
        playerAction = player1InputController->DetermineAction();
        playerMovement = player1InputController->DetermineAnalogMovement();

        escapeKeyPressed = CheckForEscapeKey();
        if (escapeKeyPressed) {
                playerAction = kPauseGame;
        }
}
else {
        playerAction = ReadKeyboard();
}
```

If the player has an HID device on his computer, reading player input is nearly identical to reading input on Mac OS 8 and 9. Because of the lack of keyboard support in the HID Manager, we must explicitly check whether the player pressed the Esc key so that we can pause the game. Fortunately, the code to do so is pretty simple, as you can see here:

```
Boolean CheckForEscapeKey(void)
{
        KeyMap currentKeyboardState;
        GetKeys(currentKeyboardState);

        Boolean result;
        result = WasKeyPressed(kEscapeKey, currentKeyboardState);
        return result;
}
```

Refer to the section, "Reading the Keyboard Directly," in Chapter 9, "Reading the Keyboard and Mouse Plus Event Handling," for the source code to the WasKeyPressed() function. If the player does not have an HID device, we must read the keyboard directly. Reading the keyboard is a little tedious, especially for movement, as you can see in the following function:

```
InputControllerAction GameApp::ReadKeyboard(void)
{
        KeyMap currentKeyboardState;
        GetKeys(currentKeyboardState);

        Boolean movedUp = false;
        Boolean movedDown = false;
        Boolean movedLeft = false;
        Boolean movedRight = false;

        // Check for pause game and attack actions
        if (WasKeyPressed(kEscapeKey, currentKeyboardState)) {
                player1InputController->SetXAxisValue(kAxisCenterValue);
                player1InputController->SetYAxisValue(kAxisCenterValue);
                return kPauseGame;
        }
        else if (WasKeyPressed (kSpaceBar, currentKeyboardState)) {
                player1InputController->SetXAxisValue(kAxisCenterValue);
                player1InputController->SetYAxisValue(kAxisCenterValue);
                return kAttack;
         }


        // Check for player movement
        if (WasKeyPressed(kUpArrow, currentKeyboardState)){
                movedUp = true;
                player1InputController->SetYAxisValue(kAxisMinimumValue);
        }

        if (WasKeyPressed(kDownArrow, currentKeyboardState)){
                movedDown = true;
                player1InputController->SetYAxisValue(kAxisMaximumValue);
        }

        if (WasKeyPressed(kLeftArrow, currentKeyboardState)){
                movedLeft = true;
```

```
                player1InputController->SetXAxisValue(kAxisMinimumValue);
        }

        if (WasKeyPressed(kRightArrow, currentKeyboardState)) {
                movedRight = true;
                player1InputController->SetXAxisValue(kAxisMaximumValue);
        }

        if ((!movedUp) && (!movedDown)) {
                player1InputController->SetYAxisValue(kAxisCenterValue);
        }

        if ((!movedLeft) && (!movedRight)) {
                player1InputController->SetXAxisValue(kAxisCenterValue);
        }

        // Determine direction of movement
        if ((movedUp) && (movedLeft))
                return kMoveUpAndLeft;
        else if ((movedUp) && (movedRight))
                return kMoveUpAndRight;
        else if ((movedDown) && (movedLeft))
                return kMoveDownAndLeft;
        else if ((movedDown) && (movedRight))
                return kMoveDownAndRight;

        // At this point, we know the movement is not diagonal
        else if (movedUp)
                return kMoveUp;
        else if (movedDown)
                return kMoveDown;
        else if (movedLeft)
                return kMoveLeft;
        else if (movedRight)
                return kMoveRight;
        else
                return kNoMovement;
}
```

After we determine the player's input, we plug it into our game's physics and animation systems. For the physics, we use the values of xAxisValue and yAxisValue to calculate the amount of force to plug into the physics system, as you can see in the following code:

```
Vector2D GameApp::CalculatePlayerForce(void)
{
        Vector2D result;

        result.SetXComponent(player1InputController->GetXAxisValue() *
                player1->GetMass() * 2.0);
        result.SetYComponent(player1InputController->GetYAxisValue() *
                player1->GetMass() * 2.0);

        return result;
}
```

The force the player applies when moving equals the amount the player moved the joystick multiplied by the player's mass times 2. I experimented with different force values, and this formula produced good movement. After calculating the force, we can call our PhysicsController class's UpdatePhysics() function to move the player, as you can see in this code:

```
void GameApp::AnimatePlayer(InputControllerAction playerAction)
{
        // Only the physics code appears here.
        // Refer to the source code on the CD-ROM for
        // the full source.

        Vector2D forceVector = CalculatePlayerForce();

        // timeStep, currentLevel, and currentTileList are
        // data members of the GameApp class
        player1PhysicsController->UpdatePhysics(playerAction, &forceVector,
                timeStep, currentLevel, currentTileList);
}
```

Updating the animation is easier than updating the physics. One call to our AnimationController() class's UpdateAnimation() call, and we're finished. Here's the function call:

```
player1AnimationController->UpdateAnimation(playerAction);
```

Moving the Enemies

Moving the enemies involves the same steps as moving the player. We determine each enemy's action, and then we update the physics and animation for each enemy. Instead of reading the joystick or keyboard as we did for the player, however, the AIController class we developed in Chapter 12, "Beginning Artificial Intelligence," tells us which action the enemy performed. We use that action to calculate the force, move the enemy, and update its animation. The following functions move the enemies:

```
void GameApp::AnimateEnemies(void)
{
        Iterator enemyListIterator(&enemyList);
        GameEnemyPtr currentEnemy = nil;
        InputControllerAction enemyAction;

        // Use the player's position to determine the enemy's action.
        short playerCenterX = player1->GetWorldX() + (kPlayerSpriteWidth / 2);
        short playerCenterY = player1->GetWorldY() + (kPlayerSpriteHeight / 2);

        do {
                // listIterator.Next provides us the link to the current missile
                currentEnemy = (GameEnemyPtr)enemyListIterator.Next();
                if (currentEnemy != nil) {
                        enemyAIController->SetModelToControl(currentEnemy);
                        enemyAction = enemyAIController-
>PerformManeuver(playerCenterX,
                                playerCenterY, currentLevel, currentTileList);
                        MoveEnemy(currentEnemy, enemyAction);
                }
        } while (currentEnemy != nil);
}

void GameApp::MoveEnemy(GameEnemyPtr enemy, InputControllerAction theAction)
{
        PhysicsController enemyPhysicsController;
        enemyPhysicsController.SetModelToControl(enemy);

        Vector2D forceVector = enemy->CalculateForce();

        enemyPhysicsController.UpdatePhysics(theAction, &forceVector, timeStep,
```

```
            currentLevel, currentTileList);

    AnimationController enemyAnimationController;
    enemyAnimationController.SetModelToControl(enemy);
    enemyAnimationController.UpdateAnimation(theAction);
}
```

Moving the Missiles

A missile gains life when the player fires his weapon. At launch, we must determine the missile's initial location and force. The missile's initial location depends on the player's position and the direction he is facing, as you can see in Figure 16-2.

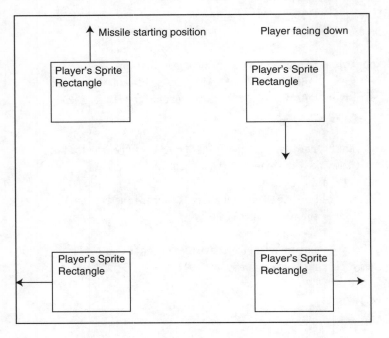

Figure 16-2

The player's direction influences the missile's initial location.

The missile's starting horizontal position can be the player's left edge, right edge, or horizontal center. It will be the left edge if the player faces left, the right edge if the player faces right, and the horizontal center if the player faces up or down, as you can see in the following function:

```
short GameApp::DetermineMissileStartX(GameSpritePtr attacker)
{
        // If the attacker faces up or down, the missile starts
```

```
// at the horizontal center of the attacker. If the attacker
// faces left, the missile starts at the left edge of the attacker.
// If the attacker faces right, the missile starts at the right
// edge of the attacker.

short leftEdge = attacker->GetWorldX();
short attackerCenterX = leftEdge + 8;
short rightEdge = leftEdge + attacker->GetSpriteWidth();

SpriteDirection missileDirection = attacker->GetSpriteDirection();

switch (missileDirection) {
        case kSpriteFacingUp:
                return attackerCenterX;
                break;

        case kSpriteFacingDown:
                return attackerCenterX;
                break;

        case kSpriteFacingLeft:
                return leftEdge;
                break;

        case kSpriteFacingRight:
                return rightEdge;
                break;

        default:
                return 0;
                break;
    }
    return 0;
}
```

Calculating the starting vertical position works in much the same way it does for
the starting horizontal position. If the player is facing up, the starting vertical position will be the top edge of the player sprite. The starting vertical position will be
the bottom edge of the sprite if the player faces left, and it will be the vertical center if the player faces left or right, as you can see in the following routine:

```
short GameApp::DetermineMissileStartY(GameSpritePtr attacker)
```

```
{
        // If the attacker faces left or right, the missile starts
        // at the vertical center of the attacker. If the attacker
        // faces up, the missile starts at the top edge of the attacker.
        // If the attacker faces down, the missile starts at the bottom
        // edge of the attacker.

        short topEdge = attacker->GetWorldY();
        short attackerCenterY = topEdge + 8;
        short bottomEdge = topEdge + attacker->GetSpriteHeight();

        SpriteDirection missileDirection = attacker->GetSpriteDirection();

        switch (missileDirection) {
                case kSpriteFacingUp:
                        return topEdge;
                        break;

                case kSpriteFacingDown:
                        return bottomEdge;
                        break;

                case kSpriteFacingLeft:
                        return attackerCenterY;
                        break;

                case kSpriteFacingRight:
                        return attackerCenterY;
                        break;

                default:
                        return 0;
                        break;
        }
        return 0;
}
```

After calculating the missile's starting position, we must give it an initial force so
that it will be able to move. What I do is determine the direction the missile is facing (the missile faces the same direction as the creature that fired it), and give it a
force in that direction. I used a constant, kBoltForceMagnitude, which represents the

initial magnitude of the force. I experimented with different values, found a value that produced realistic missile movement, and gave that value to kBoltForceMagnitude. The following code computes the initial force for the newly launched missile:

```
void GameWeapon::CalculateInitialForce(SpriteDirection missileDirection)
{
        double xComponent;
        double yComponent;

        switch (missileDirection) {
                case kSpriteFacingUp:
                        xComponent = kStandingSpeed;
                        yComponent = kBoltForceMagnitude * -1.0;
                        break;

                case kSpriteFacingDown:
                        xComponent = kStandingSpeed;
                        yComponent = kBoltForceMagnitude;
                        break;

                case kSpriteFacingLeft:
                        xComponent = kBoltForceMagnitude * -1.0;
                        yComponent = kStandingSpeed;
                        break;

                case kSpriteFacingRight:
                        xComponent = kBoltForceMagnitude;
                        yComponent = kStandingSpeed;
                        break;

                default:
                        xComponent = kStandingSpeed;
                        yComponent = kStandingSpeed;
                        break;
        }

        // currentForce is a data member of the GameWeapon class
        currentForce.SetXComponent(xComponent);
         currentForce.SetYComponent(yComponent);
}
```

After the missile launches, gravity acts upon the missile, slowing it down until it hits the ground, as you can see in Figure 16-3. Remember from Chapter 11, "Physics," that in a 2D world like our game has, gravity acts in the opposite direction of the direction the missile is moving. If gravity moved downward like it does in a 3D world, all of our game's missiles would move south, which is not what we want in this case.

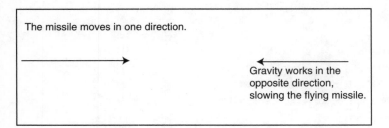

Figure 16-3

How gravity affects a flying missile.

To make the missile respond to the laws of natural physics, we determine the missile's direction and apply gravity in the opposite direction, slowing the missile. This routine applies gravity to the flying missile:

```
void GameWeapon::CalculateCurrentForce(double timeStep)
{
      // Apply gravity to the current force

      Vector2D gravityForce;

      double oldXComponent;
      double oldYComponent;

      oldXComponent = currentForce.GetXComponent();
      oldYComponent = currentForce.GetYComponent();

      double gravityMagnitude = kGravityAcceleration * GetMass() * timeStep;
      SpriteDirection missileDirection = GetSpriteDirection();

      switch (missileDirection) {
            case kSpriteFacingUp:
                  gravityForce.SetXComponent(kStandingSpeed);
                  gravityForce.SetYComponent(gravityMagnitude * -1.0);
                  break;
```

```
        case kSpriteFacingDown:
                gravityForce.SetXComponent(kStandingSpeed);
                gravityForce.SetYComponent(gravityMagnitude);
                break;

        case kSpriteFacingLeft:
                gravityForce.SetXComponent(gravityMagnitude * -1.0);
                gravityForce.SetYComponent(kStandingSpeed);
                break;

        case kSpriteFacingRight:
                gravityForce.SetXComponent(gravityMagnitude);
                gravityForce.SetYComponent(kStandingSpeed);
                break;

        default:
                gravityForce.SetXComponent(kStandingSpeed);
                gravityForce.SetYComponent(kStandingSpeed);
                break;
    }

  double newXComponent;
 double newYComponent;

 newXComponent = oldXComponent + gravityForce.GetXComponent();
 newYComponent = oldYComponent + gravityForce.GetYComponent();

 currentForce.SetXComponent(newXComponent);
 currentForce.SetYComponent(newYComponent);
}
```

Collisions

This section focuses on collisions at a higher level than we did in Chapter 11, "Physics." In our game, we must handle collisions between the following objects:

- Collisions between the player and items he can pick up in the game
- Collisions between the player and the enemies
- Collisions between the enemies and missiles

None of the enemies in the game can fire missiles. That is why we do not have to check for collisions between the missiles and the player character. There are four items the player can acquire in our game: crossbow bolts, coins, gems, and healing potions. When the player collides with an item in the level, he should pick up the item, as you can see in the following code:

```
Boolean GamePlayer::TakeItem(GameItemPtr theItem)
{
        switch (theItem->GetWhatItIs()) {
                case kBolts:
                        return (TakeBolts());
                        break;

                case kCoins:
                        return (TakeCoins());
                        break;

                case kGems:
                        return (TakeGems());
                        break;

                case kHealingPotion:
                        return (TakeHealingPotion());
                        break;

                default:
                        return false;
                        break;
        }
        return false;
}
```

When the player comes across some crossbow bolts, we first check to see whether the player has the maximum number of bolts he can carry. If he can't carry any more, we don't let the player pick up the new bolts. If he can carry additional bolts, we update the player's ammunition count to reflect the bolts he just acquired, and then we remove the bolts from the game level. The following function handles the situation in which the player acquires new crossbow bolts:

```
Boolean GamePlayer::TakeBolts(void)
{
        if (ammo >= kMaximumCrossbowAmmo) {
```

```
            return false;
        }
        else {
            ammo = ammo + kIncrementCrossbowAmmo;
            if (ammo > kMaximumCrossbowAmmo)
                ammo = kMaximumCrossbowAmmo;
            return true;
        }
    }
```

Taking coins and gems is simpler than crossbow bolts because there's no limit to the number of coins and gems the player can take. We just add to the player's score. In the current version of the game, I don't do anything with the player's score, but you could use the score to add a role-playing element to the game. For example, when the player hits a certain score, he can rise to another level, letting him inflict more damage to enemies and take more damage from enemies. The following function handles the player acquiring coins (the code for acquiring gems is remarkably similar):

```
Boolean GamePlayer::TakeCoins(void)
{
    score = score + kCoinsScore;
    return true;
}
```

Grabbing a healing potion works similarly to grabbing crossbow bolts. We check to see whether the player is at full health. If he is, we don't let the player take the potion. Otherwise, we take the potion and increase the player's health, as you can see in the following code:

```
Boolean GamePlayer::TakeHealingPotion(void)
{
    if (currentHitPoints == totalHitPoints) {
        return false;
    }
    else {
        currentHitPoints = currentHitPoints + kHealingPotionHealingValue;
        if (currentHitPoints > totalHitPoints)
            currentHitPoints = totalHitPoints;
        return true;
    }
}
```

The code that handles collisions between the player and his enemies and the code that handles collisions between the enemies and the missiles the player fires are similar. If an enemy hits the player, we reduce the player's health by the amount of damage the enemy inflicts. If a missile hits an enemy, we reduce the enemy's hit points by the amount of damage the missile inflicts. The following function shows how a player takes a hit from an enemy. The code for an enemy taking a hit is similar:

```
void GamePlayer::TakeHit(GameWeaponPtr weaponThatHit)
{
        currentHitPoints = currentHitPoints - weaponThatHit->GetDamage();
}
```

Determining the amount of damage the weapons inflict is completely arbitrary. You can let a weapon inflict as much damage as you wish. The amount of hit points creatures have in the game and the damage each weapon inflicts are values you will experiment with during the development of your game to make sure the game is balanced.

Scrolling

In Chapter 5, "Tiles and Scrolling," I covered the low-level details of scrolling the screen, so I'm not going to do it again here. This section covers scrolling at a higher level. Because scrolling the screen forces us to draw the entire screen, we want to do it as little as possible. To minimize the amount of scrolling we must do, we scroll only when the player approaches the edge of the screen. So each time through the game loop, we check the player's position. If he's too close to one of the edges of the screen, we scroll in the appropriate direction.

Another thing we must check is whether or not we actually scrolled. If the player comes to the edge of the level, there won't be any actual scrolling because there's nowhere to scroll. The scrolling functions return how many tiles we scrolled; if they return a value greater than 0, we know we scrolled.

You might wonder why it matters whether or not the screen scrolled. If the player reaches the edge of the level, can't we just draw the frame? That's what I thought when I began writing the code for this book. When I implemented the code, a problem occurred. To speed up the drawing code, I had two ways of drawing to the screen: one way when the screen scrolled and another way when the screen didn't scroll. When the player came to the edge of the level, he triggered a scroll, but there was nowhere to scroll. The sprite did not erase properly in this case, leaving remnants of itself on the screen. To have the player character's sprite show up on the screen correctly, I had to check for an actual scroll. Now you can see the revised code that scrolls the screen inside the game loop:

```
void GameApp::ScrollBackground(void)
{
        short playerScreenTop = player1->GetWorldY() - (context->GetVOffset() *
kTileHeight);
        short playerScreenBottom = playerScreenTop + player1->GetSpriteHeight();
        short playerScreenLeft = player1->GetWorldX() - (context->GetHOffset() *
kTileWidth);
        short playerScreenRight = playerScreenLeft + player1->GetSpriteWidth();

        // If we're too close to the edge of the screen, scroll
        // in the appropriate direction.

        short scrollBoundaryTop = kTileHeight * 2;
        short scrollBoundaryLeft = kTileWidth * 2;

        short tilesScrolledUp = 0;
        if (playerScreenTop < scrollBoundaryTop) {
                tilesScrolledUp = context->ScrollUp(currentLevel, kEightTiles);
        }

        short tilesScrolledLeft = 0;
        if (playerScreenLeft < scrollBoundaryLeft) {
                tilesScrolledLeft = context->ScrollLeft(currentLevel, kEightTiles);
        }

        short scrollBoundaryBottom = context->GetScreenHeight() - (kTileHeight * 2);
        short scrollBoundaryRight = context->GetScreenWidth() - (kTileWidth * 2);

        short tilesScrolledDown = 0;
        if (playerScreenBottom > scrollBoundaryBottom) {
                tilesScrolledDown = context->ScrollDown(currentLevel, kEightTiles);
        }

        short tilesScrolledRight = 0;
        if (playerScreenRight > scrollBoundaryRight) {
                tilesScrolledRight = context->ScrollRight(currentLevel, kEightTiles);
        }
```

```
      // Test if we actually scrolled. This fixes a problem
      // where fragments of the sprite do not erase when the
      // sprite approaches the edge of the level.
      if (tilesScrolledUp > 0)
              screenScrolled = true;
      else if (tilesScrolledDown > 0)
              screenScrolled = true;
      else if (tilesScrolledLeft > 0)
              screenScrolled = true;
      else if (tilesScrolledRight > 0)
              screenScrolled = true;
}
```

Rendering the Frame

When drawing the frame, we want to know whether or not the screen scrolled this
frame. For most of this book, we have been using dirty rectangle animation, which
draws only the parts of the screen that have changed since the last frame. In our
dirty rectangle animation system, we have a 2D array that marks which areas of the
screen we must draw. We go through the entire array each frame, checking
whether or not that area is dirty, and then drawing only the dirty areas.

When the screen scrolls, however, the entire screen changes. In this case, it's stupid
to check for dirty rectangles because the entire array is dirty. It's faster to just
redraw the entire screen. What we want to do is check for a screen scroll. If we have
to scroll, we draw the entire screen; if we don't scroll, we draw with dirty rectangles,
as you can see in this function:

```
void GameApp::RenderFrame(void)
{
      if (screenScrolled) {
              // Redraw the whole screen because a scroll will
              // mark all rectangles as dirty. One big draw is
              // faster than drawing the whole screen one tile at a time.
              RenderScreen();
      }
      else {
              RenderDirtyRectangles();
      }
}
```

Drawing the screen is relatively easy because the scrolling filled the back buffer with tiles. All we have to do is draw the sprites into the back buffer, then copy the back buffer to the screen. The following function draws the entire screen when a scroll occurs:

```
void GameApp::RenderScreen(void)
{
        // Get the current screen resolution
        GDHandle mainDevice = nil;
        mainDevice = GetMainDevice();
        Rect screenRect = (**mainDevice).gdRect;

        DrawMissilesOffscreen();
        DrawEnemiesOffscreen();
        DrawPlayerOffscreen();

        // Draw the entire offscreen buffer to the screen
        gameBlitter->Setup(context->GetFrontBuffer(), screenRect, screenRect);
        gameBlitter->DrawImageToScreen();

        // Let the game know we handled the scroll so we don't
        // do it again.
         screenScrolled = false;
        context->CleanDirtyRectTable();
}
```

Drawing with dirty rectangles involves a little more work. First, we must go through the dirty rectangle table and draw the tiles that are dirty. Then we draw the sprites. If we had any foreground tiles, we would draw them after the sprites, but in our game we don't have foreground tiles. The following code draws with dirty rectangles:

```
void GameApp::RenderDirtyRectangles(void)
{
        short rowCount = context->GetScreenHeight() / kTileHeight;
        short columnCount = context->GetScreenWidth() / kTileWidth;
        Rect dirtyRect;

        // Draw the dirty tiles
        for (short row = 0; row < rowCount; row++) {
                for (short column = 0; column < columnCount; column++) {
                        if (context->IsRectangleDirty(row, column)) {
```

```
                              // Draw the tile to the offscreen buffer
                              context->DrawTileFromLevelMap(currentLevel, row, col-
umn);

                              // Copy to the screen
                              dirtyRect = context->GetDirtyRect(row, column);
                              gameBlitter->Setup(context->GetFrontBuffer(),
dirtyRect, dirtyRect);

                              gameBlitter->DrawImageToScreen();
                         }
                    }
          }

          DrawMissilesOffscreen();
          DrawEnemiesOffscreen();
          DrawPlayerOffscreen();
          DrawMissilesToScreen();
          DrawEnemiesToScreen();
          DrawPlayerToScreen();

          // We did all our drawing so we can clean the table
          context->CleanDirtyRectTable();
}
```

Summary

We've done it! It took a lot of effort, but we wrote an entire game. This chapter
put the finishing touches on the game. We began the chapter by covering what it
takes to examine the player's system to see whether or not he can play the game.
The Gestalt() function tells you various aspects about the player's system. You
supply Gestalt() with an aspect you want to know, and Gestalt() returns the gory
details.

Next we examined the game loop. The game loop begins by calculating the time
that passed since the start of the previous frame. Carbon gives us three functions to
compute the elapsed time. TickCount() is the easiest to use but is the least accuracy.
Microseconds() provide more accuracy but are harder to use. UpTime() provides the
most accuracy and requires the most work if you are to use the results.

After we compute the time that elapsed since the last frame, we read input from
the player. We use the elapsed time and the player input to move the objects in the

game. The player character moves based on the player's input; the enemies move based on the artificial intelligence code we wrote in Chapters 12, "Beginning Artificial Intelligence," and 13, "Pathfinding."

The next two steps in the game loop are conditional. The background music in our game repeats to minimize the amount of memory we need to play the game. To perform the musical looping, we check once per frame to see whether we hit the end of the song. If so, we go back to the beginning of song and replay it. The next step is to check the player's position. If he is too close to the edge of the screen, we scroll the screen.

The last step in the game loop is rendering the frame. How we draw the frame depends on whether or not the screen scrolled. If the screen scrolled, we know we've rebuilt the entire back buffer during the scroll. We can just draw the sprites to the back buffer and copy the contents of the back buffer to the screen. If the screen did not scroll, we must check each tile to see whether it has to be redrawn. If so, we draw the tile. After drawing the tiles, we draw the sprites.

The game we have been working on since Chapter 4 is now finished, but don't stop reading yet. The three appendices provide you with information and tips you will find helpful when writing your own games.

CHAPTER 17

UNDERSTANDING THE GAME'S SOURCE CODE

Over the course of this book, we have built a complete game. It's not the most technically challenging game ever written, but it is a game nevertheless. Even a game as simple as the one we've made in this book has many components: graphics, animation, sound, physics, artificial intelligence, and the game logic itself. It's a lot to comprehend, considering that you do not have the familiarity with the code that I gained by writing the program. To make it easier for you to understand the game code I wrote, I have written this chapter, which describes all the classes in the game and their interactions with each other. After reading this chapter, you should have an easier time navigating through the source code files on the CD-ROM that accompanies this book.

Building the Class List

Before I describe all the classes that make up the game, I want to tell you how I assembled the list of classes. Believe it or not, the class list did not magically appear in my head. I began by deciding what type of game I wanted to write for the book. Then I made an initial list of what the game needed, which became the initial class list. I refined the list further to create the final list of classes. The sections that follow describe my process of creating the class list.

Choosing the Game to Write

When I was developing the proposal for this book, I knew that I wanted to create a working game. Many game programming books cover their topics (graphics, sound, networking, and so on) in a vacuum. The graphics examples only display graphics. The networking examples send text messages, and the AI examples use crude graphics to demonstrate the AI techniques. Although you can build on these examples to make a complete game, doing so requires much effort, especially if you're a beginner. If you've never written a game before, you may not be aware of all the little details that go into programming a computer game. By writing a full game in the book, I provide a map for the beginner that shows what it takes to develop a complete game.

Deciding on the type of game to write in the book required careful thought. I wanted it to be an action game because action games use more processor power than slower-paced games such as solitaire or checkers. Processor-intensive games force the programmer to write efficient code. The game also had to encompass all the topics I planned to cover in the book: graphics, player input, sound, physics, and artificial intelligence. The project also had to be one that I could program alone. I figured that most of the people who purchased this book would be programming alone. It wouldn't be fair if I used a team of programmers to make a game and then expected you to write a game of similar quality by yourself.

The number of requirements I had for the project limited my genre choices. Board games, turn-based strategy games, and role-playing games lacked the action element. First-person shooters, real-time strategy games, flight simulators, and adventure games were too big for one programmer to complete. After weighing my options, I chose a game that combined action and role-playing elements, somewhere between the classic game *Gauntlet* and the old *Legend of Zelda* games on Super Nintendo. This type of game would let me demonstrate all the topics I wanted to cover in the game; the game's use of 2D graphics would let me write the game alone.

Creating an Initial Class List

After choosing the kind of game I wanted to create, I had to start designing the program by listing all the classes the game would need. From a gameplay standpoint, I knew I needed classes for the player, the enemies he will encounter in the game, and items for the player to acquire. It's difficult to have a game without the player, and a *Gauntlet*-style game requires enemies for the player to fight. Because the player and enemies fight in the game, I needed a weapon class to store the various weapons the player can use in the game. Because the game world required levels to explore, I added a level class to the list. Players would want to be able to save games and resume them at another time, so I needed a saved game class. Just by considering my game's gameplay needs, I had already assembled a list of six classes, which you can see in Table 17-1.

Table 17-1   Initial Class List

Class	Description
GamePlayer	The player character in the game.table text.
GameEnemy	The creatures with whom the player will battle in the game.
GameItem	Items the player can acquire in the game.
GameWeapon	The weapons the players and enemies can use in the game.
GameLevel	The levels the player navigates in the game.
SavedGame	Games the player can save and resume playing later.

Next I moved from the game logic to the technical elements I would need in the game: graphics, sound, player input, physics, and AI. Because my game was going to be a 2D game, I needed tiles for the backgrounds and sprites for the characters, adding two more classes to the list. I wanted audio in the game, so I needed a class to play sound effects and game music. I needed a class to read player input as well as a class to implement the game world's physics. The enemies in the game would require artificial intelligence, resulting in the addition of at least one more class to the list. By walking through the game in my mind and determining the game's needs, I assembled an initial list of 12 classes. Table 17-2 lists the classes at this stage in the game's design.

Table 17-2   Class List After Technical Element Review

Class	Description
GamePlayer	The player character in the game.table text.
GameEnemy	The creatures with whom the player will battle in the game.
GameItem	Items the player can acquire in the game.
GameWeapon	The weapons the players and enemies can use in the game.
GameLevel	The levels the player navigates in the game.
SavedGame	Games the player can save and resume playing later.
GameTile	The tiles that make up the game's levels.
GameSprite	The player, enemies, and items in the game use sprites to appear on the screen.
GameSound	The sounds that play in the game.
InputController	Reads player input in the game.
PhysicsController	Implements the physics of the game world.
AIController	Implements the artificial intelligence of the game's enemies.

Building on the Initial List

From my initial list of classes, I went on to choose the technology I wanted to use to implement the various parts of the game. For graphics, I decided to use QuickDraw for the drawing and DrawSprocket for hiding the menu bar and having the game

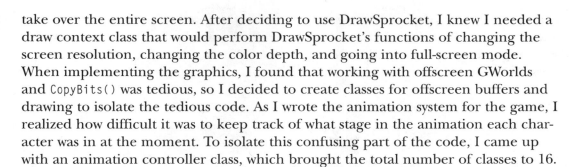

take over the entire screen. After deciding to use DrawSprocket, I knew I needed a draw context class that would perform DrawSprocket's functions of changing the screen resolution, changing the color depth, and going into full-screen mode. When implementing the graphics, I found that working with offscreen GWorlds and `CopyBits()` was tedious, so I decided to create classes for offscreen buffers and drawing to isolate the tedious code. As I wrote the animation system for the game, I realized how difficult it was to keep track of what stage in the animation each character was in at the moment. To isolate this confusing part of the code, I came up with an animation controller class, which brought the total number of classes to 16.

Initially, I thought I would need only one class for reading input from the player. One version of the class would use InputSprocket and run on Mac OS 8 and 9, and the second version would use the HID Manager and run on Mac OS X. With InputSprocket, a single input controller class worked wonderfully, but the HID Manager complicated things. To use the HID Manager, I had to write my own dialog boxes to configure the game's controls, adding another class to the growing list. Working with input devices and their elements was awkward as well, so I added classes for input devices and input device elements, bringing the total number of classes to 19.

I originally wanted to use only the Sound Manager for the game's sound, resulting in a single game sound class. After doing some research, I learned that the Sound Manager's functions to play a sound from an external file did not make it into Carbon. To play longer sounds, I had to use QuickTime. QuickTime proved to be good at playing songs, but not as good at playing short sounds such as sound effects. I had to add a second sound class: one that used the Sound Manager and one that used QuickTime, pushing the class total to 20.

The game's physics fit into one class nicely. However, I decided to use vectors to store the game characters' position, velocity, and acceleration information, which added a vector class to my class list and brought the growing class total to 21.

Artificial intelligence proved to be difficult to design. I used finite state machines and pathfinding to create the AI, and I added classes to support these two elements, pushing the class total to 23. I also needed to perform maneuvers for the game's enemies, such as chasing and patrolling; I decided to handle these actions in the original artificial intelligence class.

At this point, my list of classes had become quite long for a game that was supposed to be simple enough to program alone. I needed a central class to coordinate all the other classes and play the game, making the final number of classes 24. Now I had a list of classes, and I was ready to design all of them.

During the design process, I learned that I needed a class for the game's drawing environment, and a class to implement linked lists, pushing the class total to 26. I separated the finite state machine class into machine, state, and state transition classes to give me a final list of 28 classes, which you can see in Table 17-3.

Table 17-3 Final Class List

Class	Description
GamePlayer	The player character in the game.table text.
GameEnemy	The creatures with whom the player will battle in the game.
GameItem	Items the player can acquire in the game.
GameWeapon	The weapons the players and enemies can use in the game.
GameLevel	The levels the player navigates in the game.
SavedGame	Games the player can save and resume playing later.
GameTile	The tiles that make up the game's levels.
GameSprite	The player, enemies, and items in the game use sprites to appear on the screen.
GameSound	The sounds that play in the game that use the Sound Manager.
InputController	Reads player input in the game.
PhysicsController	Implements the physics of the game world.
AIController	Implements the artificial intelligence of the game's enemies.
DrawContext	Puts the game into full-screen mode and changes the screen resolution.
GameOffscreenBuffer	Deals with the details of working with offscreen buffers in the game.
Blitter	Deals with the details of drawing, either to an offscreen buffer or to the screen.
AnimationController	Keeps track of each character's animation stage.
ConfigurationDialog	Configures the game control's if the player uses the HID Manager.

Class	Description
InputDevice	Deals with the details of working with HID Manager input devices.
InputDeviceElement	Deals with the details of working with the elements that make up HID input devices.
GameSong	Plays musical sequences with QuickTime.
Vector2D	Implements the vectors that the physics engine uses to calculate each character's position, velocity, and acceleration.
FiniteStateMachine	Implements a finite state machine the game uses for the enemies' artificial intelligence.
Pathfinder	Implements the game's pathfinding.
GameApp	Handles the game logic. It coordinates the activity among all the other classes.
GameContext	Coordinates the game's drawing environment.
LinkedList	Handles the linked lists used in numerous places during the game.
FiniteState	Deals with one individual state in a finite state machine.
StateTransition	Handles the transition from one state to another in a finite state machine.

Designing with CRC Cards

After reading this section header, I'm sure that your first question is, "What does CRC stand for?" CRC stands for Class, Responsibilities, and Collaborators; a *CRC card* lists the responsibilities and collaborators for one class in a program.

CRC cards provide a quick and easy method for designing an object-oriented program. All you need is a stack of index cards or a notebook; no fancy computer equipment required. Take a card (or sheet of paper) and write the class name at the top. Then make two columns titled *Responsibilities* and *Collaborators*. In the *Responsibilities* column, list the functions the class should perform. In the *Collaborators* column, list the other classes with which the class interacts to perform its functions.

As an example, let's look at the `Pathfinder` class we covered in Chapter 13, "Pathfinding." A `Pathfinder` object must calculate a path from a particular location, so path calculation becomes a responsibility of the `Pathfinder` class. To compute the path, the `Pathfinder` object requires knowledge of the game world. Because we know that the `GameLevel` class contains the map of the level, the `GameLevel` class is one of the `Pathfinder` class's collaborators. We don't want the pathfinder to find a path that makes the enemy walk through walls; when the enemy encounters a wall tile, the enemy should be blocked from proceeding in that direction. The `GameTile` class stores information about tiles, so the `GameTile` class is also a collaborator of the `Pathfinder` class.

When you create CRC cards for each class in your game, you design your game's program as well as gain an understanding of how the classes interact. The *Responsibilities* column of each class tells you the functions you must write, while the *Collaborators* column tells you which classes work together.

The Game Classes' CRC Cards

To help you understand how all the different classes work and interact, I spend most of the remainder of this chapter listing the CRC cards for all the classes in the game we've developed in this book. (I know they're technically not "cards," but you get the idea.) I separated the cards into the following sections:

- Graphics
- User Input
- Sound
- Physics
- Artificial Intelligence
- Game Logic (which lists the game-specific classes)
- Utility (which lists utility classes to make development easier)

When I list the collaborators for each class, I list them from the individual class's point of view. Take the `Pathfinder` class example I gave earlier in this chapter. It needs game world data to calculate the paths, so it collaborates with the `GameLevel` and `GameTile` classes. However, the `Pathfinder` class does not appear as a collaborator for the `GameLevel` and `GameTile` classes because the `GameLevel` and `GameTile` classes do not need the `Pathfinder` class to perform their duties. If I chose not to use pathfinding in the game, I would not have to make any changes to the GameLevel and GameTile classes. In other words, collaborations may not be two-way; just because class A collaborates with class B doesn't necessarily mean that class B collaborates with class A.

Graphics Classes

This section shows the CRC cards for the graphics classes in the game: AnimationController, Blitter, DrawContext, GameContext, GameOffscreenBuffer, GameSprite, and GameTile.

Class	
AnimationController	
Responsibilities	**Collaborators**
*Update the current state of the sprite s animation.	*GameSprite

Notes

It can be confusing to determine which sprite to draw for a character in the game. Each character can face one of four directions and can be in the act of standing, running, or fighting. The actions of running and fighting contain multiple animation frames. In addition, the player can hold different weapons. The AnimationController class updates the state of each character s animation to make it easy to find out which sprite the game should draw for the current game frame.

Class

Blitter

Responsibilities	**Collaborators**
*Draw to offscreen buffer. *Draw to screen. *Set drawing mode, such as transparent drawing for sprites and straight pixel copies for tiles.	*GameOffscreenBuffer

Notes

This class simplifies calling CopyBits() to draw graphics. Like the GameOffscreenBuffer class, the Blitter class provides flexibility. For example, if I needed to write a custom blitting function to speed up my drawing, I would just have to modify the Blitter class to use my custom function instead of CopyBits().

Class

DrawContext

Responsibilities

*Set screen to full-screen mode.

*Change screen resolution and color depth.

*Restore screen after game.

Collaborators

*None

Notes

The DrawContext class is the base class for the GameContext class.

Class	
GameContext	

Responsibilities	**Collaborators**
*Draw game background.	*GameLevel
*Scroll screen.	*GameTile
*Store game s graphics, such as its tiles and sprites.	*Blitter
*Maintain the game s dirty rectangle table.	*GameOffscreenBuffer
*Store the screen s width and height.	

Notes

The GameContext class contains the game s drawing environment.

The GameContext class inherits from the DrawContext class.

Class
GameOffscreenBuffer

Responsibilities	Collaborators
*Create the buffer.	*None
*Modify its size and color depth.	
*Draw pictures into it.	

Notes

You might be wondering why I bothered to create a GameOffscreenBuffer class when I could have just used a GWorld variable. I learned not to rely on an Apple technology the hard way working on a game. When I began writing the game, DrawSprocket had its own offscreen buffers for 2D drawing, and I used them in the game. Then, Apple scrapped the DrawSprocket offscreen buffers in Mac OS X, forcing me to use GWorlds. I had to go through my code and change all the variable types to use GWorlds. If I had written a simple OffscreenBuffer class, all I would have had to change was the implementation of the OffscreenBuffer class. You end up benefiting from my previous mistakes.

Class	
GameSprite	

Responsibilities	**Collaborators**
*Store the sprite s position.	*Blitter
*Store the sprite s velocity.	*GameContext
*Store the sprite s width and height.	*GameOffscreenBuffer
*Store which frame to draw.	*AnimationController
*Draw itself offscreen.	

Notes

The GameSprite class serves as the base class for the GamePlayer, GameWeapon, GameEnemy, and GameItem classes.

Class

GameTile

Responsibilities	**Collaborators**
*Store the tile s ID so the game knows which tile to draw. *Store the tile s tile type.	*None

Notes

Related to this class is the GameTileList class, which is an array of GameTile objects. The GameTileList doesn t do anything special to warrant its own CRC card, but it does exist as a class in the game.

User Input Classes

This section shows the CRC cards for the user input classes in the game:
ConfigurationDialog, InputController, InputDevice, and InputDeviceElement.

Class
ConfigurationDialog

Responsibilities	**Collaborators**
*Allow the player to customize the game s controls. *Handle mouse clicks and key presses inside the dialog box. *Handle the player selecting each of the dialog box s items.	*InputController

Notes

The ConfigurationDialog class inherits from the MovableModalDialog class, which handles the basic functions all dialog boxes must handle. The ConfigurationDialog class does the work specific to the configuration dialog box. I use the ConfigurationDialog class with the HID Manager on Mac OS X only.

Class

InputController

Responsibilities

*Configure controls.

*Read button presses.

*Read digital movement.

*Read analog movement.

Collaborators

*InputDevice

*InputDeviceElement

*ConfigurationDialog

Notes

The InputController class collaborates with the InputDevice, InputDeviceElement, and ConfigurationDialog classes in Mac OS X only. On Mac OS 8 and 9, the InputController class uses InputSprocket, which handles the controller configuration for us. InputSprocket also saves us from having to know all the information about an input device and its elements.

Class

InputController

Responsibilities

*Configure controls.

*Read button presses.

*Read digital movement.

*Read analog movement.

Collaborators

*InputDevice

*InputDeviceElement

*ConfigurationDialog

Notes

The InputController class collaborates with the InputDevice, InputDeviceElement, and ConfigurationDialog classes in Mac OS X only. On Mac OS 8 and 9, the InputController class uses InputSprocket, which handles the controller configuration for us. InputSprocket also saves us from having to know all the information about an input device and its elements.

Class

InputDevice

Responsibilities

*Store information about an input device, such as a joystick or gamepad.

Collaborators

*None

Notes

I use the InputDevice class with the HID Manager on Mac OS X only. The InputDevice makes life easier when programming with the HID Manager.

Class

InputDeviceElement

Responsibilities	**Collaborators**
*Store information about an element in an input device, such as a button on a gamepad.	*None

Notes

I use the InputDeviceElement class with the HID Manager on Mac OS X only. The InputDeviceElement class simplifies programming the HID Manager.

Sound Classes

This section lists the CRC cards for the audio classes in the game: GameSong and GameSound.

Class	
GameSong	

Responsibilities	**Collaborators**
*Load song from disk.	*None
*Play song.	
*Pause song.	
*Resume song.	
*Stop song.	
*Loop song.	

Notes

The GameSong class plays QuickTime movies. Its use of QuickTime instead of the Sound Manager is what separates the GameSong class from the GameSound class. I need QuickTime to play the background music and the Sound Manager to play sound effects, which is why there are two sound-related classes.

Class	
GameSound	

Responsibilities	**Collaborators**
*Load sound from disk.	*None
*Play sound.	
*Pause sound.	
*Resume sound.	
*Stop sound.	
*Loop sound.	
*Set sound s volume.	

Notes

Physics Classes

This section shows the CRC cards for the physics classes in the game:
PhysicsController and Vector2D.

Class
PhysicsController

Responsibilities	Collaborators
*Calculate object s position.	*GameSprite
*Calculate object s velocity.	*GameLevel
*Calculate object s acceleration.	*GameTile
*Detect collisions.	*Vector2D
*Resolve collisions.	

Notes

The PhysicsController class handles the physics for the game.

Class

Vector2D

Responsibilities	**Collaborators**
*Add two vectors.	*None
*Subtract two vectors.	
*Multiply by a scalar.	
*Dot product.	
*Determine if two vectors are orthogonal (perpendicular).	

Notes

The game uses the Vector2D class to store each character s position, velocity, and acceleration. As you can tell from the class name, the Vector2D class stores two-dimensional vectors.

Artificial Intelligence Classes

This section displays the CRC cards for the artificial intelligence classes in the game: AIController, FiniteState, FiniteStateMachine, Pathfinder, and StateTransition.

Class
AIController

Responsibilities	Collaborators
*Tell the enemies what to do. *Perform the enemies actions (chase, flee, and patrol). *Coordinate the components of the game s AI system. *Determine whether or not the enemy needs to plan a path to reach the player.	*FiniteStateMachine *Pathfinder *GameEnemy

Notes

Class

FiniteState

Responsibilities	**Collaborators**
*Store the state itself.	*StateTransition
*Store the state s transitions.	
*Perform state transitions.	

Notes

Class

FiniteStateMachine

Responsibilities	**Collaborators**
*Perform state transitions.	**FiniteState
*Store current state.	*StateTransition

Notes

The FiniteStateMachine class performs state transitions by having the current state s FiniteState object perform the state transition.

Class

Pathfinder

Responsibilities

*Calculate paths from one place to another in the game world.

Collaborators

*GameLevel

*GameTile

*LinkedList

Notes

The LinkedList class stores the priority queue for the pathfinder.

Class

StateTransition

Responsibilities

*Store the condition that triggers the state transition.

*Store what the new state will be when the transition occurs.

Collaborators

*FiniteState

Notes

Game Logic Classes

This section shows the CRC cards for the classes that implement the game's logic: GameApp, GameEnemy, GameItem, GameLevel, GamePlayer, GameWeapon, and SavedGame.

Class	
GameApp	

Responsibilities	Collaborators
*Initialize game.	*All the other classes in the game.
*Check player s system to ensure that he can run the game.	
*Load levels.	
*Display dialog boxes to open and save games.	
*Run game loop.	
*Pause game.	
*Resume paused game.	
*Handle the player s menu selections.	
*Handle operating system events.	
*Quit the game.	

Notes

The GameApp class is the central class in the game. It makes all the other classes in the game work together.

Class

GameEnemy

Responsibilities

*Store total hit points.

*Store current hit points.

*Store point value for the player killing the enemy.

*Store the weapon the enemy uses.

*Absorb damage from player s weapon.

*Calculate view rectangle to determine whether the enemy can see the player.

*Calculate patrol rectangle.

Collaborators

*AIController

*GameWeapon

Notes

The GameEnemy class inherits from the GameSprite class.

Class

GameItem

Responsibilities

*Store what the item is.

*Store the item s effect when the player takes it.

Collaborators

Notes

The GameItem class inherits from the GameSprite class.

Class
GameLevel

Responsibilities	Collaborators
*Store which tiles make up the level. *Store the enemies that populate the level. *Store the items the player can acquire in the level. *Load level data in the game.	*GameTile

Notes

The GameLevel class uses the MapElement class to store the tiles that constitute the level and the LevelResident class to store the enemies and items that reside in the class. The MapElement and LevelResident classes do not do enough to necessitate their own CRC cards.

Class

GamePlayer

Responsibilities	**Collaborators**
*Store total hit points. *Store current hit points. *Store player s score. *Store the weapons the player has. *Store the weapon the player is currently using. *Store how much ammunition the player has. *Absorb damage from enemy s weapon.	*GameWeapon *InputController

Notes

The GamePlayer class inherits from the GameSprite class.

Class

GameWeapon

Responsibilities

*Store the type of weapon it is (see notes).

*Store the weapon s range.

*Calculate the damage it inflicts.

Collaborators

*None

Notes

Storing the weapon type allows for interesting gameplay. In a fantasy setting like this game, you can have edged weapons, blunt weapons, fire-based weapons, and cold-based weapons. Creatures can have resistance to certain types of weapons, making them more difficult to kill. You could have many types of weapons to make a really cool game.

The GameWeapon class inherits from the GameSprite class.

Class

SavedGame

Responsibilities

*Read data from the saved game file.

*Write data to the saved game file.

Collaborators

*GameLevel

*GamePlayer

Notes

Utility Class

This section lists the CRC card for the one utility class in the game: LinkedList.

Class

LinkedList

Responsibilities	**Collaborators**
*Add items to list.	*None
*Remove items from list.	
*Store the number of items in the list.	

Notes

The game has no way of knowing how many enemies or items appear in a level until the level loads. A linked list works well when you don t know the size of the list. Plus, when enemies die and the player takes items, you can easily remove them from the list, making the list smaller and quicker to navigate. I use linked lists to store the enemies, items, and flying missiles in the game world at the moment.

The LinkedList class uses two additional classes. The Link class contains one link in the linked list. The Iterator class simplifies navigating the linked list. Neither the Link class nor the Iterator class do enough to warrant individual

Header File Organization

Each class for which I created a CRC card in this chapter has its own header file. Conveniently, I used the class name to name each header file. For example, the header file for the GameSound class has the name GameSound.h. I laid out each header file in the following order:

- Included header files
- Enumerated data types
- Class declarations
- Constants

Each header file has a corresponding source code file that contains the source code for all the class's member functions. Because I used C++ to write the source code, all the source code files have the .cp extension.

Included Header Files

A fact of life when programming in C or C++ is including lots of header files. One problem in C and C++ programming is that you can include each header file once and only once. This can be a problem, especially when doing Mac Carbon programming. Virtually every file must access the Carbon.h header file. The solution is to perform conditional includes so that each header file is included just once. The following code shows an example of a conditional include:

```
#ifndef __CARBON__
  #include <Carbon/Carbon.h>
#endif
```

This statement says that if the compiler has not already included the file Carbon.h in the project, it should do so now. Apple defined the constant __CARBON__ for Carbon programs. You can define constants for your header files so that the compiler includes them once. Following is an example for my Blitter class that you can find in the file Blitter.h:

```
#define BLITTER
```

This statement defines the term BLITTER. In every file where I want to include the file Blitter.h, I write the following statement:

```
#ifndef BLITTER
        #include "Blitter.h"
#endif
```

When compiling the source code files, the first time the compiler finds a file that includes `Blitter.h`, it checks to see whether or not the term `BLITTER` has been defined. If not, it includes `Blitter.h`, which defines the term `BLITTER`. If so, the compiler moves on to the next statement because it has already included `Blitter.h`.

Enumerated Data Types

I use enumerated data types in various places throughout my code to make the code easier to understand. Wherever a class needs an enumerated data type, I define it in the header file before declaring the class. The following example shows the `InputControllerAction` data type that the `InputController` class uses:

```
enum InputControllerAction{
        kNoMovement,
        kNoButtonsPressed,
        kMoveLeft,
        kMoveUpAndLeft,
        kMoveUp,
        kMoveUpAndRight,
        kMoveRight,
        kMoveDownAndRight,
        kMoveDown,
        kMoveDownAndLeft,
        kAttack,
        kChangeWeapon,
        kPauseGame
};
```

To the computer, the `InputControllerAction` data type is just the integers 0 to 12. For somebody reading the code, the `InputControllerAction` data type transforms integers into actions the player can perform in the game. I am sure that you will agree that the value `kMoveUp` is easier to understand than the number 4 when trying to determine which way the player moved.

Class Declarations

Now it's time to declare the class by giving it a name and defining its members. I declare the class data members before the member functions. Most object-oriented software development books say that you should declare the member functions first. They believe that programmers using the class don't have to know the data members because they are not allowed to access them directly anyway. According to other books, the member functions define the way the programmer will use the class, so that's what should appear first. That argument would hold true if I were writing a game development class library that you were using blindly. However, I'm *teaching game programming*, and it is important for you to know the data members as well as the member functions for learning purposes. In reality, it doesn't matter whether you place data members before member functions or member functions before data members. I just feel more comfortable listing the data first; if you don't like this arrangement, you can move the data members so that they follow the member functions.

I declare each class's member functions in the following order:

- Constructors
- Destructor
- Accessor functions
- Other member functions, grouped by category

I wrote each class's data members in the same order I declared them in the header file. I did my best to keep related functions near each other so that you don't have to waste time scrolling through the source code. There's nothing more irritating than following the logic of a program that starts in a function at the beginning of the file and calls a function that appears at the end of the file, which in turn calls a function that appears in the middle of the file. I made it a goal to make the logic of the programs as easy as possible to follow.

After declaring each class, I created data types for pointers and handles to each class, an example of which you can see here:

```
typedef GameLevel* GameLevelPtr;
typedef GameLevel** GameLevelHandle;
```

I think pointer notation is difficult to read, which is why I declared data types for each class. Declaring data types adds only two lines of code to each class, and it makes my code clearer.

Named Constants

When looking through the code samples in this book, you've seen many values that start with the letter k: kTileWidth, kPlayerSpriteWidth, kSleepValue, and kEscapeKey to name a few. These values are named constants, some of which I defined and some of which Apple has defined. Named constants make code easier to read and modify. If I'm checking to see whether or not the player has pressed the Esc key, which of these if statements do you think is easier to understand?

```
if (keyPressed == kEscapeKey)
      PauseGame();


if (keyPressed == 0x3500)
      PauseGame();
```

Those of you who haven't memorized the virtual keycode of the Esc key (which is the hexadecimal number 0x3500, by the way) will find the first if statement easier to comprehend. To the ease of understanding, add the fact that using constants means you have to make only one change when you modify the value of something in your game—such as the sleep value in your event loop—and you can see why I used a lot of named constants in the code for this book.

I placed all the constants each class needs at the end of the header file after declaring the class. Now you know where to look if you want to change the value of one of my constants.

Summary

One of the most difficult tasks in programming is trying to understand code that someone else wrote. Figuring out what someone else wrote becomes more difficult in game programming because even the smallest games are large programs. In addition, the speed requirements for games force programmers to sacrifice code clarity for speed, both execution speed and speed of development. Because this book is supposed to teach you game programming, one of my goals is to make the source code easy to understand; I wrote this chapter to help achieve this goal.

I began the chapter by describing how I came to select the type of game I wrote for the book and how I created my list of classes for the game. Then I explained CRC cards and their use in program design. CRC cards list the tasks each class must perform along with the other classes it collaborates with to perform its tasks. I spent most of the chapter listing the CRC cards for the classes in the game we developed throughout the course of this book. The CRC cards should give you a better grasp of the game's overall design and the interaction between the game's classes.

The chapter finished with an explanation of the format I used to organize the game's header files. Each class for which I wrote a CRC card has a header file and a corresponding source code file. The header file contains the other headers this particular file needs, any enumerated data types the class needs, the class declarations, and any named constants the class requires. Now that you know the organization of the header files, you should be able to more easily navigate through the source code on the CD-ROM that comes with the book.

CHAPTER 18

Optimization

Unlike many genres of software, games have an obsession with speed. Game players want higher-quality graphics and sound, more realistic physics, and more challenging artificial intelligence—all while maintaining a high frame rate. To meet player demand, the game programmer must optimize portions of the game code to maintain acceptable speed while implementing more features.

The game we developed in the book isn't technically demanding, so it does not require much optimization work. However, the game you develop may be more ambitious than the game in this book, which will force you to optimize parts of your game code to achieve a playable game. These are the steps to take to optimize your program:

1. Write your game without worrying about optimization.
2. After you have the game working, test it on your minimum target machine to see whether or not you need to optimize.
3. If you do need to optimize, profile your code to determine where you need to optimize.
4. Optimize.

Write Your Game

Resist the urge to optimize your code while you're writing the game. When you're writing code, you don't know whether you have the need to optimize, and you don't yet know the slow spots in your code. Optimizing before you've finished the game can result in a lot of wasted effort. You might optimize a function and later realize that you have to rewrite that function. If that happens, all the time you spent optimizing the code goes down the drain.

When I say "write your game without worrying about optimization," I don't mean that you should make your code intentionally slow. I mean that you should write clear code so that you can understand what your game is doing. If it happens to be less than optimal from a speed standpoint, so be it. It's hard enough to write a game that works correctly using clear code that's easy to read. Don't make life hard by writing code that's hard to understand in the name of speed before your game even works. When your game works, you can then focus on speed.

As you are writing your game's code, it's okay to decide to use a more efficient algorithm in the game. For example, when I covered collision detection in Chapter 11, "Physics," I covered bounding boxes and pixel-perfect collision detection methods. To determine that two sprites do not collide using bounding boxes requires four tests, one for each side of the bounding box. Pixel-perfect collision detection requires a test for each pixel in the sprite. It takes 1024 tests to determine that two 32-by-32-pixel sprites did not collide. You don't have to be John Carmack to realize that bounding boxes are a faster method to determine that two sprites did not collide. Not worrying about optimization does not mean using bad algorithms. Write clear code at the start.

Test Your Game for Speed

After you complete your game and have it running, you must test the game to ensure that the game is fast enough. To do this, you must determine the computers on which you want to run your game and test the game on a computer at the low end of that spectrum. If you want your game to run on all PowerPC-based Macs, for example, you must get your hands on an old Power Mac, preferably one based on the PowerPC 601 chip. If you're writing a game only for use on Mac OS X, find an old iMac or Power Mac G3 because these machines are the low end of Macs that can run OS X.

Assuming that you own a relatively new Mac and don't own a Mac on the low end of your list of target machines, you have a few options:

- **Try a local school's computer lab.** Schools generally have lots of older machines that would be perfect for your speed tests. If you're a high school or college student, see whether you can use your school's computer lab. If you're not a student, see whether you can use a computer in the lab after school.

- **Join a Mac user group.** Most major metropolitan areas have a local Mac users group. The group may have old Macs; alternatively, one of the other group members might have an old Mac you can use for testing. Apple has a list of Mac user groups on their Apple User Groups Web page at: http://www.apple.com/usergroups

- **Buy an old Mac for testing.** This option is more attractive if you want an old Power Mac (one based on the PowerPC 601, 603e, 604, or 604e chip) than if you want to buy a G3 machine. You can find an old Power Mac for 100 to 200 dollars; G3-based machines run anywhere from 500 to 1,000 dollars.
- **Look for people on the Internet who are willing to test your game's speed.**

After you find a suitable computer for testing, play your game on this machine. If the game plays well, you don't need to speed up your game. Simpler games such as puzzle games, card games, and board games probably don't need a speed boost; action games will probably need to be optimized.

Profile Your Code

After you play your game and determine that it needs to be optimized, you must find the slow parts of the game. If you don't identify which parts of your game must run faster, all your optimization work won't increase the game's speed enough to make a difference.

A *profiler* measures the functions your game calls when it's running and creates a file telling you how many times your game called each function and how much total time the computer spent on that function. The functions on which the computer spends the most time are the functions you need to optimize.

Apple's OS X developer tools come with a variety of tools you can use to analyze your code. The Sampler program takes samples of your game while it's executing and produces a report telling you how many times Sampler saw each function on the function call stack. The gprof tool is a command-line code profiler that measures how much time your game spends in each function. Mac OS X comes with a program called Process Viewer that lets you check how much CPU time and memory your game uses. I will explain these tools in greater detail later in this chapter.

As part of the developer tools package, Apple includes many command-line utilities you may find helpful to measure your code's performance on Mac OS X. Table 18-1 lists the tools you may find useful along with a brief description of each.

Table 18-1   Mac OS X Command-Line Performance Tools

Utility	Description
top	The top utility does what the Process Viewer does, but provides more detailed information. The top tool can give you information such as how many threads your application uses, how much memory the application has for its own use, and how much memory the application shares with other programs.
sc_usage	The sc_usage tool logs all low-level operating system calls. This tool is useful for determining whether or not the operating system had to read from the hard disk and whether or not the memory page was in the cache.
fs_usage	The fs_usage tool logs all file system calls.
vmmap	The vmmap tool displays the layout of virtual memory.

To learn about these tools, run the Terminal application to access the command line; the Terminal application should be in the Utilities folder inside the Applications folder on your hard drive. When you see the command line, type the following for help on a tool:

```
man <tool name>
```

To learn about the top tool, for example, type this:

```
man top
```

The academic and professional versions of CodeWarrior come with a code profiler that's easy to use. Refer to the CodeWarrior documentation for information on using the profiler. If you're programming on Mac OS 8 or 9 with the learning edition of CodeWarrior, you can download the Instrumentation SDK from Apple's developer site. The Instrumentation SDK lets you add profiling information to your code. It hasn't been updated since 1997, so it won't work if you're coding in Mac OS X, but it's a good tool if you're programming on Mac OS 8 or 9 and don't have access to a code profiler.

Using Sampler

The Sampler application resides in the same directory as Project Builder so you shouldn't have much trouble finding and launching it. What you do next depends on whether or not your game is currently running. If it is running, you select Attach from the File menu, which brings up a list of running applications. You then choose your game from the list of running applications.

If your game is not currently running, then choose New from the File menu, which brings up a dialog box like the one shown in Figure 18-1. The Executable field, lets you choose which program you want to sample. Click the Set button to bring up an Open File dialog box from which you can choose a program to sample. Alternatively, you can type the full path name of your program on disk in the Executable field, but you will probably use the Set button. The Executable field also contains a pop-up menu (click the triangle at the right edge) that holds the locations of programs you have profiled with Sampler. If this is your first time using Sampler, the menu will have no entries.

You shouldn't have to use the Arguments field; use this field only if your game takes command-line arguments. The Working Dir field lets you specify a directory in which any files will be saved. The final question is "How would you like Sampler to observe the program?" Most of the time, you will want to choose Sample at Regular Time Intervals. If you are interested in sampling only a handful of functions, you can choose Watch for Calls to Specific Functions.

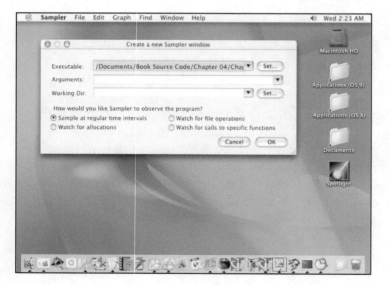

Figure 18-1

The Sampler setup dialog box

After you choose a program to sample, Sampler displays a window like the one shown in Figure 18-2. In this window, you can specify a sampling rate for this particular sampling session. The default value is 20 milliseconds; Apple recommends using a value between 10 and 50 milliseconds. Click the Launch button and then the Sample button to begin sampling; at that time, you begin playing your game.

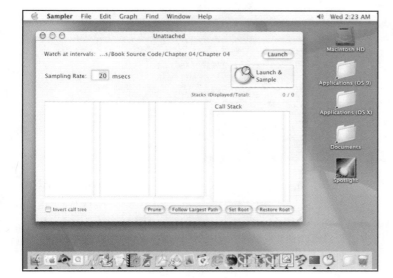

Figure 18-2

The Sampler window before starting a sample

When you're finished sampling, click the Stop Sampling button. It's important to click the Stop Sampling button before you quit playing your game. If you quit your game first, Sampler will not generate a report.

When you stop sampling, the Sampler window will look like the one in Figure 18-3. Sampler displays the Call Stack, which contains a list of the functions your game called along with the hierarchy of functions that led to each function being called. For example, if function A calls function B and function B calls function C, function A appears in the call stack every time your game calls functions A, B, or C. Sampler also displays a call tree (the three windows on the left side of Figure 18-3) telling you the functions a particular function called.

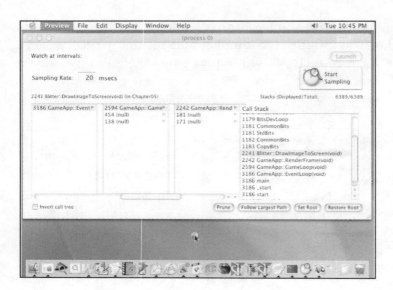

Figure 18-3

The Sampler window after sampling

Now let's interpret the results. First, let me say that to generate the window shown in Figure 18-3, I sampled the scrolling program I wrote for Chapter 5. If you look at the Call Stack window, you see a number followed by a function name. The number represents how many times that particular function appeared in the call stack during the sample. For example, in Figure 18-3, the function `DrawImageToScreen()` in the `Blitter` class appeared in the call stack 2,241 times. This does not necessarily mean that the program *called* `DrawImageToScreen()` 2,241 times. It just means that the function appeared in the call stack 2,241 times. `DrawImageToScreen()` appears in the call stack every time any other function calls `DrawImageToScreen()` as well as every time the program calls `DrawImageToScreen()` directly.

When measuring performance, the number of times a function appears in the call stack is not what's important. What *is* important is the *ratio* of the number of times a function appears in the call stack to the number of times the function that calls it appears in the call stack. For example, the function `GameLoop()` calls the function `RenderFrame()`. In Figure 18-3, `GameLoop()` appears in the call stack 2,594 times, and `RenderFrame()` appears in the call stack 2,242 times. This means that the `GameLoop()` function spends approximately 86 percent of the time (2,242 divided by 2,594) calling `RenderFrame()`. If we want to speed up the program, `RenderFrame()` is the function we want to optimize. The `RenderFrame()` function I wrote for Chapter 5 looks like this:

```
void GameApp::RenderFrame(void)
{
        // Get the current screen resolution
```

```
GDHandle       mainDevice = NULL;
mainDevice = GetMainDevice();
Rect screenRect = (**mainDevice).gdRect;

gameBlitter->Setup(GetWindowPort(screenWindow), screenRect, screenRect);
gameBlitter->DrawImageToScreen();
}
```

If we look at the Call Stack window in Figure 18-3, we see that the DrawImageToScreen() function appears in the call stack 2,241 times. The function that calls DrawImageToScreen(), RenderFrame(), appears in the call stack 2,242 times. This means that the program spends 99.9 percent of its drawing time calling DrawImageToScreen(). It now appears that DrawImageToScreen() is the function to optimize if we want to improve the speed of the program.

Although the program does spend 99.9 percent of the drawing time calling DrawImageToScreen(), DrawImageToScreen() is not the problem. The problem is that the program draws the entire screen every frame, as you can see in the RenderFrame() function just listed. As we learned in Chapter 6, "Animation," the solution is to use dirty rectangle animation to draw only the parts of the screen that change from frame to frame. If we wanted an additional speed boost than the boost that dirty rectangle animation provides, we know from using Sampler that the DrawImageToScreen() function would be the one to tune.

Keep in mind that Sampler does have some limitations. All it does is look at the call stack every 20 milliseconds (or at whatever interval you specify), meaning that it does not provide a 100 percent accurate measurement of what functions your game calls. Functions that execute faster than the sample rate don't appear in the call stack at all. For more accurate measurements, we use a code profiler such as gprof.

Using gprof

The gprof tool provides a more thorough profile of your game's code than Sampler does, but it's harder to use because it's a command-line tool and because you must do more work with the compiler. You must perform the following steps to profile your code with the gprof tool:

1. Tell the compiler to generate profiling code.
2. Compile and run your game.
3. Run the Terminal application to go to the command line.
4. Run gprof.

Generating Profiling Code

The gprof tool requires profiling code to analyze your code while it runs; you must tell the compiler to generate profiling code instead of normal code. To tell Project Builder to generate profiling code, click the Targets tab in your project and then click the target name. This action brings up your project settings. Now click the Build Settings tab. In the section Compiler Settings, look for the Generate Profiling Code check box, as shown in Figure 18-4. Enable that check box, and Project Builder will generate profiling code.

You may also want to run your game with the profiling runtime library. While you are examining your project settings, click the Executables tab (the tab two places to the right of the Build Settings tab), then click the Runtime tab. An option will come up to choose the dynamic library runtime variant. Select Profile from the list, and you will be using the profiling runtime library. Using the profiling runtime library means that gprof will generate profiling information on every function that your game calls. If you do not use the profiling library, gprof will not generate profiling information on low-level system calls that your game does not directly call.

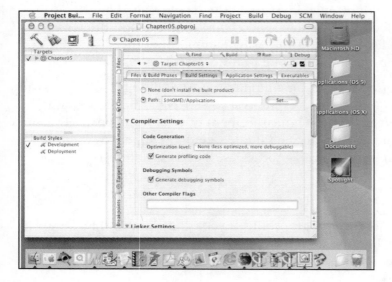

Figure 18-4

Generating profiling code in Project Builder

Compiling and Running Your Game

Telling the compiler to generate profiling code isn't going to do anything unless you recompile your code to actually generate the profiling code. First, you must clean your project, which will remove any previously compiled code. Select Clean from the Build Menu in Project Builder or click the whisk broom icon to clean the project. After cleaning the project, go to the Build menu and rebuild your project. You also may want to turn on compiler optimization when generating profiling code to gain a more accurate measurement of your game's performance.

Then play your game. Project Builder will create a file named gmon.out, which contains the profile of your code. gprof will use the gmon.out file to generate the reports that measure which functions take up the most time. You can rename the gmon.out file, but you will have an easier time when you run gprof if you don't rename the file.

Mac OS X's Command Line

Now that you have run your game, you must run gprof to view the profile of the code. Before you can run gprof, you must run the Terminal application to access the command line. The Terminal application should be in the Utilities folder inside your computer's Applications folder. If not, do a Sherlock search on your hard disk for the word *Terminal*. Figure 18-5 shows the Mac OS X command line. After you get the command line, move to the directory containing your game. This process is more difficult using the command line because you must type commands rather than using a graphical user interface as you do with most Macintosh programs. The commands you use are the cd and ls commands. The cd command changes the current directory. The ls command lists the contents of the current directory, which makes it easier for you to navigate directories.

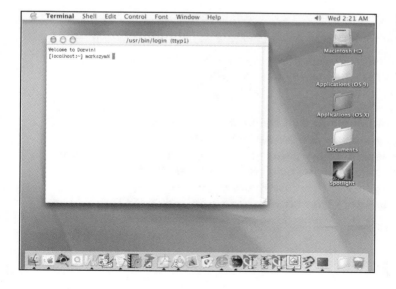

Figure 18-5

The Mac OS X command line

There are two ways to use the cd command. If you lead the directory path with a slash, the operating system will look for the directory on your startup disk, which is the hard disk for computers with one hard drive and the hard disk you chose as your startup disk on computers with multiple disk drives. For example, to navigate to the Documents folder on my hard disk, I type the following command:

cd /Documents

If you do not lead with a slash, the cd command changes the directory to a subdirectory of the current directory. Keeping with the example in the previous paragraph, if I have a folder for the game Unreal in my Documents folder, and I want to move to that folder, I type the following:

cd Unreal

If you want to navigate multiple directories with one cd command, use slashes to designate subdirectories. For example, if I have a folder named FirstLevel on my hard disk, a folder named SecondLevel inside the FirstLevel folder, and a folder named ThirdLevel inside the SecondLevel folder, I can type the following command to move directly to the ThirdLevel folder:

cd /FirstLevel/SecondLevel/ThirdLevel

If the FirstLevel folder is in the current directory, I type the following to get to the ThirdLevel folder:

cd FirstLevel/SecondLevel/ThirdLevel

TIP

If your folder or filename has spaces in it, put the folder name or filename in double quotation marks (" ") when you type it in the command line, like this:

cd "My Source Code"

Putting the string in quotation marks tells the operating system to treat the string as a single entity. If you don't put the name in quotes, the operating system will treat the words separated by spaces as separate arguments. In the preceding example, the operating system would treat the words My, Source, and Code as three separate arguments. Because the cd command takes only one argument, changing the directory like this with the command cd My Source Code will generate an error saying that you entered too many arguments.

Running gprof

Finally, we can run gprof. In its simplest form, running gprof looks like this:

```
gprof [Executable file] [gmon.out] > [Output file]
```

What complicates matters is that the executable file and the gmon.out file reside in different directories. Figure 18-6 shows the layout of the build folder of a Project Builder project.

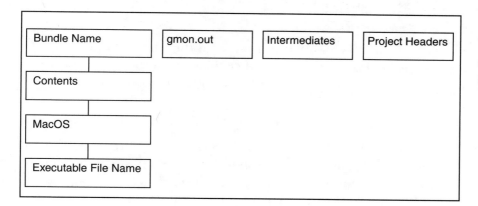

Figure 18-6

The layout of a Project Builder build folder

You'll notice that the executable file is three directories deeper than the gmon.out file. The easiest thing to do is to navigate to the Build folder of your project and then run gprof with the following command:

```
gprof "GameTitle.app/Contents/MacOS/GameTitle" > OutputFile
```

In this syntax, GameTitle is the name of your project and OutputFile is the name of the file to which gprof writes the profiling results. This command assumes that you did not change the name of the gmon.out file. If you changed the name of the file to profile.out, for example, you would run gprof like this:

```
gprof "GameTitle.app/Contents/MacOS/GameTitle" profile.out > OutputFile
```

The file OutputFile will appear in the build folder along with the gmon.out file and the application bundle. Running gprof this way is easiest because you type in only one path: the path to the executable file. If you navigate to the directory containing the executable file, you would have to type paths for the gmon.out file and the output file. In addition, you would have no easy way to get to the output file because bundles don't let you access their contents from the Finder.

After you issue the command to run `gprof`, it takes `gprof` a couple of minutes to generate the output file. The cursor moves to the left edge of the screen, and you won't be able to type any commands in the command line. Remain patient and don't panic. You haven't crashed the computer; `gprof` is doing its work. When `gprof` finishes, the cursor will move from the left edge of the screen, and you will be able to type more commands.

`gprof` has a bunch of options you can use to customize the reports that `gprof` generates. From the command line, type the following to learn about all its options:

`man gprof`

Press the Return key to scroll down so that you can read the whole manual page. I don't know why pressing the Page Down key and clicking the scrollbars do nothing. You must press the Return key repeatedly to read the entire manual listing.

Interpreting the Results

When you generate a standard profile, `gprof` produces two kinds of reports. The *flat profile* measures the amount of time your game spent calling each function. The *call graph* measures how much time your game spent in each function along with the time spent in the functions that a particular function calls.

On the CD-ROM that comes with the book, I included a file, Profiling Results.txt, which contains the output of a standard `gprof` profile. I profiled the scrolling program I wrote for Chapter 5. Profiling Results.txt is a plain text file, so you should be able to open and view it in any program that can read text documents, such as a word processor. The output file lists the call graph first and then the flat profile, but I'm going to begin the discussion with the flat profile because it's easier to understand than the call graph. The output file is pretty big; you will have to scroll down quite a bit to reach the flat profile.

The Flat Profile

The flat profile portion of the output file generated by `gprof` lists all the functions your game calls, sorted by the percentage of execution time. The functions that consume the most CPU time appear at the top of the list. The flat profile report contains seven columns, described in Table 18-2.

Table 18-2 Flat Profile Columns

Column	Description
`%time`	The percentage of the total CPU time the function consumed.
`cumulative seconds`	A running total of the amount of CPU time spent in your game.
`self seconds`	The amount of time the computer spent in this function.
`calls`	The number of times your game called this function.
`self ms/call`	The average number of milliseconds your game spent in this function each time you called it.
`total ms/call`	The average number of milliseconds your game spent in this function and the functions this particular function calls each time you call this particular function.
`name`	The name of this function.

Looking at the flat profile report for the Profiling Results.txt file, you will notice that the program spent 83.5 percent of the time calling the function `_SBCopyIdxToAny()`. If you look through the source code for the program I wrote in Chapter 5, you will not find any calls to a function named `_SBCopyIdxToAny()`. Where does this magical function appear that spends 83.5 percent of the total execution time? It's part of the `CopyBits()` function. When you call `CopyBits()`, QuickDraw calls several low-level functions, and `_SBCopyIdxToAny()` is one of these functions.

If you look through all the functions in the flat profile, you will notice that there are many low-level functions that do not appear in the source code. If you do not run your game with the profiling runtime library, the way to distinguish the functions you wrote from the low-level system calls is to look at the `calls`, `self ms/call`, and `total ms/call` columns. If those columns are blank, the function is a low-level system call that you did not write. If you used the profiling runtime library, distinguishing the functions you wrote requires more digging. Now let's search the flat profile report to determine which of the functions I wrote uses the most CPU time. If you go down the function list, you will see that the function `DrawImageToOffscreenBuffer()` is the first function that does not have blank `calls`, `self ms/call`, and `total ms/call` columns. The `DrawImageToOffscreenBuffer()` function draws a tile into the background. Because all this program does is scroll a game level, the program is going to spend a lot of time drawing tiles. If you were looking to speed up this program, the `DrawImageToOffscreenBuffer()` function would be the place to start.

The Call Graph

The call graph report in the output file generated by `gprof` measures how much time the program spent in each function and provides profiling information for both the functions that call it and the functions that it calls. The call graph report lists each function in order by its function ID (the number in brackets) so it's difficult to find the slow functions using the call graph alone. You should look at the flat profile to find the slow functions and then look at the call graph for more detailed information about these functions.

Figure 18-7 lists the call graph entry for the `DrawTileFromLevelMap()` function. There are three types of listings for a call graph entry: the primary listing, the parent listing, and the child listing.

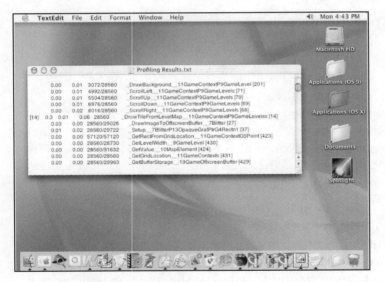

Figure 18-7

A sample call graph for a function

The *primary listing* lists information about the function itself. You can distinguish it from the parent and child listings by looking for the listing with a number in brackets in the leftmost column. Table 18-3 lists the columns in the primary listing along with a description of what each column represents. Looking at Figure 18-7, you can see that the computer spent 0.3 percent of the time in the `DrawTileFromLevelMap()` function. The computer spent 0.01 second in `DrawTileFromLevelMap()` and 0.06 second in the subroutines that `DrawTileFromLevelMap()` calls. The program called `DrawTileFromLevelMap()` 28,560 times.

Table 18-3   Primary Listing Columns

Column	Description
index	The index of the function. This is the number that appears in brackets.
%time	The percentage of the total CPU time the function consumed.
self	The amount of time the computer spent in this function.
children	The amount of time the computer spent in the subroutines that this function calls.
called	The number of times your game called the function.
name	The name of the function.

There is one *parent listing* for each function that calls the function in the primary listing. The parent listings reside above the primary listing. Table 18-4 lists the columns in the parent listing along with a description of what the column represents. When measuring performance from a parent listing, the important columns are the ratio of the called column to the total column.

Table 18-4   Parent Listing Columns

Column	Description
self	The amount of time the computer spent in the function of the primary listing when the function in the parent listing called it.
children	The amount of time the computer spent in the subroutines called by the primary listing function when the parent listing function called the primary listing function.
called	The number of times the function in the parent listing called the function in the primary listing.
total	The number of times your game called the function.
name	The name of the function in the parent listing.

If you look at Figure 18-7, you will see that my program called the function DrawTileFromLevelMap() 28,560 times. Five different functions in the program call DrawTileFromLevelMap(). DrawBackground() calls DrawTileFromLevelMap() 3,072 times. ScrollLeft() calls it 4,992 times. ScrollUp() calls it 5,504 times. ScrollDown() calls it 6,976 times, and ScrollRight() makes 8,016 calls to DrawTileFromLevelMap(). This information tells us that scrolling is responsible for the majority of calls to DrawTileFromLevelMap().

As you examine the functions in the call graph report, you will see that many functions have the name <spontaneous> as its parent listing. Low-level system calls have the name <spontaneous> in their parent listings because the profiler cannot determine the functions that call the low-level system functions. Ignore <spontaneous> parent listings because you have no control over them.

There is one *child listing* for each subroutine the function in the primary listing calls. If the function in the primary listing calls five functions, there will be five child listings. The child listings are below the primary listing. Table 18-5 lists the columns of the child listing along with a description of each column. For the purposes of measuring performance, add the self and children columns and divide by the children column of the primary listing. This calculation tells you how much time the primary listing function spends in each subroutine it calls.

Table 18-5   Child Listing Columns

Column	Description
self	The amount of time the computer spent in the function in the child listing when the function in the primary listing called it.
children	The amount of time the computer spent in the subroutines the function of the child listing calls when the function in the primary listing called it.
called	The number of times the function in the primary listing called the function in the child listing.
total	The number of times your game called the function in the child listing.
name	The name of the function in the child listing.

Looking at Figure 18-7, you will notice that the `DrawTileFromLevelMap()` function spends approximately half its time in the `DrawImageToOffscreenBuffer()` function and about half its time in the `Setup()` function from the `Blitter` class. `DrawTileFromLevelMap()` spends 0.06 second in the subroutines it calls: 0.03 second in the `DrawImageToOffscreenBuffer()` function, and 0.03 second in the `Setup()` function. The other five functions that `DrawTileFromLevelMap()` calls aren't worth the effort to optimize because the computer spends so little time in them.

One thing to remember when running your code in a profiler is that the profiler adds some overhead to your code. It takes time to measure how much time your code is spending in each function. When you make changes to your code, then run it through the profiler, you may not notice that the new code is running faster because of the time the profiling is taking.

Using Process Viewer

As is the Terminal program, the Process Viewer application is located in the Utilities folder inside your computer's Applications folder. When Process Viewer runs, it displays a window similar to the one shown in Figure 18-8. A list of running processes dominates the window. Every application you have running will appear as a process along with a bunch of operating system processes. The window displays the amount of CPU time and memory (as percentages) each process is using at the current time.

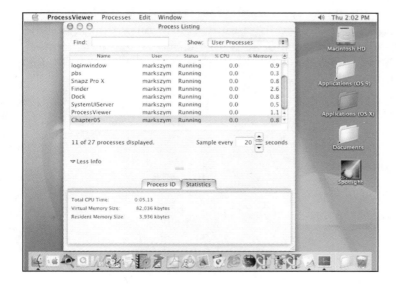

Figure 18-8

A sample Process Viewer window

At the bottom of the Process Viewer window, click the More Info triangle. Figure 18-8 shows what More Info displays. You will most likely use the Statistics tab, which tells you how much physical memory and virtual memory the application uses along with the amount of CPU time the application has used so far. As you can see from Figure 18-8, my program Chapter05 uses approximately 3.9 megabytes of physical memory and approximately 82 megabytes of virtual memory. *Virtual memory* is a portion of your hard disk that the operating system uses as memory.

Process Viewer lets you determine which processes to display in the Process Viewer window. If you want to view just one process—such as your game—type the process (application) name in the Find text box. In Figure 18-8, the window shows User Processes, but Process Viewer shows All Processes by default. All Processes shows the user processes as well as the administrator processes. User processes are all the applications you have running on your machine while administrator processes are low-level processes of interest to system administrators (the people that maintain your computer system if you work in an office). As a game developer, you're probably interested in only the user processes because your game is a user process, but you'll be okay with the default view that shows all processes.

Process Viewer does not provide much help with regard to performance if you're writing a full-screen game and have only one monitor. That's because you cannot run your game and view the Process Viewer window at the same time. When the game is running, you can't see any of Process Viewer's windows, and when you pause the game to see the Process Viewer window, the game will be using much less CPU time than when it's in normal gameplay mode. For Process Viewer to be helpful to analyze performance, you either need two monitors or a game that uses standard Mac windows. Process Viewer's biggest benefit for full-screen game developers is that it allows you to see how much memory your game uses so that you can determine the RAM requirements for your game.

Optimize Your Code

The profiler tells you what functions you need to optimize to improve your game's running speed. There are three ways you can optimize your code:

- Use a different algorithm.
- Rewrite the function in a high-level language such as C or C++.
- Rewrite the function in assembly language.

Using a different algorithm provides the greatest potential speed boost. You can use a different algorithm in conjunction with rewriting the function in either assembly language or a high-level language. You have seen examples of using a new algorithm to provide a speed boost throughout this book. For example, in Chapter 6, "Animation," I covered dirty rectangle animation. By using a new algorithm—drawing only the dirty portions of the screen instead of the entire screen—we achieved a major increase in drawing speed without resorting to assembly language.

Rewriting the function in a high-level language can provide a speed increase, but it won't have as big an effect as changing the algorithm. Writing a C or C++ function for speed makes your code more difficult to read and understand, so do it sparingly.

Hand-coding routines in assembly language can result in the fastest, most efficient code. I emphasize the word *can*. Compilers are good at handling general cases, but the programmer can make improvements for specific cases. Writing assembly language programs is difficult and beyond the scope of this book. To learn more about assembly language, go to Motorola's Web site at http://www.motorola.com. They have documentation on all the PowerPC chips, the chips that all Macs have used since 1994, and on programming the PowerPC chips in assembly language.

The PowerPC Environment

To optimize your code, you must know about the hardware to which you are coding. Modern Macs use Motorola's PowerPC chips. Table 18-6 lists the PowerPC chips that Macs use.

Table 18-6   PowerPC Chips

Chip	Description
601	The first Macs to use PowerPC chips used 601 chips. Macs sold between 1994 and 1996 use this chip.
603e	Motorola designed the 603e for laptop computers. It has the speed of a 601 chip, but uses less power.
604	The PowerPC 604 chip is a step up from the 601 and 603e. It provides extra integer units, so the 604 can execute more integer instructions at the same time.
604e	The PowerPC 604e chip is an enhanced version of the 604 chip.
750	Better known as the G3, the PowerPC 750 fuels Apple's popular iMac and iBook computers. Apple also used this chip for its desktop systems from 1997 to 1999.
7400	Better known as the G4, Apple used the PowerPC 7400 chips for its earliest G4 systems. The 7400 chip is the first to use AltiVec technology, also known as the Velocity Engine, which I cover later in this chapter.
7410	The PowerPC 7410 chip made minor improvements to the 7400, and it is used in some of Apple's G4 Macs, including iMacs with flat-panel displays.
7450	At the time I'm writing this, the PowerPC 7450 is the most powerful chip in the Macintosh line. The highest end Power Mac G4s introduced in January 2001 and the QuickSilver G4s use the 7450. The 7450 chip has its Level 2 cache on the chip itself, and adds a Level 3 cache on the backside of the processor.

At the time I'm writing this, Apple's iMac (the ones without a flat-panel screen) and iBook computers use the PowerPC 750 chip, better known as the G3. The flat-panel iMacs use the PowerPC 7410 chip while Apple's G4 Power Macs and Power Books use the PowerPC 7450 chip. Motorola is completing work on the PowerPC 8500, also known as the G5. The G5 is a 64-bit chip (all the chips listed in Table 18.6 are 32-bit chips). By the time you read this, the desktop Macs may be using the G5 chips (or whatever Apple will call the successor to the G4), and the iBooks may be using one of the G4 chips (7410 or 7450).

Figure 18-9 shows the places game data can reside inside the computer. At the top of the speed list are the PowerPC's registers. All the PowerPC chips listed in Table 18-6 have 32 integer registers and 32 floating-point registers. Each integer register can hold one integer value, which corresponds to one C language variable of type char, short, int, or long. Each floating-point register can hold one floating-point value, which corresponds to one C language variable of type float or double.

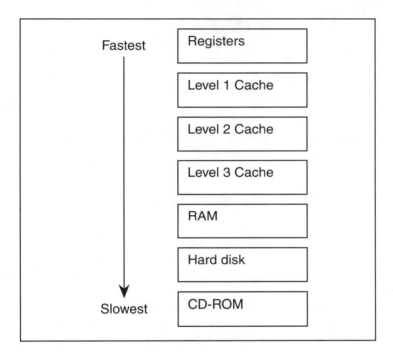

Figure 18-9

Places data can reside from fastest access to slowest.

The next fastest location is the chip's Level 1 cache, also known as an L1 cache. A *cache* is a piece of high-speed memory that holds the data and code that the program uses the most. All the PowerPC chips except the 601 have separate caches for data and instructions. Your game's variables would go in the data cache; your game's code would go in the instruction cache. The PowerPC 601 chip has a 32KB cache, where both data and instructions reside. The PowerPC 603e and 604 chips have 16KB of space for data and 16KB for instructions. All the other PowerPC chips listed in Table 18-6 have 32KB of space for data and 32KB for instruction.

The next level is the chip's Level 2 cache, also known as the L2 cache. When new data or new code flushes the L1 cache, the old data and old code falls into the L2 cache. All Macs that use the G3 or G4 processors have an L2 cache; some older Macs have it as well, but it varies from model to model. The size of the L2 cache ranges from 256KB to 2MB.

Macs that have the PowerPC 7450 chip have a Level 3 cache, also known as the L3 cache. Data and code that is flushed out of the L2 cache moves to the L3 cache. L3 caches can be either 1MB or 2MB in size.

After the L3 cache, the next fastest area is RAM, then comes hard disks, and at the bottom of the speed chain comes the CD-ROM. Large external cartridge drives such as Jaz and Peerless drives have speeds comparable to a hard disk. DVD-ROM discs have a speed similar to a CD-ROM, and Zip disks are slightly slower than CD-ROM discs.

Optimization Tips

To rehash the last section, data moves fastest in registers, then in the CPU's cache, then in RAM, then in disk. How can we use this information to improve performance? The following sections give you some pointers.

Have the Compiler Optimize Your Code

The easiest way to speed up your code is to have the compiler do it for you. Project Builder has three levels of optimization for your code. Level 1 provides the least amount of optimization. It automatically allocates variables in registers if possible.

Level 2 adds more optimizations. It performs all optimizations that don't involve a tradeoff between size and speed. Two major optimizations that Level 2 provides are common subexpression elimination and strength reduction. In *common subexpression elimination*, if the compiler sees that two statements have an identical calculation, the compiler will perform the calculation only once. Consider the following two statements:

```
result1 = (x * y) + z;
result2 = (x * y) - z;
```

The expression (x * y) is a common subexpression because the computer calculates it to determine the values of result1 and result2. With Level 2 optimization, the compiler will change the code to this:

```
temp = x * y;
result1 = temp + z;
result2 = temp - z;
```

By using common subexpression elimination, the computer multiplies the variables x and y only once.

Strength reduction optimizes loops by substituting less time-consuming operations in your loops. Consider the following for loop:

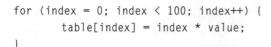

```
for (index = 0; index < 100; index++) {
      table[index] = index * value;
}
```

A compiler that uses strength reduction would replace the product inside the `for` loop with an addition like this:

```
temp = 0;
for (index = 0; index < 100; index++) {
      table[index] = temp;
      temp = temp + value;
}
```

Substituting the addition for the multiplication saves two to four processor cycles. Multiply that by the 100 times you enter the loop, and the compiler saved you 200 to 400 clock cycles. The length of a clock cycle depends on the clock speed of your CPU; its approximate value is (1 / (1,000,000 * MHz of the CPU) seconds). For example, on a 100MHz computer, a clock cycle is approximately one hundred millionth of a second. Saving two to four clock cycles in a loop you call 100 times will not provide a huge speed increase, but saving a few clock cycles in a function you call tens of thousands of time will provide a noticeable increase in performance.

Level 3 adds even more optimization, making your code run faster at the expense of making the code larger. It inlines functions and unrolls loops. An *inline function* works like a C language macro. Instead of calling the function, the compiler inserts the function's statements into the code. Consider the `RenderFrame()` function in the `GameApp` class for the scrolling program I wrote for Chapter 5. The code for the function looks like this:

```
void GameApp::RenderFrame(void)
{
      // Get the current screen resolution
      GDHandle       mainDevice = NULL;
      mainDevice = GetMainDevice();
      Rect screenRect = (**mainDevice).gdRect;

      gameBlitter->Setup(GetWindowPort(screenWindow), screenRect, screenRect);
      gameBlitter->DrawImageToScreen();
}
```

The `Setup()` function for the `Blitter` class looks like this:

```
void Blitter::Setup(CGrafPtr destBuffer, Rect sourceRect, Rect destRect)
{
```

```
            // Sets up the parts of the sprite blitter that
            // change from frame to frame
            SetupSourceRect(sourceRect);
            SetDestinationBuffer(destBuffer);
            SetupDestinationRect(destRect);
}
```

If the compiler inlined the Setup() function, the RenderFrame() function would look like this:

```
void GameApp::RenderFrame(void)
{
            // Get the current screen resolution
            GDHandle        mainDevice = NULL;
            mainDevice = GetMainDevice();
            Rect screenRect = (**mainDevice).gdRect;

            // Inlined portion of the code
            gameBlitter->SetupSourceRect(screenRect);
            gameBlitter->SetDestinationBuffer(GetWindowPort(screenWindow));
            gameBlitter->SetupDestinationRect(screenRect);

            gameBlitter->DrawImageToScreen();
}
```

As you can see, inlining a function makes your code larger, but you avoid the overhead of calling the function, which saves time. Inlining the function provides a speed boost only if you call the function many times. The overhead of one function call is not much, but the overhead of making thousands of function calls can be significant.

Loop unrolling duplicates statements inside a loop so that you make fewer checks to see whether you should exit the loop. Consider this for loop, which fills the screen with tiles:

```
for (short row = 0; row < kRowsOnScreen; row++) {
        for (short column = 0; column < kColumnsOnScreen; column++) {
                DrawTile(row, column);
        }
}
```

Using loop unrolling, the compiler would transform the loop to something like this:

```
for (short row = 0; row < kRowsOnScreen; row++) {
        for (short column = 0; column < kColumnsOnScreen; column+= 4) {
                DrawTile(row, column);
                DrawTile(row, column + 1);
                DrawTile(row, column + 2);
                DrawTile(row, column + 3);
        }
}
```

By unrolling the loop, the program goes through the inner loop 75 percent less often, which means it checks the conditions in the two for loops 75 percent less often. On the newest Macs, loop unrolling does not provide much time savings, but every bit of improvement helps.

CodeWarrior has four levels of optimization for your game's code. Read the documentation that comes with CodeWarrior for more information about the optimization options for your code.

Load Graphics and Sound Effects into RAM

Because reading data from disk is the slowest way to read data, you should load as much of your graphics and sound data as you can into RAM. Avoid reading data from disk while the game is in action. Read from disk at the beginning of the game and when loading a new level—as most commercial games do. That's why they take so long to load and require so much memory to play; they have lots of sound and graphics, and they load this information into memory when you first run the game.

The game we developed in this book had two kinds of visual data and two kinds of audio data to read from disk: tiles, sprites, music, and sound effects. We want to load the sound effects and sprites into RAM at the start of the game along with the first set of tiles and the first piece of background music. We use the sprites and sound effects throughout the entire game, so we need them in memory at all times. When the player kills an enemy, we want the sound effect of the enemy dying to occur immediately. If we were to load the sound effect from disk and then play it, the sound would come too late.

The game music we use is too large to load into memory all at once, so we have one piece of music in RAM at one time. We use one piece of music for a particular level, and then load a new piece of music from disk when the player reaches a new level. We don't want to read a large music file from disk during the game.

Our game doesn't have too many sets of tiles, so we could conceivably load them all into RAM at the start of the game. I chose to be memory efficient, however; only the set of tiles that the current level is using is loaded into RAM.

Don't Use More Than Eight Parameters in a Function

Mac compilers load the first eight parameters to a function into registers. By limiting yourself to a maximum of eight parameters, you ensure that the compiler loads all your function's parameters into registers, where they will be read fastest. This should not be too much of a burden; I have never written a function with more than six parameters.

Keep Data You Use Together Near Each Other in Memory

If data stays near each other in memory, the chances of it staying in one of the caches (L1, L2, or L3) improves. Now what can you do to keep data that works together near each other in memory? The easiest thing you can do is to declare variables that work together in the same function. For example, if you had two pieces of data, piece1 and piece2, that work together, declare them near each other like this:

```
long piece1;
long piece2;
```

If you declared piece1, declared 50 other variables, and then declared piece2, the two pieces of data will be separated by the 50 variables you declared between piece1 and piece2. If you explicitly allocate memory for the data, it's not enough to just declare the variables at the same time. You must allocate the memory at the same time for the two pieces to be near each other in memory.

How you access a large piece of data can also have a big impact on whether the data stays in the cache. Let's look at an example of something we do in the program we created in the book—filling the screen with tiles—to see what we can do to keep data close together in memory. There are two possible ways to do this: The first way is to fill the screen column by column like this:

```
for (short column = 0; column < kColumnsOnScreen; column++) {
    for (short row = 0; row < kRowsOnScreen; row++) {
        DrawTile(row, column);
```

```
        }
    }
```

Alternatively, we can fill the screen row by row like this:

```
for (short row = 0; row < kRowsOnScreen; row++) {
        for (short column = 0; column < kColumnsOnScreen; column++) {
                DrawTile(row, column);
        }
}
```

Which method do you think does a better job of keeping the data near each other? Filling the screen row by row does a better job because each row is next to the previous one in memory. Filling the screen column by column means skipping a number of bytes equal to the width of the screen each time we draw a tile, and then backtracking to the beginning when we start a new column. The two pieces of code do the same thing, and they're just as easy to read, but reading columns in the inner for loop does a better job of keeping your tiles in the cache, improving your drawing performance.

Avoid Conversions Between Integer and Floating-Point Numbers

If you have two integers with the values 18 and 5, and you divide them, you will get the result 3 instead of 3.6. To get the actual result of 3.6, you must convert the integers to floating-point values and then do the division. The problem with converting integers to floating-point numbers and vice versa is that there is no direct path between the integer registers and the floating-point registers. When you convert an integer that's in a register to a floating-point number, the value must travel from the integer register to RAM and then to the floating-point register. Having to travel through RAM slows things down. The best solution to this problem is to declare all the variables involved in a calculation to be the same data type so you do not need to perform any type conversions. If these variables happen to be integers, avoid division because division requires a floating-point number for accurate results.

Place the Expected Result in the if Portion of an if-then-else Statement

The PowerPC uses branch prediction to enhance performance. For example, if you have a while or a for loop, the computer predicts that the condition will be true and moves to execute the code inside the loop. This makes sense because the condition can be false only once, and can be true many times.

For an if-then-else statement, the computer predicts that the condition in the if clause will be true. Should the condition be false, the computer has to backtrack from its incorrect prediction, causing a minor slowdown. If you know that a condition will be true a majority of the time, put it in the if clause.

Use Floating-Point Multiplication Instead of Division

Consider this statement that uses floating-point division:

```
x = y / 100.0;
```

Rewrite this statement to use multiplication, like this:

```
x = y * .01;
```

Floating-point multiplication is much faster than division; even though the preceding two statements do the exact same thing, the second statement executes faster than the first one. On PowerPC chips, floating-point multiplication takes three to six clock cycles, depending on the chip. Floating-point division takes anywhere from 17 to 35 clock cycles, depending on the chip and the precision of the numbers. More precise results take more clock cycles. On floating-point data, multiplication is 6 to 12 times faster than division.

Position Multiple Conditions Wisely

Let's say that we have an if statement with two conditions like the following code:

```
if ((condition1) && (condition2)) {
      DoSomething();
}
```

When evaluating this statement, if condition1 is false, the computer doesn't bother to check condition2 because the expression is already false. If you know that condition1 is usually true and condition2 is usually false, you can gain a little speed by rewriting the if statement like this:

```
if ((condition2) && (condition1)) {
    DoSomething();
}
```

The computer evaluates conditions that you OR together in a similar manner. If the first condition is true, the compiler doesn't check the other conditions. In this case, you want the condition that is most likely to be true first in the collection of conditions. Consider an if statement like this one:

```
if ((condition1) || (condition2) || (condition3)) {
    DoSomething();
}
```

Make sure that condition1 is the condition that is most likely to be true.

AltiVec

Motorola introduced AltiVec (Apple calls it the Velocity Engine) with the PowerPC 7400 chip, meaning that all Macs with a G4 processor (and future Macs with G5 processors) have an AltiVec unit. AltiVec is a vector unit with 32 vector registers. Whereas the PowerPC's floating-point and integer registers can store just one variable, the vector registers can store multiple variables in one register. Each vector register is 128 bits long, meaning that one register can store sixteen 8-bit numbers, eight 16-bit numbers, or four 32-bit numbers. You can perform the same operations—addition, subtraction, multiplication, division, assignment—on vector variables that you can with integer and floating-point variables, but using vector variables lets you perform multiple calculations at once. Figure 18-10 provides an example of adding two vectors that contain eight 16-bit integers. In the calculation in Figure 18-10, the computer performs eight additions with one statement. Adding two vector registers takes the same amount of time as adding two integer registers, so the calculation in Figure 18-10 is eight times faster than adding the integers separately. You should be able to see AltiVec's potential to improve the speed of Mac games.

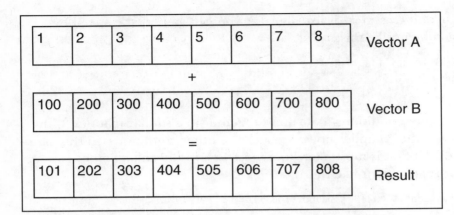

Figure 18-10

An example of adding two vector registers together

> **NOTE**
>
> Don't confuse AltiVec's use of the term *vector* with my discussion of vectors in Chapter 11, "Physics." AltiVec vectors are just a group of numbers. They do not have to contain direction as mathematical vectors do. Although you could store mathematical vectors inside an AltiVec vector, the Velocity Engine does not limit you to mathematical vectors. If AltiVec did limit you to mathematical vectors, it would not have much benefit.

Apple wrote Quartz, Mac OS X's graphics engine, to take advantage of AltiVec acceleration. Because QuickDraw sits on top of Quartz, QuickDraw uses AltiVec on G4 computers running Mac OS X. This means that all the graphics code in Chapters 4, 5, and 6 that uses QuickDraw automatically takes advantage of the Velocity Engine on G4 Macs running OS X. Because most Macs with Velocity Engine capability will be running Mac OS X, we get improved performance without having to write special code. If you are interested in programming for AltiVec, read the following sections.

Should I Use AltiVec?

When deciding whether or not to write AltiVec code, ask yourself the following questions:

1. Does my game perform many (hundreds or thousands) calculations?
2. Does my game work with large amounts of data?
3. Does my game need a speed boost on G4 Macs?

If the answer to these questions is *yes*, you should consider writing special AltiVec code. In the realm of game development, sound and 3D graphics are the areas that will benefit most from AltiVec. As you know from reading Chapter 10, "Sound," sounds require a lot of data, which would provide a resounding *yes* to question number 2. 3D graphics require many calculations and can always use a speed boost, so you can use higher-quality graphics on high-end machines.

Generating AltiVec Code in Your Compiler

For your game to use any AltiVec code that you write, you must tell the compiler to generate AltiVec code. In Project Builder, you must go into your project's build settings (an example of which you can see in Figure 18-11) and place the following statement in the Other Compiler Flags field:

```
-faltivec -force_cpusubtype_ALL
```

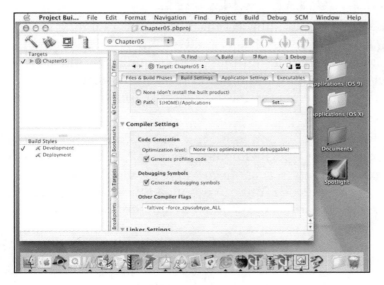

Figure 18-11

Project Builder build settings using AltiVec.

In CodeWarrior, enable the AltiVec Programming Model check box in the PPC Processor panel in your project's settings, as shown in Figure 18-12. In the figure, notice that the Generate VRSAVE Instructions check box has been enabled for you. Leave this option enabled to keep the vector registers from being trashed by the operating system and other applications.

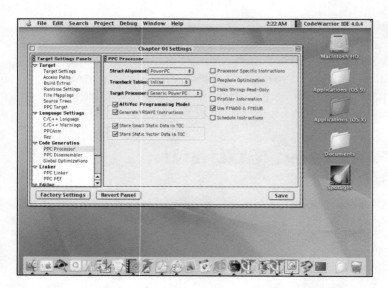

Figure 18-12

CodeWarrior project settings using AltiVec.

Programming with AltiVec

You can program AltiVec in C, C++, or assembly language. The programming is similar no matter what language you choose. The C and C++ functions correspond to one assembly language statement. This means that programming with AltiVec is low-level programming, and is difficult to do. You will write AltiVec code using the same criteria you use to write a routine in assembly language: sparingly, and only in code that could use a speed boost.

The following sections provide an introduction to writing AltiVec code. It is by no means an exhaustive treatment on the Velocity Engine. Motorola has two reference books for AltiVec: *AltiVec Technology Programming Interface Manual* and *AltiVec Technology Programming Environments Manual.* You can download these books from Motorola's Web site (http://www.motorola.com) and learn all there is to know about AltiVec.

Checking for the Availability of AltiVec

As I stated earlier, the Velocity Engine runs only on G4 (and future chips that Motorola introduces)Macs, so you must determine whether the player's computer has AltiVec capability before you call any AltiVec functions. To do this, call the Gestalt() function on the processor features and check the results against the constant gestaltPowerPCHasVectorFunctions, as shown in the following function:

```
Boolean IsAltiVecAvailable(void)
{
     long processorAttributes;
```

```
     OSErr error;
     Boolean result;

     error = Gestalt(gestaltPowerPCProcessorFeatures, &processorAttributes);

     if (error != noErr)
          return false;

     result = processorAttributes & gestaltPowerPCHasVectorFunctions;
     return result;
}
```

Declaring Variables

AltiVec adds the new data types listed in Table 18-7. As you can see from the table, most of the new data types just add the word vector to existing C language data types.

Table 18-7 AltiVec Data Types

Data Type	Description
vector unsigned char	16 elements of type unsigned char.
vector char	16 elements of type char.
vector unsigned short	Eight elements of type unsigned short.
vector short	Eight elements of type short.
vector unsigned int	Four elements of type unsigned int.
vector int	Four elements of type int.
vector float	Four elements of type float.
vector pixel	Eight 16-bit color pixels. To use AltiVec with 8-bit color pixels, use the type vector unsigned char. To use AltiVec with 32-bit color pixels, use the type vector unsigned int.
vector bool char	You use the vector bool types when comparing two vectors. The vector bool char type stores the result of a comparison between two vectors containing 8-bit numbers.
vector bool short	The vector bool short type stores the result of a comparison between two vectors containing 16-bit numbers.
vector bool int	The vector bool int type stores the result of a comparison between two vectors containing 32-bit numbers.

If you wanted a group of numbers with data type short in a vector, you could declare the variable like this:

```
vector short testVector;
```

In this case, the variable testVector would contain eight numbers of data type short. To make it easier to access each of the eight numbers, you can create a data structure that includes an array of short variables along with the vector short variable, as shown in the following code:

```
typedef union
{
        vector short theVector;
        short vectorElements[8];
} ShortVector;
```

We can then declare the variable testVector to be of type ShortVector. If we wanted to find the third number of the variable testVector, we would do the following:

```
short value = testVector.vectorElements;
```

Data structures for the other vector types look similar to the one for ShortVector, substituting the appropriate data type for the vector variable and the array. Remember to change the size of the array if necessary to ensure that the size of the array is 16 bytes, which is the size of all AltiVec vectors.

Loading and Storing Variables

After you declare a variable of one of AltiVec's vector types, you must move data into the variable. To give a vector initial values, you can just put them in parentheses after you declare the variable, as shown here:

```
vector int myVector = (1, 3, 5, 8);
```

To load a vector with data from another place in memory, use the function vec_ld(). vec_ld(). The second parameter is a pointer containing the data you want to load in the vector. It can be either a pointer to an AltiVec vector or a pointer to a traditional C language data type. The first parameter is an offset from this pointer. To load from the beginning of the data to which the pointer points, pass 0 as the first parameter. The following code demonstrates the use of the vec_ld() function:

```
vector short destination1;
vector short destination2;
vector short destination3;
```

```
vector short* source;

// Assume that source has data in it already.

// Load the three vectors. AltiVec vectors are 16 bytes long
// so we increment the offset by 16 for the second and third vectors.
destination1 = vec_ld(0, source);
destination2 = vec_ld(16, source);
destination3 = vec_ld(32, source);
```

vec_ld() loads an entire vector. If you want to load only one element of a vector, use the function vec_lde(). The major difference in calling vec_lde() from calling vec_ld() is that in vec_lde() the second parameter cannot be a pointer to an AltiVec vector. It must be a pointer to a C language data type.

If you plan on using a newly loaded vector only briefly, use the function vec_ldl() instead of vec_ld(). The vector you load by calling vec_ldl() will be the first data the computer flushes from the cache when new data enters the cache. Now why would you want this to happen? If you're not going to use the vector much, you would rather have the computer flush the vector out of the cache instead of the data you use more often. vec_ldl() allows you to keep important data in the cache longer, which improves your game's performance.

The AltiVec load functions allow you to load a vector with data from memory. The Velocity Engine's store functions do the opposite; they let you store a vector you created into a location in memory. Just as with the load functions, there are three store functions: vec_st() stores an entire vector, vec_ste() stores one element of a vector and vec_stl() stores a vector in such a way that it is the first data the computer flushes from the cache.

vec_st() takes three parameters. The first parameter contains the vector you want to store. The third parameter is a pointer to where you will store the vector. It can either be a pointer to a Velocity Engine vector or a pointer to a C language data type. The second parameter is the offset from the pointer. The following code demonstrates the use of the vec_st() function:

```
vector short source1;
vector short source2;
vector short source3;
vector short* destination;

// Assume that the source vectors have data in them already.
```

```
// Store the three vectors. AltiVec vectors are 16 bytes long
// so we increment the offset by 16 for the second and third vectors.
vec_st(source1, 0, destination);
vec_st(source2, 16, destination);
vec_st(source3, 32, destination);
```

Arithmetic Operations

To add two AltiVec vectors, you typically call the function vec_add(). The following function adds two vectors full of short integers:

```
ShortVector VectorSum(ShortVectorPtr vector1, ShortVectorPtr vector2)
{
      ShortVector result;
      result.theVector = vec_add(vector1->theVector, vector2->theVector);
      return result;
}
```

The vec_add() function does not prevent overflow. For example, if you added the short integers 20,000 and 15,000, you would get the value 2,232, not 35,000. That's because the highest positive value a short integer can store is 32,767. The computer stores the number 32,768 as 0. To prevent overflow on addition, use the function vec_adds(). When an overflow occurs with vec_adds(), the computer keeps the value at the highest possible value for the particular data type. Adding the short integers 20,000 and 15,000 would result in the value 32,767 if you used vec_adds(). To get the actual value of 35,000, you would need to change the data type from short to int.

To subtract two vectors, you normally call the function vec_sub(). You can see an example of vector subtraction in the following function:

```
ShortVector VectorDifference(ShortVectorPtr vector1, ShortVectorPtr vector2)
{
      ShortVector result;
      result.theVector = vec_sub(vector1->theVector, vector2->theVector);
      return result;
}
```

Just like with vec_add(), the vec_sub() function does not prevent overflow. The function vec_subs() will stop the overflow and use the smallest possible value for the particular data type.

Multiplying two vectors is more complicated than adding and subtracting vectors for two reasons. First, there are different multiplication functions for each type of data you can have in the vector. Table 18-8 lists the Velocity Engine's multiplication functions. Second, the multiplication functions don't just do multiplication; they perform an addition as well. The following formula shows what the multiplication functions do:

```
result = (vectorA * vectorB) + vectorC;
```

The exception to this is the vec_nmsub() function, which subtracts vectorC instead of adding it.

Table 18-8   AltiVec Multiplication Functions

Function	Description
vec_madd()	Multiply four 32-bit floating-point numbers.
vec_madds()	Multiply eight numbers of type short. vec_madds() saturates (uses the highest possible value for a short, 32,767) like the function vec_adds does to deal with overflow.
vec_mladd()	Multiply eight 16-bit integers.
vec_mradds()	Multiply eight numbers of type short. vec_mradds() saturates (uses the highest possible value for a short, 32,767) like the function vec_adds does to deal with overflow.
vec_msum()	Multiply either sixteen 8-bit integers or eight 16-bit integers.
vec_msums()	Multiply eight 16-bit integers and store the result as four 32-bit integers. vec_msums() saturates (uses the highest possible value for a 32-bit integer) like the function vec_adds does to deal with overflow.
vec_mule()	Multiply the even elements of 8-bit or 16-bit integers. For 8-bit integers, vec_mule() multiplies elements 0, 2, 4, 6, 8, 10, 12, and 14. For 16-bit integers, vec_mule() multiplies elements 0, 2, 4, and 6.
vec_mulo()	Multiply the odd elements of 8-bit or 16-bit integers. For 8-bit integers, vec_mulo() multiplies elements 1, 3, 5, 7, 9, 11, 13, and 15. For 16-bit integers, vec_mulo() multiplies elements 1, 3, 5, and 7.
vec_nmsub()	Multiply four 32-bit floating-point numbers.

The function vec_msums() deserves special attention. It takes two vectors composed of eight 16-bit integers, multiplies them, then adds them to a third vector made up of four 32-bit integers. What vec_msums() does is take the first two elements of the products of vectorA and vectorB, adds them, then adds that sum to the first element of vectorC. vec_msums() repeats this three more times to fill the rest of the destination vector, as you can see in Figure 18-13.

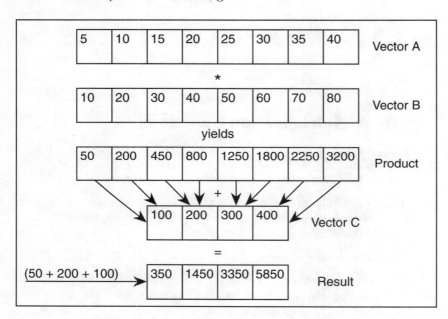

Figure 18-13

How vec_msums() *multiplies two vectors containing eight 16-bit integers into a vector containing four 32-bit vectors.*

Now let's see a little source code that multiplies two vectors of type ShortVector():

```
ShortVector VectorSum(ShortVectorPtr vector1, ShortVectorPtr vector2)
{
        ShortVector result;
        vector short zeroVector = (0, 0, 0, 0, 0, 0, 0, 0);

        // We just want to multiply, not do a multiply and add.
        result.theVector = vec_msum(vector1->theVector, vector2->theVector,
                                zeroVector);

        return result;
}
```

In AltiVec, you can perform division only on vectors containing floating-point numbers. To perform division, you take the vector you want to be the divisor and use its reciprocal (1/v for a vector v) by calling `vec_re()`. You multiply the dividend vector by its reciprocal to get the quotient. The following code segment demonstrates division:

```
// Divide vector1 by vector2;
vector float vector1;
vector float vector2;

// Assigning values to the vectors omitted

vector float divisor;
vector float result;

divisor = vec_re(vector2);
result = vec_madd(vector1, divisor);
```

Boolean Operations

AltiVec has functions for providing bitwise Boolean operations on vectors. The function `vec_and()` performs a bitwise AND between two vectors. The function `vec_or` performs a bitwise OR between two vectors. The function `vec_xor()` performs a bitwise XOR (exclusive OR—either A or B, but not both A and B) between two vectors.

You can perform these Boolean operations on all Velocity Engine vector types except for type `vector pixel`. However, the two vectors must have the same type. For example, you cannot call `vec_and()` on one vector with type `vector int` and another with type `vector unsigned int`.

Comparing Two Vectors

As part of its arsenal of functions, the Velocity Engine has a series of functions to compare two AltiVec vectors, as you can see in Table 18-9. Figure 18-14 shows the results of running the comparison functions on two sample vectors. When running the comparison functions on two vectors, the two vectors must have the same data type (Table 18-7 lists the data types).

100	90	80	70	60	50	40	30	Vector A

100	10	20	30	40	50	60	70	Vector B

True	False	False	False	False	True	False	False	vec_cmpeq()

True	True	True	True	True	True	False	False	vec_cmpge()

False	True	True	True	True	False	False	False	vec_cmpgt()

True	False	False	False	False	True	True	True	vec_cmple()

False	False	False	False	False	False	True	True	vec_cmplt()

Figure 18-14

Running AltiVec's comparison functions on two vectors.

Table 18-9 AltiVec Vector Comparison Functions

Function	Description
vec_cmpeq()	Compares two vectors and determines whether each element in vector A is equal to the corresponding element in vector B.
vec_cmpge()	Compares two vectors and determines whether each element in vector A is greater than or equal to the corresponding element in vector B.
vec_cmpgt()	Compares two vectors and determines whether each element in vector A is greater than the corresponding element in vector B.
vec_cmple()	Compares two vectors and determines whether each element in vector A is less than or equal to the corresponding element in vector B.
vec_cmplt()	Compares two vectors and determines whether each element in vector A is less than the corresponding element in vector B.
vec_cmpb()	Compares two vectors containing floating-point numbers and determines whether each element in vector A falls within the bounds specified in the corresponding element in vector B.

The following function determines whether or not the elements of two vectors are equal:

```
vector bool short TestForEquality(ShortVectorPtr vector1,
                                    ShortVectorPtr vector2)
{
      vector bool short result;

      result. = vec_cmpeq(vector1->theVector, vector2->theVector);

      return result;
}
```

As you can see from the `TestForEquality()` function, the vector comparison functions return a result of type `vector bool`. Comparing vectors that have 8-bit numbers return type `vector bool char`. Comparing vectors that have 16-bit numbers return type `vector bool short`, and comparing vectors containing 32-bit numbers return type `vector bool int`.

When running the comparison tests for less than, greater than, less than or equal to, and greater than or equal to, the functions test the first parameter against the second parameter. As an example, the following function shows a test for greater than:

```
vector bool short TestForGreaterThan(ShortVectorPtr vector1,
                                       ShortVectorPtr vector2)
{
      // Test if each element in vector1 is greater than the
      // corresponding element in vector 2.

      vector bool short result;

      result. = vec_cmpgt(vector1->theVector, vector2->theVector);

      return result;
}
```

The `vec_cmpb()` function is the most confusing of the AltiVec comparison functions, so it requires some additional explanation. The `vec_cmpb()` function performs two comparisons on vectors containing floating-point numbers. First, `vec_cmpb()` tests each element in vector A (the first parameter) against the corresponding element in vector B (the second parameter). If the element of vector A is less than or equal to the corresponding element in vector B, vec_cmpb() sets the high bit in the destination vector to 0; otherwise it sets the high bit to 1. Second, vec_cmpb() tests each element in vector A against the *negative* of the corresponding element in vector B. If the element of vector A is greater than or equal to the negative of vector B's element, vec_cmpb() sets the second highest bit in the destination vector to 0; otherwise it sets the bit to 1. Figure 18-15 shows an example of vec_cmpb().

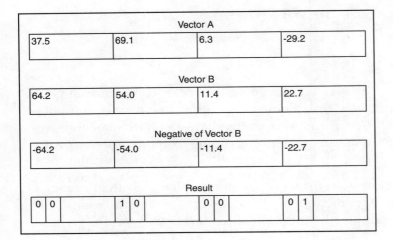

Figure 18-15

Example of vec_cmpb()

Permute Functions

When working with AltiVec, you may have to create a new vector containing elements of two other vectors. The vec_perm() function allows you to do this. This function takes three parameters. The first two parameters contain the two vectors from which you're creating the new vector. The third parameter is the permute vector. The permute vector has data type vector unsigned char, and it tells you which byte to use in the new vector. Values from 0 to 15 come from the first vector and values 16 to 31 come from the second vector. Figure 18-16 provides an example of using vec_perm().

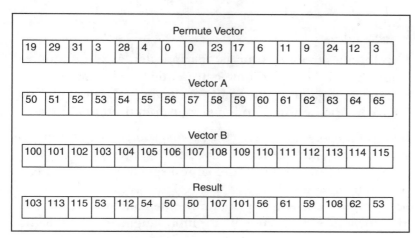

Figure 18-16

Example of
`vec_perm( )`

Creating the permute vector takes time; permutating vectors is not something you will want to do often in your game. The only exception to this rule is if you use genetic algorithms for your game's artificial intelligence. Genetic algorithms take a population and breed them to create new members. For example, if you were writing a strategy game with genetic algorithms, you would create a population of game players in which each player has a different strategy for playing the game. You would play many games with these players to determine which strategies were best. Then you would breed two game players that have the best strategies to create a new player with its own strategy, which might be something *you* never envisioned. By playing and breeding multiple players usually thousands of times, intelligence emerges without you having to explicitly program it.

What does permutating vectors have to do with genetic algorithms? The breeding of two parents to create a new child involves taking pieces of each parent and placing them in the child, which is the equivalent of permutating a vector. You could store your population members in AltiVec vectors, and use `vec_perm( )` for breeding.

Summary

This chapter dealt with techniques to make your game run faster. As you undoubtedly now know, optimization is a difficult and time-consuming process. Because of this, you should avoid tuning your game's code until your game runs properly; you should profile your code to determine where to focus your optimization efforts.

After you determine the locations of your game's slow spots, you can begin optimizing. There are three ways you can optimize your code. The first method is to rewrite the algorithm, which is the method with the largest speed potential. The second method is to tune your high-level language code. The easiest way to tune high-level language code is to have the compiler optimize the code for you. The final method is to rewrite portions of your code in assembly language, which is the most difficult way to increase your game's speed.

When writing optimized code, it's important to know your computer hardware. On PowerPC Macs, the 32 integer and 32 floating-point registers are fastest, so it's important to get your variables into those registers. Next on the speed list is the cache, which is high-speed memory that stores frequently used data and code. All PowerPC Macs have Level 1 cache, most have Level 2 cache, and some have Level 3 cache. Keeping the data you use often near each other in memory increases the chances of the data staying in the cache. Next on the speed list is RAM which is the slowest. For speed reasons, you should avoid reading data from disk while the game is in progress. Load the sound and graphics you need into RAM before the game begins.

AltiVec is a technology Motorola added to the G4 processors. AltiVec provides the capability of working with multiple pieces of data in a single instruction. If your game performs many calculations or uses lots of data, writing portions of your code with AltiVec can produce significant speed gains when your code runs on G4 processors.

Motorola's Web site (http://www.motorola.com) is the best source of information for optimizing PowerPC Mac programs. It has reference manuals for all the PowerPC chips, help for programming in PowerPC assembly language, and information about the AltiVec programming environment.

CHAPTER 19

GAME
DEVELOPMENT
TIPS

In the last chapter, we discussed techniques to optimize your game's code. In this chapter, we will learn techniques to optimize the game development process so that you can complete your games more quickly. Normally, this type of material appears in a software engineering book instead of a game development book, but with games becoming larger and larger, game developers need techniques to manage the complexity. Sitting in front of the computer and cranking out code isn't going to work with the size of modern games. We game developers can learn lessons from the software engineering community, which has a great deal of experience developing large computer programs.

The System Development Process

Every nontrivial program has the following phases:

- Requirements
- Analysis
- Design
- Construction
- Maintenance

The following sections explain each phase and how it pertains to game development. Keep in mind that systems analysts came up with the system development process to help create large business computer systems, not games, but much of the system life cycle applies to game development as well.

Requirements Phase

You will never guess what the requirements phase entails. Believe it or not, in the requirements phase, you make a list of your program's requirements. This phase is where games differ most from business systems. Businesses have specific needs that their computer systems fill whereas games generally don't have any formal requirements.

For game development, you describe the game and its features in the requirements phase. Some things to specify in the requirements phase include:

- Genre: Are you making an action game? a role-playing game? a strategy game? a completely new genre?
- Is the game single player, multiplayer, or both?
- Will the game have 2D or 3D graphics?
- Features your game will have that distinguish it from other games in the genre. If all you are doing is rehashing an existing game, you should suspend development until you can come up with some features that make your game unique. You're going to be spending months creating your game; you might as well create an original game instead of copying somebody else's game.

You will find this to be the easiest phase because you get to describe all the cool things you want to put in your game without having to worry about how to implement them. One thing to remember is that just because you include a feature in the requirements phase doesn't mean that you have to have it in the final product. If you want to include a fancy graphics feature in your game, but you find that it makes the game too slow to play, you can (and probably should) scrap the feature.

Analysis Phase

In the analysis phase, you build a model of the system from which you design the programs for the system. This phase is where you perform the typical game design duties. Some items to specify in the analysis phase include:

- The game's story, if it has one.
- The units in the game such as the player characters, enemies, other units, and items the player can acquire.
- Levels or missions in the game.
- If you use an object-oriented language such as C++ or Objective C to program your game, include a list of your game's classes and a description of what each class does.
- If you use a nonobject-oriented programming language such as C, include a list of your game's data structures and a description of each structure.

Design Phase

You design your program's code in the design phase. If you write your game in an object-oriented language such as C++ or Objective C, you flesh out your initial class declarations in the analysis phase by listing all the data members and member functions for each class. If you write your game in a structured programming language such as C, you list all your game's data structures and functions.

Along with listing your game's functions, you should provide a description of what each function does. You move from this description to working code in the construction phase. Remember that you can make changes if you need to during the construction phase. For example, if you design a function but during construction find that the code would be easier to understand if you split that function into two separate functions, then split the function. The work you do in the requirements, analysis, and design phases is supposed to make the construction phase easier. Don't handcuff your game's construction by being rigid with your game's design.

Construction Phase

The construction phase is where you begin coding. It has three stages:

- Coding
- Testing
- Debugging

In the coding stage, you write your programs from the design you created in the design phase. In the testing stage, you test your code to ensure that it is correct. There are two types of testing to perform: unit testing and system testing. You test each individual function with unit testing, and then you test how all the functions work together using system testing.

Games must survive an additional level of testing to which business programs are not subjected. They must be played to make sure that the game is fun to play. The game must also be balanced, that is, the game must be easy enough for the player to pick up quickly and have fun while being enough of a challenge for him to continue playing. People who write business systems don't have to worry whether their programs are fun for the people using them. As long as the programs work correctly and are easy to use, the system developers have done their jobs.

Every programmer makes mistakes, which introduce errors into the program. In the debugging stage, you locate the errors and fix them. Then you must retest to make sure that your fixes work. Eventually, you eliminate most of the bugs and have a finished product.

Maintenance Phase

When you finish the construction phase, you move into the maintenance phase, where you make changes to the program after it's a finished product. As computer game players, you're familiar with the maintenance phase. The maintenance phase in game development is where you release patches for the games. Patches fix bugs that went undetected in the construction phase, and they may add functionality to a game, such as adding multiplayer support to a single-player game.

Your goal should be to have no bugs in your game so that you don't have to release patches to fix errors. The best way to ensure that your game ships with no bugs is to take the time to test it thoroughly before you release the game. The problem in many commercial games is that the publisher sets a deadline to finish the game, usually to have the game on store shelves during the big Christmas shopping season. The publisher rushes the developer to finish the game by the deadline, so the developer doesn't have the time to find and fix all the bugs. Then the developer has to write a patch to fix the bugs he could have fixed if he hadn't been rushed to meet the deadline. Don't make this mistake. Release your game when it's ready so that you do not have to write patches to fix errors.

What Does It All Mean to Me?

Now that you know the phases of developing a system, how can you use this information to develop games faster? The time you spend in the requirements, analysis, and design phases will save you time in the construction and maintenance phases. The mistake most beginning game programmers make is that they are too eager to start writing code. They get an idea in their heads and skip the requirements, analysis, and design phases. When they hit a wall and their code does not work, the code is so hard to comprehend that it takes a long time to discover what's wrong with the code and fix the errors without messing up other parts of the game.

Performing the requirements, analysis, and design phases before you write any code provides you with several advantages. First, it forces you to think deeply about your game. This thought can show you that a feature you wanted in your game won't work in the game or will take too long to add to the game. Finding out that something won't work before you write any code is cheaper from a time standpoint than writing the program and then discovering that the feature will not work.

Second, all this planning makes coding easier. If you design your data structures and functions, your header files are practically written for you. Describing what each function does makes it easier to code the function than coding off the top of your head.

Third, performing upfront requirements, analysis, and design gives your game focus. It provides you with a roadmap for the construction of your game, telling you what you need to do to complete your game. If you've ever taken a road trip, you know that having a map makes it easier to determine where you are and where you have to go. Skimping on upfront design is like taking a long trip without a map. It will lead to the programming equivalent of making wrong turns and missing highway exits, which will make you take more time to reach your destination, a finished game.

Writing Clear Code

From reading this book, you should be able to tell that games contain a great deal of code and data. It can be difficult to keep track of all the code and remember what every function does. The best thing you can do to help you remember what everything does is to write clear code. Clear code makes it blatantly obvious what the code is doing so that you don't have to expend much effort trying to understand the code. The next sections provide some practical tips for making your code easier to understand.

Use Meaningful Variable Names

Name your variables so that you can tell what the variable does by its name alone. As an example, let's look at the data members for the Blitter class I developed for this book:

```
class Blitter
{
        protected:
                CGrafPtr sourceBuffer;
                CGrafPtr destinationBuffer;
                Rect sourceRect;
                Rect destinationRect;
                short drawingMode;
                long transparentColor;
}
```

The variable names tell you what each variable does. For example, the variable transparentColor gives you a clue that this variable stores the color that the Blitter class uses as the transparent color when drawing. Imagine how hard it would be to understand the Blitter class if I had named the variables like this:

```
class Blitter
{
        protected:
                CGrafPtr sb;
                CGrafPtr db;
                Rect sr;
                Rect dr;
                short mode;
                long tc;
}
```

Somebody looking at the code for the first time will not be able to determine that `tc` is an abbreviation for transparent color. If you wrote this code and then looked at it again six months later, you probably wouldn't be able to figure it out either. The other abbreviations would be just as difficult to decipher. The variable name `mode` isn't much better; it's a vague name that does not tell you what it does in the game. You'd want to find out where I live, track me down, and beat the crap out of me if I used variable names like this throughout the entire book. To the computer, the two `Blitter` class declarations are identical; to somebody reading the declarations, these code snippets are radically different; the first declaration is superior because of its use of clear variable names.

Use Descriptive Function Names

Just as you do with variable names, give your functions names that clearly describe what the function does. Let's look at the declaration for one of the `Blitter` class's functions:

```
virtual void DrawImageToScreen(void);
```

What do you think this function does? If you guessed that it draws an image to the screen, you guessed correctly. You must have psychic powers! Now imagine that I called the function `Copy()` because it calls `CopyBits()`. You would think that the function copied something, but you wouldn't think that it drew an image to the screen.

By combining good variable names and good function names, you can minimize the amount of comments in your programs. With descriptive variable and function names, you can figure out what the code does just by looking at the source code; most of the comments you would normally write become redundant, just as the comment in the following code is redundant at the beginning of the `DrawImageToScreen()` function:

```
void DrawImageToScreen(void)
{
        // Draws an image from the offscreen buffer to the screen

        // Rest of code here
}
```

The comment looks stupid because it just rehashes what the function name says. Save your comments for pieces of code that require an explanation.

Have Good Code Layout

You use paragraphs, punctuation, spaces, and capital letters in your normal writing to make your text easy to read. Imagine how difficult this book would be to read if I didn't use any spaces or punctuation. Code layout is the programming equivalent of using punctuation marks and paragraphs. Let's look at two identical functions with different layouts to see the difference between good and bad layout:

```
void Blitter::DrawImageToScreen(void)
{
// Make sure the source and destination buffers exist.
CGrafPtr theSource = GetSourceBuffer();
CGrafPtr theDestination = GetDestinationBuffer();
if ((theSource == nil) || (theDestination == nil))
return;
CGrafPtr oldPort;
GDHandle oldGDevice;
// Save previous drawing area
GetGWorld (&oldPort, &oldGDevice);
// Set drawing area to the screen
SetGWorld (theDestination, GetMainDevice());
// Lock the pixels
PixMapHandle thePixMap = GetGWorldPixMap(theSource);
Boolean canLockPixels = LockPixels(thePixMap);
// Draw from the offscreen GWorld to the window
if (canLockPixels){
// Source and destination rectangles and drawingMode
// are data members of the Blitter class.
CopyBits(GetPortBitMapForCopyBits(theSource),
GetPortBitMapForCopyBits(theDestination), &sourceRect, &destinationRect, drawingMode,
nil);
```

```
        }
        // OS X windows are double buffered. We check if the destination
        // is double buffered. If so, we flush the port buffer so the
        // drawing will show on the screen in OS X.
        RgnHandle theVisibleRegion;
        if (QDIsPortBuffered(theDestination)) {
        theVisibleRegion = NewRgn();
        GetPortVisibleRegion(theDestination, theVisibleRegion);
        QDFlushPortBuffer(theDestination, theVisibleRegion);
        DisposeRgn(theVisibleRegion);
        }
        // restore graphics port and GDevice
        SetGWorld(oldPort, oldGDevice);
        }
```

```
void Blitter::DrawImageToScreen(void)
{
        // Make sure the source and destination buffers exist.
        CGrafPtr theSource = GetSourceBuffer();
        CGrafPtr theDestination = GetDestinationBuffer();
        if ((theSource == nil) || (theDestination == nil))
                return;

        CGrafPtr oldPort;
        GDHandle oldGDevice;

        // Save previous drawing area
        GetGWorld (&oldPort, &oldGDevice);

        // Set drawing area to the screen
        SetGWorld (theDestination, GetMainDevice());

        // Lock the pixels
        PixMapHandle thePixMap = GetGWorldPixMap(theSource);
        Boolean canLockPixels = LockPixels(thePixMap);

        // Draw from the offscreen GWorld to the window
        if (canLockPixels){
                // Source and destination rectangles and drawingMode
```

```
                // are data members of the Blitter class.
                CopyBits(GetPortBitMapForCopyBits(theSource),
                        GetPortBitMapForCopyBits(theDestination),
                        &sourceRect, &destinationRect, drawingMode, nil);


        }

        // OS X windows are double buffered. We check if the destination
        // is double buffered. If so, we flush the port buffer so the
        // drawing will show on the screen in OS X.
        RgnHandle theVisibleRegion;

        if (QDIsPortBuffered(theDestination)) {
                theVisibleRegion = NewRgn();
                GetPortVisibleRegion(theDestination, theVisibleRegion);
                QDFlushPortBuffer(theDestination, theVisibleRegion);
                DisposeRgn(theVisibleRegion);
        }

        // restore graphics port and GDevice
        SetGWorld(oldPort, oldGDevice);
}
```

I'm sure you will agree that the second function's layout is superior to the first. The first function uses no blank lines or indentation at all, which makes the code difficult to read. It's the programming equivalent of writing a ten-page term paper with only one paragraph in it. The second function indents the code inside the if statements so that it's easy to tell that those statements execute when the condition in the if statement is true. It uses white space to separate groups of related statements.

For good layout, you should indent statements that execute inside a loop. You should also use blank lines to separate groups of related statements. You don't have to use the exact layout I use in my code, but you should format your code in a way that makes it easy for you to read the code and follow its logic.

Have Each Function Perform One Task

When each function performs only one task, it makes the function's name accurate. If my `DrawImageToScreen()` function does anything besides draw the image to the screen, it will confuse the reader because the function name implies that it only draws an image to the screen.

Writing your functions to do only one thing can also speed up the development of future games. If each function performs one well-defined task, the chances of you being able to reuse the code in another game increase. The more code you reuse, the less original code there is to write, which will allow you to finish the new game faster. As an example, the `DrawContext` class we developed in this book deals with switching screen resolution and hiding the menu bar. Every full-screen game you create will have the same requirements, so you can reuse the entire class in another game.

Break Large Functions into Several Smaller Functions

You saw this tip in action if you looked at the `GameLoop()` function in any of the programs I wrote in the book, but if you didn't, here's one version of the function:

```
void GameApp::GameLoop(void)
{
        timeStep = CalculateTimeStamp();

        InputControllerAction playerAction;
        InputControllerAction playerMovement;


        playerAction = player1InputController->DetermineAction();
        playerMovement = player1InputController->DetermineAnalogMovement();


        AnimatePlayer(playerAction);
        AnimatePlayer(playerMovement);

        AnimateEnemies();
        AnimateMissiles();
        CollisionDetection();
```

```
        PlayMusic();
        ScrollBackground();
        RenderFrame();
}
```

If I put all the code involved in the game loop into one function, that function would be huge. Even though this function would do only one thing—run the game loop—it would be difficult to manage because of the amount of work a game performs in a game loop. By breaking the game loop into smaller elements such as reading the player input, animating the characters, detecting collisions, and rendering the frame, we make the GameLoop() function clearer.

Using lots of smaller functions makes unit testing easier, because smaller functions are easier to test than larger ones. Smaller functions make it easier to isolate the source of errors, and they can even help performance. If you can isolate the slow portions of the game to a single function, and optimize that function, you can increase performance while keeping most of your code easy to read.

Having many small functions also helps you manage complexity in your game. Games have a lot of elements: graphics, sound, physics, AI, game logic, and networking to name a few. Trying to handle it all at once can be an overwhelming job, but things become more manageable if you focus on just one portion. Breaking things up into many small functions lets you develop your game one function at a time. Think of it as baby-stepping your way through the game development process.

You will notice that I used this approach when developing the game in this book. I started out by drawing something to the screen, then I added one feature at a time: scrolling, animation, reading user input, sound, physics, AI, and files. Eventually, a complete game emerged. Writing the entire game at once would have been a lot to handle (the book would have been one enormous chapter), but writing a program that draws a picture to the screen as a starting point was relatively easy. Adding one feature at a time made things easier on me. When I added audio to the game, I just had to worry about the sound code, instead of having to consider the other aspects of the game.

Use Constants Instead of Hard-Coding Values

Hard-coding values such as 16, 77, and "Player died" makes your code difficult to understand and change. What does the number 16 represent? You can't tell from the value alone. Instead, declare a constant variable with the value 16 and use that:

```
const short k16BitColor = 16;
```

The constant's name makes it clear that it represents 16-bit color. If I pass this constant to the function `NewGWorld()` to create an offscreen buffer, you can easily tell that I want to create a 16-bit color GWorld. Passing the literal value 16 makes your intention less clear.

If you look at the drawing code in the book, you'll notice that I use the constants `kTileWidth` and `kTileHeight` quite a bit. I used 32-by-32 pixel tiles so both constants have the value 32. If I wanted to change the size of the tiles, all I would have to do is change the `kTileWidth` and the `kTileHeight` constants. If I used the literal value 32 instead of the constants `kTileWidth` and `kTileHeight`, I would have to search my source code files for every instance of the value 32, decide whether it was the tile height, tile width, or another value, and then make the appropriate change. As you can well imagine, doing this would be time consuming and error prone.

Create Your Own Data Types

The C, C++, and Objective C programming languages give you the capability to create your own data types by using the `typedef` and `enum` statements. The `typedef` statement lets you give an existing data type a new name. For example, this declaration creates a data type called `WeaponType` that uses integer values:

```
typedef int WeaponType;
```

I can then use this new data type to create weapon variables like this:

```
WeaponType machineGun;
WeaponType crossbow;
```

To the computer, declaring the variable this way is equivalent to declaring integer variables, but to the reader of the code, this data type makes the code easier to read.

The `enum` statement lets you create an enumerated data type, which gives integer values their own names, allowing you to interpret an integer as a game-specific data type. I used an enumerated data type to list the tile types in the game, as you can see here:

```
enum GameTileType
{
    kWallTile = 1,
    kFloorTile,
    kDoorTile,
```

```
        kTrapTile,
        kForegroundTile,
        kEntranceTile,
        kExitTile
};
```

In Chapter 6, " Animation," when I wrote the functions to determine whether or not a sprite could move in a particular direction, I checked to see whether the next tile was a wall, as you can see in the following code snippet:

```
mapIndex = (rowToTest * theLevelWidth) + columnToTest;
tileNum = currentLevel->levelMap[mapIndex].GetValue();
tileAttribute = theTileList->tileTable[tileNum].GetTileType();
if (tileAttribute == kWallTile)
        return false;
```

Using the enumerated data type GameTileType with the value kWallTile makes the code easier to understand than not using the constant. Consider this version of the if condition:

```
if (tileAttribute == 1)
        return false;
```

Crash Causes and Remedies

The most noticeable bugs in computer programs are those that cause the program to crash; games are no different in this regard. The following sections list the most common causes of crashes and provide steps you can take to avoid them.

Accessing Null Pointers

The biggest cause of programs crashing involves accessing null (also known as nil) pointers. A *null pointer* points to location zero in memory, which is where the operating system's data begins. Writing data or accessing the data in location zero will make your game blow up immediately.

The way to avoid using null pointers is to make sure that each pointer is not null before you do anything with the pointer. In the BlitImageToScreen() function I've been using as an example in this chapter, I check to make sure that the source and destination buffers are not null before I draw, as you can see in the following code snippet:

```
// Make sure the source and destination buffers exist.
CGrafPtr theSource = GetSourceBuffer();
CGrafPtr theDestination = GetDestinationBuffer();
if ((theSource == nil) || (theDestination == nil))
        return;
```

If you discover that a pointer you want to use is null, do not use it. Leave the function, and if you need to, exit the game. It's better to exit the game than crash, especially on Mac OS 8 and 9, where a crash means restarting the computer. During development, when you find null pointers, go through your code and make sure you have code that sets the pointer to valid data. For example, in the code above, I would check to make sure I have code that sets the source and destination buffers to valid graphics ports before I do any drawing.

Going Past Array Bounds

When you go past the bounds of an array, you cannot be sure what piece of memory you're accessing or overwriting, and the results are usually disastrous. For example, in your graphics code, if you go past the bounds of an offscreen buffer when drawing from the buffer to the screen, garbage will appear on the screen instead of your game's graphics. Going past the bounds of an array is easy to do in C, C++, and Objective C because array indices start at 0 instead of 1. The following code shows just how easy it is to move past the bounds of the array:

```
int table[100];
for (int index = 1; index <= 100; index++)
        table[index] = index;
```

When this loop hits array index 100 and tries to set its value, it will write past the end of the array and will probably crash the program. The trick is to rewrite the for loop like this:

```
for (int index = 0; index < 100; index++)
        table[index] = index;
```

Using Uninitialized Data

When you attempt to use a variable whose contents you have not initialized, you're playing with fire. You have no idea what the value will be each time you run the program. This is a difficult error to track down because sometimes the code will run and sometimes it will crash. The solution is to give each variable an initial value, either when you declare the variable or just before you use the variable, as you can see in the following code:

```
int myData = 0;
Boolean isDone;

// Do other stuff

isDone = false;
while (!isDone) {
        // Do something
}
```

Another related problem is accessing data whose memory you have not allocated, which hit me when I was developing the code for this book. In the BlitImageToScreen() function, I initially wrote the following code to flush the port buffer:

```
RgnHandle theVisibleRegion;

if (QDIsPortBuffered(theDestination)) {
        GetPortVisibleRegion(theDestination, theVisibleRegion);
        QDFlushPortBuffer(theDestination, theVisibleRegion);
}
```

When I wrote this code in CodeWarrior, it ran fine on Mac OS X 10.0.4 (the code would execute only on Mac OS X), but it crashed when I moved the program to Project Builder. What complicated matters is that the code ran well the first time through, but crashed the second time through. When I upgraded to Mac OS X 10.1, the CodeWarrior version began to crash as well, and I could not understand what could be causing the error. The cause of the crash was that I had not allocated memory for the variable theVisibleRegion. I had to add two lines, as you can see here:

```
RgnHandle theVisibleRegion;

if (QDIsPortBuffered(theDestination)) {
        theVisibleRegion = NewRgn();
        GetPortVisibleRegion(theDestination, theVisibleRegion);
        QDFlushPortBuffer(theDestination, theVisibleRegion);
        DisposeRgn(theVisibleRegion);
}
```

By allocating memory for the variable theVisibleRegion with a call to NewRgn(), the code stopped crashing.

Memory Leaks

Throughout the book, I've alerted you to functions you need to call to avoid memory leaks. Now let's go into more detail on memory leaks. The memory in a computer is like a library. When you allocate memory for a variable, you're checking out a portion of memory. When you forget to free the memory when you're finished with it, it's like forgetting to return a library book. Instead of paying a fine of five cents per day, the RAM library has a hole in it. One small memory leak won't cause a problem, but if you continue to leak memory, eventually there will be no memory available when your program asks for memory, and a crash will ensue. Memory leaks can be difficult to find because the program appears to crash at random times.

When you declare most variables in a C language function, the compiler automatically disposes of the variable at the end of the function so you don't have to worry about it. Following are some variable declarations you don't have to worry about:

```
int x;
float y;
char message[50];
```

However, if your program explicitly allocates memory, either by the standard C language function `malloc()`, the C++ language function `new()`, or by the Mac OS calls `NewPtr()` or `NewHandle()`, you must explicitly dispose of the memory, or you will create a memory leak. I can create a variable like this in a C++ program:

```
int* value;
value = new int;
```

If I do so, however, I must dispose of the memory by calling the `delete()` function:

```
delete value;
```

In the previous section, notice that in my fix of the program by calling `NewRgn()`, I added a call to `DisposeRgn()` after I used the variable `theVisibleRegion` to avoid a memory leak.

As you've seen throughout this book, the Macintosh operating system has many functions that allocate memory. For each of these functions, there's a matching function that disposes of the memory. Remember to pair a dispose memory function with each function that allocates memory.

Mac Debugging Tools

No matter how much upfront design work you do on your game, you will have to do some debugging. Even the smallest games have thousands of lines of code, making it virtually impossible for you to write it all correctly the first time. The tool you will use most for your debugging is the debugger that comes with your compiler. In Chapter 2, "Project Builder," I showed you how to use Project Builder's debugger. CodeWarrior's debugger works similarly to Project Builder's, so I'm not going to spend this section rehashing material I have already covered.

Sometimes, problems occur for which a source-level debugger such as Project Builder's provides no help. You are then forced to use other tools. For debugging Mac OS 8 and 9 programs, Apple provides MacsBug, a low-level debugger. MacsBug can help you find a bug that crashes the source-level debugger or find errors that occur when you run your game but don't occur when you step through the code in a source-level debugger. MacsBug does require knowledge of assembly language, so it's not the easiest tool to use. You can download MacsBug and its manual from Apple's developer Web site (**http://www.apple.com/developer**).

Spotlight is a third-party debugging tool that you will find helpful for debugging applications on Mac OS 8 and 9. When your program does something to crash the computer, Spotlight generates a log telling you about the error and where the error happened. Spotlight also stops executing the program, which saves you the aggravation of having to restart your computer. The time you save by not having to reboot your machine every time your game crashes is worth the price of Spotlight. Spotlight also detects any memory leaks your game has. I included a 30-day demo of Spotlight for you to try on the CD-ROM that accompanies this book.

Apple's developer tools for Mac OS X include a slew of tools for debugging and testing your game. MallocDebug keeps track of all memory allocations in your program and checks your code for memory leaks. I will go into much more detail on MallocDebug in the next section. ObjectAlloc keeps track of every memory allocation and deallocation in your game. The program itself is pretty easy to use, but finding the information you want can be difficult. I introduce you to the ObjectAlloc program later in this chapter.

If you have two computers capable of running Mac OS X, the DebugNubController program can help you. It allows you to debug a program on one machine that is running on a second machine.

Along with the `MallocDebug`, `ObjectAlloc`, and `DebugNubController` tools that have graphical user interfaces, Mac OS X has command-line debugging tools. Table 19-1 lists these tools.

Table 19-1   Mac OS X Command-Line Debugging Utilities

Utility	Description
heap	The `heap` utility lists all the objects that your game has allocated in the game's memory heap.
leaks	The `leaks` tool lists all the memory leaks in an application.
fs_usage	The `fs_usage` tool logs all file system calls.
vmmap	The `vmmap` tool displays the layout of virtual memory.

All four of these command-line debugging utilities require you to know the application's process ID. Because of this, you should first run the `top` utility from the command line (run the Terminal application to launch the command line). The `top` tool lists all the programs running along with their process IDs. Create another command-line window by selecting New from the Shell menu; this will keep you from having to memorize process IDs. Now you can run the command-line debugging tools. For online help on the command-line tools, use the `man` utility from the command line. For example, to learn more about the `heap` program, type the following:

`man heap`

CAUTION

The `leaks` tool has one major flaw. It does not detect leaks when you allocate memory using the Carbon function `NewHandle()`. `leaks` *does* detect a couple of memory leaks that `MallocDebug` does not. You should start with `MallocDebug` to check for memory leaks in your game, then use `leaks` when you have fixed all the memory leaks that `MallocDebug` detects. The two tools work together; `MallocDebug` detects most memory leaks, and `leaks` detects the ones that `MallocDebug` misses.

Using MallocDebug

MallocDebug is a tool that tells you the amount of memory your game uses and the amount of memory each function in your game allocates. It also can search your code for memory leaks. In the next three sections, I introduce you to MallocDebug and show you how to use it to find errors in your code.

On Mac OS X you have different reasons for wanting to know how much memory your game uses than on Mac OS 8 and 9. On Mac OS 8 and 9, the user decides how much memory to give an application. If your game uses more memory than the user gave it, the program will crash. The amount of RAM and hard disk space on the player's computer are the only limits to how much memory your game can allocate. If you exhaust the player's RAM, the operating system will allocate memory on his hard disk. As we learned last section, the hard disk is much slower to access than memory. You want to be efficient with memory usage so the operating system does not have to allocate any memory on the hard disk.

Running MallocDebug

You will make things easier on yourself if you run MallocDebug first and then launch your game from MallocDebug. To attach a running program to MallocDebug, you must link your program to the MallocDebug library when you compile it. Because it's so much simpler to run MallocDebug before launching the game, that's what we will do here.

MallocDebug resides in the same folder as Project Builder, so you should have no trouble finding MallocDebug. After launching MallocDebug, select New Window from the File menu to display the window shown in Figure 19-1. Use the Browse button to find your game and then click the Launch button. Your game will run, and the Launch button will change to a Stop button. Don't click the Stop button until you are finished looking at your game. Clicking the Stop button quits your game and erases all the data about your game from the window.

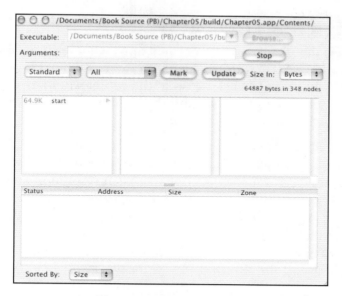

Figure 19-1

The MallocDebug *window before you run your game.*

I will use my scrolling program example from Chapter 5 to demonstrate the use of MallocDebug. After choosing Start from the File menu to go into full-screen mode, I paused the game. If you do the same with the Chapter 5 program or with a program you wrote, you will notice that the MallocDebug window does not change to reflect the memory you allocated. To see the memory MallocDebug has allocated, you must click the Update button, which will make the MallocDebug window look like the one in Figure 19-2.

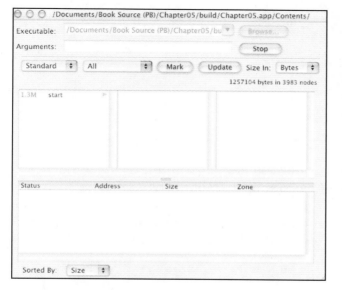

Figure 19-2

The MallocDebug *window after running your game and clicking the Update button.*

Interpreting the Results

All Figure 19-2 tells you is that the program allocated approximately 1.3MB of memory in a function called start() with two blank windows. We need to dig a little deeper. Select the start() function by clicking on it; the center window will show a function called _start(). Select that function, and the rightmost window will show three functions: main(), moninit(), and _keymgr_dwarf2_.

Let's look at main(). Click it, and you will see that the program allocates 1.1MB of RAM in the function InitApp() and 120KB of RAM in the function EventLoop(). Your allocation totals may be different depending on your screen resolution and color depth; I used an 800-by-600-pixel screen with 16-bit color for Figure 19-3. Select InitApp(), and you will see a bunch of functions, as shown in Figure 19-3. Looking at the figure, you will see that the InitApp() function allocates most of its memory when it creates the background and tile storage: 502KB in the function CreateBackground() and 327KB in the function CreateTileStorage().

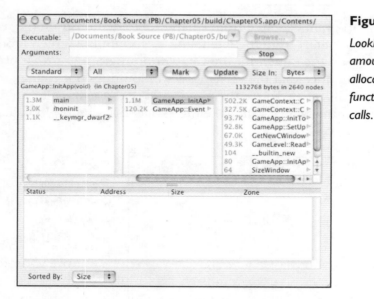

Figure 19-3

Looking at the amount of memory allocated in the functions InitApp() *calls.*

Working with MallocDebug is similar to working with the Sampler tool explained in the last chapter. Instead of measuring the number of times a function appears in the call stack, as Sampler does, MallocDebug measures the amount of memory allocated in each function. If you look at the functions that appear in the rightmost window and add the memory allocated in each, you will have the total amount in the window to its left.

At the bottom of Figures 19-2 and 19-3, you will see four headings: Status, Address, Size, and Zone, all with no data. This is one of the frustrating parts of working with MallocDebug. The bottom-left corner of the window has a drop-down list called Sorted By with the Size option selected. Even though you want to sort by size, you must explicitly select this option each time you select a function to browse in the MallocDebug window to have data appear in the columns of the bottom window. Select the InitApp() function, then choose to sort by size, and your MallocDebug window will look like the one in Figure 19-4. The bottom window now lists every allocation your game made in the InitApp() function, starting with the largest allocation. Choosing to sort by time displays the allocations in the order the computer made them.

Figure 19-4

Look at each memory allocation for a function.

If you double-click one of the individual allocations in the bottom window, the Memory Viewer Panel appears, as shown in Figure 19-5. The Memory Viewer Panel displays the memory at the location you double-clicked. In this window, you can look at the memory and see whether it looks like it should. Figure 19-5 shows that the memory at the location I double-clicked contains the hexadecimal (the memory displays its values in hexadecimal, rather than decimal numbers) digits F and C repeatedly, which isn't much help to you because you have no idea what the memory should look like in a program you didn't write. I can't tell you how the memory in the programs you write should look. As the person who wrote your code, you should know your variables and what types of values your variables should have.

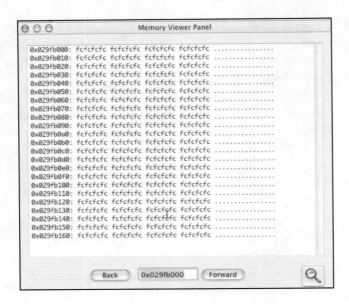

Figure 19-5

MallocDebug's *Memory Viewer Panel*

Detecting Memory Leaks

Although it is nice to know how much memory your game uses so that you can determine system requirements, I'm sure that you would like to know how to use MallocDebug to detect memory leaks. Searching for memory leaks is easy (fixing them may not be so simple). From the second drop-down list at the top of the window, select either Leaks or Definite Leaks. Choose Leaks to compile a list of all definite memory leaks and all possible memory leaks. Choose Definite Leaks to compile a list of only definite memory leaks. Figure 19-6 shows all the leaks for my scrolling program when I chose Leaks. From the figure, it looks like I'm leaking 12.6KB of memory, 9.5KB in the function EventLoop() and 3.1KB in the function InitApp().

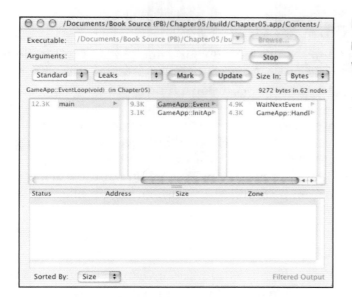

Figure 19-6

MallocDebug's *Leaks window*

Let's see whether our leaks are definite leaks or just possible leaks. Select Definite Leaks from the drop-down menu at the top of the screen. My MallocDebug window went empty when I selected Definite Leaks, so I know I don't have any definite memory leaks. I should double-check the areas of the code that MallocDebug pinpointed as possible leaks when I selected Leaks just to make sure that I'm not actually leaking memory.

The terms "possible leak" and "definite leak" are self-explanatory, but I should explain how MallocDebug classifies leaks. When you make memory allocations in your programs, the computer maintains a list of pointers to the blocks of memory you allocated. If MallocDebug finds a block of allocated memory that has no pointers to it, MallocDebug classifies that block as a definite memory leak. If a block of allocated memory has no pointers to the start of the block, but has pointers to other places in the block, MallocDebug classifies the block as a possible memory leak. In this case it is a possible leak because the pointers to other places in the block could be old pointers or random pointers (in which case, it is a memory leak), or it could simply be a pointer that points to the middle of the block (in which case it is not a memory leak).

To see whether your program trashed any memory, choose Trashed from the second drop-down menu at the top of the screen. If you run this command on my scrolling program, you should find no trashed memory. Writing past the bounds of an array is the most common cause of trashing memory.

Using ObjectAlloc

The ObjectAlloc program allows you to look at your game's memory allocations in greater detail than you can with MallocDebug. Although MallocDebug can tell you that the computer allocated *x* bytes of memory inside a function, ObjectAlloc can tell you the total number of times the function allocated memory. ObjectAlloc also provides a report of every memory allocation your game makes and gives you the capability to examine each and every allocation. I would not recommend starting your debugging with ObjectAlloc. Project Builder's (or CodeWarrior's) debugger is the best starting point, followed by MallocDebug. However, if you want to track every memory allocation your program makes to hunt down an elusive bug, ObjectAlloc is the tool for you.

Running ObjectAlloc

ObjectAlloc resides in the same folder as MallocDebug and Project Builder, so you should be able to find it easily. Launch ObjectAlloc by double-clicking the ObjectAlloc icon. ObjectAlloc brings up an Open File dialog box asking you which application you want to observe with ObjectAlloc. After selecting your program , a window like the one in Figure 19-7 appears.

Figure 19-7

The ObjectAlloc *window*

At this point, nothing is happening because the program you are testing has not launched yet. At the top of the window, you will notice five buttons; click the one on the left (the one with the triangle) to run your program and have `ObjectAlloc` start measuring it.

Global Allocations Tab

When you begin measuring your program, the `ObjectAlloc` window will look similar to the one in Figure 19-8 because `ObjectAlloc` defaults to displaying the Global Allocations tab. The Global Allocations tab displays every memory allocation your game has made. It lists the category, the current allocations, the peak number of allocations, the total number of allocations, and a graph representing the number of allocations.

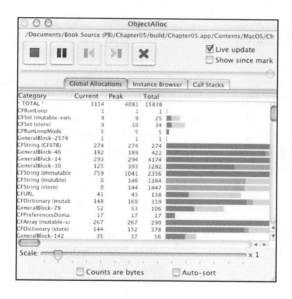

Figure 19-8

`ObjectAlloc`'s
Global Allocations tab

The Category column is difficult to understand because it doesn't directly relate to anything in your code. The categories that start with the letters *CF* are Mac OS X Core Foundation classes. The ones labeled *GeneralBlock* are general memory allocations. The number next to each GeneralBlock category represents the number of bytes of memory for each allocation. In Figure 19-8, the listing `General Block-2574` means that that particular allocation allocated 2574 bytes at a time.

The Current column measures the current number of memory allocations in a particular category. The Peak column measures the highest total of memory allocations during the time your game has run, and the Total column measures the total number of allocations for each category. By default, ObjectAlloc measures the number of allocations. If you enable the Counts Are Bytes check box, ObjectAlloc measures the number of allocated bytes instead of the number of memory allocations.

The graph provides a graphical view of the memory allocations. The entire graph measures the total number of allocations. The leftmost portion of the graph (the part of the graph that is blue) measures the current number of allocations. The purple portion of the graph (I know the figure is in black and white; trust me that the lighter portion of each bar is purple) measures allocations you made that were deallocated. The Scale slider allows you to change what one line of the graph represents. By default, it's 1, which means that each line in the graph measures one allocation. The scale can range from 0.5 to 8192.

You can sort the contents inside the window by enabling the Auto-Sort check box. By default, ObjectAlloc will sort by Category. You can change the sort criteria by clicking the column heading you want to sort by (Category, Current, Peak, or Total).

If you want to look at a particular allocation in time, you can move the slider located just above the Global Allocations tab to start looking at that particular moment in time. You can use the third and fourth buttons at the top of the window to step one allocation backward and forward respectively. With these buttons, you can look at each individual memory allocation your game makes, which is a potentially powerful tool for you to understand how your game is running.

Instance Browser Tab

To look deeper at each allocation, click the Instance Browser tab (see Figure 19-9). When using the Instance Browser tab, you must pause the execution of the program by clicking the pause button (the second button in the row of five buttons at the top of the window).

Figure 19-9

ObjectAlloc's
Instance Browser tab

The left pane of the Instance Browser tab lists every category of allocation. Three panes occupy most of the top portion of the window along with one pane on the bottom. To look at a category of allocations, select it. The middle window should display one or more memory addresses. Selecting one of these addresses will fill the rightmost column with a list of events and the bottom window with the memory contents at that address.

The rightmost column will have either one or two events. It will have an AllocationEvent because the computer allocated memory. If the memory was freed, a FreeEvent will also appear; otherwise the allocated memory is still in use.

If you select one of the events, an Event Inspector window appears as shown in Figure 19-10. The Event Inspector tells you the event, when it occurred, the size of the allocation, and a trace of the call stack which lists the hierarchy of functions that made the allocation or freed the memory. You can also bring up the Event Inspector window by selecting Inspector from the Edit menu.

Figure 19-10

ObjectAlloc's *Event Inspector window*

Call Stacks Tab

It wouldn't be a Mac OS X development tool if we couldn't look at call stacks. In ObjectAlloc, clicking the Call Stacks tab does this for us, making the ObjectAlloc window look like the one in Figure 19-11.

Figure 19-11

ObjectAlloc's *Call Stacks tab*

Notice that every allocation starts with a function called start(). To view the call stack for a particular allocation, click the triangle to expand the call stack; continue to click triangles until you see a function you recognize.

If you look at Figure 19-11, you will see that GeneralBlock-270 made 664 allocations totaling 179,280 bytes. 662 of these allocations occurred somewhere in the main() function; of these 662 allocations, 654 appeared in the EventLoop() function and 8 appeared in the InitApp() function. Of the 654 memory allocations in the EventLoop() function, 465 occurred in the GameLoop() function, 135 in HandleEvent(), and 54 in WaitNextEvent().

Retrieving Crash Information

Mac OS X has a nice little feature that creates a log file when your program crashes. To create a crash report, you must run the Console program. It should reside in the Utilities folder inside your Applications folder. Run the Console program and choose Preferences from the Console menu. Under the Crashes tab, enable the Log Crash Information check box. If you want to see the crash log immediately after your game crashes, enable the Automatically Display Crash Logs check box.

Figure 19-12 shows a crash log for the scrolling program I wrote in Chapter 5. If you want to recreate this log, go into the DrawImageToScreen() function and comment out the calls to NewRgn() and DisposeRgn(). The crash log displays the error that caused the crash, each thread in the program, and the state of each register at the time of the crash.

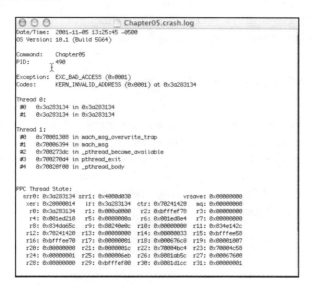

Figure 19-12

A sample crash log

My scrolling program does not use multiple threads and the commented-out version crashes early in the program, so the crash report does not contain tons of information. The most interesting part in this case is the error code near the top of the report, which says that I used an invalid kernel address in the code. As I mentioned in the "Using Uninitialized Data" section earlier in this chapter, the problem with the code is that I used a handle for which I did not allocate any memory, so the handle points to a bad address.

Where to Go for Help

There will be bugs in your game that are difficult to find and fix even if you use all the tools mentioned in the preceding sections. You can spend hours, days, and even weeks going through your code, making no apparent progress. This is the most frustrating part about computer programming. If you find yourself in this situation, the next sections will give you some hope.

Think about Something Else

If you have spent days being consumed with a bug in your game, take a break and think about something else. Work on another part of your game. Play a game, watch some TV, listen to some music, or do anything to take your mind off the problem. Getting away from the problem will clear your mind and let the subconscious part of your brain work on the problem. If your subconscious doesn't come up with a solution, you will at least be able to look at your problem with a fresh perspective. This fresh perspective will allow you to look at your code in a new way, which can make a stubborn bug appear obvious.

Search the Web

The chances are pretty good that you are not the first programmer to have the problem you're having. Go on the Internet and see whether someone else has had this problem. Google's Usenet archives let you search Usenet message boards; Apple's game development mailing list lets you search every message written to the list. In the best scenario, someone else will have posted a message with an identical problem and received a solution that will solve your problem, too. Refer to Appendix B, "Game Development Resources," for a list of relevant mailing lists and Usenet boards.

Ask for Help

If you're lucky enough to know someone who has Mac programming experience, let him look at your code and see whether he can figure out the problem. At this stage of your problem, you have a blind spot from being too close to your code, which is keeping you from solving the problem. Somebody looking at your code for the first time might be able to see the problem because he doesn't have the blind spot you built by thinking about the problem for days.

For those of you who don't personally know a Mac programmer (count me among the people who don't personally know a Mac programmer), use the Internet. There are multiple Usenet message boards about Mac programming, an Apple mailing list where Apple software engineers lurk, and a game programming message board on the iDevGames site where people can post questions about Mac game programming. Post a message describing your problem—include any source code if you know where the problem lurks—and someone may be able to help you. Mac programmers are generally a helpful group, and if they can't solve your problem, they can give you areas to look, which may help you solve your problem. Appendix B, "Game Development Resources," contains a list of resources you can use to find help for your problems.

Summary

This chapter covered areas you will rarely see covered by a game programming book: tips and techniques to improve the programs you write so that you can finish your games. I began the chapter by covering the system life cycle. In the requirements phase, you list your game's features. You perform the traditional game design duties in the analysis phase. The design phase involves designing all your game's data structures and functions. You write your code, test it, and fix any errors in the construction phase. When you complete your game, it enters the maintenance phase, which involves writing patches to fix bugs or add features to the completed game. By spending time at the beginning of your project in the requirements, analysis, and design phases, you reduce the time you spend in the construction and maintenance phases, resulting in faster development. Don't be too rigid in your upfront design. If you have to make a design change during construction, feel free to make it if it will make construction go more smoothly.

After covering the system life cycle, I moved on to discuss some techniques for writing clearer code. Clear code is easy to read and understand, making the process of finding problems in your game simpler. You can reduce complexity in your game by using many small functions, each of which performs one task. Many small functions make it easy to isolate trouble areas in your code and allow you to develop your game one feature at the time. In each individual function, you should use variable and function names that describe what the variable or function does. Format your code to make it easy to read. Indent code inside a loop. Group related statements together and use blank lines to separate statement groups.

I spent most of the remaining part of the chapter discussing Mac OS X's debugging tools. `MallocDebug` tells you the amount of memory your game uses and detects memory leaks. `ObjectAlloc` goes into more detail on your game's memory allocation, letting you step through each allocation. If the debugging tools aren't enough, the Internet has resources to help you. There are Usenet groups, message boards, and mailing lists where you can post questions and receive solutions for your programming problems. When all else fails, let other programmers help you.

APPENDIX A

Installing Programs from the CD-ROM

The CD-ROM that accompanies this book comes packed with programs to help you develop Macintosh games. The CD-ROM includes the source code for the programs I've presented in the book, third-party development tools, graphics, music, sound effects and Mac games to provide a diversion when you need a break from programming. This appendix provides guidance for moving the programs from the CD-ROM to your hard drive. From there, the individual programs have documentation that provides additional information on how to use them.

Most of the programs on the CD-ROM have been compressed with Aladdin System's StuffIt program so I could fit more programs on the CD-ROM. To expand the compressed files, you need Aladdin's StuffIt Expander. It should be on your computer already, but if it isn't, you can download it for free from Aladdin's Web site at **http://www.aladdinsys.com**. Double click any of the compressed files to expand them.

Using the Book's Source Code

I have two folders for the source code I wrote for this book. The first folder contains all the CFM Carbon programs I wrote in CodeWarrior. If you are running Mac OS 8 or 9, this is the folder you should use. Inside the folder is a list of folders, one for each chapter that has source code. Drag a chapter folder to the place you want the folder to reside on your hard disk. This will install that chapter's program on your hard disk. The project files are CodeWarrior Pro 5 projects. If you have a version of CodeWarrior (CodeWarrior Pro 6 or later) that has Carbon stationery to make Carbon programs, you should create new projects and add the source code files to the new project. All of the programs in this folder will run on Mac OS 8 and 9. Most of them run in Classic mode on Mac OS X; Chapters 4, 5, 6, and 9 run natively in Mac OS X.

The second folder contains all the Mach-O Carbon programs I wrote in Project Builder. If you use Project Builder to develop your games, or you create Mach-O Carbon programs with CodeWarrior, you should use this folder. Inside the folder is a list of folders, one for each chapter that has source code. Drag a chapter folder to the place you want the folder to reside on your hard disk. This will install that chapter's program on your hard disk. If you use CodeWarrior to write your Mac OS X programs, you must create a new project and add the source code files to the project. The code in this folder runs on Mac OS X only.

Installing Third-Party Software

Most of the third-party software included on the CD-ROM can be installed by double-clicking the compressed file located on the CD-ROM. Expanding the compressed file either installs the program on your hard disk or expands to an installer program you can run to install the software. Consult each program's Read Me file to learn more about using that particular program.

The third-party programs included on the CD-ROM fall into three categories: demos, shareware, and freeware. I included a list of the programs with their category on the CD-ROM for you to consult. "Demo" programs are demonstration versions of commercial software designed to entice you to purchase the full version. The demos have limits such as missing features or running for a specified period of time. In most cases, you can use the demo however you want. Normally, the demos don't work well enough to use alone for longer than 30 days without buying the full version.

"Shareware" programs take a try-before-you-buy approach. You try the program, and if you want to use it, you pay the author to register the program. The registration fees in most cases are reasonable—much less than what you would pay for a similar commercial product. If you like any of the shareware products on this CD-ROM and use them, please register them. Otherwise, you are stealing the program. The authors of the programs worked hard to develop them, and they have placed their trust in you to do the right thing and register the program if you like it.

"Freeware" programs are free for you to use without any further registration requirements. I hope that was clear enough.

APPENDIX B

GAME DEVELOPMENT RESOURCES

As much as it pains me to say it, this book does not contain the total sum of knowledge in the field of Mac game programming. Believe it or not, there is more for you to learn. This appendix lists sources of information that will help you continue your game development journey.

Books

This list of books is by no means exhaustive. There are hundreds of books on game programming, 3D graphics, and artificial intelligence on the market today—some of which you will find very helpful—but I'm not going to urge you to buy a book just because I heard other people say it was good. I've personally read all the books in this list and can heartily recommend them to you.

OpenGL Red Book

Eventually, you will want to jump into 3D game development, and on the Macintosh, this means learning OpenGL. The ultimate guide to learning OpenGL is *OpenGL Programming Guide* by the OpenGL Architectural Review Board, better known as the *Red Book* because the cover of the book happens to be red. Until I finish my masterpiece on 3D Macintosh game programming, you will have to use the Red Book to quench your thirst for OpenGL knowledge.

Macintosh C Carbon

K. J. Bricknell's *Macintosh C Carbon* provides hands-on instruction of Carbon programming. It also contains sample programs that illustrate the text in the book. With Bricknell's book, you will learn to program user-interface elements such as windows, dialog boxes, and menus. *Macintosh C Carbon* also covers graphics and sound, but because you have already read this book, the graphics and sound chapters will have less use than they would have if you were starting from scratch. You can download an electronic version from *MacTech* magazine's Web site, listed later in this appendix. If you want a printed version, you can find it at your local bookstore under the title *Carbon Programming* (Sams Publishing).

Inside Macintosh

In the mid 1990s, Apple published a series of reference books for writing Macintosh programs, called the *Inside Macintosh* series. Each volume in the series covered a different aspect of programming the Macintosh, such as graphics, sound, networking, files, and user interface. You might think that the series is out of date, but much of the material still applies if you use Carbon for your games. Here's a list of the titles with the most benefit for game developers:

- *Imaging with QuickDraw*
- *Sound*
- *Macintosh Toolbox Essentials*
- *More Macintosh Toolbox*
- *Files*
- *Networking with Open Transport*

You can download the *Inside Macintosh* series of books from Apple's developer Web site. Refer to the "Web Sites" section later in this appendix for the address of the Apple site.

Game Programming Gems

Charles River Media publishes the *Game Programming Gems* series of books. At the time I'm writing this, the publisher is working on volume 3 of the series. Rather than having each chapter build on the one before it as this book does, the *Game Programming Gems* books contain a collection of standalone articles—gems—covering various aspects of game programming, such as 3D graphics, artificial intelligence, and mathematical techniques. I own the first volume of the series, and it contains the best material on game AI that I have seen. None of the material in the books is Mac specific, but most of it applies to the Mac. You can view the table of contents for each book in the series at the publisher's Web site (**http://www.charlesriver.com**).

Game Design: Theory and Practice

Richard Rouse's *Game Design: Theory and Practice* is a book dedicated to game design. It contains interviews with famous game designers such as Sid Meier and Will Wright along with analysis of classic games such as *Tetris*, the *Sims*, and *Myth*. The book shows you what it takes to write a design document for your game and teaches you about gameplay, storytelling, and level design. After reading *Game Design: Theory and Practice*, you will be able to design better games—and the Mac market can always use more well-designed games.

Code Complete

Steve McConnell's *Code Complete* contains no material on game programming, but I still recommend this book to all of you who do not own it. This book provides lots of practical techniques you can use to write better programs, which will allow you to finish your games sooner.

Magazines

Computer books take months and even years to write; trust me, they involve a lot of hard work. Sometimes, computer books can be obsolete by the time they arrive on store shelves because computer technology changes so rapidly. Computer magazines, on the other hand, provide more timely information. The following sections list some interesting computer magazines.

Game Developer

Game Developer is the premiere game development magazine in print. Each month, *Game Developer* provides you with the latest game development news, reviews, technical articles, and game postmortems. To subscribe to *Game Developer*, go to their Web site at **http://www.gdmag.com**.

MacTech

MacTech is the only print magazine I know of that covers Macintosh programming. Although *MacTech* does not have many game development articles, it does have articles on Macintosh technologies such as QuickTime, Navigation Services, and Carbon events, which game developers use. *MacTech* comes out monthly, and you can try one issue for free at their Web site, **http://www.mactech.com**.

Journal of Graphics Tools

The *Journal of Graphics Tools* comes out four times a year. Each issue usually contains three or four papers on computer graphics. The papers are more technical than the articles you will find in *Game Developer* or *MacTech*, but they are more practical than the papers that appear in academic journals. Go to the ACM Web site, listed in the next section, for more information on the magazine.

ACM Publications

The Association for Computer Machinery (ACM) is a computer society where computer science professors, researchers, and other computer professionals exchange technical information. The ACM has many publications, the ones of greatest interest to game developers being

- *Transactions on Graphics*
- *Journal of Experimental Algorithmics*
- *intelligence*
- *Transactions on Networking*
- *Transactions on Modeling and Computer Simulation*

The material in these publications is cutting edge; computer professionals write the articles for other professionals, meaning that these publications are not easy to read. The book you are holding now reads like a children's book in comparison to these publications. If you're interested in pushing the state of the art in computer gaming, you should read these publications.

In addition to publishing magazines, the ACM has special interest groups covering fields such as graphics and artificial intelligence. The group you would be most familiar with is SIGGRAPH, the graphics group. Every year, SIGGRAPH has a conference where people present research papers in computer graphics.

To subscribe to the ACM publications, you must join the ACM. Technically, you can avoid joining, but the subscription costs for nonmembers are so expensive, it's cheaper to join the ACM. ACM also has a digital library subscription that enables you to access all the publications electronically. This subscription is a little pricey, but they have generous student discounts if you happen to be a student. To learn more, go to **http://www.acm.org**.

IEEE Computer Society Publications

Like the ACM, the Institute of Electrical and Electronics Engineers (IEEE) Computer Society exists for computer professionals to publish research papers and exchange technical information. The IEEE Computer Society publishes many magazines. The ones you would find most interesting include

- *Transactions on Visualization and Computer Graphics*
- *Computer Graphics and Applications*
- *Intelligent Systems*
- *Transactions on Pattern Analysis and Artificial Intelligence*

The IEEE Computer Society has a digital library just like the one offered by the ACM to which you can subscribe to electronically access all the society's publications. The subscription costs are so outrageous for non-members that you really should join the society to subscribe to the magazines. Like the ACM, the IEEE Computer Society has generous membership discounts for students. To learn more, go to **http://computer.org**.

Web Sites

There's no faster way to publish technical information than on the World Wide Web. As you can imagine, there are hundreds of sites dedicated to game development, and I detail the ones of greatest interest to Mac developers in the following sections.

CAUTION

The World Wide Web is a volatile place. Web sites come and go and change addresses all the time. When I put this list together, all the URLs pointed to working sites with updated information. By the time you read this, some of the sites may have moved or disbanded.

Apple's Developer Page

The first place on the Internet every Mac programmer should go is Apple's developer page, located at **http://www.apple.com/developer**. No other site has so much for the Mac programmer. It contains tools, development kits, documentation, and sample code. The site even offers a game developer page, which currently is pretty weak, but you never know when it might improve.

At the Apple developer site, you can join Apple's Developer Connection. You can become an online member for free, which lets you download the latest tools before they become available on the regular developer site. Apple also has other membership plans that give you perks such as monthly CD-ROMs, early versions of upcoming operating system releases, technical support incidents, and hardware discounts, but these plans can be expensive.

iDevGames

The best place for Mac game programming information is the iDevGames site, located at **http://www.idevgames.com**. It contains articles, source code, game assets such as sounds and graphics, and development news—and the material is Mac specific. In addition, this site has a message board where you can post Mac game development questions. If it weren't for this site, I would not be writing this book. The publisher saw some articles I wrote for the iDevGames site and asked me to submit a proposal for this book.

GameDev.net

GameDev.net, which you can find at **http://www.gamedev.net**, is the best site I have seen for general game programming information. It has hundreds of articles on topics such as graphics, sound, physics, networking, and artificial intelligence. It also has message boards on various aspects of game development. Most of the material is platform independent, so you can use it for Mac games.

Gamasutra

Gamasutra is yet another game development site, but it focuses more on the commercial game developer than do sites such as iDevGames and GameDev.net. Gamasutra contains lots of articles about game programming, game design, art, and music as well as articles about the business side of game development. This site also reprints many articles from *Game Developer* magazine, so if you don't have the money to subscribe to the magazine, you can find some of the articles online here. Go to **http://www.gamasutra.com** to view the Gamasutra site.

Motorola

Motorola develops the PowerPC chips that power Macs. (Yes, I'm being paid by the number of times I use the word *power*; it's an obscure part of my publishing deal.) From the Motorola site, you can download books on all the PowerPC chips, PowerPC assembly language, and AltiVec. If you want to write fast code for your Macintosh, check this site out. The Motorola Web site has the URL **http://www.motorola.com**. Look in the Semiconductors section for PowerPC programming information.

Game AI Page

I wonder what this page covers. If you guessed that it provides information about artificial intelligence in video games, give yourself a gold star. You can get another gold star if you can guess the URL. You're right! It's at **http://www.gameai.com**.

Game Developer's Conference Papers

Every spring, game developers from all over the world flock to California for the Game Developer's Conference. Game developers give presentations, vendors display their products, and people come to schmooze. If you're too busy or too financially strapped to attend the conference, there's help. The Game Developer's Conference's Web site, located at **http://www.gdconf.com**, has electronic versions of the presentations for you to download so that you can get a lot of the technical information at the conference without having to go to California. Go to the Archives section at the Game Developer's Conference Web site to access the papers.

IGDA

The International Game Developers Association (IGDA) is a game developer's trade group. IGDA hopes to be for game developers what the American Medical Association is for doctors. You can use this group to connect with other game developers from around the world. You can find the IGDA Web site at **http://www.igda.org**.

FlipCode

FlipCode is a general game programming site, similar to GameDev.net. It does not have as much information as GameDev.net, but it has enough articles to keep you busy. You can reach the FlipCode site at **http://www.flipcode.com**.

Game Programming Patterns Page

Design patterns provide a common vocabulary for problems in software development. The pattern lists a common problem and the solution to the problem so that software developers don't have to spend their time reinventing the same solutions to common programs. The Game Programming Patterns page has design patterns for game programming. The URL is **http://www.totempole.net/patterns/gamepat-**

terns.html. The solutions are general; you won't find any code listings here. However, that's a good thing because you can implement the solutions in the language and on the computer platform you choose.

At this site, you can also access the Game Engineering Process Patterns page. Set your browser to **http://www.totempole.net/patterns/gameprocess.html**. Although the Engineering page is not as large as the Game Programming Patterns page, it contains some techniques that can speed up the development of your game.

Erasmatazz

Chris Crawford, a famous computer game designer from the 1980s and the creator of the Game Developer's Conference, created this site. On this site, you can read Crawford's game design newsletters, *The Journal of Computer Game Design* and *Interactive Entertainment Design*, download his book *The Art of Computer Game Design*, download his storytelling tool Erasmatron, and download some old Mac games he developed. The URL for Erasmatazz is **http://www.erasmatazz.com**.

Chris Hecker's Page

Chris Hecker has a Web page that you will find interesting if you're into physics. The site contains the physics articles he wrote for *Game Developer* magazine, and a bibliography of books for you to read if you want to add realistic physics to your games. The URL is **http://www.d6.com/users/checker**.

Graphics Papers

The Graphics Papers site has a database of graphics papers. You type in a subject, and the site will give you a list of papers about that subject along with where you can find it on the Internet. It also contains links to sites that have graphics papers. One such link lets you download old SIGGRAPH presentations. The URL for the Graphics Papers site is **http://www.graphicspapers.com**.

AI on the Web

This site has a collection of links about artificial intelligence. It contains many links to university research sites, where you can download AI papers. It also contains a list of AI books and journals that you can read to learn more about artificial intelligence. The URL for the AI on the Web page is **http://www.cs.berkeley.edu/~russell/ai.html**.

Usenet

Sometimes, you may encounter a problem and not be able to find a solution in a book, magazine, or Web pages. Usenet message boards come to the rescue, letting you post questions and comments on a million topics. Strangely enough, there are Usenet groups on game programming and on Mac programming. Table B-1 lists the Mac programming groups, and Table B-2 lists the game programming groups. To view Usenet message boards from the World Wide Web and to search the archives of the Usenet groups, go to **http://groups.google.com**.

Table B-1   Mac Programming Usenet Groups

Group*	Description
codewarrior	This group covers programming with CodeWarrior.
games	A group for your Mac game development questions
help	A group for you to go to with your Mac programming problems
misc	If you have a Mac programming message that does not fit in one of the other groups in this table, submit it to this group.
tools	This group deals with Mac development tools. If you have a problem with Project Builder, this is the group to post a question about it.

* All the Mac programming Usenet groups have the prefix `comp.sys.mac.programmer`.

Table B-2   Game Development Usenet Groups

Group*	Description
design	A game design newsgroup
industry	A group to discuss the game development industry
programming.algorithms	Ask your questions about game programming algorithms in this group.
programming.misc	This group covers every aspect of game programming other than algorithms.

* All the game development Usenet groups have the prefix `comp.games.development`.

Mailing Lists

Apple hosts many mailing lists about different aspects of Macintosh development. People post programming questions to the mailing list and receive answers to their questions. Apple engineers frequent many of the lists so that they can help you with problems not covered in the documentation. Table B.3 lists the mailing lists of greatest interest to game developers. To view a list of all the mailing lists Apple hosts so that you can subscribe to these lists, go to **http://lists.apple.com/mailman/listinfo**.

Table B-3   Apple Mailing Lists

List	Description
mac-games-dev	A mailing list about Macintosh game development
mac-opengl	A mailing list about writing OpenGL programs on the Mac
carbon-development	A mailing list about developing programs in Carbon
openplay-development	A mailing list about OpenPlay, Apple's open-source cross-platform networking library. The list tends to spend more time on questions developing OpenPlay itself rather than questions on using OpenPlay, but it's the best place to go with OpenPlay questions.
projectbuilder-users	A mailing list about using Project Builder, Apple's IDE for developing Mac OS X programs
coreaudio-api	A mailing list about programming with Core Audio, Apple's API for programming sound on Mac OS X. The Sound Manager, which I covered in Chapter 10, "Sound," sits on top of Core Audio on Mac OS X.

Keep in mind that every message posted to the mailing list winds up in the mailboxes of hundreds of people. Treat the other people on the list with respect, and don't get into e-mail arguments. Make sure that your questions are relevant to the list. For example, don't post a problem you're having compiling a program with Project Builder on the game development mailing list; post it to the Project Builder list. Search the archives of the list to see whether someone has already asked a similar question. By checking the archives first, you can find your answer quicker—and you avoid flooding people's mailboxes with repetitive e-mails. People tire of answering the same questions over and over again.

APPENDIX C

CD-ROM Contents

As I have mentioned many times this CD-ROM comes with the book. In addition to the source code for all the programs I wrote for the chapters in the book, the CD-ROM contains programs you should find helpful as you develop your own games. This appendix provides a list of the programs that appear on the CD-ROM along with a brief description of each program.

Development Tools

The process of developing a game requires many things: You have to program the game, debug the game, and test the game. In addition to these tasks, your game will require graphics and sound files. The following tools, which I've included on the CD-ROM, will help you write your game.

- **CodeWarrior 7.0 Demo**
  The CD-ROM contains a 30-day demo of CodeWarrior 7.0, so don't install it until you are ready to do some serious programming. CodeWarrior lets you write both CFM and Mach-O Carbon programs using C, C++, or Java. If you want to write CFM Carbon programs that run on Mac OS 8, 9, and X, CodeWarrior is the tool for you.

- **Graphic Converter**
  This neat little shareware program does what its title suggests. Do you want to use 16-bit color in your game, but your artist gave you 32-bit color artwork? Graphic Converter makes the conversion to 16-bit color for you. Do you need to get a PICT resource out of a Photoshop file? Graphic Converter can convert the file for you. Graphic Converter performs all kinds of conversions on graphics files and also functions as a 2D paint program, making it well worth the registration fee. Graphic Converter runs on Mac OS 7, 8, 9, and X.

- **Spotlight Demo**
  If you program with Mac OS 8 or 9, you will find Spotlight to be a lifesaver. When your game is about to crash the computer, Spotlight stops the game and tells you where the problem occurred in the program, saving you from rebooting your Mac. Spotlight also detects any memory leaks your game has. Try the 30-day demo and see whether you like it.

- **QC Demo**
  QC is a tool to test Mac OS 8 and 9 programs for memory errors. When your game is ready to ship, run it through QC to determine whether or not it is as error-free as you thought it was. Like Spotlight, the QC demo lasts for 30 days.

- **Snapz Pro**
  Snapz Pro is a shareware program that allows you to take screenshots of your games and record game action to QuickTime movies.

- **Amapi**
  Amapi is a 3D modeling program. The CD-ROM contains two versions of Amapi. Version 4 is free, but does not run natively in Mac OS X. Version 6.1 is a demo version that runs natively in Mac OS X and contains features not present in the free version.

- **Groove Maker Demo**
  Groove Maker is a program that lets nonmusicians create soundtracks for games. The demo lets you play around with the program to see whether or not it's right for you. This version of Groove Maker runs natively in Mac OS X.

- **SndSampler**
  SndSampler is a shareware tool for recording and editing sounds. This version does not run natively in Mac OS X.

- **Kinky Beep**
  Kinky Beep is a nice little shareware utility you can use to make sound effects for your games. This version does not run natively in Mac OS X.

- **Nanosaur Source Code**
  Brian Greenstone of Pangea generously allowed me to include the source code for his Mac game *Nanosaur* so that you can see what the source code for a commercial 3D game looks like. He also let me include the *Oreo Terrain* program, a level editor for *Nanosaur*. Refer to the Read Me file that comes with the Nanosaur source code on the CD-ROM to see what you can and cannot do with the source code.

- **Player PRO**
  Player PRO is a library that lets Mac programs play MOD files. Remember from Chapter 10, "Sound," that MOD files provide a way of playing music without taking up much disk space.

- **Quesa**
  Quesa is an open-source version of Apple's QuickDraw 3D technology. Apple introduced QuickDraw 3D in the mid-1990s as its 3D graphics technology. QuickDraw 3D was good technology with bad timing. When Apple intro-

duced QuickDraw 3D, most Macs did not have a 3D accelerator, and QuickDraw 3D did not run well on Macs without a 3D accelerator. By the time 3D accelerators became common on Macs, Apple switched from QuickDraw 3D to OpenGL. Quesa is higher level than OpenGL so if you are new to 3D graphics, Quesa provides a nice way to learn the subject. Quesa code runs on Mac OS 8, 9, and X along with Windows and Linux. You can learn more about Quesa at the Quesa Web site (**http://www.quesa.org**).

- **SpriteWorld**
  SpriteWorld is a graphics and animation library for creating 2D games. By using SpriteWorld, you can focus on adding features to your game instead of worrying about things like scrolling and sprite animation. You can learn more about SpriteWorld at the SpriteWorld Web site (**http://www.sprite-world.org**).

uDevGame Contest Entries

The Mac game programming Web site (**http://www.iDevGames.com**) sponsors the uDevGame game programming contest. Look at the Contests section of the iDevGames site for more information about the contest. Contestants have a short time—a couple of months—to write a complete Mac game; the best entries receive game development prizes. I have included the games and source code for three of the four finalists of the inaugural uDevGame contest.

- **Evolution**
  Evolution is a Mac OS X strategy game for two-players—you can play either against the computer or another human—where the object is to fill the game board with amoebae. The author of *Evolution*, Sacha Saxer, wrote the game in Objective C using Cocoa. If you are interested in Cocoa for game development, take a look at *Evolution*'s source code.

- **GL Fighters**
  GL Fighters is a cool-looking two-person fighting game. The game is a bit rough with regard to user interface (because of the time constraints of the contest), but it has a really interesting look. David Rosen wrote *GL Fighters* using OpenGL. Refer to the source code to learn more about OpenGL programming. *GL Fighters* does not run natively in Mac OS X.

- **Silly Balls**

  Silly Balls is an action game reminiscent of the classic game *Marble Madness*. William Thimbleby, the author of *Silly Balls*, wrote the game using OpenGL. By looking at the source code for *Silly Balls*, you can learn how to use OpenGL to develop a game. *Silly Balls* does not run natively in Mac OS X.

Games

Game programming is long, hard work. Sometimes you need a break to recharge your batteries. I've included these games from the top Mac game companies to provide you with enough "ready-to-run" entertainment to help get you through the programming of your own first game.

- **Airburst**

  Airburst is an action game that plays like a combination of the classic games *Breakout* and *Pong*. The game has been Carbonized, so it runs on Mac OS 8, 9, and X. The version on the CD-ROM lets you play two of the eleven types of *Airburst* games.

- **Avernum 2**

  Avernum is an old-school, fantasy role-playing game along the lines of the old *Ultima* and *Wizardry* series of games. *Avernum 2* does not run natively in Mac OS X.

- **Battle-girl Demo**

  Battle-girl is a fast-paced arcade game, as you will see when you test the demo I've included on the CD-ROM. *Battle-girl* does not run natively in Mac OS X.

- **Captain Bumper Demo**

  Captain Bumper is an action-packed arcade that runs on Mac OS 8.6 and above, including OS X. The demo lets you play two levels in the game.

- **Colibricks**

  Colibricks is a shareware game that plays similarly to the classic *Breakout*. You can play six levels without registering; if you register, you can play 50 levels. *Colibricks* runs natively on Mac OS X as well as on Mac OS 8 and 9.

- **Deimos Rising**

  Deimos Rising is the sequel to the classic Mac shareware game *Mars Rising*. If that doesn't mean anything to you, let me tell you that *Deimos Rising* is an action-packed, shoot'em-up arcade game. *Deimos Rising* runs on Mac OS 8.6

and above and runs natively in Mac OS X. The version I've included on the CD-ROM lets you play four levels. Registering gives you the remaining eight levels.

- **Gridz Demo**
  Gridz is a strategy game in which you lead an army of robots into battle against other robots. *Gridz* does not run natively in Mac OS X.

- **Jiggy**
  Jiggy is a combination action/puzzle game in which you put jigsaw puzzles together in a race against the clock. The shareware version of *Jiggy* that I've included on the CD-ROM contains ten puzzles. Registering the game gives you 25 additional puzzles to solve. *Jiggy* runs on Mac OS 8.6 and above; it also runs natively in Mac OS X.

- **Otto Matic Demo**
  Otto Matic is the latest game from Pangea Software, creators of the Mac games *Nanosaur*, *Bugdom*, and *Cro-Mag Rally*. The demo lets you play the first level of the game. *Otto Matic* runs natively in Mac OS X.

- **Wing Nuts Demo**
  Wing Nuts is a fast-paced shoot-em-up arcade game that has been Carbonized, which means that it runs on Mac OS 8.6, 9, and X. I'm sure you have noticed that the Mac has a lot of action arcade games from looking at the list of games included on the CD-ROM.

Game Assets

Games require a great deal of graphics and sound. To help meet your game's graphics and sound needs, Carlos Camacho, the founder of iDevGames, has supplied us with a bunch of game assets you can use in your games, such as background tiles, sound effects, and background music. In addition, Ari Feldman has donated some arcade game graphics you can use if you're developing an arcade game.

Index

G

License Agreement/Notice of Limited Warranty

By opening the sealed disc container in this book, you agree to the following terms and conditions. If, upon reading the following license agreement and notice of limited warranty, you cannot agree to the terms and conditions set forth, return the unused book with unopened disc to the place where you purchased it for a refund.

License:

The enclosed software is copyrighted by the copyright holder(s) indicated on the software disc. You are licensed to copy the software onto a single computer for use by a single user and to a backup disc. You may not reproduce, make copies, or distribute copies or rent or lease the software in whole or in part, except with written permission of the copyright holder(s). You may transfer the enclosed disc only together with this license, and only if you destroy all other copies of the software and the transferee agrees to the terms of the license. You may not decompile, reverse assemble, or reverse engineer the software.

Notice of Limited Warranty:

The enclosed disc is warranted by Premier Press, Inc. to be free of physical defects in materials and workmanship for a period of sixty (60) days from end user's purchase of the book/disc combination. During the sixty-day term of the limited warranty, Premier Press will provide a replacement disc upon the return of a defective disc.

Limited Liability:

THE SOLE REMEDY FOR BREACH OF THIS LIMITED WARRANTY SHALL CONSIST ENTIRELY OF REPLACEMENT OF THE DEFECTIVE DISC. IN NO EVENT SHALL PREMIER PRESS OR THE AUTHORS BE LIABLE FOR ANY OTHER DAMAGES, INCLUDING LOSS OR CORRUPTION OF DATA, CHANGES IN THE FUNCTIONAL CHARACTERISTICS OF THE HARDWARE OR OPERATING SYSTEM, DELETERIOUS INTERACTION WITH OTHER SOFTWARE, OR ANY OTHER SPECIAL, INCIDENTAL, OR CONSEQUENTIAL DAMAGES THAT MAY ARISE, EVEN IF PREMIER AND/OR THE AUTHORS HAVE PREVIOUSLY BEEN NOTIFIED THAT THE POSSIBILITY OF SUCH DAMAGES EXISTS.

Disclaimer of Warranties:

PREMIER AND THE AUTHORS SPECIFICALLY DISCLAIM ANY AND ALL OTHER WARRANTIES, EITHER EXPRESS OR IMPLIED, INCLUDING WARRANTIES OF MERCHANTABILITY, SUITABILITY TO A PARTICULAR TASK OR PURPOSE, OR FREEDOM FROM ERRORS. SOME STATES DO NOT ALLOW FOR EXCLUSION OF IMPLIED WARRANTIES OR LIMITATION OF INCIDENTAL OR CONSEQUENTIAL DAMAGES, SO THESE LIMITATIONS MIGHT NOT APPLY TO YOU.

Other:

This Agreement is governed by the laws of the State of Indiana without regard to choice of law principles. The United Convention of Contracts for the International Sale of Goods is specifically disclaimed. This Agreement constitutes the entire agreement between you and Premier Press regarding use of the software.